Exploring America's Past

Beginnings to 1914

JOHN A. GARRATY

Gouverneur Morris Professor Emeritus of History
Columbia University

HOLT, RINEHART AND WINSTON
Harcourt Brace & Company
Austin • New York • Orlando • Atlanta • San Francisco • Boston • Dallas • Toronto • London

John A. Garraty is a distinguished historian and writer and the Gouverneur Morris Professor Emeritus of History at Columbia University. His books include the widely adopted college textbook *The American Nation.* He has held Guggenheim, Ford, and Social Science Research Council Fellowships. Professor Garraty is a former president of the Society of American Historians, editor of the forthcoming *American National Biography,* and coeditor of the *Encyclopedia of American Biography*.

Executive Editor
Sue Miller

Managing Editor
Jim Eckel

Editorial Staff

Pupil's Edition
Steven L. Hayes, *Editor*
Hadley Lewis Watson, *Associate Editor*
Margaret Thompson, *Associate Editor*
Melissa Langley, *Assistant Editor*

Multimedia
Tracy C. Wilson, *Editor*
Joni Wackwitz, *Associate Editor*
Edward D. Connolly, Jr., *Associate Editor*
Christopher J. Parker, *Associate Editor*
Robert A. Partain, *Associate Editor*
Dwonna N. Goldstone, *Assistant Editor*
Kevin N. Christensen, *Assistant Editor*
Laura H. Twohey, *Assistant Editor*

Fact Checking
Bob Fullilove, *Associate Editor*

Copy Editing
Nancy Katapodis Hicks, *Copy Editor*
Joseph S. Schofield IV, *Copy Editor*

Ancillaries
W. H. Bass III, *Editor*
Anthony Pozeck, *Associate Editor*

Editorial Permissions
Ann Farrar

Art, Design, and Photo
Diane Motz, *Art Director, Book*
Candace Moore, *Senior Designer*
Tonia Klingensmith, Lisa Walston, *Designers*
Bob Prestwood, Holly Trapp, Anne Wright, *Design Staff*
Debra Schorn, *Image Services*
Susan Michael, *Art Director, Multimedia*
Peggy Cooper, *Photo Research Manager*
Bob McClellan, Mavournea Hay, Kristin Hay, Sam Dudgeon, Victoria Smith, *Photo Team*
Cortex Communications Inc., *Photo Permissions*
Joe Melomo, *Design Manager, Media*

Production and Manufacturing
Gene Rumann, *Production Manager*
Leanna Ford, *Production Assistant*
Nancy Hargis, *Senior Production Coordinator*
Shirley Cantrell, *Production Coordinator*
Jenine Street, *Manufacturing Coordinator*
Laura Cuellar, *Manufacturing Assistant*

Electronic Publishing
Carol Martin, *EP Manager*
Kristy Sprott, *Project Manager*
Barbara Hudgens, *EP Supervisor*
JoAnn Brown, David Hernandez, Heather Jernt, Mercedes Newman, Rina May Ouellette, Michele Ruschhaupt, Charles Taliaferro, Ethan Thompson, *EP Staff*

Multimedia
Randy Merriman, *Vice President*
Kate Bennett, *Associate Director*
Debra Dorman, *Sr. Technology Projects Editor*
Lydia Doty, *Technology Projects Editor*
William L. Clark, *Associate Technology Project Editor*
Virgil McCullough, *Production Manager*
Armin Gutzmer, *Manager of Training and Technical Support*
Cathy Kuhles, *Technical Assistant*
Kathy Blanchard, *Executive Secretary*
Roslyn Degollado, *Intern*

Management of Information Systems
Ian Christopher, *Sr. System Support Specialist*

Book cover: *background scenic,* Mark Segal/Panoramic Images; *eagle,* Art Wolfe/Tony Stone Images; *flag,* SuperStock

For acknowledgments, see page 745, which is an extension of the copyright page.

Printed in the United States of America

ISBN 0-03-050532-1

1 2 3 4 5 6 7 8 9 032 00 99 98 97

REVIEWERS

CONTENT REVIEWERS

Sterling Stuckey
University of California, Riverside
African American

Michael M. Benedict
Ohio State University
Civil War and Reconstruction, American constitutional

Beverly Jones
North Carolina Central University
Reconstruction

William Bravman
University of Maryland
Africa, social and cultural

Paul A. Gilje
University of Oklahoma
Colonial America

Herbert T. Hoover
University of South Dakota
American West, American Indian

Dorothee E. Kocks
University of Utah
American West

Robert Remini
University of Notre Dame
American studies

Marvin Lunenfeld
State University of New York
Spain

Jan E. Lewis
Rutgers University
America to 1830, family, women

Neil Foley
University of Texas at Austin
Southwestern, borderlands, Texas

Carl H. Moneyhan
University of Arkansas at Little Rock
South, Civil War and Reconstruction

Wyatt Wells
Harvard University
U.S. economic

Mary C. Brennan
Southwest Texas State University
Postwar U.S.

Raymond M. Hyser
James Madison University
Gilded Age, Progressive Era, business

Julie Greene
University of Colorado at Boulder
U.S. political and labor

Noel Pugach
University of New Mexico
U.S. diplomatic

Maureen Flanagan
Michigan State University
20th-century U.S.

Eileen Boris
Howard University
American women, U.S. social and cultural

H. W. Brands
Texas A&M University
U.S. diplomatic

Marilyn Young
New York University
U.S.-East Asian relations

Nan Elizabeth Wookruff
Penn State University
20th-century U.S.

Thomas A. Schwartz
Vanderbilt University
U.S. foreign relations

David Helgren
San Jose State University

Mark C. Smith
University of Texas at Austin
American studies

EDUCATIONAL REVIEWERS

Linda A. Boaen
Baird Magnet School
Fresno, California

Daniel E. Fee
South Jefferson Central School District
Adams, New York

Marilyn Kretzer
Johnston Middle School
Houston, Texas

Jeri Goodspeed-Gross
Grass Middle School
West St. Paul, Minnesota

Tom Harris
Oak Park Middle School
Leesburg, Florida

Maureen Lewis
Yelm Middle School
Yelm, Washington

James H. Curtis
Corbett Junior High School
Schertz, Texas

Pat Tobbe
Newburg Middle School
Louisville, Kentucky

David Burns
Thomas A. Edison High School
Alexandria, Virginia

Tammy Kowalczyk
Corbett Junior High School
Schertz, Texas

Nancy Lehmann-Carssow
Lanier High School
Austin, Texas

Donny L. Branam
Dobie Middle School
Austin, Texas

Irving Kohn
Fort Myers Middle School
Fort Myers, Florida

Jacqueline Lazenby
Marysville Middle School
Marysville, Ohio

Deborah K. Lofton
Blackstock Junior High School
Oxnard, California

Roberta D. Martinez
Blackstock Junior High School
Oxnard, California

Michelle Susberry Range
Hudtloff Junior High School
Tacoma, Washington

Trisha Sims
Hyde Park Baptist High School
Austin, Texas

Kristin Truman
Hunterdon Central Regional High School
Flemington, New Jersey

Roberto C. Vasquez
Covington Middle School
Austin, Texas

Devon I. Weyler
Lamberton Middle School
Carlisle, Pennsylvania

Lisa M. Williams
Lamberton Middle School
Carlisle, Pennsylvania

Barry Bienstock
Horace Mann School
Bronx, New York

Exploring America's Past

Beginnings to 1914

CONTENTS

The Granger Collection, New York

Members of a mestizo *family in New Spain*

The Granger Collection, New York

Bostonians watch the Battle of Bunker Hill.

Thomas Jefferson, author of the Declaration of Independence, became the third president of the United States.

The Granger Collection, New York

Many slaves had to wear tags when they were off the plantation.

CHAPTER 9

The North and Manufacturing

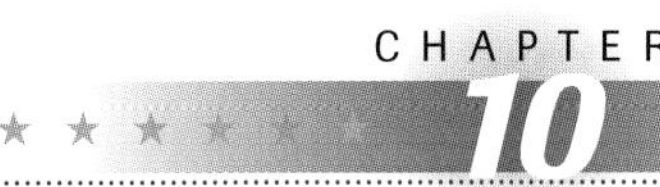

CHAPTER 10

The South and King Cotton

UNIT 4

Seeking Growth and Change

CHAPTER 11

Conflicts and Reform

Woolaroc Museum, Bartlesville, Oklahoma

Removal to Indian Territory

Thomas Moran's painting, Grand Canyon of the Yellowstone.

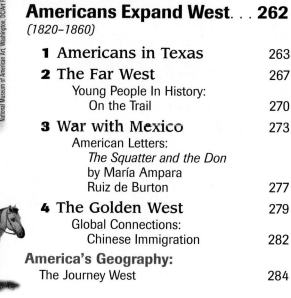

Many children accompanied their parents on the long and difficult journey west during the 1800s.

CHAPTER 12

UNIT 5

CHAPTER 13

CHAPTER 14

Former slaves during Reconstruction

UNIT 7

America Becomes a World Power 404

(1865–1920)

CHAPTER 18

Jane Addams is shown here celebrating the 40th anniversary of Hull House with children from the settlement house.

CHAPTER 19

Reference Section

CATTLE TRAILS AND WESTERN RAILROADS TO 1890

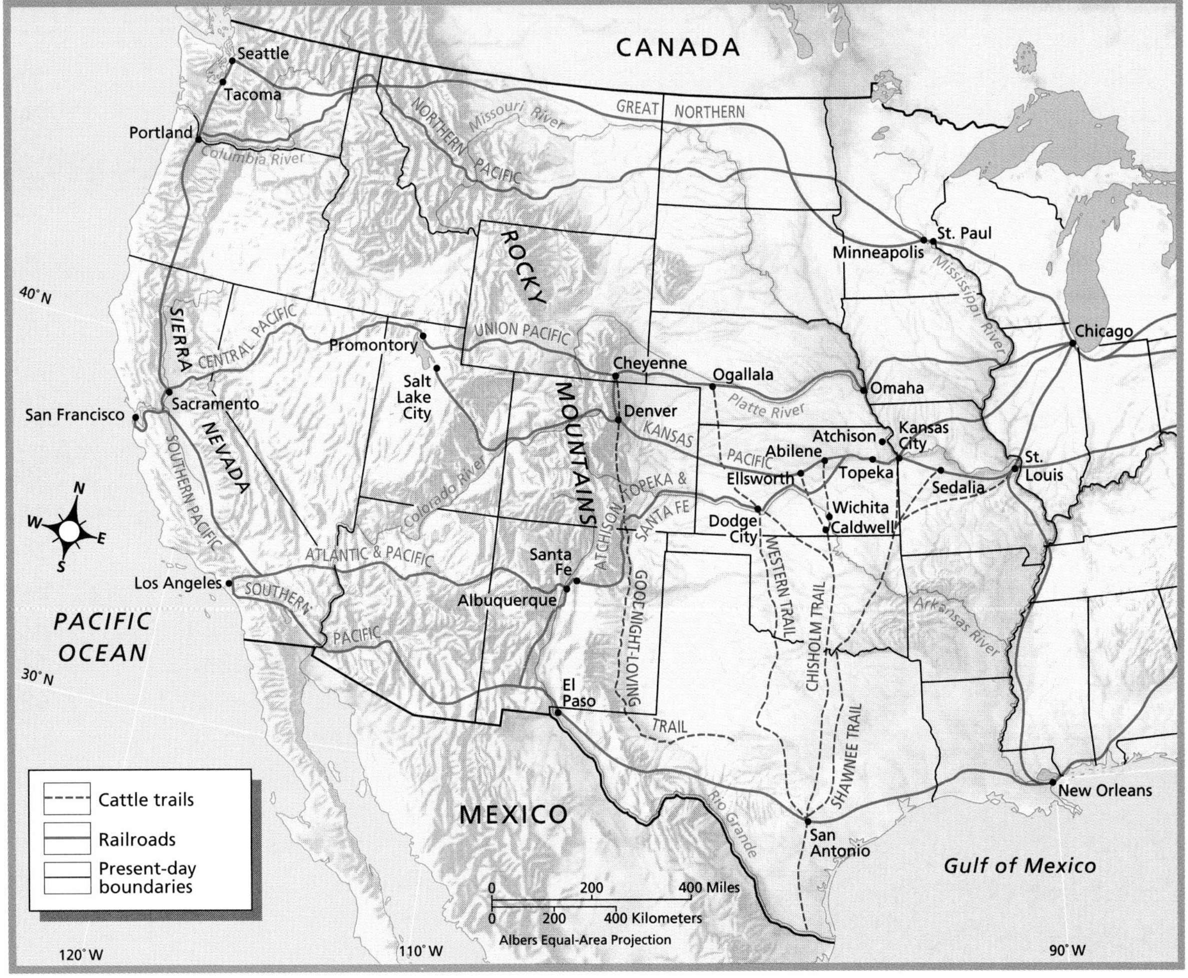

MAPS

COLONIAL PRODUCTS, 1700s

St. Lawrence River
Lake Ontario
Lake Erie
Portsmouth
Albany
Boston
Newport
New Haven
New York
Philadelphia
Baltimore
Jamestown
Norfolk
New Bern
Wilmington
Charles Town
Savannah
ATLANTIC OCEAN
40°N
35°N
30°N
25°N
70°W
75°W
80°W
N
S
E
W
Tobacco
Wheat, flour, bread
Rice
Fish
Indigo
Rum
Timber
Furs
Extent of settlement
0 100 200 Miles
0 100 200 Kilometers
Albers Equal-Area Projection

CHARTS

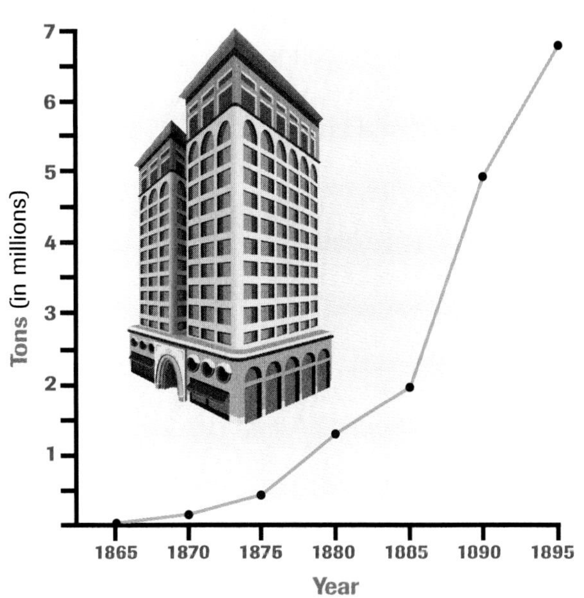
Steel Production, 1865–1895
Tons (in millions)
1
2
3
4
5
6
7
1865
1870
1875
1880
1885
1890
1895
Year

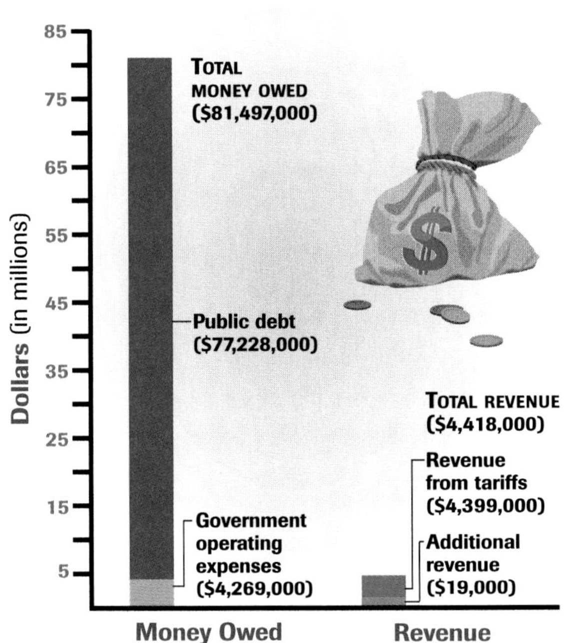
The U.S. Government's Finances 1789–1791
Dollars (in millions)
5
15
25
35
45
55
65
75
85
TOTAL MONEY OWED ($81,497,000)
Public debt ($77,228,000)
Government operating expenses ($4,269,000)
TOTAL REVENUE ($4,418,000)
Revenue from tariffs ($4,399,000)
Additional revenue ($19,000)
Money Owed
Revenue

FEATURES

These children lived on a prosperous southern plantation in the 1800s.

To the Student

Exploring America's Past is a multimedia program. Your textbook is one piece of that program. The program also includes CD-ROMs and videodiscs. As you look through your textbook, you will notice references to material on the CD-ROM. Each resource's location is indicated by a component button and a key word or phrase.

COMPONENT BUTTON ——  Profile

KEY PHRASE —— • **Abraham Lincoln**

Locating Items on the CD-ROM

Follow these easy steps to locate material on the *Exploring America's Past CD-ROM:*

1. Select the appropriate unit on the CD-ROM **Timescape** by clicking on the image that matches the one that appears next to the Themes in American History box at the beginning of each textbook chapter. Then click on the appropriate chapter:

UNIT 1
Chapters 1, 2, 3, and 4

UNIT 2
Chapters 5, 6, and 7

UNIT 3
Chapters 8, 9, and 10

UNIT 4
Chapters 11 and 12

UNIT 5
Chapters 13, 14, and 15

UNIT 6
Chapters 16 and 17

UNIT 7
Chapters 18 and 19

2. When the **Tool Book** appears, select the component that matches the button in the chapter:

Readings

Glossary

Simulation

Gazetteer

Skill Builder

3. If you have selected an Interactive Map, a Time Line, or a Simulation, you will arrive at the beginning of the activity.
4. For all other components, you will arrive at a base screen. To find a specific item, click on the word LIST to view a menu of items. When you have located the title that matches the key word or phrase in your textbook, click the item and it will appear on the screen.

▶ Searching On-Line

The **Tool Book** is a good way to access material when you know the specific database item you want. But what about when you want to find information on a general topic? There are two methods you can use to search for information on the *Exploring America's Past CD-ROM*. The first method is through a menu-driven search. The second method is through a free search. These methods can be used alone or in combination with each other.

The Menu-Driven Search. The menu-driven search enables you to access the database through six broad search categories: TIME PERIOD, REGION, THEMES, MEDIA/COMPONENT, CHAPTER, and KEY TOPIC. Although it is possible to search the database using only one category, your search will be very general. If, for example, you select Chapter 1 from the CHAPTER category, you will get a list of every database item associated with Chapter 1. That would be a very long list!

You can narrow your search by using AND and OR to combine up to three search categories. AND and OR are known as Boolean operators. Boolean operators help you narrow or expand your search. In most cases you will want to begin your search by using AND to find specific matches. If this search is unsuccessful, you can use OR to broaden the search. You will come up with different search results depending on how you position AND and OR. Let's look at an example to see what we mean.

Suppose that you want to collect information on Abraham Lincoln's presidency. There are several ways that you can build a search. One possibility would be to use AND to combine the following search categories:

TIME PERIOD: 1850–1900
AND
REGION: United States
AND
KEY TOPIC: Presidents/Presidency

This search will find any database item that meets *all three* criteria. The diagram on the next page presents this idea graphically. The gray area represents the items that meet all three criteria—that is, any item associated with a U.S. president who served between 1850 and 1900.

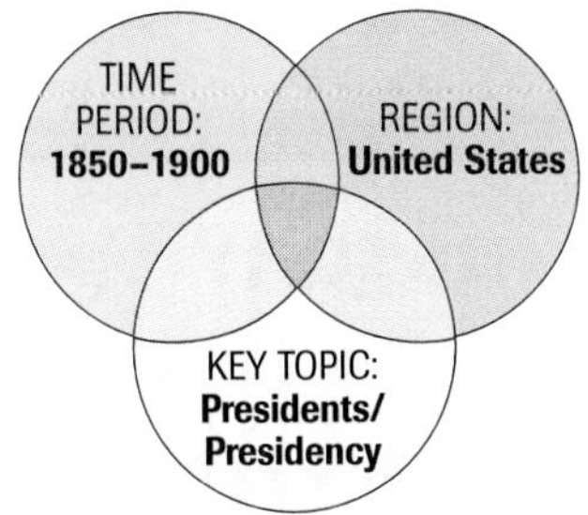

Items related to Abraham Lincoln's presidency fall in the gray area and would thus be included on the search-results list. However, the list will also include items on *any president* who served between 1850 and 1900.

Using Free Search to Narrow Your Search. If your first search attempt yields too much information that is not directly related to your search topic, you can narrow your search by changing one of the categories to FREE SEARCH. In the above example, for instance, you might replace the REGION category with FREE SEARCH: Abraham Lincoln.

TIME PERIOD: 1850–1900
AND
KEY TOPIC: Presidents/Presidency
AND
FREE SEARCH: Abraham Lincoln

This search will locate only those items related to Abraham Lincoln's presidency.

Expanding Your Search. Since the above search includes the KEY TOPIC: Presidents/Presidency category and the AND Boolean operator, it will not call up information on Lincoln's life before he ran for president. Suppose that you decide you want more information on Abraham Lincoln's political life than just his years as president. You can broaden your search by using the OR operator:

KEY TOPIC: Presidents/Presidency
OR
KEY TOPIC: Politics/Political Parties
AND
FREE SEARCH: Abraham Lincoln

As the diagram at the top of the next column illustrates, this search will locate any items related to Lincoln's political career.

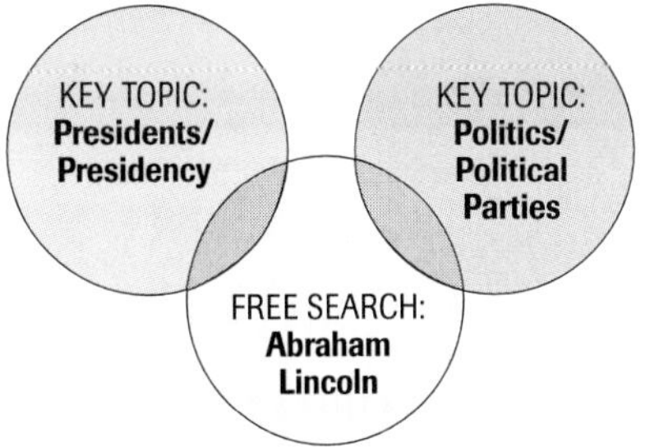

Using all ORs will yield very different results. For example, if you replace the AND in the above search with an OR, you will locate all of the items on the database related to the presidency and individual presidents, all of the items related to politics and political parties, and all of the items related to Abraham Lincoln, regardless of time period or region of the world:

Tips for Using Free Search. How you phrase your FREE SEARCH entry will determine whether your search is broad or narrow. If you type in Presidents you will locate all of the items that are associated with any of the presidents. However, if you type in President Abraham Lincoln, you will locate only those items associated with President Lincoln.

If for some reason there are no exact matches to what you typed in, FREE SEARCH will automatically alert you to this fact and break your search down into the separate words. It will then retrieve every item associated with President, every item associated with Abraham, and every item associated with Lincoln.

One final note about FREE SEARCH—it does not care whether you use lowercase or uppercase letters. PRESIDENTS, PrEsIdEnTs, presidents, and PRESidents will all be treated the same.

Have **FUN** using the CD-ROM!

THEMES IN AMERICAN HISTORY

Exploring America's Past begins every chapter with a set of theme questions. These questions are drawn from seven broad themes central to American history: Global Relations, Constitutional Heritage, Democratic Values, Technology and Society, Geographic Diversity, Cultural Diversity, and Economic Development. These themes provide a framework for the historical events in each chapter. This framework will help you understand the connections between historical events and see how past events relate to the social, political, and economic challenges our nation faces today.

As you begin each chapter, examine the theme questions and answer them based on your own experiences or prior knowledge. As you read the chapter, explore how the theme questions relate to the chapter's history. By tracing the themes through the book, you will be able to see how each theme has developed over time.

• Global Relations

From the time thousands of years ago, when the first Asian nomads crossed a land bridge to the North American continent, America has been involved in global events. The Global Relations theme invites you to trace ways in which our nation's political, social, and economic development has affected—and been affected by—other countries and their people.

• Constitutional Heritage

No study of American history would be complete without examining the U.S. Constitution, the document that provides the legal framework for our democratic government. The Constitutional Heritage theme will help you understand the Constitution's origins and how it has evolved through constitutional amendments, Supreme Court rulings, and congressional actions. This theme also explores how individuals and different groups in the nation's history have influenced the Constitution and have been affected by it. Finally, this theme asks you to consider how the relationship between Americans and their government has changed over time.

• Democratic Values

Throughout our history, Americans have struggled to define, possess, and protect individual rights and personal freedoms, such as the freedom of speech and religion, the right to vote, and the right to privacy. The Democratic Values theme examines how changing social, economic, and political conditions have influenced the theory and practices of these rights and freedoms. This theme also explores the many conflicts that have arisen over these democratic values, and Americans' attempts to resolve these conflicts.

• Technology and Society

From the Hopi and Zuñi Indians' use of adobe bricks in building cliff villages hundreds of years ago to the computers that help you with school assignments and personal projects today, technology has influenced every aspect of our culture and society. The Technology and Society theme explores technological developments and their influence on the U.S. economy and life.

• Geographic Diversity

The Geographic Diversity theme explores ways in which the nation's vast and diverse geography has played an important role in American history. The theme examines how the development of the nation's resources has helped shape its economy, society, and politics. In addition, the Geographic Diversity theme traces how public and government attitudes about resources and the environment have changed over time.

- **Cultural Diversity**

Our nation's rich and unique culture comes from its many different ethnic, racial, and religious groups. The Cultural Diversity theme examines America's experiences in dealing with diverse culture groups from the time of the Spanish explorers to recent immigration from around the world.

- **Economic Development**

President Calvin Coolidge said in 1925 that "the business of America is business." The Economic Development theme asks you to explore the close relationship between history and economics that has shaped the United States. This theme traces the relationship between government, business, and labor in America. It examines how the growth of a strong national economy has influenced the country's domestic and foreign politics, as well as individual lives and American society in general.

GEOGRAPHY THEMES

History and geography share many common elements. History describes the events that have taken place from ancient times until the present day. Geography describes how physical environments affect human events and how people influence the environment around them. To describe a series of events without placing them in their physical settings is to tell only part of the story. Geographers have developed five themes—location, place, region, movement, and human-environment interaction—to organize information.

▶ **Location** describes a site's position. This is the spot on the earth where something is found, often expressed in terms of its position in relation to other places.

▶ **Place** refers to the physical features and human influences that define a particular site on the earth and make it different from other sites. Physical features include landscape, climate, and vegetation. Human influences include land use, architecture, and population size.

▶ **Region** is the common cultural or physical features of an area that distinguishes it from other areas. One region may be different from another area because of physical characteristics, such as landforms or climate, or because of cultural features, such as dominant languages or religions.

▶ **Movement** describes the way people interact as they travel, communicate, and trade goods and services. Movement includes human migration as well as the exchange of goods and ideas.

▶ **Human-environment interaction** deals with the ways in which people interact with their natural environments, like clearing forests or building cities. This theme is particularly important to the study of history in that it shows how people shape and are shaped by their surroundings.

unit 1 

AMERICAN BEGINNINGS (BEGINNINGS–1763)

Chapter 1
Worlds Meet (Beginnings–1500)

Chapter 2
Empires in the Americas (1500–1700)

Chapter 3
The English Colonies (1607–1752)

Chapter 4
Colonial Life and Government (1650–1763)

This painting shows how one artist imagined an early American Indian settlement might have looked before the Indians came into contact with Europeans.

Courtesy of the Witte Museum, San Antonio, Texas

Linking Past to Present
American Indian Rituals

Every year around July 4th a group of middle-school-aged girls gather in brightly colored clothing to participate in a ritual that has been practiced in their community for centuries. Although the girls live in the United States, this celebration does not focus on American independence from Great Britain. Instead, these Apache girls are celebrating their passage from childhood into adulthood. For four days, all the members of the local Apache community will sing, dance, eat, make crafts, and perform traditional rituals.

Throughout the United States many young American Indians participate in similar rituals that celebrate the passage through four stages of life—infancy, childhood, adulthood, and old age. The Apache ceremony signifies the important place that women have traditionally held in the community. Apache children trace their heritage through their mother's family line.

The process of carrying on the Apache traditions often requires memorizing hours of songs and stories. The songs sung over the four-day ceremony are never written down or recorded because they are considered to be sacred. These songs must be memorized by the performers and passed down verbally from one generation to the next.

In continuing to participate in these types of ceremonies, modern American Indians try to maintain a link to a world that was changed forever when Europeans came to the Native Americas around 1500. As you read this unit, you will learn what little we know about Native American civilizations before that time and how they were changed by contact with Europeans.

It is hard to be certain how closely modern rituals follow those of American Indians before 1500. Many of the rituals that are performed today have probably changed gradually over time. The July date of the Apache ceremony, for example, was determined by events in the late 1800s. At that time the Apaches were only allowed to gather in large groups around the time of American Independence Day. As you will learn, however, we do know that many parts of such rituals, including stories told, food prepared, crafts made, and styles of dances performed, resemble those observed by the first Europeans who encountered Native Americans some 500 years ago.

Many young American Indians, like this girl from Oklahoma, wear traditional clothing for special ceremonies.

Travelpix/FPG International

CHAPTER 1

Worlds Meet
(Beginnings–1500)

THEMES IN AMERICAN HISTORY

Cultural Diversity:
How might cross-cultural interactions change a society?

Geographic Diversity:
How might people adapt to their physical environment?

Global Relations:
How might the growth of trade affect a society's development?

• **Video Opener**

• **Skill Builder**

In his novel Alaska, *writer James A. Michener imagined what the first travelers to North America were like:*

"On small sleds with runners of antler and bone, the travelers dragged behind them . . . bone needles, skins not yet sewn into clothing, shallow bowls carved from heavy wood or bone, long-handled cooking spoons of ivory. . . . Men and women alike knew hundreds of rules for surviving an arctic winter."

image above: *Early Native American pottery*

Section 1
THE FIRST AMERICANS

Multimedia Connections

Explore these related topics and materials on the CD–ROM to enrich your understanding of this section:

Gazetteer
- Bering Strait
- Mesoamerica
- North America
- South America

Media Bank
- Tlingit Artifact
- American Indian Music

Profiles
- Leif Eriksson

Atlas
- American Landscape

Readings
- Creation Myths

Sometime around A.D. 1000, European explorer Leif Eriksson established a camp in Newfoundland. Eriksson visited many nearby areas, including a region with "wheatfields growing wild . . . also those trees which are called maple." Could this have been part of what is now the United States? We do not know. We do know, however, that the explorers met people in this land. These people were descendants of ancient travelers who arrived long before the Europeans.

As you read this section you will find out:

- **How the first Americans arrived, and where they came from.**
- **How hunter-gatherers differed from farming communities.**
- **What some early American societies were like.**

The Great Migration

Today Asia is separated from North America by the Bering Strait, a body of water between Alaska and Siberia more than 50 miles wide. When the first people arrived in North America from Asia, however, instead of water there was dry land. The earth was then passing through a great **Ice Age**, a period when the weather was much colder than it is now. During the Ice Age, moisture that in warmer times would have fallen as rain and drained back into the oceans fell as snow instead.

Gradually, far more snow piled up in the northern regions of the earth than could melt. Vast ice fields called **glaciers** formed. So much water was trapped in these glaciers that the water level of the oceans dropped sharply, exposing a land bridge across what is now the Bering Strait.

Eventually, animals and plants passed across the land bridge and spread throughout North America. The bones of ancient Asian elephants, called mammoths, have been found in dozens of places in the United States. Following the animals came people—the first Americans. No one knows exactly when the first Americans arrived because no historian made written records of the adventures of these pioneers. The early Americans were probably following the great herds of wild game.

Scholars disagree as to when these overland crossings began. Estimates range from 12,000 to more than 50,000 years ago. They ended about 10,000 years ago as melting glaciers signaled the end of the Ice Age. Although the Bering land bridge gradually disappeared beneath the rising ocean, some **migration**, or movement from one place to another, continued in small boats until possibly as late as 1000 B.C.

MIGRATION TO THE AMERICAS

Learning from Maps. Early nomadic peoples from Asia took thousands of years to spread throughout the Americas.

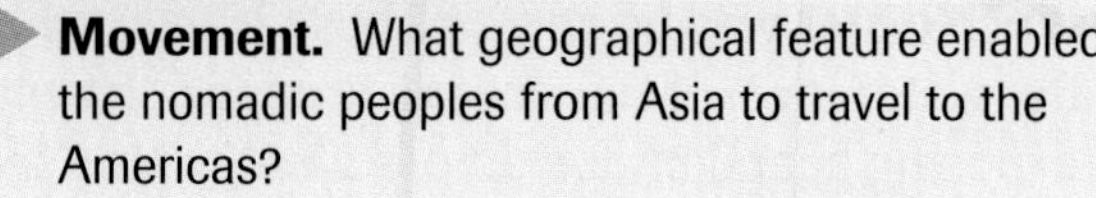

Movement. What geographical feature enabled the nomadic peoples from Asia to travel to the Americas?

• Maps

Early Societies

Once in North America, the first Americans and their descendants moved slowly to the south and east, following the game animals. They eventually settled in places as far apart as present-day New England and the southern tip of South America. Thousands of years and many generations passed before they spread over all this land.

As they advanced, the early Americans formed **societies**, each with its own distinct **culture**. Societies are groups of people that live and work together and that have common values and customs. The culture of a society consists of those common values and customs—such as language, government, and family relationships. The objects that the people create are also part of their culture.

Whenever these early Americans migrated, they

had to adapt to the different environments they encountered. Some groups made their homes in fertile valleys, others in tropical rain forests. Some settled in the mountains or in deserts. Some hunted game and gathered wild plants, roaming constantly in search of food. These **hunter-gatherers**, as they are now known, generally traveled in small groups. Their homes were usually natural shelters like caves, or tepees they carried with them as they wandered. Where climate and soil were favorable, others took up farming. Farmers soon built permanent shelters and gradually gave up their roaming ways. Farming communities were generally larger than the communities of hunter-gatherers.

The Maya built many detailed statues in Mesoamerica such as this one, which still stands in Honduras.

Maize, or corn, was the most important food crop grown in the Americas. Groups in present-day Mexico were growing it perhaps as early as 8000 B.C. As supplies of maize increased, the farmers began to trade the surplus with other communities. Around 3500 B.C. the desert people of what is now the southwestern United States also began to grow maize. Experts believe that these early farmers learned this technique from contact with their southern neighbors.

Early Native Americans used arrowheads like these to hunt big game.

• Mammoth

The success of agriculture in Mexico and Central America—the region often known as Mesoamerica—enabled the area to support many millions of people. As the population grew, large cities and complex societies gradually formed.

One of the most important Mesoamerican societies was that of the Maya, who thrived from about A.D. 300 to 800. The Maya developed a complex irrigation system that enabled them to produce enough food to support their large population. They also had a system of writing that used **glyphs**, or pictures. Researchers who study these glyphs have uncovered much of the history of the Maya and other early peoples.

• Uncovering the past

North American Societies

Scholars believe that by 1492 there were 1 to 2 million people living in what is now the United States and Canada. Today we refer to these people and their descendants as Native Americans or American Indians. They were not a single group with a common culture, however. Native Americans were organized into a wide variety of tribes, each with its own culture. Because environment had a strong effect on cultural development, tribes within a common geographic area tended to share many characteristics. For that reason, experts often group tribes by **culture area**. A culture area is a geographic region whose residents share common cultural traits.

The eastern culture areas. The Cayuga, Mohawk, Oneida, Onondaga, and Seneca

NATIVE AMERICAN CULTURE AREAS

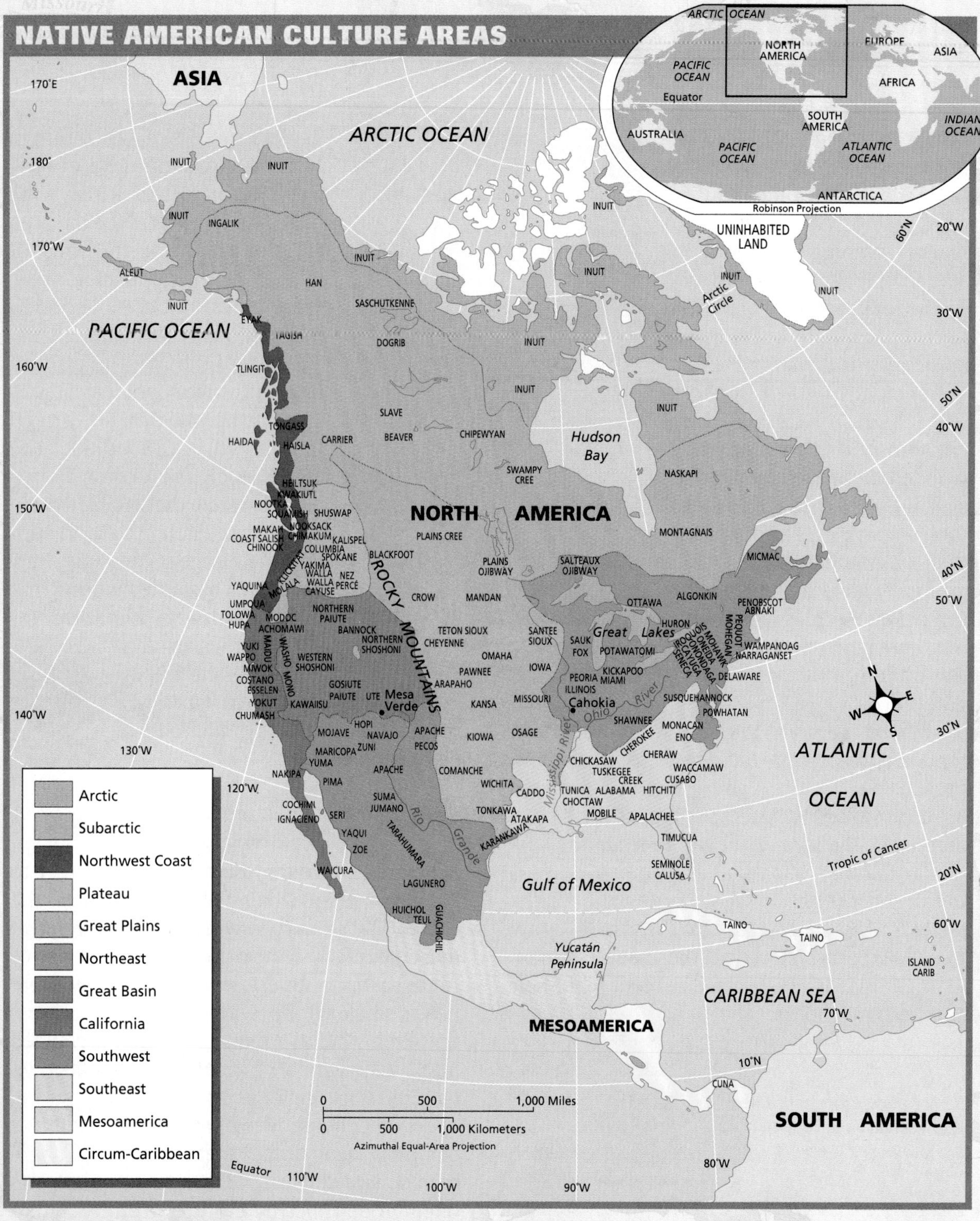

- Arctic
- Subarctic
- Northwest Coast
- Plateau
- Great Plains
- Northeast
- Great Basin
- California
- Southwest
- Southeast
- Mesoamerica
- Circum-Caribbean

0 500 1,000 Miles
0 500 1,000 Kilometers
Azimuthal Equal-Area Projection

Learning from Maps. Before 1500, many different Native American cultures inhabited the Americas. Many of these thriving cultures had adapted to a wide range of climatic and geographical regions.

• Maps

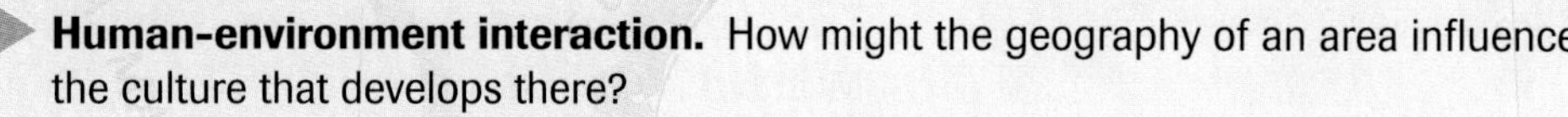

▶ **Human-environment interaction.** How might the geography of an area influence the culture that develops there?

tribes of the *Northeast* culture area lived in the densely wooded central region of what is now New York State. Later, they banded together as the Five Nations, or **Iroquois League**.

The Iroquois League was powerful because of its brave warriors and the alliances among its communities. As in many tribes, Iroquois men usually hunted while the women farmed. Iroquois women also played important roles in tribal decision making. For example, women were in charge of nominating members to the tribal council. They also had a voice in declaring war and making treaties.

This ruin of a cliff dwelling at Mesa Verde, Colorado, is one of the most well-preserved examples of an ancient southwestern community. Over the years the cliffs helped protect the structure from harm.

• Indian Ruins

The various peoples of the *Southeast* culture area were mostly farmers. They lived in the lower Mississippi River valley. Europeans later called these groups the "Five Civilized Tribes," which included the Cherokee, Chickasaw, Choctaw, Creek, and Seminole.

These peoples used timber from the dense forests around them to make everything from farming tools to fences to small houses. They also wove fine baskets. The Creek formed well-organized towns, with their homes arranged around a public square and a council house.

The western culture areas. In the *Southwest* culture area the Hopi and the Zuni people built with adobe—sun-baked brick plastered with mud. Their homes looked somewhat like modern apartment buildings. Some were four stories high and contained quarters for perhaps 1,000 people, along with storerooms for grain and other crops. These homes were usually built against cliffs, both to make construction easier and to help with defense against enemies. Later European explorers called these adobe homes **pueblos**, meaning "towns."

In the *California* culture area, groups such as the Miwok and the Hupa lived off acorns, fish, deer, and other plants and animals. This area was so fertile that it supported the densest population in what is now the United States. Most of the people lived in groups so small they are often called tribelets rather than tribes.

The Kwakiutl, Nootka, and Chinook of the *Northwest Coast* culture area lived mostly on salmon and other fish. Magnificent forests of redwood, pine, and cedar supplied lumber for their homes, canoes, and totem poles.

Farther inland, the *Plateau* culture area lay between the Cascade and Rocky Mountains. The people of this region, such as the Modoc, Nez Percé, and Cayuse, lived in small villages along the numerous, fast-flowing mountain rivers of the region. They ate mostly fish. Although their villages were independent, the people stayed in close contact with one another through river trade.

The *Great Basin* culture area was also located in mountainous country, but life was much harsher than in the Plateau area. Tribes such as the Shoshoni and the Ute wandered in small bands through dry, rugged lands. They gathered berries and nuts and hunted small animals such as rabbits and snakes. The Great Basin peoples are sometimes referred to as the "diggers" because they often had to dig for roots to survive.

The Great Plains and far north. In the 1400s most of the residents of the dry, treeless grassland known as the *Great Plains* were traveling farmers and hunters of small game. This included groups such as the Pawnee. When the soil in one spot wore out, they moved on. This changed after European explorers and settlers introduced horses to the Americas. Horses transformed the Great Plains tribes into hunting societies that lived off the mighty buffalo.

Far to the north lived the people of the *Arctic* and *Subarctic* culture areas. They included the Inuit, who became known to Europeans as Eskimos, an Indian word meaning "eaters of raw meat." They hunted seals, walruses, and whales. Some groups fished for salmon and hunted caribou. Because trees did not grow that far north, the Inuit often lived in igloos built of blocks of packed snow. The Inuit were probably the people Leif Eriksson and his followers met when they first arrived in North America.

• Viking Sagas

This finely crafted gold, silver, and bronze jewelry was worn by a person from the native land of Leif Eriksson, one of the first known Europeans to visit North America. Well known as great warriors and explorers, the Scandinavians were also skilled craftspeople.

The Granger Collection, New York

Section 1 Review

• Glossary

IDENTIFY and explain the significance of the following: Ice Age, glaciers, migration, societies, culture, hunter-gatherers, maize, glyphs, culture area, Iroquois League, pueblos

LOCATE and explain the importance of the following: Bering Strait, Mesoamerica

• Gazetteer

REVIEWING FOR DETAILS

1. How did hunter-gatherer and farming societies differ?
2. What were some of the main traits of people in each culture area?

REVIEWING FOR UNDERSTANDING

3. **Geographic Literacy** Describe how the first North Americans arrived on the continent.
4. **Writing Mastery:** *Describing* Imagine you are a member of an early American society. Write a poem describing some aspects of your daily life.
5. **Critical Thinking:** *Cause and Effect* Why did lifestyles in the Native American culture areas vary so much?

Section 2
THE LURE OF TRADE

Multimedia Connections

Explore these related topics and materials on the CD-ROM to enrich your understanding of this section:

Atlas

- Medieval Trade Routes

Gazetteer

- Europe
- Africa
- Asia

Media Bank

- Medieval Church
- Medieval Life
- Marco Polo
- Western Africa
- Medieval Warfare
- Astronomy
- Astrolabe
- Manorial Life
- Diamond Sutra
- Italian Port

Profiles

- Ibn Battuta
- Mansa Musa
- Marco Polo
- Zheng He

Readings

- Marco Polo
- King Mbemba

In 1271 the emperor of China invited Italian merchants Niccolò and Maffeo Polo to visit his country. Niccolò's teenage son, Marco, went along. They returned home some 25 years later with amazing stories about the places they had been. As Europeans read Marco Polo's account of his travels, their interest in Asian goods grew. Many years passed, however, before Europe took a leading role in trade and exploration.

As you read this section you will find out:

- **Where global trade was most active before A.D. 1000.**
- **How religion influenced the growth of trade and cross-cultural interactions.**
- **How the Commercial Revolution and new technologies affected Europe.**

Europe in the Year 1000

If Leif Eriksson's crew could make their way to North America, why did no other Europeans do so for such a long time? There were several reasons for the delay.

Nations as we know them did not yet exist. True, there were kings of regions like England and France, but these rulers had relatively little power. Instead, land was divided up into sections called **manors**, which were ruled by nobles known as lords.

Each manor was a tiny world in itself. Peasants called **serfs** worked the lord's fields. Serfs labored to feed themselves and their families, but a large part of what they produced went to the lord of the manor. The manors were practically independent—the manor community produced nearly everything its members ate, wore, or used.

The residents of the manors also had to help protect the land from outside invaders. Between A.D. 600 and 1000 the manors faced constant attacks from Scandinavians and eastern European groups.

Manor life did have advantages. Everyone knew what to expect of everyone else. But it was a narrow existence in a small world. Most people lacked not only the wealth and free time to explore but also the urge to do so.

African Trading Kingdoms

While Europeans and the people of the Americas were living in relative isolation, people in Africa and Asia were exploring new lands and establishing extensive trade networks. By the 700s some Africans on the east coast were trading with Arab peoples across the Red Sea.

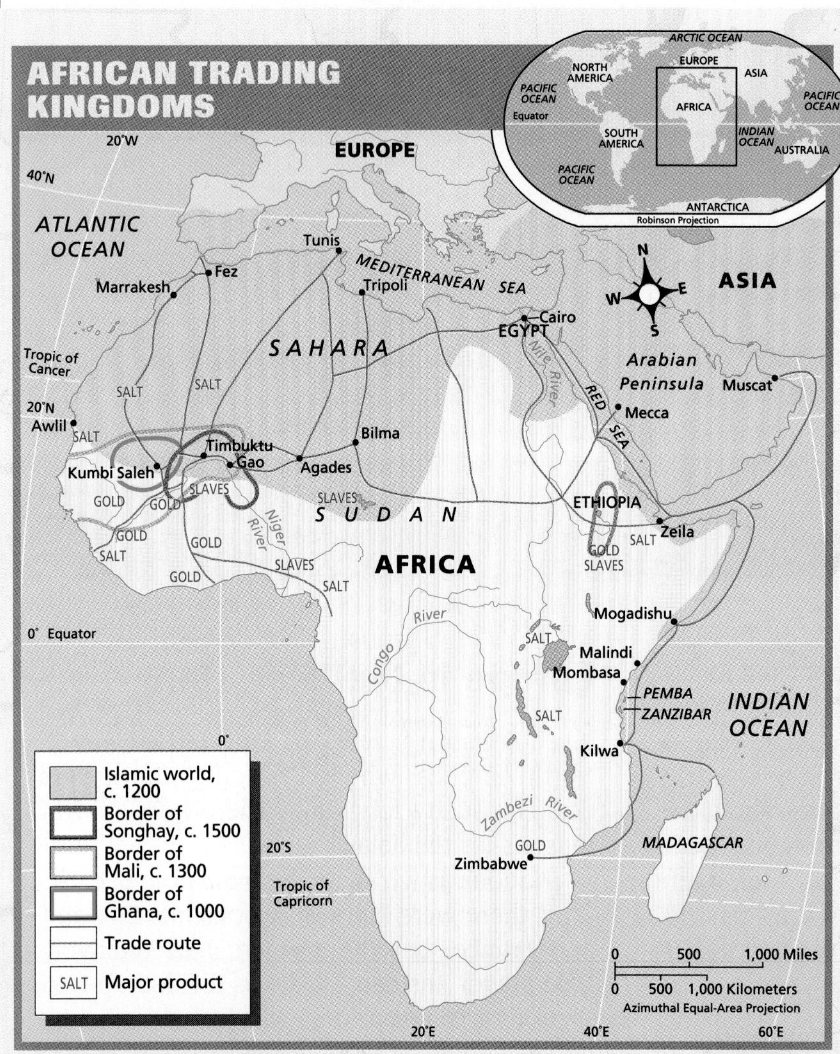

Learning from Maps.
The African trade routes allowed the exchange of goods and knowledge between cultures.

Region. According to the map, what three products come from the region west of the Niger River, south of Mali, and bordered to the south and west by the Atlantic Ocean?

• Maps

Other trade routes brought the desert peoples of the north into contact with the inhabitants of West Africa. Merchants from North Africa traveled south across the Sahara Desert to the kingdoms of Ghana and Mali. In these kingdoms, the merchants exchanged cloth, salt, and copper for gold and also for slaves needed to work in desert salt mines. According to one African historian, merchants from the Arabian Peninsula, attracted by gold, "came with many caravans of camels" to the trading cities.

Trade with these Arab peoples had a great influence on life in the African kingdoms, and African cultures had a strong influence on the Arabs. On the African east coast, for example, new languages developed. One of the most important was Swahili (swah-HEE-lee), a mixture of African Bantu languages and Arabic.

The most significant cultural change resulting from these trading ties, however, was the spread of the Islamic religion.

Islam and Trade

In 610 Muhammad, a merchant who lived in the Arabian Peninsula, reported experiencing a holy vision. He founded a religion called Islam and dedicated his life to preaching the message of God, whom he called Allah. Like Judaism and Christianity, Islam emphasized the existence of only one god, honor toward parents, and kindness to others. Above all, the faith stressed devotion to Allah. Islam soon attracted many followers, who became known as **Muslims**.

After Muhammad's death, his followers organized his teachings into a holy book called the Qur'an (kuh-RAN), which Muslims carried with them as they spread the faith through trade and conquest. Muslim merchants soon controlled trade between Asia and Africa.

Sometimes the spread of the Muslim faith and culture caused problems. The powerful African empire of Ghana became divided over religion as the number of Muslim residents increased. The king, Tunka Manin, supported Ghana's traditional religion, which taught that the world was run by numerous spirits found in nature. This idea conflicted with the Muslim belief in one supreme god.

In 1076 Muslims from North Africa invaded the kingdom of Ghana and made it a Muslim nation. Internal religious conflict continued, however. As Ghana declined, it was gradually replaced by the Muslim kingdom of Mali.

This early brass statue from Benin, West Africa, shows an African man blowing a horn.

• Mansa Musa

• Views of Africa

The Granger Collection, New York

Trade caravans like this one moved Asian goods across the desert to Europe. Although demand for Asian goods was high, the journey to get such goods was often difficult.

• Commerce

Mali reached its peak under the leadership of Mansa Musa, a Muslim who ruled from 1307 to 1332. In 1324 Mansa Musa made a **pilgrimage**, or religious journey, to Mecca, the holy city of Islam. He also used the trip to show off Mali's great wealth and to expand its trading connections. Ibn Fadl Allah al Omari (ib-uhn FAHD AH-lah ah oo-MAHR-ee), an attendant to the Egyptian pharaoh, recalled his impression of Mansa Musa:

> **"He is the king who is the most powerful, the richest, the most fortunate, and the most feared by his enemies and the most able to do good to those around him."**

Stories of Mansa Musa's magnificent kingdom spread as far as western Europe. An atlas prepared for King Charles V of France pictured Mansa Musa, sitting on a throne holding a large gold nugget.

Cultures Cross

The growth of trade brought many different cultures into contact. In their vast travels, Muslim traders took elements of their culture to distant lands. They also brought new ideas back to their own civilization. Knowledge gained from Muslim mapmakers improved the maps of the known world. The city of Timbuktu (tim-buhk-TOO) in Mali became a center of learning in the Muslim world. It contained 180 Islamic schools and three universities. The university libraries housed large collections of Greek, Roman, and Arabic manuscripts on subjects such as religion, poetry, astronomy, and medicine.

Muslims also came into contact with other Asian cultures. Ideas from China and India, for example, helped Arab mathematicians perfect their numbering system and advance the study of algebra. As in Africa, such knowledge spread across Asia largely as a result of cross-cultural trade.

Contact between China and the Arab world existed for centuries along a network of trade routes known as the **Silk Road**. However, China's rulers tried to keep foreign contacts to a minimum, so few outsiders were allowed to enter the country and few Chinese ever left. Thus, most merchants did not travel over the entire Silk Road. Instead, goods passed from one trader to another in the numerous towns that grew up along the routes.

Camel caravans carried Chinese silk, tea, spices, porcelain, and cotton linens over mountains and deserts, all the way to the Mediterranean Sea. When Europeans encountered all the products of this vast trading network, they began to expand their interest in world trade.

Through Others' Eyes

Chinese Trading Voyages

In the early 1400s the emperor of China sponsored seven large naval expeditions to expand trade and increase China's reputation in the world. These voyages spanned Southeast Asia and reached west to the Arabian Peninsula and Africa. Although the Chinese typically viewed other peoples as "barbarians," they were favorably impressed by Islamic culture. In 1432 one expedition member recorded his impressions of Mecca, one of the most important cities in the Muslim world:

> *"The people of this country are stalwart [strong] and fine-looking. . . . The customs of the people are pacific [peaceful] and admirable. There are no poverty-stricken families. They all observe the precepts [rules] of their religion, and law-breakers are few. It is in truth a most happy country."*

Although China's naval expeditions ended in 1433, they had a lasting effect on Europe. The Chinese voyages increased European explorers' desire to find a water route for trade with East Asia.

The Crusades

What helped thrust Europeans into further contact with the rest of the world, however, was the **Crusades**, a series of religious wars. These wars were fought for control of Palestine, an area in Southwest Asia that was sacred to Muslims, Jews, and Christians.

Since the early 600s Palestine had been ruled by Muslims. Around the year 1000, the Muslim ruler of Palestine began persecuting Christians in the region. In 1095 Pope Urban II summoned Catholics to launch a crusade (from the Latin word for "cross") to drive the Muslims out of Palestine.

Thousands of European people eagerly responded to the pope's call. They sewed crosses to their garments and marched off to Palestine. This Crusade failed, but in 1099, a second wave of Crusaders captured the city of Jerusalem. However, the Muslims did not willingly give up a region that was equally holy to their faith. On and off for the next 200 years, war raged in and around Palestine.

Gradually, the Muslims pushed the Christians back. The Muslim sultan

Saladin's forces recaptured the city of Jerusalem in 1187. Europeans organized several more crusades to try to regain the lost territory. Finally, Acre, the last Christian city in the region, surrendered to the Muslims in 1291.

These Crusades caused great changes in how Europeans thought and acted. The Crusaders returned from Palestine with new interests and tastes, which they communicated to friends and family. In addition, Europeans had been trading for Asian goods in the eastern Mediterranean for many years. With increasingly more contact between Europeans and Asians, the desire for Asian goods such as spices, cotton and silk cloth, and Chinese plates and vases quickly spread across Europe.

Christians and Muslims fought many bloody battles during the Crusades.

Europe Stirs to New Ideas

In the 1300s shortly after the end of the last Crusade, the first of many waves of a deadly disease known as the **Black Death** struck Europe. The Black Death swept across the continent, killing somewhere between 25 and 50 percent of Europe's population.

Economic recovery. By the 1400s, however, Europeans had begun to recover from this terrible disaster. Trade revived between Europe and Asia and fed a growing European economy. To pay for desired Asian products, Europeans produced more goods of their own. They manufactured more woolen cloth, trapped more fur-bearing animals, and cut more lumber. This rapid growth in the European economy produced what became known as the **Commercial Revolution**.

Other factors also contributed to the Commercial Revolution. With the great decrease in population caused by the Black Death, by the 1400s it took fewer farmers to produce enough food to meet society's needs. Since farming now required fewer workers, many people left the manors for towns. Towns grew into cities filled with **artisans**, people who crafted items by hand.

• Crusades

Life generally became more exciting—and also more uncertain and dangerous. Trade between East and West made merchants and bankers more important. They needed strong rulers who would build roads, protect trade routes against robbers, and keep the peace. Merchants and bankers lent money to these rulers, who used the funds to raise armies to protect their lands.

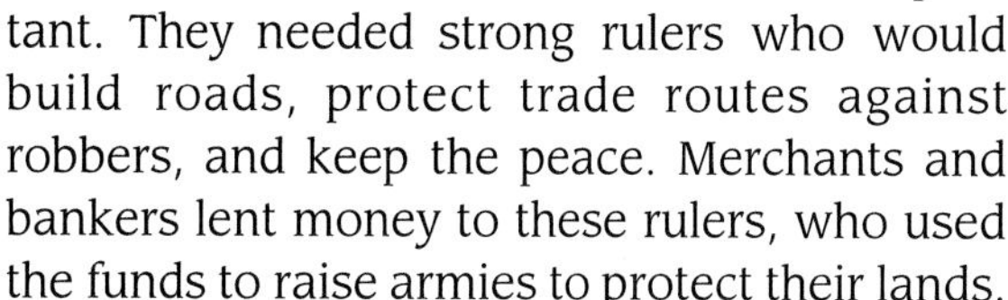

Merchants and kings helped one another. The kings became more powerful, and the merchants grew richer. As a result, the European economy expanded. At the same time, the power of the Catholic Church began to decline, but the religious ideals that inspired the Crusades were not forgotten.

Printing. Advances in printing technology during the 1450s made by Johannes Gutenberg of Germany helped to break down some barriers for people. (Printing was originally a Chinese invention.) With Gutenberg's press, a printer could make any number of copies of a book simply by setting the type once. It was no longer necessary to copy manuscripts by hand. Books became much cheaper. As a result, many more people learned to read. They improved their minds with the powerful new knowledge found in books.

The Granger Collection, New York

This engraving shows how Europeans made books after the printing press was invented. Although the printing press made the process faster, it still took many workers to make books.

• **Medieval Technology**

New technologies. Leif Eriksson and his crew had crossed the Atlantic with just a few crude instruments to guide them by the stars and sun. In cloudy weather they could only guess their location and hope for the best. By the 1400s great improvements had been made in designing and sailing ships. The compass had been invented in China and introduced to European mariners by Arab traders. Its magnetized needle always pointed north, which enabled sailors to know their direction even when the sun and stars were hidden by clouds.

Sailors were also using the **astrolabe**, an instrument that helped them figure out a ship's **latitude**—that is, its distance north or south of the equator. These instruments made navigation more accurate. Soon larger ships were being designed and built. The stage was set for Europeans to explore many other parts of the world.

Section 2 Review

• **Glossary**

• **Gazetteer**

IDENTIFY and explain the significance of the following: manors, serfs, Muslims, Mansa Musa, pilgrimage, Silk Road, Crusades, Black Death, Commercial Revolution, artisans, astrolabe, latitude

LOCATE and explain the importance of the following: Ghana, Mali, Timbuktu

REVIEWING FOR DETAILS

1. What regions were most active in world trade before A.D. 1000?
2. How did religion affect trade and cross-cultural interactions?
3. What impact did the Commercial Revolution and new technologies have on Europe?

REVIEWING FOR UNDERSTANDING

4. **Geographic Literacy** How might the location of the Arabian Peninsula have helped increase the role of Muslim merchants in world trade?
5. **Critical Thinking:** *Drawing Conclusions* Why might the existence of manors have discouraged trade among various parts of Europe?

Section 3
EUROPEANS LOOK TO THE SEA

Multimedia Connections
Explore these related topics and materials on the CD-ROM to enrich your understanding of this section:

Gazetteer
- Portugal
- Spain
- Hispaniola

Media Bank
- *Niña, Pinta,* and *Santa María*
- Vasco da Gama

Readings
- Taino

Profiles
- Bartolomeu Dias
- Kublai Khan
- Prince Henry
- Queen Isabella
- Vasco da Gama

As Europeans extended their trading ties, they began to look for other routes to East Asia. At first, they sought a water route around Africa. Some bold adventurers had different ideas, however. They talked of reaching the East by sailing west. An Italian sailor who worked for Spain actually tried to prove it could be done. The unexpected outcome to his voyage secured his place in history and changed the world forever.

As you read this section you will find out:

- **Why Europeans wanted to find a water route to East Asia.**
- **How Columbus planned to get to East Asia.**
- **What Columbus thought about the land and peoples he encountered.**

Getting Around Africa

Italian merchants had long held control over Europe's trade with Asia. Ships sailed from Venice, Naples, and other Italian ports carrying products such as cloth and furs to Constantinople. They brought back the silks, spices, and other Asian goods that had arrived there over the Silk Road.

By the 1300s Asian wars began to disrupt this trade by making travel extremely dangerous. The trading caravans had to crawl through bandit-filled mountain passes and trek across burning deserts where roving bands of robbers might strike at any time.

Some Europeans thought that they could avoid these dangers and not have to deal with Italian merchants if they could find an all-water route around Africa to East Asia. No one had ever sailed from Europe all the way to

East Asia. Furthermore, no European they knew of had ever seen the southwest coast of Africa.

Prince Henry of Portugal, later known as Henry the Navigator, created a research center for navigators and sailors. Geographers and mapmakers came there from many lands. Their information about tides and the position of the stars in different regions was of great value to Henry's captains.

Armed with this information and financed by Henry, brave Portuguese sailors gradually explored the African coast. In 1445 one of them, Dinís Dias, reached the great western bulge where Africa's coast turns to the east and then to the south.

Vasco de Gama and his crew met with the representatives of India. They arrived there after sailing around Africa.

• **Prince Henry**

By the 1470s, Portuguese ships had reached and crossed the equator. In 1488 Bartolomeu Dias managed to sail around the southern tip of the continent, only to turn back when the crew panicked, afraid to venture into the unknown seas ahead. Finally, in 1498, Vasco da Gama sailed around southern Africa and on to India.

Columbus's Voyage

Meanwhile, another explorer traveled in a different direction. His name was Cristoforo Colombo, or as we know him today, Christopher Columbus. Instead of sailing around Africa, Columbus thought he could reach Asia by sailing west. By the late 1400s few educated people believed that the world was flat. They did not think that a ship sailing too far to the west would reach the edge and "fall off." They did not know, however, that there was land between Europe and East Asia.

Christopher Columbus in his later years.

• **Columbus**

By most navigators' estimates it was at least 10,000 miles by sea from Europe to Asia. A western voyage seemed out of the question because no ship could carry enough food and water to make such a journey across the open ocean. Columbus disagreed; he thought (incorrectly) that it was barely half that distance. He approached the rulers of several countries, hoping to find a sponsor. Finally, the Spanish monarchs, Ferdinand and Isabella, agreed to fund the voyage.

On Friday, August 3, 1492, Columbus's little fleet, the *Niña,* the *Pinta,* and the *Santa María,* set sail from Palos, Spain. After a stopover in the Canary Islands, off the coast of northwestern Africa, the ships headed into the unknown. For more than a month they sailed westward, always toward the setting sun, always alone, never another sail in sight.

As one day followed another into October, Columbus's crew began to grumble. They had not seen land for more than three weeks, and before them lay only the endless ocean. They urged Columbus to turn back. He refused.

Soon the breeze freshened and the three ships picked up speed. Then, broken branches, land birds, and other hopeful signs began to appear. Excitement mounted, in part because Ferdinand and Isabella had promised a large cash reward to the sailor who first sighted land.

At last, by moonlight at around 2:00 A.M. on October 12, the *Pinta*'s lookout, Rodrigo de Triana, spotted the white foam of waves breaking on a distant shore. *"Tierra! Tierra!"* he shouted. "Land! Land!"

Encounters in America

When day broke, Columbus and his companions approached the land, which was a small island in what we now call the Bahamas. He was certain that he had reached the Indies, the name the Europeans gave to the lands and islands of East Asia. Now he would earn the title promised him by Ferdinand and Isabella—Admiral of the Ocean Sea. He named the island San Salvador, or "Holy Savior," out of gratitude for reaching it safely. Columbus, however, found no spices there, no silks or rugs. Except for tiny bits that some inhabitants wore in their noses, he found none of the gold he expected.

The local inhabitants called the island Guanahaní (gwahn-uh-HAHN-ee). Because Columbus thought that he was in the Indies, he called them Indians—a label by which all Native Americans were thereafter mistakenly described. The Indians came forth bearing gifts. Columbus in turn gave them some beads, bits of cloth, and tiny brass bells. "They have so little to give," Columbus recorded, "but will give it all for whatever we give them."

By hand gestures the Indians told Columbus that many other islands lay to the west and south. He pushed on. Everywhere they went, Columbus and his men were thrilled by the strange new plants and animals they saw, including beautiful, multicolored parrots. In a letter later sent to a friend, Columbus described the terrain:

> **"These islands are of a beautiful appearance and . . . adorned [decorated] with a great variety of exceedingly lofty trees . . . as verdant [green] and flourishing as they exist in Spain in the month of May, some covered with flowers, others loaded with fruit."**

The explorers soon reached Cuba. At every harbor, Columbus expected to find an Asian merchant fleet. Some of the local people told him that gold could be found at *Cubanacan,* by which they meant "in the middle of Cuba." Columbus thought they were saying *El Gran Can*—in Spanish, "the Great Khan"—so he sent a delegation headed by

History Makers

Isabella (1451–1504)

The Granger Collection, New York

The queen who co-sponsored Christopher Columbus's voyage was one of Spain's most important rulers. The beautiful queen with the reddish blond hair and blue-green eyes dazzled Columbus. For many years Isabella remained equally impressed by the dashing explorer. As his voyages failed to produce the wealth she hoped for, however, the queen became less supportive. No topic brought more conflict between Isabella and Columbus than did treatment of Native Americans.

Columbus believed that the best way to convert Indians to Christianity was to enslave them. Isabella disagreed. She thought that the Indians should want to become Christians, not be forced to do so. One of her last wishes before her death was that future Spanish rulers treat the Native Americans "without any injury to them or their subjects, but command that they are treated well."

COLUMBUS'S VOYAGES, 1492–1504

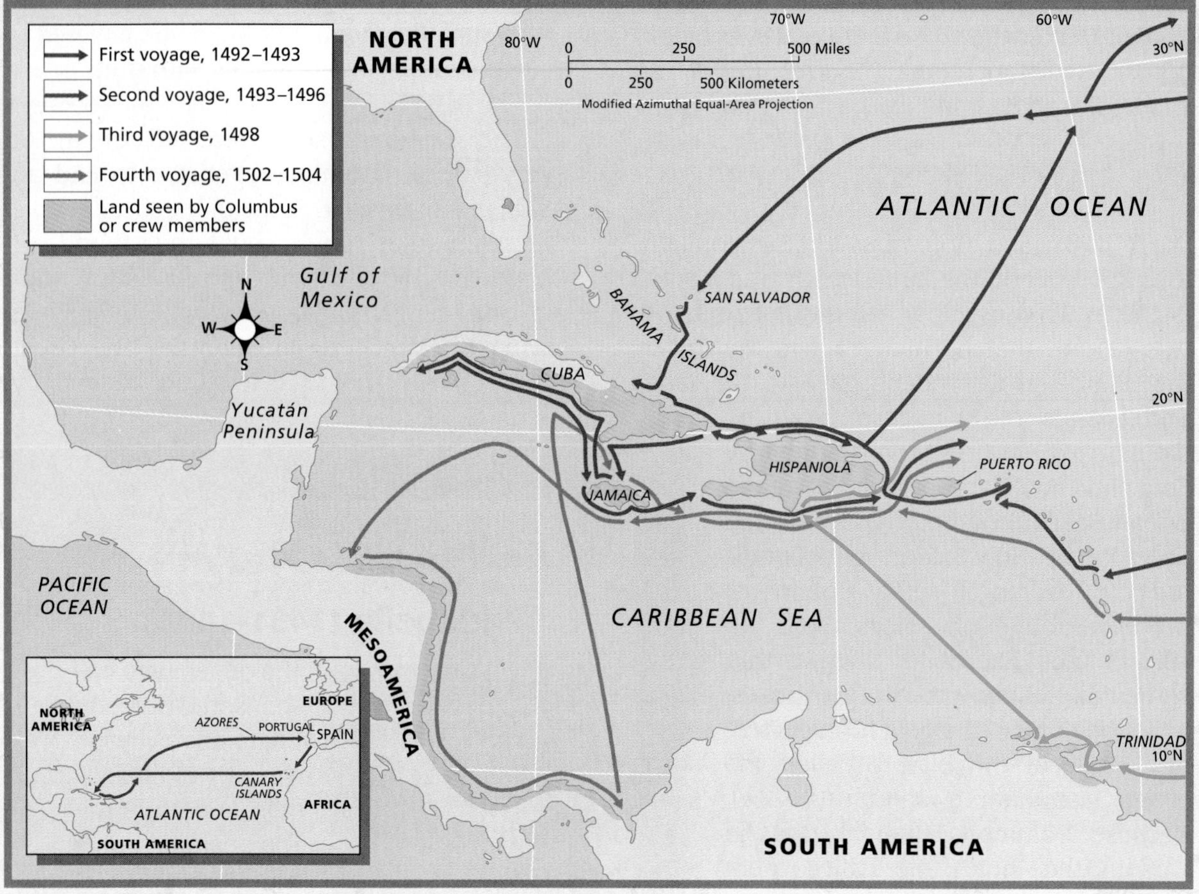

Learning from Maps. During his four voyages, Columbus became familiar with the lands in and around the Caribbean Sea.

Location. On which voyage did Columbus reach Trinidad?

• **Maps**

interpreter Luis de Torres to pay his respects to the emperor of China, Kublai Khan! Of course, they found only tropical forests and a small village.

In December 1492 Columbus reached an island that he named Hispaniola (his-puhn-YOH-luh), the "Spanish Isle." It is the present site of Haiti and the Dominican Republic. There the inhabitants had large amounts of gold. One chief even gave Columbus a belt with a solid gold buckle.

The Spaniards could not find the source of the gold, but there was enough of it to convince them that there must be mines nearby. When the *Santa María* ran aground and had to be abandoned, Columbus left some of his crew on the island and ordered them to build a fort with the remains of the ship. He then sailed home on the *Niña*.

Reaction in Europe

When Columbus landed at Palos, Spain, on March 15, 1493, crowds lined his route. People gazed in wonder at the Indians, birds, and plants he brought to show the king and queen. When he reached Barcelona, Ferdinand and Isabella showered honors upon him. They appointed him their **viceroy**, or representative, in the Indies.

No one yet had a clear picture of where these new territories were. Columbus had claimed them for Spain, but the Portuguese, who already owned the Azore Islands, insisted that any lands found west of Africa and south of the Canary Islands belonged to them.

The two Catholic countries turned to Pope Alexander VI to decide the issue. In May 1493 the Pope divided the ocean about 400 miles west of the Azores. Lands west of the **Line of Demarcation** were to belong to Spain, those to the east to Portugal. In 1494 Spain and Portugal signed the **Treaty of Tordesillas** (tawrd-uh-SEE-uhs), which moved the line about 700 miles farther west. When Brazil, which extends well east of the Line of Demarcation, was first explored in 1500, it became Portuguese.

Columbus made three more round-trips across the Atlantic. On one he claimed the island of Trinidad off the northern coast of South America. On another trip he explored the coast of Central America from Honduras to Panama and spent several months stranded on the island of Jamaica. He obtained some wealth, but far less than he had hoped for. Eventually, the king took away much of his power. The explorer died, almost forgotten, in 1506. He never accepted the fact that he had not reached Asia.

The Granger Collection, New York

This engraving shows Native Americans meeting Columbus and his crew after the Europeans landed on Cuba.

Section 3 Review

• Glossary

• Gazetteer

• Time Line

IDENTIFY and explain the significance of the following: Henry the Navigator, Bartolomeu Dias, Vasco da Gama, Christopher Columbus, Ferdinand and Isabella, viceroy, Line of Demarcation, Treaty of Tordesillas

LOCATE and explain the significance of the following: San Salvador, Hispaniola

REVIEWING FOR DETAILS

1. Why did Europeans want to find a way to reach East Asia by sea?
2. How did Columbus plan to reach East Asia?

REVIEWING FOR UNDERSTANDING

3. **Geographic Literacy** How did Columbus's voyage change many people's ideas about the earth's geography?
4. **Writing Mastery:** *Expressing* Imagine that you are Christopher Columbus. Write a journal entry expressing your feelings about the land and the people you have encountered.
5. **Critical Thinking:** *Drawing Conclusions* When Columbus first returned to Europe, he was hailed as a hero, yet he died almost forgotten. Why might some people have considered his explorations a failure?

CHAPTER 2

The Granger Collection, New York

Empires in the Americas (1500–1700)

THEMES IN AMERICAN HISTORY

Cultural Diversity:
Why might conflicts develop between different cultures?

Economic Development:
How might owning overseas colonies affect a country's economy?

Global Relations:
Why might nations compete to establish overseas colonies?

Before one Spanish expedition sailed to the Americas, a man approached its captain with a request. "[Take] my son Antonio among your troops," he pleaded, "that when he is old, he may have a tale to tell." Like young Antonio, countless other Spaniards participated in the conquest of the Americas. The tales they sent back to Spain told of a world that would be changed forever.

• Video Opener

• Skill Builder

image above: *Diego Rivera's* Colonial Domination

Section 1

Spanish Conquest in the Americas

Multimedia Connections

Explore these related topics and materials on the CD–ROM to enrich your understanding of this section:

Media Bank

- Vasco Núñez de Balboa
- Cortés Meets Moctezuma
- Francisco Pizarro

Gazetteer

- Spain
- Florida
- Panama
- Brazil
- Guam
- Pacific Ocean
- Mexico

Profiles

- Hernán Cortés
- Malintzin
- Moctezuma II

Readings

- Aztec and Inca

The Spanish artisan looked up at the dark sky and nodded. Finally, no moonlight, all the better to shape the glowing red steel as it left the fire. When done, he passed the new blade to his young assistant, who rubbed it with a fresh animal kidney to darken the metal. Later, the engraver carved a fancy pattern on the base, and the craft worker added a heavy handle. A sword was born! Using such weapons, the Spaniards conquered a land later called "America."

As you read this section you will find out:

- **How America got its name.**
- **How the explorations of Balboa and Magellan contributed to Spain's knowledge of the world.**
- **How Spaniards conquered the Aztec.**

A New Name for an Old Land

In the years following Columbus's voyage, other explorers ventured across the ocean and gradually came upon more lands. One of these navigators was an Italian named Amerigo Vespucci (vuh-SPOO-chee), who made at least two trips along the coast of present-day South America.

Vespucci's written description of his adventures attracted the attention of many mapmakers and geographers. He called the places he had visited a "New World, because our ancestors had no knowledge of them." In 1507 the German mapmaker who published Vespucci's account suggested that the "new land" be called America in his honor. The idea caught on, and by 1600 most Europeans referred to the new regions as America.

The Conquistadores

Soldier-explorers, or **conquistadores**, helped Spain establish and expand its empire in the Americas. They conquered and claimed vast new lands for the Spanish monarch.

The conquistadores had different reasons for undertaking this dangerous work. Simple desire for wealth encouraged many. As one conquistador announced upon his arrival in the Americas in 1504, "I came here to get gold, not to till the soil like a peasant." Once they actually found "gold and precious stones" in the new region, some conquistadores became incredibly greedy.

Many conquistadores also had religious goals. They felt a deep sense of mission, or special purpose—a belief that God had appointed them to convert Native Americans to Christianity. These conquistadores were determined to carry out this task, even if completing it meant using deadly force.

Others sought adventure. They enjoyed the challenge of exploration. When one conquistador landed in present-day Florida, he exclaimed, "Thanks be to Thee, O Lord, Who has permitted me to see something new."

Conquistadores faced almost unimaginable dangers in the Americas—Indians determined to protect their lands and cultures, tropical diseases, and exhausting marches. Many soldiers died in this "New World" far from their homes. Those who survived, however, often reaped political, financial, and emotional rewards.

Balboa's Journey

Two other explorers soon added to Amerigo Vespucci's knowledge of the Americas. The first was Vasco Núñez de Balboa (NOON-yays day bahl-BOH-uh), the governor of a Spanish settlement in what is now Panama.

In 1513 Balboa set out with about 200 Spanish soldiers and several hundred American Indians to explore the area. The party had to cross deep rivers and trudge through rain forests swarming with insects and poisonous snakes. After marching for more than three grueling weeks, they finally neared the top of some mountains. Balboa ordered the men to stop and he hiked alone to the summit. Before him, glittering in the sun as far as he could see, stretched a seemingly endless ocean.

After giving thanks to God, the expedition pushed onward until it reached the shore. Balboa waded into the sea with his sword in hand and took possession of the "new" ocean for Spain.

Balboa's discovery that another great body of water lay beyond the Americas suggested that it was in fact a very long way from Europe to Asia. To get there by sailing west, a captain would have to find a passage through the **isthmus**, or small neck of land, that connected the larger land masses. The Isthmus of Panama was relatively narrow, so it seemed likely that somewhere a water passage, or strait, led from the Atlantic to the ocean that Balboa had discovered.

Many maps used by Spanish explorers, like this one of Central America, placed the Southern Hemisphere at the top.

Magellan's Voyage

In 1519 a clever Portuguese explorer named Ferdinand Magellan (muh-JEL-uhn) learned even more about the Americas when he set out to claim a group of islands in the Indies for Spain. He hoped to find a strait through the "New World" to shorten his long voyage.

Magellan was a short and powerful man. He wore a full beard and, because of an old battle wound, walked with a noticeable limp. One impressed sailor described him as "tough, tough, tough."

In September 1519 Magellan left Spain with five ships and about 240 sailors. They crossed the Atlantic Ocean to present-day Brazil, then sailed southward along the coast, searching always for a water passage to the West.

The captains of the other ships eventually became angry with Magellan, claiming that he would not discuss his plans with them. A **mutiny**, or rebellion, soon broke out. Magellan quickly crushed the revolt and put some of the leaders to death. Then he continued to sail on.

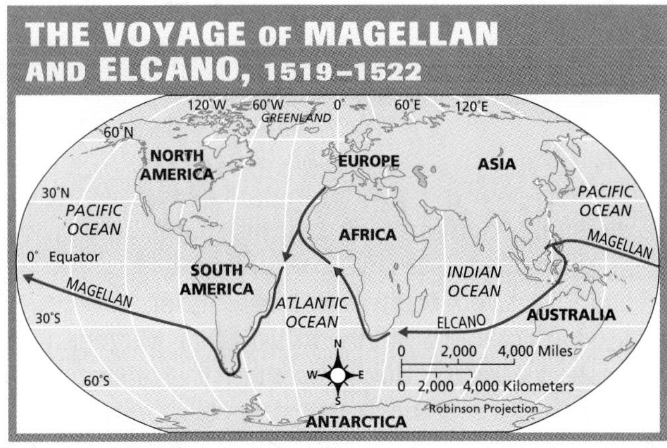

Learning from Maps.
After Ferdinand Magellan died in the Far East, Juan Sebastián de Elcano became the fleet's new leader.

• Maps

Movement. How many miles did the Magellan-Elcano expedition sail on their voyage?

The Granger Collection, New York

Ferdinand Magellan said good-bye to his wife and son—for the last time—shortly before he began his risky voyage.

Finally, the voyagers reached a break in the coast near the southern tip of South America. As the fleet entered a narrow passage between the shore and the island of *Tierra del Fuego,* or "the land of fire," fierce storms and huge waves tossed the ships around wildly. The sailors on one ship, shaken and discouraged, fled homeward.

The other ships battled strong winds and powerful currents for 38 days. At last they made it through the passage, which we now call the Strait of Magellan, into a broad and calm sea. Magellan broke down and cried with joy when he saw the smooth water. He named this ocean *el Mar Pacífico,* which means "the peaceful sea," because it seemed so calm.

Magellan then pointed his fleet northwest. For more than three long months the explorers sailed on, spotting only two islands, both uninhabited. Food supplies ran dangerously low. One sailor recorded:

"We ate biscuit . . . swarming with worms. . . . We drank yellow water that had been putrid [polluted] for many days. . . . Rats were sold

for a half ducat [gold coin] apiece, and even so, we could not always get them."

Although not very tasty, the stringy rat meat provided essential vitamins and minerals. When even this food ran out, the hungry sailors ate leather from the rigging, then sawdust. Many died, most of them from a disease called scurvy.

In early March 1521 the ships reached the island known today as Guam. After getting food and water from the inhabitants, Magellan pushed on to the present-day Philippine Islands. He became involved in a local war and died during battle. Juan Sebastián de Elcano (el-KAHN-oh) then took command.

Elcano's fleet wandered in the western Pacific for many months. Eventually, only one ship remained to sail across the Indian Ocean, around the southern tip of Africa, and home to Spain. In September 1522, almost three years after the expedition had set out, Elcano and 17 other surviving European sailors reached Spanish soil once again. They were the first to **circumnavigate**, or travel around, the entire earth. Their great sea voyage proved that sailing west from Europe to Asia was more dangerous, much farther, and more expensive than anyone had imagined.

Cortés and the Aztec

While Magellan and Elcano sailed around the world, Spain extended its presence in the "New World." By 1519 Spaniards had explored most of the islands in the Caribbean Sea and had collected much information about Indians there and in Mesoamerica.

The Aztec Empire. By the early 1500s the Aztec Empire was the most powerful Indian state in Mesoamerica. Its territory stretched from the Gulf of Mexico to the Pacific Ocean and from present-day Guatemala to the center of modern Mexico.

The Aztec had a written language and a wide knowledge of mathematics, astronomy,

Mercado/AMI/Art Resource, NY

The Aztec held many of their religious services and sacred ceremonies at stone temples. This embroidered cloth shows a soaring temple in Tenochtitlán.

• **Sports and Pastimes**

and architecture. Great stone temples dotted many of their tidy, well-run towns. Their capital city, Tenochtitlán (tay-NAWCH-tee-TLAHN), housed about 300,000 people.

The Aztec dominated other local Indians. In the Aztec religion, human sacrifices had to be offered to the gods to ensure their goodwill. For this purpose, Aztec rulers killed thousands of captives taken in wars. They also forced other Indians they had defeated to make large payments of crops or gold.

Cortés and Moctezuma. In 1519 a conquistador named Hernán Cortés set out to explore Mesoamerica and possibly make contact with the Aztec. He sailed from present-day island of Cuba with about 600 soldiers. Shortly after Cortés landed, he met a young Aztec woman called Malintzin (mah-LINT-suhn). She became his interpreter, guide, and adviser. Malintzin told Cortés that many Indians in the area hated the Aztec and might fight against them.

With this valuable information, Cortés led his large force inland from the coast. Many Indians who resented Aztec rule joined him on the way, just as Malintzin had predicted. By the time Cortés neared Tenochtitlán, he commanded a very large army.

The Aztec emperor at that time, Moctezuma (MAWK-tay-soo-mah) II, was a delicate, well-mannered man of about 40. His people treated him with great respect. They spoke to him with eyes lowered, not daring to look at his face.

Like many Mesoamericans, Moctezuma may have believed in the prophecy of Quetzalcoatl (ket-SAHL-kwaht-uhl). This legend told of a powerful god who would someday come from the east to rule the Aztec. Moctezuma may have thought that Cortés, with his steel armor and large warhorses, was Quetzalcoatl.

In an effort to persuade Cortés to turn back from Tenochtitlán, Moctezuma sent the Spaniards a large disc of gold and some valuable jewelry. This tactic backfired. An Aztec account described the Spaniards' reaction:

> **"They picked up the gold and fingered it like monkeys; they seemed to be transported by joy. . . . They longed and lusted for gold. Their bodies swelled with greed . . . ; they hungered like pigs for that gold."**

When Cortés and his men finally reached Tenochtitlán, Moctezuma did not openly resist

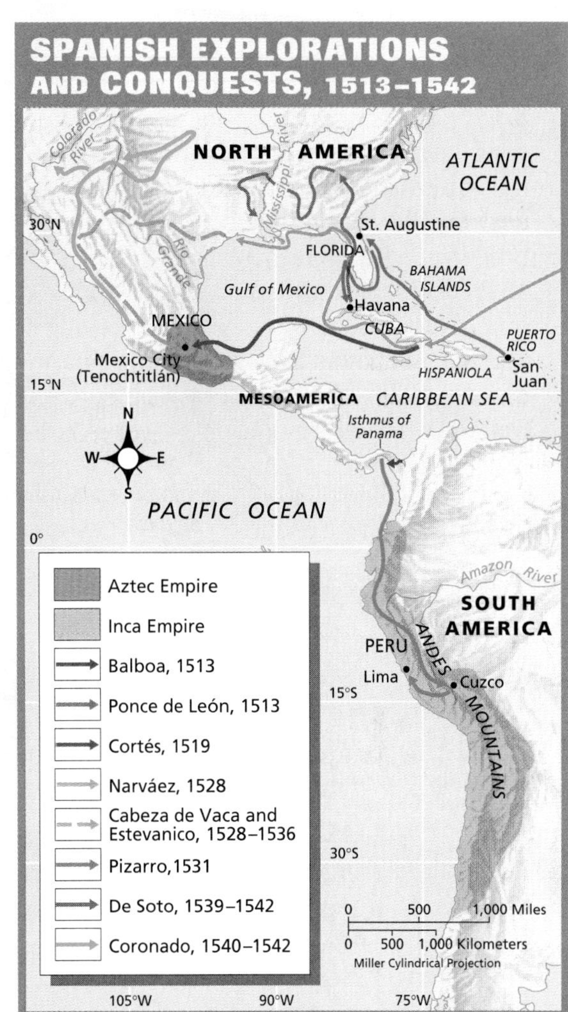

Learning from Maps. Spanish explorers claimed lands from Peru in South America to the Rio Grande in North America.

• Maps

Region. Which Spanish explorer first claimed the western coast of South America?

them. He gave them lodging in one of his palaces and provided them with delicious food. Cortés responded to this hospitality by taking Moctezuma prisoner. Although the quiet emperor remained on the throne, in reality Cortés controlled the Aztec Empire.

In 1520 the Aztec rebelled and drove the invaders out of the city. Moctezuma died during the harsh fighting. The Spaniards soon regrouped, however. Aided by their Indian allies, they recaptured Tenochtitlán roughly a year later. Cortés renamed the capital Mexico City and destroyed Aztec artifacts, houses, and temples. By 1539 Cortés controlled much of present-day Mexico. Spanish soldiers would continue to conquer more of the region in the years to come.

• Aztec Warriors

Aztec weapons such as this gold inlaid spear-thrower were no match against the Spanish.

Courtesy Trustees of The British Museum

One powerful but unexpected factor aided the Spaniards' conquest of the Aztec and other Mesoamerican Indians—the introduction of diseases from Europe. Indians in the Americas had no **immunity**, or resistance, to European illnesses like smallpox, measles, and typhus. Once struck and weakened, Indians found it almost impossible to defend themselves. The Spaniards took advantage of this weakness and gained huge amounts of land and gold as a result.

A new chance for conquest. Cortés's adventures caused a sensation in Spain. When conquistador Francisco Pizarro (puh-ZAHR-oh) reported the existence of another rich Indian society on the western coast of present-day South America, the Spanish king hoped for another profitable conquest. He gave Pizarro permission to explore the land, a region that Pizarro and other conquistadores had named "Peru" on an earlier visit. The rulers of this region, a people called the Inca, suffered much the same fate as the Aztec.

• Pizarro and the Inca

Section 1 Review

• Glossary

IDENTIFY and explain the significance of the following: Amerigo Vespucci, conquistadores, Vasco Nuñez de Balboa, isthmus, Ferdinand Magellan, mutiny, circumnavigate, Hernán Cortés, Malintzin, Moctezuma II, immunity

• Gazetteer

LOCATE and explain the importance of the following: Isthmus of Panama, Tenochtitlán

REVIEWING FOR DETAILS

1. Where did the name "America" come from?
2. How did Cortés conquer the Aztec Empire?

REVIEWING FOR UNDERSTANDING

3. **Geographic Literacy** How did the explorations of Balboa and Magellan expand Europeans' geographic knowledge?
4. **Writing Mastery:** *Describing* Imaginc that you are a Spanish conquistador in Mexico during the conquest of the Aztec. Write a letter to your family describing your experiences.
5. **Critical Thinking:** *Cause and Effect* How did the Aztec treatment of their Indian subjects contribute to the fall of their empire?

Section 2

SPAIN AND NEW SPAIN

Multimedia Connections

Explore these related topics and materials on the CD-ROM to enrich your understanding of this section:

Profiles

- Alvar Núñez Cabeza de Vaca
- Bartolomé de Las Casas
- Estevanico

Readings

- *El Dorado*
- Fiery Sermon

Atlas

- De Soto's Explorations
- Wealth of Spanish America

Gazetteer

- New Spain
- Arkansas
- Texas
- Arizona
- New Mexico
- California

Media Bank

- Spanish Medieval Music
- Treasure from the Americas
- Spanish Explorer
- Bartolomé de Las Casas

One observant priest noticed that Europeans were always hungry in the Americas. "In Spain . . . a man's stomach will hold out from meal to meal . . . ," he commented, "but in Mexico and other parts of America we found that two or three hours after a good meal . . . our stomachs would be ready to faint." Although he spoke of the Spaniards' hunger for food, the same could be said for the conquistadores' always unsatisfied appetite for more land and riches.

As you read this section you will find out:

- **How Spain governed and expanded its American empire.**
- **What daily life was like in New Spain.**
- **Why the Golden Age of Spain ended.**

Governing New Spain

The Spaniards created a system of government for their colonies to help control their vast American empire. The monarch ruled over Spain itself and the entire Spanish Empire. Royal assistants made up the **Council of the Indies**. Based in Spain, the group nominated colonial officials and drafted and administered laws relating to Spain's colonies in the Americas.

Viceroys ruled the Spanish colonies. The viceroy for New Spain—a territory that included Mexico and parts of the present-day United States—lived in Mexico City. As the monarch's personal representatives, viceroys had great power. This included the ability to issue local orders and regulations. In addition to this authority, a wide ocean separated the viceroys from Spain.

In practice they did more or less as they wanted. As one worried Spaniard wrote:

> **"Our people, transported across an ocean to such strange, changing, and distant worlds . . . leave [Spain] meeker than lambs, [but] change as soon as they arrive there [America] into wild wolves, forgetting all the royal commands."**

Though the Fountain of Youth was only a myth, Juan Ponce de León's search for it had a powerful hold on artists' imaginations.

• European Exploration

The Spanish Empire in North America

As viceroys established local governments in the Americas, conquistadores pushed further into lands that now make up part of the United States. They planted their social and cultural traditions as they went.

The Southeast. The earliest recorded Spanish landing in the present-day United States took place in the spring of 1513, when Juan Ponce de León (PAWN-say day lay-AWN) arrived to look for precious metals. He called the lush green area Florida, after *Pascua florida,* the Feast of Flowers at Easter time.

Ponce de León may have heard an Indian tale about the Fountain of Youth, a spring that supposedly prevented its bathers from growing old. Searching for this miraculous water was almost certainly not his main objective in the Americas, however. He explored the eastern shore of Florida and gradually made his way south and west around the tip of the huge peninsula. Then he returned home.

Hernando de Soto, a Spanish conquistador who had acquired a fortune while serving in Peru, led a large force through the country beyond Florida between 1539 and 1542. De Soto's expedition included a small number of women. While fighting almost constant battles with local Indians, de Soto journeyed north into present-day Georgia and the Carolinas and west through what would later become Tennessee, Alabama, Mississippi, and Arkansas.

In 1565 a Spanish conquistador named Pedro Menéndez de Avilés (may-NAYN-days day ah-BEE-lays) founded the town of St. Augustine on the northeastern coast of Florida. St. Augustine is believed to be the oldest permanent European settlement in the present-day United States.

The Southwest. Spanish conquistadores also began to explore the area that now makes up the southwestern United States. In 1528 Pánfilo de Narváez (PAHM-fee-loh day nahr-BAH-ays) landed on the western coast of Florida with about 400 soldiers. He marched north, planning to collect gold along the way and then meet his ships at a harbor on the Gulf of Mexico. He soon ran into trouble. Illness and fierce fighting with Apalachee Indians greatly reduced his force, and when Narváez reached the coast, he could not find his fleet.

Hoping to reach distant Mexico, the Spaniards built five rickety boats, using old shirts as sails. Many died as they slowly drifted westward. A little over a month after setting out, the survivors washed ashore on or near present-day Galveston Island, Texas. Local Karankawa Indians soon attacked them.

No one knows the exact fate of the vast majority of these explorers. Only four ever returned to Spanish civilization. Among the tiny group were Álvar Núñez Cabeza de Vaca (kah-BAY-sah day BAH-kah), the treasurer of the original party, and Estevanico (e-stay-bah-NEE-koh), a North African. They spent roughly seven years traveling across southern Texas and northeastern Mexico. Acting as medicine men, they journeyed through Indian lands and reached Mexico City in 1536.

In 1540 Francisco Vásquez de Coronado led a force of Spaniards and Mexican Indians through what would become Arizona, New Mexico, Texas, Oklahoma, and Kansas. As with some other Spanish expeditions, his large group contained a number of women. Coronado hoped to find the mythical Seven Cities of Cibola, said to be full of gold, but he never succeeded.

Over time, Spanish influence spread farther into the desert regions north of Mexico. In 1598 Juan de Oñate (ohn-YAH-tay) the son of a very wealthy conquistador, journeyed there to settle in what is now New Mexico with about 400 soldiers, some accompanied by their families.

After his soldiers fought and defeated the Indians who lived in the Acoma pueblos, Oñate claimed a huge area for Spain. That same year he founded San Gabriel, which was the only Spanish settlement in the area for nearly a decade. Sometime around 1610 the Spaniards built Santa Fe, which became the area's capital. Today it is the oldest capital city in the United States.

California. As the Spanish conquered land and built settlements in the regions that now make up the southwestern United States, they also began to explore present-day California. Juan Rodríguez Cabrillo (kah-BREE-yoh) explored parts of the California coast for Spain around 1542, reaching the bays at present-day San Diego and Monterey.

Hoping to establish firm control over California, the Spaniards began to think of building colonies there. By 1602 Sebastián Vizcaíno (bees-kah-EE-noh), a wealthy Spanish merchant, had sailed up the Pacific coast as far north as Monterey Bay. He recommended that the Spaniards establish a military base there to protect their claim to the region.

History Makers

Estevanico (?–1539)

The Granger Collection, New York

Though historians know little about Estevanico's early life, most agree that he was from North Africa. He arrived in the Americas during 1528 as part of Spain's ill-fated Narváez expedition. Estevanico acted as a scout and healer on the survivors' long, difficult journey to Mexico City.

When the four weary explorers reached Spanish civilization in 1536, they reported that Indians along their route had described rich cities to the north. The viceroy begged Cabeza de Vaca and the other Spaniards to go and find them, but the men refused. Only Estevanico volunteered for the dangerous job.

Estevanico led a small expedition through Mexico and into present-day New Mexico, where Zuni Indians killed him for crossing a sacred cornmeal line. Estevanico was the first African to explore what is now the United States, and his journeys helped later explorers traveling through the Southwest.

Spanish America

As Spanish explorers spread throughout New Spain, a Hispanic American civilization slowly developed. It included some elements from the Catholic religion, Indian agriculture, and Spanish military and political organizations.

Missions. As the frontier of Spanish settlement expanded north of Mexico, Catholic priests founded church communities called **missions**. They hoped to use the missions to convert the Indians, develop distant territories, and provide a structure of Spanish government. By 1630 these priests had established some 25 missions north of the Rio Grande.

The missions were towns unto themselves, each built around a church. As time passed, large Indian villages clustered around the missions. Indians did the vast majority of the work that supported the missions. They tended large herds of cattle and grew various crops. They also wove woolen cloth and made products such as leather goods, wine, and soap.

Life for mission Indians was hard and strict. They had to give up their own religions, become Catholics, and obey the priests' orders. Those who did not willingly fit into this system often felt the lash of the whip.

Colonial life. Some Spanish soldiers eventually became civilian **colonists**, or people who leave their home countries to establish new settlements elsewhere. Using the labor of Indians and enslaved Africans, these colonists ran farms, ranches, and mines. They were joined by other Spaniards, who flooded into the Americas during the 1500s and 1600s.

• Labor in Spanish America

The Spanish social structure in New Spain was based largely on race. Those with Spanish blood—*peninsulares* (pay-neen-soo-LAHR-es), or Spaniards born in Spain, and *criollos* (kree-OHL-yohs), their American-born descendants—formed the upper class. *Mestizos* (me-STEE-zohs), people of mixed Spanish and Indian blood, fell beneath them. Next came Indians who had adopted Spanish ways, then mulattoes (muh-LA-tohs), or people of mixed European and

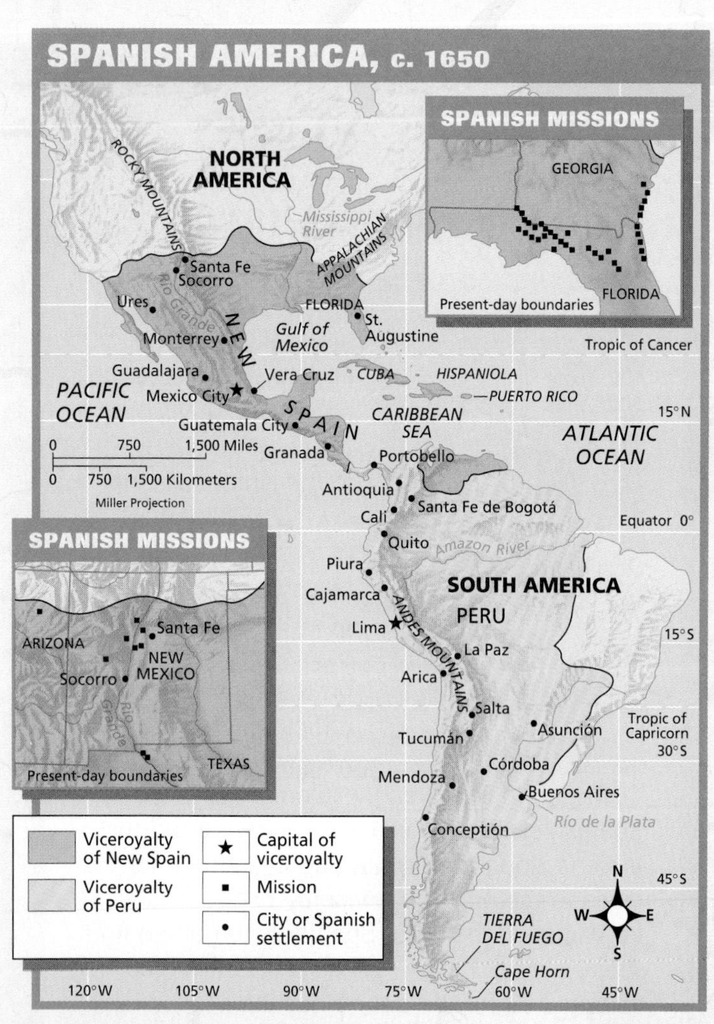

Learning from Maps.
By the mid-1600s the Spanish had claimed a vast area and established many cities and missions in the Americas.

Location. How far was it between the northernmost and southernmost Spanish cities?

• Maps

Although isolated, church complexes like the San Jose Mission in Texas helped the Spaniards control the frontier.

• Junípero Serra

African ancestry. Free or enslaved black Africans were at the bottom.

On the northern frontier of New Spain, however, these divisions were somewhat less rigid. Talented and energetic people from the lower ranks of society could, with persistence and luck, sometimes achieve positions of wealth and influence.

Women occupied an important role in New Spain. They helped men settle the land and shared all the hardships of pioneering. An observer remembered one woman's difficult journey to her new home in Spanish America:

> **"She forced herself to ride in a chair atop a saddled mule, and she rode over the rough places and bad passes in these roads as easily and successfully as any of the company."**

In New Spain, married women could legally possess property and pass it to their heirs. Some women even owned and operated large ranches. In New Mexico Juana Luján (loo-HAHN) maintained an enormous spread with pastures, a garden, fields, an orchard, and livestock corrals.

Few women in New Spain ran big estates or owned large amounts of property, however. Most women worked hard inside homes owned by their fathers, husbands, or brothers. The high death rate for men in New Spain meant that women often had to take control if one of their close male relatives died suddenly.

Many wealthy Spanish women were educated at home or in convent schools, where they learned to read and write. This privilege did not extend to all women in New Spain, however. Most Indian, African, and *mestizo* women never received any schooling. Even women from the upper classes did not have access to colleges or universities. Those who wanted to concentrate on their studies often entered convents and became nuns, such as Mexican poet Juana Inés de la Cruz.

Some Spanish children in New Spain spent their days in school. Others worked with their parents. A young boy sometimes joined his father in the fields or on errands. A young girl often helped with shopping or baking. If the family was wealthy, Indian servants or enslaved Africans did most of these jobs.

Members of a mestizo *family work together in this 1775 oil painting.*

• Women in New Spain

The End of the Golden Age

The Golden Age of Spain began in the early 1500s and brought the country great prosperity. By the 1530s Spain ruled a greater empire than any other European nation. The Portuguese controlled the enormous region that would become Brazil, but the red and gold Spanish flag flew on staffs all over the West Indies and from present-day Argentina to New Mexico. With a huge empire, a strong army, and a thriving artistic life, the Spanish Empire seemed all-powerful.

There were some flaws with Spain's success, however. Spain's own economy, particularly its ability to produce goods, was weak and inefficient.

Art Resource, NY

Denied the chance to study at a university, Juana Inés de la Cruz entered a convent in the mid-1600s and became a nun and poet.

• Juana Inés de la Cruz

Because of poor soil and bad farming methods, Spanish farmers did not raise enough food to support the rest of the population. Spain even had to purchase wheat from other parts of Europe.

Manufactured articles also had to be imported, because Spain had almost no industry. Instead of using gold and silver from its colonies to finance manufacturing, the Spanish government bought what it needed abroad. It paid for these imports with its treasure. In addition, all this gold and silver often caused severe **inflation**, or a sharp rise in prices.

As long as the precious metals from abroad continued to stream in, Spain could cope with its problems. When the flow slowed to a trickle in the mid-1600s, Spain's Golden Age came to an end.

Section 2 Review

• Glossary

IDENTIFY and explain the significance of the following: Council of the Indies, Juan Ponce de León, Hernando de Soto, Pedro Menéndez de Avilés, Álvar Núñez Cabeza de Vaca, Estevanico, Francisco Vásquez de Coronado, Juan de Oñate, Juan Rodríquez Cabrillo, Sebastián Vizcaíno, missions, colonists, Juana Inés de la Cruz, inflation

• Gazetteer

LOCATE and explain the importance of the following: Mexico City, Florida, St. Augustine, Santa Fe, Rio Grande

REVIEWING FOR DETAILS

1. How did Spain control its new territories and enlarge its empire in the Americas?
2. What was daily life like for the residents of New Spain?
3. Why did Spain's Golden Age come to an end?

REVIEWING FOR UNDERSTANDING

4. **Writing Mastery:** *Creating* Imagine that you are an Indian living at a Spanish mission. Create a poem or short story about your experiences there.
5. **Critical Thinking:** *Synthesizing Information* How might Spain's distance from its colonies have affected government in New Spain?

Section 3
THE STRUGGLE FOR EMPIRES

Multimedia Connections

Explore these related topics and materials on the CD–ROM to enrich your understanding of this section:

Atlas
- Early European Settlements

Profiles
- Sir Walter Raleigh

Readings
- French and Dutch in America

Biographies
- Queen Elizabeth

Media Bank
- New Amsterdam, c. 1626
- Virginia Coastal Map

As reports of Spain's success in the Americas spread through Europe, other countries began to think of establishing their own settlements across the ocean. But what room had Spain left for other nations? One English observer surveyed the situation and wrote sadly, "[If only] they that be Englishmen/Might have been the first of all." Despite Spain's head start, many European countries soon decided to enter the race for empire.

As you read this section you will find out:

- **How England clashed with Spain in Europe and the Americas.**
- **How the English attempted to build a colony in North America.**
- **How the arrival of Europeans affected American Indians.**

England Enters America

When the news of Columbus's explorations reached England, Spain seemed too powerful to be challenged directly. The English concentrated on looking for a northern sea route to East Asia instead.

Early explorations in North America. In 1497 John Cabot, an Italian employed by the king of England, searched for such a passage along the coast of Newfoundland. A year later he sailed south, possibly as far as Chesapeake Bay. Cabot's voyages gave England a claim to regions in North America. The king rewarded Cabot by granting him trade privileges and a small financial reward.

English fishers also reached America about the same time, sailing in the icy waters near Newfoundland. Some may have established temporary camps ashore to salt or dry their catch. Though they did not build permanent settlements, they helped establish an English presence in North America that the country would draw on in the years to come.

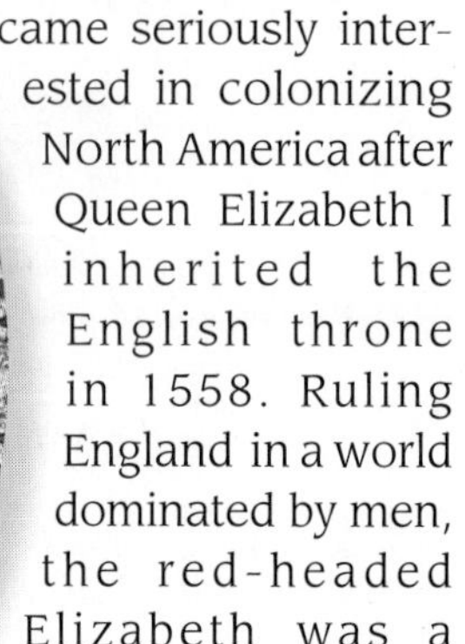

A talented leader and diplomat, Queen Elizabeth I spoke four languages.

Conflicts with Spain. The English only became seriously interested in colonizing North America after Queen Elizabeth I inherited the English throne in 1558. Ruling England in a world dominated by men, the red-headed Elizabeth was a careful, clever leader. Well aware of England's limited strength compared to Spain's, she proceeded with a great deal of caution.

England could weaken Spain without actually going to war by striking Spanish merchant ships on the high seas. In those days, a ship far from land was at the mercy of any more-powerful vessel. There was no way to call for help if suddenly attacked. A fast English ship could easily overtake a slow Spanish vessel loaded with treasure. Then Elizabeth's eager sailors could swarm aboard, kill the crew, remove the gold and silver, and sink the ship.

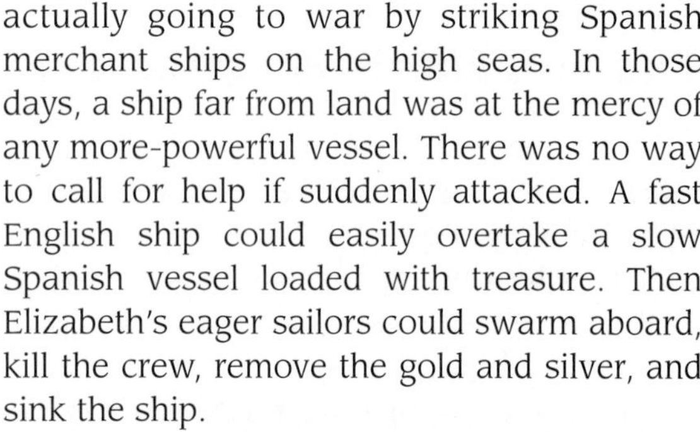

The Spanish considered such attackers pirates, and rightly so. Ignoring this opinion, Elizabeth encouraged English captains to roam the trade routes between Spain and its American colonies in search of easy prey. Besides weakening Spain, these attacks provided England with a great deal of gold and silver.

Francis Drake was one of the most famous of what the English affectionately called their "**sea dogs**," or sailors who preyed on Spanish ships. In 1578 Drake sailed through the Strait of Magellan on a handsome ship he later named the *Golden Hind*. In the Pacific Ocean, he captured a Spanish galleon carrying a fortune in silver. Then he went up the west coast of the Americas, possibly as far as present-day Vancouver, before crossing the Pacific and sailing home.

When Drake reached England in 1580, the *Golden Hind* was packed with Spanish treasure. Spain's forceful king, Philip II, demanded that Drake be punished. Instead, Elizabeth made him a knight.

Drake, now Sir Francis Drake, sailed again in 1585. This time he terrorized Spanish towns in the Caribbean Sea. Philip was furious! He disliked Elizabeth and he feared economic competition from the English. Philip also wanted the Protestant England to become Catholic, like Spain. So he collected what was probably the most powerful fleet the world had yet seen—some 130 ships armed with more than 3,000 cannons and carrying nearly 30,000 men. In 1588 this mighty **Spanish Armada** sailed from Spain to invade England.

As the Spanish fleet approached, Elizabeth urged her sailors to fight for the glory of England:

> **"I have placed my chiefest strength and safeguard in the loyal hearts and good will of my subjects. . . . By your valor [courage] in the field, we shall shortly have a famous**

The Granger Collection, New York

The Vanguard, *an English warship, attacks the Spanish Armada in a surprising show of strength and strategy.*

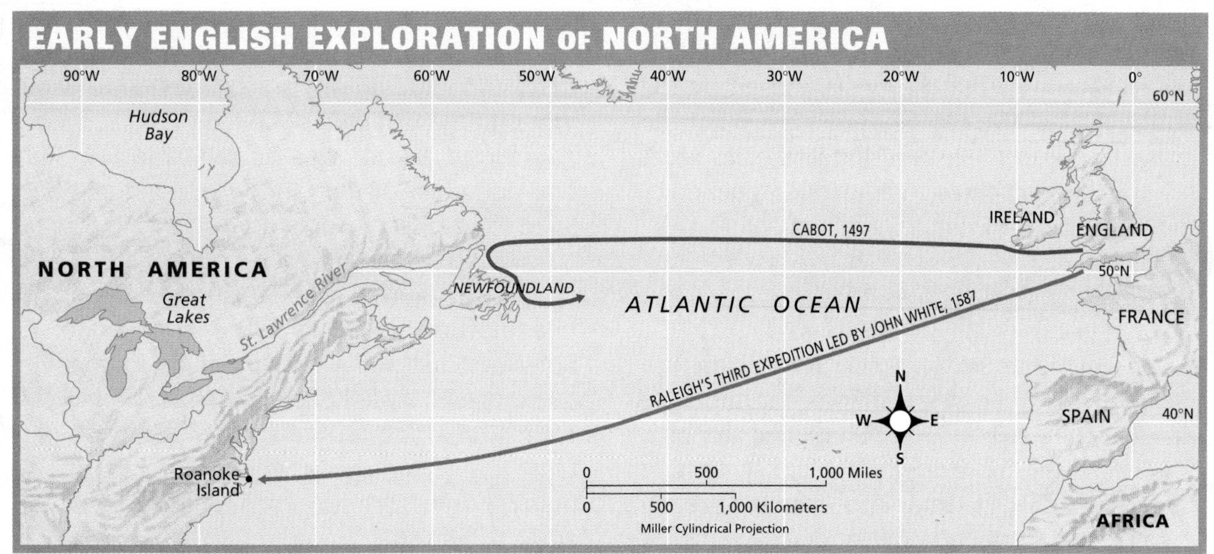

Learning from Maps. Despite threats from Spain and the failure of the Roanoke settlement, the English continued to explore North America.

Location. What body of land did Cabot reach on his voyage to North America?

• **Maps**

victory over the enemies of my God, of my kingdom, and of my people."

The English ships were smaller than the Spanish vessels and easier to maneuver. They sank many of the Spanish vessels, and storms finished off still more. Only about half of the Armada struggled back to Spanish ports, and most of these ships were too damaged to be of any use. Now England was ready to carve a place for itself in the Americas.

A False Start at Roanoke Island

Even before the defeat of the great Spanish Armada, Elizabeth had begun to think of building a colony in North America. In 1578 she issued a **charter**, or document granting certain rights and powers, to an English navigator named Sir Humphrey Gilbert. This charter gave him permission to establish a settlement in the Americas. Gilbert and a small party of colonists landed on Newfoundland in 1583, but they did not stay. Gilbert drowned on the way home when his ship went down in a storm.

In 1585 Gilbert's half-brother, Sir Walter Raleigh, sent about 100 men to the Americas. They landed on an island off of present-day North Carolina and named it Roanoke. The settlers soon built a fort, but they made no effort to plant crops. When Sir Francis Drake stopped by in 1586 after his raid on the Spanish in the Caribbean, most of the colonists went back to England with him.

The next year Raleigh sent about 118 settlers—including a number of women—to Roanoke. Most of them knew nothing of the country and had no previous experience as colonists. Just a few weeks after

The Granger Collection, New York

John White led the second Roanoke expedition. To show others what the land was like, he painted watercolors of American animals, like this land crab.

they had arrived, their leader sailed back to England for more supplies. He intended to return promptly, but the crisis caused by the attack of the Armada delayed him. When he did get back in 1591, the island was deserted. No one has ever discovered what happened to the inhabitants of Roanoke's "lost colony."

Indian-European Relations

When Columbus stepped onto San Salvador in October 1492, he gave thanks for the safe arrival of his ships. Then he claimed the land for Ferdinand and Isabella. He did so despite the obvious fact that the island already belonged to someone—the "Indians" gathered on the beach.

Later explorers—French, Dutch, Swedish, and English—dismissed the Native Americans they encountered in much the same way. What many people have called the "discovery" of a "New World" was actually the invasion and conquest of the land where Indians had lived for thousands of years.

First contact. We must use historical imagination to picture the first contacts between Europeans and American Indians. In these "new" lands, Europeans must have felt 10 feet tall. Here were discoveries to be made, fame and fortune to be won. At the beginning, many Europeans felt confident that Indians could offer little or no effective resistance. How could they resist good Christians, the Europeans asked. Of what use were spears and arrows against soldiers wearing steel and armed with guns and cannons?

It is possible that many Indians believed that the Spaniards, with their prancing war horses and shiny armor, represented the god Quetzalcoatl. The powerful European strangers might have looked down from their huge floating fortresses on the Indians' frail canoes. In contrast to the Indians' simple weapons, the foreigners had flaming, roaring "firesticks" that could strike down an animal or human across great distances.

The Columbian Exchange. In reality, of course, Europeans were not so mighty, and Indians were not so powerless. Each had things to teach and learn. The result was what historian Alfred Crosby, Jr., has called the **Columbian Exchange**. This term refers to the transfer of ideas, plants, animals, and diseases between the Americas and Europe, Africa, and Asia.

Europeans learned vital survival skills from Indians—how to live, travel, hunt, and fight in a different environment. Europeans also gained

Through Others' Eyes

The Race for Empires

Like the English, the French envied the success of the Spanish in the Americas. How, they asked, had Spaniards managed to "steal" the "New World" for themselves when the French could sail and hunt and fight better than any other people? Some French leaders feared that Spain would control the world if other European nations did not build their own colonies overseas. One French scholar of the time explained why his nation decided to enter the colonial race:

> *"The French above all were spurred [motivated] by a desire to do likewise in areas that had not been reached by [the Spaniards], for the French did not esteem [consider] themselves less than [the Spaniards], neither in navigation . . . nor in any other calling. The French persuaded themselves that [the Spaniards] had not discovered all, and that the world was large enough to reveal even stranger things than those already known."*

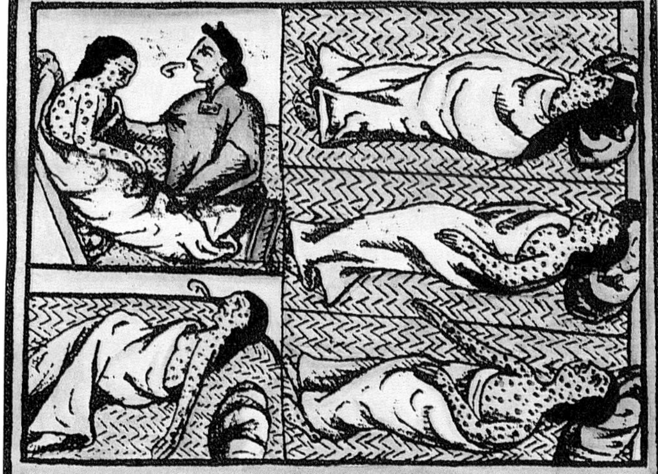

In this book illustration from the1500s, a medicine man attempts to cure an Aztec of the smallpox he caught from the Spaniards. Diseases were the greatest threat to Indians.

important new plants, like corn and potatoes, from Indians.

Indians also received new knowledge and material from Europeans. They acquired highly useful devices, like shovels and steel traps, from European settlers.

Disease played a tragic role in the Columbian Exchange. Many Indians died in battle trying to resist the European conquest of the Americas. The introduction of European diseases, however, accounted for many more Indian deaths than did Spanish military campaigns.

The germs that caused these diseases came to the Americas from Europe, where people had suffered from them for countless generations. Although many people in Europe died each year from diseases like smallpox, most Europeans had developed considerable immunity to them. The native inhabitants of the Americas lacked such immunity. One European described the result:

> **"Within a few days after our departure from every such town, the people began to die very fast . . . in some towns about 20, in some towns 40, . . . in one six score [120]. The disease also was so strange, that they neither knew what it was, nor how to cure it."**

There are no records of early Indian populations, so it is difficult to know exactly how many Indians died from European diseases. Estimates of deaths run in the millions.

Section 3 Review

• Glossary

• Gazetteer

• Time Line

IDENTIFY and explain the significance of the following: John Cabot, Elizabeth I, Sir Francis Drake, sea dogs, Spanish Armada, Sir Walter Raleigh, charter, Columbian Exchange

LOCATE and explain the importance of the following: Newfoundland, Roanoke Island

REVIEWING FOR DETAILS

1. How did England and Spain come into conflict in the Americas and Europe, and what was the result?
2. What kind of efforts did England make to establish a permanent settlement in North America?
3. How did contact with Europeans affect American Indians?

REVIEWING FOR UNDERSTANDING

4. **Geographic Literacy** How did the Europeans both adapt to America's environment and change it?
5. **Critical Thinking:** *Drawing Conclusions* Why do you think the English experienced so much difficulty building a permanent colony on Roanoke Island?

The Columbian Exchange

The exchange of goods across the Atlantic Ocean that Christopher Columbus started in 1492 changed the world forever. Not since the Bering land bridge was covered by water in ancient times had there been any exchange to speak of between the Western Hemisphere (the Americas) and the Eastern Hemisphere (Europe, Asia, and Africa). Plants and animals developed that were unique to each hemisphere.

When people began to journey between the hemispheres they transported goods with them. Many plants and animals we consider "American" today were actually brought over by Europeans, Asians, and Africans. Likewise, many items we now associate with other countries actually originated in the Americas.

The state of Kentucky has long been known as the "Bluegrass State" because of the 8,000-square-mile region where the bluish-green grass grows. Kentucky Bluegrass originated as a European pasture and meadow grass. It was transplanted to North America in the 1700s.

The Americas

Food Plants

corn, white potatoes, tomatoes, pumpkins/squash, beans (navy, lima, kidney, string), peppers (bell, chili), pineapples, peanuts, pecans, cashews, avocados, papayas, cocoa beans, vanilla beans, sweet potatoes, wild rice, cassava roots (tapioca)

Other Plants

cotton, tobacco, marigolds

Animals and Insects

turkeys, hummingbirds, rattlesnakes, gray squirrels, guinea pigs, muskrats, potato beetles

Today dogs and cats are the most common domestic pets in America. For centuries before contact with Europeans, American Indians kept dogs as companions and helpers. People in the Eastern Hemisphere raised both dogs and cats. There were no domestic cats in North America, however, until the first common "house cats" were brought over by Europeans around 1750.

CLIMATE	VEGETATION
Humid Tropical	Tropical rain forest
Tropical Savanna	Tropical grasslands with scattered trees
Desert	Sparse, drought-resistant plants, many barren, rocky or sandy areas
Steppe	Grassland, few trees
Mediterranean	Scrub, woodland, grassland
Humid Subtropical	Mixed forest
Marine West Coast	Temperate evergreen forest
Humid Continental	Mixed forest
Subartic	Northern evergreen forest
Tundra	Moss, lichens, low shrubs
Highland	Forest to tundra vegetation, varies with altitude

NUTRITIONAL VALUE OF CROPS (in millions of calories per acre)

Chief Crops of the Americas		Chief Crops of Europe, Asia and Africa	
Cassava roots (tapioca)	24.45	Rice	18.03
White potatoes	18.56	Oats	13.59
Corn	18.03	Barley	12.60
Sweet potatoes and yams	17.54	Wheat	10.37

Many American plants were more nutritious than were many of the major food crops of Europe, Asia, and Africa. **Human-Environment Interaction:** What effect might raising new crops with higher nutritional values have on the population of a region?

Source: *The Columbian Exchange*

Europe, Asia, and Africa

Food Plants
wheat, oats, barley, soybeans, Asian rice, radishes, lettuce, onions, okra, chickpeas, olives, grapes, peaches, pears, oranges, lemons, coffee, watermelons, bananas, sugarcane

Other Plants
dandelions, crabgrass, couchgrass, bluegrass, roses, daisies

Animals and Insects
cows, horses, hogs, goats, sheep, chickens, rabbits, elephants, house cats, Mediterranean fruit flies, Japanese beetles, sparrows, starlings, mice, rats

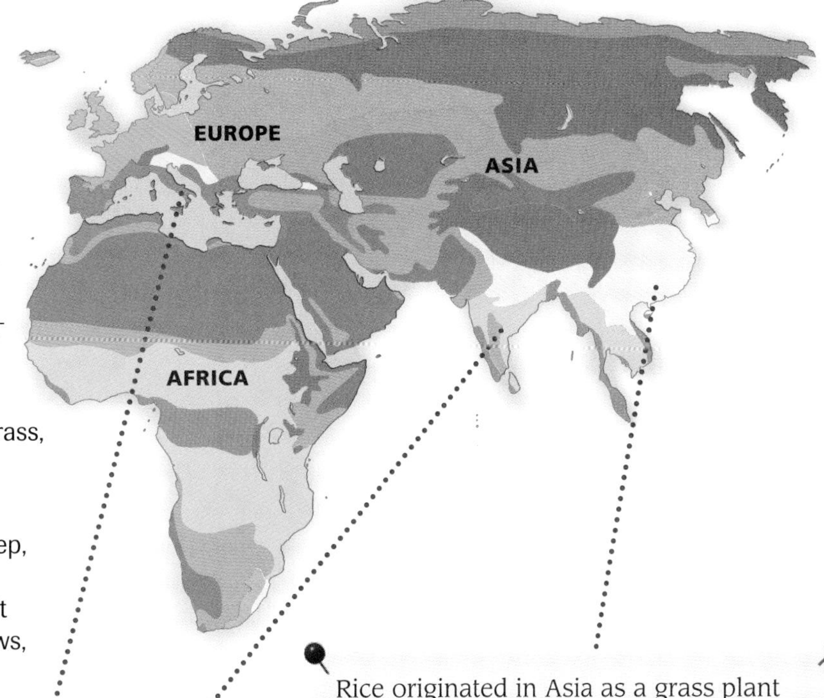

Rice originated in Asia as a grass plant and became an important food source throughout the Eastern Hemisphere. Eventually, rice also became a popular food product in the Americas. **Place:** Rice grows particularly well in both East Asia and southeastern North America. Why might that be so?

Many popular Italian and Indian dishes today include tomatoes and peppers, products imported from the Americas. Although tomatoes were transplanted to Europe in the 1500s, few Europeans ate them until after 1800. People thought the colorful plants were poisonous and grew them only for decoration.

To learn more *about the Columbian Exchange, go to the interactive map, "The Columbian Exchange," on the CD-ROM.*

• **Columbian Exchange**

CHAPTER 3

Courtesy The Pilgrim Society

The English Colonies (1607–1752)

THEMES IN AMERICAN HISTORY

Global Relations:
How might events in one country affect the founding of colonies overseas?

Cultural Diversity:
Why might a country's colonies develop different cultures?

Geographic Diversity:
How might a region's geography affect the development of a colony?

• Video Opener

• Skill Builder

The men, women, and children were sick and weary from their long voyage. Finally, in November 1620, these colonists reached America. One colonist, William Bradford, later described their landing: "They fell upon their knees and blessed the God of Heaven who had brought them over the vast and furious ocean." Bradford wondered, "What could now sustain them but the Spirit of God and His grace?"

image above: *Henry Bacon's* Landing of Pilgrims

Section 1
JAMESTOWN

Multimedia Connections

Explore these related topics and materials on the CD–ROM to enrich your understanding of this section:

Gazetteer

- Virginia
- Jamestown
- Roanoke Island

Simulation

- Building a Colony

Readings

- Colonial Narrative Accounts

Profiles

- John Rolfe
- John Smith
- Pocahontas

Media Bank

- John Smith
- Woodlands Indian Pipe
- Population of Jamestown

Before returning to England, Captain Newport made sure that the colonists were settled into the place they had named Jamestown. Just a few days after Newport left, the colony's president, Edward Wingfield, wrote that "an Indian came to us from the great Powhatan with the word of peace." The Powhatan messenger reassured Wingfield "that he desired greatly our friendship . . . that we should sow and reap in peace." Whether the colonists and American Indians could live together peacefully remained to be seen.

As you read this section you will find out:

- **How Jamestown was financed.**
- **What hardships early settlers faced.**
- **What the relationship was between the colonists and the local American Indians.**

Merchant Adventurers

Despite the setback of the failed Roanoke colony, many people in England, particularly wealthy merchants, remained interested in colonization. The experiences of men like Humphrey Gilbert and Walter Raleigh had proven that founding a colony was expensive and risky. Most English merchants and manufacturers were cautious businesspeople, not daring adventurers or court favorites. Instead of outfitting expeditions as individuals, they organized what they called **joint-stock companies**. These companies were ancestors of modern-day corporations. They were owned by many stockholders who shared in the profits and losses.

In 1606 James I, who had become king after the death of Queen Elizabeth I, gave the joint-stock London Company a charter to develop a huge area of North America. The region was named Virginia in honor of Elizabeth, who, because she had never married, was known as the Virgin Queen. By 1609 the London Company's grant of land extended along the Atlantic coast from the Hudson River in present-day New York to North Carolina, and west "from Sea to Sea"—that is, all the way to the Pacific Ocean!

• New Hopes in America

The Settlement of Jamestown

A few days before Christmas 1606, three London Company ships set sail for Virginia. The voyage had three purposes—to prepare the way for larger groups of colonists, to search for precious metals, and to find a trade route to East Asia. The ships reached the coast of Virginia in April 1607. They sailed up a river, which the settlers named after King James. Then the 105 men who decided to stay in the new colony built a fort, which they called Jamestown.

From the start, life at Jamestown was an endless series of troubles. The settlement was easy to defend, but it was also swampy and infested with disease-bearing mosquitoes. Illness soon struck the colonists who were already weak and sick from the long ocean voyage. By the end of the summer, almost half of the settlers were dead, and many of the rest were sick with malaria. When the first supply ship arrived in December, fewer than 40 colonists were alive to greet it.

The ship brought 120 more English settlers to Jamestown, but few of the newcomers survived for very long. They were poorly prepared for the challenge of living in a wilderness, and they had few of the practical skills needed by pioneers, such as carpentry and farming. Expecting to find that wealth practically grew on trees, they did not realize that it was necessary to work hard merely to stay alive.

John Smith. Luckily, one colonist, John Smith, had the courage to take command. Smith was a short, bearded man of action. Although he was only in his mid-twenties, Smith had seen far more of the world than had the other settlers. He had fought in several wars against the Turks in

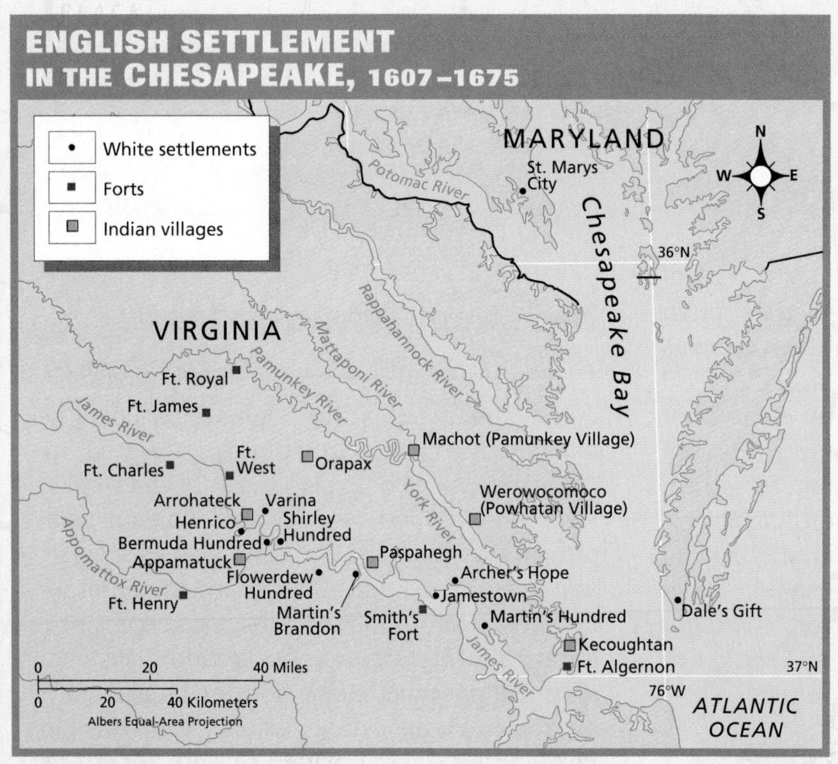

Learning from Maps. Early English settlments and forts often were located near Indian villages. This brought the cultures into close contact, and conflicts frequently erupted.

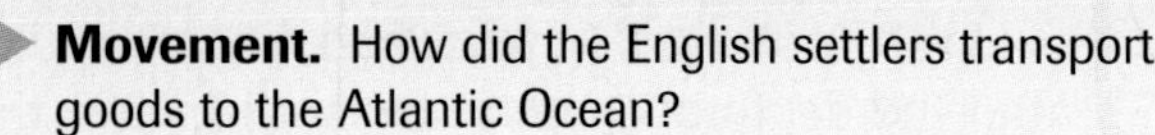

▶ **Movement.** How did the English settlers transport goods to the Atlantic Ocean?

• Maps

Nova Britannia.
OFFERING MOST
Excellent fruites by Planting in
Virginia.
Exciting all ſuch as be well affected
to further the ſame.

The London Company continually tried to rebuild Jamestown's declining population by recruiting new settlers. Posters such as this one appealed to potential colonists' hope of financial gain and sense of adventure.

eastern Europe. In one battle, he was captured and sold into slavery. However, he managed to kill his master and escape. After many other remarkable adventures, he found himself in Virginia.

Smith put all his worldly experience and resourcefulness to work in Jamestown. After becoming president of the colony's council in 1608, Smith made hard work and strict discipline the rule. He stopped the colonists from searching for gold and obtained food for them by trading with the 32 tribes of the powerful Powhatan Confederacy.

The Powhatan. The Powhatan possessed the food and knowledge of the land that the colonists lacked. The Indians showed them how to catch fish and how to grow corn. Without this help, Jamestown might not have survived.

In spite of the colonists' need for friendship with the Powhatan, relations between the two groups soon became strained. When the Powhatan no longer wanted to help Jamestown, the settlers forced their cooperation by threatening them. Smith even took food from them at gunpoint! The Powhatan responded by raiding Jamestown and killing settlers who ventured too far into the forest.

Hard Times in Jamestown

In 1609 the London Company again tried to help the struggling colony. It sent about 500 more settlers, including the first women, to Jamestown. This did not solve the colony's problems, however.

The starving time. Conditions in Jamestown continued to worsen. The winter of 1609–10 became known as the "starving time." As Smith described it, there remained only:

> **"sixtie men, women and children, most miserable and poore creatures; and those were preserved for the most part, by roots, herbes, acornes, walnuts, berries, now and then a little fish . . . yea, even the very skinnes of our horses."**

At one point, the colonists almost decided to abandon the settlement and return to England.

Things began to improve in 1611 when Thomas Dale, a military man with a reputation for sternness, arrived to run the colony. During the next five years, Jamestown was more like a military camp than a civilian community.

Around 1619, women started coming to Jamestown in greater numbers. Single women often married male settlers in mass wedding ceremonies.

The Granger Collection, New York

The colonists disliked Dale, but under his leadership they did essential work likc plant corn and repair the fort. The colony survived but remained unprofitable.

New hopes. Among their other problems, the colonists struggled to produce something they could sell in Europe. They had hoped to find gold, but there was none. Instead, they found another type of "gold"—a native plant called tobacco.

American Indians had been growing and smoking tobacco for centuries. In the late 1500s Sir Walter Raleigh had made smoking fashionable in English high society. Many people, however, argued that smoking was unhealthy. King James published *Counterblaste to Tobacco,* which criticized smoking as:

> **"This filthie noveltie . . . a custome loathsome [disgusting] to the eye, hatefull to the Nose, harmefull to the braine, [and] dangerous to the Lungs."**

Thousands of English people ignored his warning, and the demand for tobacco soared.

The type of tobacco native to Virginia was too bitter for English taste. Colonist John Rolfe solved that problem in 1612 when he introduced a sweeter variety from the West Indies. The settlers now had something they could sell in England. Large farms called **plantations** gradually developed because of the great profits made by growing tobacco.

History Makers

Pocahontas

Pocahontas, also known as Matoaka, was one of Jamestown's most famous figures. The daughter of a Powhatan chief, Pocahontas led a life of adventure.

Detail from the National Portrait Gallery, Smithsonian Institution, Washington DC/Art Resource, NY

In 1608 her father captured John Smith. The Powhatan were ready to kill him, but Pocahontas begged her father to spare Smith's life. Smith lived to tell the tale of his rescue by the daring 13-year-old.

Later, in 1612, English settlers took Pocahontas hostage to ensure peace with the Powhatan. In Jamestown she converted to Christianity and took the name Rebecca. She also fell in love with tobacco planter John Rolfe. Their marriage in 1614 brought a truce between the Powhatan and the colony. When the newlyweds visited England, Pocahontas was treated with the respect due a princess and was presented to the English king and queen. Tragically, Pocahontas died of smallpox in England at the age of 22.

Bloodshed in Jamestown

The tobacco economy grew partly because of the relatively peaceful relations with the Powhatan. The tensions between the settlers and the Powhatan had eased in 1614, when John Rolfe married Pocahontas, a daughter of the Powhatan chief. Tobacco farming and the arrival of new settlers in Virginia, however, resulted in demands for more and more Indian land.

The strained relationship between the English and the Powhatan began to worsen, particularly after the deaths of Pocahontas and her father. Pocahontas's uncle, Opechancanough (OH-puh-chan-kuh-noh), then became the new Powhatan leader.

Historians have attempted to piece together Opechancanough's long and fascinating life. They believe that in 1561, when Opechancanough was a teenager, Spanish explorer Pedro Menéndez de Avilés stopped in the Chesapeake area. Menéndez was impressed by Opechancanough and persuaded his father to let the youth sail to Spain. He promised that the boy would return with riches.

Over time, the young Indian learned Spanish, became a Catholic, and acquired the Spanish name Don Luis. After many years, he persuaded the authorities to send him back to his homeland as a missionary. He arrived with a group of priests in 1570.

Once back in the Chesapeake area, however, he gave up Christianity. After several conflicts with the priests, he killed them and then changed his name to Opechancanough.

Later, Opechancanough watched the growth of Jamestown with deep concern. By 1620 there were more than 2,000 settlers in the colony. Their increasing numbers were beginning to threaten the Powhatan's control of the region. In 1622 Opechancanough launched a sudden attack that killed almost a third of the settlers, including John Rolfe. War followed, and the English struck back with equal fierceness.

This bloodshed and other problems caused King James to cancel the London Company's charter in 1624. He put Virginia under royal control, but the fighting continued. Finally, in 1644, when Opechancanough was about 100 years old, the English captured and killed him. This ended the last Powhatan resistance.

C Smith taketh the King of Pamavnkee prisoner 1608

Courtesy of the John Carter Brown Library at Brown University

Some historians believe this sketch—from John Smith's account of his life in Virginia—shows him threatening Opechancanough.

Section 1 Review

• Glossary

• Gazetteer

IDENTIFY and explain the significance of the following: joint-stock companies, James I, John Smith, John Rolfe, plantations, Pocahontas, Opechancanough

LOCATE and explain the importance of the following: Virginia, Jamestown

REVIEWING FOR DETAILS

1. How was settlement in Jamestown financed?
2. How would you describe the relationship between the Virginia colonists and American Indians?

REVIEWING FOR UNDERSTANDING

3. **Geographic Literacy** What hardships did early settlers in Virginia face?
4. **Writing Mastery:** *Persuading* Imagine that you are a leader of Jamestown during the "starving time." Write a speech convincing the settlers not to abandon the colony.
5. **Critical Thinking:** *Generalizations and Stereotypes* What ideas or opinions might the Virginia colonists have held about American Indians that would have led them to believe they had a right to Indian land?

Section 2
The New England Colonies

Multimedia Connections

Explore these related topics and materials on the CD–ROM to enrich your understanding of this section:

Gazetteer
- Boston
- Connecticut
- New Hampshire
- Plymouth

Profiles
- William Bradford

Readings
- Mayflower Compact

Biographies
- Anne Bradstreet

Atlas
- Great Migration

Media Bank
- Anne Bradstreet
- Founding of Connecticut
- Puritan Meeting House
- Puritan Life
- Puritans in England
- Settling New England

In the 1630s merchant ships leaving for Massachusetts regularly sailed out of the ports of England. Colonists heading for New England packed the decks of ships such as the *Bevis*. In 1638 the *Bevis* sailed from Southampton. On board were Abigail and Benjamin Carpenter from the small village of Hartwell. Their four sons, all under the age of 10 years old, and Benjamin's elderly father traveled with them. Would they survive the voyage and prosper in Massachusetts?

As you read this section you will find out:

- **Who the Pilgrims were, and why they came to America.**
- **How Puritan communities were organized.**
- **What role religion played in New England.**

Religion and Colonization

While many people came to America for economic reasons, others had religious motives. In the early 1500s, almost a century before the first English colonists arrived in Jamestown, a religious movement called the **Reformation** had swept through Europe.

Catholics and Protestants. Before the Reformation, most western Europeans were Catholics. In 1517 Martin Luther, a German monk, published criticisms of many of the Roman Catholic Church's ideas and practices. Thousands of people supported his attempt to reform Catholicism. These protesters became known as Protestants.

Protestants founded a variety of new Christian churches. In England, King Henry VIII established the Church of England, also known

The Granger Collection, New York

Squanto showed the Pilgrims how to fertilize their fields with fish remains to produce a larger crop yield.

as the Anglican Church. The Church of England retained many Catholic ceremonies, including the mass, however.

Some English Protestants thought that the Anglican Church was still too Catholic. They wanted to "purify" it by removing all traces of Catholicism. These people became known as **Puritans**. Even more radical Protestants wanted to separate from the Church of England entirely. These **Separatists**, as they were called, eventually founded **sects**, or new religious groups.

Members of these sects, as well as Catholics, were often persecuted in England because of their beliefs. Some of them began to think of America as a place where they might practice their faith openly.

Pilgrims found Plymouth. The **Pilgrims** were the first English Separatists to come to America seeking religious freedom. (A pilgrim is someone who has religious motives for making a journey.) They had left England for Holland in 1608 to escape persecution, but life in Holland disappointed them. After they obtained permission to settle within the London Company's grant, they returned to England. In September 1620 a party of 35 Pilgrims and 66 other colonists sailed on the *Mayflower*, bound for Virginia.

They never reached their destination. On November 9 they sighted land on Cape Cod in present-day Massachusetts. A few of the Pilgrams had read John Smith's description of the area, which he had called New England. They decided to settle on Cape Cod because winter was approaching. They were outside the London Company's grant, so the Pilgrims drew up a document, the **Mayflower Compact**, to provide a legal basis for their colony, which they named Plymouth. As had happened in Jamestown, disease swept through the community. Within six months almost half of the colonists had died.

Fortunately, the Pilgrims had the help of two English-speaking American Indians, Samoset (SAM-uh-set), a Pemaquid Indian, and Squanto (SKWAHN-toh), a Pawtuxet Indian. They taught the Pilgrims how to plant corn, showed them where to hunt and fish, and helped them arrange a peace treaty with the powerful Wampanoag tribe. The Pilgrims worked hard,

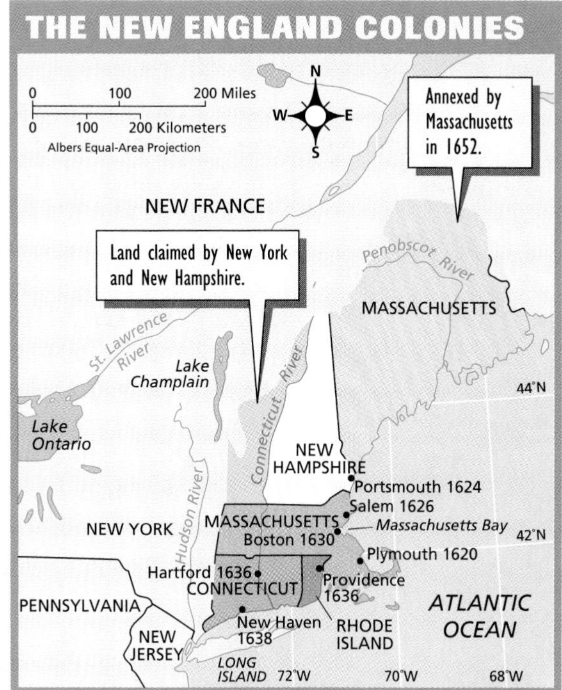

Learning from Maps.
Within 20 years, colonists settled throughout New England.

Location. What town is near the Connecticut River?

• **Maps**

planted crops, and in the autumn gathered a good harvest. The settlers then came together to give thanks for their survival.

• Pilgrims

The Puritans

In addition to the Plymouth colony, a few English fishing settlements and trading posts had been established along the New England coast. Large-scale colonization did not begin in the region until the Puritans arrived in the 1630s, however.

Unlike the Separatist Pilgrims, the Puritans wanted only to reform the Anglican Church. But as persecution in England increased, they came to doubt that reform was possible. John Winthrop, a Puritan leader, hoped to build a model Christian community in America:

> **"We must consider that we shall be like a City upon a Hill; the eyes of all people are on us. . . . We shall be made a story and a byword throughout the world."**

In 1629 King Charles I gave a group of Puritan merchants permission to organize a joint-stock company called the Massachusetts Bay Company. One year later, a 17-ship convoy carrying almost 1,000 Puritan men, women, and children arrived in New England. While few of these Puritans were wealthy, most had some education and had enough money to pay for their own passage and to later set themselves up in the new colony.

John Winthrop, the first colonial governor of Massachusetts, founded the settlement that became Boston. His son and grandson were both colonial governors of Connecticut.

• John Winthrop

Massachusetts Historical Society

Anne Pollard immigrated to America when she was a child. She prospered in the Puritan colony, living to be 105 years old.

The climate in Massachusetts was very different from that in Virginia. New England winters were harsh, but the cold weather discouraged the spread of malaria and other diseases that killed so many Virginians. After a difficult first year, the Puritans prospered. Most lived longer than people in England or Virginia.

The colder climate also meant that New Englanders could not grow semitropical crops, such as tobacco. This discouraged the development of large plantations like those in Virginia. Although New England land was stony and hilly, it was very fertile. Many people who lived inland became farmers. Those in seacoast towns often became merchants, craftspeople, or fishermen.

Puritan groups that wanted to found new towns received large tracts of land from the colonial government. They centered their towns around a plot of public grazing land called a **common**. Each town usually had a school and a meetinghouse, which often served as both a church and a town hall. Each family received a small plot of land for a house. Outside the town lay fields where townspeople grew crops. The rest of the land remained town property, to be given out to new settlers as the town grew.

The Puritans founded several communities centered around their chief town, Boston. By 1640 more than 20,000 people had come to New England. They were part of a movement called the **Great Migration**. They eventually settled other colonies in Connecticut, Rhode Island, New Hampshire, and Long Island, New York.

Global Connections

The Great Migration

The Puritans who went to New England were part of a larger movement known as the Great Migration. Life in England was increasingly difficult for Puritans after 1625. King Charles I forced them out of positions in the Anglican Church and the government. In 1629 he dissolved Parliament and ruled alone for 11 years. During that time some 60,000 Puritans left England. Only about one third went to New England, however. Another 20,000 settled colonies in the Caribbean, and the rest went to other countries in Europe.

While some Puritans built colonies in America, others remained in England to challenge royal authority. When Charles summoned a new Parliament in 1640 to raise taxes, Puritan members demanded reforms. Charles resisted, and England soon plunged into civil war. Parliament's army, led by Puritan Oliver Cromwell, defeated the king in 1646. The Puritans held power in England for the next 12 years. During this time, their colonies in America continued to grow and prosper.

Church and Community

Puritans believed that they had formed a **covenant**, or sacred agreement, with God to build a society based on the Bible's teachings. They worked and worshiped together, seeking to create such an ideal community. The church, family, education, and government were institutions the Puritans used to create and sustain their vision of a perfect godly society.

The church was the most important part of the Puritan community. On Sundays, everyone was expected to attend. Services, which included praying and listening to long sermons, lasted much of the day.

Unlike the early colonists in Jamestown, who were mostly single men, Puritans encouraged families to emigrate. The head of a family, usually the father, was responsible for making sure that its members lived up to Puritan ideals.

Puritans also used education as a way of maintaining social and religious unity. They wanted everyone to be able to read the Bible and understand Puritan ways. For this reason, Massachusetts required towns with at least 50 families to establish a public school.

Providing well-educated ministers for future generations was particularly important to Puritans. Therefore, in 1636 they founded Harvard, the first college in all the English colonies.

The Puritans discussed community issues at town meetings. This idea of political participation also extended to the colony's government. At first, all political power was in the hands of the General Court, made up of a small group of men from the colony. The General Court, however, soon gave greater privileges, including the right to vote for governor and for members of the Court, to all male church members. This gave Puritans in Massachusetts much more political influence than people had in England at the time.

• **Roger Williams**

The Narragansett Indians sheltered Roger Williams after he was exiled. He bought land from them and founded Providence, Rhode Island.

The Granger Collection, New York

Conflicts in New England

Although the Puritans had left England to obtain religious freedom, they did not tolerate **dissenters**, people who disagreed with commonly held opinions. Religious dissenters were no more welcome in the Massachusetts colony than they were in England. Members of other religious sects were often expelled from the colony and sometimes were even executed.

Roger Williams. Even among themselves, Puritans had little liking for disagreement. Roger Williams, a minister, questioned many Puritan ways. He insisted that the colonists had no right to land in Massachusetts until either they or the king purchased it from local American Indians. To the authorities, Williams's argument threatened the colony's existence.

In 1635 the Massachusetts General Court ordered Williams to leave. He went south and the next year founded Rhode Island. There he put his ideas about religious freedom and fair treatment of Indians into practice. In 1644 he received a charter for his colony.

Anne Hutchinson. Anne Hutchinson led another major dissent against Puritan beliefs. She held meetings in her home to discuss religious questions. For example, she argued that going to church and praying were less important than leading a holy life.

Hutchinson began to attract a number of followers, including important members of the colony. One supporter described her as "a woman that preaches better . . . than any . . . learned scholars." Hutchinson's teachings and popularity greatly alarmed Puritan officials. They felt even more

Anne Hutchinson was tried by the Massachusetts General Court for her religious views. The record of her trial still exists today.

• **Anne Hutchinson**

threatened because a woman expressing such independent ideas challenged the authority of Puritan men. One minister called her:

> **"a dangerous instrument of the Devil, raised up by Satan amongst us. . . . The misgovernment of this woman's tongue has been a great cause of this disorder."**

In 1637 Hutchinson was expelled from Massachusetts. She and her followers then joined the Williams group in Rhode Island. Later, she and her six youngest children moved to the Dutch colony of New Netherland. In 1643 she was killed by Indians. Some Puritans believed her death was divine punishment for her sins.

Salem. One of the most extreme examples of the Puritans' attempt to maintain absolute control over their community was in the Salem witch trials of 1692. Like most people in the 1600s, Puritans believed in the existence of witchcraft. The trouble began in Salem when several girls began to act strangely. Three women were accused of bewitching the girls and were arrested. Soon, other townspeople reported that evil forces were tormenting them. Hundreds of people—mostly women—were accused of being witches. Some 30 were found guilty, and 19 were hanged before Governor William Phips stopped the trials and forbade further executions.

The Salem panic severely shook the colony. A few years later, ashamed officials issued a public apology. The Salem witch trials had highlighted some of the worst aspects of Puritan New England—suspicion, intolerance, and the community's pressure on residents to follow a strict code of behavior.

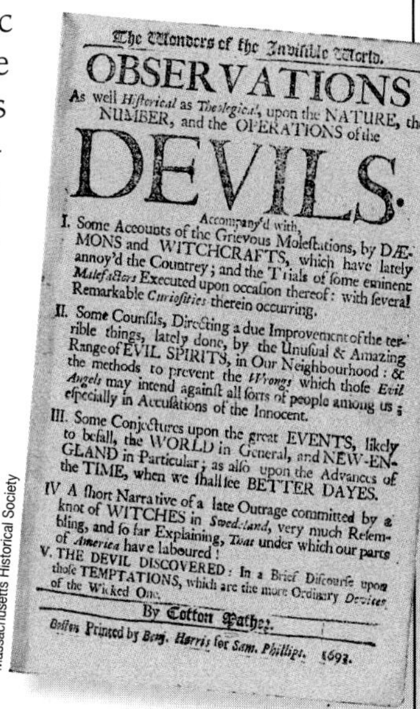
The Wonders of the Invisible World.
OBSERVATIONS
As well *Historical* as *Theological*, upon the NATURE, the NUMBER, and the OPERATIONS of the
DEVILS.
Accompany'd with,
I. Some Accounts of the Grievous Moleſtations, by DÆMONS and WITCHCRAFTS, which have lately annoy'd the Countrey; and the Trials of ſome eminent *Malefactors* Executed upon occaſion thereof: with ſeveral Remarkable *Curioſities* therein occurring.
II. Some Counſils, Directing a due Improvement of the terrible things, lately done, by the Unuſual & Amazing Range of EVIL SPIRITS, in Our Neighbourhood: & the methods to prevent the *Wrongs* which thoſe *Evil Angels* may intend againſt all ſorts of people among us; eſpecially in Accuſations of the Innocent.
III. Some Conjectures upon the great EVENTS, likely to befall, the WORLD in General, and NEW-ENGLAND in Particular; as alſo upon the Advances of the TIME, when we ſhall ſee BETTER DAYES.
IV A ſhort Narrative of a late Outrage committed by a knot of WITCHES in *Swedeland*, very much Reſembling, and ſo far Explaining, *That* under which our parts of *America* have laboured!
V. THE DEVIL DISCOVERED: In a Brief Diſcourſe upon thoſe TEMPTATIONS, which are the more Ordinary *Devices* of the Wicked One.
By Cotton Mather.
Boston Printed by *Benj. Harris* for *Sam. Phillips*. 1693.

Massachusetts Historical Society

Cotton Mather was an important minister in Boston. He wrote on religious matters, including this pamphlet, The Wonders of the Invisible World. *His writings and views on witchcraft had an impact on the Salem witch trials.*

• Salem Witch Trials

Section 2 Review

• Glossary

• Gazetteer

IDENTIFY and explain the significance of the following: Reformation, Puritans, Separatists, sects, Pilgrims, Mayflower Compact, John Winthrop, common, Great Migration, covenant, dissenters, Roger Williams, Anne Hutchinson

LOCATE and explain the importance of the following: Massachusetts, Rhode Island, Salem

REVIEWING FOR DETAILS

1. Why did the Pilgrims come to America?
2. How did the Puritans organize their communities?
3. What role did religion play in Puritan society?

REVIEWING FOR UNDERSTANDING

4. **Geographic Literacy** Where did the Puritans spread in North America, and why did they move there?
5. **Critical Thinking:** *Cause and Effect* How can the Protestant Reformation be linked to the colonization of America? Explain your answer.

Section 3
THE SOUTHERN COLONIES

Multimedia Connections

Explore these related topics and materials on the CD–ROM to enrich your understanding of this section:

Gazetteer

- Florida
- Maryland
- Georgia
- North Carolina
- South Carolina

Readings

- Making the Atlantic Crossing

Profiles

- James Oglethorpe

Media Bank

- Colonial Savannah
- Colony of Maryland
- Life in the Carolinas
- Settling the Southern Colonies

In 1669 widows were among the few women who could claim economic independence. Unlike single and married women, widows could own property. To remarry meant that widows would risk losing their independence. Margaret Preston took steps to protect her property before she remarried. Her future husband, William Perry, signed a document guaranteeing that some of her money, a slave, her household goods, and a horse would remain hers to do with as she pleased.

As you read this section you will find out:

- **How the Virginia colony developed.**
- **What changes Bacon's Rebellion brought to Virginia.**
- **What new southern colonies were founded.**

Life in Virginia

Life in Virginia was very different from life in a New England community. There were few towns in Virginia because planters relied on rivers for transporting goods. Oceangoing vessels could sail up the James and other rivers, bringing European products directly to the plantations and taking away cured tobacco for sale in England. The plantations could be widely separated because the buying and selling of goods took place on each planter's dock. There were few schools because the population was so scattered. In fact, most families educated their children at home.

In general, most early Virginia settlers were more concerned with making money than in establishing families. Those interested in forming a family faced several difficulties, including the fact that there were about six times as many men as women. The high death rate also affected family life. It was common for one marriage partner to die and for the surviving partner to marry a second or even a third time.

Children frequently were raised by step-parents or, if orphaned, by strangers. Because life was short and uncertain, most parents were careful to make arrangements for their children in their wills. Colonist Susan English, who had three children, provided:

> **"whereas there wilbe charge in bringing upp the abovesaid Children both for diet Cloathing and scooling I desire . . . that whosoever bringeth upp the children unto the age of discresion [good judgment] with all things necessary and fitting shall have the male cattle for soe long tyme as the Children be with them."**

The London Company realized that families were essential if Virginia was to prosper, so it worked hard to bring over female settlers. Over time men no longer outnumbered women and a stable family life developed.

Life in early Virginia involved hard work for the entire family. Women were usually responsible for child care.

Labor Problems in Virginia

The London Company campaigned constantly to attract settlers. It gave colonists who paid their own way or that of others 50 acres of land for each "head" (person) transported. This grant was called a **headright**.

Many people who could not afford the cost of passage to America got there by becoming **indentured servants**. They signed contracts called indentures, agreeing to work for a period of time—generally four or five years—to pay for the voyage. These contracts could be bought and sold. About 75 percent of the early Virginia colonists were at one time under indenture.

Indentured servants had to work without wages for whoever owned their indentures. The owner also received the headright for bringing the newcomer to Virginia. In other words, the person who paid the servant's passage received both land and the labor needed to farm it.

When servants completed their time of service, their employers were supposed to provide them with clothes, food, and other basic supplies. In the early years, disease killed more than two thirds of the indentured servants before their contracts expired. Despite the risks, people still came to Virginia in search of economic opportunity.

Indenture was not the only labor system in Virginia. In 1619 a Dutch ship arrived with 20 Africans on board. Historians are not sure whether these first Africans were sold as indentured servants or as slaves. As more Africans were brought to Virginia, however, many were treated as slaves. In this way, race began to be a factor in determining one's status in the colony, and the institution of slavery took root in Virginia.

Until the 1690s planters preferred indentured servants to enslaved Africans as a labor source, in part because it cost much more to buy a slave. However, planters soon found that using indentured servants had drawbacks.

Once the servants worked off their debt, many became independent planters who competed with their former employers.

The newly independent planters often found that they only had access to poor land. In addition, the increase in crop production caused the price of tobacco to fall. This left many small planters in debt and dissatisfied. They had come to America seeking a better way of life but were not getting what they expected.

The Granger Collection, New York

Nathaniel Bacon (right) confronts Sir William Berkeley (left), Virginia's governor. Bacon was only 29 years old when he led the rebellion against Berkeley's government.

Bacon's Rebellion

The discontent of small planters in Virginia erupted in 1676. They had begun to eye land that was guaranteed to the Powhatan in a 1646 treaty. Fighting soon broke out between the farmers and the Indians. Nathaniel Bacon, a newcomer to the colony, raised a large force and asked the governor of Virginia, Sir William Berkeley, to authorize him to begin a war with the Indians. Berkeley, however, wanted to keep peace with the Indians and refused Bacon's request.

Defying the governor, Bacon's force massacred peaceful Indians and attacked others at random. When Berkeley declared him a rebel, Bacon and his men turned against the government. Bacon drove the governor out of Jamestown and burned the town. In October 1676, however, Bacon became ill and died, and **Bacon's Rebellion** soon collapsed.

Although the rebellion failed to get more land for the settlers, it led to major changes in Virginia. In 1619 most male settlers had been given the right to vote for representatives to an assembly called the **House of Burgesses**. This was the first elected English governmental body in the colonies. Since 1661, however, Berkeley had refused to call an election. As a result of Bacon's Rebellion, new elections finally were held.

The rebellion also contributed to increased use of enslaved Africans by many tobacco farmers. Planters became less willing to employ indentured servants who might later become troublemakers like Bacon's rebels. Instead, planters increasingly used slaves, who could never become economic competitors. Planters also realized that the children of slaves would provide labor for the future.

Slavery was common in the Spanish and English colonies in the Caribbean. In early Virginia, some Africans were enslaved. Others, however, were indentured servants who would eventually become independent planters.

Colonial Williamsburg Foundation

Gradually, Virginia became almost entirely dependent on slave labor.

New Colonies in the South

Although it had a shaky start, Virginia was much more stable by the mid-1630s. By 1641 the colony's population had reached 7,500 and tobacco exports were topping 1 million pounds a year. Virginia's prosperity encouraged other English developers to found new colonies in the region.

Maryland. In 1632 King Charles I gave several million acres of land around Chesapeake Bay to a Catholic noble named George Calvert, Lord Baltimore. Most colonies were controlled by joint-stock companies. Lord Baltimore, however, was the **proprietor**, or single owner, of his colony.

In 1634 the first settlers arrived in the colony, which was named Maryland after Queen Mary, the wife of Charles I. After Calvert died, his son, Cecilius, Second Lord Baltimore, founded Maryland as a refuge for Catholics, but Protestants were also admitted. The Maryland **Toleration Act of 1649** guaranteed religious freedom to all Christians.

Although the death rate among the early settlers was high, life in Maryland was somewhat easier than it had been for the first colonists at Jamestown. The Maryland colony was successful because its settlers carefully planned their activities and avoided many of the mistakes that Jamestown colonists had made. Following the example of the Virginia planters, the settlers in Maryland turned to growing tobacco.

The Carolinas. In 1663 Charles II, who had become king after the death of his father, gave the land between Virginia and Spanish Florida to eight noblemen, including Sir George Carteret. The proprietors called this colony Carolina, Latin for "Charles." They hoped to attract settlers from the more established colonies. Although a number of Virginians did drift into the northern part of the grant, settlement there was scattered. There were few roads and practically no towns, churches, or schools.

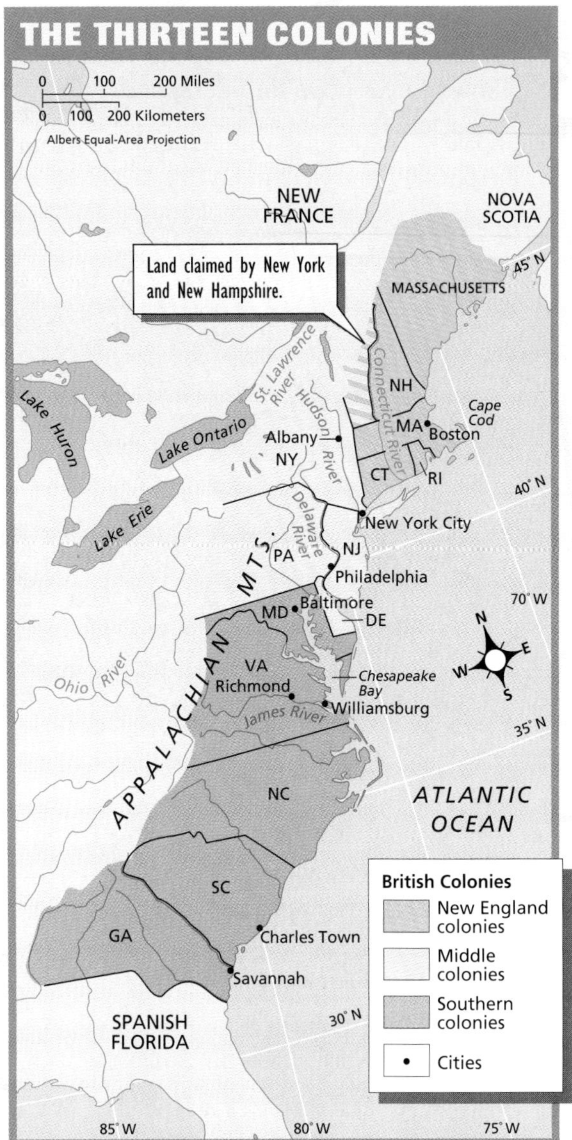

Learning from Maps. English settlements filled the Atlantic coast between the borders of Spanish Florida and New France.

Movement. What geographical barrier stopped westward expansion in the southern colonies?

The proprietors then brought settlers from the West Indies to thc southern part of their grant, promising them that:

> **"any man whatever that is but willing to take . . . pains may be assured of a most comfortable subsistence [life], and . . . raise his fortunes far beyond what he could ever hope for in England."**

Charles Town (now Charleston) was founded in 1670. It soon became a busy trading center, as well as the social and political center of the new colony.

In 1719, however, the settlers rebelled against the proprietors' government and asked the king to take control of the colony. Ten years later the area was officially separated into two royal colonies, North and South Carolina.

Georgia. The last of the southern colonies was not founded until 1733. A group of charitable Englishmen, led by James Oglethorpe, hoped Georgia would be a colony where debtors and other poor people could make a new start in life.

Few English settlers came to Georgia, however. Some prospective settlers feared the Spanish, who also claimed the region. Others resented Oglethorpe's strict rules, which included bans on liquor and slaves. In 1752 the colony's trustees turned Georgia over to the Crown.

Maryland Historical Society, Baltimore

In 1648 Margaret Brent became the first woman to demand the vote in the English colonies. A major landowner, she was active in colonial affairs and served as attorney for important colonists.

Section 3 Review

• Glossary

• Gazetteer

IDENTIFY and explain the significance of the following: headright, indentured servants, Bacon's Rebellion, House of Burgesses, proprietor, Cecilius Calvert, Toleration Act of 1649, James Oglethorpe

LOCATE and explain the importance of the following: Maryland, Charles Town, North Carolina, South Carolina, Georgia

REVIEWING FOR DETAILS

1. How did Bacon's Rebellion change life in Virginia?
2. What new southern colonies were founded, and why?

REVIEWING FOR UNDERSTANDING

3. **Geographic Literacy** How did the geography of Virginia influence the colony's development?
4. **Writing Mastery:** *Creating* Imagine that you are a proprietor of a colony. Create an advertisement to attract settlers.
5. **Critical Thinking:** *Making Comparisons* What were the major differences between the Virginia and Massachusetts colonies?

Section 4
THE MIDDLE COLONIES

Multimedia Connections

Explore these related topics and materials on the CD–ROM to enrich your understanding of this section:

Media Bank

- Life in Colonial New York
- Settling the Middle Colonies

Atlas

- Middle Colonies

Profiles

- William Penn

Gazetteer

- New York
- New Jersey
- Pennsylvania
- Delaware

Four English warships anchored in the harbor. The Dutch waited to see if the ships would fire on the town. The arrival of the English was not unexpected. Other countries had threatened New Netherland before, but up until now the Dutch had managed to drive out the Swedish and hold off the English. Governor Peter Stuyvesant (STY-vi-suhnt) was determined to unite the New Netherland colonists and fight off the enemy. Tension mounted as a crowd of colonists gathered in the harbor.

As you read this section you will find out:

- **How New Netherland became New York.**
- **Why Pennsylvania was settled.**
- **What colonies were created from parts of New York and Pennsylvania.**

England Seizes the Dutch Colonies

The English claimed the entire area between Newfoundland and Florida on the basis of John Cabot's 1497 voyage. They considered the Dutch in their colony of New Netherland to be intruders on English soil. The fact that Dutch merchants were buying Virginia tobacco and selling it elsewhere irritated English tobacco merchants, who felt that the tobacco trade was rightfully theirs.

In 1664 King Charles II gave his brother James, the Duke of York, a grant that included New Netherland. Then he sent four English warships to attack the colony's capital of New Amsterdam.

New Netherland was governed by Peter Stuyvesant, a colorful character with a long military career. In one battle, he had been wounded in the right leg, which had to be amputated. As a result, hc walked on a decorated wooden leg.

For 17 years, Stuyvesant ruled New Netherland. Because its settlers came from many regions, numerous languages were spoken there. This diversity sometimes created cultural conflicts. New Netherland also had financial troubles. Over the years, Stuyvesant's attempts to raise taxes and to create a solidly Dutch society angered some of the colonists.

When the English warships arrived in 1664, New Amsterdam's inhabitants pushed Stuyvesant aside and surrendered the town without firing a shot. Most of the residents, including ex-governor Stuyvesant, continued to live in the colony, which was renamed New York in honor of James of York.

James then handed out generous land grants to his friends. The largest grant, which included all the land between the Hudson and Delaware Rivers, went to Sir George Carteret, who had just become one of the proprietors of Carolina, and to Lord John Berkeley. This grant became the colony of New Jersey.

To attract settlers, Carteret and Berkeley offered land on easy terms. They also promised settlers religious freedom and the right to elect a legislature. In the 1670s members of a religious sect known as **Quakers** purchased the western part of the colony. The proprietors sold the rest of the colony in 1684. In 1702 the two sections were combined.

The Wrath of Peter Stuyvesant, painting by Asher B. Durand from The Collection of The New-York Historical Society.

Peter Stuyvesant, the governor of New Netherland, had a commanding presence. He had spent much of his life in leadership positions in military and political service.

• Peter Stuyvesant

Quakers Found Colonies

In 1681 Charles II awarded another large grant in America to an unlikely candidate, William Penn. Although he was wealthy and of high social status, Penn was also a Quaker.

William Penn took an active role in the founding of his colony. He visited it twice, making sure that the colony was developing as he had planned. One of his most important accomplishments was the signing of the treaty shown in this painting. Penn's treaty with these American Indians established a friendly relationship between the colonists and their Indian neighbors.

Quakers stressed religious tolerance, simplicity, and kindness toward others. They were opposed to warfare and any use of force. They also emphasized the authority of the individual in religious, social, and political matters. Because of this belief, many English people thought the Quakers were religious radicals. Therefore, Quakers were often imprisoned, tortured, or even hanged.

To protect Quakers from such persecution, Penn wanted to create a refuge for them in America. Charles II was agreeable because he owed a large sum of money to Penn's father, who had died in 1670. To cancel this debt, Charles gave Penn the region between New Jersey and Maryland, suggesting that it be called Pennsylvania in honor of Penn's father.

Penn was deeply religious. He decided to make Pennsylvania "a holy experiment" in Christian living and self-government. In his plan for the settlement of the colony, Penn declared:

> **"Governments, like clocks, go from the motion men give them; and as governments are made and moved by men, so by them they are ruined. . . . Let men be good, and the government cannot be bad; if it be ill, they will cure it."**

Like Roger Williams, Penn insisted that Indians be paid for their land and be treated fairly by the colonists. Unlike most proprietors, Penn came to America to oversee the laying-out of his colony's capital, Philadelphia, an ancient name meaning "brotherly love."

To attract settlers to his colony, Penn wrote glowing accounts of its soil and climate and circulated them throughout Europe. These, along with his promises of a voice in government and religious liberty, lured settlers from many lands. Among them were large numbers of Germans, who became known as the Pennsylvania Dutch because of the way English settlers pronounced *Deutsch*, meaning "German."

Pennsylvania prospered from the beginning. Farmers produced large crops of wheat and other foodstuffs. In 1682 Penn obtained another grant of land on Delaware Bay. When Pennsylvania expanded westward, this region received the right to have its own colonial assembly in 1704. It eventually became the colony of Delaware.

Section 4 Review

• Glossary

IDENTIFY and explain the significance of the following: Peter Stuyvesant, Quakers, William Penn

LOCATE and explain the importance of the following: New York, New Jersey, Pennsylvania, Philadelphia (See the map on page 55.)

• Gazetteer

REVIEWING FOR DETAILS

1. How and why did England take the Dutch colony of New Netherland?
2. Why was Pennsylvania founded?

• Time Line

REVIEWING FOR UNDERSTANDING

3. **Geographic Literacy** What colonies were created from New York and Pennsylvania?
4. **Writing Mastery:** *Informing* Write a paragraph telling settlers what to expect if they come to William Penn's colony.
5. **Critical Thinking:** *Making Comparisons* How was English treatment of Dutch settlers in New Netherland similar to English treatment of American Indians in the colonies? How did treatment of the two groups differ?

CHAPTER 4

Colonial Life and Government (1650–1763)

THEMES IN AMERICAN HISTORY

Constitutional Heritage:
How might one society's system of government influence another's?

Economic Development:
How might trade affect government policies and foreign relations?

Democratic Values:
How might shared experiences help create a common culture?

• Video Opener

• Skill Builder

In 1729 writer Daniel Defoe described the great importance of international trade:

"How miserable, how dejected [sad], do a People look, (however prosperous before,) if by any Accident of an unprosperous *War*, or an *ill manag'd Peace*, Trade receives a Blow! And how cheerfully do men Fight in a War, and Work in a Peace, if the Channels of Trade are but kept open, and a free Circulation of Business is preserved!"

image above: *A colonial family*

Section 1

THE ENGLISH COLONIAL SYSTEM

Multimedia Connections

Explore these related topics and materials on the CD-ROM to enrich your understanding of this section:

Gazetteer

- Boston, Massachusetts

Media Bank

- Virginia House of Burgesses
- Regional Trade
- Colonial City
- English History, 1625–1765

Readings

- Frontier and City Life

Early one April morning in 1689, a group of angry citizens gathered in Boston. They planned to rebel against new laws that English officials had forced on them without their consent. The colonists were upset because they had come to expect a certain degree of freedom in governing their own affairs. Although colonial policies were still shaped by the needs of the Crown, in general England allowed the colonists to rule themselves.

As you read this section you will find out:

- **Who carried out the English Crown's policies in the colonies.**
- **Why the Dominion of New England failed.**
- **How the English government tried to control trade in the colonies.**

Governing the Colonies

Technically, the English colonies belonged to the king or queen personally, not to the government. Of course, the king or queen did not personally manage the affairs of the colonies. Colonial policy was set by the royal advisers, who made up what was called the **Privy Council**. This council, in turn, was subject to **Parliament**, the lawmaking body of England.

Each colony also had a government that carried out English policies and enforced the laws of England. Colonial governments were modeled after the English government and attended to all sorts of local matters that were of no direct concern to England. At the head of each colony was a governor who represented the king and made sure that English laws were enforced. Some governors were American-born, but most were sent over from England.

The Granger Collection, New York

Sir Richard Onslow leads a meeting of the English House of Commons in London's Westminster Hall around 1700.

Colonial governors received orders and policies from London and put them into effect. When local problems arose, however, the government had the power to handle them directly.

Governors were assisted by councils that had roughly the same powers and duties that the Privy Council had in England. In most of the colonies, members of the councils were appointed, not elected by the voters.

Elected bodies made local laws. These colonial assemblies, or legislatures, were modeled on the House of Commons, the elected branch of Parliament. On paper, they had only limited powers. The colonial governor or the government in England could cancel any law passed by a colonial assembly.

In practice, however, the assemblies had a great deal of power. Since they set taxes in the colonies, the assemblies controlled how money was raised and spent. Frequently, this power to tax and spend gave a colonial assembly control over the governor. For example, an assembly could refuse to spend money on projects that the governor wanted unless he agreed to approve laws that the assembly supported. An assembly might even attach a sentence providing money for the governor's salary to a bill he had threatened to disallow, or cancel. Then if the governor disallowed the bill, he did not get paid!

Governors, however, could call the assemblies into session and dismiss them without explanation. A governor could also order new elections for the legislators. The governor could not, however, make the legislators pass a law that a majority did not want to support.

The Dominion of New England

Most colonists liked the fact that England's empire was divided into so many separate parts. The system allowed each colony a great deal of control over its own affairs. But English leaders felt differently. They believed that combining the colonies into a few regional groups would make them easier to manage.

The most serious attempt to unify a group of colonies occurred after the death of King Charles II in 1685. Since Charles had no children who could be heirs to the throne, his brother James became king. In 1686 James created the **Dominion of New England**, which included Connecticut, Massachusetts, Rhode Island, and New Hampshire. Two years later, New York and New Jersey were added.

Sir Edmund Andros, a soldier who had formerly been colonial governor of New York, was appointed governor of the Dominion. Andros had a great deal of power. He could enact laws on his own, including tax laws. He ruled almost like a dictator, deciding by himself most questions of importance.

The colonists in the Dominion resented this loss of their independence. One angry New Englander described what life was like under Andros:

> **"It was now plainly affirmed [declared true], both by some in open Council, and by the same in private . . . , that the people in New England were all slaves, and the only difference between them and slaves is their not being bought and sold."**

Fortunately for the citizens of the Dominion, Andros did not last very long. King James II proved to be extremely unpopular in England. He ignored laws that Parliament had passed and adopted a strongly pro-Catholic policy that alarmed many Protestants.

When James's second wife, Queen Mary of Modena, gave birth to a son who would be raised a Catholic, leaders in Parliament staged a revolt that soon became known as the **Glorious Revolution**. They invited James's Protestant daughter Mary and her Dutch husband, William of Orange, to be crowned king and queen of England.

James fled first to France and then to Ireland. Meanwhile, William and Mary crossed the English Channel from the Netherlands in November 1688 to take the throne. News of the Glorious Revolution did not reach Boston until the following April, but when word finally arrived, it encouraged the colonists to take action. Angry colonists arrested Andros and other Dominion officials. Leading citizens took over the government. The Dominion soon fell apart. English authorities gave up the idea of a united Dominion of New England.

The Navigation and Trade Acts

Although the colonists enjoyed a great deal of local self-government, the English continued to establish general policies for their American possessions. Colonies were expected to benefit the countries that owned them. One way the colonies did this was by strengthening their home country's **balance of trade**, the

Many colonists were pleased when William and Mary were crowned the new rulers of England. This 1689 woodcutting illustrating their coronation was re-created on song-sheets and other items celebrating the event.

The Granger Collection, New York

• **Dominion**

Goods came in and out of busy shipping ports like this one in Bristol Quay, England. The men in this picture are probably unloading sugar products.

relationship between what a nation buys from and what it sells to foreign countries (not including its own colonies). The goal was to maintain a favorable balance of trade—to **export**, or sell, more than it would **import**, or buy, from other countries.

Regulating trade. The economic program designed to achieve a favorable balance of trade was called **mercantilism**. Mercantilists hoped to maintain their country's wealth by tightly controlling trade. To make sure that the colonies produced and sold things that England needed, Parliament passed many laws regulating the buying and selling of goods. These laws were known as the **Navigation and Trade Acts**. The first act was passed in 1651, and they continued to be enacted up through the mid-1700s.

These regulations required that all goods passing between England and the colonies be transported in ships built either in the colonies or in England. The owners of the ships also had to be English or American, as did the captain and most of the crew. For example, a Boston merchant could own a ship made in Philadelphia or London and carry goods from Virginia to New York or to any port in England or the English West Indies. The merchant, however, could not use a Dutch-made ship or hire a French captain.

European goods could be brought into the American colonies only after being taken to an English port. American colonists could import French wine, for instance, but it had to be taken to England first. Of course, once in England the wine could only be carried to the colonies in an English or colonial ship.

Colonial producers could sell certain products only within English territory. These **enumerated articles**, as they were called, were things that England needed but could not produce at home. Sugar, tobacco, furs, timber, and cotton were among the most important enumerated articles. The restrictions on these goods applied to both the colonies and to England. English sugar planters in the West Indies and tobacco planters in Virginia and Maryland could not sell their crops in France, Spain, or the Netherlands. In return, consumers in England could not buy sugar or tobacco produced in the French, Spanish, or Dutch colonies. Many colonial products, such as fish and wheat, were not enumerated because England already produced enough of them. Colonists could sell them anywhere.

Parliament also put restrictions on a few colonial handmade products that competed with similar English goods. For example, colonists could make fur hats and woolen cloth for local sale, but they were not allowed to export these products.

The English argued that these laws were fair to both the home country and the colonists. If the colonies produced raw materials that England needed, and if England manufactured items that the colonies needed, each would benefit.

Smuggling in the colonies. This trade system worked reasonably well for many decades. The success of the trading system was partly because most colonists were farmers, and many others worked as fishers, shipbuilders, or merchants. These colonists did not produce large amounts of manufactured goods. England, on the other hand, was one of the leading producers of manufactured goods in the world.

The Navigation and Trade Acts were not enforced very strictly, however, and smuggling was common. The colonies were far from England. America had a long coastline with many out-of-the-way harbors and tiny coves where small ships could slip in under cover of night and unload illegal goods.

For many years the English government did not try very hard to prevent smuggling. England was getting all the colonial products it needed. It hardly seemed worth the cost and effort to stop shippers who tried to sneak past the English navy with tobacco bound for the West Indies, or with French wine or silk that had not been taken first to England. Thus, while on paper the English government had great power, in practice it allowed the colonies a great deal of independence.

Courtesy of the Free Library of Philadelphia

Many colonial American women spun their own yarn from wool. Since wool was an enumerated article, colonists could not export any extra yarn or cloth they produced. They could sell such products locally, however.

Section 1 Review

• Glossary

IDENTIFY and explain the significance of the following: Privy Council, Parliament, Dominion of New England, Edmund Andros, Glorious Revolution, balance of trade, export, import, mercantilism, Navigation and Trade Acts, enumerated articles

REVIEWING FOR DETAILS

1. Who was responsible for carrying out the Crown's policies in the colonies?
2. Why was the Dominion of New England unsuccessful?
3. How did the English government try to control colonial trade?

REVIEWING FOR UNDERSTANDING

4. **Writing Mastery:** *Expressing* Imagine that you are a citizen of the Dominion of New England. Write a letter to a member of Parliament expressing why you are unhappy living under the Dominion.
5. **Critical Thinking:** *Drawing Conclusions* Overall, do you think the Navigation and Trade Acts limited the colonial economy? Explain your answer.

Section 2
THE COLONIAL ECONOMY

Multimedia Connections

Explore these related topics and materials on the CD–ROM to enrich your understanding of this section:

Media Bank

- Colonial Exports
- Colonial Tobacco
- West Indies Sugar Production

Gazetteer

- West Africa
- British West Indies
- Great Britain

Readings

- Slavery in the West Indies

Profiles

- Eliza Lucas Pinckney

Atlas

- Atlantic Slave Trade
- British West Indies

One of the first truly "self-made" Americans was the multitalented Benjamin Franklin. He started his career at age 12, working in a print shop. At 42 he was rich enough to retire from his business. In his essay "Advice to a Young Tradesman," Franklin explained how to earn a fortune in America. "The way to wealth," he wrote, ". . . is as plain as the way to market." Franklin's words were timely indeed. By the mid-1700s commerce was becoming a key to prosperity in the colonies.

As you read this section you will find out:

- **What the major economic products of the colonies were.**
- **Why trade networks developed.**
- **What life was like on the Middle Passage.**

The Southern Economy

The colonists needed manufactured goods such as farm tools, furniture, guns and ammunition, pots and pans, books, and glassware. They had to get most of these goods by producing crops that England or other countries could use. Crops that farmers raise in large quantities to sell are called **staple crops**.

The southern colonies had an advantage in growing staple crops because of their warm climate. Tobacco provided a staple crop for the colonists of Virginia, Maryland, and North Carolina. When American tobacco first became popular in England, its price was very high. For a time, anyone with even a small plot of land could make a good living growing tobacco. Although tobacco prices eventually fell, farmers were still able to make good profits from the crop.

In parts of South Carolina and later in Georgia, rice was the chief staple crop. Since rice needs plenty of water, it grew well in the swamps and low-lying lands along the Atlantic coast. The fields were flooded by building locks and dams to trap river water.

Slaves provided the main source of labor in the rice fields. Plantation owners tried to purchase slaves from West Africa. West African farmers were highly skilled and knowledgeable about growing rice. West Africans also seemed to have more resistance to the tropical diseases common in the rice fields.

South Carolina farmers also grew indigo, a plant that produced a blue dye used by English cloth manufacturers. Indigo was first grown in the South by Eliza Lucas (later Pinckey), whose father was a colonial official in the English West Indies. While still in her teens, Lucas ran three large plantations owned by her father.

Lucas experimented with many crops. It took her several years to perfect southern indigo. By 1746, however, she and other South Carolina planters were exporting 40,000 pounds of the crop. The following year that amount more than doubled.

The Northern Economy

The economy of the northern colonies was more diverse than that of the southern colonies. The climate from Pennsylvania to Massachusetts Bay and New Hampshire was too cold to grow most of the southern staple crops. Throughout most of the colonial period, there was no demand in Europe for wheat and other grains that grew well in the northern colonies.

One northern product that *was* highly valued in Europe was fur. Colonists hunted and trapped beavers, raccoons, foxes, and other animals for their own use, for sale locally, and for export. They sold the pelts in Europe, where they were made primarily into coats or hats. In addition, the colonists traded with the Indians for furs.

Northerners also did a great deal of fishing to earn a living, particularly in the waters off Newfoundland. Many English sailors fished that area too, so there was no market in England for fish exported from the colonies. However, dried and salted fish could be sold easily in southern Europe for good profits, and fish was not an enumerated article.

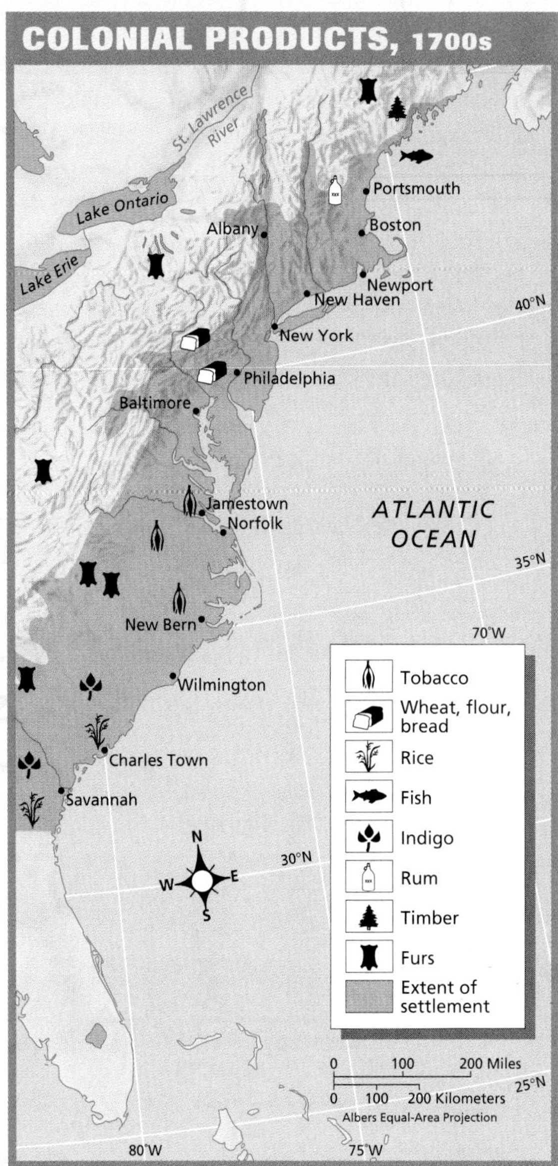

Learning from Maps. The thirteen colonies provided Great Britain with a wide variety of raw materials.

• Maps

Region. What were the southern colonies' greatest resources?

Shipbuilding and foreign commerce were also important economic activities in the northern colonies. Merchants and shipowners in Boston, New York, and Philadelphia competed vigorously with English shippers for the trade with Europe. Northern cities such as New York and Boston also became centers of the slave trade in the mainland colonies.

This northern concentration on trade developed because northern colonists generally produced much more food than they could eat. Since there was no market for American grain in England, they began to look elsewhere for buyers. The most promising market seemed to be the sugar-producing islands of the West Indies. From there a complex system of trade developed that linked many parts of Great Britain's empire. (In 1707 England and Scotland united to form the United Kingdom of Great Britain.)

Trade Networks and Slavery

The islands in the Caribbean were all small. Nearly every acre of the fertile soil in these islands was devoted to raising sugarcane. Since producing sugar required a great deal of labor, the islands were heavily populated, mostly by enslaved Africans. This large population required large amounts of food.

Most sugar planters drove their slaves mercilessly. Many slaves were literally worked to death. As a result, West Indian plantation owners also needed a constant supply of new slaves from Africa.

Colonial merchants and ship captains soon discovered that they could make good profits by shipping grain and fish to the sugar islands. Merchants also sold cattle for plowing and hauling, and lumber for building. They could invest their profits in sugar and carry it to England. Then the merchants could buy English manufactured goods for sale at home for yet another profit.

Complex trade networks soon developed, linking the northern colonies, England, the sugar islands, the southern colonies, and Africa. There were many types of trade routes. For example, American merchants frequently bought molasses in the West Indies instead of sugar. Molasses is what is left over after the sugar has been boiled out of sugarcane juice. It was considered almost a waste product in the islands and so it was very inexpensive.

The Americans took this molasses to the mainland, most often to Rhode Island and Massachusetts, where it was

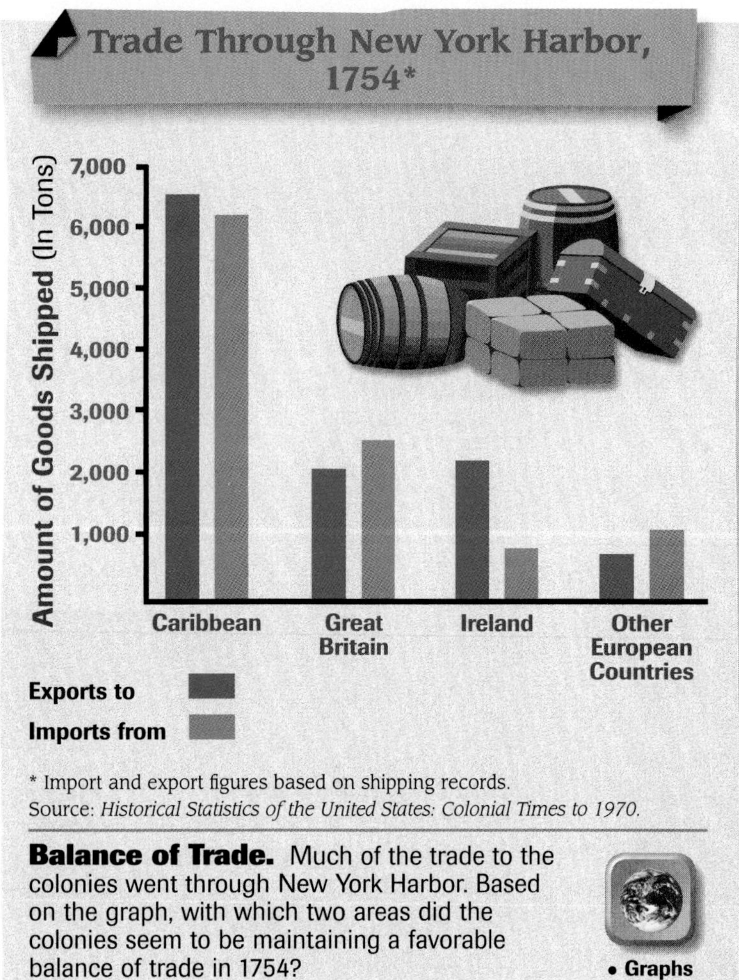

* Import and export figures based on shipping records.
Source: *Historical Statistics of the United States: Colonial Times to 1970.*

Balance of Trade. Much of the trade to the colonies went through New York Harbor. Based on the graph, with which two areas did the colonies seem to be maintaining a favorable balance of trade in 1754?

• Graphs

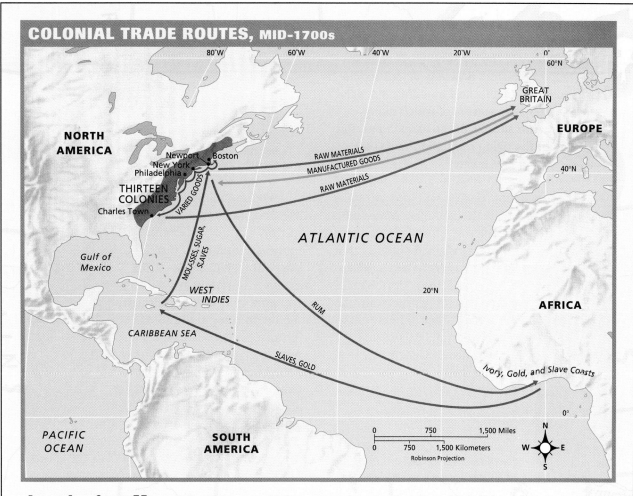

COLONIAL TRADE ROUTES, MID-1700s

Learning from Maps. The thirteen colonies exported raw materials such as timber, tobacco, and furs to Great Britain. The colonies took the molasses and sugar they imported from the West Indies and made them into rum, which the colonists then shipped to Africa.

Region. What did Great Britain export?

• **Maps**

made into rum, a powerful liquor. The rum was then shipped to West Africa, where it was traded for slaves. The slaves, in turn, were taken to the West Indies.

The Middle Passage

The transporting of enslaved Africans to the Americas was called the **Middle Passage**. This trip, which normally took between six and nine weeks, was a horrifying experience for the Africans. Most captains packed as many Africans as possible below deck. Although Parliament set limits on the number of slaves that could be carried on the ships, such regulations were rarely enforced.

On some ships there was hardly any room for the chained people to move once they were all below deck. Under such conditions, the death toll was often very high, particularly if smallpox or some other disease broke out. Olaudah Equiano (oh-LOW-duh ek-wee-AHN-oh), a slave who later bought his freedom, recalled his experience on the Middle Passage around 1755:

> **"The closeness of the place and the heat of the climate, added to the number in the**

ship, which was so crowded that each had scarcely room to turn himself, almost suffocated us. . . . The air soon became unfit for respiration from a variety of loathsome [disgusting] smells, and brought on a sickness among the slaves, of which many died. . . . The shrieks of the women and the groans of the dying rendered [made] the whole a scene of horror."

This cutaway of a slave ship shows how the crew planned to pack as many enslaved Africans as possible in the hold below deck. Many people died as the result of this "tight-pack" system.

• Middle Passage

On some ships nearly half the Africans died before reaching the colonies. Many who survived the passage never fully recovered their health. Some historians estimate that less than half of the more than 10 to 15 million people removed from Africa ever became useful workers in the Americas. The others either died during the passage or were disabled for the rest of their lives.

Sailor and former slave Olaudah Equiano wrote a book about his life entitled Equiano's Travels.

• Equiano

Overcrowding could be bad business as well as terribly cruel and inhumane. Contagious disease on board ship could strike enslaved Africans as well as captains and crew. Despite the death rate on the Middle Passage, however, the trade networks proved very profitable for most of the merchants involved. Profits ranged anywhere from 10 to 100 percent. To those Europeans and colonists involved in the slave trade, African lives were far less important than the money the traders made.

Section 2 Review

• Glossary

IDENTIFY and explain the significance of the following: staple crops, Eliza Lucas, Middle Passage, Olaudah Equiano

REVIEWING FOR DETAILS

1. What major economic goods were produced by the southern colonies and the northern colonies?
2. Why did colonial trade networks develop?

REVIEWING FOR UNDERSTANDING

3. **Geographic Literacy** Why did the northern colonies not grow large amounts of tobacco, indigo, and rice?
4. **Writing Mastery:** *Describing* Imagine that you are an enslaved African transplanted to the colonies. Write a paragraph describing your experiences on the Middle Passage.
5. **Critical Thinking:** *Synthesizing Information* If most slaves wound up in southern colonies, how did northern cities such as New York and Boston become centers of the slave trade?

Section 3
An American Culture

Multimedia Connections
Explore these related topics and materials on the CD–ROM to enrich your understanding of this section:

Media Bank

- Colonial Population
- Orrery
- Benjamin Franklin
- Sir Issac Newton

Biographies

- Benjamin Banneker

Profiles

- Jonathan Edwards

Readings

- Religion in the Colonies
- Sermons of the Great Awakening
- Franklin's Kite Experiment

George Whitefield lifted his finger and paused. The crowd grew tense. Then a clap of thunder crashed. Whitefield fell to his knees in prayer. When the storm passed, the sun revealed a magnificent rainbow. This dramatic scene in 1740 was one of many that took place after George Whitefield arrived from Europe to spread Christianity. This religious movement, along with many new scientific ideas from Europe, challenged how colonists viewed the world around them.

As you read this section you will find out:

- **What impact the Great Awakening had on the colonies.**
- **How the Scientific Revolution shaped American thought and culture.**
- **How colonists gained an education with few schools available.**

The Great Awakening

The Christian religion had played an important part in the founding of several colonies and in the lives of many colonists, particularly the Quakers and the Puritans. In other areas, however, religious faith had little impact on daily life. Then in the 1730s a series of events later called the **Great Awakening** sparked new interest in Christianity.

Whitefield and Edwards. In 1739 a young minister from Great Britain named George Whitefield visited America. Over the next 30 years, Whitefield traveled to America several more times. During his visits, he preached in towns and cities large and small, from Savannah, Georgia, to York, Maine. He became one of the most popular voices of the Great Awakening.

The talented preacher George Whitefield gained followers and influenced ministers throughout the colonies.

Detail from the National Portrait Gallery, Smithsonian Institution, Washington, DC/Art Resource, NY

Whitefield was a small, fair-skinned man with deep-blue eyes. While preaching, he radiated energy and enthusiasm. He spread a message that anyone could be saved by repenting of his or her sins and trusting in Jesus Christ. He stirred intense religious emotion in his listeners everywhere. During his sermons, thousands of colonists confessed their sins and promised to try to lead better lives.

Next to Whitefield, one the best-known preachers of the Great Awakening was New England minister Jonathan Edwards. In his most famous sermon, "Sinners in the Hands of an Angry God," Edwards compared humans to the lowliest of creatures found in nature. He warned his listeners:

> **"The God that holds you over the pit of hell, much as one holds a spider or some loathsome insect over the fire, . . . is dreadfully provoked: His wrath [anger] towards you burns like fire."**

As his listeners trembled, Edwards told them the good news that God was also merciful and would still allow them into Heaven if they accepted God's forgiveness for their sins.

Effects of the Awakening. Many ministers followed in the steps of Whitefield and Edwards. As they did, waves of religious enthusiasm swept through towns from Georgia to New England.

On the frontier, where the settlers were spread thinly over wide areas, people traveled for miles to attend religious services. In Virginia and the Carolinas, and later in western Pennsylvania and New York, frontier ministers rode from place to place on horseback. They preached and held meetings wherever a group could be brought together. Methodist and Baptist preachers were particularly successful at gaining converts on the frontier.

African Americans were among the many Methodist and Baptist converts. Until the Great Awakening there had been few efforts to convert slaves to Christianity. The message of the Great Awakening offered the hope of salvation even to those who were enslaved.

The religious excitement of the Great Awakening continued until about the 1770s. The movement had important political consequences. People who came to realize that they had choices in their religious lives began to seek the same freedom in their political activities.

The Search for Knowledge

By the 1750s many colonists were also caught up by the spirit of a European movement known as the **Scientific Revolution**. This movement, which had begun in the 1500s, encouraged people to improve themselves and the world around them by careful study.

Two great scientific advances set the stage for the Scientific Revolution. One was the improvement of the telescope by the Italian scientist Galileo in 1609, which

Galileo Galilei's telescope helped people to see the stars and encouraged other scientists to examine the mysteries of the universe.

Scala/Art Resource, NY

American Letters

Benjamin Franklin's *Autobiography*

Benjamin Franklin's life story has been one of the best-selling autobiographies of all time. In the following passage, Franklin reveals how he developed a formula to help people improve themselves. The book was originally published as a series that came out in parts over several years.

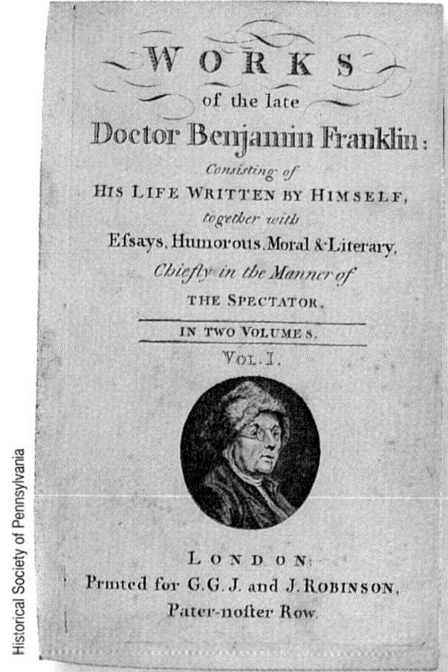

WORKS
of the late
Doctor Benjamin Franklin:
Consisting of
HIS LIFE WRITTEN BY HIMSELF,
together with
Eſsays, Humorous, Moral & Literary,
Chiefly in the Manner of
THE SPECTATOR.
IN TWO VOLUMES.
VOL. I.

LONDON:
Printed for G.G.J. and J. ROBINSON,
Pater-noſter Row.

Historical Society of Pennsylvania

An early volume of Benjamin Franklin's best-selling Autobiography

It was about this time that I conceiv'd the bold and arduous [difficult] Project of arriving at moral Perfection. I wish'd to live without committing any Fault at anytime; I would conquer all that either Natural Inclination [tendency], Custom, or Company might lead me into. As I knew, or thought I knew, what was right and wrong, I did not see why I might not *always* do the one and avoid the other. But I soon found I had undertaken a Task more Difficulty than I had imagined: while my Care was employ'd in guarding against one Fault, I was often surpris'd by another. Habit took the Advantage of Inattention. Inclination was sometimes too strong for Reason. I concluded at length, . . . that the contrary Habits must be broken and good Ones acquired and established, before we can have any Dependence on a steady uniform Rectitude of [virtuous] Conduct. For this purpose I therefore contriv'd [developed] the following Method.

. . . I included after . . . Names of Virtues all that at that time occurr'd to me as necessary or desirable, and annex'd to each a short Precept [rule], which fully express'd the Extent I gave to its Meaning.

These Names of Virtues with their Precepts were:

• Franklin

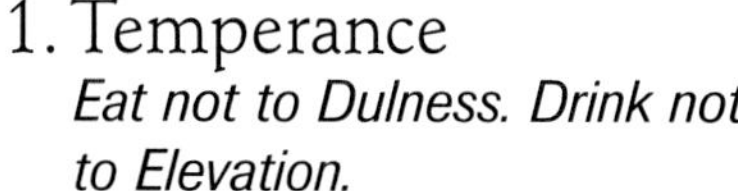

1. Temperance
   Eat not to Dulness. Drink not to Elevation.
2. Silence
   Speak not but what may benefit others or your self. Avoiding trifling [unimportant] Conversation.
3. Order
   Let all your Things have their Places. Let each Part of your Business have its Time.
4. Resolution
   Resolve to perform what you ought. Perform without fail what you resolve.
5. Frugality
   Make no Expense but to do good to others or yourself: i.e. [that is] Waste nothing.
6. Industry
   Lose no Time. Be always employ'd in something useful. Cut off all unnecessary Actions.
7. Sincerity
   Use no hurtful Deceit. Think innocently and justly; and, if you speak, speak accordingly.
8. Justice
   Wrong none, by doing Injuries or omitting the Benefits that are your Duty.
9. Moderation
   Avoid extremes. Forbear [keep from] resenting Injuries so much as you think they deserve.
10. Cleanliness
    Tolerate no Uncleanliness in Body, Clothes or Habitation.

made it easier to study the universe. The other advance, late in the 1600s, was Sir Isaac Newton's development of theories about motion. These theories explained why the stars and planets behave as they do.

The work of Galileo, Newton, and other scientists changed the way educated people thought and the value they gave to knowledge. The orderly movements of the planets suggested that the universe was like a gigantic clock. It was complicated, but it operated according to fixed laws of nature. If laws or rules governed the universe, many people argued, surely no mystery of nature was beyond human understanding.

Self-Taught Americans

In America, it was easy to believe that thought and study would push the frontiers of knowledge forward. Explorers and scientists were finding rivers, mountains, plants, and animals that were new to them. Americans were developing new ideas and ways of doing things.

Much of this learning took place outside of organized schools. Colonial America had only a few colleges. Most Americans taught themselves or were taught at home. Benjamin Franklin, one of the greatest American thinkers of the colonial period, had only two years of formal schooling.

Early writers. Benjamin Franklin, who first gained fame as a printer and publisher, advised Americans, "Either write things worthy [of] reading, or do things worth the writing." Many Americans, such as Mary Katherine Goddard, were doing both. At various times Goddard managed newspapers in Providence, Baltimore, and Philadelphia. In 1775 she became postmaster of Baltimore, probably the first colonial woman to hold such a position.

Phillis Wheatley, a slave in Boston, began writing poetry at an early age. She was the first African American woman to have a collection of her work published. In one of her earliest poems, "To the University of Cambridge, in New England," she celebrated the value of learning:

> **"Students, to you 'tis giv'n to scan**
> **the heights**
> **Above, to traverse [cross] the**
> **etheral [heavenly] space,**
> **And mark the systems of revolving**
> **worlds."**

Young People In History

Apprentices

The Granger Collection, New York

A master potter teaches the skills of the craft to a group of apprentices.

Many children in colonial America learned trades by working with a skilled craftsperson. These trainees were called apprentices. Although most apprentices were boys, some were girls. Children usually began apprenticeships at about age 13 or 14, and their training might last as long as seven or eight years. The craftsperson, called a master, taught the apprentice the skills needed in their trade. The young pupil practiced by working alongside the master. At first, apprentices might work as assistants. As their skills grew they worked on their own under the masters' watchful eyes.

Even Benjamin Franklin started out as an apprentice—first in candlemaking and then in printing. While few apprentices enjoyed Franklin's success, apprenticeship offered a young person with no land and little education a way to earn a living in the colonies.

Detail from The Pierpont Morgan Library/Art Resource, NY

Poet Phillis Wheatley's works encouraged learning, good moral character, and religious devotion—three subjects of interest to many colonial Americans.

• Phillis Wheatley

Colonial scientists. Phillis Wheatley's poem reflects the Scientific Revolution's focus on education. Even many colonial scientists, however, had little or no formal education.

Benjamin Banneker, whose father was a slave and whose mother was a free African American, taught himself astronomy and surveying. Banneker also produced a widely used almanac that helped farmers plan their crops. Later in his career, Banneker helped lay out the boundaries of the District of Columbia.

Another surveyor and astronomer of the period was David Rittenhouse, a clockmaker from Pennsylvania. During the course of his work, he improved the making of clocks, telescopes, and other instruments. He also built a mechanical model that closely copied the movements of the sun and planets.

John Bartram traveled far and wide collecting unusual plants for his garden outside Philadelphia. He sent carefully packed samples of his discoveries to the leading European naturalists and they sent him their own unusual finds. Distinguished visitors from Europe often came to see Bartram's collection, as did many well-known Americans like Benjamin Franklin. Such sharing of information was another way colonists spread their knowledge throughout the colonies.

The Granger Collection, New York

The Franklin stove was one of many new inventions for use in American colonial homes. Ben Franklin himself sketched this design of the stove.

Section 3 Review

• Glossary

IDENTIFY and explain the significance of the following: Great Awakening, George Whitefield, Jonathan Edwards, Scientific Revolution, Benjamin Franklin, Mary Katherine Goddard, Phillis Wheatley, Benjamin Banneker

REVIEWING FOR DETAILS

1. How did the Great Awakening affect the colonies?
2. What effects did the Scientific Revolution have on American thought and culture?
3. With few schools in America, how did colonists gain an education?

REVIEWING FOR UNDERSTANDING

4. **Writing Mastery:** *Creating* Imagine that you are an early American writer. Write a poem or short story that expresses the importance of learning in the American colonies.
5. **Critical Thinking:** *Synthesizing Information* How might shared experiences such as the Great Awakening and the Scientific Revolution have contributed to the creation of a common American culture?

Section 4

EXPANDING WESTWARD

Multimedia Connections

Explore these related topics and materials on the CD–ROM to enrich your understanding of this section:

Gazetteer

- Ohio River valley
- Great Lakes
- Pittsburgh
- Quebec

Atlas

- King Philip's War
- North America in 1754
- French and Indian War

Readings

- Seven Years' War

Media Bank

- Yankee Doodle Dandy
- Battle of Quebec

Profiles

- Metacom

On July 7, 1742, the Iroquois leader Canassateego headed a delegation of Indians meeting with Pennsylvania officials who wanted to expand British settlement into the Ohio River valley. The British knew that French leaders had similar desires. Fearing that the French were gaining the loyalty of American Indians in the valley, the Pennsylvanians tried with little success to secure the delegates' trust. Tensions over this region would eventually end in war.

As you read this section you will find out:

- **How trade influenced relations among American Indian groups.**
- **What events led to the French and Indian War.**
- **How the French and Indian War affected Great Britain's empire.**

Conflict Over Land and Trade

As the British colonists expanded westward, they met resistance from both American Indians and French colonists. Of course, conflict with Indians was not new. In Puritan New England, the Wampanoag led by Metacom, whom the Puritans called King Philip, attempted in 1675 to halt settlement after several of their warriors were killed by settlers. In a series of deadly raids, they destroyed some 12 villages. The colonists struck back with equal force. In August 1676 Metacom was killed, and the war was soon over.

The colonists' final victory in what the British later called King Philip's War was aided by the Mohawk, who were members of the Iroquois League. In the mid-1600s the Iroquois, who at that time were allies of the Dutch in New Netherland, had gained control

Through Others' Eyes

Colonial Traders

By the mid-1700s many tribes in the Ohio River valley were suffering the ill effects of contact with some French and British traders. For this reason, many opposed white settlement in the area for fear it would destroy their culture. Particularly damaging had been the introduction of alcohol. In 1753 Oneida chief Scarouady pled with his British allies to prevent dishonest traders from ruining the tribes:

> *"The rum ruins us. We beg you would prevent its coming in such quantities by regulating the traders. When these whisky traders come they bring thirty or forty caggs [kegs] and put them down before us and make us drunk, and get all the skins that should go to pay the debts we have contracted for goods bought of the fair traders, and by this means we not only ruin ourselves but them [the traders] too. These wicked whisky sellers, when they have once got the Indians in liquor, make them sell their very clothes from their backs. In short, if this practice be continued we must inevitably [certainly] be ruined."*

of the trade in beaver pelts in the northeast. In 1649 the Iroquois had defeated the Huron, who were allies of the French.

For decades thereafter the Iroquois prospered through a mixture of war, diplomacy, and trade policy. They acted as middlemen in the profitable fur trade, gathering pelts from other tribes and selling them to the English. However, they also cooperated with the French when Iroquois leaders felt it was in their best interest to do so.

Trouble in Ohio Country

In 1718 Alexander Spotswood, then lieutenant governor of Virginia, had warned British authorities, "The French have built so many forts that the British settlements almost seem surrounded." He advised the British to protect their claims by encouraging settlement along the Great Lakes. Likewise, by 1750 French Canadians were complaining about British activities on Lake Ontario:

> **"It is there that the English hand out rum to the Indians, even though the King of France has forbidden this trade. It is there that the English try to win over all the Indian nations. . . . As long as the English occupy Fort Oswego, we must distrust even those Indians who are most loyal to the French."**

Although the Great Lakes area continued to be a source of conflict between the two sides, it was only after each tried to establish military posts deep in the Ohio River valley that a final, decisive war broke out.

Conflict over forts. In 1752 the French governor of Canada, the Marquis Duquesne de Menneville, ordered the construction of a new chain of forts running from Lake Erie south to the Ohio River, in what is now western Pennsylvania. The French actions alarmed many people in the British colonies, including

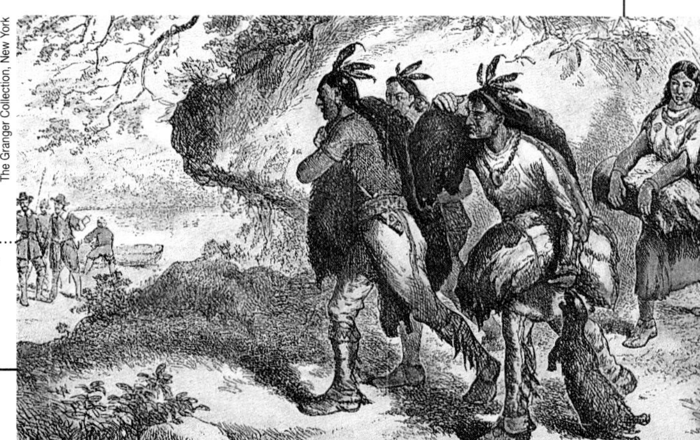

The Granger Collection, New York

Native Americans from many tribes traded valuable beaver pelts with Europeans. Sometimes this trade led to wars between tribes.

Lieutenant Governor Robert Dinwiddie of Virginia.

When Dinwiddie learned what the French were doing, he sent a planter and land surveyor named George Washington to warn them that they were trespassing on Virginia property. In November 1753 Washington set out with a party of six to find the French commander. After weeks of tramping through icy forests, Washington encountered the French and delivered Dinwiddie's message. Duquesne rejected it with disgust.

Fort Duquesne. In early 1754 Dinwiddie sent another group of Virginians to build a British fort where the Monongahela and Allegheny Rivers join to form the Ohio River. Dinwiddie then appointed Washington as lieutenant colonel of the Virginia **militia**, a group of citizens organized for military service. He ordered Washington to lead a force to protect the incomplete post against French attack.

Before Washington could reach the site, the French drove off the construction party. Then they completed the post themselves, naming it Fort Duquesne. Washington marched toward Fort Duquesne. Along the way he won a brief battle with a small French party. The main French force then advanced against Washington. He set up a defensive post, Fort Necessity, but the French easily surrounded it. After an all-day battle Washington had to surrender. The French commander then allowed Washington and his men to go free. They returned to Virginia, leaving the disputed territory in French hands.

• Years of War

NORTH AMERICA IN 1763

British | Russian | French | Unclaimed | Spanish

ARCTIC OCEAN, UNCLAIMED, Hudson Bay, NEWFOUNDLAND, PACIFIC OCEAN, Disputed, CANADA, Great Lakes, St. Lawrence River, FRENCH, Mississippi River, Ohio River, LOUISIANA, THIRTEEN COLONIES, ATLANTIC OCEAN, Rio Grande, FLORIDA, Gulf of Mexico, NEW SPAIN, WEST INDIES, CARIBBEAN SEA

0 500 1,000 Miles; 0 500 1,000 Kilometers; Azimuthal Equal-Area Projection

Learning from Maps. Wars in Europe soon spilled over into North America and radically changed the colonial borders.

Place. What country had the smallest land claims in 1763?

• Maps

The French and Indian War

After Washington's retreat the war began in earnest. In all of North America there were no more than 70,000 French settlers. The population of the British colonies was about 1.5 million. This gave the British a definite advantage. For about two years, however, the French won most of the battles. Many of the Indians sided with them, because, unlike the British, the French usually did not try to force the Indians to give up their lands or their ways of life.

The British were not easily discouraged, however. The tide began to turn after a brilliant British politician, William Pitt, took over management of the war effort. British troops finally captured Fort Duquesne in 1758. They changed its name to Fort Pitt, which is why the modern city on the site is named Pittsburgh.

Gradually, other key French posts were taken. The most decisive battle occurred at the French city of Quebec in 1759. The battle took place outside of the city on a field called the Plains of Abraham. Both the British commander, General James Wolfe, and the

British general Edward Braddock was killed trying unsuccessfully to recapture Fort Duquesne in 1755.

• Fort Duquesne

French commander, General Louis Joseph de Montcalm, were killed in the fight, which ended with the surrender of the city to the British.

By this time, the conflict had spread throughout the world, including Europe, where it became known as the Seven Years' War. Spain entered the conflict on the side of France in 1762, only to see its colonies in Cuba and the Philippine Islands overwhelmed by the British.

The British were victorious almost everywhere. When the war ended in 1763, the British were able to redraw the map of the world. France had to surrender Canada and most of its claims in the Mississippi and Ohio River valleys. Spain turned over Florida and the Gulf Coast as far as the Mississippi River to the British. The British colonists were delighted. The French threat to the Ohio River valley had been removed. Spain had been pushed back from the southern frontier.

All was not yet settled, however. Although some of the colonies had contributed men and money to the conflict, British soldiers and sailors had done most of the fighting. The Royal Treasury paid most of the bills. In the long run, these and other factors would cause growing conflict between the British government and its colonists. Yet in 1763 most colonists felt loyal to the king and grateful to Great Britain.

Section 4 Review

• Glossary

IDENTIFY and explain the significance of the following: Metacom, Marquis Duquesne de Menneville, George Washington, militia

LOCATE and explain the importance of the following: Ohio River valley, Great Lakes

• Gazetteer

REVIEWING FOR DETAILS

1. How did trade increase conflict among American Indian groups?
2. What triggered the French and Indian War? How did the war affect control of North America?

• Time Line

REVIEWING FOR UNDERSTANDING

3. **Geographic Literacy** Why might the Ohio River valley have become an area of conflict between the French and the British?
4. **Writing Mastery:** *Persuading* Imagine that you are an American Indian from the Ohio River valley. Write a speech persuading your tribe to side with either the French or the British.
5. **Critical Thinking:** *Recognizing Point of View* Most descriptions of the early Iroquois come from the French and their Indian allies, who described the Iroquois as brutal warriors. Why might such sources be biased?

unit 2

THE NEW AMERICAN NATION (1755–1801)

Betsy Ross and her assistants make the first American flag in 1776. The "Stars and Stripes" was officially adopted as the flag of the United States in 1777.

Linking Past to Present
American Principles

"I pledge allegiance to the flag of the United States of America." Millions of American middle-school students recite these words every day before classes begin. Many started out memorizing these words as soon as they were old enough to go to school, at which point the students often did not quite understand what the words meant. "With liberty and jelly for all," recited one elementary student at the end of the Pledge.

The Pledge of Allegiance originated in 1892, when Francis Bellamy wrote it to celebrate the 400th anniversary of Columbus's voyage. Almost immediately, students began to recite the Pledge in schools. Before long, all students were required to say the Pledge, but controversy soon followed.

In the 1930s members of certain religious groups said that reciting the Pledge went against their sacred beliefs. In 1943 the U.S. Supreme Court ruled that forcing people to recite the Pledge against their religious beliefs was contrary to the principles upon which this nation was founded. Although some political leaders today still support the idea of requiring students to say the Pledge, it remains a voluntary action.

Paul S. Conklin

These teenagers are observing artwork in the rotunda of the U.S. Capitol Building in Washington, D.C.

The issues the Pledge has raised and the process by which these issues have been debated would never have been imaginable to people 300 years ago. As you read this unit, you will learn how a group of people living in North America under European rule joined together to create a system of government unlike anything the world had witnessed before. They founded a nation based on two things—individual freedom of expression and government by the people.

In most societies before 1776, if a ruler ordered the people to recite a pledge they had little choice but to obey or be severely punished. There was no system by which they could challenge the word of the ruler. As you will learn, however, in the eastern part of North America those principles of government began to change with a rebellion that started in the late 1700s.

CHAPTER 5

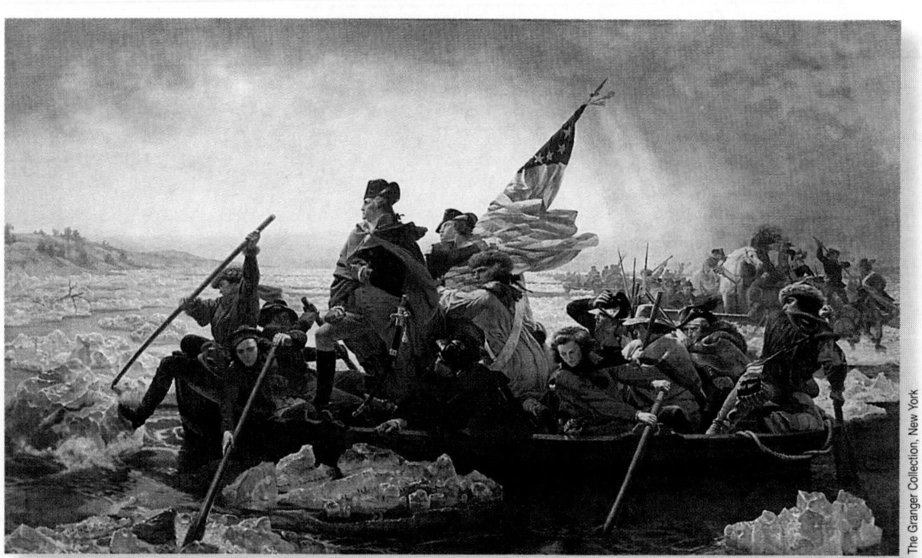
The Granger Collection, New York

Americans Seek Independence (1755–1783)

Economic Development:
How might economic conditions contribute to political revolution?

Democratic Values:
Why might colonists break away from their home country?

Global Relations:
Why might nations support a revolution in another country's colonies?

• Video Opener

• Skill Builder

The spring of 1775 did not dawn hopeful for James Thacher, a young doctor who lived near Boston. British soldiers had "actually commenced [started] hostilities against our people," he confided to his journal. He went on to describe the call that echoed through colonial towns: "To Arms! To Arms!" *The American Revolution had begun.*

image above: Washington Crossing the Delaware

Section 1
RESISTING BRITISH RULE

Multimedia Connections

Explore these related topics and materials on the CD–ROM to enrich your understanding of this section:

Media Bank
- Samuel Adams
- Keeping the People Informed

Atlas
- Pontiac's Rebellion

Profiles
- Pontiac
- Samuel Adams

Gazetteer
- Great Britain
- Appalachian Mountains
- New York
- Massachusetts

"We will not submit to any tax!" rebel leader Samuel Adams shouted. "We are free, and we want no King!" Shortly after his radical speech, British warships sailed into Boston's harbor. The vessels carried troops, sent to put down a revolt in Massachusetts. This alarmed Boston's citizens, most of whom supported the king. Their loyalty would be tested as Britain tried to force the colonists into line.

As you read this section you will find out:

- **How the end of the French and Indian War affected Native Americans and colonists.**
- **How Britain attempted to raise money in America.**
- **How the colonists resisted British attempts to control them.**

Conflict Across the Appalachians

The end of the French and Indian War changed the lives of American Indians living west of the Appalachian Mountains. After his country's victory, the British commander in the colonies raised the price of goods traded to Indians. He also refused to give presents or feasts in exchange for trade and the use of Indian land, standard practices with the French. These policies angered the Seneca, Ottawa, Miami, and other Indians of the Ohio River valley. The tribes also had to deal with white settlers, who began pouring into the area after the French defeat in North America.

In 1763 Pontiac, an Ottawa chief, organized Indians to protect their land. They began a war to drive the settlers back across the Appalachians. The Indian force fought for about two years, destroying most of the British forts along the frontier. After their siege of Fort Detroit failed, however, the Indians soon halted their attacks. **Pontiac's Rebellion** came to an end.

Realizing that it would be difficult to protect settlers, the British government issued the **Proclamation of 1763**, which closed the area west of the Appalachian Mountains to newcomers. This initially benefited Indians, but it frustrated colonists who believed that the frontier was their only opportunity to own land. Many simply ignored the new policy and continued to move into the region.

Pontiac urged Indians from different tribes in the Ohio River valley to work together against the British. The rebellion slowed British settlement in the area.

Paying for Defense

The British soon found themselves in financial trouble. Great Britain had borrowed huge sums to pay for the French and Indian War and had stationed more than 10,000 soldiers in the colonies to enforce the Proclamation of 1763. To ease the burden, British officials wanted the colonists to start paying for their own protection and government.

New taxes. In April 1764 Parliament passed what became known in America as the Sugar Act. This law set **duties**, or import taxes, on foreign sugar, textiles, and other goods entering the colonies. Britain also cracked down on smuggling to make sure that everyone paid the duties.

In March 1765 Parliament approved the **Stamp Act**. The law enabled the British to collect money by selling stamps, which had to be purchased and attached to all printed matter in the colonies. This even applied to common items like land deeds, marriage licenses, and newspapers.

Angry protests. The colonies erupted in opposition when colonists learned the terms of the Stamp Act. They were outraged about being taxed without having representatives in Parliament and began to take up the cry, "No taxation without representation."

In October 1765, representatives from nine colonies attended the Stamp Act Congress in New York City. This organization issued a statement that colonists could be taxed only by those legislatures in which they had direct representation. Many colonists also refused to import some British goods.

Opponents of the Stamp Act began to join groups called Sons of Liberty and Daughters of Liberty. Like many other colonists, members of these organizations believed in action rather than talk. Protests over the Stamp Act led to riots in several colonies.

The repeal of the Stamp Act. The colonists' refusal to import certain goods was

The Stamp Act was Britain's first direct tax on its American colonies. Enraged by the law, many colonists burned the stamps in public to show their displeasure.

Many colonists celebrated the "death" of the hated Stamp Act, whose "funeral" is shown in this cartoon. Members of Parliament grieve while carrying a small coffin.

so effective that British merchants urged Parliament to back down. In March 1766 Parliament decided to **repeal**, or officially withdraw, the hated Stamp Act. Parliament did not want this to seem like a surrender, so it passed the Declaratory Act. This law stated that the colonies remained under Parliament's control. Many colonists ignored the new act's message, however. They did not accept the principle that Parliament was supreme.

American Resistance Grows

After repealing the Stamp Act, Britain needed a new supply of money. Thus, Charles Townshend, the country's finance minister, attempted to tax the colonies yet again.

The Townshend Acts. In 1767 Parliament passed the **Townshend Acts**, which placed duties on some items colonists imported from Great Britain—glass, lead, paper, paint, and tea. Customs officials used **writs of assistance**, or special search warrants, to help them collect the taxes and stop smuggling. These writs of assistance allowed agents to search any ship, warehouse, or home without reason.

Many colonists saw Parliament's move as another violation of their rights. They decided to **boycott**, or refuse to buy, British goods. Colonial merchants stopped importing British products. Colonial women began spinning and weaving cloth in their homes rather than purchasing British cloth. The Sons of Liberty also staged more protests.

In New York further conflict arose when townspeople refused to obey the Quartering Act, which required colonists to quarter, or house and supply, British soldiers. In response, Britain suspended the New York assembly.

The largest protest came from Boston, where the Massachusetts legislature called on the colonies to resist the Townshend Acts. Britain dismissed the Massachusetts assembly and moved a large number of soldiers, called "Redcoats" because of their bright red uniforms, into Boston.

The Boston Massacre. The soldiers' presence soon led to trouble. On March 5, 1770, a large crowd began yelling insults at a squad of Redcoats guarding the customhouse. People hurled snowballs, some packed around stones. The British soldiers panicked and fired

Trouble often broke out when British soldiers gathered in colonial towns to enforce Parliament's laws.

• Poor Old England

into the mob. Three colonists were killed, and two others died later. An African American sailor named Crispus Attucks was among the dead. Boston's radicals, led by Samuel Adams, called this incident the **Boston Massacre**. Shortly afterward, the British commander and eight soldiers were arrested and charged with murder. Despite angry calls for revenge, the soldiers received a fair trial. Boston lawyer John Adams, Samuel Adams's cousin and himself a critic of British policy, defended the soldiers. Most were found to have acted in self-defense.

Trouble Over Tea

In March 1770 Parliament repealed all the Townshend duties except the tax on tea. This helped restore calm in the colonies. The new British prime minister, Lord North, also promised not to raise any more money by taxing the colonists.

Many colonial radicals like Samuel Adams remained active, however. Adams and his supporters believed that:

> **"among the natural rights of the colonists are these: first, a right to life; second, to liberty; third, to property; together with the right to support and to defend them in the best manner they can."**

Adams thought Britain's actions threatened the colonists' rights. He and other colonists formed **Committees of Correspondence** to share information about resistance to the British. Similar groups sprang up in other colonies. Without intending to, these committees gradually became a kind of informal central government for the colonies.

The tea business. After a few years of peace, new problems erupted in the colonies. The British East India Company, an important business, was in financial trouble. It had a huge amount of unsold tea in its warehouses. In May 1773 Parliament passed a **Tea Act**

• Crispus Attucks

Many colonists blamed the British for the terrible violence in Boston. In this painting of the Boston Massacre by Paul Revere, British troops fire on the colonists.

allowing the firm to sell its product directly to the American colonies. Using its own agents, the company bypassed American tea sellers and saved the money that merchant "middlemen" normally took.

Americans greatly resented the Tea Act. Local tea merchants lost business. Other colonists thought the law set a terrible example—that Parliament had the power to give a British business control of an industry and disrupt trade in America. Despite its popularity, colonists began to boycott tea.

When ships carrying the British East India Company's tea arrived in America, public protest soared to new heights. In Charleston, South Carolina, a crowd persuaded the firm's tea agents to resign. The tea went into storage, but it could not be sold without an agent. In New York and Philadelphia the captains of the tea ships did not even try to unload their cargo. Rather than risk trouble, they sailed back to England.

The Granger Collection, New York

Samuel Adams worried that the British East India Company's cheap tea would be a temptation to colonists. To destroy the tea he helped organize the Boston Tea Party.

The Boston Tea Party. Massachusetts governor Thomas Hutchinson was determined that Boston would accept tea from the British East India Company. When three tea ships arrived in November, he insisted that their captains prepare to unload the cargo soon for public sale.

While the vessels lay at anchor in Boston Harbor, Samuel Adams and other activists stirred up the public at mass meetings. Angry crowds gathered in the streets, and the tension grew for more than two weeks. Finally, on the night of December 16, 1773, townspeople disguised as Mohawk Indians boarded the ships. Bostonian George Hewes described the daring event that became known as the **Boston Tea Party**:

> **"In about three hours . . . we had thus broken and thrown overboard every tea chest to be found in the ship, while those in the other ships were disposing of the tea in the same way."**

The protesters continued their work until they had destroyed huge amounts of the British East India Company's tea.

The Intolerable Acts

Britain's reaction to the Boston Tea Party was swift and severe. Parliament passed four new laws to reclaim its control and punish Massachusetts. Many colonists called these the **Intolerable Acts**.

Under the first law, no ship could enter or leave Boston Harbor until the townspeople had paid for the tea they had ruined. The second act canceled Massachusetts's charter.

Now town meetings could be held only with the governor's permission. The third law moved trials involving Massachusetts officials charged with criminal activity to Britain. Lastly, a new Quartering Act required residents of Boston to shelter British soldiers in their homes. To enforce all of these laws, General Thomas Gage, commander of the British troops in North America, soon replaced Thomas Hutchinson as the governor of Massachusetts.

Even though the British government's response was aimed primarily at Massachusetts, it outraged people from all the colonies. Increasingly, British actions seemed to threaten the colonists' liberty. In June 1774 the Massachusetts Committee of Correspondence sent out a call for a meeting of colonial leaders.

Many colonists saw King George III as an uncaring leader who was out of touch with colonial problems.

The Granger Collection, New York

• **King George III**

Three months later, delegates from all the colonies except Georgia met in Philadelphia for the **First Continental Congress**. The Congress expressed its loyalty to Britain but demanded the repeal of all British taxation laws. The group banned all trade with Britain until Parliment met its demands.

The delegates set up a Continental Association to enforce this ban. They also advised the colonists to begin forming militias and agreed to meet again the following May if their demands had not been met. Their meeting concluded with this warning: "We have for the present only resolved to pursue . . . peaceable measures." In Britain, King George III, who had lost all patience with the colonists, summed up the crisis. "The Colonies," he wrote, "must either submit or triumph."

Section 1 Review

• **Glossary**

IDENTIFY and explain the significance of the following: Pontiac's Rebellion, Proclamation of 1763, duties, Stamp Act, repeal, Townshend Acts, writs of assistance, boycott, Samuel Adams, Boston Massacre, Committees of Correspondence, Tea Act, Boston Tea Party, Intolerable Acts, First Continental Congress

REVIEWING FOR DETAILS

1. What conflicts arose between American Indians and colonists after the end of the French and Indian War, and what was the outcome?
2. How did Britain try to use its colonies to make money?
3. How did the colonists respond to British attempts at control?

REVIEWING FOR UNDERSTANDING

4. **Writing Mastery:** *Informing* Imagine that you live in Boston. Write a letter to a friend agreeing or disagreeing with colonists' actions at the Boston Tea Party.
5. **Critical Thinking:** *Recognizing Point of View* Why do you think the British believed they were justified in their new colonial policies?

Section 2
LIBERTY OR DEATH

Multimedia Connections

Explore these related topics and materials on the CD–ROM to enrich your understanding of this section:

Media Bank

- "The Pennsylvania Song"
- Two Continental Congresses
- Revolutionary War Soldiers

Readings

- Revolutionary War Armies

Profiles

- Patrick Henry
- Peter Salem

Gazetteer

- Lexington
- Concord
- Boston

The Redcoats had driven the rebels from Breed's Hill! Bostonians loyal to the British cheered when they heard the news. Their celebration ended, however, when the British soldiers straggled back to town. That evening the wounded filled the streets, and the consequences of war became clear to everyone. As Henry Hulton explained, "The lamentations [grief-filled cries] of the women and children over their husbands and fathers, pierced one to the soul."

As you read this section you will find out:

- **Why the battles at Lexington and Concord were significant.**
- **What role the Second Continental Congress played.**
- **How geography influenced the colonists' military strategy in Boston.**

Lexington and Concord

Conflict over the Intolerable Acts turned Massachusetts into an armed camp. General Gage and his troops occupied Boston. Citizens in the surrounding towns and villages responded by forming militia companies. Parliament soon declared Massachusetts to be in a state of rebellion. The British government sent 6,000 more soldiers to join Gage and ordered him to arrest the rebel leaders.

The "shot heard round the world." On the night of April 18, 1775, Gage sent 700 troops to destroy a militia's supply of weapons in Concord, a town west of Boston. He wanted his soldiers to stop in nearby Lexington and capture rebels Samuel Adams and John Hancock on the way. The colonists learned of these plans. Paul Revere and

Paul Revere was a silversmith and artist who became active in the independence movement. He became famous after his "midnight ride" to warn colonists of a British attack.

The Granger Collection, New York

William Dawes rode through the night, calling out, "The British are coming!" to warn the nearby towns.

The first British soldiers reached Lexington at dawn. Waiting for them were about 70 **Minutemen**—members of rebel militias who were ready for action on a minute's notice. British major John Pitcairn rode forward and ordered them to move off, sneering "Disperse [leave] . . . rebels! You dogs, run!" Suddenly, someone—no one knows who—fired "the shot heard round the world." More shots followed, and when the smoke cleared, eight Minutemen lay dead. Ten other rebel colonists and one British soldier were also wounded.

The British retreat. The British marched on to Concord. After more fighting they destroyed whatever supplies the colonists had not carried off or hidden. Then the British turned back toward Boston. Outside Concord, Minutemen from nearby towns rapidly gathered. All along the road to Boston the angry colonists hid behind trees and in hollows, showering the British with bullets when they passed. Thousands of local citizens picked up their muskets and followed the sound of gunfire to join in the fight. One British soldier described the terrifying journey:

> **"All the hills on each side of us were covered with rebels . . . so that they kept the road always lined and a very hot fire on us without intermission. We . . . returned their fire as hot as we received it; but when we arrived within a mile of Lexington our ammunition began to fail, and the light companies were so fatigued . . . they were scarce able to act."**

By the time they reached Boston, the British had more than 270 **casualties**—people killed, wounded, or missing. The colonists lost less than 100 of some 3,800 militiamen. The battles at Lexington and Concord marked the beginning of the American Revolution.

The Second Continental Congress

Less than a month after the bitter clashes at Lexington and Concord, delegates to the

Trying to frighten and confuse the Minutemen waiting on the Lexington town green, the British troops screamed loudly as they went into battle.

The Granger Collection, New York

Second Continental Congress met in Philadelphia. Massachusetts radicals Samuel Adams, John Adams, and John Hancock joined the assembly, as did Benjamin Franklin of Pennsylvania. Virginia sent its fiery speaker Patrick Henry, who had recently urged the colonists to take up arms against the British in a dramatic speech:

> **"Gentlemen may cry peace, peace—but there is no peace. The war is actually begun! . . . Is life so dear, or peace so sweet, as to be purchased at the price of chains and slavery? Forbid it, Almighty God! I know not what course others may take; but as for me, give me liberty, or give me death!"**

Henry favored immediate independence from Great Britain, but not all the delegates took such an extreme position. Given the number of conflicting opinions, the Congress decided not to break away from Britain. The delegates did issue a "Declaration of the Causes and Necessity of Taking Up Arms" and also created an official military force, the **Continental Army**. The Congress appointed Virginia delegate George Washington to command the army.

Washington accepted this new assignment eagerly and set out at once for Massachusetts. Before he reached the colony, however, word came that an important battle had just occurred.

The Battle of Bunker Hill

On June 16, 1775, the colonial militia moved in on Bunker Hill and Breed's Hill, which overlooked Boston from the north. The colonists spent the night digging an earthen fort to protect their position on Breed's Hill. The British discovered their presence the next morning. General William Howe, who had replaced Gage, quickly sent British troops to drive the rebels from the hill.

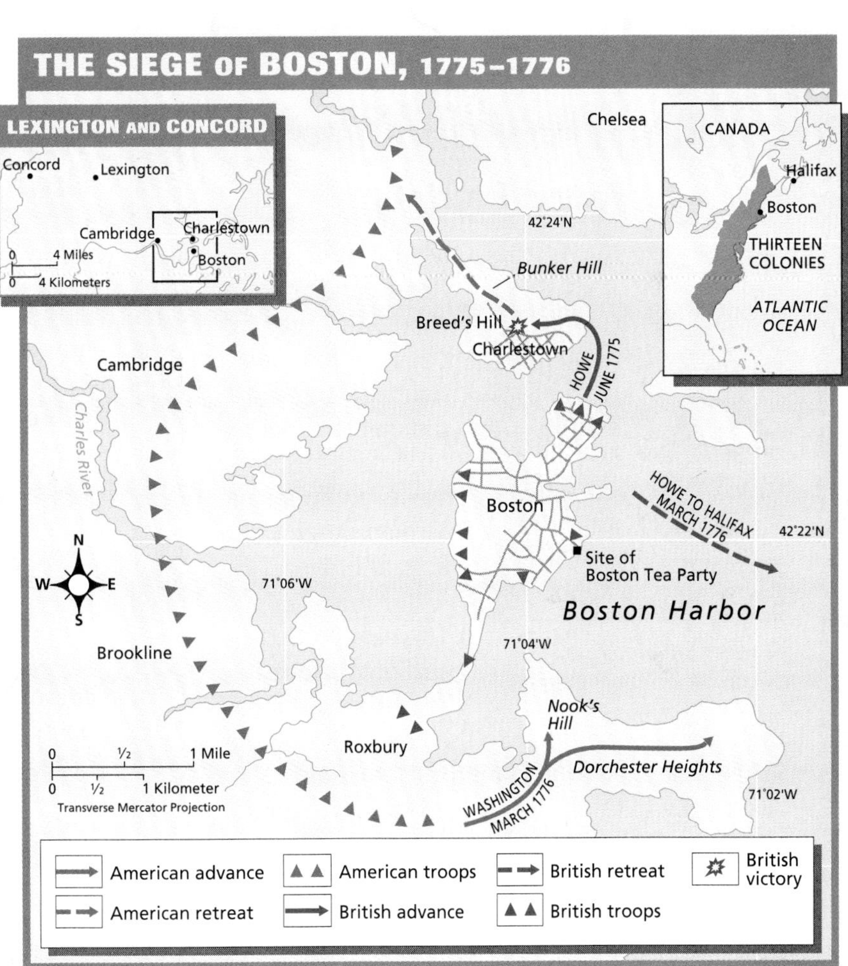

Learning from Maps.
After the British drove the American forces from Breed's Hill, the Americans took up positions around Boston. When Washington's troops occupied Dorchester Heights in March 1776, the British decided to retreat by sea.

Location. What does Dorchester Heights overlook?

• Maps

The colonists on Breed's Hill were tired and hungry after their night's work. They expected fresh militia to come and reinforce them, but none arrived. Now these civilian soldiers faced professional British troops.

Across the bay, hundreds of Bostonians watched from their windows and rooftops as the battle began. The British, loaded down with heavy packs, advanced up the hill in three broad lines. To save ammunition, an American commander ordered his men: "Don't one of you fire until you see the whites of their eyes." When the Americans finally did shoot, their musket balls tore through the enemy. The British fell back, leaving the field littered with dead and dying men.

Twice more the British charged with fixed bayonets. Inside the fort the Americans ran low on ammunition. They loaded their guns with nails and pieces of glass and fired off one last round of shots. Then the British came over the wall, forcing the Americans to retreat. The British victory at what became known as the **Battle of Bunker Hill** was a very costly one. More than 1,000 British soldiers and some 400 American militiamen were killed or wounded.

Young People In History

Young Patriots

A young drummer boy accompanies older Patriots.

Many young Americans contributed to the cause of independence. They beat the call to arms on drums, became spies, and performed other acts of bravery.

In April 1777, 16-year-old Sybil Ludington rode more than 30 miles through the night to warn the colonists that the British had landed at Danbury, Connecticut. Alerted by her call, the townspeople escaped the enemy advance.

As a teenager, James Forten signed on an American ship and carried gunpowder to the deck during battle. When the British captured his vessel, he faced a terrible danger. Would they enslave him because he was African American? The captain's son, however, liked Forten and asked for his release. Forten chose to be imprisoned with his fellow Americans, saying, "I'm a prisoner for my country, and I'll never be a traitor to her."

The Olive Branch Petition

Despite the bloodshed at Lexington, Concord, and Bunker Hill, many colonists still hoped for peace. In July 1775, after much debate, the Second Continental Congress sent the **Olive Branch Petition** to King George III. It asked him to protect the colonies against further actions by Parliament until a compromise could be worked out. The document got its name from the olive branch, a traditional symbol of peace.

King George was furious with the colonists and declared them to be in open rebellion. To isolate America, he ordered a **blockade**, or naval measure that used ships to cut off a country's trade and supplies. Now it was up to Washington and his army to fight the British.

Washington's First Victory

After Washington arrived in Boston with his army, he pinned down the British troops. He decided not to attack the city until he had better artillery.

In May 1775 Ethan Allen and the "Green Mountain Boys," a militia from present-day Vermont, had captured Fort Ticonderoga in northern New York. This gave the rebels a valuable supply of cannons—if they could move them to Boston. Colonel Henry Knox, a young artillery officer, hoped to do so. He and his men dragged about 50 cannons nearly 300 miles, using sleds and oxen. They reached Washington's camp with the heavy equipment in January 1776.

Overjoyed, Washington had the cannons hauled up Dorchester Heights, overlooking Boston from the south. From this position the colonists could bombard the British in the city below. General Howe realized that his troops were in a dangerous position. On March 17, 1776, the entire British army sailed off to Britain's naval base in Nova Scotia. More than 1,000 colonists went with the British army. They preferred exile to rebellion against king and country. Some also feared for their lives if they remained. For the time being, Washington had driven British troops from the American colonies.

The Granger Collection, New York

As British troops struggled up Breed's Hill in the humid June heat, Bostonians streamed to the city's rooftops to watch the important battle unfold.

• Home Front

Section 2 Review

• Glossary

• Gazetteer

IDENTIFY and explain the significance of the following: Minutemen, casualties, Second Continental Congress, Patrick Henry, Continental Army, William Howe, Battle of Bunker Hill, Olive Branch Petition, blockade

LOCATE and explain the importance of the following: Lexington, Concord, Bunker Hill, Breed's Hill

REVIEWING FOR DETAILS

1. What was significant about the fighting at Lexington and Concord?
2. What actions did the Second Continental Congress take?

REVIEWING FOR UNDERSTANDING

3. **Geographic Literacy** How did Boston's geography influence the colonists' military strategy against the British?
4. **Writing Mastery:** *Persuading* Imagine that you are part of the militia that fought in Lexington. Draw up a flyer persuading other colonists to take up arms against the British.
5. **Critical Thinking:** *Drawing Conclusions* If you had been a delegate to the Second Continental Congress, would you have favored immediate independence or a more cautious approach? Explain your answer.

Section 3

Declaring Independence

Multimedia Connections

Explore these related topics and materials on the CD-ROM to enrich your understanding of this section:

Media Bank

- Harassing Loyalists
- Loyalist Recruiting Poster

Readings

- *Common Sense*

Profiles

- Thomas Paine

Gazetteer

- Virginia
- South Carolina
- Connecticut

Caesar Rodney rode hard through the night to reach Philadelphia. His word would decide Delaware's position in the congressional vote on independence. He had to make it in time! Rodney soon got the chance to give his "voice in the matter of Independence." Like so many others, he voted to break away from Britain. The Americans had made their fateful choice.

As you read this section you will find out:

- **What effect Thomas Paine's *Common Sense* had on colonists.**
- **What the main parts of the Declaration of Independence are.**
- **How the Declaration of Independence has affected the United States and other countries.**

The Impact of *Common Sense*

By early 1776 the call for independence was gaining ground. A few colonists still believed that King George III was under the influence of bad advisers. More people in the colonies, however, thought George was cruel and unfair.

Thomas Paine, an Englishman who had recently come to America, helped convince the colonists that the king was wrong. In January 1776 he published a pamphlet called *Common Sense*. In it, Paine attacked not only the king but also the whole idea of monarchy. Americans had a natural right to rule themselves, Paine insisted:

> **"A government of our own is our natural right; and when a man seriously reflects on the precariousness [uncertainty] of human**

affairs, he will become convinced that it is infinitely wiser and safer to form a constitution of our own in a cool, deliberate manner, while we have it in our power, than to trust such an interesting event to time and chance."

Common Sense was an immediate best-seller throughout the colonies. As a colonist from South Carolina explained, "It made independents of the majority of the country."

COMMON SENSE;
ADDRESSED TO THE
INHABITANTS
OF
AMERICA,
On the following interesting
SUBJECTS.
I. Of the Origin and Design of Government in general, with concise Remarks on the English Constitution.
II. Of Monarchy and Hereditary Succession.
III. Thoughts on the present State of American Affairs.
IV. Of the present Ability of America, with some miscellaneous Reflections.
Man knows no Master save creating HEAVEN,
Or those whom choice and common good ordain.
THOMSON.
PHILADELPHIA Printed:
NEW-YORK, Reprinted and Sold, by JOHN ANDERSON, the Corner of Beekman's-Slip.

Historical Society of Pennsylvania

The Granger Collection, New York

Common Sense author Thomas Paine lived in poverty in England before meeting Benjamin Franklin, who convinced him to try life in America.

Congress Burns Its Bridges

By June 1776 nearly all the members of the Second Continental Congress were ready to act. On June 7 Richard Henry Lee of Virginia introduced a resolution for independence. Before passing it, the Congress appointed a committee to prepare a statement that explained the need for independence. The committee members were Benjamin Franklin, John Adams, Roger Sherman of Connecticut, Robert Livingston of New York, and Thomas Jefferson of Virginia. Jefferson was the main author of this statement, the **Declaration of Independence**.

On July 2 the delegates approved Lee's resolution. Two days later, on July 4, many of them signed the Declaration of Independence. They were burning their bridges behind them. "I am well aware of the toil and blood and treasure that it will cost us," Adams wrote to his wife Abigail, "to maintain this declaration and support and defend these states."

In the colonies, reaction to the Declaration was mixed. People who supported the British, called **Loyalists** or Tories, strongly opposed the Declaration. They regarded the **Patriots**, people who favored independence, as rebels. To the Patriots, however, a Tory was "a creature whose head is in England, [and] whose body is in America."

In British eyes, the Declaration's signers were traitors. If the "Americans" lost the war, these rebel leaders could expect the treatment commonly given traitors—death.

The Declaration of Independence

The Declaration of Independence is one of the best-known and most influential political documents ever written. It consists of two parts. The first restates the ideas of English philosopher John Locke. He believed human beings formed governments to protect their natural rights. If a government failed to do its job, or fulfill its "contract," the people could abolish it and create a new one—by force if necessary. The second part of the Declaration leveled several charges against George to prove that he had broken this "contract" with the colonists.

The Declaration includes the famous words, "all men are created equal." Over the years, people have debated what Jefferson meant by this phrase. Jefferson's noble principle did not apply to everyone in the 1700s. Despite their many contributions to the Revolution, women lacked full legal equality. So did African Americans, free and enslaved. Many African Americans had joined the fight for American independence before the delegates even signed the Declaration. Caesar Ferrett, Samuel Craft, and Prince Estabrook, for example, were among the militiamen at Lexington. Nevertheless, Jefferson's equality did not apply to African Americans, thousands of whom were held in slavery. New Englander Samuel Hopkins noted:

> **"Our struggle for liberty . . . while the poor Negroes look on and hear . . . that slavery is more to be dreaded than death, and [that] we are resolved to live free or die, . . . leads them to attend to their own wretched situation more than otherwise they could."**

Despite these contradictions between its intent and practice, the Declaration's case for equality deeply influenced political thinking. Later American reformers used Jefferson's words in their arguments to abolish slavery and to increase rights for women and African Americans. The Declaration also inspired people in many other countries as they struggled for freedom.

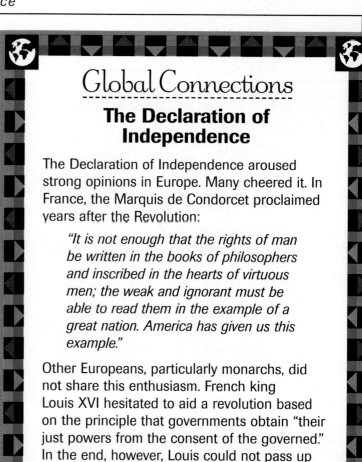

Global Connections

The Declaration of Independence

The Declaration of Independence aroused strong opinions in Europe. Many cheered it. In France, the Marquis de Condorcet proclaimed years after the Revolution:

> *"It is not enough that the rights of man be written in the books of philosophers and inscribed in the hearts of virtuous men; the weak and ignorant must be able to read them in the example of a great nation. America has given us this example."*

Other Europeans, particularly monarchs, did not share this enthusiasm. French king Louis XVI hesitated to aid a revolution based on the principle that governments obtain "their just powers from the consent of the governed." In the end, however, Louis could not pass up the opportunity to weaken the British Empire by helping the American rebels.

Section 3 Review

• Glossary

IDENTIFY and explain the significance of the following: Thomas Paine, Thomas Jefferson, Declaration of Independence, Loyalists, Patriots, John Locke

REVIEWING FOR DETAILS

1. How did the colonists react to Thomas Paine's *Common Sense*?
2. What are the two main sections of the Declaration of Independence?
3. How has the Declaration of Independence affected political thinking in the United States and other countries?

REVIEWING FOR UNDERSTANDING

4. **Writing Mastery:** *Persuading* Imagine that you are a political writer. Produce a short pamphlet persuading colonists to revolt against the British or to remain loyal.
5. **Critical Thinking:** *Determining the Strength of an Argument* How strong an argument did Jefferson present to justify a revolution against British rule in the colonies? Explain your answer.

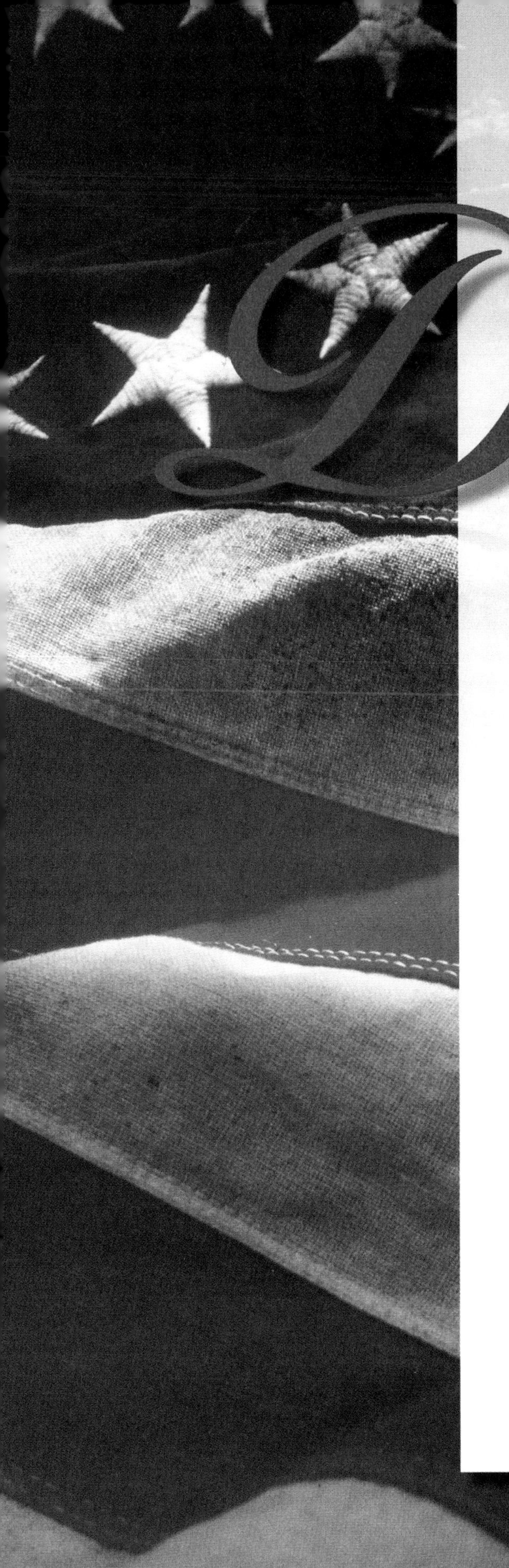

DECLARATION OF INDEPENDENCE

In Congress, July 4, 1776

THE UNANIMOUS DECLARATION OF THE THIRTEEN UNITED STATES OF AMERICA,

When in the Course of human events, it becomes necessary for one people to dissolve the political bands which have connected them with another, and to assume among the Powers of the earth, the separate and equal station to which the Laws of Nature and of Nature's God entitle them, a decent respect to the opinions of mankind requires that they should declare the causes which impel them to the separation.

Thomas Jefferson wrote the first draft of the Declaration of Independence in a little more than two weeks.

In the first paragraph, the signers state that it is important to justify why the colonists must break their political ties with Britain.

impel: force

endowed: provided

We hold these truths to be self-evident, that all men are created equal, that they are endowed by their Creator with certain unalienable Rights, that among these are Life, Liberty and the pursuit of Happiness. That to secure these rights, Governments are instituted among Men, deriving their just powers from the consent of the governed, That whenever any Form of Government becomes destructive of these ends, it is the Right of the People to alter or to abolish it, and to institute new Government, laying its foundation on such principles and organizing its powers in such form, as to them shall seem most likely to effect their Safety and Happiness. Prudence, indeed, will dictate that Governments long established should not be changed for light and transient causes; and accordingly all experience hath shown, that mankind are more disposed to suffer, while evils are sufferable, than to right themselves by abolishing the forms to which they are accustomed. But when a long train of abuses and usurpations, pursuing invariably the same Object evinces a design to reduce them under absolute Despotism, it is their right, it is their duty, to throw off such Government, and to provide new Guards for their future security.—Such has been the patient sufferance of these Colonies; and such is now the necessity which constrains them to alter their former Systems of Government. The history of the present King of Great Britain is a history of repeated injuries and usurpations, all having in direct object the establishment of an absolute Tyranny over these States. To prove this, let Facts be submitted to a candid world.

usurpations: wrongful seizures of power

despotism: unlimited power

tyranny: oppressive power used by a government or ruler

candid: fair

Here the Declaration lists the charges that the colonists had against King George III. How does the language in the list appeal to people's emotions?

He has refused his Assent to Laws, the most wholesome and necessary for the public good.

He has forbidden his Governors to pass Laws of immediate and pressing importance, unless suspended in their operation till his Assent should be obtained; and when so suspended, he has utterly neglected to attend to them.

He has refused to pass other Laws for the accommodation of large districts of people, unless those people would relinquish the right of Representation in the Legislature, a right inestimable to them and formidable to tyrants only.

relinquish: release, give up

inestimable: priceless

formidable: causing dread

Why do you think the king had his legislatures in the colonies meet in places that were hard to reach?

He has called together legislative bodies at places unusual, uncomfortable, and distant from the depository of their Public Records, for the sole purpose of fatiguing them into compliance with his measures.

He has dissolved Representative Houses repeatedly, for opposing with manly firmness his invasions on the rights of the people.

He has refused for a long time, after such dissolutions, to cause others to be elected; whereby the Legislative Powers, incapable of Annihilation, have returned to the People at large for their exercise; the State remaining in the mean time exposed to all the dangers of invasion from without, and convulsions within.

annihilation: destruction

convulsions: violent disturbances

naturalization of foreigners: the process by which foreign-born persons become citizens

appropriations of land: setting aside land for settlement

He has endeavored to prevent the population of these States; for that purpose obstructing the Laws of Naturalization of Foreigners; refusing to pass others to encourage their migration hither, and raising the conditions of new Appropriations of Lands.

He has obstructed the Administration of Justice, by refusing his Assent to Laws for establishing Judiciary Powers.

tenure: term

He has made Judges dependent on his Will alone, for the tenure of their offices, and the amount and payment of their salaries.

He has erected a multitude of New Offices, and sent hither swarms of Officers to harass our People, and eat out their substance.

a multitude of: many

He has kept among us, in times of peace, Standing Armies without the Consent of our legislature.

He has affected to render the Military independent of and superior to the Civil Power.

He has combined with others to subject us to a jurisdiction foreign to our constitution, and unacknowledged by our laws; giving his Assent to their acts of pretended legislation:

What wrongful acts does the Declaration state have been committed by the king and the British Parliament?

For quartering large bodies of armed troops among us:

quartering: lodging, housing

For protecting them, by a mock Trial, from Punishment for any Murders which they should commit on the Inhabitants of these States:

For cutting off our Trade with all parts of the world:

For imposing taxes on us without our Consent:

For depriving us in many cases, of the benefits of Trial by Jury:

For transporting us beyond Seas to be tried for pretended offences:

For abolishing the free System of English Laws in a neighboring Province, establishing therein an Arbitrary government, and enlarging its Boundaries so as to render it at once an example and fit instrument for introducing the same absolute rule into these Colonies:

The "neighboring Province" that is referred to here is Quebec.

arbitrary: not based on law

render: make

For taking away our Charters, abolishing our most valuable Laws, and altering fundamentally the Forms of our Governments:

For suspending our own Legislature, and declaring themselves invested with Power to legislate for us in all cases whatsoever.

He has abdicated Government here, by declaring us out of his Protection and waging War against us.

abdicated: given up

He has plundered our seas, ravaged our Coasts, burnt our towns, and destroyed the lives of our people.

He is at this time transporting large armies of foreign mercenaries to complete the works of death, desolation and tyranny, already begun with circumstances of Cruelty & perfidy scarcely paralleled in the most barbarous ages, and totally unworthy the Head of a civilized nation.

foreign mercenaries: soldiers hired to fight for a country not their own

perfidy: violation of trust

He has constrained our fellow Citizens taken Captive on the high Seas to bear Arms against their Country, to become the executioners of their friends and Brethren, or to fall themselves by their Hands.

He has excited domestic insurrections amongst us, and has endeavored to bring on the inhabitants of our frontiers, the merciless Indian Savages, whose known rule of warfare, is an undistinguished destruction of all ages, sexes and conditions.

insurrections: rebellions

Notice that the Declaration has 18 paragraphs beginning with "He has" or "He is." What is the effect of this repetition?

In every stage of these Oppressions We have Petitioned for Redress in the most humble terms: Our repeated Petitions have been answered only by repeated injury. A Prince, whose character is thus marked by every act which may define a Tyrant, is unfit to be the ruler of a free People.

petitioned for redress: asked formally for a correction of wrongs

Nor have We been wanting in attention to our British brethren. We have warned them from time to time of attempts by their legislature to extend an unwarrantable jurisdiction over us. We have reminded them of the circumstances of our emigration and settlement here. We have appealed to their native justice and magnanimity, and we have conjured them by the ties of our common kindred to disavow these

unwarrantable jurisdiction: unjustified authority

magnanimity: generous spirit

conjured: urgently called upon

usurpations, which, would inevitably interrupt our connections and correspondence. They too have been deaf to the voice of justice and of consanguinity. We must, therefore, acquiesce in the necessity, which denounces our Separation, and hold them, as we hold the rest of mankind, Enemies in War, in Peace Friends.

consanguinity: common ancestry
acquiesce: consent to

We, therefore, the Representatives of the united States of America, in General Congress, Assembled, appealing to the Supreme Judge of the world for the rectitude of our intentions, do, in the Name, and by Authority of the good People of these Colonies, solemnly publish and declare, That these United Colonies are, and of Right ought to be Free and Independent States; that they are Absolved from all Allegiance to the British Crown, and that all political connection between them and the State of Great Britain, is and ought to be totally dissolved; and that as Free and Independent States, they have full Power to levy War, conclude Peace, contract Alliances, establish Commerce, and to do all other Acts and Things which Independent States may of right do. And for the support of this Declaration, with a firm reliance on the Protection of Divine Providence, we mutually pledge to each other our Lives, our Fortunes and our sacred Honor.

rectitude: rightness

In this paragraph, the signers state their actual declaration of independence. What rights would the new United States of America now have as an independent nation?

Congress adopted the final draft of the Declaration of Independence on July 4, 1776. A formal copy, written on parchment paper, was signed on August 2, 1776.

About two months before his participation on the committee to prepare the Declaration, John Adams received a letter from his wife, Abigail Adams. The last sentence said, "If particular care and attention is not paid to the ladies, we are determined to foment [start] a rebellion and will not hold ourselves bound by any laws in which we have no voice, or representation." Did the writers of the Declaration listen to her advice?

John Hancock
Button Gwinnett
Lyman Hall
George Walton
William Hooper
Joseph Hewes
John Penn
Edward Rutledge
Thomas Heyward, Jr.
Thomas Lynch, Jr.
Arthur Middleton
Samuel Chase
William Paca
Thomas Stone
Charles Carroll of Carrollton
George Wythe
Richard Henry Lee
Thomas Jefferson
Benjamin Harrison
Thomas Nelson, Jr.
Francis Lightfoot Lee
Carter Braxton
Robert Morris
Benjamin Rush
Benjamin Franklin
John Morton
George Clymer
James Smith

George Taylor
James Wilson
George Ross
Caesar Rodney
George Read
Thomas McKean
William Floyd
Philip Livingston
Francis Lewis
Lewis Morris
Richard Stockton
John Witherspoon
Francis Hopkinson
John Hart
Abraham Clark
Josiah Bartlett
William Whipple
Matthew Thornton
Samuel Adams
John Adams
Robert Treat Paine
Elbridge Gerry
Stephen Hopkins
William Ellery
Roger Sherman
Samuel Huntington
William Williams
Oliver Wolcott

Section 4
INDEPENDENCE IS WON

Multimedia Connections

Explore these related topics and materials on the CD–ROM to enrich your understanding of this section:

Biographies
- John Paul Jones

Media Bank
- Mercy Otis Warren
- John Paul Jones
- Joseph Brant
- Baron Fredrick von Steuben
- Battle of Trenton
- Francis Marion

Gazetteer
- Saratoga
- Yorktown

Atlas
- Victories of John Paul Jones

Readings
- Indians and the War
- Occupied New York

Profiles
- Benedict Arnold
- Bernardo de Gálvez
- Deborah Sampson
- Mercy Otis Warren
- Nathan Hale

It was September 1776. Lord Richard Howe, a British naval officer, waited for his guests. He had invited the Patriots to informal peace talks. The Americans sent Benjamin Franklin, John Adams, and Edward Rutledge to meet with him. As they talked, relations became strained. "Is there no way of turning back this step of independence?" Howe asked. The Americans said that things had gone too far. Disappointed, Howe thanked them for coming. The war would continue.

As you read this section you will find out:

- **How Washington's army fared in the middle colonies.**
- **Why the Battle of Saratoga was the turning point in the Revolution.**
- **How the British were defeated in the South.**

Americans at War

The Patriots had declared their independence, and now they would have to fight for it. This task went to George Washington's Continental Army. Washington soon turned his inexperienced troops into orderly units. At first, there were 28 regiments, each with eight companies of about 90 men. Washington removed officers who could not maintain discipline and appointed new ones. He made the soldiers construct barracks and taught them to march in step. Washington's endless list of tasks and stern approach made him unpopular with many troops. Some Europeans, including Count Casimir Pulaski and Thaddeus Kosciusko of Poland, and Baron Friedrich von Steuben of Prussia, helped train the army.

More than 5,000 African Americans served in the Continental Army. Jehu Grant, the escaped slave of a Loyalist, described why he enlisted:

> **"When I saw . . . the people all engaged for the support of freedom, I could not but . . . be pleased with such [a] thing. . . . These considerations induced me to enlist into the American army, where I served faithful about ten months."**

Women also contributed to the Continental Army's success. In addition to those who ran farms and businesses, many women acted as nurses, did laundry, and cooked for the soldiers. Some even fought in the ranks. Among them were Mary Ludwig Hays and Deborah Sampson. Hays carried water to the troops, earning her the nickname Molly Pitcher. When her husband fell in battle, she took his place loading cannons. Sampson disguised herself as a man in order to enlist with Washington's troops and became the most famous woman to fight in the Continental Army.

Mary Ludwig Hays showed great courage when she loaded cannons and carried water during battle.

• Deborah Sampson

• Molly Pitcher

America's Darkest Hour

After they retreated from Boston, the British decided to capture New York. If successful, this would crush the Revolution by splitting the colonies in two.

A loss at New York. In late June 1776, General Howe sailed just south of New York City with about 10,000 troops. Two months later the British attacked Long Island, where Washington had moved much of his army. Howe outmaneuvered the Patriots and struck from two directions. Washington barely managed to withdraw his battered troops across the East River to safety on Manhattan Island. Howe then drove the Americans to the north end of Manhattan and took control of New York City. Large numbers of Loyalists welcomed the British with open arms. After further fighting, Washington retreated across the Hudson River into New Jersey. Many of his soldiers had been captured, and others had deserted. Just weeks after the Patriots had declared their independence, their cause seemed doomed!

Victories at Trenton and Princeton. During this dark hour, Washington devised a daring plan. Howe had settled down for the winter in New York City, but he left about 1,400 soldiers in Trenton, New Jersey. These **mercenaries**, or hired fighters, were called Hessians because some of their leaders came from the German state of Hesse-Cassel.

On Christmas night, in the middle of a snowstorm, Washington led his troops across the ice-choked Delaware River, nine miles north of Trenton. At dawn the American soldiers overwhelmed the astonished Hessians and took more than 900 prisoners. The surprise was so complete that only about 30 Hessians and few, if any, Patriots died in the brief **Battle of Trenton**.

American Letters

The Crisis

Thomas Paine

In late 1776 the American cause seemed almost hopeless. Washington's appeals for more troops and supplies went unheard. Thomas Paine, author of Common Sense, *traveled with the army on its long retreat. In December he wrote a new pamphlet,* The Crisis, *to rouse Americans to the cause of freedom.*

These are the times that try men's souls. The summer soldier and the sunshine patriot will, in this crisis, shrink from the service of his country; but he that stands it now deserves the love and thanks of man and woman. Tyranny, like hell, is not easily conquered; yet we have this consolation [comfort] with us—that the harder the conflict, the more glorious the triumph. What we obtain too cheap, we esteem [honor] too lightly: It is dearness only that gives everything its value. Heaven knows how to put a proper price upon its goods; and it would be strange indeed if so celestial [heavenly] an article as freedom should not be highly rated. Britain, with an army to enforce her tyranny, has declared that she has a right not only to tax but "to bind us in all cases whatsoever," and if being bound in that manner is not slavery, then there is not such a thing as slavery upon earth. . . .

. . . I turn . . . to those who have nobly stood and are yet determined to stand the matter out. I call not upon a few, but upon all; not in this state or that state, but on every state. Up and help us. . . . Throw not the burden of the day upon Providence, but "show your faith by your works," that God may bless you. It matters not where you live, or what rank of life you hold, the evil or the blessing will reach you all. . . . The heart that feels not now is dead; the blood of his children will curse his cowardice who shrinks back at a time when a little might have saved the whole. . . . But he whose heart is firm, and whose conscience approves his conduct, will pursue his principles unto death. . . .

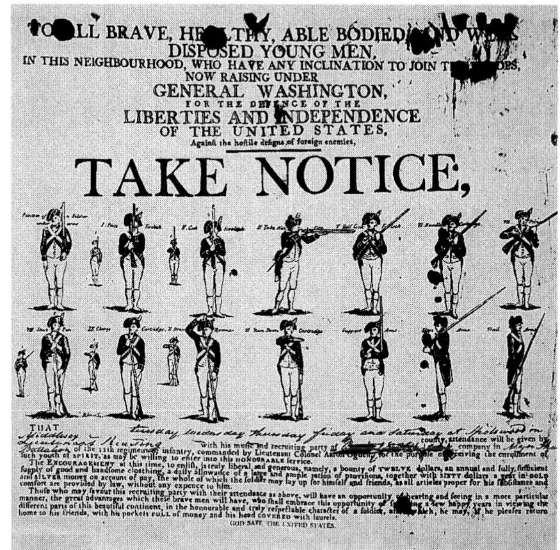

Recruitment poster for the Continental Army, led by General Washington

There are cases which cannot be overdone by language, and this is one. There are persons, too, who see not the full extent of the evil which threatens them; they solace [assure] themselves with hopes that the enemy, if he succeed, will be merciful. It is the madness of folly to expect mercy from those who have refused to do justice. . . .

. . . By perseverance [determination] and fortitude [endurance] we have the prospect of a glorious issue [result]; by cowardice and submission, the sad choice of a variety of evils—a ravaged country—a depopulated city—habitations [homes] without safety and slavery without hope. . . . Look on this picture and weep over it! And if there yet remains one thoughtless wretch who believes it not, let him suffer it unlamented [without grief].

Washington quickly struck again, this time at nearby Princeton, where he drove two British regiments from the town. Then he made camp for the winter at Morristown, New Jersey, about 30 miles west of New York. Washington's victories at Trenton and Princeton did wonders to raise American spirits during this difficult time.

A New British Strategy

The war began again in the spring of 1777. The British developed a complicated strategy for the upcoming battles. A British army under the command of General John "Gentleman Johnny" Burgoyne would march south from Canada into New York. At the same time, Howe would march north from New York City to meet Burgoyne. The British hoped this would threaten New England and draw Washington's Continental Army northward, where large numbers of Redcoat forces could defeat the Patriots.

Howe never fully understood his role in the plan, however, and did not carry it out. He decided to attack Philadelphia, home of the rebel Congress, instead. Howe moved his troops by sea to Delaware Bay and soon landed in Pennsylvania. Washington hurried south as soon as he learned of Howe's location.

When the two armies clashed just southwest of Philadelphia at Brandywine Creek, the Americans lost very badly. Howe then marched into Philadelphia. The American cause of independence once again seemed to be in danger of defeat.

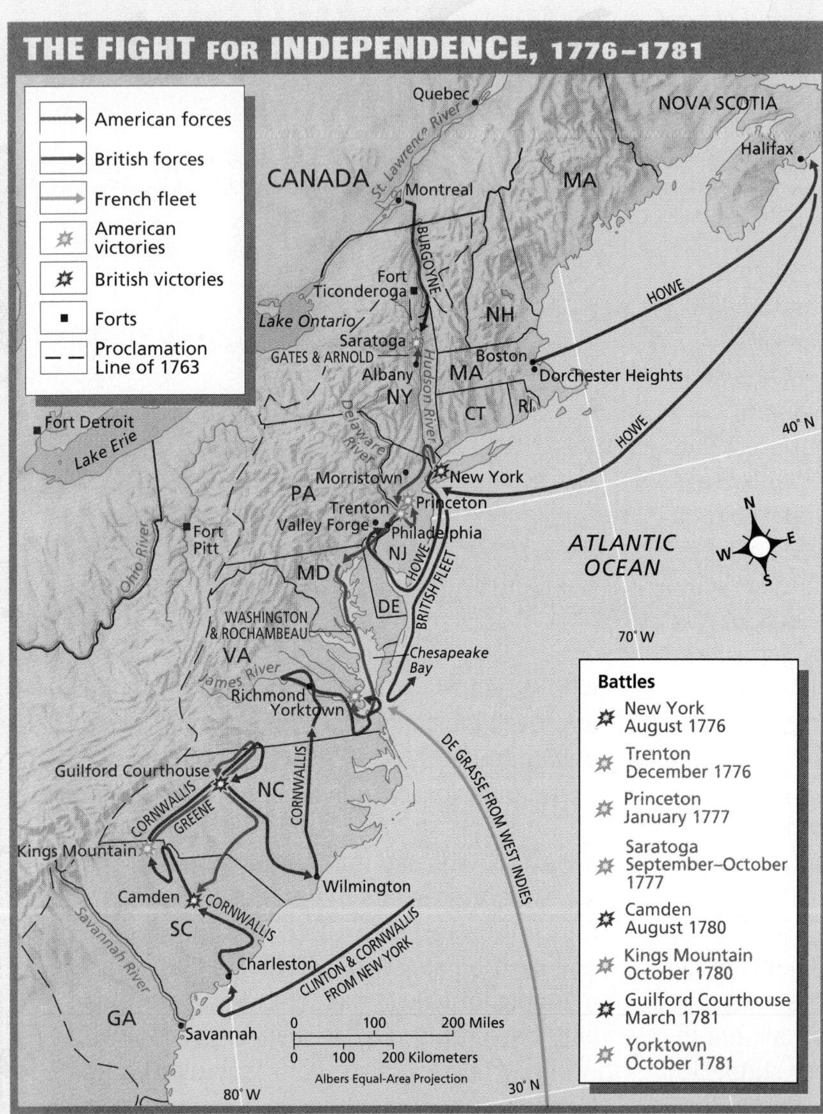

Learning from Maps.
The Revolutionary War was fought across the vast area of the thirteen colonies. British troops could be transported on ships of the British fleet, while the American army had to move on foot.

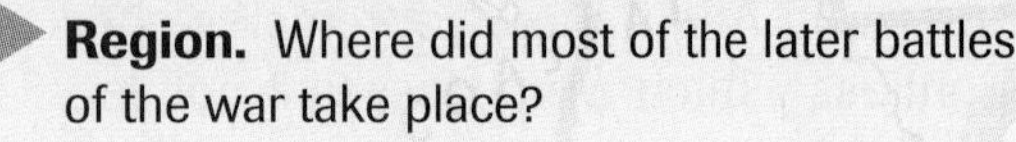

▶ **Region.** Where did most of the later battles of the war take place?

• **Maps**

The Ganger Collection, New York

Dressed in a fancy uniform, General John "Gentleman Johnny" Burgoyne surrenders to the Patriots. American and British officers later marked the event with a formal dinner.

• Battle of Saratoga

Turning Point at Saratoga

Meanwhile, General Burgoyne, unaware that Howe would not be meeting him, marched southward from Canada with more than 7,200 troops. Burgoyne's army recaptured Fort Ticonderoga on July 5. Then their advance slowed to a crawl. The retreating Patriots burned bridges and chopped down huge trees to block the paths through the heavily forested region. With each passing day, more and more American militias gathered near Saratoga, New York, under the command of American general Horatio Gates.

On September 19 and October 7, 1777, Gates delivered crushing blows to Burgoyne's force. Baroness von Riedesel, whose husband commanded the German troops with the British, described the defeated army's retreat:

> **"Fires had been kindled in every direction, and many tents left standing to make the enemy believe that the camp was still there. We traveled continually the whole night. Little Frederica [von Riedesel's daughter] was afraid and would often begin to cry. I was therefore obliged to hold a pocket handkerchief over her mouth, lest our whereabouts should be discovered."**

With supplies running low and no help in sight, Burgoyne surrendered his force on October 17. The **Battle of Saratoga** proved to be the turning point in the war.

New Hopes and Hard Times

The Battle of Saratoga again raised the hopes of many Americans. It also brought aid from abroad. Without this assistance, the United States might never have been born.

Aid from abroad. When news of Saratoga reached Paris in early 1778, France officially recognized the government of the United States of America. France also signed a treaty of alliance and declared war on Great Britain.

The French were eager to weaken Britain, their longtime enemy. They had been helping the rebels with loans and supplies from the start of the war, and many French officers had already come to America to fight. After the Battle of Saratoga the French army and navy joined in the American Revolution directly, greatly strengthening the forces against the British.

Spain also declared war on Great Britain. Bernardo de Gálvez, the governor of Spanish Louisiana and Florida, sent weapons, supplies, and money. Later he captured the British fort at Pensacola, Florida.

The winter at Valley Forge. Before much aid reached the colonies, Washington's army had to get through the winter of 1777–78 at Valley Forge, near Philadelphia. Supplies of food and clothing were scarce. One Patriot described the difficult, painful experience:

> **"Thousands were without blankets, and were obliged to warm themselves over fires all night. . . . It was not uncommon to track the march of the men over ice and frozen ground by the blood from their naked feet."**

In spite of such hardships, the tattered army made it through the winter.

Supplies ran so low at Valley Forge that many soldiers did not have enough clothing to leave their tents. Roughly 25 percent of the troops died during the cold winter.

• Valley Forge Diary

The March Toward Victory

After Saratoga, the British concentrated their efforts in the South. The Americans had control of New England and by 1779 they had won major victories in the West. The British thought they would have a better chance in the South, which reportedly contained many Loyalist militia units. Using their great navy, the British captured the ports of Savannah, Georgia, in 1778 and Charleston, South Carolina, in 1780. General Lord Charles Cornwallis had the responsibility of conquering the rest of the southern colonies. In August 1780 he defeated an American army at Camden, South Carolina.

Cornwallis soon faced trouble, however. Roving bands of Patriot **guerrillas**, or fighters who use hit-and-run tactics, began picking away at the British forces. These bands were led by Francis Marion and Thomas Sumter. Marion was called the "Swamp Fox" because he and his soldiers usually disappeared into the nearest swamp when the British attacked.

In March 1781 Cornwallis defeated an American force at Guilford Courthouse in North Carolina. It was a costly victory. Cornwallis lost about one third of his soldiers in the battle and became short of supplies. He quickly retreated to the coast, where the British navy could support him.

• Heroes and Traitors

Victory at Yorktown

By May 1781 Cornwallis had marched north into Virginia. He established his army at Yorktown, choosing a peninsula with harbor access at the mouth of the York River. A Patriot force under French general Lafayette took up positions outside Yorktown.

Washington, and Comte de Rochambeau (raw-shahm-boh) a French general, gave up a plan to attack New York City and marched south to Yorktown. Their combined forces arrived in September 1781. Over 16,000 French and American troops on the peninsula stood ready to prevent the more than 7,000 British soldiers from escaping over land. Off the coast, French warships blocked any help or escape by sea.

On October 9 Washington's artillery began to batter the British position in the **Battle of Yorktown**. Cornwallis sent off a last, desperate message to his commander. "If you cannot relieve me very soon, you must be prepared to hear the worst."

No assistance came. On October 19 Cornwallis surrendered. His troops marched out of Yorktown, while the band played "The World Turned Upside Down."

The fighting was over. The British still controlled New York City, Charleston, Savannah, and some frontier posts, but they no longer had the will to continue the war. In Great Britain, public opposition to the war had grown. In March 1782 Parliament voted, in effect, to give up "farther prosecution of offensive war on the continent of North America." About two weeks later Lord North resigned as prime minister. Although they still had to sign a peace treaty with the British, the Americans had won their independence.

General Charles Cornwallis surrenders at the Battle of Yorktown. The Americans had defeated the British!

Section 4 Review

• Glossary

• Time Line

IDENTIFY and explain the significance of the following: mercenaries, Battle of Trenton, John Burgoyne, Horatio Gates, Battle of Saratoga, Charles Cornwallis, guerrillas, Francis Marion, Battle of Yorktown

REVIEWING FOR DETAILS

1. What successes and failures did Washington's army have in New York, New Jersey, and Pennsylvania?
2. In what way can the Battle of Saratoga be considered the turning point in the American Revolution?

REVIEWING FOR UNDERSTANDING

3. **Geographic Literacy** Why was Washington able to defeat the British at Yorktown?
4. **Writing Mastery:** *Creating* Imagine that you are a soldier in Washington's army. Write a journal entry, song lyric, or poem about your experiences at New York, Trenton, or Valley Forge.
5. **Critical Thinking:** *Drawing Conclusions* Do you think the Patriots could have won the Revolution without help from foreign nations? Give facts to support your opinion.

Loyalists in America

A variety of people in the colonies supported the British during the Revolutionary War. It is difficult, however, to estimate exactly how many American colonists remained loyal to Britain. Some Patriots considered any person who did not actively support their cause to be a Loyalist. As a result, many people who tried to stay neutral during the war, including religious groups like the Quakers, were considered Loyalists.

Other Loyalist activity was very direct. Loyalist newspapers were published throughout the colonies. Loyalist military units, called Provincial Corps, were organized in several areas. New York was the leading colony for Loyalist activity, with five Loyalist newspapers and 18 Provincial Corps.

Many Loyalists fled the colonies during the war. After the British surrendered, thousands more Loyalists emigrated to escape persecution by Patriots. The majority went to Canada, while others went to Great Britain and the Caribbean Islands.

Sites of Loyalist Activity, 1775–1783

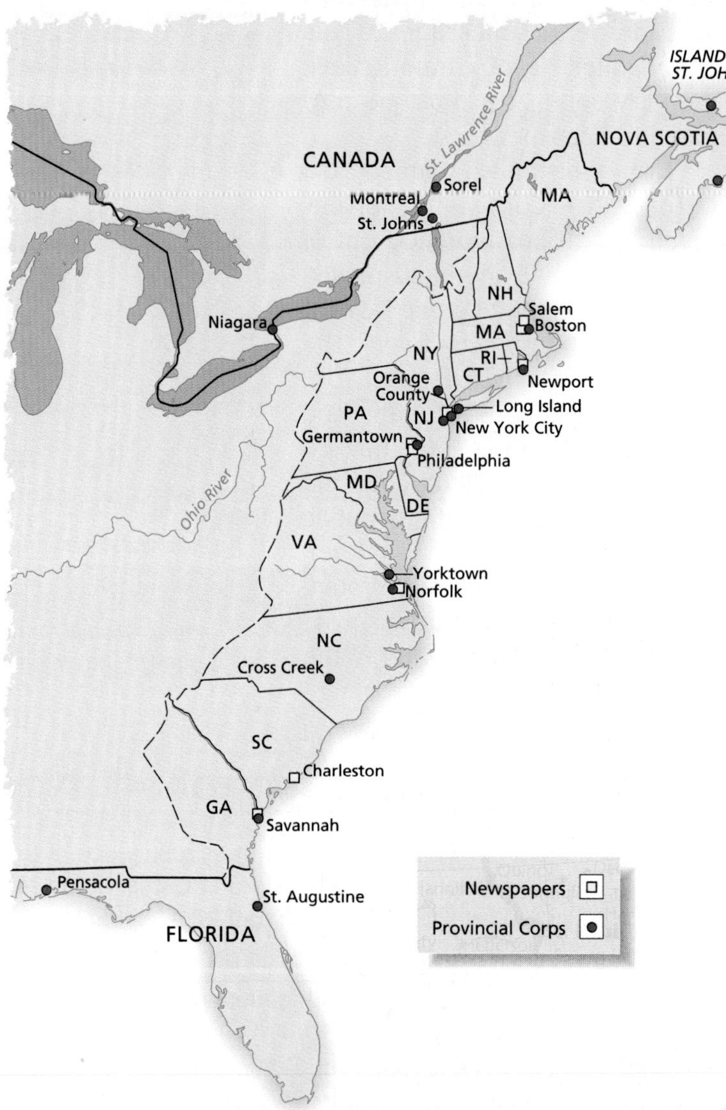

Some cities with many Loyalists had both newspapers and Provincial Corps. **Place:** Which colonial cities housed both Loyalist newspapers and Provincial Corps? What was the primary Loyalist activity in cities outside of the thirteen colonies?

Loyalist Resettlement, 1770–1780s

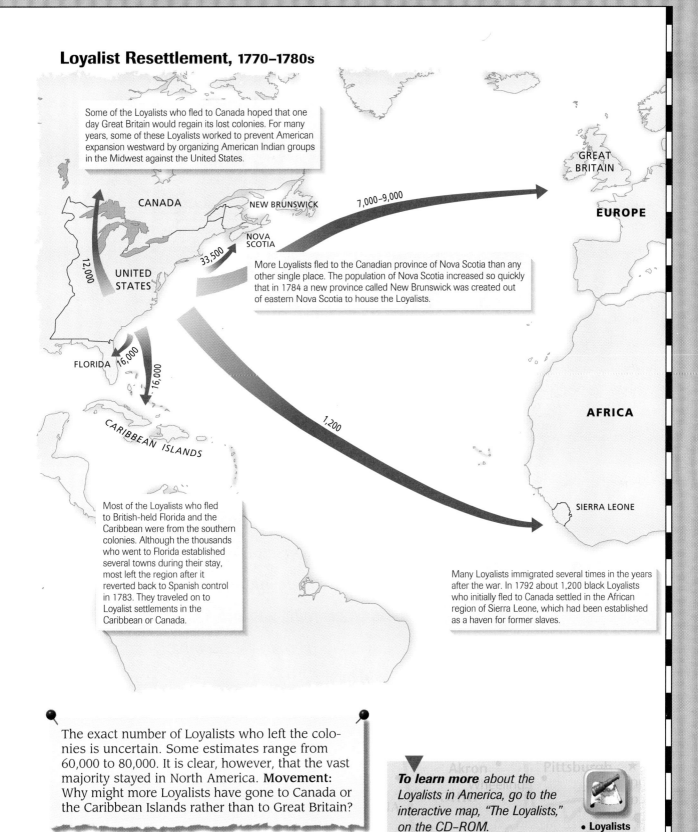

Some of the Loyalists who fled to Canada hoped that one day Great Britain would regain its lost colonies. For many years, some of these Loyalists worked to prevent American expansion westward by organizing American Indian groups in the Midwest against the United States.

CANADA
NEW BRUNSWICK
NOVA SCOTIA
UNITED STATES
12,000
33,500
7,000–9,000
GREAT BRITAIN
EUROPE
FLORIDA
16,000
16,000
CARIBBEAN ISLANDS
1,200
AFRICA
SIERRA LEONE

More Loyalists fled to the Canadian province of Nova Scotia than any other single place. The population of Nova Scotia increased so quickly that in 1784 a new province called New Brunswick was created out of eastern Nova Scotia to house the Loyalists.

Most of the Loyalists who fled to British-held Florida and the Caribbean were from the southern colonies. Although the thousands who went to Florida established several towns during their stay, most left the region after it reverted back to Spanish control in 1783. They traveled on to Loyalist settlements in the Caribbean or Canada.

Many Loyalists immigrated several times in the years after the war. In 1792 about 1,200 black Loyalists who initially fled to Canada settled in the African region of Sierra Leone, which had been established as a haven for former slaves.

The exact number of Loyalists who left the colonies is uncertain. Some estimates range from 60,000 to 80,000. It is clear, however, that the vast majority stayed in North America. **Movement:** Why might more Loyalists have gone to Canada or the Caribbean Islands rather than to Great Britain?

***To learn more** about the Loyalists in America, go to the interactive map, "The Loyalists," on the CD-ROM.*

• **Loyalists**

CHAPTER 6

Forming a New Nation (1776–1789)

THEMES IN AMERICAN HISTORY

Constitutional Heritage:
Why might people want to have a basic set of written laws with which to govern their country?

Democratic Values:
Why might people choose a democratic form of government?

Economic Development:
How might economic issues influence people's political beliefs?

• **Video Opener**

• **Skill Builder**

Benjamin Franklin acknowledged that the U. S. Constitution had flaws. "When you assemble . . . men to have the advantage of their joint wisdom," he wrote, "you inevitably [certainly] assemble . . . all their prejudices, their passions. . . . Can a perfect production be expected?" Whatever its imperfections, Franklin concluded, the document gave the young nation a government it badly needed.

image above: Drafting the Constitution

Section 1
Moving Toward Self-Government

Multimedia Connections

Explore these related topics and materials on the CD–ROM to enrich your understanding of this section:

Readings

- Iroquois Great Law of Peace
- What Is an American?

Media Bank

- Ohio River Flatboat

Profiles

- Benjamin Franklin

Glossary

- English Bill of Rights
- Magna Carta
- town meetings

Gazetteer

- Great Britain
- Virginia
- Maryland
- Appalachian Mountains

Many Americans realized that victory in the American Revolution would allow them to create an entirely new form of government. Patriot John Adams called this chance "a phenomenon [remarkable event] in the political world." He observed, "We must realize the theories of the wisest writers, and invite the people to erect the whole building with their own hands." The American experiment in the tricky art of self-government had begun.

As you read this section you will find out:

- **What traditions and ideas influenced government in America.**
- **What elements many of the first state constitutions had in common.**
- **Why state leaders created a national government but limited its power.**

Thinking About Government

Even before the Revolution ended, Americans began to develop an independent system of government, one shaped by many political and intellectual traditions. Some of these traditions were based in English experience. In 1215 English nobles had forced King John to sign Magna Carta, a document that limited the power of the monarch. It declared that the monarch could not collect taxes without the consent of an advisory body. Magna Carta thus provided the basis for establishing parliamentary democracy in Great Britain. Another model for American government was the English Bill of Rights of 1689, which declared that the monarch could not make or suspend any law, create any tax, or maintain an army in peacetime without the consent of Parliament.

Voting rights varied greatly from state to state. While most state constitutions did not extend the vote to women, for example, New Jersey gave women the vote between 1790 and 1807.

The Granger Collection, New York

Other ideas came from European philosophy. The **Enlightenment**, a movement during the 1700s that grew out of the Scientific Revolution, influenced many American leaders. Philosophers of the Enlightenment used reason to investigate and to try to improve government and society. For example, in his book *The Social Contract,* philosopher Jean-Jacque Rousseau (roo-soh) studied many different forms of government and concluded that the best was one in which everyone was equal.

American leaders also drew on colonial traditions, such as New England town meetings. In these gatherings, ordinary citizens participated in community government by voicing their opinions on important issues.

State Governments and Constitutions

During the Revolution, Patriots wanted to make the colonies into independent states. In order to remove British political controls, leaders in each colony either revised their old royal charter or wrote a new state **constitution**—a set of laws that defines the basic structure and powers of a government.

Under the new constitutions, powerful state legislatures replaced the colonial assemblies. Because the colonists feared government abuses, however, most constitutions put some controls on the legislature. Many established short terms of office, in part so that voters could quickly get rid of unpopular representatives. One North Carolina man expressed many colonists' fears of a powerful central government:

> **"The more experience I acquire, the stronger is my conviction [belief] that *unlimited power can not be safely trusted* to any man or set of men on earth. . . . Power of all kinds has an irresistible propensity [tendency] to increase a desire for itself."**

The new constitutions assigned little power to the state executive. In addition, most state constitutions limited the power of judges by placing them under the control of the legislature.

Many of the state constitutions contained a bill of rights. These guaranteed that the state governments would not violate the rights and freedoms of their citizens.

The constitutions reflected Americans' desire for a **republican** form of government, or one in which the people hold the power and give elected representatives the authority to make and carry out laws. The constitutions greatly expanded **suffrage**, or voting rights, for white men. Suffrage varied from state to state, even for white men. In Pennsylvania, for example, all free men who paid taxes could vote. But in South Carolina, men had to own a certain amount of property to vote.

Most of the states did not extend suffrage to African Americans, American Indians, and women. During the next few decades, however, supporters of the antislavery movement convinced most northern states to ban slavery in their territory and to give voting rights to free African American men.

The Articles of Confederation

Setting up the state governments proved easier than forming a central structure. This was an old problem. In 1754 Benjamin Franklin had drafted the **Albany Plan of Union**, a proposal for permanently uniting the colonies. He believed that common interests made it worthwhile for the colonies to have some sort of common government. At the time, his plan attracted little support.

During the 1760s and 1770s, however, citizens responded to the need for group action with the Stamp Act Congress and the boycott of British goods. When the Revolution finally came, Franklin made the case for unity. "We must all hang together," he said, "or assuredly we shall all hang separately."

The Second Continental Congress eventually agreed with Franklin. It became, in effect, America's first government. It operated a postal service, planned finances, and even printed paper money. The Congress also appointed American **diplomats**, or officials who conducted government relations with foreign countries.

By November 1777 Congress had also written a constitution called the **Articles of Confederation**. This document was America's first national constitution. The Articles stressed the independence of the separate states. It established the United States of America as only "a firm league of friendship"—a loose alliance of states.

The Articles of Confederation created a single national governing body called the **Confederation Congress** and generally gave it the powers that had been granted to the Second Continental Congress. Each of the 13 states had one vote in Congress and was

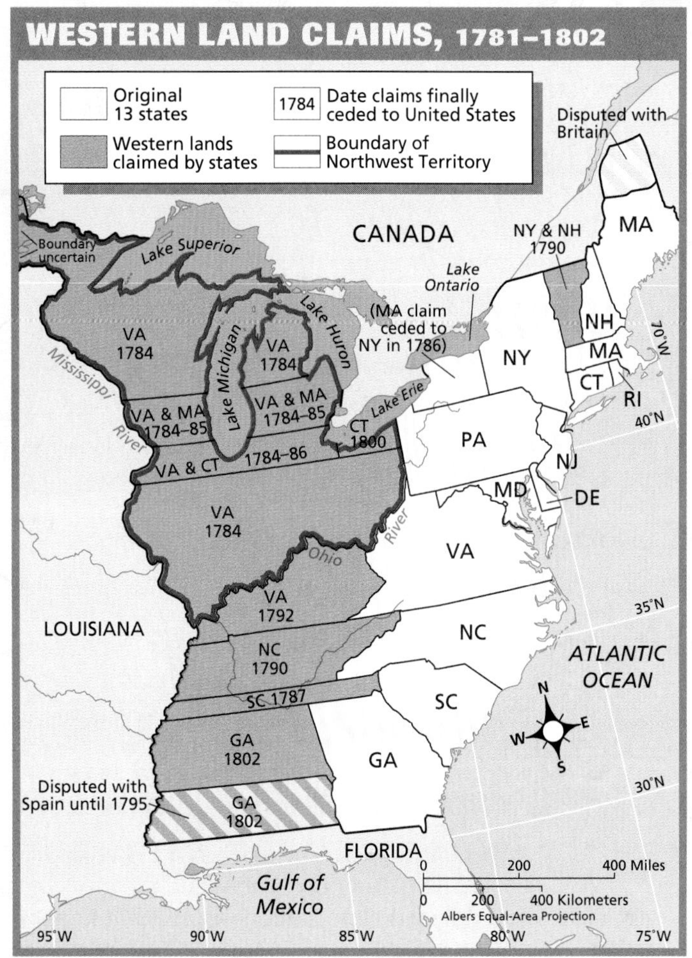

Learning from Maps. Many of the original 13 states had western land claims, some of which were larger than the states themselves. Most of these claims were eventually ceded to the United States.

• Maps

Location. What state claimed the greatest amount of western land?

supposed to contribute money for national defense and other expenses.

The Articles had serious weaknesses, however. Congress could not take action on certain important matters, such as declaring war or making treaties, without approval by nine states. The Articles also did not specify how Congress was to exercise or enforce many of the powers it did have. For example, Congress could decide how much money it needed and how much each state should pay, but it could not make them pay.

The states reserved other powers as well, like the authority to print their own money. They could also establish their own policies for **interstate commerce**, or business and trade between states.

Rivalries among several states held up **ratification**, or formal approval, of the Articles of Confederation. After deciding that the document could not go into effect until all the states had accepted it, Congress distributed copies in late 1777. Maryland and other states without large western land holdings would not ratify it until all state claims to lands beyond the Appalachian Mountains were turned over to the new United States. Virginia and a few other states with huge land claims refused to do so, unwilling to lose money from western land sales.

Eventually, only two states—Maryland and Virginia—continued to fight over this issue. In January 1781 Virginia finally agreed to give up some of its claims in a bid for national unity. Maryland then ratified the Articles soon after.

The Granger Collection, New York

Benjamin Franklin, a scientist and political leader, conducted electrical experiments with lightning.

Section 1 Review

• Glossary

IDENTIFY and explain the significance of the following: Enlightenment, constitution, republican, suffrage, Albany Plan of Union, diplomats, Articles of Confederation, Confederation Congress, interstate commerce, ratification

REVIEWING FOR DETAILS

1. What did many of the first state constitutions have in common?
2. Why did state leaders establish a national government but limit its power?

REVIEWING FOR UNDERSTANDING

3. **Geographic Literacy** Why might different amounts of western land ownership lead to conflict between states?
4. **Writing Mastery:** *Informing* Imagine that you are a historian. Write a paragraph explaining how Magna Carta, the English Bill of Rights of 1689, the Enlightenment, and New England town meetings influenced American government.
5. **Critical Thinking:** *Synthesizing Information* How did the state constitutions and the Articles of Confederation display Americans' fear of powerful government?

Section 2
EXPERIMENTS IN SELF-GOVERNMENT

Multimedia Connections

Explore these related topics and materials on the CD–ROM to enrich your understanding of this section:

Media Bank

- Shays at the Court
- Defeat of Shays's Rebellion
- Town of Cincinnati in 1800
- Classroom Equipment

Simulation

- The Democracy Project

Gazetteer

- Ohio
- Indiana
- Illinois
- Michigan
- Wisconsin
- Massachusetts

Profiles

- Daniel Shays

Readings

- Schooling in Early America

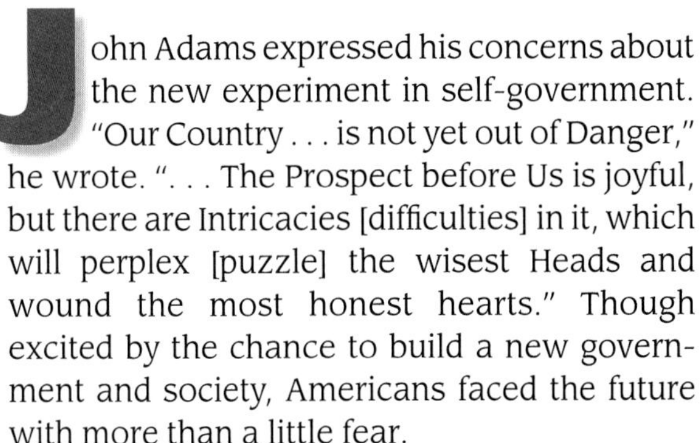

John Adams expressed his concerns about the new experiment in self-government. "Our Country . . . is not yet out of Danger," he wrote. ". . . The Prospect before Us is joyful, but there are Intricacies [difficulties] in it, which will perplex [puzzle] the wisest Heads and wound the most honest hearts." Though excited by the chance to build a new government and society, Americans faced the future with more than a little fear.

As you read this section you will find out:

- **How the United States developed the territory beyond the Appalachian Mountains.**
- **What economic problems the new nation faced.**
- **Why Massachusetts farmers revolted against their state government.**

The Confederation Congress Succeeds

Despite its initial failure to secure ratification, the Confederation Congress had some successes. For example, it appointed diplomats to work out a complicated treaty with Great Britain and developed western lands.

The Treaty of Paris of 1783. One of Congress's most important achievements was the **Treaty of Paris of 1783**. Negotiated by an American delegation in France, it officially ended the Revolutionary War and signaled Britain's recognition of U.S. independence. It also enlarged American territory.

The Treaty of Paris required the British to remove their armed forces from the new country. In return, the United States agreed to restore the rights of American Loyalists.

Congress also promised to ask the states to return seized Loyalist property, although few states actually did. Finally, the United States promised to let British subjects try to recover prewar debts owed them by Americans.

Once the treaty established the borders of the United States, Congress turned to organizing the Trans-Appalachian West, or the land between the Appalachian Mountains and the Mississippi River. To do this, Congress passed laws called land ordinances.

The Land Ordinance of 1785. Congress established a plan for the orderly sale of the country's western territory with the **Land Ordinance of 1785**. The law called for the land to be surveyed and divided into townships six miles on a side. Each township was split into sections of 640 acres. These pieces could then be sold. The law also required that one particular section per township be reserved to support a public school.

The Northwest Ordinance. The Land Ordinance of 1787, better known as the **Northwest Ordinance**, was a plan to create a government for the region north of the Ohio River and west of Pennsylvania. This area became known as the Northwest Territory.

The law provided that the land be divided into smaller territories. After 5,000 free men of voting age had settled in a territory, they could then elect a legislature and send a nonvoting delegate to Congress. The Northwest Ordinance outlined the next step:

> **"Whenever any of the said States shall have sixty thousand free inhabitants therein, such State shall be admitted . . . into the Congress of the United States, on an equal footing with the original States in all respects whatever."**

In addition, the law required new states to establish a republican form of government. It provided that "there shall be neither slavery nor involuntary servitude in the [Northwest Territory] otherwise than in the

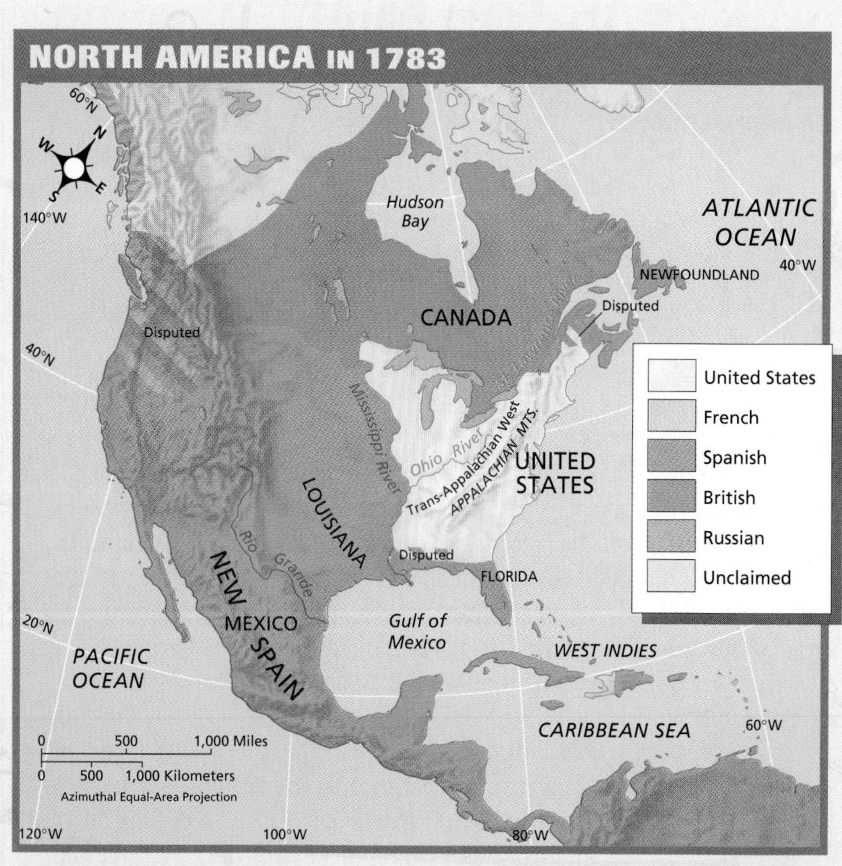

Learning from Maps.

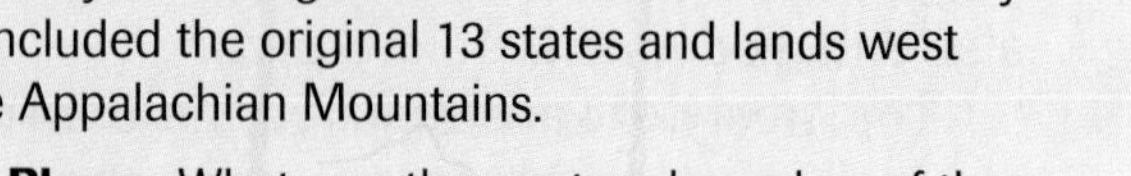
The Treaty of Paris granted the United States territory that included the original 13 states and lands west of the Appalachian Mountains.

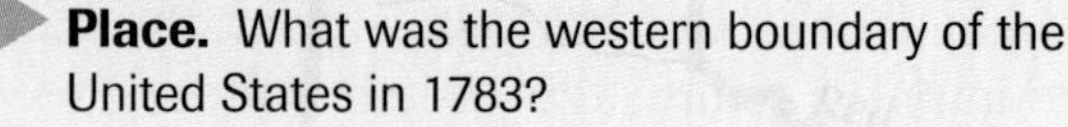
Place. What was the western boundary of the United States in 1783?

• **Maps**

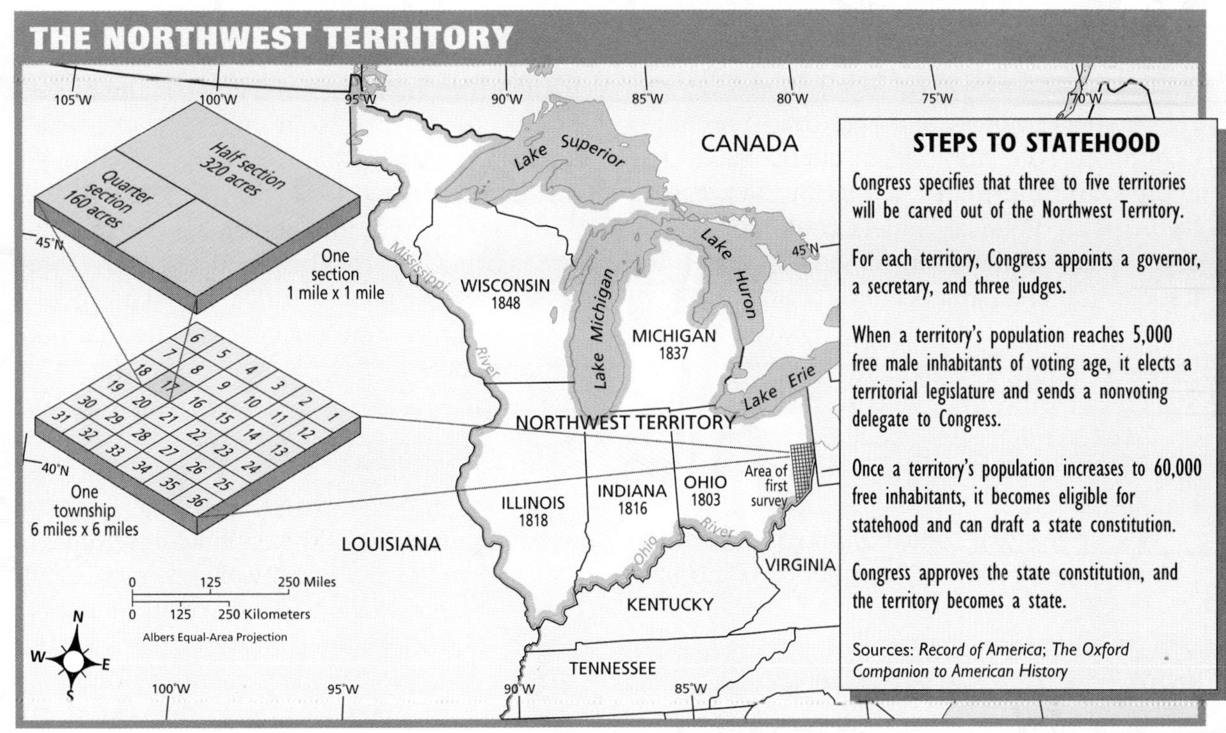

Learning from Maps. The Northwest Territory was divided into townships of six square miles. Each township was subdivided into 36 sections of 640 acres.

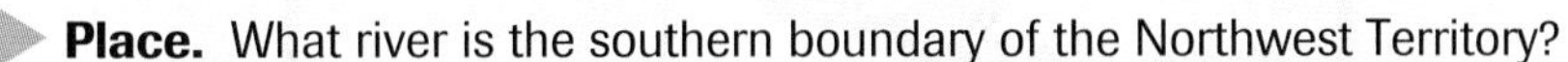
Place. What river is the southern boundary of the Northwest Territory?

• Maps

punishment of crimes." This represented a great triumph for Americans who opposed slavery. However, it also showed the need to compromise with those who favored the institution because the ordinance allowed the return of slaves who had escaped into the Northwest Territory.

Under the Northwest Ordinance, the states of Ohio, Indiana, Illinois, Michigan, and Wisconsin eventually were formed. As the nation expanded westward, it used the same basic method to admit new states.

Trade Problems

Peace quickly brought out the weaknesses of a national government that was only a "league of friendship" among the states. Instead of helping each other, as friends would, the states competed fiercely.

Interstate commerce. Under the Articles of Confederation, Congress had no power to regulate trade between states. Each state set its own interstate commerce policies, which sometimes clashed with those of its neighbors. By the mid-1780s there were 13 different sets of trade regulations in the United States!

Like many other American businesspeople, a group of concerned Philadelphia merchants argued that Congress should be given the power to oversee interstate commerce. They insisted that national considerations must be placed ahead of state interests in order to avoid quarrels:

> **"If Congress should think fit to act upon it, . . . a regard to *national interest* [well-being] may get the better of that jealous spirit which on other occasions has hitherto [until now] defeated the wisest**

plan for redeeming our *national credit* & *character*."

To give Congress authority over interstate commerce, all the states would have to approve **amendments**, or official changes, to the Articles. Political leaders could not reach unanimous agreement, however, and the trade problem continued.

International trade. The Articles also denied Congress the power to collect **tariffs**, or taxes on imported goods. This affected international trade and hurt many American businesses.

During the war, British manufacturers did not sell their products in America. Colonial businesses therefore had started supplying goods. With peace restored, the British began to offer their manufactured items in the United States at low prices in order to win back customers. Americans might have controlled this trend by taxing British imports. Again, Congress lacked the power to do so. The states could not stop the practice, either. If one state taxed the goods, British merchants could simply ship their products to a state that had no tariff laws.

The Money Problem

Under the Articles, states were supposed to cover the expenses of the national government. This system never worked well, however. Most states tended to pay only for things that benefited them directly. For example, North Carolina and Georgia, both open to attacks by American Indian or Spanish forces, agreed to contribute money for defense along the frontier. South Carolina, however, was geographically protected from these dangers by North Carolina and Georgia and thus refused to pay.

Since Congress could not force the states to contribute money, it soon had serious financial problems. Desperate to pay its bills, Congress printed more and more paper money. Under the Articles, state governments could issue paper currency too, and all did so. Because there was so much money in circulation, it fell in value. Fearing that merchants and bankers would refuse to accept the new money, people lost confidence in it. When the central or state governments printed large amounts of paper money, steep inflation resulted.

Not all Americans disliked this inflation, however. It helped **debtors**, or people who owe money, pay off their accounts. For example, a farmer who borrowed $10 when wheat sold for 25 cents a bushel had to sell

Global Connections

American Trade with China

The end of the American Revolution brought peace–and conflict–to American merchants. Resentful at the war's outcome and determined to prevent the new nation from succeeding, Great Britain closed markets formerly open to American businesses. Britain also restricted trade between the United States and the British West Indies, a large market for American goods of all sorts.

American merchants soon found a new trading partner–China. Before the Revolution, Great Britain had refused to allow American ships to sail to China. Independence removed that obstacle, of course, and American merchants quickly took advantage of their new opportunity. The *Empress of China* left the Atlantic coast in 1784 carrying ginseng, a root popular in China. After sailing for several months, it reached the trading city of Canton, becoming one of the first American ships ever to enter Chinese waters. This voyage launched a profitable trading relationship between the United States and China.

The Smithsonian Institution, Museum of American History, National Numismatic Collection

State currency used in America

40 bushels to pay the $10 back. If inflation drove the price of wheat up to 50 cents a bushel, the farmer had to sell only 20 bushels to pay the debt. This meant that **creditors**, or people to whom money is owed, would be repaid with currency that had only half the purchasing power of that which they had lent.

Shays's Rebellion

Events in Massachusetts soon gave many Americans more cause to worry. Unlike other state governments, the Massachusetts legislature would not print enough paper money to meet popular demands. In addition, state leaders raised taxes, a move that particularly hurt small property owners. Poor farmers who could not pay these taxes had their farms seized by the government. Anger grew, and farmers began to demonstrate peacefully against what they called the "gross [terrible] mismanagement of our rulers."

Daniel Shays eventually emerged as a leader of the protests. He was a former Patriot who had fought at Ticonderoga, Bunker Hill, and Saratoga. In September 1786 Shays gathered a group of protesters in Springfield, Massachusetts. They forced the state supreme court to shut down, hoping to postpone or end legal judgments against poor farmers. Then in January 1787 Shays and his followers attacked the Springfield **arsenal**, or arms storage center, to get weapons. The governor sent more than 4,000 militia to guard the building and defeated the rebel force. Shays lost later battles as well and fled to Vermont. By late February the uprising had collapsed.

Although **Shays's Rebellion** failed in the short run, it led to improvements for many Massachusetts farmers. Soon after the disturbance, the state legislature enacted some of the rebels' demands.

Section 2 Review

• Glossary

• Gazetteer

IDENTIFY and explain the significance of the following: Treaty of Paris of 1783, Land Ordinance of 1785, Northwest Ordinance, amendments, tariffs, debtors, creditors, arsenal, Shays's Rebellion

LOCATE and explain the importance of the following: Trans-Appalachian West, Northwest Territory

REVIEWING FOR DETAILS

1. How did Congress develop the region beyond the Appalachian Mountains?
2. What economic problems did the United States encounter after the Revolution?

REVIEWING FOR UNDERSTANDING

3. **Geographic Literacy** How might the acquisition of the Northwest Territory have benefited the United States?
4. **Writing Mastery:** *Persuading* Imagine that you are a poor Massachusetts farmer. Write a short letter to convince your neighbors to join in Shays's Rebellion.
5. **Critical Thinking:** *Cause and Effect* How did weaknesses in the Articles of Confederation cause economic and political problems?

Section 3
"We the People"

Multimedia Connections

Explore these related topics and materials on the CD–ROM to enrich your understanding of this section:

Profiles

- James Madison
- George Washington
- William Paterson
- Edmund Randolph

Media Bank

- Federal System
- Requirements for Federal Office
- Dolley Madison
- Abigail Adams
- James Madison
- Edits to the Constitution
- Remember the Ladies

Biographies

- Abigail Adams
- Benjamin Banneker

Glossary

- Electoral College

Before long, many American leaders concluded that their first experiment in self-government was not working well. In 1787 they met in Philadelphia to try to find some solutions. Philadelphia was a crowded, hot, smelly city. The humidity was almost unbearable, and biting flies swarmed everywhere. Some delegates had occasional outbursts of temper, but by the end of the steamy summer, they had created a very important document—the U.S. Constitution.

As you read this section you will find out:

- **Why political leaders decided to hold the Constitutional Convention.**
- **How the delegates settled major disagreements.**
- **How the delegates viewed the role of each branch of government.**

A Meeting in Philadelphia

Along with widespread economic problems, Shays's Rebellion forced some Americans to consider the future of the Confederation Congress and republican government itself. They referred to life under the Articles of Confederation as a "parade of horribles" and asked some difficult questions. Did allowing the people to rule mean that they would resort to violence whenever their government did something they disliked? Would debtors try to get out of paying their debts whenever they gained control of the legislature?

These concerns led some political leaders and businesspeople to consider **reforms**, or improvements, to the Articles. After a series of meetings, they called for a gathering of representatives from all the states to discuss the national government.

Congress reluctantly approved this proposal, and every state but Rhode Island agreed to send delegates to the meeting. Like many other leaders, George Washington was pleased with this development. In a letter to a friend, he wrote of his hope that the delegates would closely examine the Articles:

• Road to Philadelphia

> **"My wish is that the Convention . . . probe the defects [faults] of the Constitution [the Articles] to the bottom, and provide radical [extreme] cures, whether they are agreed to or not. A conduct like this will stamp wisdom and dignity on the proceedings."**

On May 25, 1787, the delegates gathered for the first session of what became known as the **Constitutional Convention**. They met at the Pennsylvania State House in a simply furnished room described as "neat but not elegant."

The delegates elected Washington as the presiding officer of the gathering. They also decided to keep the proceedings secret until they had completed their work. This encouraged people to speak frankly about difficult issues. Despite the secrecy, Virginia delegate James Madison decided to keep careful notes. A leading Patriot, he had helped write Virginia's constitution and knew the importance of precise record-keeping. Madison's notes give us a thorough account of the speeches and events at the convention.

Representation: Conflict and Compromise

Just four days after the start of the convention, Virginia delegate Edmund Randolph presented a set of resolutions that would create a new system of government instead of merely revising the Articles of Confederation. Drafted in part by Madison, this **Virginia Plan** proposed that the "league of friendship" among the states become a truly national government.

The Virginia Plan provided for a central government with three separate branches. There was to be an executive and a **bicameral**, or two-house, legislature. The plan also mentioned a system of national courts.

The Virginia Plan suggested that state population determine representation in both houses of the legislature. Members of the legislature would then choose the executive. Not surprisingly, delegates from states with large populations favored the Virginia Plan because it gave them a great deal of influence. The plan, however, made those from states with small populations very uneasy. They feared that the heavily populated states would take control of the new government.

In mid-June, William Paterson offered the **New Jersey Plan**, a set of resolutions written by delegates from states with small populations. This plan proposed to continue the one-state, one-vote system used under the Articles. After just a few days of debate, however, the delegates rejected the New

George Washington oversees the Constitutional Convention.

• Signing of the Constitution

Jersey Plan and decided to continue their discussions using the Virginia Plan as the model for the new government.

This defeat of the New Jersey Plan did not mean that all was well. The delegates from the smaller states dug in their heels on the question of representation by population. The fight dragged on for weeks and threatened to break up the convention. The delegates finally accepted what is often called the **Great Compromise**. It established that population would determine representation in the national legislature's lower house, while each state would have an equal vote in the legislature's upper house.

The Question of Slavery

Even after approving the Great Compromise, the delegates continued to clash over whether or not slaves should be counted in a state's population. Many northern delegates felt that allowing southerners to include slaves gave the slave states an unfair political advantage and encouraged slavery. Southern delegates insisted that slaves be counted in a state's population. They hoped this would give the South more votes in the legislature.

After a heated debate, the delegates agreed to the **Three-Fifths Compromise**. It established a system of counting "the whole Number of free Persons" and three fifths of "all other Persons," meaning slaves, for the purposes of representation. In another compromise related to slavery, the delegates permitted the importation of slaves until 1808. The delegates also wrote a clause that required states to return any "Person held to Service or Labor" who managed to escape into their territory.

It is clear today that when the delegates spoke of "We the People," they were not referring to slaves. Nowhere did the U.S. Constitution contain the words *slave* or *slavery.*

Some of the participants at the convention probably felt uneasy about allowing slavery to exist in a nation that proclaimed "all men are created equal." Others, however, believed that African Americans were inferior. Along with the delegates, nearly all white people at the time shared this **prejudice**, or unreasonable opinion unsupported by facts. Many delegates also thought that individual states should decide the issue of slavery. Of course, some delegates—northern and southern—were themselves slaveholders. Whatever their personal feelings about slavery, they voted to protect their own economic and political interests.

History Makers

Roger Sherman (1721–1793)

Few delegates at the Constitutional Convention could match the public service of Connecticut's Roger Sherman. As a member of the Second Continental Congress, Sherman had helped draft both the Declaration of Independence and the Articles of Confederation. Sherman regarded the convention as fundamentally important to the nation's future.

The Granger Collection, New York

His commitment to continuing the fragile convention led Sherman to help write and to introduce in early June 1787 what became known as the Great Compromise. He did not offer much explanation of the plan, however, and at first it received little attention. After weeks of standstill, however, the delegates looked at the proposal again. They adopted the Great Compromise in mid-July and went on to complete the U.S. Constitution.

This antislavery painting shows "Liberty" extending knowledge to freed slaves.

In the end, many delegates believed that they had to accept the existence of slavery if they wanted to form a truly united nation. The delegates feared that if they threatened slavery or its supporters, some of the southern states would not join the Union.

The delegates' actions at Philadelphia led some free African Americans to step up their work against slavery and the slave trade. They argued that all African Americans should be free. A few years after the convention, black scientist Benjamin Banneker expressed regret that the nation's leaders showed so little concern for African Americans:

> **"If your love for . . . those inestimable [very great] laws . . . was founded on sincerity, you could not but be solicitous [concerned], that every individual, of whatever rank or distinction, might with you equally enjoy the blessings thereof."**

Forming a Government

The delegates eventually wrote a constitution that described the powers and shape of the new government. It would consist of three main parts: a **legislative branch** to write the laws; an **executive branch** to carry out the laws; and a **judicial branch** to interpret the laws. The Constitution also outlined various processes and procedures, such as making treaties and electing government officials.

The legislature. The delegates at the convention intended to make the national legislature the most powerful part of the new government. They were determined to prevent it from being controlled by a monarch or prime minister.

The delegates assumed that the lower house, or the **House of Representatives**, would act on behalf of the people. They intended that the upper house, or the **Senate**, would give the executive advice and consent on appointments and foreign treaties.

The presidency. One of the most important results of the convention was the creation of a powerful executive branch. When the delegates thought about the new office, they were torn in different directions. Some did not even want an executive official. Others wanted a national leader, but not one who was too powerful. Nor did they want a figurehead, someone who appeared to rule but had no real

In the early 1790s, Benjamin Banneker published a popular almanac and also wrote a well-known letter defending the intellectual capabilities of African Americans.

power. The delegates finally decided on a strong executive—a president who would act as the head of state.

Everyone expected that the first president would be George Washington. This was one reason why the delegates gave the presidency so much power. They admired and trusted him so much that they made the office worthy of his talents. Washington could not be president forever, of course. To create a way of

The Articles of Confederation and the Constitution

ARTICLES	CONSTITUTION
Executive Branch	
• No executive to administer and enforce legislation; Congress had sole authority to govern • Executive committee to oversee government when Congress out of session	• President administers and enforces federal laws
Legislative Branch	
• A unicameral (one-house) legislature	• A bicameral (two-house) legislature
• Each state had one vote, regardless of population	• Each state has equal representation in the Senate; each state represented according to population in the House of Representatives
• Nine votes (of the original 13) to enact legislation	• Simple majority to enact legislation
Judicial Branch	
• No national court system	• National court system, headed by Supreme Court
• Congress to establish temporary courts to hear cases of piracy	• Courts to hear cases involving national laws, treaties, the Constitution, cases between states, between citizens of different states, or between a state and citizens of another state
Other Matters	
• Admission to the Confederation by 9 votes (of 13)	• Congress to admit new states; all must have a republican form of government
• Amendment of Articles by unanimous vote	• Amendment of the Constitution by two-thirds vote of both houses of Congress or by national convention and ratified by three fourths of the states
• The states retained independence	• The states accept the Constitution as the supreme law of the land

A Better Foundation. The Constitution fixed some of the weak points of the Articles of Confederation. How did the documents differ in terms of the executive branch? How might the Constitution's provisions regarding the executive branch have remedied some of the weaknesses of the Articles?

choosing his successor, the delegates worked out a complicated system called the Electoral College. (See the Constitution Handbook on page 141.)

The judiciary. The Constitution established a system of national courts that would be separate from those of the individual states. The document specifically mentioned only a "supreme" court, but it also allowed for the creation of lower courts. The delegates left it up to Congress to determine the number of judges on the Supreme Court and the actual structure of the lower courts.

"The Supreme Law of the Land"

A brief article in the Constitution established the document as "the supreme Law of the Land." It replaced the Articles' "league of friendship" with a national government.

The Constitution divided power between state and national governments in a system known as **federalism**. For example, the delegates gave the national government the authority to collect tariffs and other taxes on goods, regulate interstate and international trade, coin money, and maintain an army and a navy. The delegates allowed states to keep many of their powers. The states still had the right to tax their citizens, control public education, punish criminals, and make all sorts of local regulations.

The U.S. Constitution fixed many problems of the Articles. The Constitution's Preamble neatly summarized the intent of these changes. The "People" were creating "a more perfect Union." It would "promote the general Welfare" by supplying the national unity lacking under the Articles.

The noble bald eagle became a symbol for the United States.

Section 3 Review

• Glossary

IDENTIFY and explain the significance of the following: reforms, Constitutional Convention, James Madison, Virginia Plan, bicameral, New Jersey Plan, Great Compromise, Three-Fifths Compromise, prejudice, legislative branch, executive branch, judicial branch, House of Representatives, Senate, federalism

REVIEWING FOR DETAILS

1. What factors encouraged political leaders to hold the Constitutional Convention?
2. How did the delegates decide major disputes?
3. What were to be the roles of each branch of government?

REVIEWING FOR UNDERSTANDING

4. **Writing Mastery:** *Expressing* Write a paragraph expressing your opinion about the way the delegates dealt with slavery at the Constitutional Convention.
5. **Critical Thinking:** *Drawing Conclusions* Why did the delegates create a system of government based on federalism?

Section 4

THE "MORE PERFECT UNION"

Multimedia Connections

Explore these related topics and materials on the CD-ROM to enrich your understanding of this section:

Gazetteer

- New York City

Biographies

- Alexander Hamilton

Profiles

- John Hancock
- Paul Revere

Atlas

- Federalists and Antifederalists

Media Bank

- *Federalist Papers*
- Samuel Adams

As states ratified the new Constitution, many Americans rejoiced at what they hoped would finally be a successful attempt at self-government. Celebrations often began with large, noisy parades. Some cities lit towering bonfires. Philadelphia threw a huge party for its citizens. An observer reported that 17,000 people gathered "to celebrate . . . the constitution of the United States, and that they separated at an early hour, without intoxication, or a single quarrel."

As you read this section you will find out:

- **Why Federalists supported the Constitution.**
- **Why Antifederalists opposed the Constitution.**
- **How the first presidential election took place.**

Federalists and Antifederalists

In September 1787 the delegates completed the Constitution and sent copies to each state. The document would become law when 9 of the 13 states had ratified it.

In the months following the Constitutional Convention, popular interest in the document was high. People everywhere read and discussed the proposal. They elected representatives to state ratifying conventions, where the final decision to approve or disapprove the Constitution would be made.

Different opinions. Since the Constitution involved so many important changes, it did not have everyone's approval. Supporters of the new Constitution called themselves **Federalists**. Many were wealthy lawyers, merchants, and planters. Those who opposed the new Constitution became known as **Antifederalists**. They tended to come from rural areas and were generally less wealthy than Federalists.

The Federalists argued that the Constitution would strike a good balance between national unity and state independence. They believed that a strong central government would help prevent disturbances like Shays's Rebellion. Federalists also thought that the Constitution represented a new age of democracy. For example, one New Jersey farmer declared:

> **"What a glorious spectacle would the adoption of this constitution exhibit! . . . We should probably have the honor of teaching mankind . . . THAT MAN HIMSELF IS ACTUALLY CAPABLE OF GOVERNING HIMSELF."**

The Antifederalists disapproved of the Constitution because they felt the powerful new central government might destroy the states' independence. They also feared the power of the wealthy over poorer citizens. As one Massachusetts Antifederalist described the situation, if the Federalists win, "they will swallow up all us little folks." The Constitution, another excited Antifederalist wrote, was "a beast, dreadful and terrible," which "devours, breaks into pieces, and stamps [the states] with his feet."

A bill of rights. Like the Articles of Confederation, the Constitution did not contain a bill of rights to guarantee certain freedoms. Foremost among these rights were freedom of speech, freedom of the press, and freedom of religion. Under the Articles, the central government had been weak. In addition, many of the state constitutions contained bills of rights. A national bill of rights had not seemed important, but now some people feared for their freedoms.

Ratifying the Constitution

As political leaders considered the new Constitution, no one knew what to expect. In some states the Federalists had a clear majority, but in others the Antifederalists ruled public opinion.

An easy start. Delaware was the first state to ratify the Constitution. In December 1787 Delaware delegates voted unanimously to approve the document. By early January 1788 Pennsylvania, New Jersey, Georgia, and Connecticut also had ratified the Constitution by large margins.

Ratification by just nine states would be enough to adopt the Constitution. But how effective could the government be if populous states like Massachusetts, New York, and Virginia refused to join the United States?

The Pennfylvania Packet, *and Daily Advertifer.*

[Price Four-Pence.] WEDNESDAY, September 19, 1787. [No. 2690.]

WE, the People of the United States, in order to form a more perfect Union, eftablifh Juftice, infure domeftic Tranquility, provide for the common Defence, promote the General Welfare, and fecure the Bleffings of Liberty to Ourfelves and our Pofterity, do ordain and eftablifh this Conftitution for the United States of America.

ARTICLE I.

Sect. 1. ALL legiflative powers herein granted fhall be vefted in a Congrefs of the United States, which fhall confift of a Senate and Houfe of Reprefentatives.

Sect. 2. The Houfe of Reprefentatives fhall be compofed of members chofen every fecond year by the people of the feveral ftates, and the electors in each ftate fhall have the qualifications requifite for electors of the moft numerous branch of the ftate legiflature.

No perfon fhall be a reprefentative who fhall not have attained to the age of twenty-five years, and been feven years a citizen of the United States, and who fhall not, when elected, be an inhabitant of that ftate in which he fhall be chofen.

Reprefentatives and direct taxes fhall be apportioned among the feveral ftates which may be included within this Union, according to their refpective numbers, which fhall be determined by add-

This Pennsylvania newspaper was one of many that reprinted the full text of the Constitution for its readers. The preamble to the Constitution is shown here.

Citizens of New York City celebrate the state's ratification of the U.S. Constitution on July 26, 1788.

The Granger Collection, New York

Difficult battles. The Massachusetts convention met in January 1788 and debated the Constitution for nearly a month. At first, the Antifederalists seemed to have a majority. Samuel Adams and John Hancock were delegates. Because they were famous supporters of states' rights, many people thought they were Antifederalists.

The Federalists, however, proved to be clever politicians. They eventually convinced Hancock to support the Constitution. He even made an important suggestion that helped persuade delegates in Massachusetts and other states to ratify it. If there were objections to the Constitution, he proposed, delegates should accept it and later submit amendments to improve the document.

In Boston Paul Revere organized a mass meeting to urge ratification. This show of support in Samuel Adams's home district helped sway him to approve the Constitution in spite of his doubts. After some additional negotiation between Hancock and Adams, the Massachusetts convention voted 187 to 168 to ratify. By late June, Maryland, South Carolina, and New Hampshire had also voted to accept the document. At last the Constitution had been ratified! Shortly thereafter, by a close margin, Virginia became the tenth state to join the Union. By the beginning of July only New York, North Carolina, and Rhode Island had yet to approve the document.

Orphaned as a teenager, Alexander Hamilton worked as a store clerk in the West Indies. Friends and relatives, impressed by his intelligence, decided to send him to school in America.

New York was most important. Because of the state's location, the nation would be split into two parts if New York did not ratify the Constitution and enter the Union. However, the Antifederalists outnumbered the Federalists at the New York ratifying convention by more than two to one! Defeat for the ratification of the Constitution seemed certain.

A number of factors helped the New York Federalists improve their chances of success. A series of newspaper essays, now known as the *Federalist Papers,* explained and defended the Constitution. They were written by Alexander Hamilton and John Jay, both New York Federalists, and James Madison of Virginia.

• Federalists Papers

New York's central location also placed the Antifederalists there in a difficult position. They realized that New York needed the United States as much as the United States needed New York. Moreover, popular opinion in New York City favored the Constitution. Local leaders threatened to break away from the state and join the Union on their own if the New York delegates rejected the Constitution. In late July 1788 enough Antifederalists supported the Constitution to ratify it, 30 to 27.

REDEUNT SATURNIA REGNA.
On the erection of the Eleventh PILLAR of the great National DOME, we beg leave moſt ſincerely to felicitate "OUR DEAR COUNTRY."
DEL.
PEN.
N.JER.
GEOR.
CON.
MASSA.
MARY.
S° CARO.
N.HAMP.
VIRG.
N.YORK.
N.CARO.
The foundation good—it may yet be SAVED.
The FEDERAL EDIFICE.

Collection of The New-York Historical Society

This cartoon celebrates ratification while also criticizing North Carolina's and Rhode Island's refusal to ratify the Constitution.

The United States of America

Now the new system of federal government would have its chance. Although North Carolina did not ratify the Constitution until November 1789, and Rhode Island held out until May 1790, by that time the new government had been firmly established.

The states began to select their representatives and senators in the fall of 1788. By January 1789 almost all of the state legislatures had chosen their presidential electors. On April 6 the new Congress gathered for the formal counting of the electoral votes in New York City, the temporary national capital. No one was surprised that George Washington was the unanimous choice of the electors. John Adams became vice president.

In late April, Washington stood on the balcony of Federal Hall, at the corner of Broad and Wall Streets, and took the oath of office as president. When he finished, the city rang with the sound of church bells, and the evening sky blazed with the largest display of fireworks the nation had ever seen. The 13 states had at last become one country! What would Americans make of their new Union?

Section 4 Review

• Glossary

• Time Line

IDENTIFY and explain the significance of the following: Federalists, Antifederalists, John Hancock, Alexander Hamilton, John Jay, John Adams

REVIEWING FOR DETAILS

1. Why did Federalists favor the Constitution?
2. Why did Antifederalists dislike the Constitution?
3. When was the new government launched? Who served as the first president?

REVIEWING FOR UNDERSTANDING

4. **Geographic Literacy** Why was ratification of the Constitution by New York so important?
5. **Critical Thinking:** *Making Comparisons* How was the fight for ratification in Massachusetts similar to that in New York?

CONSTITUTION HANDBOOK

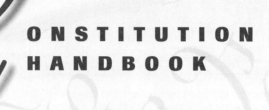

The delegates who assembled in the spring of 1787 to revise the Articles of Confederation included many of the most capable leaders in the country. Convinced that the Confederation was not strong enough to bring order and prosperity to the new nation, the delegates abandoned all thought of revising the Articles. Instead, they proceeded to draw up a completely new Constitution. Patrick Henry called this action "a revolution as radical as that which separated us from Great Britain." Out of their long political experience, their keen intelligence, and their great learning, these framers of the Constitution created a blueprint for a truly united nation—the new United States of America.

An observer once referred to the U.S. Constitution as "the most wonderful work ever struck off at a given time by the brain and purpose of man." Revised, modified, and amended, the Constitution has served the American people for more than 200 years. It has become a model for representative government throughout the world. The Constitution has successfully survived the years for two reasons. First, it lays down rules of procedure and guarantees of rights and liberties that must be observed, even in times of crisis. Second, it is a "living" document, capable of being revised to meet changing times and circumstances.

"To Form a More Perfect Union"

The framers of the Constitution wanted to establish a strong central government, one that could unite the country and help it meet the challenges of the future. At the same time, however, they feared a government that was too strong. The memories of the troubled years before the American Revolution were still fresh. The framers knew that uncontrolled power in the hands of individuals, groups, or branches of government could lead to tyranny.

The framers' response was to devise a system of government in which power is divided between the states and the federal government and then further divided within each government. In *The Federalist* Number 51, James Madison described the advantages of such a system:

> *"In the compound republic of America, the power surrendered by the people is first divided between two distinct governments, and then the portion allotted [given] to each subdivided among distinct and separate departments. Hence a double security arises to the rights of the people. The different governments will control each other, at the same time that each will be controlled by itself."*

The seven Articles that make up the first part of the Constitution provide the blueprint for this system. The framers divided the government into three branches—the legislative branch (Congress), the executive branch (the president and vice president), and the judicial branch (the federal courts)—each with specific powers. As a further safeguard, the framers wrote a system of checks and balances into the Constitution. Articles I, II, and III outline the checks and balances and the powers of each branch of government.

Article IV outlines the relations between the states and between the states and the federal government. Among the issues addressed are each state's recognition of other states' public records and citizens' rights, the admission of new states, and the rights and responsibilities of the federal government in relation to the states.

Article V specifies the process by which the Constitution can be amended. The framers purposely made the process slow and difficult. They feared that if the amendment process was too easy, the Constitution—the fundamental law of the land—would soon carry no more weight than the most minor law passed by Congress.

Article VI includes one condition that addressed the immediate concerns of the framers and two conditions that have lasting significance. The short-term condition promises that the United States under the Constitution will honor all public debts entered into under the Articles of Confederation. The two long-term conditions declare the Constitution is the "supreme Law of the Land" and prohibit religion being used as a qualification for holding public office.

Article VII is the framers' attempt to ensure ratification of the Constitution. Under the Articles of Confederation, amendments had to be approved by all 13 original states. Realizing that it would be difficult to get the approval of all the states, the framers specified that the Constitution would go into effect after ratification by only nine states.

Protecting Individual Liberty

The framers' opposition to a strong central government was in part a concern over states' rights. It was also rooted in the desire to protect individual liberties. American colonists had always insisted on the protection of their civil liberties—their rights as individuals.

The Articles of the Constitution contain many important guarantees of civil liberties. On a broad level, the separation of powers and the system of checks and balances help safeguard citizens against the abuse of government power. The Articles also contain conditions that speak directly to an individual's right to due process of law. For example, Section 9 of Article I prohibits both *ex post facto* laws and bills of attainder.

An *ex post facto* law is a law passed "after the deed." Such a law sets a penalty for an act that was not illegal when it was committed. A bill of attainder is a law that punishes a person by fine, imprisonment, or seizure of property without a court trial. If Congress had the power to adopt bills of attainder, lawmakers could punish any American at will, and that person could do nothing to appeal the sentence. Instead, the Constitution provides that only the courts can impose punishment for unlawful acts, and then only by following the due process of law.

Section 9 of Article I also protects a citizen's right to the writ of *habeas corpus.* The writ of *habeas corpus* is a legal document that forces a jailer to release a person from prison unless the person has been formally charged with, or convicted of, a crime. The Constitution states that "the Privilege of the Writ of Habeas Corpus shall not be suspended, unless when in Cases of Rebellion or Invasion the public Safety may require it."

The Constitution also gives special protection to people accused of treason. The framers of the Constitution knew that the charge of treason was a common device used by rulers to get rid of people they did not like. Rulers could bring the charge of treason against people who merely criticized the government. To prevent such use of this charge, Section 3 of Article III carefully defines treason and the circumstances under which a person may be charged with it:

> *"Treason against the United States, shall consist only in levying War against them, or in adhering to their Enemies, giving them Aid and Comfort. No Person shall be convicted of Treason unless on the Testimony of two Witnesses to the same overt [obvious] Act, or on Confession in open Court."*

The Article also protects the relatives of a person accused of treason. Only the convicted person can be punished. No penalty can be imposed on the person's family.

The Bill of Rights

Despite the safeguards written into the Articles of the Constitution, some states initially refused to ratify the document because it did not offer greater protection to the rights of individuals. These states finally agreed to ratification after they had been promised that a bill of rights would be added to the Constitution by amendment.

In 1789 the first Congress of the United States wrote the ideals of the Declaration of Independence into the Bill of Rights, the first 10 amendments to the Constitution. Among other things, the Bill of Rights protects persons against any action by the federal government that may deprive them "of life, liberty, or property, without due process of law."

Among the guarantees of liberty in the Bill of Rights, several are particularly important. The First Amendment guarantees freedom of religion, speech, the press, and assembly, and the right to petition. The Fourth Amendment forbids "unreasonable searches and seizures" of any person's home. The Fifth, Sixth, and Eighth Amendments protect individuals from random arrest and punishment by the federal government. The Bill of Rights was ratified by the states in 1791. It has remained one of the best-known features of the Constitution.

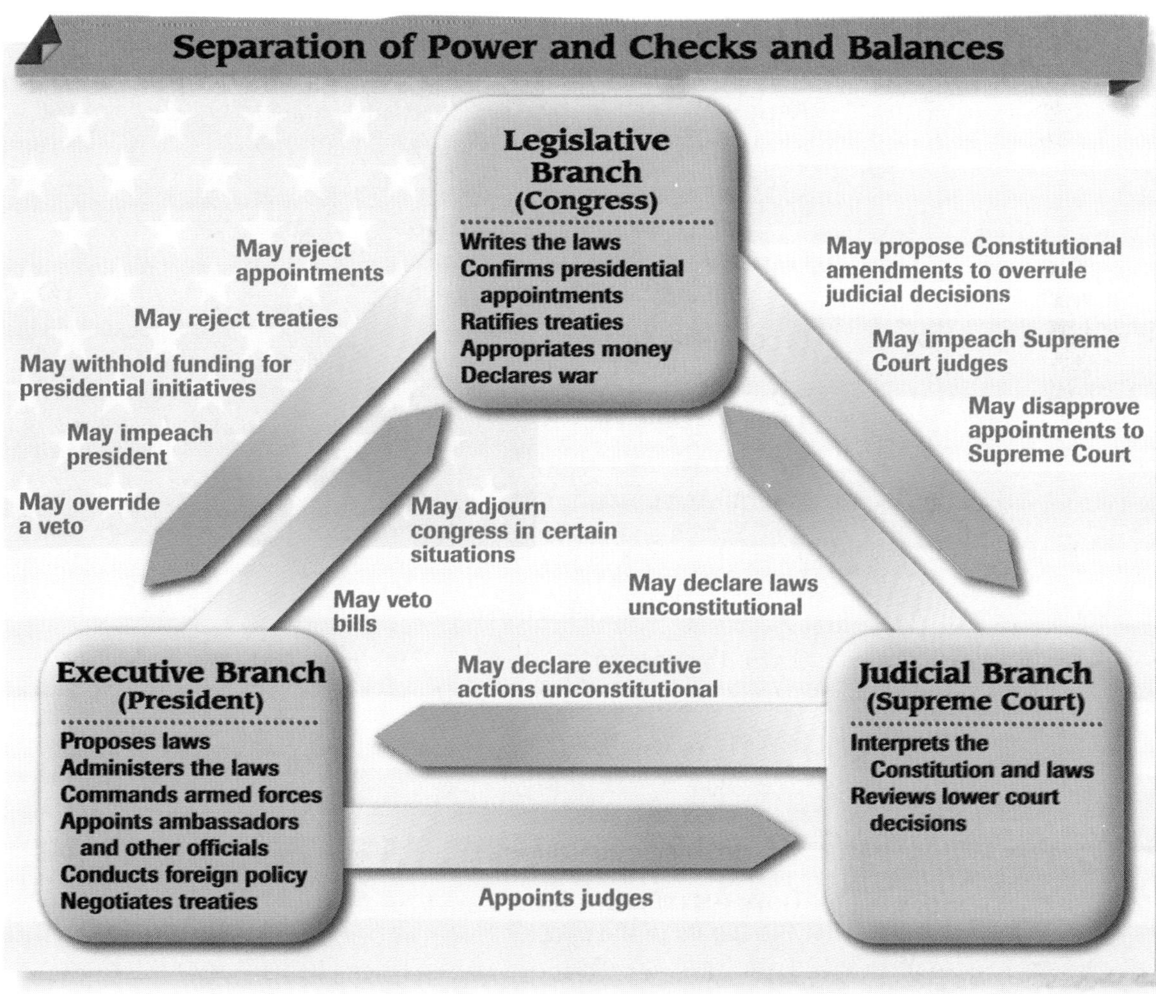
Separation of Power and Checks and Balances
Legislative Branch (Congress)
Writes the laws
Confirms presidential appointments
Ratifies treaties
Appropriates money
Declares war
May reject appointments
May reject treaties
May withhold funding for presidential initiatives
May impeach president
May override a veto
May propose Constitutional amendments to overrule judicial decisions
May impeach Supreme Court judges
May disapprove appointments to Supreme Court
May adjourn congress in certain situations
May veto bills
May declare laws unconstitutional
Executive Branch (President)
Proposes laws
Administers the laws
Commands armed forces
Appoints ambassadors and other officials
Conducts foreign policy
Negotiates treaties
May declare executive actions unconstitutional
Appoints judges
Judicial Branch (Supreme Court)
Interprets the Constitution and laws
Reviews lower court decisions

Contents of the Constitution

PREAMBLE

"We the People of the United States, in Order to form a more perfect Union, establish Justice, insure domestic Tranquility, provide for the common defence, promote the general Welfare, and secure the Blessings of Liberty to ourselves and our Posterity, do ordain and establish this Constitution for the United States of America."

*Parts of the Constitution that have been ruled through are no longer in force or no longer apply because of later amendments.

Preamble
The short and dignified Preamble explains the goals of the new government under the Constitution.

Section 1. All legislative Powers herein granted shall be vested in a Congress of the United States, which shall consist of a Senate and House of Representatives.

Legislative Branch
Article I explains how the legislative branch, called Congress, is organized. The chief purpose of the legislative branch is to make the laws. Congress is made up of the Senate and the House of Representatives. The decision to have two bodies of government solved a difficult problem during the Constitutional Convention. The large states wanted the membership of Congress to be based entirely on population. The small states wanted every state to have an equal vote. The solution to the problem of how the states were to be represented in Congress became known as the Great Compromise.

Section 2. The House of Representatives shall be composed of Members chosen every second Year by the People of the several States, and the Electors in each State shall have the Qualifications requisite for Electors of the most numerous Branch of the State Legislature.

No Person shall be a Representative who shall not have attained to the Age of twenty five Years, and been seven Years a Citizen of the United States, and who shall not, when elected, be an Inhabitant of that State in which he shall be chosen.

Representatives and direct Taxes shall be apportioned among the several States which may be included within this Union, according to their respective Numbers~~, which shall be determined by adding to the whole Number of free Persons, including those bound to Service for a Term of Years, and excluding Indians not taxed, three fifths of all other Persons~~. The actual Enumeration shall be made within three Years after the first Meeting of the Congress of the United States, and within every subsequent Term of ten Years, in such Manner as they shall by Law direct. The Number of Representatives shall not exceed one for every thirty Thousand, but each State shall have at Least one Representative; ~~and until such enumeration shall be made, the State of New Hampshire shall be entitled to chuse three; Massachusetts eight; Rhode Island and Providence Plantations one; Connecticut five; New York six; New Jersey four; Pennsylvania eight; Delaware one; Maryland six; Virginia ten; North Carolina five; South Carolina five; and Georgia three~~.

The number of members each state has in the House is based on the population of the individual state. Each state has at least one representative. In 1929 Congress fixed the size of the House at 435 members. Today, if each member of the House were to represent only 30,000 Americans, the House would have more than 8,600 members.

When vacancies happen in the Representation from any State, the Executive Authority thereof shall issue Writs of Election to fill such Vacancies.

The House of Representatives shall chuse their Speaker and other Officers; and shall have the sole Power of Impeachment.

Section 3. The Senate of the United States shall be composed of two Senators from each State~~, chosen by the Legislature thereof~~, for six Years; and each Senator shall have one Vote.

Every state has two senators. Senators serve a six-year term. Every two years, one third of the senators reach the end of their terms. In any election, at least two thirds of the senators stay in office. This system ensures that there are experienced senators in office at all times.

Immediately after they shall be assembled in Consequence of the first Election, they shall be divided as equally as may be into three Classes. The Seats of the Senators of the first Class shall be vacated at the Expiration of the second Year, of the second Class at the Expiration of the fourth Year, and of the third Class at the Expiration of the sixth Year, so that one third may be chosen every second Year; ~~and if Vacancies happen by Resignation, or otherwise, during the Recess of the Legislature of any State, the Executive thereof may make~~

~~temporary Appointments until the next Meeting of the Legislature, which shall then fill such Vacancies~~.

No Person shall be a Senator who shall not have attained to the Age of thirty Years, and been nine Years a Citizen of the United States, and who shall not, when elected, be an Inhabitant of that State for which he shall be chosen.

The only duty that the Constitution assigns to the vice president is to preside over meetings of the Senate. Modern presidents have given their vice presidents more responsibilities.

The Vice President of the United States shall be President of the Senate, but shall have no Vote, unless they be equally divided.

The Senate shall chuse their other Officers, and also a President pro tempore, in the Absence of the Vice President, or when he shall exercise the Office of President of the United States.

The Senate shall have the sole Power to try all Impeachments. When sitting for that Purpose, they shall be on Oath or Affirmation. When the President of the United States is tried, the Chief Justice shall preside: And no Person shall be convicted without the Concurrence of two thirds of the Members present.

The House charges a government official of wrongdoing, and the Senate acts as a court to decide if the official is guilty.

Judgment in Cases of Impeachment shall not extend further than to removal from Office, and disqualification to hold and enjoy any Office of honor, Trust or Profit under the United States: but the Party convicted shall nevertheless be liable and subject to Indictment, Trial, Judgment and Punishment, according to Law.

Congress decided that elections will be held on the Tuesday following the first Monday in November of even-numbered years. The Twentieth Amendment states that Congress shall meet in regular session on January 3 of each year. The president may call a special session of Congress whenever it is necessary.

Section 4. The Times, Places and Manner of holding Elections for Senators and Representatives, shall be prescribed in each State by the Legislature thereof; but the Congress may at any time by Law make or alter such Regulations, except as to the Places of chusing Senators.

~~The Congress shall assemble at least once in every Year, and such Meeting shall be on the first Monday in December, unless they shall by Law appoint a different Day.~~

Section 5. Each House shall be the Judge of the Elections, Returns and Qualifications of its own Members, and a Majority of each shall constitute a Quorum to do Business; but a smaller Number may adjourn from day to day, and may be authorized to compel the Attendance of absent Members, in such Manner, and under such Penalties as each House may provide.

Congress makes most of its own rules of conduct. The Senate and the House each have a code of ethics that members must follow. It is the task of each house of Congress to discipline its own members. Each house keeps a journal, and a daily, unofficial publication called the *Congressional Record* details what happens in congressional sessions. The general public can learn how their representatives voted on bills by reading the *Congressional Record.*

Each House may determine the Rules of its Proceedings, punish its Members for disorderly Behaviour, and, with the Concurrence of two thirds, expel a Member.

Each House shall keep a Journal of its Proceedings, and from time to time publish the same, excepting such Parts as may in their Judgment require Secrecy; and the Yeas and Nays of the Members of either House on any question shall, at the Desire of one fifth of those Present, be entered on the Journal.

Neither House, during the Session of Congress, shall, without the Consent of the other, adjourn for more than three days, nor to any other Place than that in which the two Houses shall be sitting.

The framers of the Constitution wanted to protect members of Congress from being arrested on

Section 6. The Senators and Representatives shall receive a Compensation for their Services, to be ascertained by Law, and paid out of the Treasury of the United States. They shall in all Cases, except Treason, Felony and Breach of the Peace, be privileged from Arrest during their Attendance at the Session of their respective Houses, and in going to and returning from the same; and for any Speech or Debate in either House, they shall not be questioned in any other Place.

No Senator or Representative shall, during the Time for which he was elected, be appointed to any civil Office under the Authority of the United States, which shall have been created, or the Emoluments whereof shall have been encreased during such time; and no Person holding any Office under the United States, shall be a Member of either House during his Continuance in Office.

false charges by political enemies who did not want them to attend important meetings. The framers also wanted to protect members of Congress from being taken to court for something they said in a speech or in a debate.

Section 7. All Bills for raising Revenue shall originate in the House of Representatives; but the Senate may propose or concur with Amendments as on other Bills.

The power of taxing is the responsibility of the House of Representatives. The framers felt that because members of the House are elected every two years, representatives would listen to the public and seek its approval before passing taxes.

Every Bill which shall have passed the House of Representatives and the Senate, shall, before it become a Law, be presented to the President of the United States; If he approve he shall sign it, but if not he shall return it, with his Objections to that House in which it shall have originated, who shall enter the Objections at large on their Journal, and proceed to reconsider it. If after such Reconsideration two thirds of that House shall agree to pass the Bill, it shall be sent, together with the Objections, to the other House, by which it shall likewise be reconsidered, and if approved by two thirds of that House, it shall become a Law. But in all such Cases the Votes of both Houses shall be determined by yeas and Nays, and the Names of the Persons voting for and against the Bill shall be entered on the Journal of each House respectively. If any Bill shall not be returned by the President within ten Days (Sundays excepted) after it shall have been presented to him, the Same shall be a Law, in like Manner as if he had signed it, unless the Congress by their Adjournment prevent its Return, in which Case it shall not be a Law.

The veto power of the president and the ability of Congress to override a presidential veto are two of the important checks and balances in the Constitution.

Every Order, Resolution, or Vote to which the Concurrence of the Senate and House of Representatives may be necessary (except on a question of Adjournment) shall be presented to the President of the United States; and before the Same shall take Effect, shall be approved by him, or being disapproved by him, shall be repassed by two thirds of the Senate and House of Representatives, according to the Rules and Limitations prescribed in the Case of a Bill.

Section 8. The Congress shall have Power To lay and collect Taxes, Duties, Imposts and Excises, to pay the Debts and provide for the common Defence and general Welfare of the United States; but all Duties, Imposts and Excises shall be uniform throughout the United States;

To borrow Money on the credit of the United States;

To regulate Commerce with foreign Nations, and among the several States, and with the Indian Tribes;

To establish an uniform Rule of Naturalization, and uniform Laws on the subject of Bankruptcies throughout the United States;

To coin Money, regulate the Value thereof, and of foreign Coin, and fix the Standard of Weights and Measures;

To provide for the Punishment of counterfeiting the Securities and current Coin of the United States;

To establish Post Offices and post Roads;

The framers of the Constitution wanted a national government that was strong enough to be effective. This section lists the powers given to Congress. The last sentence in Section 8 (see page 140) contains the famous "elastic clause"—so called because it has been stretched (like elastic) to fit many different circumstances. The clause was first disputed when Alexander Hamilton proposed a national bank. Thomas Jefferson said that because the Constitution did not give Congress the power to establish a bank, it could not do so. Hamilton argued that the bank was "necessary and proper" in order to carry out other powers of Congress, such as borrowing money and regulating currency. This argument was tested in the courts in 1819 in the case of *McCulloch* v. *Maryland*, when Chief Justice Marshall ruled in favor of the federal government. Powers given to the government by the "elastic clause" are called implied powers.

To promote the Progress of Science and useful Arts, by securing for limited Times to Authors and Inventors the exclusive Right to their respective Writings and Discoveries;

To constitute Tribunals inferior to the supreme Court;

To define and punish Piracies and Felonies committed on the high Seas, and Offences against the Law of Nations;

To declare War, grant Letters of Marque and Reprisal, and make Rules concerning Captures on Land and Water;

To raise and support Armies, but no Appropriation of Money to that Use shall be for a longer Term than two Years;

To provide and maintain a Navy;

To make Rules for the Government and Regulation of the land and naval Forces;

To provide for calling forth the Militia to execute the Laws of the Union, suppress Insurrections and repel Invasions;

To provide for organizing, arming, and disciplining, the Militia, and for governing such Part of them as may be employed in the Service of the United States, reserving to the States respectively, the Appointment of the Officers, and the Authority of training the Militia according to the discipline prescribed by Congress;

To exercise exclusive Legislation in all Cases whatsoever, over such District (not exceeding ten Miles square) as may, by Cession of particular States, and the Acceptance of Congress, become the Seat of the Government of the United States, and to exercise like Authority over all Places purchased by the Consent of the Legislature of the State in which the Same shall be, for the Erection of Forts, Magazines, Arsenals, dock-Yards, and other needful Buildings; —And

To make all Laws which shall be necessary and proper for carrying into Execution the foregoing Powers, and all other Powers vested by this Constitution in the Government of the United States, or in any Department or Officer thereof.

Although Congress has implied powers, there are also limits to its powers. Section 9 lists powers that are denied to the federal government. Several of the clauses protect the people of the United States from unjust treatment. For example, Section 9 guarantees the writ of *habeas corpus* and prohibits bills of attainder and *ex post facto* laws (see page 132).

Section 9. ~~The Migration or Importation of such Persons as any of the States now existing shall think proper to admit, shall not be prohibited by the Congress prior to the Year one thousand eight hundred and eight, but a Tax or duty may be imposed on such Importation, not exceeding ten dollars for each Person~~.

The Privilege of the Writ of Habeas Corpus shall not be suspended, unless when in Cases of Rebellion or Invasion the public Safety may require it.

No Bill of Attainder or ex post facto Law shall be passed.

No Capitation, or other direct, Tax shall be laid, unless in Proportion to the Census or Enumeration herein before directed to be taken.

No Tax or Duty shall be laid on Articles exported from any State.

No Preference shall be given by any Regulation of Commerce or Revenue to the Ports of one State over those of another: nor shall Vessels bound to, or from, one State, be obliged to enter, clear, or pay Duties in another.

No Money shall be drawn from the Treasury, but in Consequence of Appropriations made by Law; and a regular Statement and Account of the Receipts and Expenditures of all public Money shall be published from time to time.

No Title of Nobility shall be granted by the United States: And no Person holding any Office of Profit or Trust under them, shall, without the Consent of the Congress, accept of any present, Emolument, Office, or Title, of any kind whatever, from any King, Prince, or foreign State.

Section 10. No State shall enter into any Treaty, Alliance, or Confederation; grant Letters of Marque and Reprisal; coin Money; emit Bills of Credit; make any Thing but gold and silver Coin a Tender in Payment of Debts; pass any Bill of Attainder, ex post facto Law, or law impairing the Obligation of Contracts, or grant any Title of Nobility.

Section 10 lists the powers that are denied to the states. In our system of federalism, the state and federal governments have separate powers, share some powers, and are each denied other powers. The states may not exercise any of the powers that belong to Congress.

No State shall, without the Consent of the Congress, lay any Imposts or Duties on Imports or Exports, except what may be absolutely necessary for executing its inspection Laws: and the net Produce of all Duties and Imposts, laid by any State on Imports or Exports, shall be for the Use of the Treasury of the United States; and all such Laws shall be subject to the Revision and Controul of the Congress.

No State shall, without the Consent of Congress, lay any Duty of Tonnage, keep Troops, or Ships of War in time of Peace, enter into any Agreement or Compact with another State, or with a foreign Power, or engage in War, unless actually invaded, or in such imminent Danger as will not admit of delay.

Section 1. The executive Power shall be vested in a President of the United States of America. He shall hold his Office during the Term of four Years, and, together with the Vice President, chosen for the same Term, be elected, as follows.

Executive Branch

The president is the chief of the executive branch. It is the job of the president to enforce the laws. The framers wanted the president's and vice president's term of office and manner of selection to be different from those of members of Congress. They decided on four-year terms, but they had a difficult time agreeing on how to select the president and vice president. The framers finally set up an electoral system, which varies greatly from our electoral process today. The Twelfth Amendment changed the process by requiring that separate ballots be cast for president and vice president. The rise of political parties has since changed the process even more.

Each State shall appoint, in such Manner as the Legislature thereof may direct, a Number of Electors, equal to the whole Number of Senators and Representatives to which the State may be entitled in the Congress: but no Senator or Representative, or Person holding an Office of Trust or Profit under the United States, shall be appointed an Elector.

~~The Electors shall meet in their respective States, and vote by Ballot for two Persons, of whom one at least shall not be an Inhabitant of the same State with themselves. And they shall make a List of all the Persons voted for, and of the Number of Votes for each; which List they shall sign and certify, and transmit sealed to the Seat of the Government of the United States, directed to the President of the Senate. The President of the Senate shall, in the Presence of the Senate and House of Representatives, open all the Certificates, and the Votes~~

~~shall then be counted. The Person having the greatest Number of Votes shall be the President, if such Number be a Majority of the whole Number of Electors appointed; and if there be more than one who have such Majority, and have an equal Number of Votes, then the House of Representatives shall immediately chuse by Ballot one of them for President; and if no Person have a Majority, then from the five highest on the List the said House shall in like Manner chuse the President. But in chusing the President, the Votes shall be taken by States, the Representation from each State having one Vote; A quorum for this Purpose shall consist of a Member or Members from two thirds of the States, and a Majority of all the States shall be necessary to a Choice. In every Case, after the Choice of the President, the Person having the greatest Number of Votes of the Electors shall be the Vice President. But if there should remain two or more who have equal Votes, the Senate shall chuse from them by Ballot the Vice President~~.

In 1845 Congress set the Tuesday following the first Monday in November of every fourth year as the general election date for selecting presidential electors.

The Congress may determine the Time of chusing the Electors, and the Day on which they shall give their Votes; which Day shall be the same throughout the United States.

The youngest elected president was John F. Kennedy; he was 43 years old when he was inaugurated. (Theodore Roosevelt was 42 when he assumed office after the assassination of McKinley.) The oldest elected president was Ronald Reagan; he was 69 years old when he was inaugurated.

No Person except a natural born Citizen, ~~or a Citizen of the United States, at the time of the Adoption of this Constitution~~, shall be eligible to the Office of President; neither shall any Person be eligible to that Office who shall not have attained to the Age of thirty five Years, and been fourteen Years a Resident within the United States.

In Case of the Removal of the President from Office, or of his Death, Resignation, or Inability to discharge the Powers and Duties of the said Office, the Same shall devolve on the Vice President, and the Congress may by Law provide for the Case of Removal, Death, Resignation or Inability, both of the President and Vice President, declaring what Officer shall then act as President, and such Officer shall act accordingly, until the Disability be removed, or a President shall be elected.

Emolument means "salary, or payment." In 1969 Congress set the president's salary at $200,000 per year. The president also receives an expense account of $50,000 per year. The president must pay taxes on both.

The President shall, at stated Times, receive for his Services, a Compensation, which shall neither be increased nor diminished during the period for which he shall have been elected, and he shall not receive within that Period any other Emolument from the United States, or any of them.

The oath of office is administered to the president by the chief justice of the U.S. Supreme Court. Washington added "So help me, God." All succeeding presidents have followed this practice.

Before he enter on the Execution of his Office, he shall take the following Oath or Affirmation:—"I do solemnly swear (or affirm) that I will faithfully execute the Office of President of the United States, and will to the best of my Ability, preserve, protect and defend the Constitution of the United States."

The framers wanted to make sure that an elected representative of the people controlled the nation's military. Today, the president is in charge of the army, navy, air force, marines, and coast guard. Only Congress, however, can decide if the United States will declare war. This section also contains the basis for the formation of the president's cabinet. Every president, starting with George Washington, has appointed a cabinet.

Section 2. The President shall be Commander in Chief of the Army and Navy of the United States, and of the Militia of the several States, when called into the actual Service of the United States; he may require the Opinion, in writing, of the principal Officer in each of the executive Departments, upon any Subject relating to the Duties of their respective Offices, and he shall have Power to grant Reprieves and Pardons for Offenses against the United States, except in Cases of Impeachment.

He shall have Power, by and with the Advice and Consent of the Senate, to make Treaties, provided two thirds of the Senators present concur; and he shall nominate, and by and with the Advice and

Consent of the Senate, shall appoint Ambassadors, other public Ministers and Consuls, Judges of the supreme Court, and all other Officers of the United States, whose Appointments are not herein otherwise provided for, and which shall be established by Law: but the Congress may by Law vest the Appointment of such inferior Officers, as they think proper, in the President alone, in the Courts of Law, or in the Heads of Departments.

Most of the president's appointments to office must be approved by the Senate.

The President shall have Power to fill up all Vacancies that may happen during the Recess of the Senate, by granting Commissions which shall expire at the End of their next Session.

Section 3. He shall from time to time give to the Congress Information of the State of the Union, and recommend to their Consideration such Measures as he shall judge necessary and expedient; he may, on extraordinary Occasions, convene both Houses, or either of them, and in Case of Disagreement between them, with Respect to the Time of Adjournment, he may adjourn them to such Time as he shall think proper; he shall receive Ambassadors and other public Ministers; he shall take Care that the Laws be faithfully executed, and shall Commission all the Officers of the United States.

Every year the president presents to Congress a State of the Union message. In this message, the president explains the legislative plans for the coming year. This clause states that one of the president's duties is to enforce the laws.

Section 4. The President, Vice President and all civil Officers of the United States, shall be removed from Office on Impeachment for, and Conviction of, Treason, Bribery, or other high Crimes and Misdemeanors.

Section 1. The judicial Power of the United States, shall be vested in one supreme Court, and in such inferior Courts as the Congress may from time to time ordain and establish. The Judges, both of the supreme and inferior Courts, shall hold their Offices during good Behaviour, and shall, at stated Times, receive for their Services, a Compensation, which shall not be diminished during their Continuance in Office.

Section 2. The judicial Power shall extend to all Cases, in Law and Equity, arising under this Constitution, the Laws of the United States, and Treaties made, or which shall be made, under their Authority;—to all Cases affecting Ambassadors, other public Ministers and Consuls;—to all Cases of admiralty and maritime Jurisdiction;—to Controversies to which the United States shall be a Party;—to Controversies between two or more States;—~~between a State and Citizens of another State~~;—between Citizens of different States;—between Citizens of the same State claiming Lands under Grants of different States, ~~and between a State, or the Citizens thereof, and foreign States, Citizens or Subjects~~.

Judicial Branch
The Articles of Confederation did not set up a federal court system. One of the first things that the framers of the Constitution agreed upon was to set up a national judiciary. With all the laws that Congress would be enacting, there would be a great need for a branch of government to interpret the laws. In the Judiciary Act of 1789, Congress provided for the establishment of lower courts, such as district courts, circuit courts of appeals, and various other federal courts. The judicial system provides a check on the legislative branch; it can declare a law unconstitutional.

In all Cases affecting Ambassadors, other public Ministers and Consuls, and those in which a State shall be Party, the supreme Court shall have original Jurisdiction. In all the other Cases before mentioned, the supreme Court shall have appellate Jurisdiction, both as to Law and fact, with such Exceptions, and under such Regulations as the Congress shall make.

The Trial of all Crimes, except in Cases of Impeachment, shall be by Jury; and such Trial shall be held in the State where the said Crimes shall have been committed; but when not committed within any State, the Trial shall be at such Place or Places as the Congress may by Law have directed.

Congress has the power to decide the punishment for treason, but it can punish only the guilty person. "Corruption of Blood" means punishing the family of a person who has committed treason. It is expressly forbidden by the Constitution.

Section 3. Treason against the United States, shall consist only in levying War against them, or in adhering to their Enemies, giving them Aid and Comfort. No Person shall be convicted of Treason unless on the Testimony of two Witnesses to the same overt Act, or on Confession in open Court.

The Congress shall have Power to declare the Punishment of Treason, but no Attainder of Treason shall work Corruption of Blood, or Forfeiture except during the Life of the Person attainted.

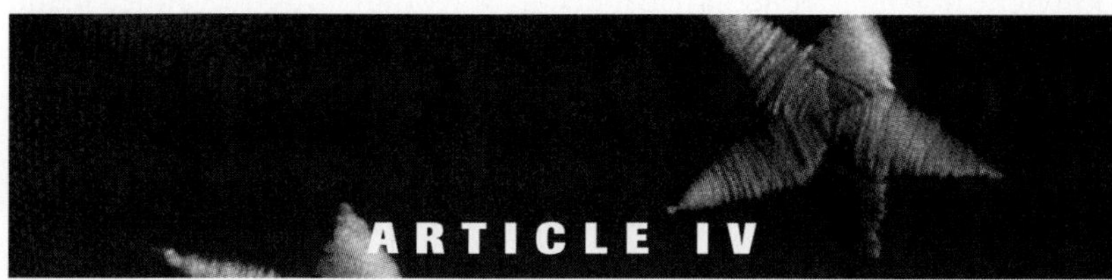

ARTICLE IV

The States
States must honor the laws, records, and court decisions of other states. A person cannot escape a legal obligation by moving from one state to another.

Section 1. Full Faith and Credit shall be given in each State to the public Acts, Records, and judicial Proceedings of every other State. And the Congress may by general Laws prescribe the Manner in which such Acts, Records and Proceedings shall be proved, and the Effect thereof.

Section 2. The Citizens of each State shall be entitled to all Privileges and Immunities of Citizens in the several States.

A Person charged in any State with Treason, Felony, or other Crime, who shall flee from Justice, and be found in another State, shall on Demand of the executive Authority of the State from which he fled, be delivered up, to be removed to the State having Jurisdiction of the Crime.

~~No Person held to Service of Labour in one State, under the Laws thereof, escaping into another, shall, in Consequence of any Law or Regulation therein, be discharged from such Service or Labour, but shall be delivered up on Claim of the Party to whom such Service or Labour may be due~~.

Section 3 permits Congress to admit new states to the Union. When a group of people living in an area that is not part of an existing state wishes to form a new state, it asks Congress for

Section 3. New States may be admitted by the Congress into this Union; but no new State shall be formed or erected within the Jurisdiction of any other State; nor any State be formed by the Junction of two or more States, or Parts of States, without the Consent of the Legislatures of the States concerned as well as of the Congress.

The Congress shall have Power to dispose of and make all needful Rules and Regulations respecting the Territory or other Property belonging to the United States; and nothing in this Constitution shall be so construed as to Prejudice any Claims of the United States, or of any particular State.

Section 4. The United States shall guarantee to every State in this Union a Republican Form of Government, and shall protect each of them against Invasion; and on Application of the Legislature, or of the Executive (when the Legislature cannot be convened) against domestic Violence.

permission to do so. The people then write a state constitution and offer it to Congress for approval. The state constitution must set up a representative form of government and must not in any way contradict the federal Constitution. If a majority of Congress approves of the state constitution, the state is admitted as a member of the United States of America.

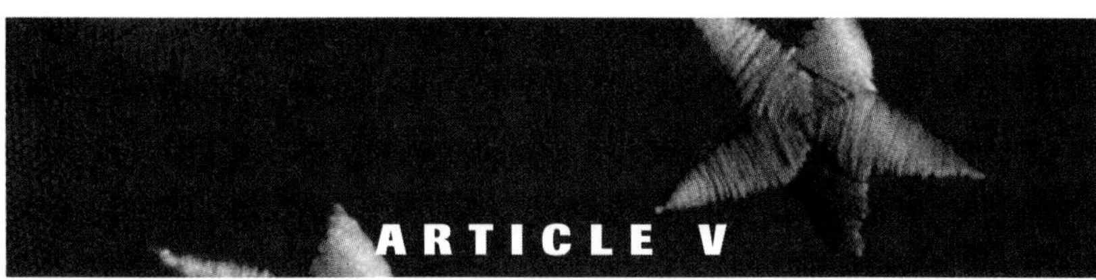

The Congress, whenever two thirds of both Houses shall deem it necessary, shall propose Amendments to this Constitution, or, on the Application of the Legislatures of two thirds of the several States, shall call a Convention for proposing Amendments, which, in either Case, shall be valid to all Intents and Purposes, as Part of this Constitution, when ratified by the Legislatures of three fourths of the several States, or by Conventions in three fourths thereof, as the one or the other Mode of Ratification may be proposed by the Congress; Provided that ~~no Amendment which may be made prior to the Year One thousand eight hundred and eight shall in any Manner affect the first and fourth Clauses in the Ninth Section of the first Article; and that~~ no State, without its Consent, shall be deprived of its equal Suffrage in the Senate.

The Amendment Process

America's founders may not have realized just how enduring the Constitution would be, but they did set up a system for changing or adding to the Constitution. They did not want to make it easy to change the Constitution. There are two different ways in which changes can be proposed to the states and two different ways in which states can approve the changes and make them part of the Constitution.

All Debts contracted and Engagements entered into, before the Adoption of this Constitution, shall be as valid against the United States under this Constitution, as under the Confederation.

This Constitution, and the Laws of the United States which shall be made in Pursuance thereof; and all Treaties made, or which shall be made, under the Authority of the United States, shall be the supreme Law of the Land; and the Judges in every State shall be bound thereby, any Thing in the Constitution or Laws of any State to the Contrary notwithstanding.

National Supremacy

One of the biggest problems facing the delegates to the Constitutional Convention was the question of what would happen if a state law and a federal law conflicted. Which law would be followed? Who would decide? The second clause of Article VI answers those questions. When a federal law and a state law disagree, the federal law overrides the state law. The Constitution is the "supreme Law of the Land." This clause is often called the "supremacy clause."

The Senators and Representatives before mentioned, and the Members of the several State Legislatures, and all executive and judicial Officers, both of the United States and of the several States, shall be bound by Oath or Affirmation, to support this Constitution; but no religious Test shall ever be required as a Qualification to any Office or public Trust under the United States.

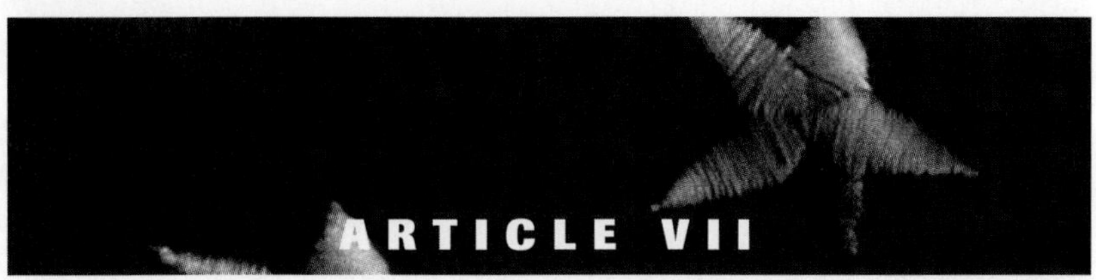

ARTICLE VII

Ratification
The Articles of Confederation called for all 13 states to approve any revision to the Articles. The Constitution required that 9 out of the 13 states would be needed to ratify the Constitution. The first state to ratify was Delaware, on December 7, 1787. Almost two and a half years later, on May 29, 1790, Rhode Island became the last state to ratify the Constitution.

The Ratification of the Conventions of nine States, shall be sufficient for the Establishment of this Constitution between the States so ratifying the Same.

Done in Convention by the Unanimous Consent of the States present the Seventeenth Day of September in the Year of our Lord one thousand seven hundred and Eighty seven and of the Independence of the United States of America the Twelfth. In witness whereof We have hereunto subscribed our Names,

George Washington—
President and deputy from Virginia

NEW HAMPSHIRE
John Langdon
Nicholas Gilman

DELAWARE
George Read
Gunning Bedford, Jr.
John Dickinson
Richard Bassett
Jacob Broom

MASSACHUSETTS
Nathaniel Gorham
Rufus King

MARYLAND
James McHenry
Daniel of St. Thomas Jenifer
Daniel Carroll

CONNECTICUT
William Samuel Johnson
Roger Sherman

NEW YORK
Alexander Hamilton

VIRGINIA
John Blair
James Madison, Jr.

NEW JERSEY
William Livingston
David Brearley
William Paterson
Jonathan Dayton

NORTH CAROLINA
William Blount
Richard Dobbs Spaight
Hugh Williamson

PENNSYLVANIA
Benjamin Franklin
Thomas Mifflin
Robert Morris
George Clymer
Thomas FitzSimons
Jared Ingersoll
James Wilson
Gouverneur Morris

SOUTH CAROLINA
John Rutledge
Charles Cotesworth Pinckney
Charles Pinckney
Pierce Butler

GEORGIA
William Few
Abraham Baldwin

Attest:
William Jackson, Secretary

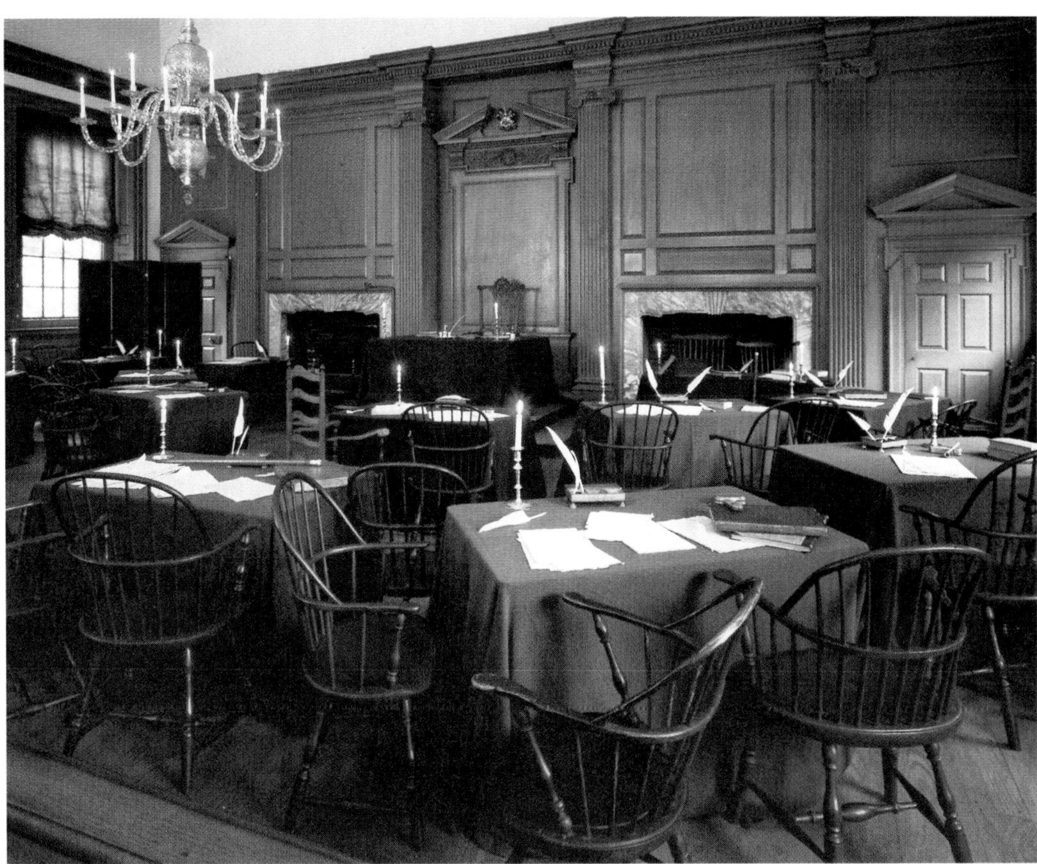

The delegates signed the Constitution in the Independence Hall Assembly Room. The room has been preserved so it looks much like it would have in 1787.

Articles in addition to, and Amendment of the Constitution of the United States of America, proposed by Congress, and ratified by the Legislatures of the several States, pursuant to the fifth Article of the original Constitution.

[The First through Tenth Amendments, now known as the Bill of Rights, were proposed to the states for ratification on September 25, 1789, and declared in force on December 15, 1791.]

Bill of Rights
One of the conditions set by several states for ratifying the Constitution was the inclusion of a Bill of Rights. Many people feared that a stronger central government might take away basic rights of the people that had been guaranteed in state constitutions. If the three words that begin the preamble—"We the people"—were truly meant, then the rights of the people needed to be protected.

First Amendment

Congress shall make no law respecting an establishment of religion, or prohibiting the free exercise thereof; or abridging the freedom of speech, or of the press; or the right of the people peaceably to assemble, and to petition the Government for a redress of grievances.

The First Amendment protects—among other freedoms—freedom of speech—and forbids Congress to make any "law respecting an establishment of religion" or restraining the freedom to practice religion as one chooses.

Second Amendment

A well regulated Militia, being necessary to the security of a free State, the right of the people to keep and bear Arms, shall not be infringed.

Third Amendment

No Soldier shall, in time of peace, be quartered in any house, without the consent of the Owner, nor in time of war, but in a manner to be prescribed by law.

A police officer or sheriff may only enter a person's home with a search warrant, which allows the law official to look for evidence that could convict someone of committing a crime.

Fourth Amendment

The right of the people to be secure in their persons, houses, papers, and effects, against unreasonable searches and seizures, shall not be violated, and no Warrants shall issue, but upon probable cause, supported by Oath or affirmation, and particularly describing the place to be searched, and the persons or things to be seized.

The Fifth, Sixth, and Seventh Amendments describe the procedures that courts must follow when trying people accused of crimes. The Fifth Amendment guarantees that no one can be put on trial for a serious crime unless a grand jury agrees that the evidence justifies doing so. It also says that a person cannot be tried twice for the same crime.

Fifth Amendment

No person shall be held to answer for a capital, or otherwise infamous crime, unless on a presentment or indictment of a Grand Jury, except in cases arising in the land or naval forces, or in the Militia, when in actual service in time of War or public danger; nor shall any person be subject for the same offence to be twice put in jeopardy of life or limb; nor shall be compelled in any criminal case to be a witness against himself, nor be deprived of life, liberty, or property, without due process of law; nor shall private property be taken for public use, without just compensation.

The Sixth Amendment makes several guarantees, including a prompt trial and a trial by a jury chosen from the state and district in which the crime was committed. The Sixth Amendment also states that an accused person must be told why he or she is being tried and promises that an accused person has the right to be defended by a lawyer.

Sixth Amendment

In all criminal prosecutions, the accused shall enjoy the right to a speedy and public trial, by an impartial jury of the State and district wherein the crime shall have been committed, which district shall have been previously ascertained by law, and to be informed of the nature and cause of the accusation; to be confronted with the witnesses against him; to have compulsory process for obtaining witnesses in his favor, and to have the Assistance of Counsel for his defence.

The Seventh Amendment guarantees a trial by jury in cases that involve more than $20, but in modern times, usually much more money is at stake before a case is heard in federal court.

Seventh Amendment

In Suits at common law, where the value in controversy shall exceed twenty dollars, the right of trial by jury shall be preserved, and no fact tried by a jury, shall be otherwise re-examined in any Court of the United States, than according to the rules of the common law.

Eighth Amendment

Excessive bail shall not be required, nor excessive fines imposed, nor cruel and unusual punishments inflicted.

Ninth Amendment

The enumeration in the Constitution, of certain rights, shall not be construed to deny or disparage others retained by the people.

The Ninth and Tenth Amendments were added because not every right of the people or of the states could be listed in the Constitution.

Tenth Amendment

The powers not delegated to the United States by the Constitution, nor prohibited by it to the States, are reserved to the States respectively, or to the people.

Eleventh Amendment

[Proposed March 5, 1794; declared ratified January 8, 1798]

The Judicial power of the United States shall not be construed to extend to any suit in law or equity, commenced or prosecuted against one of the United States by Citizens of another State, or by Citizens or Subjects of any Foreign State.

Twelfth Amendment

[Proposed December 9, 1803; declared ratified September 25, 1804]

The Electors shall meet in their respective states, and vote by ballot for President and Vice-President, one of whom, at least, shall not be an inhabitant of the same state with themselves; they shall name in their ballots the person voted for as President, and in distinct ballots the person voted for as Vice-President, and they shall make distinct lists of all persons voted for as President, and of all persons voted for as Vice-President, and of the number of votes for each, which lists they shall sign and certify, and transmit sealed to the seat of the government of the United States, directed to the President of the Senate;—The President of the Senate shall, in the presence of the Senate and House of Representatives, open all the certificates and the votes shall then be counted;—The person having the greatest number of votes for President, shall be the President, if such number be a majority of the whole number of Electors appointed; and if no person have such majority, then from the persons having the highest numbers not exceeding three on the list of those voted for as President, the House of Representatives shall choose immediately, by ballot, the President. But in choosing the President, the votes shall be taken by states, the representation from each state having one vote; a quorum for this purpose shall consist of a member or members from two-thirds of the states, and a majority of all the states shall be necessary to a choice~~. And if the House of Representatives shall not choose a President whenever the right of choice shall devolve upon them, before the fourth day of March next following, then the Vice-President shall act as President, as in the case of the death or other constitutional disability of the President.~~ —The person having the greatest number of votes as Vice-President, shall be the Vice-President, if such number be a majority of the whole number of Electors appointed, and if no person have a majority, then from the two highest numbers on the list, the Senate shall Choose the Vice-President; a quorum for the purpose shall consist of two-thirds of the whole number

The Twelfth Amendment changed the election procedure for president and vice president. This amendment became necessary because of the growth of political parties. Before this amendment, electors voted without distinguishing between president and vice president. Whoever received the most votes became president, and whoever received the next highest number of votes became vice president. A confusing election in 1800, which resulted in Thomas Jefferson's becoming president, caused this amendment to be proposed.

of Senators, and a majority of the whole number shall be necessary to a choice. But no person constitutionally ineligible to the office of President shall be eligible to that of Vice-President of the United States.

Although some slaves had been freed during the Civil War, slavery was not abolished until the Thirteenth Amendment took effect.

Thirteenth Amendment

[Proposed January 31, 1865; declared ratified December 18, 1865]

Section 1. Neither slavery nor involuntary servitude, except as a punishment for crime whereof the party shall have been duly convicted, shall exist within the United States, or any place subject to their jurisdiction.

Section 2. Congress shall have power to enforce this article by appropriate legislation.

In 1833 the Supreme Court ruled that the Bill of Rights limited the federal government but not the state governments. This ruling was interpreted to mean that states were able to keep African Americans from becoming state citizens: if African Americans were not citizens, they were not protected by the Bill of Rights. The Fourteenth Amendment defines citizenship and prevents states from interfering in the rights of citizens of the United States.

Fourteenth Amendment

[Proposed June 16, 1866; declared ratified July 28, 1868]

Section 1. All persons born or naturalized in the United States, and subject to the jurisdiction thereof, are citizens of the United States and of the State wherein they reside. No State shall make or enforce any law which shall abridge the privileges or immunities of citizens of the United States; nor shall any State deprive any person of life, liberty, or property, without due process of law; nor deny to any person within its jurisdiction the equal protection of the laws.

Section 2. Representatives shall be apportioned among the several States according to their respective numbers, counting the whole number of persons in each State, ~~excluding Indians not taxed~~. But when the right to vote at any election for the choice of electors for President and Vice President of the United States, Representatives in Congress, the Executive and Judicial officers of a State, or the members of the Legislature thereof, is denied to any of the ~~male~~ inhabitants of such State, ~~being twenty-one years of age~~, and citizens of the United States, or in any way abridged, except for participation in rebellion, or other crime, the basis of representation therein shall be reduced in the proportion which the number of such ~~male~~ citizens shall bear to the whole number of ~~male~~ citizens ~~twenty-one years of age~~ in such State.

Section 3. No person shall be a Senator or Representative in Congress, or elector of President and Vice President, or hold any office, civil or military, under the United States, or under any State, who, having previously taken an oath, as a member of Congress, or as an officer of the United States, or as a member of any State legislature, or as an executive or judicial officer of any State, to support the Constitution of the United States, shall have engaged in insurrection or rebellion against the same, or given aid or comfort to the enemies thereof. But Congress may by a vote of two-thirds of each House, remove such disability.

Section 4. The validity of the public debt of the United States, authorized by law, including debts incurred for payment of pensions and bounties for services in suppressing insurrection or rebellion, shall not be questioned. But neither the United States nor any State shall assume or pay any debt or obligation incurred in aid of insurrection or rebellion against the United States~~, or any claim for the loss of emancipation of any slave~~; but all such debts, obligations and claims shall be held illegal and void.

Section 5. The Congress shall have power to enforce, by appropriate legislation, the provisions of this article.

Fifteenth Amendment

[Proposed February 27, 1869; declared ratified March 30, 1870]

The Fifteenth Amendment extended the right to vote to African American men.

Section 1. The right of citizens of the United States to vote shall not be denied or abridged by the United States or by any State on account of race, color, or previous condition of servitude.

Section 2. The Congress shall have power to enforce this article by appropriate legislation.

Sixteenth Amendment

[Proposed July 12, 1909; declared ratified February 25, 1913]

The Congress shall have power to lay and collect taxes on incomes, from whatever source derived, without apportionment among the several States, and without regard to any census or enumeration.

Seventeenth Amendment

[Proposed May 13, 1912; declared ratified May 31, 1913]

The Seventeenth Amendment required that senators be elected directly by the people instead of by the state legislature.

The Senate of the United States shall be composed of two Senators from each State, elected by the people thereof, for six years; and each Senator shall have one vote. The electors in each State shall have the qualifications requisite for electors of the most numerous branch of the State legislatures.

When vacancies happen in the representation of any State in the Senate, the executive authority of such State shall issue writs of election to fill such vacancies: *Provided,* That the legislature of any State may empower the executive thereof to make temporary appointments until the people fill the vacancies by election as the legislature may direct.

~~This amendment shall not be so construed as to affect the election or term of any Senator chosen before it becomes valid as part of the Constitution.~~

Eighteenth Amendment

[Proposed December 18, 1917; declared ratified January 29, 1919; repealed by the Twenty-first Amendment December 5, 1933]

Although many people felt that prohibition was good for the health and welfare of the American people, the amendment was repealed 14 years later.

~~**Section 1.** After one year from the ratification of this article the manufacture, sale, or transportation of intoxicating liquors within, the importation thereof into, or the exportation thereof from the United States and all territory subject to the jurisdiction thereof for beverage purposes is hereby prohibited.~~

~~**Section 2.** The Congress and the several States shall have concurrent power to enforce this article by appropriate legislation.~~

~~**Section 3.** This article shall be inoperative unless it shall have been ratified as an amendment to the Constitution by the legislatures of the several States, as provided in the Constitution, within seven years from the date of the submission hereof to the States by the Congress.~~

Abigail Adams was disappointed that the Declaration of Independence and the Constitution did not specifically include women. It took almost 150 years and much campaigning by suffrage groups for women to finally achieve voting privileges.

Nineteenth Amendment

[Proposed June 4, 1919; declared ratified August 26, 1920]

The right of citizens of the United States to vote shall not be denied or abridged by the United States or by any State on account of sex.

Congress shall have power to enforce this article by appropriate legislation.

In the original Constitution, a newly elected president and Congress did not take office until March 4, which was four months after the November election. The officials who were leaving office were called "lame ducks" because they had little influence during those four months. The Twentieth Amendment changed the date that the new president and Congress take office. Members of Congress now take office on January 3, and the president takes office on January 20.

Twentieth Amendment

[Proposed March 2, 1932; declared ratified February 6, 1933]

Section 1. The terms of the President and Vice-President shall end at noon on the 20th day of January, and the terms of Senators and Representatives at noon on the 3d day of January, of the years in which such terms would have ended if this article had not been ratified; and the terms of their successors shall then begin.

Section 2. The Congress shall assemble at least once in every year, and such meeting shall begin at noon on the 3d day of January, unless they shall by law appoint a different day.

Section 3. If, at the time fixed for the beginning of the term of the President, the President elect shall have died, the Vice-President elect shall become President. If a President shall not have been chosen before the time fixed for the beginning of his term, or if the President elect shall have failed to qualify, then the Vice-President elect shall act as President until a President shall have qualified; and the Congress may by law provide for the case wherein neither a President elect nor a Vice-President elect shall have qualified, declaring who shall then act as President, or the manner in which one who is to act shall be selected, and such person shall act accordingly until a President or Vice-President shall have qualified.

Section 4. The Congress may by law provide for the case of the death of any of the persons from whom the House of Representatives may choose a President whenever the right of choice shall have devolved upon them, and for the case of the death of any of the persons from whom the Senate may choose a Vice-President whenever the right of choice shall have devolved upon them.

~~**Section 5.** Sections 1 and 2 shall take effect on the 15th day of October following the ratification of this article.~~

~~**Section 6.** This article shall be inoperative unless it shall have been ratified as an amendment to the Constitution by the legislatures of three-fourths of the several States within seven years from the date of its submission.~~

Twenty-first Amendment

[Proposed February 20, 1933; declared ratified December 5, 1933]

The Twenty-first Amendment is the only amendment that has been ratified by state conventions rather than by state legislatures.

Section 1. The eighteenth article of amendment to the Constitution of the United States is hereby repealed.

Section 2. The transportation or importation into any State, Territory, or possession of the United States for delivery or use therein of intoxicating liquors, in violation of the laws thereof, is hereby prohibited.

~~**Section 3.** This article shall be inoperative unless it shall have been ratified as an amendment to the Constitution by conventions in the several States, as provided in the Constitution, within seven years from the date of the submission hereof to the States by the Congress.~~

Twenty-second Amendment

[Proposed March 21, 1947; declared ratified February 26, 1951]

From the time of President Washington's administration, it was a custom for presidents to serve no more than two terms of office. Franklin D. Roosevelt, however, was elected to four terms. The Twenty-second Amendment made into law the old custom of a two-term limit for each president, if re-elected.

Section 1. No person shall be elected to the office of the President more than twice, and no person who has held the office of President, or acted as President, for more than two years of a term to which some other person was elected President shall be elected to the office of the President more than once. ~~But this Article shall not apply to any person holding the office of President when this Article was proposed by the Congress, and shall not prevent any person who may be holding the office of President, or acting as President, during the term within which this Article becomes operative from holding the office of President or acting as President during the remainder of such term.~~

~~**Section 2.** This article shall be inoperative unless it shall have been ratified as an amendment to the Constitution by the legislatures of three-fourths of the several States within seven years from the date of its submission to the States by the Congress.~~

Twenty-third Amendment

[Proposed June 16, 1960; declared ratified March 29, 1961]

Until the Twenty-third Amendment, the people of Washington, D.C., could not vote in presidential elections.

Section 1. The District constituting the seat of Government of the United States shall appoint in such manner as the Congress may direct:

A number of electors of President and Vice-President equal to the whole number of Senators and Representatives in Congress to which the District would be entitled if it were a State, but in no event more than the least populous state; they shall be in addition to those appointed by the States, but they shall be considered, for the purposes of the election of President and Vice-President, to be electors appointed by a State; and they shall meet in the District and perform such duties as provided by the twelfth article of amendment.

Section 2. The Congress shall have power to enforce this article by appropriate legislation.

Twenty-fourth Amendment

[Proposed August 27, 1962; declared ratified January 23, 1964]

Section 1. The right of citizens of the United States to vote in any primary or other election for President or Vice-President, for electors for President or Vice-President, or for Senator or Representative in Congress, shall not be denied or abridged by the United States or any State by reason of failure to pay any poll tax or other tax.

Section 2. The Congress shall have power to enforce this article by appropriate legislation.

The illness of President Eisenhower in the 1950s and the assassination of President Kennedy in 1963 were the events behind the Twenty-fifth Amendment. The Constitution did not provide a clear-cut method for a vice president to take over for a disabled president or upon the death of a president. This amendment provides for filling the office of the vice president if a vacancy occurs, and it provides a way for the vice president to take over if the president is unable to perform the duties of that office.

Twenty-fifth Amendment

[Proposed July 6, 1965; declared ratified February 10, 1967]

Section 1. In case of the removal of the President from office or of his death or resignation, the Vice-President shall become President.

Section 2. Whenever there is a vacancy in the office of the Vice-President, the President shall nominate a Vice-President who shall take office upon confirmation by a majority vote of both Houses of Congress.

Section 3. Whenever the President transmits to the President pro tempore of the Senate and the Speaker of the House of Representatives his written declaration that he is unable to discharge the powers and duties of his office, and until he transmits to them a written declaration to the contrary, such powers and duties shall be discharged by the Vice-President as Acting President.

Section 4. Whenever the Vice-President and a majority of either the principal officers of the executive departments or of such other body as Congress may by law provide, transmit to the President pro tempore of the Senate and the Speaker of the House of Representatives their written declaration that the President is unable to discharge the powers and duties of his office, the Vice-President shall immediately assume the powers and duties of the office as Acting President.

Thereafter, when the President transmits to the President pro tempore of the Senate and the Speaker of the House of Representatives his written declaration that no inability exists, he shall resume the powers and duties of his office unless the Vice-President and a majority of either the principal officers of the executive department or of such other body as Congress may by law provide, transmit within four days to the President pro tempore of the Senate and the Speaker of the House of Representatives their written declaration that the President is unable to discharge the powers and duties of his office. Thereupon Congress shall decide the issue, assembling within forty-eight hours for that purpose if not in session. If the Congress, within twenty-one days after receipt of the latter written declaration, or, if Congress is not in session, within twenty-one days after Congress is required to assemble, determines by two-thirds vote of both Houses that the President is unable to discharge the powers and duties of his office, the Vice-President shall continue to discharge the same as Acting President; otherwise, the President shall resume the powers and duties of his office.

Twenty-sixth Amendment

[Proposed March 10, 1971; declared ratified July 5, 1971]

Section 1. The right of citizens of the United States, who are eighteen years of age or older, to vote shall not be denied or abridged by the United States or by any State on account of age.

Section 2. The Congress shall have power to enforce this article by appropriate legislation.

The Voting Act of 1970 tried to set the voting age at 18. But the Supreme Court ruled that the act set the voting age for national elections only, not state or local elections. This ruling would make necessary several different ballots at elections. The Twenty-sixth Amendment gave 18-year-old citizens the right to vote in all elections.

Twenty-seventh Amendment

[Proposed September 25, 1789; declared ratified May 7, 1992]

No law, varying the compensation for the services of the Senators and Representatives, shall take effect, until an election of Representatives shall have intervened.

Federalism

Powers Delegated to the National Government	Powers Shared by National and State Governments	Powers Reserved for the States
Declare war	Maintain law and order	Establish and maintain schools
Maintain armed forces	Levy taxes	Establish local governments
Regulate interstate and foreign trade	Borrow money	Conduct corporate laws
Admit new states	Charter banks	Regulate business within the state
Establish post offices	Establish courts	Make marriage laws
Set standard weights and measures	Provide for public welfare	Provide for public safety
Coin money		Assume other powers not delegated to the national government or prohibited to the states
Establish foreign policy		
Make all laws necessary and proper for carrying out delegated powers		

Sharing Power. Under the system of federalism, the national and state governments share political power. "Delegated powers" are given to the national government. "Reserved powers" are given to the states. Why might it be beneficial to have the national government establish post offices? Why might it be beneficial to have the state governments establish and maintain schools?

CHAPTER 7

From the Collections of Henry Ford Museum & Greenfield Village

Launching the United States (1789–1801)

THEMES IN AMERICAN HISTORY

Constitutional Heritage:
Why might people disagree over the interpretation of the Constitution?

Global Relations:
How might conflict between two countries affect a third country?

Economic Development:
Why might one country loan money to other countries?

• Video Opener

• Skill Builder

French immigrant Michel Guillaume Jean de Crèvecoeur expressed his views on his new home and its citizens:

"Americans are the western pilgrims who are carrying along with them that great mass of arts, sciences, vigor, and industry which began long since in the east; they will finish the great circle. The Americans . . . are incorporated into one of the finest systems of population which has ever appeared."

image above: *Passing the cup of freedom*

Section 1
First Steps

Multimedia Connections

Explore these related topics and materials on the CD–ROM to enrich your understanding of this section:

Atlas

- U.S. Regions, 1790

Profiles

- George Washington

Biographies

- Alexander Hamilton

Readings

- African Americans in the 1700s
- Children in the New Republic

Media Bank

- Amending the U.S. Constitution
- Bill of Rights Stamp
- Alexander Hamilton

President George Washington would have preferred to serve without pay, as he had during the Revolutionary War. Congress, however, voted him an annual salary of $25,000 and rented him a three-story mansion in New York City, the new national capital. Martha Custis Washington described the house as "handsomely furnished, all new." The Washingtons lived in grand style, serving the best food at official dinners and driving around town in a horse-drawn carriage.

As you read this section you will find out:

- **How the president and Congress launched the new government.**
- **How Alexander Hamilton planned to strengthen the nation's finances.**
- **Why Hamilton and Jefferson clashed over the need for a national bank.**

The New Nation

New York City was still a small town of about 30,000 people in 1789. Like other towns in the United States, New York City was alive with excitement as the new government took office. People wondered what the future would bring. Americans had their constitution, but what would they do with democracy?

This new government seems simple when compared to the enormous federal government of today. It was not so simple, however, to design and staff it in 1789.

Establishing precedents. Washington had few **precedents**, or earlier examples, to follow. He knew that as the first president, every time he made a decision he was establishing a precedent for future presidents. This was a big responsibility.

Many people lined the streets of Trenton, New Jersey, to watch George Washington on his way to New York City to be inaugurated as the first president of the United States.

The Constitution had given the office of president a great deal of power. A strong and determined leader, Washington wanted to use this power to the fullest to ensure liberty and order in the new nation. Yet he also wanted to calm citizens who were worried about the possible misuse of presidential power. For that reason, Washington was particularly careful not to overstep his authority. He sincerely believed in the separation of powers. It was the job of Congress to make the laws. His job as the chief executive was to execute, or carry out, those laws.

The cabinet. Washington's first task was to appoint officials to run the government departments. He also had to decide what jobs needed to be done and how the work should be organized and supervised. This task required cooperation with Congress, which had to pass laws to create government positions and to provide money to pay salaries. It was also up to the Senate to approve Washington's appointments.

In 1789 Congress created three main executive departments: a Treasury Department, a State Department, and a War Department. Each department was headed by a secretary appointed by the president. Washington soon began to meet with the department secretaries for advice. This small group of department heads became the first **cabinet**.

Today the State Department is in charge of government relations with foreign countries. In 1789, however, it also had to manage all domestic affairs except those handled by the War and Treasury Departments. Yet Thomas Jefferson, the first secretary of state, had a staff of only five clerks! The War Department, headed by General Henry Knox, maintained a small army and navy. In peacetime just a few people were needed to carry out military functions. Only the Treasury Department, run by Alexander Hamilton, had a fairly large staff. It collected taxes and tariffs. Under Hamilton's direction, the department made a farsighted economic plan for the United States.

President Washington and his cabinet (left to right) Henry Knox, Alexander Hamilton, Thomas Jefferson, and Edmund Randolph

Washington also made several other important executive appointments. Attorney General Edmund Randolph served as the president's legal adviser, and Postmaster General Samuel Osgood ran the Post Office.

Jefferson and Hamilton

At cabinet meetings, Jefferson was very independent-minded and often disagreed with Hamilton. Hamilton was a bundle of energy with wide-ranging interests. He was eager to increase his influence. Knox tended to agree with Hamilton's suggestions. Gradually, Hamilton became Washington's most important adviser.

Hamilton's ideas about government and human nature were controversial and remain so today. He had a low opinion of the average person's honesty and judgment. He believed that most people were selfish and easily misled by sly, power-hungry leaders.

Hamilton favored the rich but did not trust them much more than what he called "the mass of the people." If the rich had power, they would control the rest of society, Hamilton believed. If the poor had power, they would use it to seize the property of the rich. A good government, he thought, was one that balanced rival interests between rich and poor. This attitude was not unusual. However, Hamilton went beyond most political thinkers of his day. He thought that the selfish desires of the rich could be used to strengthen the government and the whole nation.

Although Jefferson found much to admire in Hamilton, he strongly criticized Hamilton's political beliefs:

> **"Hamilton was, indeed, a singular [unique] character. Of acute [sharp] understanding, disinterested, honest, and honorable in all private transactions, amiable [friendly] in society, and duly [properly] valuing virtue in private life, yet so bewitched [fascinated] and perverted [misguided] by the British example as to be under thorough conviction [belief] that corruption [dishonesty] was essential to the government of a nation."**

Presidential Lives

George Washington

George Washington was considered by many to be very dignified. After one visit with the president, Abigail Adams wrote,

> *"I found myself much more deeply impressed [by the Washingtons] than I ever did before their Majesties of Britain."*

To many people, Washington seemed too formal to be a real person. He was more like a statue on a pedestal than a human being. This was because he was so aware of his responsibilities that he could hardly ever relax. Americans considered him the greatest hero of the Revolution. He felt that he had to live up to this high image.

Such expectations made Washington's life difficult. After his inauguration he wrote a friend, "I greatly fear that my countrymen will expect too much from me." He often complained about the burdens of his office. He looked forward to the day when he could retire to Virginia. Washington never neglected his duties, however. He was probably the best first president the nation could have had.

First Lady Martha Washington entertained many important political leaders at the presidential mansion in New York City.

• Martha Washington

Jefferson believed that Hamilton wished to undo the gains of the Revolution and go back to a less democratic form of government. He even thought that Hamilton wanted to make the United States into a monarchy, perhaps with George Washington as king.

Jefferson wanted to keep the government as small as possible. In his opinion, the best way to keep government small was to keep society simple. He believed that the United States was a free country because it was a nation of farmers. The population was spread out and people managed their own affairs. Countries with crowded seaports and industrial towns needed more government controls to preserve order. "When we get piled upon one another in large cities," Jefferson said, "we shall become corrupt."

Hamilton, on the other hand, disagreed with this idea. He wanted the nation to have a mixed economy, and he did everything in his power to encourage business growth.

Financing the New Nation

One of the main reasons government leaders had decided to strengthen the national government by crafting the Constitution had been the poor financial condition of the United States. During and after the Revolution, the government had accumulated a **national debt**. The amount of the debt the country owed was estimated at $77 million. This national debt included loans from foreign countries and treasury certificates. These certificates, often called **bonds**, represented money that the government borrowed from private citizens. Bond holders could cash in the bonds at a later date to earn a profit. The debt also included payments promised to soldiers and money owed to merchants and manufacturers. Many other countries hesitated to make any new loans to the United States because they were not sure if the American experiment in government would succeed.

New taxes. Using its new power to tax, Congress placed tariffs of about 5 percent on many foreign goods entering the country. This law was quite similar to the measures Parliament had employed in the 1760s to raise money in America. Those laws had been a major cause of the Revolution. Americans paid these new taxes, although somewhat reluctantly, because these taxes were passed by their representatives, not an outside power.

These taxes were used to meet the day-to-day expenses of the government. They did not raise enough money to pay off all the national debt, however.

Hamilton's plan. It was the responsibility of Secretary of the Treasury Hamilton to find a way to pay off the national debt. He proposed gradually raising enough money through **excise taxes**—taxes on goods produced and consumed inside the country.

Hamilton also had the task of restoring the credit of the government. Investors were afraid the government would not be able to pay off its debts. Some investors even doubted that the U.S. experiment in democracy would succeed. They considered the United States a poor credit risk and were unwilling to lend it money. As a result, government bonds had fallen far below face value. Many people sold their bonds at a loss—sometimes selling a $1,000 bond for as little as $150—to investors who were willing to take a risk. Such buyers, called **speculators**, were gambling that someday the government would be able to pay off its bonds at full value. If this happened, they would make huge profits.

Hamilton proposed doing just that. A speculator who had bought a $1,000 bond for $500 would receive the full $1,000. Hamilton believed that paying off the nation's debts at face value would restore the nation's credit. He also reasoned that his plan would encourage investment in the United States and thus boost the economy.

Some Americans believed this policy was unfair to former soldiers and other Patriots who had sold their bonds cheaply. Hamilton pointed out, however, that the speculators had paid what the bonds were worth at the time they bought them. They had taken the risks and were entitled to the profits. After some hesitation, Congress approved Hamilton's proposal and passed it into law.

Hamilton also wanted the United States to take over $21.5 million of the $25 million in debts owed by individual states. Jefferson and most southern congressmen opposed this idea. The largest state debts were owed by New England states. Most southern states had already managed to pay off their debts and did not want the federal government to take on the debts of those states that had not yet paid.

Jefferson and other southerners went along with Hamilton's plan only after he agreed to use his influence to get Congress to locate the permanent national capital in the South. Maryland and Virginia donated land for the new capital. Despite this compromise, the controversy over the debt revealed a growing split between Hamilton, a New Yorker, and Jefferson, a Virginian.

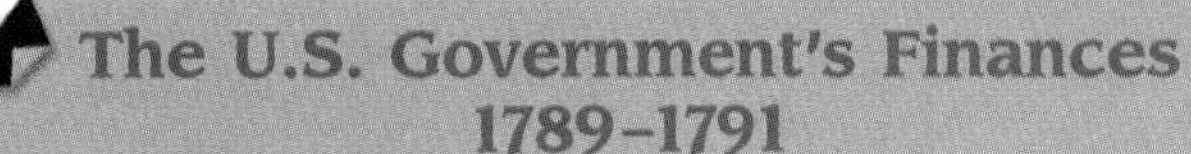

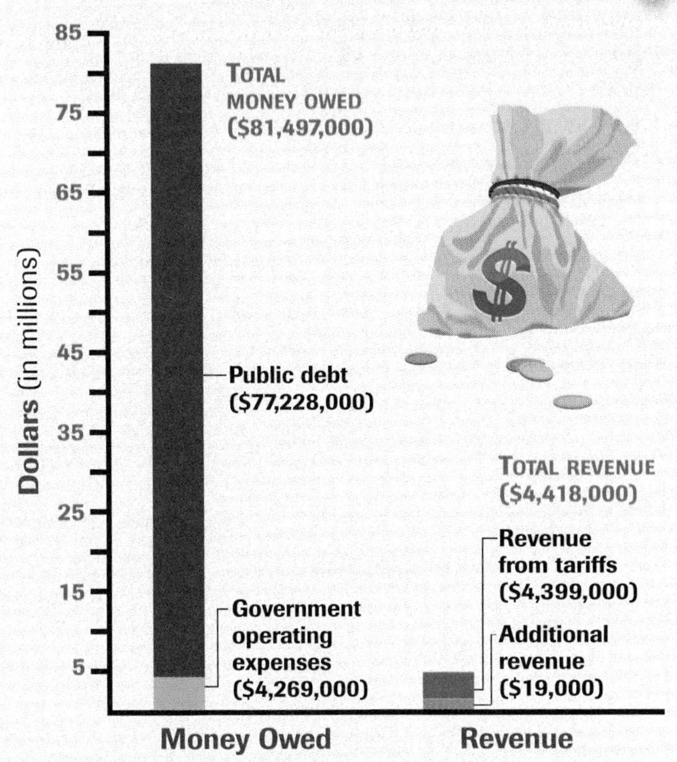

Source: *Historical Statistics of the United States.*

Government Finances. One of the most pressing problems of Washington's administration was the federal government's finances. How much more money did the government owe than it took in between 1789 and 1791?

The Bank of the United States. Jefferson also objected to Hamilton's proposal to create the **Bank of the United States**, a national bank with branches in major American cities. In 1790 there were very few banks of any kind in the country. Hamilton argued that the government could deposit money received from taxes into the bank. The bank would print paper money, called **bank notes**, to represent the money it had on deposit. It could also make loans to merchants and manufacturers, which might expand trade. Hamilton believed that this bank would benefit the entire nation.

The First Bank of the United States was built in Philadelphia. Alexander Hamilton fought a long battle to have this bank established.

In 1791 Congress passed a bank bill, but Washington did not sign it immediately. He could find nothing in the Constitution authorizing Congress to create a bank. So he asked his advisers if they thought the bill was constitutional. Hamilton said the bill was constitutional. He believed that Congress could establish a bank as long as the Constitution did not clearly oppose it. This interpretation of the Constitution is known today as **loose construction**. Jefferson, on the other hand, insisted that Congress could not form the bank, because the Constitution did not specifically say that Congress had the power to do so. This interpretation is known today as **strict construction**. Washington decided to support Hamilton and sign the bank bill.

• Construction

Hamilton was a financial genius. Under his guidance, the national debt was financed and the credit of the United States was soon as good as that of any nation in the world. Many people found the national bank to be a valuable institution. Hamilton was second only to Washington in establishing the shape and power of the new federal government.

Section 1 Review

• Glossary

IDENTIFY and explain the significance of the following: precedents, cabinet, national debt, bonds, excise taxes, speculators, Bank of the United States, bank notes, loose construction, strict construction

REVIEWING FOR DETAILS

1. What actions did the president and Congress take to launch the new government?
2. What was Hamilton's plan to handle the national debt and strengthen the nation's finances?
3. Why did Hamilton favor a national bank and Jefferson oppose it?

REVIEWING FOR UNDERSTANDING

4. **Writing Mastery:** *Expressing* Imagine that you are a newspaper editor. Tell your readers whether or not Hamilton's plan to repay the bonds at their full value is fair.
5. **Critical Thinking:** *Making Comparisons* Why do you think Jefferson and Hamilton had different views about society and government?

BILL OF RIGHTS

First Amendment	Guarantees freedom of speech, religion, and the press and the right to assemble peacefully and to petition the government.
Second Amendment	Acknowledges the necessity of state militias and the right of people to keep and bear arms.
Third Amendment	Forbids troops being quartered in a person's home without consent as stated by law.
Fourth Amendment	Forbids search and seizures without a warrant, which may be issued only with probable cause.
Fifth Amendment	Ensures that a person must be indicted by a grand jury before being tried for a serious criminal offense; prohibits persons from being tried twice for the same crime; protects people from being forced to testify against themselves; and guarantees that no person be denied life, liberty, or property without due process of law.
Sixth Amendment	Guarantees the right to a speedy trial with an impartial jury in all criminal cases, the right to know all charges, the right to obtain and question all witnesses, and the right to legal counsel.
Seventh Amendment	Guarantees a trial in most civil cases.
Eighth Amendment	Prohibits excessive bail or fines and forbids cruel and unusual punishment.
Ninth Amendment	Protects individual rights not stated in the Constitution.
Tenth Amendment	Reserves for the states and the people the powers not specifically delegated to the government or prohibited by the Constitution.

Section 2
A Time of Troubles

Multimedia Connections

Explore these related topics and materials on the CD-ROM to enrich your understanding of this section:

Gazetteer

- Haiti

Atlas

- Ohio Valley, 1750–1811

Media Bank

- Northwest Indian Life
- Battle of Fallen Timbers

Readings

- Indian Confederacy

Profiles

- Toussaint L'Ouverture
- Edmond Genet
- Thomas Pinckney
- Anthony Wayne

In the summer of 1794, David Bradford and his neighbors gathered to debate a new tax on whiskey. To these farmers in western Pennsylvania, the new tax seemed as unjust as British taxes before the Revolution. In the spirit of 1776, local farmers vowed resistance. Like the Patriots of that earlier time, the farmers threatened tax collectors and formed militias. Britain's King George III had used troops against the rebel Patriots. Many wondered if President Washington would treat these Pennsylvania farmers any differently.

As you read this section you will find out:

- **How the French Revolution affected American politics.**
- **Why western farmers rebelled.**
- **What parting advice President Washington gave to the nation.**

Trouble Abroad

Events on the other side of the Atlantic Ocean intensified the political conflicts that developed over Hamilton's economic policies. The American Revolution had been popular in France, in part because it weakened France's chief rival, Great Britain. It also seemed a great step forward for the republican ideals that many French people supported.

The French Revolution. The American Revolution, along with Enlightenment ideas of personal liberty, helped inspire the **French Revolution**, which began in 1789. The French Revolution, in turn, was greeted with enormous enthusiasm in America.

This enthusiasm slackened, however, after Revolutionary extremists, or radicals, gained control of France. The extremists began to

Global Connections

The American Revolution

Inspired in part by the ideas and success of the American Revolution, the French demanded more rights from their government. When their demands were not met, the angry citizens revolted. On July 14, 1789, Parisians stormed the Bastille—a hated prison-fortress. This marked the beginning of the French Revolution. The monarchy was toppled and replaced by a republican government.

In 1791 the freed slave François-Dominique Toussaint L'Ouverture (TOO-san loo-vuhr-TOOHR) led slaves and free people of African-European ancestry to rise up against France on the Caribbean colony they named Haiti. Other revolutions were also brewing in Latin America. In Mexico in 1810 a creole priest named Miguel Hidalgo y Costilla led a rebellion against the Spanish government. Simon Bolívar and José de San Martín led uprisings against the Spanish Crown in South America between 1809 and 1824. Out of their efforts came independence for the countries of Venezuela, Ecuador, Colombia, Argentina, Chile, and Peru.

make harsh changes to the society. They executed thousands of men and women, including King Louis XVI and Queen Marie Antoinette. As one French noble described:

> **"Troops of women and men armed with pikes [long spears] and muskets were everywhere hunting the men of the [king's] Bodyguard. . . . The barbarous horde [crowd] manifested [showed] a savage pleasure, some of them . . . dancing round the bodies."**

Then in 1793 war broke out between France and Great Britain. Many Americans, including Thomas Jefferson, were sympathetic to France. French help had made it possible for America to win its independence. In fact, the 1778 treaty of alliance with France was still in effect. The United States seemed duty-bound to side with France. Other Americans, including Alexander Hamilton, considered the leaders of the French Revolution too radical and favored the British.

American neutrality. Washington took a more balanced view. He issued the **Neutrality Proclamation**, warning Americans not to favor either side. The United States would try to be "friendly and impartial [fair]" to both. He did not believe the United States would benefit from war with either France or Great Britain.

Maintaining neutrality proved difficult. The French government ignored Washington's proclamation and sent over a special diplomatic representative, Edmond Genet (zhuh-ne). He arrived in America in April 1793. Genet quickly persuaded a number of Americans who owned merchant ships to become **privateers**—armed private ships authorized to attack enemy shipping—and to attack British ships on the high seas. Genet even tried to organize private American

This anti-French cartoon shows President Washington in his federal chariot heading off an invasion of French Revolutionary leaders.

Spain's refusal to allow Americans to load and unload cargo at the important seaport of New Orleans greatly affected the trade of western farmers.

• **Spanish Land Claims**

armies to attack British Canada and Spanish Florida and Louisiana, because France was at war with Spain as well as Great Britain. Washington finally demanded that the French government recall Genet.

Washington's troubles were not over. The navies of both France and Great Britain began to seize American merchant ships on the Atlantic. Both countries ignored U.S. claims of neutrality. In a single year, several hundred American vessels loaded with valuable goods were captured. As time passed this disruption caused serious financial problems for many Americans involved in trade overseas.

New Treaties

In 1794 Washington sent John Jay to Britain to try to work out a solution to all the conflicts that had developed between the two nations. Jay had done well negotiating the Treaty of Paris that ended the American Revolution.

Jay's Treaty. Jay got the British to agree to withdraw their troops from forts on the western frontier of the United States. Britain also promised to improve trade relations and to pay damages to the shipowners whose vessels had been seized. In turn, the United States agreed to pay debts owed to British merchants prior to the Revolution.

These terms, however, failed to meet the expectations of many Americans. The British ignored the American view of the rights of neutral nations during wartime and continued seizing American merchant ships. In addition, the British would not agree to pay for slaves they had taken during the Revolutionary War.

Many Americans disliked **Jay's Treaty**. Mobs of angry citizens gathered to protest its ratification. Nevertheless, Washington decided to accept the treaty. He realized that the United States had made some gains in the treaty and that time was on the nation's side. With each year the United States became richer and stronger. A war with Great Britain, or any other European nation, would cost much and could gain little. After a long debate, the Senate accepted these arguments and voted to ratify the treaty.

Pinckney's Treaty. The United States obtained an additional and very unexpected benefit from Jay's Treaty. It improved relations with Spain. Before the war, relations between the two

People opposed to Jay's Treaty express their feelings by burning an image of John Jay.

• **John Jay**

countries had not been good. The Spanish government had refused to recognize the boundary between Florida and the United States. Spain also controlled the west bank and mouth of the Mississippi River, including the city of New Orleans.

The Spanish refused to allow Americans to load and unload cargo freely at New Orleans. This was an economic burden on western farmers who needed to transfer their farm products from river craft to oceangoing ships. The farmers wanted Spanish authorities to grant them the **right of deposit**—the right to transfer their goods without paying a duty.

When Spanish authorities read Jay's Treaty, they suspected that the published version was incomplete because many treaties of the time had secret clauses. Perhaps there was a clause calling for a British-American alliance. Spain decided to try to improve relations with the United States.

In 1795 Spain signed a treaty accepting the American version of the Florida boundary line. The treaty also recognized Americans' right to navigate freely on the Mississippi River and granted them the right of deposit at New Orleans. This agreement became known as **Pinckney's Treaty** because it was negotiated for the United States by Thomas Pinckney.

The Treaty of Greenville. On the western frontier, American settlers were pushing past the Appalachian Mountains. The Indian tribes of the region north of the Ohio River resisted the invasion of American settlers who moved into the area after 1783. The tribes joined together in a confederacy and pledged not to sell any territory to the settlers. By the late 1780s, however, 10,000 settlers were pouring into the Ohio Valley each year. They disregarded the fact that the land had always been owned by Indians. These settlers demanded that the U.S. government protect them.

The leader of the Indian confederacy was Michikinikwa (mi-chee-ken-EEK-wah), or Little Turtle, chief of the Miami. He successfully defeated the troops Washington sent to the region in 1790 and 1791. In August of 1794 the

Chief Little Turtle tried to negotiate a settlement with General Anthony Wayne in 1794 before bloody fighting resumed between the Indians and American troops.

• Little Turtle

confederacy, now led by the Shawnee chief Blue Jacket, was defeated in the **Battle of Fallen Timbers**. After the battle, American commander "Mad Anthony" Wayne ordered his troops to set the Indians' cornfields and homes on fire. The Indians lost everything. In 1795 more than 90 leading chiefs were forced to sign the **Treaty of Greenville**, turning over the entire southern half of present-day Ohio to the American settlers.

The Whiskey Rebellion

Washington faced a much different problem when western farmers protested an excise tax Congress had placed on whiskey that was distilled, or manufactured, in the United States. The tax was one of the measures designed by Hamilton to raise money to pay off the nation's debts. It triggered what is known as the **Whiskey Rebellion**.

The tax angered frontier farmers who usually distilled a large part of their surplus rye and other grain into whiskey. The farmers did this because whiskey was cheaper to ship to market than bulky farm products.

Farmers in western Pennsylvania rioted in 1794 to protest the whiskey tax. They bullied tax collectors, tried to prevent courts from meeting, and marched on Pittsburgh.

Washington promptly called 12,900 militia troops to duty. He put Virginia governor Henry Lee in charge of the military, with Alexander Hamilton as the civilian leader. When the soldiers finally reached the troubled area, however, not a single "rebel" could be found. No one dared to stand up before this huge force, which was larger than any American army had been during the Revolutionary War! The "rebellion" had ended, or perhaps it would be more accurate to say that it had disappeared.

Some historians believe that Washington overreacted to the Whiskey Rebellion. Perhaps he did. Still, there was a difference between his swift and painless enforcement of the law and the bloodshed of Daniel Shays's rebellion only eight years earlier. This time there was a strong central government backed by the new Constitution.

Washington's Farewell Address

By 1796 Washington could justly feel that he had set the United States well on its way as an independent nation. Jay's and Pinckney's Treaties had improved American relations with Great Britain and Spain. The new nation was growing. Kentucky had enough people to become a state by 1792. Tennessee entered the Union in 1796, and Ohio would soon follow.

Besides his sense of having completed his main tasks, Washington was tired after serving two terms as president. Political bickering was beginning to affect his reputation as a national hero. Although he surely could have been elected to a third term had he wished to be, Washington decided to retire.

His Farewell Address of September 1796 was drafted with the help of Hamilton and James Madison. It contained his parting advice to the American people. That advice can be boiled down to three ideas—unity at home, good national credit, and neutrality abroad. To prevent political disunity, Washington warned:

> **"In contemplating [thinking about] the causes which may disturb our Union, it occurs as matter of serious concern that any ground should have been furnished for characterizing [political] parties by geographical discriminations [divisions]: Northern and Southern; Atlantic and Western; whence [from where] designing [scheming] men may endeavor [try] to**

During the Whiskey Rebellion some Pennsylvania farmers tarred and feathered tax inspectors to show their dissatisfaction with the new tax laws.

excite a belief that there is a real difference of local interests and views."

Washington advised the government to use the nation's credit "as sparingly [little] as possible . . . by shunning [avoiding] occasions of expense." He urged Americans not to pass on to future generations "the burden which we ourselves ought to bear."

As for neutrality, Washington advised, "Observe good faith and justice toward all nations. Cultivate peace and harmony with all." Washington supported fair dealings with all foreign countries rather than a permanent policy of alliances or isolation.

As the first president, Washington made decisions that shaped the highest office in the land. He set up a cabinet of advisers. He restored the credit of the United States and avoided foreign wars. When he left office, he recommended neutrality and national unity. Would those who came after him be able to follow this advice?

This oil painting from 1810 illustrates the association many Americans made between George Washington and the ideals of liberty.

Section 2 Review

• Glossary

IDENTIFY and explain the significance of the following: French Revolution, Neutrality Proclamation, Edmond Genet, privateers, Jay's Treaty, right of deposit, Pinckney's Treaty, Battle of Fallen Timbers, Treaty of Greenville, Whiskey Rebellion

REVIEWING FOR DETAILS

1. Why did Americans disagree over the nation's policy toward France?
2. What advice did Washington give to the nation as he left office?

REVIEWING FOR UNDERSTANDING

3. **Geographic Literacy** Why might western Pennsylvania farmers have opposed the whiskey tax more strongly than similar farmers in a less mountainous area?
4. **Writing Mastery:** *Expressing* Write a short speech supporting or criticizing Edmond Genet's actions.
5. **Critical Thinking:** *Synthesizing Information* How might the fact that Great Britain was a more powerful nation than Spain have affected Jay's and Pinckney's Treaties?

Section 3

John Adams's Presidency

Multimedia Connections

Explore these related topics and materials on the CD–ROM to enrich your understanding of this section:

Readings

- What Is an American?
- Election of 1796
- John Adams

Media Bank

- Settlers Moving West
- Clothing Styles, 1776–1812
- Farm Life
- Abigail Adams

Profiles

- John Adams

Charles Pinckney (Thomas's brother), John Marshall, and Elbridge Gerry listened to the French secret agents' list of demands. The three Americans had been sent to France to iron out the two nations' differences. But instead of negotiating, the French agents demanded a bribe! The Americans were furious. This was not how things were done in America. Finally, one of the Americans burst out angrily, "No, no! Not a sixpence!"

As you read this section you will find out:

- **How the rise of political parties affected government.**
- **What problems the nation had overseas during John Adams's presidency.**
- **How Americans' rights and freedoms were threatened at home.**

The Election of 1796

The election of a president to succeed Washington was the first in which **political parties** played a role. Political parties are groups of people who organize to help elect government officials and to try to influence government policies.

The first political parties developed around Alexander Hamilton and Thomas Jefferson. Members of Congress who favored Hamilton's financial policies took the name of the **Federalist Party**. The Federalists began to vote as a group on most issues.

Those who opposed Hamilton and his ideas began to call themselves the **Democratic-Republican Party**, or Republicans for short. (This party has no historical connection to the Republican Party of today.) Jefferson was one of their best-known leaders.

By 1796 Hamilton was probably the most powerful figure in the Federalist Party. Because he had been born in the West Indies, however, he could not, under the Constitution, run for president. Therefore, the Federalists settled on Vice President John Adams as their candidate for president. Jefferson was the Republican favorite.

For vice president, the Federalist leaders decided to run Thomas Pinckney of South Carolina, who had negotiated the treaty with Spain. The Republican candidate for vice president was Senator Aaron Burr of New York.

The campaign to succeed Washington was a bitter one. A typical campaign advertisement for Jefferson ran:

> **"*Who shall be President of the United States?*... THOMAS JEFFERSON is a firm REPUBLICAN,—JOHN ADAMS is an avowed [openly declared] MONARCHIST.... Will you, by your votes, contribute to [help] make the avowed friend of monarchy, President?... *Adams* is a fond admirer of the British Constitution, and says it is the first wonder of the world. *Jefferson* likes better our Federal Constitution, and thinks the British full of deformity, corruption, and wickedness."**

Hamilton also disliked Adams. This was partly because as vice president, Adams had opposed some of Hamilton's ideas. However, Hamilton dared not openly oppose his party's presidential candidate. Instead, he worked out a clever but shady scheme. He persuaded a few Federalist electors in South Carolina not to vote for Adams. Then, if Pinckney got even one more electoral vote than Adams, he would be president and Adams vice president!

Unfortunately for Hamilton, news of his plan leaked out. A large number of Federalist electors who were friendly to Adams reacted by not voting for Pinckney. When the electoral votes were counted, Adams had 71 and Pinckney only 59. Jefferson, who had the united support of the Republican electors, received 68 votes. So Jefferson, not Pinckney, became the new vice president!

The 1796 election revealed that the Constitution's method for electing a president did not work well in a system that had political parties. It put two rivals, Adams and Jefferson,

Some Americans feared that the Federalist-Republican rivalry threatened to tear down the very foundations that the new country was built upon.

Although John Adams won the presidency in 1796, he had to deal with the Republicans, not only in Congress but also in his own administration. His vice president, Thomas Jefferson, was from the opposing party.

in the uncomfortable position of serving together as president and vice president.

The XYZ Affair

From the beginning of his presidency, John Adams had to deal with the same international problems that had troubled George Washington. France was still at war with Great Britain. French leaders were angry at the United States for agreeing to Jay's Treaty. French warships and privateers were stopping American merchant ships on the high seas and seizing their cargoes.

Agents in France. Washington had tried without success to reach an agreement with France, but Adams decided to try again. In October 1797, three U.S. diplomats arrived in France to meet with the French foreign minister, Charles-Maurice de Talleyrand.

Instead of meeting with Talleyrand, the Americans met and exchanged letters with three of his secret agents. These agents said that Talleyrand would not discuss the issues until he received a large bribe. In addition, he expected the United States to make a large loan to France and to apologize for harsh remarks about France that Adams had made in a speech to Congress.

Adams was very upset by the diplomats' report, which substituted the letters X, Y, and Z for the names of the agents. Adams shared the report with the members of Congress, who became angry and made it public.

News of the **XYZ affair** created a public outcry. "Millions for defense, but not one cent for tribute [forced payment]" became a Federalist slogan. Popular feeling against France grew bitter. For the next two years the United States and France waged an undeclared naval war in the Atlantic.

Congress began making preparations for war. It created a Department of the Navy and set aside money for new warships. It also

The Granger Collection, New York

This cartoon of American diplomats refusing a bribe from the "monster" France expressed the general outrage over the XYZ affair.

The Granger Collection, New York

The United States dismantled most of its military forces after the Revolution. International events, however, proved the need for continuous military forces. As tensions increased between the United States and France, President Adams moved to increase the strength of American naval forces. This etching from 1800 shows workers building the warship Philadelphia.

increased the size of the army. Washington came out of retirement to command this force, with Hamilton second in command. Suddenly, Adams, who had been elected president by a close vote, became a national hero.

War or peace. Adams wanted to be re-elected president in 1800. He knew that his strong stand on the XYZ affair had made him very popular. Americans saw him as the defender of the nation's honor. If he could win the dispute with France, he would almost certainly be re-elected. Adams was not willing to rush into a war with France, however. When he learned that Talleyrand was eager to repair the damage caused by the XYZ affair, Adams decided to negotiate.

Late in 1799 he sent three new diplomats to Paris. After months of discussion they signed a treaty known as the Convention of 1800. Adams had stopped the threat of a full-fledged war with France. He had also seriously divided his political party, however, because many Federalists wanted the conflict to continue so that Adams would gain more public support and be re-elected.

The Alien and Sedition Acts

Taking advantage of the war scare and the public anger over the XYZ affair, in the summer of 1798 the Federalists pushed several laws through Congress. These laws are known as the **Alien and Sedition Acts**. They were aimed at foreigners in the United States and at Republicans who were supposedly trying to weaken the government.

One of these laws increased the length of time foreigners had to live in the United States before they could become citizens. Others gave the president the power to jail or to **deport**—order out of the country—foreigners he considered "dangerous to the peace and safety of the United States."

Just as severe was the Sedition Act. This law made it a crime for anyone to "write, print, utter, or publish" statements discrediting the government, members of Congress, or the president. The Sedition Act was an attempt to frighten the Republicans into silence. In practice, it was used to protect Adams but allowed the press to attack Jefferson freely.

This engraved cartoon from 1798 illustrates the level of hostile debate the Sedition Act caused in Congress. Representative Roger Griswold (right) is shown attacking Matthew Lyon, who was one of many Republicans prosecuted under the new law.

Such an attack on freedom of speech and the press was a threat to everything the American Revolution had sought to protect. In 1798 the American experiment in republican government was little more than 20 years old. Was it about to come to an end?

Attacks on the Alien and Sedition Acts

Vice President Jefferson reacted swiftly against the Alien and Sedition Acts, which he believed were unconstitutional. He wrote several statements called resolutions that explained his reasoning. The Kentucky legislature, where the Republicans had a majority, voted to approve the first resolution in November 1798. The Virginia legislature passed a similar resolution written by James Madison.

The **Virginia and Kentucky Resolutions** argued that the federal government had overstepped its power. When Congress went beyond its legal powers, what could be done?

Jefferson had a simple answer. The Constitution, he wrote, was a contract made by the separate states that gave certain powers to the federal government. If Congress passed a law the Constitution did not give it the power to pass, any state could declare the law unconstitutional.

If put into practice, this idea could have put an end to the United States as one nation. If any state could refuse to obey a law of Congress, the national government might soon collapse. Fortunately, the other states, which were mostly controlled by Federalists, did not respond favorably to Jefferson's resolutions. Federalists believed that no state should have the power to decide whether a law was unconstitutional.

Congress eventually repealed the Alien and Sedition Acts. The Virginia and Kentucky resolutions are important, however, because they put forth an argument for **states' rights**—the belief that the states, not the federal government, hold ultimate political power.

The Election of 1800

Republicans used the Alien and Sedition Acts to attack Adams and the Federalists during the hotly contested presidential election of 1800. The Republican Party once again nominated Jefferson for president and Aaron Burr for vice president. The Federalists ran Adams and Charles Pinckney.

In the campaign the Republicans were united, the Federalists badly divided. Hamilton disliked Adams so much that he published the pamphlet "The Public Conduct and Character of John Adams," in which he described Adams as jealous, conceited, and ill-tempered. According to Hamilton, Adams was totally unfit to be president. Adams returned Hamilton's dislike in full.

Hamilton, of course, had no intention of helping Adams get re-elected. Once again he tried to manage the Federalist electors so that the Federalist candidate for vice president got more votes than Adams. Again this trick failed. Adams received 65 electoral votes, Pinckney only 64. However, Jefferson beat them both with 73 votes.

Although victorious, the Republicans faced a problem. Because they were well organized, all their electors had voted for Burr as well as Jefferson. He, too, had 73 electoral votes. The electors had intended that Burr be vice president. A tie meant that the House of Representatives would have to choose between them. For an entire week the House could not come to a decision. Finally, a few representatives changed their votes, giving Jefferson the presidency. Burr became vice president.

The Granger Collection, New York

This campaign banner was used by Jefferson supporters in the election of 1800. It read, "Thomas Jefferson—President of the U.S.A." and "John Adams—no more."

To avoid future ties for president and vice president, the Twelfth Amendment was added to the Constitution. Thereafter, the electors voted separately for president and vice president. Despite the problems that plagued the election of 1800, the young nation was able for the first time to transfer power peacefully between different parties.

Section 3 Review

• Glossary

• Time Line

IDENTIFY and explain the significance of the following: political parties, Federalist Party, Democratic-Republican Party, XYZ affair, Alien and Sedition Acts, deport, Virginia and Kentucky Resolutions, states' rights

REVIEWING FOR DETAILS

1. What effect did the rise of political parties have on government?
2. What foreign problems did the United States face during John Adams's presidency?
3. How did the Federalists try to control criticism of their policies?

REVIEWING FOR UNDERSTANDING

4. **Writing Mastery:** *Expressing* Imagine that you are the campaign manager for one of the political parties. Write a short paragraph either attacking or defending Adams's presidency.
5. **Critical Thinking:** *Cause and Effect* What problems might have arisen from choosing a president and vice president from different parties?

unit 3

BUILDING A STRONG NATION (1790–1860)

Chapter 8
Expansion and War (1801–1830)

Chapter 9
The North and Manufacturing (1790–1860)

Chapter 10
The South and King Cotton (1790–1860)

This image shows a busy urban marketplace in the 1800s. Such marketplaces developed along with the rise of cities after the Revolutionary War.

Linking Past to Present
Young Consumers

"And now a word from our sponsor. . . ."

The commercial shows middle-school-aged students using some product that the sponsoring company would like viewers to buy. Such advertisements can be found every day on television and in print advertisements. They are increasingly common today as Americans between the ages of 6 and 14 together have billions of dollars in spending money.

Many students earn spending money by doing chores at home. As a result, more and more teenagers have become consumers, or buyers of products, in recent years. Many teenagers read consumer magazines like *Zillions,* which offers comparisons of products and tips on money management for its readers.

Young consumers spend their money on a wide variety of products. Some even invest for future earnings. Some do both, like the young consumers who recently purchased "collector's editions" of a popular comic book. Many bought one copy to read and a second one to preserve so that it would increase in value over time.

The students who earn money and buy products are all participating in a type of economy that came to dominate American society in the early 1800s. As you read this unit, you will learn that until that time, the economy was largely driven by the ownership of land, not the earning of wages and the buying of manufactured products.

Most Americans who lived around 1800 made or traded everything they needed. They spent most of their time working on their own land and in their homes. As you will learn, however, changes began to take place in the northern American economy that eventually made wage earning and consumer purchasing the norm.

This girl is helping her mother buy food at an outdoor market.

CHAPTER 8

The Granger Collection, New York

Expansion and War

(1801–1830)

THEMES IN AMERICAN HISTORY

Cultural Diversity:
How might cultural differences lead to unrest within a country?

Global Relations:
Why might governments find it difficult to maintain control of overseas territories?

Economic Development:
How might economic issues affect U.S. relations with other nations?

• Video Opener

• Skill Builder

In less than 25 years, the young American government had gained a huge amount of land. Louisiana, once a French property, was now part of the United States, as was Florida, a former Spanish settlement. Even decades later, travelers marveled at the diversity of America. "There are many soils and many climates included within the . . . United States," one British woman remarked, ". . . many countries."

image above: *New Orleans around 1800*

Section 1
JEFFERSON AS PRESIDENT

Multimedia Connections

Explore these related topics and materials on the CD–ROM to enrich your understanding of this section:

Biographies

- Sacagawea

Profiles

- Thomas Jefferson
- Zebulon Pike

Media Bank

- Clark's Buffalo-Skin Shirt
- Slave Revolt in Saint Domingue
- Lewis & Clark Meeting Indians
- Drawings from Clark's Journal
- Bird from Clark's Journal
- President Thomas Jefferson
- Burr-Hamilton Duel
- Chief Justice John Marshall

Readings

- Jefferson's Inaugural Address

The Shoshoni Indian girls bent over the berries that grew on the banks of the Missouri River. Suddenly a war party of Hidatsa Indians swept down. They captured the girls, keeping some and selling others. Sacagawea (sak-uh-juh-WEE-uh) was among those sold by the Hidatsa. Drawing on her skills as an interpreter, Sacagawea later became "the outstanding Indian woman in the West," guiding an important American expedition through dangerous territory.

As you read this section you will find out:

- **Why President Jefferson clashed with the Supreme Court.**
- **Why the Louisiana Purchase was important to the United States.**
- **What the Lewis and Clark expedition achieved.**

The Republicans in Charge

Thomas Jefferson viewed his election as a kind of second American Revolution. In his opinion, it had halted the Federalists' attempt to make the United States a monarchy. In his inaugural address, Jefferson emphasized unity by pointing out how important majority rule was in a democracy like the United States. He reminded victorious Republicans, however, that minority groups had rights too, and that "to violate [them] would be oppression." Political differences, he said, could be smoothed over by discussion and compromise, "Let us, then, fellow-citizens, unite with one heart and one mind. . . . We are all Republicans, we are all Federalists."

In practice, Jefferson made few drastic changes in the direction of the national government. Some Federalist laws, such as the

Alien and Sedition Acts and the Whiskey Tax, were either repealed or allowed to expire. President Jefferson came to recognize that some Federalist laws provided many benefits for the nation. Jefferson continued Alexander Hamilton's policy of paying off the national debt to ensure good credit. He also made no effort to do away with the Bank of the United States, which had proven to be a useful financial institution.

Presidential Lives

Thomas Jefferson

When Thomas Jefferson became president, he was nearly 58 years old. He was a tall, lanky man. His red hair was streaked with gray. Although he had been born a Virginia aristocrat, Jefferson looked more like a country squire than the leader of a nation. He had always been painfully shy, which sometimes caused him to appear reserved. However, when Jefferson discussed such topics as science, mathematics, architecture, music, and art, his eyes lit up and he talked with great ease.

The Granger Collection, New York

Jefferson had little taste for fancy ceremony. He once greeted the French representative to the United States wearing a dressing gown and slippers! At that time, important government officials usually dressed in powdered wigs, satin coats covered with medals, and silver-buckled shoes. Jefferson saw ordinary citizens and foreign diplomats each in their turn. He told them all, "Nobody shall be above you, nor you above anybody."

Jefferson and the Courts

One problem Jefferson encountered in his first term involved the courts. He was annoyed that so many judges were Federalists. Since the judges had been appointed before Jefferson took office, there was little he could do about the situation.

Supreme Court Chief Justice John Marshall, whom Jefferson particularly disliked, had been appointed by President John Adams after he had been defeated in the election of 1800 but before Jefferson had taken office. At the same time, Adams had appointed many other judges and court officials who were unfriendly to the Republicans. Some of these officials were called the "midnight judges" because Adams had signed the papers appointing them during the final hours of his presidency.

In the confusion of Adams's last hours, however, some of these papers had not been distributed, and Jefferson refused to let them be released to the appointees. William Marbury, whom Adams had appointed as a justice of the peace, asked the Supreme Court to order Jefferson's secretary of state, James Madison, to issue his appointment papers.

The case of ***Marbury* v. *Madison*** in 1803 provided a great test for the Court. The chief justice ruled that he could not force the president to give the appointment to Marbury. Marshall explained that the part of the Judiciary Act of 1799 that allowed the Supreme Court to give such an order was **unconstitutional**, or in violation of the Constitution.

• Marshall Court

Marshall established for the Court the power of **judicial review**—the right to declare an act of Congress unconstitutional. This meant that the Supreme Court had the final say in interpreting the Constitution.

more alarming to most Americans than the loss of ships and cargoes was the loss of American sailors.

As the war in Europe continued, Great Britain stepped up its longtime practice of **impressment**—forcing sailors suspected of being British subjects to serve in the Royal Navy. Conditions in the British navy were terrible. Sailors had to live in extremely cramped quarters and obey strict rules of conduct. As a result, the desertion rate was very high. British warships often stopped American merchant ships on the high seas to search for deserters.

• Trouble

American relations with Great Britain became even more strained in June 1807. The British frigate *Leopard* stopped the *Chesapeake,* an American naval ship. The British claimed that four men aboard were British deserters. When the American commander refused to allow the British to search his ship, the *Leopard* opened fire. The *Chesapeake* surrendered, and the British snatched the four sailors off the ship. Only one turned out to be a British deserter. The incident encouraged many Americans to call for war.

The Embargo Act

Instead of going to war, Jefferson tried to put economic pressure on both Great Britain and France. In December 1807 he persuaded Congress to pass the **Embargo Act**. An **embargo** is a government order prohibiting trade—in this case, all exports from the United States. Jefferson hoped that by depriving Britain and France of goods they needed, the embargo would make them stop violating America's neutral rights. He also reasoned that if American ships did not carry goods on the high seas, no American sailor could be forced into a foreign navy.

This was, of course, an extreme measure to avoid war. Stopping foreign trade caused massive unemployment among sailors and among workers who had been making goods that were usually exported. The busy American shipbuilding industry nearly came to a halt.

New Englanders particularly resented the Embargo Act. One man who signed himself "A lover of his Country" wrote to Jefferson on July 4, 1808:

> **"Mr. President if you know what is good for your future welfar[e] you will take off the embargo that is now such a check upon American commerce. . . . Your friend as long as you act with propriety [properness] toward your country but when you depart from that I am your enehmy [enemy]."**

Because many Americans considered the embargo unwise and unfair, they did not hesitate to break the law. Trade by sea between one American port and another was allowed. Therefore, many captains claimed that they were making such a voyage but went to Europe or the West Indies instead.

Despite these violations and the smuggling of American goods into Canada, the Embargo Act seriously hurt the American economy. The value of goods imported into the United States

The Granger Collection, New York

The British impressment of American sailors aboard the Chesapeake *increased support for a war against Great Britain.*

in 1808 was less than half what it was in 1807. Exports dropped from $108 million in 1807 to $22 million in 1808.

Drifting Toward War

Early in 1809, after James Madison had been elected president, Congress responded to the protests over loss of trade. Congress replaced Jefferson's earlier Embargo Act with the **Non-Intercourse Act**. This law restored trade with all foreign countries *except* France and Great Britain and ports under their control. It also gave the president the power to open trade with either France or Great Britain if such trade "shall cease to violate the neutral commerce of the United States."

The Non-Intercourse Act was just as hard to enforce as the Embargo Act. A ship's captain could, for example, set out officially for the Netherlands and when he reached the English Channel change course for Great Britain or France. Finally, in 1810 Congress removed all restrictions on trade with Great Britain and France. However, Congress provided that if either nation stopped attacking American merchant ships, the president could cut off trade with the other nation.

National Portrait Gallery, Smithsonian Institution, Washington, DC/Art Resource, NY

Kentucky senator Henry Clay was one of the most outspoken War Hawks in Congress.

This action was an attempt to get each side to be the first to respect American neutral rights. The British, however, ignored the new American policy and continued to impress American sailors. The policies of Jefferson and Madison had failed. More and more Americans began calling for war with Great Britain.

The War Hawks

Most of the people who favored war were southerners and westerners. Their leaders belonged to a new breed of young Republicans in Congress known as **War Hawks**. Two of the most famous were John C. Calhoun of South Carolina and Henry Clay of Kentucky. In a speech to the Senate in February 1810, Clay made his views clear. "I prefer the troubled ocean of war," he said, "to the calm, decaying pool of dishonorable peace."

Although many War Hawks were angered by the impressment of American sailors, they were more concerned with expanding the boundaries of the United States. Some hoped to take Florida from Spain, now Great Britain's ally in the long war against Napoleon. Others hoped to gobble up British-owned Canada. The War Hawks

The Plumb-pudding in danger, —or State Epicures taking un Petit Souper. "the great Globe itself, and all which it inherit," is too small to satisfy such insatiable appetites.

During the early 1800s many countries such as the United States were caught in the middle as the British and the French "carved up the world" between them.

also blamed the Spanish and British for helping Indians resist the advance of American settlers.

The situation was particularly tense in the Northwest Territory. The huge area that American Indians turned over to land-hungry settlers in the Treaty of Greenville of 1795 was not enough to satisfy the settlers for long. One of the settlers' leaders was General William Henry Harrison, governor of the Indiana Territory. Harrison considered Indians to be "wretched savages" who were blocking the forward march of what he called "civilization." He used trickery, bribery, and military force to push Indians off their land.

In 1809 Harrison reached a treaty agreement with the chiefs of a few Indian tribes in the territory. The tribes gave up 3 million acres in return for about $10,000—less than half a cent an acre. The U.S. government was selling similar land for at least $2 an acre.

Tecumseh and the Prophet

Even before Harrison made this deal, a brilliant leader had been rising among the Indians of the Ohio Valley. He was Tecumseh (tuh-KUHM-suh) of the Shawnee nation. Tecumseh was furious when he heard how the Native Americans had been cheated. He believed that God, "the Great Spirit," had created the land for Indians to *use* but not to *own.* At a meeting with Harrison, Tecumseh argued that Indians had no right to sell the land. "Sell a *country!"* he cried. "Why not sell the air, the clouds and the great sea?"

Tecumseh offered Indian support in any war against the British if the United States would give up its claims to the lands purchased by the 1809 treaty. Harrison told Tecumseh frankly that the president would never agree to this.

Despite this rejection, however, Tecumseh continued his efforts to unite all the Indian nations east of the Mississippi to resist white expansion. He was a marvelous speaker and worked tirelessly for his cause. Even Harrison admitted that Tecumseh was "one of those . . . geniuses which spring up occasionally to produce revolutions."

Tecumseh traveled up and down the frontier of the United States talking to the Sauk, the Fox, and the Potawatomi in the north as well as the Creek, the Choctaw, and the Cherokee in the south. Everywhere he spoke for unity among Native Americans:

> **"White people . . . have driven us from the great salt water, forced us over the mountains, and would shortly push us into the lakes. But we are determined to go no farther. The only way to stop this evil is for all red men to unite."**

Shawnee leader Tecumseh struggled to maintain American Indian independence against Americans like William Henry Harrison. Tecumseh believed the only way the Indians could succeed was for the various tribes to unite.

The brutal Battle of Tippecanoe severely weakened American Indian control over land in the Midwest. Among white settlers, however, it made a hero of General William Henry Harrison.

Tecumseh was aided in his crusade by his brother Tenskwatawa (ten-SKWAHT-uh-wah), known as the Prophet. The Prophet attracted many Indians to the confederacy, but he was an ineffective leader. General Harrison marched with about 1,000 troops toward Tenskwatawa's village of Prophetstown in the fall of 1811. Tecumseh, who was away at the time, had cautioned Tenskwatawa to avoid a fight until the confederacy was ready. But the Prophet attacked anyway.

The **Battle of Tippecanoe** took place in present-day Indiana, near where Tippecanoe Creek joins the Wabash River. The battle was fierce and extremely bloody, but Harrison defeated the Indians. The returning Tecumseh was stricken with grief and anger. He knew that the defeat had destroyed his confederacy.

Section 2 Review

• Glossary

IDENTIFY and explain the significance of the following: impressment, Embargo Act, embargo, Non-Intercourse Act, War Hawks, William Henry Harrison, Tecumseh, Battle of Tippecanoe

REVIEWING FOR DETAILS

1. How did Great Britain and France threaten American neutrality?
2. How did Jefferson and Madison try to defend America's neutrality?
3. Why was the push to declare war on Great Britain strongest on the frontier?

REVIEWING FOR UNDERSTANDING

4. **Geographic Literacy** How was the American Indian view of land different from that of the white settlers? What conflicts arose from this difference?
5. **Critical Thinking:** *Generalizations and Stereotypes* What stereotype of Indians did William Henry Harrison hold? How might this view have influenced the way he treated them?

Section 3

THE WAR OF 1812

Multimedia Connections

Explore these related topics and materials on the CD-ROM to enrich your understanding of this section:

Gazetteer

- Fort Detroit
- Lake Erie
- Potomac River

Media Bank

- Time Line: War of 1812
- Battles of the War of 1812
- Naval Warfare, War of 1812
- Bombardment of Fort McHenry

Profiles

- Oliver Hazard Perry

Maryland lawyer and poet Francis Scott Key had been on board the British warship for days. Now he watched as British vessels gleefully bombed Baltimore's Fort McHenry. Would the fort or the American flag that flew overhead survive the attack? Dawn revealed the stars and stripes, tattered but proud! A few days later Key recalled the battle in a poem. It began with, "Oh, say, can you see, by the dawn's early light. . . . " His stirring words eventually became the national anthem.

As you read this section you will find out:

- **How the early battles progressed.**
- **How British attacks in America affected the course of the war.**
- **Why the Battle of New Orleans was significant.**

Early Battles

In June 1812 Congress finally declared war on Great Britain. The first American victories in the War of 1812 occurred at sea. Great Britain was still fighting France, so the Royal Navy could not spare its entire fleet to fight the Americans. Its Atlantic fleet was still much larger than the American navy.

Early in the war, however, the tiny American navy won some important victories against the British. For example, in August 1812, the frigate *Constitution* defeated the British frigate *Guerrière* in a battle off the Maine coast. Then it defeated the British frigate *Java* in another famous battle.

After these early losses, British captains avoided single-ship battles with American frigates. Instead, the British established a naval blockade just as it had during the Revolution.

The Fight for Canada

At the start of the war, Canada seemed an easy target to some Americans. The population of Canada was small, compared to that of the United States. Yet when an American force commanded by General William Hull crossed into Canada from Fort Detroit in July 1812, Indians led by Tecumseh attacked the soldiers. Hull then withdrew to Fort Detroit, pursued by a small Canadian force under General Isaac Brock. Hull soon surrendered. By the end of 1812, the British controlled Lake Erie and most of present-day Indiana and Illinois.

In light of these setbacks, President Madison put General Harrison in command of the army on the northwest frontier. Before a new American invasion of Canada could be launched, however, a British naval squadron had to be cleared from Lake Erie.

The U.S. troops who accomplished this task were under the command of Oliver Hazard Perry. At least 10 percent of these sailors were African American. In September 1813, in the **Battle of Lake Erie**, Perry's force defeated the British forces. "We have met the enemy, and they are ours," Perry informed Harrison.

Now Harrison was able to recapture Fort Detroit and advance into Canada. At the Thames River in southern Canada he defeated the British and their Indian allies on October 5, 1813.

The **Battle of the Thames** allowed the United States to win back the Great Lakes region. Perhaps more significantly, however, the battle resulted in the death of Tecumseh. Without this great leader, the Indian confederacy collapsed.

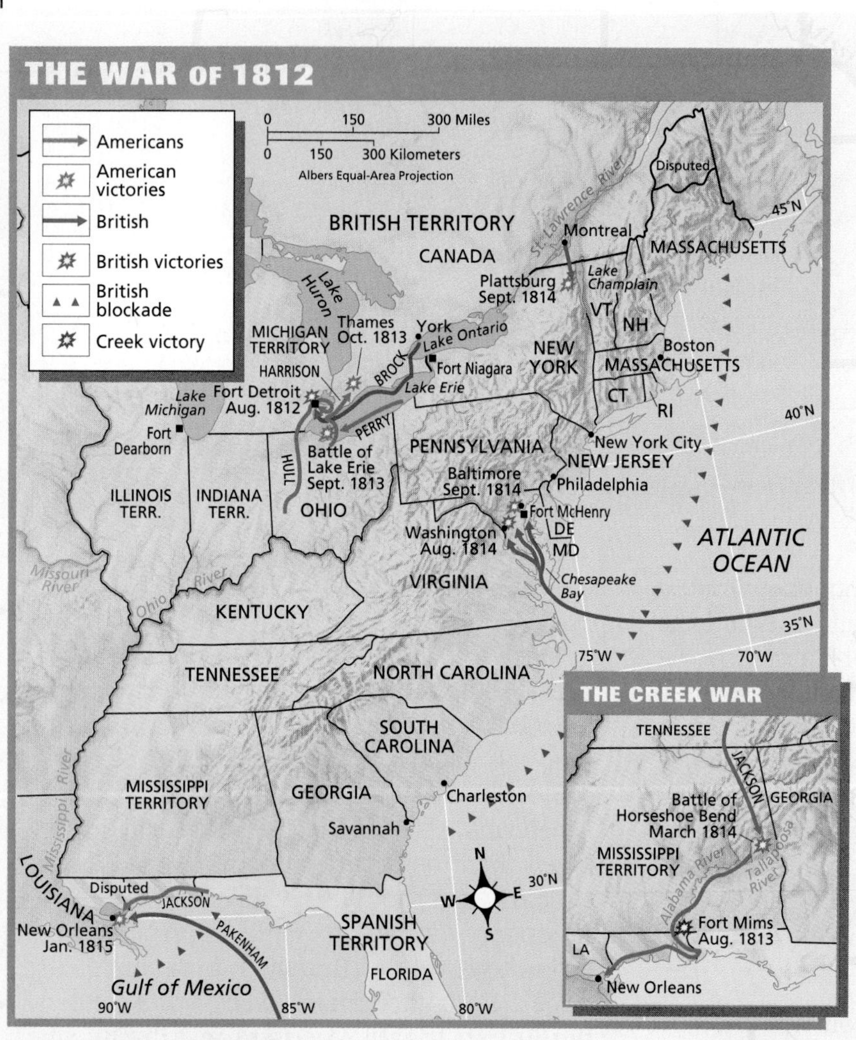

Learning from Maps.
The War of 1812 lasted nearly three years. Battles took place all over the United States.

Place. Which forts were located on the Great Lakes? What battles were fought on the Great Lakes?

• Maps

Southern Battles

In March, 1814, Creek Indian forces that had been aiding the British were defeated by the Tennessee militia. American general

The Granger Collection, New York

This engraving shows the burning of Washington after the British marched through the city.

• **Early View**

Andrew Jackson led a force of 2,000 troops in a series of armed conflicts that ended with the **Battle of Horseshoe Bend**. After this defeat, in which about 750 Creek people were killed, the tribe was forced to give up 20 million acres of land that they controlled.

The defeats suffered by the British were humiliating. The greatest blow to British pride was when U.S. forces burned York, the capital of British Canada. Afterward, the British set out to inflict the same on the U.S. capital and to draw U.S. forces away from Canada. In August 1814 a force of some 4,000 British troops came ashore southeast of Washington. The troops marched into Washington and set fire to all the public buildings, including the Capitol and the White House.

President James Madison was out with the forces trying to halt the British advance. He escaped by fleeing up the Potomac River. First Lady Dolley Madison, protected by a slave, got away from the White House minutes before the British entered. She wrote to her sister as she was leaving:

> **"We have had a battle . . . and here I am still, within sound of the cannon! Mr. Madison comes not. May God protect us! A wagon has been procured [found], and I have had it filled with . . . the most valuable portable articles. . . . I insist on waiting until the large picture of General Washington is secured, and it requires to be unscrewed from the wall."**

First Lady Dolley Madison helped save many articles from the White House before it was burned by the British.

• **Dolley Madison**

The British had no intention of stopping in Washington. On September 13, British warships opened fire on Fort McHenry, which guarded the entrance to Baltimore Harbor. After a whole day and night of firing on the fort with no success, the British fleet withdrew. Baltimore was safe.

The Battle of New Orleans

After being stopped at Baltimore, the British unleashed a greater attack aimed at New Orleans. In late 1814 a force of 7,500 British troops landed on the Louisiana coast and marched through the swampy country without being discovered.

On December 23, 1814, about 2,000 British troops were only seven miles from New Orleans when a muddied messenger burst in to warn General Andrew Jackson, who was in charge of defending the city. Although somewhat surprised, Jackson declared, "Gentlemen, the British are below. We must fight them tonight!" He ordered every available unit forward—a total of about 2,400 men. They included Jackson's regular troops, along with hastily organized militia units. Among the militia were several hundred free African Americans, a band of Choctaw Indians, and a group of pirates.

The Granger Collection, New York

The Battle of New Orleans was the greatest victory for the United States in the War of 1812, even though the war was officially over by the time the battle took place.

Jackson's troops attacked the British at about 8:00 P.M. After two hours of fighting, he decided to fall back before the British could receive reinforcements. His men built an earthen defensive wall behind a canal only five miles from New Orleans.

When the British commander, General Edward Pakenham, finally attacked on January 8, 1815, his men were mowed down by a hail of iron and lead. Over 2,000 British soldiers were killed or wounded. When the smoke cleared, even the toughest veterans were stunned by the sight of the battlefield. "The field was entirely covered with . . . bodies," one Kentucky soldier reported. Only 71 Americans were killed or wounded, however, in this **Battle of New Orleans**.

The loss of life at New Orleans was particularly tragic because the war was officially over before the battle was even fought! This important news had not even reached the United States, however, because communications were slow. Nevertheless, Jackson and his men had won the greatest land victory of the war, and it made the general a popular hero.

Section 3 Review

• Glossary

• Gazetteer

IDENTIFY and explain the significance of the following: Battle of Lake Erie, Battle of the Thames, Battle of Horseshoe Bend, Dolley Madison, Andrew Jackson, Battle of New Orleans

LOCATE and explain the importance of the following: Fort Detroit, Lake Erie, Fort McHenry

REVIEWING FOR DETAILS

1. What was the outcome of early battles at sea?
2. How did British strategy affect the course of the war?

REVIEWING FOR UNDERSTANDING

3. **Geographic Literacy** British forces invaded the United States in three places. How might geography have made this strategy difficult to carry out?
4. **Writing Mastery:** *Describing* Imagine that you are a newspaper reporter after the Battle of New Orleans. Write an article describing the battle's significance.
5. **Critical Thinking:** *Making Comparisons* How was the War of 1812 similar to the American Revolution? How were the two conflicts different?

Section 4
PEACE AND NEW BOUNDARIES

Multimedia Connections
Explore these related topics and materials on the CD–ROM to enrich your understanding of this section:

Media Bank

- *The County Fair*
- Map of New Orleans, 1815
- American Patriotism

Gazetteer

- Belgium

Atlas

- Territorial Expansion, 1820

Readings

- Adams-Onís Treaty
- Monroe Doctrine
- Washington Irving

James Gallatin felt a little shy. Imagine him, just a teenager, at a Christmas dinner to celebrate the treaty that would end the War of 1812! He quickly reminded himself that he was there to assist his father, Albert Gallatin, one of the American diplomats who had negotiated the deal with British officials. After the elaborate meal, which featured roast beef, he described the event in his diary. "It was a scene to be remembered," he wrote. "God grant that there may be always peace between the two nations."

As you read this section you will find out:

- **What effects the War of 1812 had on the United States.**
- **How the United States annexed Florida.**
- **Why the Monroe Doctrine was significant.**

Negotiating Peace

In August 1814, British and American diplomats met at Ghent in Belgium to negotiate an end to the war. The discussions dragged on for months. Finally, everyone realized that the reasons for fighting had disappeared. With Napoleon temporarily defeated, the British no longer needed to stop American ships from carrying goods to Europe or to impress American sailors into the Royal Navy. On Christmas Eve 1814, the delegates signed the **Treaty of Ghent**. Though neither side could claim victory, peace was restored. The treaty did not even mention the issues of neutral rights and impressment. Indeed, it had few concrete terms, but it was generally popular among Americans.

News of the treaty came shortly after the Hartford Convention, a meeting of New

This image of the signing of the Treaty of Ghent on Christmas Eve 1814 was painted by Amedee Forestier 100 years after the signing. The treaty set the terms for the end of the War of 1812.

England Federalists called in December 1814 to protest the war. With peace restored, the goals of the convention were pointless. The Federalists appeared out of date and almost unpatriotic, and their power gradually declined. In the 1816 presidential election, the Federalist candidate, Rufus King, got only 34 votes in the Electoral College to James Monroe's 183 votes.

The War of 1812 not only helped bury the Federalists, it also convinced the nations of Europe that the United States was here to stay. The British in particular began to treat America with greater respect. After the war, conflicts between the two nations were solved by diplomats.

In 1815 Great Britain and the United States signed an agreement ending certain restrictions on America's trade with the British Empire. In 1817 the two nations signed the **Rush-Bagot Agreement**, which provided that neither country would maintain a fleet of warships on the Great Lakes. The **Convention of 1818** set the boundary between the Louisiana Purchase and British Canada at 49° north latitude from northern Minnesota to the Rocky Mountains. The agreement also called for joint control of the disputed area of Oregon Country.

The Annexation of Florida

The Florida question, however, was not as easy to settle. Southerners had hoped that the War of 1812 would pry Florida from Spanish control. By the end of the war, the United States had staked a claim to an area called West Florida, though Spain disputed the claim.

Settlers who lived along the southern frontier of the United States complained of raids by Seminole Indians from Spanish Florida. The settlers also complained that many of their slaves were escaping to Spanish territory.

Late in 1817, President James Monroe sent General Jackson to defeat the Seminole. Ignoring the boundary line, Jackson pursued them into Florida at the head of an army of 2,000 U.S. troops. When the Seminole fell back, avoiding a battle, a furious Jackson seized two British traders and put them on trial for encouraging the Seminole raids. The two men were found guilty and executed. Jackson then captured two Spanish forts, including Pensacola, the capital of West Florida.

Luis de Onís, the Spanish minister to the United States, bitterly protested Jackson's behavior. Most Americans, however, supported Jackson's actions. President Monroe did not want to go against popular sentiment.

Therefore, Secretary of State John Quincy Adams told Onís that Jackson had only acted to protect the security of the United States. Adams also suggested that if Spain could not control what went on in its colony of Florida, it should turn the colony over to the United States.

In the **Adams-Onís Treaty**, signed in February 1819, Spain gave up claims to West Florida and agreed to **cede**, or surrender, the rest of Florida to the United States. Spain also abandoned its claims to the Oregon Country. In return, the United States agreed to pay the $5 million in claims for damages that Americans had against the Spanish government in Florida. In addition, the United States agreed to a boundary between the Louisiana Purchase and Spanish Mexico, giving up any claims to the land that would later become Texas.

The Adams-Onís Treaty was a great triumph for the United States. Adams later said that the day he and Onís signed the treaty was "the most important day of my life." In little more than 40 years the young nation had grown from a string of settlements along the Atlantic coast to a huge country nearly an entire continent wide. Adams believed "the whole continent appears to be destined . . . to be peopled by one nation."

Revolution in Latin America

The Adams-Onís Treaty was just one sign that the great Spanish Empire in the Americas was falling apart. Revolutionary leaders like Simón Bolívar in Venezuela, José de San Martín in what became Argentina, Bernardo O'Higgins in Chile, and Miguel Hidalgo y Costilla in Mexico inspired the people to throw off their colonial masters. By 1822 most of Spain's colonies in the Americas had declared their independence.

These revolutions delighted many people in the United States. The new nations seemed to be copying the example of their North American neighbor. Once free from Spain's control, these new nations would be open to ships and goods from the United States.

Great Britain also profited from Spain's declining influence by greatly increasing its trade with the new republics. British leaders soon found themselves in a difficult position,

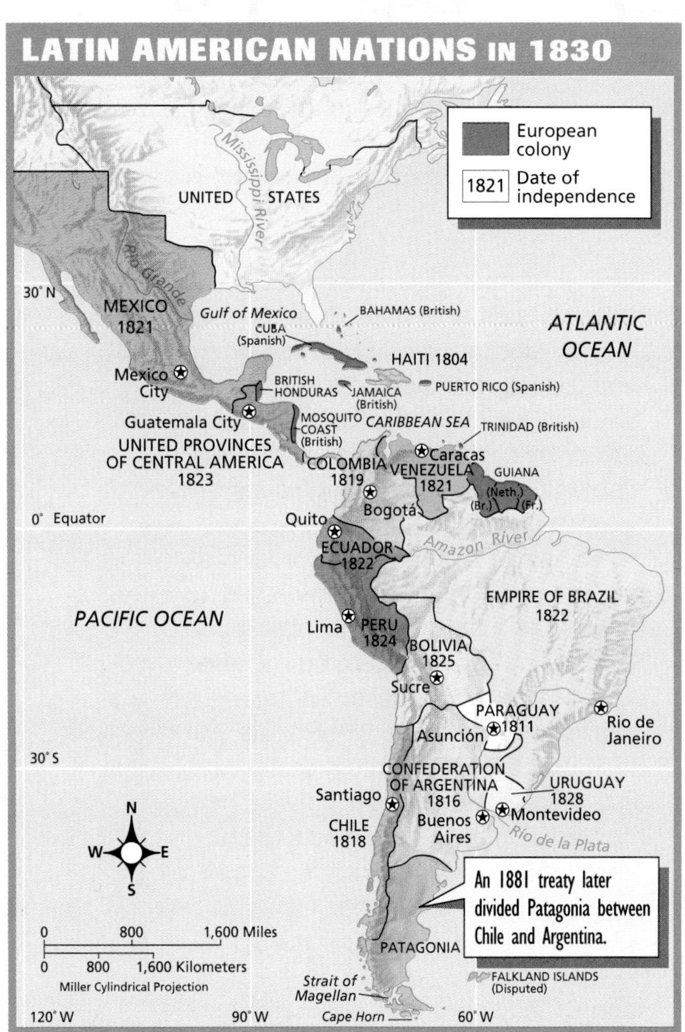

Learning from Maps.
Many countries in Latin America became independent in the early 1800s.

Place. Which nations became independent from 1820 to 1825?

• **Maps**

Many Latin American leaders like Simón Bolívar of Venezuela helped their countries break free from Spanish rule.

• Simón Bolívar

however. They worried about the possibility that other European monarchs might help the king of Spain regain control of his colonies.

In 1823 British foreign minister George Canning proposed that the United States and Great Britain issue a joint declaration. This statement would declare that the two countries would not try to annex any of Spain's former or current colonies and would warn other nations not to try to restore Spanish control in Latin America.

Canning's statement, however, was not one the United States wished to make. The island of Cuba was still a Spanish colony. Someday, the United States might be interested in taking it over. Canning's plan would rule out this possibility. The United States was also reluctant to do anything to help the British increase trade with the new Latin American republics.

The Monroe Doctrine

John Quincy Adams advised President Monroe to issue a statement of his own that dealt with entirely American interests. On December 2, 1823, in a speech to Congress, the president announced what came to be known as the **Monroe Doctrine**. Its main point declared:

> **"that the American continents, by the free and independent condition which they have assumed and maintain, are henceforth not to be considered as subjects for future colonization by any European powers."**

Monroe went on to say that the United States would "consider any attempt" by the European powers to create new colonies in the Americas "as dangerous to our peace and safety." In return, America would not become involved in European affairs.

European leaders were both amused and annoyed by Monroe's declaration. They knew that British seapower was really what would

Through Others' Eyes

The Test of Time

The Monroe Doctrine continued to influence U.S.–Latin American relations into the 1900s. While some U.S. presidents ignored the policy, others used it as an excuse to interfere in Central and South America. Although Europeans and some Latin Americans protested against U.S. involvement, other people from Latin America believed the Monroe Doctrine was important to their countries' protection. For example, in 1916, Simón Planas Suárez, a Venezuelan diplomat, expressed his support for the Monroe Doctrine:

> *"If all our republics were great Powers, strong and wealthy, the Monroe Doctrine would . . . probably be unnecessary. . . . But unfortunately such is not the case. . . . Consequently, the shield which has protected the Latin-American people against possible conquests of their territory by European nations has been the Monroe Doctrine, which . . . faithfully represents the sentiment of all America without distinction of race or latitude."*

keep the European monarchies out of the Americas. The new Latin American nations generally approved of Monroe's ideas and hoped he was sincere. However, some Latin Americans wondered if the United States could really help them in times of crisis.

At the time, the Monroe Doctrine merely announced that America was taking its place on the world diplomatic stage. Later, when the United States became powerful enough to back its words with actions, it was clear that President Monroe had issued a kind of second Declaration of Independence. This one said to the nations of Europe: "Hands off the Western Hemisphere." The Monroe Doctrine became one of the most important statements of U.S. foreign policy ever issued.

The Era of Good Feelings

The Monroe Doctrine was one sign of **nationalism**, or national pride, that swept the United States after the War of 1812. Albert Gallatin, America's minister to France, described this mood:

> **"The war had renewed & reinstated the National feelings & character, which the Revolution had given. . . . The people . . . are more American: they feel & act more as a Nation."**

President Monroe seemed to symbolize the emergence of this national spirit. He had been elected in 1816 without major opposition in part because the Federalists were so unpopular after the War of 1812. When Monroe ran for re-election four years later, no one ran against him. The Federalist Party soon collapsed.

In 1817 President Monroe made a goodwill tour of New England, which had been a Federalist strong point. Yet everywhere he went, enthusiastic crowds greeted the president warmly. As one Boston newspaper wrote, an "Era of Good Feelings" had begun.

National Portrait Gallery, Smithsonian Institution, Washington, DC/Art Resource, NY

President Monroe

• James Monroe

Section 4 Review

• Glossary

• Time Line

IDENTIFY and explain the significance of the following: Treaty of Ghent, James Monroe, Rush-Bagot Agreement, Convention of 1818, Adams-Onís Treaty, cede, Monroe Doctrine, nationalism

REVIEWING FOR DETAILS

1. What were the results of the War of 1812?
2. What was the significance of the Monroe Doctrine?

REVIEWING FOR UNDERSTANDING

3. **Geographic Literacy** How did the location of Florida contribute to its annexation by the United States?
4. **Writing Mastery:** *Expressing* Write a letter to a friend expressing the feelings that swept the nation in the years following the War of 1812.
5. **Critical Thinking:** *Drawing Conclusion* What factors might have led President Monroe to decide to issue the Monroe Doctrine?

CHAPTER 9

The North and Manufacturing (1790–1860)

THEMES IN AMERICAN HISTORY

Technology and Society:
How might new technology affect the growth of industry?

Economic Development:
What impact might the growth of industry have on a country's economy?

Global Relations:
How might immigration affect the development of a society?

Poet Thomas Man described the early effects of factories in the United States:

"For Liberty our fathers fought,
Which with their blood, they dearly bought.
The factory system sets at naught.
A slave at morn, a slave at eve,
It doth my innermost feelings grieve;
The blood runs chilly from my heart,
To see fair Liberty depart."

• Video Opener

• Skill Builder

image above: *American steam locomotive, 1829*

Section 1

FROM FARMS TO FACTORIES

Multimedia Connections

Explore these related topics and materials on the CD–ROM to enrich your understanding of this section:

Media Bank

- Inventions, 1760–1850
- Making Straw Hats
- Cooper's Shop

Gazetteer

- Rhode Island

Biographies

- Samuel Slater

Readings

- *American Notes*

Profiles

- Eli Whitney

In 1801 a young inventor named Eli Whitney took 10 guns to Washington. Before an amazed group of officials, Whitney took the guns apart. He mixed the parts so that it was not possible to know which trigger went with which barrel, and so on. Then, choosing pieces at random, he reassembled the parts into 10 new guns. This demonstration began a new era of industrial expansion that dramatically changed the American way of life.

As you read this section you will find out:

- **How and where the Industrial Revolution began.**
- **Why most American factories were located in the Northeast.**
- **How mass production changed industry.**

The Turn Toward Manufacturing

Since the first English settlements were established in the 1600s, land had been the chief source of wealth in America. This was still the case in the early 1800s. Most people wanted to own land, even if only a small plot. Owning land was a sign of freedom, independence, and stability in society. It seemed as if Americans' preference for farm life might prohibit interest in expanding industry.

Support for manufacturing. The American Revolution had brought the nation political independence. Economic independence was more complicated, however. As soon as the Revolution ended, the British began selling cloth, chinaware, and every sort of manufactured product at bargain prices to win back

American customers. American consumers eagerly purchased these goods, and American producers lost business.

A small but very determined group of Americans saw the advantages of developing manufacturing. Alexander Hamilton was an important spokesperson for this group. Hamilton and others favored a mixed economy, one in which manufacturing existed side by side with agriculture. Some people argued that manufacturing would make America independent of European suppliers.

Because the United States was mainly an agricultural nation, Americans continued to depend on foreign-made goods for many years. However, the conflicts with Britain that led to the War of 1812 made overseas trade almost impossible. As foreign products became less available, quick profits could be made by anyone who could manufacture goods that previously had been imported.

Many Americans came to believe that manufacturing should be an important part of the economy. They realized that if Americans could produce more manufactured goods, they would be less dependent on foreign sources. Even Thomas Jefferson, who had opposed government assistance to industry, wrote in 1816:

> **"To be independent for the comforts of life we must fabricate [make] them ourselves. We must now place the manufacturer by the side of the agriculturist. . . . Shall we make our own comforts or go without them at the will of a foreign nation? . . . Experience has taught me that manufactures are now as necessary to our independence as to our comfort."**

The Industrial Revolution. Great Britain had been able to dominate the world market for many years because British manufacturers had largely shifted their work from hand tools to power-driven machinery. Historians have labeled this shift the **Industrial Revolution**, a period of great industrial expansion.

The process began in Great Britain in the 1700s. The first steps toward industrialization came in the **textiles**, or cloth, industry. Before industrialization, most families made much of their own clothing. Almost every home had a spinning wheel for making thread, and some also had a loom for weaving cloth. It took much longer to spin thread, however, than it took to weave the thread into cloth. This meant that one weaver used all the thread that several spinners could produce.

Americans imported many items from overseas, such as this British-made water pitcher, which celebrates the first U.S. census in 1790.

Sometime around 1764 James Hargreaves, a British weaver, built a hand-operated mechanical spinning wheel called the spinning jenny. Some people say the machine was named after Hargreaves's wife. Others say the name came from "gin," a short form of the word *engine.* Spinning jennies were relatively small, inexpensive, and easy to build. Before long, many textile manufacturers had adopted Hargreaves's useful invention.

The spinning jenny increased output, but it did not greatly reduce the price of cotton cloth. Because cotton fibers were not very strong, cotton could not be used very easily to make long threads for weaving cloth. By 1769 a former barber named Richard Arkwright solved this problem. He invented a spinning machine, called a water frame, that produced much stronger cotton thread. With the widespread use of the water frame, the price of textiles fell dramatically.

Arkwright's spinning machine was much too large to fit into people's homes, however. He set up his machines in mills along streams, where water could be used to power the new

James Hargreaves's spinning jenny greatly improved cloth production. This woman is working with an advanced version of Hargreaves's jenny.

equipment. Instead of taking the work to the people in their homes, Arkwright brought people to the work in the mills. In this way, Arkwright and others like him created Britain's first factories.

The Factory Comes to America

Arkwright's spinning machines proved so successful that British cloth was soon being exported to every part of the world. The British government had no intention of losing the competitive advantage that resulted from its new industrial methods. The British would not allow the export of textile-making machinery, and workers who were familiar with the machines could not leave the country.

Despite government opposition, a number of skilled workers did manage to make their way to America. One of the most important was Samuel Slater, who at one time had worked for Arkwright. When Slater decided to come to America, he memorized the designs for the new cotton-spinning machinery.

Slater arrived in New York in 1789. He soon met Moses Brown, whose family had been engaged in commerce and small-scale manufacturing in Providence, Rhode Island, for generations. Slater formed a partnership with Brown and another investor, William Almy, who was Brown's son-in-law. Slater agreed to produce cotton-spinning machines in Pawtucket, Rhode Island. By 1793 the task was complete.

Slater's machines spun cotton thread that was better than homespun cotton. Soon, Slater was operating his own factories as well as designing them for other people.

Slater's factories made nothing but thread. Brown and Almy sold some of this thread at their store in Providence. The rest of the thread was supplied to workers, who wove it into cloth on looms in their homes. The weavers returned the cloth to Brown and Almy, who paid them a set price per yard for the cloth they wove. Brown and Almy then sold the cloth in their store. This system of take-home work remained an important part of production long after factories became widespread. In addition to cloth, many products such as hats and shoes were produced in a similar manner.

Encouraged by Slater's success with these textile producers, other Americans began to build factories. Much of this early industry developed in the northeastern United States. The location of the new factories and the towns

Samuel Slater's factory in Pawtucket, Rhode Island, relied on nearby waterfalls for power. Most early factories were built in similar locations to take advantage of waterpower.

that grew up around them was influenced by the region's geography.

Since the machinery in the factories was driven by waterpower, the factories were built beside swiftly moving streams and rivers, where waterwheels turned the machinery. Particularly ideal were sites in the Northeast where rivers drop from the Appalachian foothills to the Atlantic Coastal Plain in small waterfalls. Owners built factories all along the northeastern seaboard to take advantage of this power source.

Mass Production

America contained vast reserves of many natural resources that were useful to the manufacturing process. Forests provided lumber for buildings and machines, and iron could be used to make tools and nails. Although the natural resources existed in good supply, changes had to take place before manufacturers could produce large numbers of identical goods in great quantities, a process known as **mass production**.

Industrial **technology**—the use of tools to produce goods or to do work—used in the late 1700s seems quite inefficient by modern standards. Most items were made by skilled artisans, thus each item was slightly different from the other. If part of an item broke, it took a long time to fix because an artisan would have to craft a new part from scratch. In some cases the entire item would have to be rebuilt.

Using this system of production, most manufacturing was very slow. For example, it took the new government arsenal at Springfield, Massachusetts, two years to turn out only 245 muskets. When war threatened between the United States and France in the 1790s, Congress purchased 7,000 muskets from foreign sources. At this point, several inventors, the most famous of whom was Eli Whitney, stepped in to try to improve the nation's industrial technology.

Whitney believed that he could manufacture muskets by using **interchangeable parts**. This meant that all the parts for a certain model of the gun would be exactly the same and could be used with the pieces of any other gun of the same model. Thus, when a part on a gun broke, that part could be fixed more quickly than before. Whitney explained the key to his strategy:

> **"One of my primary objects is to form the tools so the tools themselves shall fashion the work and give to every part its just proportion—which when once accomplished, will give expedition [speed], uniformity [sameness], and exactness to the whole."**

In 1798 Whitney signed a government contract and received an advance payment of $5,000 to get his business started. It took him over two years to build the equipment that would enable him to turn out identical parts. Within a few months of starting production, his shop near New Haven, Connecticut, had produced 500 muskets.

Whitney's and others' demonstrations of the importance of interchangeable parts revolutionized manufacturing in America. Soon, machine parts could be replaced with relative ease, making industrial production more efficient and economical.

Before the invention of interchangeable parts, most mechanical items had to be forged by hand by artisans like these. It took them a long time to craft new items from scratch when one broke. The process saved time and labor.

Section 1 Review

• Glossary

IDENTIFY and explain the significance of the following: Industrial Revolution, textiles, Samuel Slater, mass production, technology, Eli Whitney, interchangeable parts

REVIEWING FOR DETAILS

1. How and where did the Industrial Revolution begin?
2. How did mass production change the way goods were made?

REVIEWING FOR UNDERSTANDING

3. **Geographic Literacy** Why did most early American factories develop in the Northeast?
4. **Writing Mastery:** *Classifying* Write a paragraph explaining the advantages and disadvantages of having workers produce goods in factories rather than in their homes.
5. **Critical Thinking:** *Making Comparisons* How do mass-produced items differ from products crafted by artisans? What might have been some advantages and disadvantages of the two types of production?

Section 2
LIFE IN THE FACTORIES

Multimedia Connections

Explore these related topics and materials on the CD–ROM to enrich your understanding of this section:

Profiles
- Sarah Bagley
- Francis Cabot Lowell

Media Bank

- Cyrus H. McCormick
- Chuck Factory
- Mill Workers

Simulation
- Choosing a Factory Site

Readings
- Rules for Boardinghouses

In the 1830s Sarah Monroe helped launch one of the first organizations for female workers. Monroe explained, "If it is unfashionable for the men to bear oppression in silence, why should it not also become unfashionable with the women?" As factories increased production, many workers grew unhappy with labor conditions. Some organized to protest wage cuts or increased working hours. Although few of these early efforts were very successful, they provided workers with a way to voice their concerns about the new industrial era.

As you read this section you will find out:

- **Who worked in factories.**
- **What working and living conditions were like for mill workers.**
- **Why workers organized unions.**

Recruiting a Labor Force

The northeastern section of the United States—the New England states, plus New York, New Jersey, and Pennsylvania—soon became the nation's major manufacturing area. In large cities like New York and Boston, one could find a variety of industries. In smaller factory towns, the economy often centered around one industry. For example, Lynn, Massachusetts, was a center for the shoe industry, while Danbury, Connecticut, focused on hat manufacturing.

In the 1790s the first American factories were just being built. The question of who would work in these factories soon arose. In Great Britain most early factory jobs were filled by tenant farmers who had been thrown out of work when owners fenced the land in order to raise sheep. This process has come to be known as the **enclosure movement**. In America, however, most farmers still owned their own land. Most artisans, such as carpenters and shoemakers, owned their own workshops. Few Americans worked for wages, and still fewer were willing to work in factories.

The early textile manufacturers solved this problem in two ways. One was by employing children. Samuel Slater's first spinning machines were operated by seven boys and two girls ranging in age from 7 to 12. Slater employed these children because their small hands could operate the machinery easily. He paid them between 25 and 55 cents a week, much less than adults in Rhode Island, who usually earned over $3 a week.

Child labor seemed perfectly reasonable to most people. Farm children had always worked, and poor families were delighted to have any money their children could earn. Factories sometimes employed entire families.

The Lowell Girls

Another method of attracting factory workers was developed by Francis Lowell, a Boston merchant. In 1810 Lowell went to Britain, where he spent the next two years visiting spinning and weaving mills. He was deeply impressed by their efficiency. Like Slater, he carefully memorized the layout of the mills, hoping to be able to reproduce them in New England.

By the time Lowell returned to the United States, the War of 1812 had broken out. British goods were no longer available. Lowell organized a group of investors called the Boston Associates and hired a young engineer named Paul Moody to help him build power looms copied from designs he had seen in Britain.

The Associates built a factory at Waltham, Massachusetts, where they could use the waterpower of the Charles River. The looms were finished in 1814, and production started the following year. This factory spun cotton into thread and also wove it into cloth with machines.

Lowell was determined not to employ poor families. Instead, he hired young unmarried women from nearby farms. Many of these young women planned to work for wages for only a short time to earn extra money for their families before they got married.

Young People In History

Factory Workers

"Families wanted—Ten or Twelve good respectable families consisting of four or five children each, from nine to sixteen years of age, are wanted to work in a cotton mill." This was the text of an 1828 advertisement in Rhode Island. Such ads were quite common in the early 1800s. During that time, many children worked in factories to help their families make ends meet.

Some early textile mills preferred to hire children to work in the same mills as their parents. That way the parents could oversee their children's work. Some reformers, however, worried that mill life was unhealthy for children, as it kept them out of school and exposed them to dangerous working conditions. Children were often mistreated by factory supervisors. Others lost limbs and some were even killed in industrial accidents. Still, child labor continued in many factories until the 1900s.

The Granger Collection, New York

Young workers head to the factory.

The Granger Collection, New York

Many women wrote articles for the Lowell Offering, *a magazine produced by female factory workers.*

At first, life in the factory community seemed both profitable and interesting to many **Lowell girls**, as the female workers were called. They lived in company dormitories, where their activities were closely supervised. Lucy Larcom began working at Lowell when she was about 11 years old. "I liked it better than going to school," she recalled years later. Larcom added:

• **Home to Factory**

> **"I regard it as one of the privileges of my youth that I was permitted to grow up among those active, interesting girls. . . . They were earnest and capable, ready to undertake anything that was worth doing. . . . They gave me a larger, firmer ideal of womanhood."**

The success of Lowell's business system encouraged other manufacturers to construct similar mills. Conditions varied from mill to mill. As time passed, however, living and working conditions in many mill towns became harsh as owners tried to increase profits by demanding more work from employees. Some workers became unhappy with their situation. In 1845 a Lowell girl, now known only as Julianna, expressed what many factory workers were feeling:

> **"Crowded into a small room, which contains three bed and six females, . . . what chance is there for *studying?* and much less so for thinking and reflecting? . . . Incarcerated [Held captive] within the walls of a factory . . . drilled there from five [A.M.] until seven o'clock [P.M.], year after year . . . what *will* be the natural, rational result? What but ignorance, misery, and *premature decay* of both *body* and *intellect?*"**

Efforts to Help Workers

Sarah Bagley, another Lowell girl, became so unhappy with the system that in 1844 she founded the Lowell Female Labor Reform Association to campaign for laws improving working conditions in factories. Bagley organized branches of the Association in other New England factory towns. She also published articles attacking the "cotton lords" who controlled the textile mills.

A group called the Lowell Female Labor Reform Association was one of many new **labor unions**, or organizations workers form to improve their conditions. Although there had been some labor

Young women like these often learned how to make thread at home before going off to work in textile mills.

The Granger Collection, New York

• **Working Conditions**

organizations since the colonial period, few had been very successful. In the 1830s and 1840s, however, many skilled workers joined unions. They protested long hours and low wages or wage reductions.

Sometimes workers would stage a **strike**—a refusal to work until their demands for improved conditions were met. Few early strikes were successful, however. The courts and other authorities tended to view unions as illegal attempts to "control" wages. They usually sided with the employers.

The harsh conditions and long hours of factory work caused a number of reformers to try to improve the lives of these workers. Seth Luther, a carpenter and textile worker, was one of the most outspoken critics of the factory system. In particular, he criticized the employment of children in factories. Instead of working, he argued, every child should receive a good education at public expense. Luther also called for shorter work hours and better working conditions for all laborers.

Many less-radical reformers supported the movement to reduce the workday from the usual dawn-to-darkness routine to 10 hours. Employers, however, had much more influence with legislators, and the 10-hour movement made slow progress. In 1840, however, the federal government did set a 10-hour limit on the workday of its employees.

Many people in Lynn, Massachusetts, showed up to express their support for a strike by shoe-factory workers. The strike parade included some 800 female workers, some 4,000 male workers and firefighters, a military unit, and a band.

The Granger Collection, New York

Section 2 Review

• Glossary

IDENTIFY and explain the significance of the following: enclosure movement, Francis Lowell, Lowell girls, Sarah Bagley, labor unions, strike, Seth Luther

REVIEWING FOR DETAILS

1. What groups of people worked in early factories?
2. What were working and living conditions like at the mills?
3. Why did some workers organize unions?

REVIEWING FOR UNDERSTANDING

4. **Writing Mastery:** *Creating* Write a poem or short story expressing how some Lowell girls might have felt about their lives.
5. **Critical Thinking:** *Recognizing Point of View* What might have been some of the factors affecting Seth Luther's view of the factory system?

Section 3

LIFE IN THE CITIES

Multimedia Connections

Explore these related topics and materials on the CD-ROM to enrich your understanding of this section:

Gazetteer

- Germany
- Ireland

Media Bank

- Immigrant Music
- Occupations, Boston, 1850
- Cartoon of Immigrant Woman
- Immigrant Culture

Atlas

- Boston, 1850

Shortly after moving to America, Englishwoman Alice Barlow wrote to her family overseas to describe her new home. "Tell my old friends," she declared, ". . . if they were here, they would know nothing of poverty." The new home she described was overflowing with opportunity. Barlow's husband had already found a job in a textile factory. The nation's cities attracted thousands of people like the Barlows who were seeking prosperity and a better life.

As you read this section you will find out:

- **Why Irish and German immigration increased.**
- **What problems emerged as urban population grew.**
- **How the rise of a middle class affected women.**

Immigration from Europe

Sometimes when early factory workers organized strikes, they were replaced by **immigrants**—foreign-born people who had recently moved to the United States. The number of immigrants, particularly Europeans, coming to America was increasing yearly.

Between 1790 and 1820, only about 234,000 immigrants had entered the United States. During the next 30 years almost 2.5 million people crossed the Atlantic bound for America. Nearly all of these immigrants came to the United States because they were poor and hoped to earn a better living.

The majority came from Ireland, Germany, and Great Britain. In the 1840s disease destroyed most of the potato crop in Ireland. Facing starvation, thousands of Irish people came to the United States. Many Germans

moved to escape political turmoil caused by a failed revolution in 1848. Others came to gain religious freedom or better jobs.

Most immigrants settled among people of similar national, religious, and ethnic backgrounds. While about half the German immigrants were Protestant, about one third were Catholic and one fifth were Jewish. Most Irish immigrants were Catholic. They established many new Catholic churches in the nation's large cities. By the mid-1800s Catholicism was one of the largest religious denominations in the United States.

Some Americans opposed unlimited immigration because they believed that too many newcomers would destroy American institutions. They were called **nativists** because they wanted to keep the country for "native Americans." They conveniently forgot, however, that the only real native Americans were American Indians. Fear of competition for jobs fueled the anger of many nativists, such as Boston resident Jesse Chickering, who complained in 1850:

> **"The increased competition for employment has diminished the facility [ease] of obtaining it. . . . In many employments the foreigners, at first compelled [forced] by necessity to labor for small wages, have at length almost excluded the natives."**

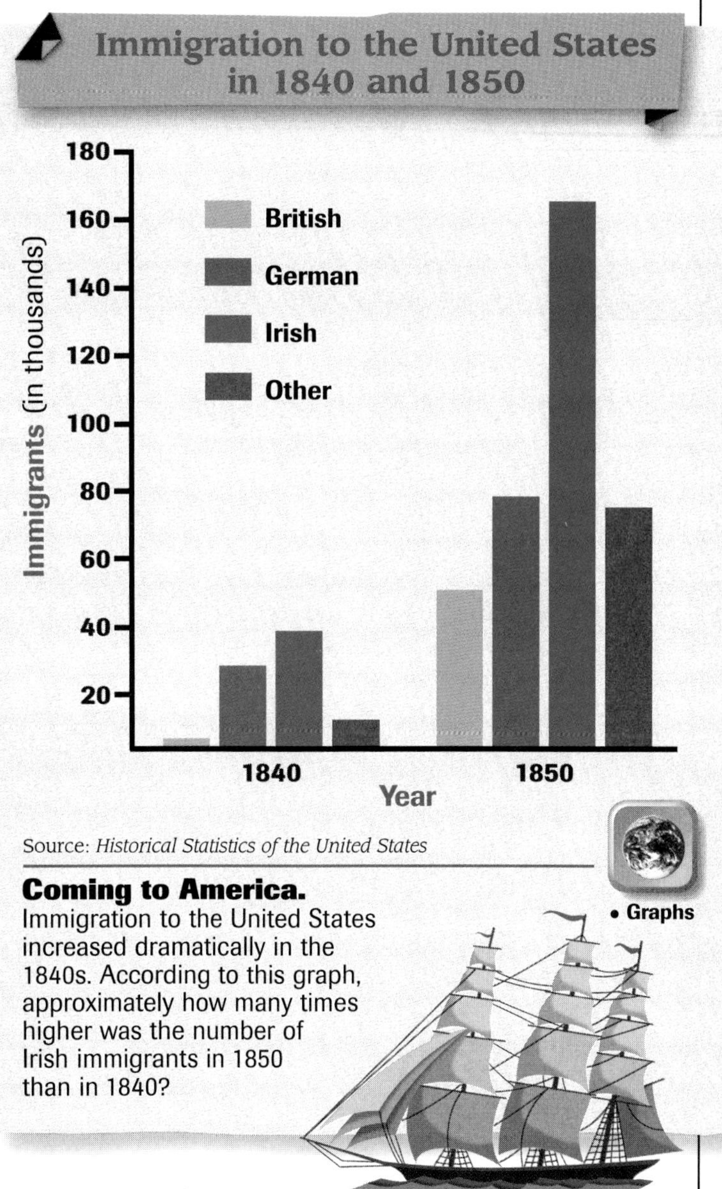

Coming to America. Immigration to the United States increased dramatically in the 1840s. According to this graph, approximately how many times higher was the number of Irish immigrants in 1850 than in 1840?

Most nativists were members of various Protestant churches. They were particularly hostile to the Irish Catholics, who were arriving in large numbers. Most of the Irish immigrants were poor, unskilled, and willing to work for less money than most native-born workers.

In 1834 a nativist mob burned a Catholic convent near Boston. Similar violent incidents occurred in other parts of the country. In 1849 some nativists went so far as to form a new, anti-immigrant political party, later known as the American Party. Members of the secretive organization were often called **Know-Nothings** because when asked about the organization, they replied, "I know nothing about it."

City Life in America

While many immigrants who came to America between 1820 and 1850 became farmers, a significant number settled in the cities of the Northeast. They were not the only people coming to the cities, however.

By the mid-1800s, many cities were becoming very crowded. This painting shows downtown New York City around the 1850s. At that time, New York was already becoming a bustling city.

Urban growth. When they grew up, many children of American farmers moved to towns and cities. The expanding industrial economy offered them many new job opportunities in all areas of trade and commerce.

Free African Americans also came to the northern cities in large numbers. However, many white factory employers refused to hire black workers for well-paying, skilled jobs. Most unions excluded black workers entirely. Thus, many urban African Americans worked in service industries instead of factories. In New York, Philadelphia, and Boston, many African American men found jobs as house servants, waiters, barbers, coachmen, shoe shiners, and porters. African American women often worked as laundresses, dressmakers, seamstresses, and cooks.

• African Americans in the North

With all these new arrivals, the number of people living in towns and cities rose from about 5 percent of the U.S. population in 1790 to about 18 percent in 1850. In 1790 there were only 24 urban centers in the United States with a population of 2,500 or more. By 1850 there were about 235.

Urban problems. American cities underwent many growing pains during this period. As cities grew, slums developed because the cities could not absorb people as fast as the newcomers arrived. Large apartment buildings were broken up into many small units. People even lived in attics and cellars.

In these buildings several families often lived crowded together in single dwellings. Rents were usually low, but because there were so many apartments in each building, the owners could make very large profits. Little, if any, of the profits went to keeping the buildings in repair. They were often unsanitary and unsafe.

Since few city streets were paved, there was always mud in rainy weather. This gave rise to an often-told joke about the poor condition of city streets: A passing citizen offers

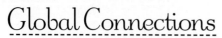

Global Connections

German Immigrants

The immigrants we refer to as "Germans" were not all from a single country known as Germany. In the mid-1800s Germany as we know it was not yet a unified nation like France or Great Britain. Instead, it was a group of independent countries in which the citizens spoke a common German language.

When French emperor Napoleon tried to conquer Europe in the early 1800s, many people in the German-speaking countries realized how vulnerable they were on their own. One group in particular, known as Liberals, wanted to create a unified government under a constitutional system.

In 1848 Liberals launched a revolution for constitutional reform. Anti-Liberals not only defeated the revolutionaries but also began a campaign to silence Liberal supporters. To escape harsh new restrictions, thousands of "Germans" fled their homelands for the United States.

help to a man who has sunk up to his neck in a huge mud puddle. "No need to worry," replies the man. "I have a horse under me."

Polluted water and the lack of sanitation often led to epidemics of contagious diseases. One of the most dreaded diseases was cholera, which attacks the intestinal system. During cholera epidemics, poor people living in dirty, crowded apartments died by the thousands. Some people, therefore, thought the disease was a punishment for poverty.

Most American cities did not have police or fire departments. Even the largest cities had no more than a few police officers, who usually did not have uniforms to identify them. Volunteer fire companies put out fires. Cash prizes were sometimes awarded to the companies that responded most quickly to alarms, causing much competition between these associations. When fires broke out, fire companies sometimes fought each other rather than the blaze.

Urban attractions. Despite its problems, many people found the hustle and bustle of city life exciting. The cities were the cultural centers of American life. More theaters and concert halls were built. Book and magazine publishing prospered. Cafes, taverns, and libraries attracted artists, writers, and crowds of ordinary people searching for excitement, adventure, and jobs.

The Middle Class

The beginnings of industrialization had both positive and negative effects on families living in cities. As the American economy moved steadily from an agricultural base to manufacturing, family life changed. The industrial changes in the Northeast brought dramatic improvements in the average family's standard of living. By 1840 the industrial surge had increased personal income in the region about 35 percent above the national average. As a result of this change, a new social class developed between the rich and the poor—the **middle class**.

Middle-class families were usually headed by a father who owned a small business or worked in a management or other professional job created by the new economy. Middle-class wives usually did not work

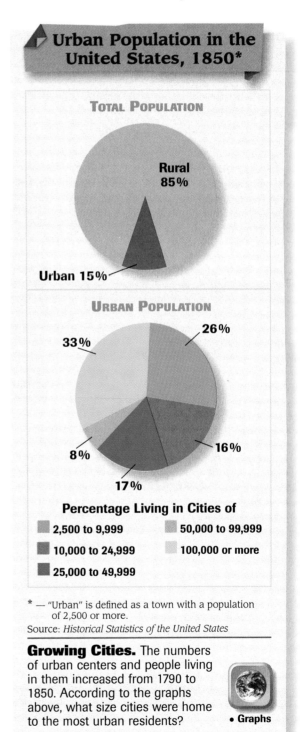

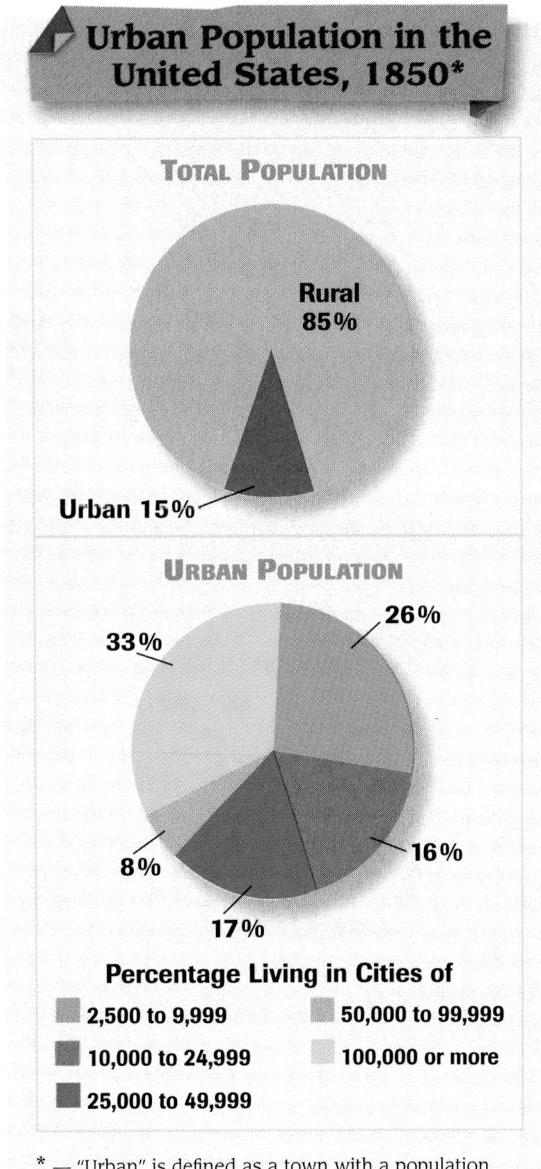

* — "Urban" is defined as a town with a population of 2,500 or more.

Source: *Historical Statistics of the United States*

Growing Cities. The numbers of urban centers and people living in them increased from 1790 to 1850. According to the graphs above, what size cities were home to the most urban residents?

• Graphs

outside of the home. A middle-class woman's lifestyle was normally determined by her husband's wealth and by the type of job he held.

• Household Chores

The wives of wealthy city husbands had a great deal of leisure time compared to farm women or working-class women. This was because they could employ servants and buy items they needed.

The fact that many middle-class women had more time on their hands increased their interest in education. Several all-female academies were founded to educate women. One of the best was Catharine Beecher's school in Hartford, Connecticut.

Beecher wrote and lectured extensively on women's education. She also founded the American Women's Educational Association and other teacher-education institutions. Beecher's goal was to establish teacher-training schools run by master teachers. As she explained in 1835 in *An Essay on the Education of Female Teachers*:

> **"When these teachers shall have succeeded in training classes of teachers on the best system their united wisdom can devise, there will be instructors prepared for other seminaries [schools] . . . ; and thus a regular and systematic course of education can be disseminated [spread] through the nation."**

Beecher and other supporters of female education believed that the future of the nation lay in the hands of its women.

A middle-class family relaxes at home around 1840. Many prosperous and educated families would entertain themselves in the evenings by having one member of the family read to everyone else.

Section 3 Review

• Glossary

IDENTIFY and explain the significance of the following: immigrants, nativists, Know-Nothings, middle class, Catharine Beecher

REVIEWING FOR DETAILS

1. Why did many Irish and German immigrants come to America?
2. How did the rise of a middle class affect women's lives?

REVIEWING FOR UNDERSTANDING

3. **Geographic Literacy** What were some of the problems that emerged as urban areas grew?
4. **Writing Mastery:** *Describing* Imagine that you are an immigrant living in an American city. Write a letter to a family member overseas describing your new community.
5. **Critical Thinking:** *Generalizations and Stereotypes* "Look at the hordes of . . . Irish thieves and vagabonds roaming about our streets," exclaimed a nativist in the 1840s. How does this statement reflect a use of stereotypes?

Section 4
TRANSPORTATION AND GROWTH

Multimedia Connections

Explore these related topics and materials on the CD–ROM to enrich your understanding of this section:

Gazetteer

- Lake Erie

Profiles

- Daniel Boone
- Robert Fulton

Atlas

- National Road

Media Bank

- St. Louis Waterfront
- First Locomotive
- Transportation Methods
- Tom Thumb and Horse Car

Writer Mark Twain described one of the many inventions that radically altered American life in the 1800s: "She is long and sharp and trim and pretty. She has two fancy-topped chimneys . . . and a fanciful pilothouse. . . . The furnace doors are open and the fires glaring bravely." The mysterious creature was a steamboat. Such improvements in transportation encouraged the growth of business and brought the nation's people closer together.

As you read this section you will find out:

- **How the government tried to improve overland transportation.**
- **What effect canals and steamboats had on water travel.**
- **What advantages railroads offered over other forms of travel.**

New Roads and Turnpikes

As cities expanded, they became so large that it was no longer easy to walk from one end to the other. By the 1830s New York City had dozens of carriages, each drawn by two or four horses with seating for 12 passengers. In the winter some drivers replaced their wheels with runners, turning the carriages into sleighs. Carriages could soon be found in most cities, and service between many cities was also available.

In the countryside, nearly all roads were unpaved. They turned into seas of mud after every heavy rain and were bumpy and rough in dry weather. Most long roads were built by private companies. The builders collected tolls, or fees, from people who used them. The tollgate was usually a pike, or pole, blocking the road. When the traveler paid the toll, the

The National Road made travel overland much easier, as these travelers experienced in the 1850s. As a result, thousands more people moved west of the Appalachian Mountains.

The Granger Collection, New York

pike was raised or turned aside to let the traveler pass. These toll roads were thus called **turnpikes**.

Overland travel was both expensive and slow. In the early 1800s it cost more to haul a ton of goods several miles overland than to bring the same ton all the way across the Atlantic Ocean! This was one reason why rebellious Pennsylvania farmers in the 1790s turned their surplus corn into whiskey.

To improve overland transportation, the federal government began construction of the **National Road** in 1811 at Cumberland, Maryland. The route crossed over the mountains in southwestern Pennsylvania and ended at the site of present-day Wheeling, West Virginia. Gradually, it was extended west to Vandalia, Illinois.

The road was a remarkable engineering achievement. It had a foundation of solid stone and a top of gravel, and it carried countless numbers of wagons and carts. The road was constructed so well that some of its bridges are still in use today.

Canals

The easiest means of moving goods and people was by water. The problem was that few American rivers and lakes were connected. Fortunately, many could be joined by digging **canals**, or artificial waterways.

Goods were carried along canals on barges. These barges were towed by horses or mules, which walked alongside the canal. It was much easier for animals to pull heavy loads on canal barges than it was to pull them over dry land. Thus, canal transportation was much cheaper than transportation by road.

Canals were expensive to build, however, and could not be constructed without great financial support. In 1817 New York governor DeWitt Clinton, who had been a member of the state canal commission, persuaded the state legislature to build a canal running from the Hudson River across the state all the way to Lake Erie. As Clinton explained it, the canal:

> **"will create the greatest inland trade ever witnessed. The most fertile and extensive regions of America will avail [make use] themselves of its facilities for a market. All their surplus . . . will concentrate in the city of New York."**

This engraving shows a section of the Erie Canal at Lockport, New York, in 1838.

The Granger Collection, New York

The route of the **Erie Canal** would pass through the Mohawk Valley, a gap in the Appalachian Mountains where the land was fairly level. This meant that the water would not have to be raised and lowered very much by canal locks.

In 1817 work on "Clinton's Big Ditch" began. Much of the digging was done by Irish immigrants. The first section was opened in 1819. In 1825 the Erie Canal was completed. The canal was an engineering wonder: some 363 miles long, 40 feet wide, and 4 feet deep. It cost the state $7 million, an enormous amount of money at the time.

However, as Clinton had predicted, the canal attracted so much traffic that the tolls collected soon paid its cost. The cost of shipping goods fell from $100 a ton before the canal was built to $5 a ton afterward. The canal became the busiest route for goods and people moving west.

When people in other states saw how profitable the Erie Canal was, they hurried to build canals of their own. By 1840 more than 3,300 miles of canals had been built throughout the country, farther than the distance across the continent.

The canals united the different sections of the country and stimulated their economies. Farm crops could now be shipped cheaply to distant markets. Products manufactured in the East no longer had to be lugged over the Appalachian Mountains by wagon.

Steamboats

Although much more economical, travel by canal was slow—mules pulling a barge could only cover about one mile an hour. What water transportation needed was a new

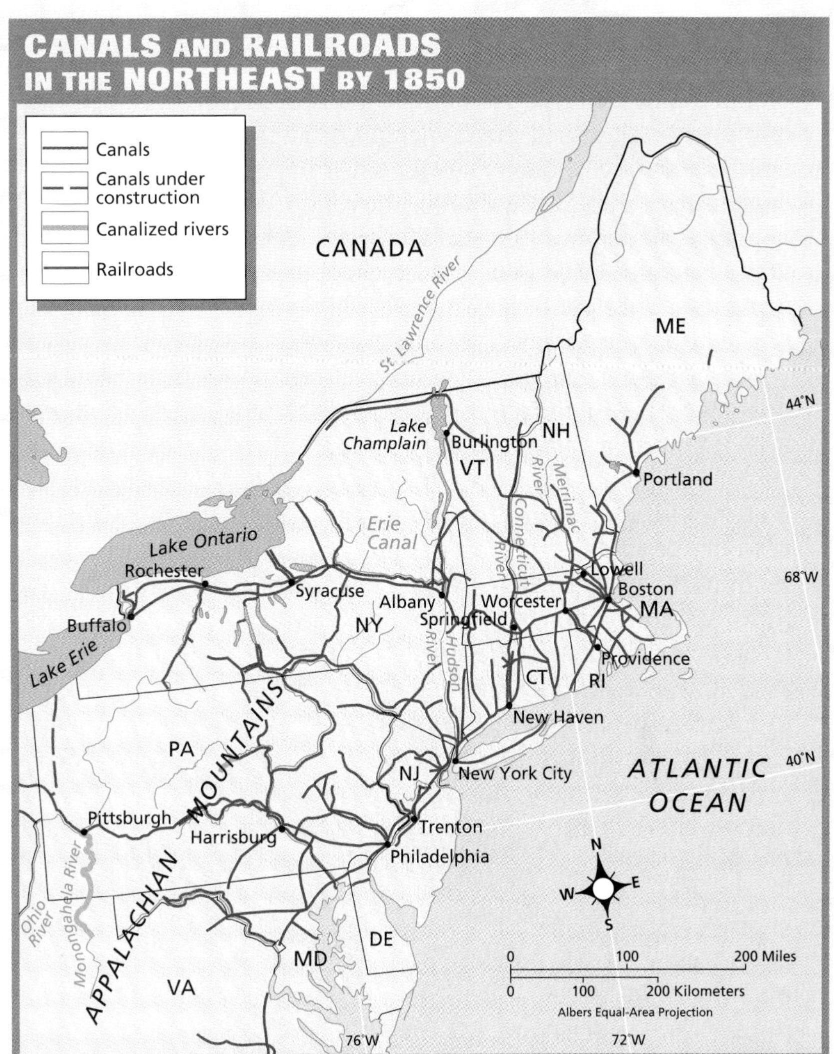

Learning from Maps.
By 1850 much of the Northeast was connected by railroads and canals. People and goods could move more easily.

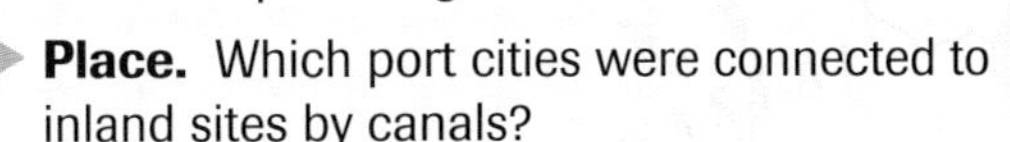
Place. Which port cities were connected to inland sites by canals?

source of power. British technology supplied the answer. In the 1760s a Scottish man named James Watt invented a practical steam engine. Watt's invention, which used the energy of burning wood and coal, was used to run machines in factories. Steam power meant that factories no longer had to be located near dams or swiftly moving rivers.

If steam could drive machines, could it also be used to move boats? One of the first Americans to ask this question was John Fitch, a silversmith and clockmaker. In 1787 Fitch launched a steamboat propelled by 12 paddles on the Delaware River. Among the many spectators who witnessed the launching of Fitch's smoke-belching monster were several delegates from the Constitutional Convention in nearby Philadelphia. Shortly afterward, Fitch built a second, larger boat, which carried passengers and freight between Philadelphia and Burlington, New Jersey.

For another 20 years, however, steamboats were neither efficient nor reliable. Then Robert Fulton, an artist turned inventor, built a steamboat on the East River in New York City. Fulton called it the *Clermont*, but those who had watched it being built called it "Fulton's Folly," believing it would never work. In August 1807 the *Clermont* made its first voyage, up the Hudson River from New York City to Albany. The 130-mile trip took 32 hours, compared to a time of four days by sailing ship.

An associate of Fulton's, Nicholas Roosevelt, built the *New Orleans* in Pittsburgh in 1811. This boat soon made the 1,950-mile trip from Pittsburgh to New Orleans in just 14 days. Previously the journey had taken four to six weeks. An even more dramatic breakthrough occurred in 1815 when the steamboat *Enterprise* sailed up the Mississippi River from New Orleans to Pittsburgh against the current. Before that time, a trip upstream from New Orleans to Pittsburgh took more than four months. Soon, dozens of steamboats were churning up and down the western rivers of the United States.

By the 1830s steamboats had become an important part of the transportation system. One European traveler noted:

> **"The essential point is . . . that they should be numerous; . . . well commanded or not, it matters little, if they move at a rapid rate, and are navigated at little expense. The circulation of steamboats is as necessary to the West, as that of the blood is to the human system."**

Railroads

Soon after the canals and steamboats, there came an even more significant transportation advance—the railroad. One of the first steam-driven locomotives, the Tom Thumb, was built by Peter Cooper for the Baltimore & Ohio Railroad in 1830. Cooper raced the Tom Thumb against a horse-drawn coach. The locomotive swept ahead right from the start. It broke down before the finish line, however, and the horse won the race.

Despite this unimpressive beginning, trains had many advantages over canals and steamboats. They could go practically anywhere that tracks could be put down. They were much faster,

Many steamboats like these traveled the Mississippi River in the mid-1800s. Steam travel also decreased the amount of time it took to travel across the oceans.

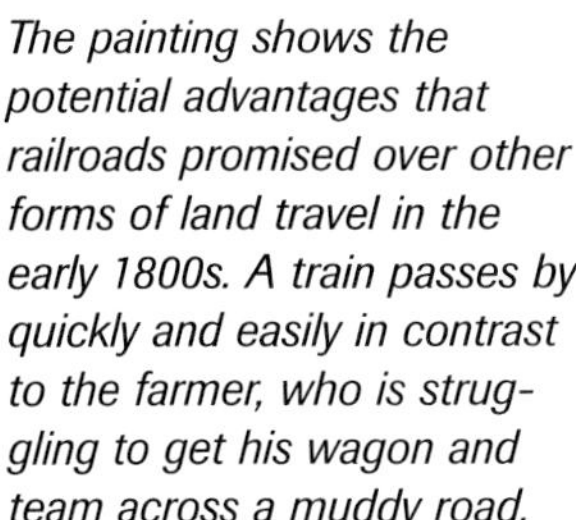

The painting shows the potential advantages that railroads promised over other forms of land travel in the early 1800s. A train passes by quickly and easily in contrast to the farmer, who is struggling to get his wagon and team across a muddy road.

and they could haul greater loads. Perhaps most importantly, trains could operate all year round in the northern states, where many canals and rivers were frozen solid in the winter months.

In the beginning many Americans considered trains dangerous. The sparks from the engines sometimes set fields on fire and frightened farm animals. Many early engines often jumped the tracks. The long-term advantages of railroads, however, could not be resisted. During the 1840s about 9,000 miles of track were built, mostly in the Northeast.

Railroads gave the economy a great boost. Besides reducing travel time and cost, they allowed many other businesses to expand. The demand for iron for engines and rails greatly increased the mining and smelting of iron. Remote areas boomed once the railroads reached them. Farmers increased output as railroads allowed them to quickly ship their goods to distant markets.

The railroads expanded the transportation growth that began with turnpikes. This **Transportation Revolution** made it easier for people in one region to meet and to do business with people in other regions. The Transportation Revolution began a process of linking the nation closer together that continues to the present.

Section 4 Review

• Glossary

• Time Line

IDENTIFY and explain the significance of the following: turnpikes, National Road, canals, DeWitt Clinton, Erie Canal, Robert Fulton, Transportation Revolution

REVIEWING FOR DETAILS

1. What did the U.S. government do to improve overland transportation?
2. How did canals and steamboats affect transportation?
3. In what ways were railroads an improvement over other forms of transportation?

REVIEWING FOR UNDERSTANDING

4. **Geographic Literacy** How did geography interfere with travel by land and water? How were these obstacles overcome using technology?
5. **Critical Thinking:** *Synthesizing Information* How did the Transportation Revolution help unite the nation?

CHAPTER 10

The South and King Cotton (1790–1860)

THEMES IN AMERICAN HISTORY

Cultural Diversity:
How might different people's common experiences contribute to forming a common culture?

Economic Development:
How might geography affect a regional economy?

Technology and Society:
Why might people be interested in making technological advances?

• Video Opener

• Skill Builder

African American abolitionist Henry Highland Garnet looked at the sea of faces before him. "Slavery!" he hissed. "How much misery is comprehended [included] in that single word." Garnet continued, "Awake, awake; millions of voices are calling you! Your dead fathers speak to you from their graves." He ended his speech with a singular call: "Resistance! Resistance! *RESISTANCE!"*

image above: *Romantic view of a plantation*

Section 1

COTTON IN THE SOUTH

Multimedia Connections

Explore these related topics and materials on the CD–ROM to enrich your understanding of this section:

Atlas

- Agriculture and Slavery

Readings

- Cotton Kingdom

Media Bank

- Pre-Civil War South

Profiles

- Eli Whitney
- John C. Calhoun

In the early 1800s cotton controlled the fortunes of most white southerners. One traveler noticed this when he stopped at a quiet Georgia inn and the manager immediately asked him about the price of cotton. "She said . . . there was an academy to which her daughter went when cotton was thirty cents per pound," he remembered. "But . . . as cotton had fallen to fifteen cents she could not afford to buy an instrument, and supposed her daughter must forget her music."

As you read this section you will find out:

- **What difficulties southern farmers faced in growing cotton.**
- **Why southern farmers moved westward.**
- **Why the demand for slaves rose after the invention of the cotton gin.**

The Birth of the Cotton Kingdom

In the years immediately following the American Revolution, some people thought that the falling price of tobacco signaled the end of plantation agriculture—and slavery. They believed both institutions would gradually die out in the new nation.

A troublesome crop. When there arose a new demand for cotton, however, many Americans became convinced that slavery had a future in the United States. Cotton could be grown profitably with slave labor. The efficient new spinning machines common in British factories by the 1790s had lowered the cost of cotton goods. As the price of these products went down, people could buy more of them. This increased the demand for cotton.

At first, few southern farmers could meet this demand. Not all varieties of cotton could be grown easily in the United States. Green-seed cotton, however, was hardy enough to grow almost anywhere in the South. The fibers of this plant were short and tightly woven around its seeds in pods called "bolls." It took a long time for even a skilled person to pick the seeds from a single pound of this cotton. People wished someone would invent a machine for removing the pesky seeds.

Eli Whitney and the cotton gin. In 1792, some nine years before he demonstrated his guns with interchangeable parts, Eli Whitney decided to take a job as a tutor on a Georgia plantation. There he talked with a number of farmers. They mentioned their interest in growing cotton and showed him how hard it was to remove the seeds from the bolls.

Curious, Whitney studied the cotton plant carefully. After only a short period of thinking and experimenting in the spring of 1793, he had designed and built a **cotton gin**, a machine that separated the seeds from the fibers. The machine consisted of a wooden box with a handle. When stuffed with cotton, the gin used stiff brushes and rollers fitted with wire teeth to pull the fibers through narrow slits and free them from the seeds. One person turning the handle could remove the seeds from 50 pounds of cotton in less than a day! In addition, the cotton gin was inexpensive and easy to copy. Most farmers could build their own or buy one. Whitney's gin quickly made it profitable to grow cotton in the South.

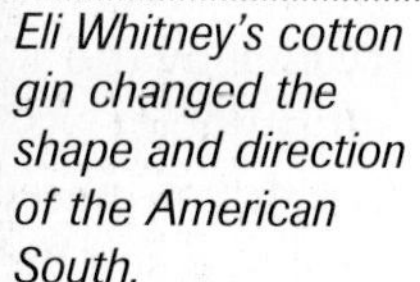

Eli Whitney's cotton gin changed the shape and direction of the American South.

The Granger Collection, New York

The Granger Collection, New York

This engraving shows how workers ran cotton through a gin to separate fibers from seeds.

The Cotton Boom

All over the South, farmers began to plant cotton, hoping to make money from the growing demands for the crop. In 1793 farmers grew about 10,000 bales, or large bundles. In 1801 production reached 100,000 bales, and by 1835 it had passed the 1 million mark.

A crop for the North. The availability of southern cotton soon contributed to the rapid growth of the northern textile industry. People everywhere benefited from cheap cotton clothing, which was cool in the summer and much easier to keep clean than woolen garments. Other businesses related to textiles, such as shipping, also boomed because of the ready supply of cheap southern cotton.

Cotton expands westward. As cotton farming became more profitable, people pushed westward in search of more fertile land. They flocked into Alabama, Mississippi, Tennessee, Arkansas, Louisiana, and Texas. In these areas, farmers also raised large quantities of corn, wheat, cattle, and other food products, but cotton was their key to prosperity. Before long, there was a recognizable **cotton belt**, a huge agricultural region largely devoted to the production of cotton, across the southern United States.

Although not all farmers prospered, a great many who moved westward to grow cotton became very wealthy. It was much less expensive to use slaves to work the cotton fields than to hire workers. According to one observer, these cotton farmers made "oceans of money." Cotton farmer E. N. Davis evaluated his chances of success and determined that the odds were good:

> **"I shall make a crop with the hands and finish the work the ensuing [following] fall and winter. My hands are doing a good business, averaging me some 200 Acres of Land per day. If . . . [the cotton] comes on the Market soon it will be a small fortune."**

Whenever they conducted business off the plantation, many slaves had to wear tags such as these indicating their occupation.

The whole region prospered. Southern exports of cotton to the Northeast, Great Britain, and other markets paid for badly needed manufactured goods.

Slavery expands westward. As the cotton belt expanded, the demand for slaves grew. The great cotton boom increased farmers' desire for workers who would plant, weed, and harvest the crop and then gin and bale the fluffy white fibers.

Under the terms of the compromise delegates had reached at the Constitutional Convention, Congress banned the importing of slaves in 1808. Although some illegal importation of slaves continued, the market for American-born slaves increased dramatically. This increased the price of slaves, and many slaveholders in the Upper South started to sell slaves to eager pioneers in the Lower South.

• Southern Defense

Section 1 Review

• Glossary

IDENTIFY and explain the significance of the following: Eli Whitney, cotton gin, cotton belt

REVIEWING FOR DETAILS

1. Why was growing and selling cotton difficult for southern farmers?
2. Why did the demand for slaves rise after Whitney invented the cotton gin?

REVIEWING FOR UNDERSTANDING

3. **Geographic Literacy** Why did white southern farmers move westward in the early 1800s?
4. **Writing Mastery:** *Describing* Imagine that you are an Alabama cotton farmer. Write a letter to a relative in Massachusetts and describe how the cotton gin has changed things on your farm.
5. **Critical Thinking:** *Cause and Effect* How did the development of efficient spinning machines in Great Britain affect agriculture in the American South?

Section 2
The World Cotton Built

Multimedia Connections

Explore these related topics and materials on the CD-ROM to enrich your understanding of this section:

Gazetteer
- Richmond
- Lexington
- New Orleans

Interactive Map
- The Cotton Plantation

Profiles
- Mary Boykin Chesnut

Media Bank
- Southern Population, 1850
- Slaveholding Families, 1850
- Small Southern Farm

In 1860 Alabama resident Daniel R. Hundley wrote one of the first studies of the southern population. He divided southerners into groups such as "The Southern Gentlemen," "The Middle Class," "Cotton Snobs," "The Southern Yankee," "The Southern Yeoman," "Poor White Trash," and "The Negro Slaves." While Hundley's study was largely shaped by his own biased views as a wealthy landowner, his book reflected the diversity of people that could be found in southern society.

As you read this section you will find out:

- **What social groups existed within the white southern population.**
- **What kind of industries there were in the South.**
- **What life was like for free African Americans in the South.**

The Planters

Unlike popular images often portrayed in movies and books, most white people in the South did not live on large, beautiful plantations or hold slaves. In fact, most white southerners had no slaves at all.

A small group of slaveholders dominated southern society, however. These were the **planters**, people who owned plantations and who held more than 20 slaves. In 1850 there were about 46,000 planters in a southern population of almost 9 million. Planters were often quite rich since they usually owned a large amount of fertile land on which enslaved African Americans worked. Thus, slaves played an essential role in creating planters' large fortunes.

Planters' lives varied greatly. While most had between 20 and 50 slaves, a few held as

This engraving shows the "big house" and slave quarters on a Mississippi sugar plantation.

many as 3,000. Planters typically lived in simple two-story houses with columned front porches, but a few had mansions with fancy trim.

Katherine Lumpkin left a description of her grandfather's 1,000-acre estate in Georgia, which included a workforce of about 50 slaves. Lumpkin called the plantation "a community and business rolled into one." In addition to the "big house," or main residence, there were:

> **"slave quarters, stables, and spring-house [storage place], and the work radiating out into the fields from this hub of activity."**

Separate buildings held the carpentry shop and the smokehouse. Lumpkin's was not even a particularly large plantation!

The White Majority

Most other white southerners lived and worked in rural areas. They made up the groups below the planters on the South's social ladder.

Small farmers. Small farmers were the largest group in white southern society. Because plantations took the best soil, small farmers often had to make do with land in hilly regions or other less favorable locations.

Like the planters, small farmers' wealth and social status varied. The majority, however, had no slaves. Those who did rarely held more than one or two, or perhaps a slave family with a couple of children. This was largely because slaves were very costly. In 1850 a slave could cost $1,000. These small farmers often labored alongside their slaves in the fields.

Young People In History

Plantation Children

During the early years of childhood, white and slave children often played together. There were glaring differences between the lives of the children from the start, however. The slaveholder's children wore fancy clothing. Wealthy planters imported expensive clothes for their children from fashionable stores in Europe. Slave children made do with whatever the master gave them, often plain dresses for boys and girls alike.

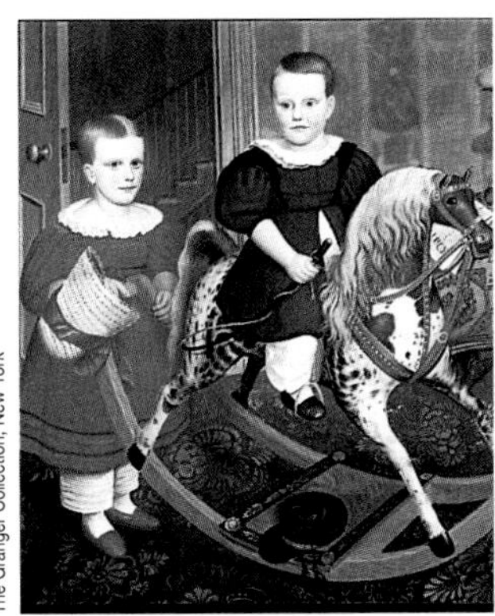

These children, who lived on a wealthy southern plantation in the 1800s, were provided with the fanciest of toys.

Slavery eventually disrupted the lives of both white and slave children, causing a painful break between former playmates. Sometimes it became obvious when a black teenager had to call a slaveholder's new baby "Young Massa" or "Young Missus." Other times it became obvious when a white child left for school and a slave child went to work in the nursery or fields.

The work for small farmers and slaves was extremely difficult. Farmers and slaves spent all day in the hot sun, doing the backbreaking work of plowing, planting, and harvesting crops. In addition to cotton, most small farmers in the South raised corn or other grain, vegetables, and barnyard animals. They depended on most of these for food and sold whatever was left over. The women in the family spun cotton into thread, wove the thread on a simple loom, then turned the homespun cloth into shirts, dresses, and other garments.

Most small farmers hoped to one day be as wealthy as the planters. Many who had no slaves were enthusiastic supporters of slavery, hoping to someday have enough money to obtain slaves of their own.

Other rural whites. This was not true, however, in remote mountain valleys and in other isolated areas, where the poorest whites resented both slaves and slaveholders. Planters and small farmers commonly looked down on these poor whites. Very poor white people made up a large part of southern society. They often lived on some of the least productive soil. They survived by fishing, hunting, and tending small garden patches. One traveler described them as "poverty-stricken vagabonds [tramps] . . . without . . . reliable means of livelihood [income] . . . [and] having almost no property but their own bodies."

Manufacturing and the Urban South

Although the South devoted most of its resources to agriculture, there was some manufacturing in the region. Textiles, tobacco products, and iron played important roles in economic growth, particularly in the cities of the Upper South. Other businesses, such as sugar refineries, ropemaking companies, and cotton presses, dotted the region as well.

Many of the textile mills in the South were located on the streams and rivers of the eastern

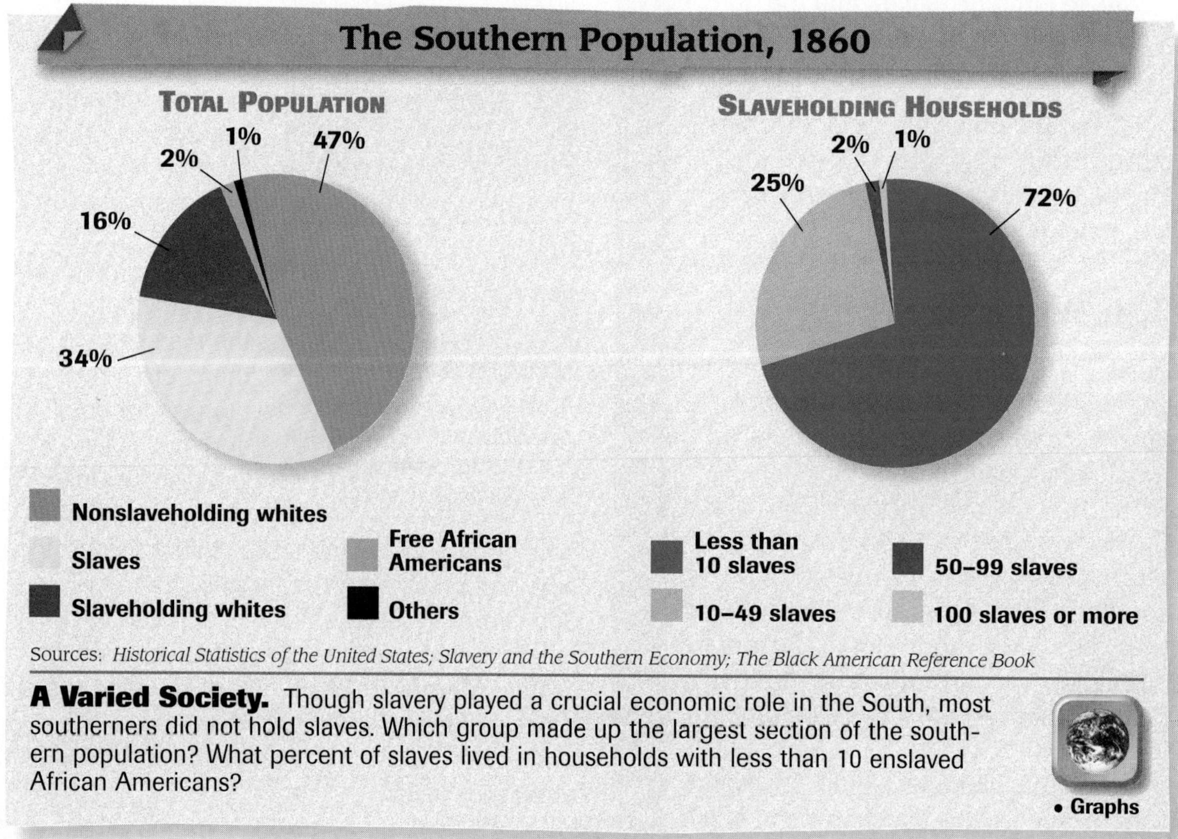

Sources: *Historical Statistics of the United States; Slavery and the Southern Economy; The Black American Reference Book*

A Varied Society. Though slavery played a crucial economic role in the South, most southerners did not hold slaves. Which group made up the largest section of the southern population? What percent of slaves lived in households with less than 10 enslaved African Americans?

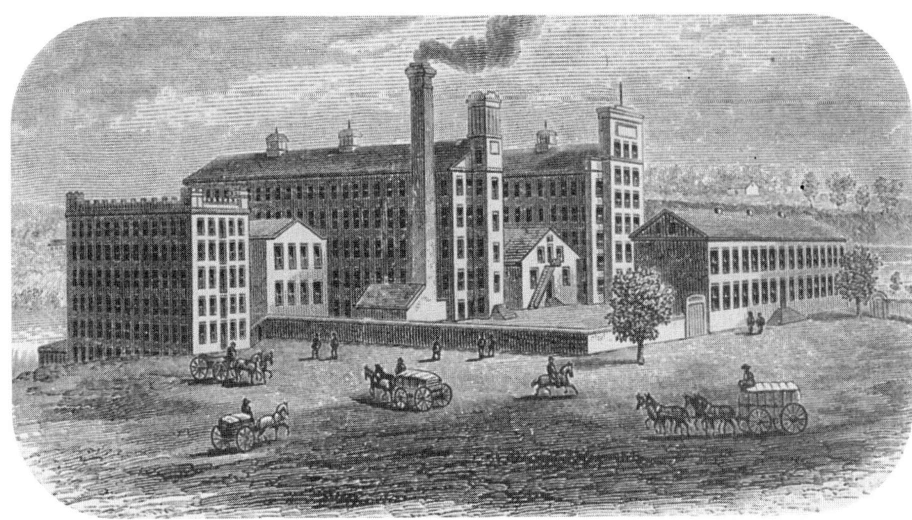

Manufacturing businesses like this textile mill in Columbus, Georgia, were rare in the South before 1860, even though the southern states produced most of the cotton used in textile mills.

slopes of the Appalachian Mountains. One of the best known and most efficient was William Gregg's cotton mill in South Carolina. It employed about 300 workers by 1850, many of them women or teenagers.

Tobacco companies were clustered in the Upper South. In the 1850s Richmond, Virginia, had about 50 companies manufacturing tobacco products. Many of the tobacco workers were slaves, either purchased by the companies or hired from individual slaveholders. Kentucky had ropemaking plants in Louisville and Lexington. Cotton presses, which compressed the fluffy crop into 500-pound bales, also existed in many southern cities. The New Orleans Levee Steam Cotton Press, which employed more than 100 slaves in 1850, was one of the largest.

Iron manufacturing was also an important industry in the South. The **Tredegar Iron Works** of Richmond was the largest iron company in the region. It made steam engines and other iron products. The Tredegar Iron Works sometimes competed successfully with northern iron mills. Like other southern firms, it used slave labor.

Many southerners dreamed of great industrial growth in their region. "With slave labor that . . . is absolutely reliable," reported a New Orleans newspaper, "manufactured fabrics can be produced so as to compete successfully with the world."

Southern cities and manufacturing grew at a slow pace, however. In 1860 the total amount of manufactured goods in all the southern states put together was less than that of Massachusetts alone! The northern states had over 10 times more people working in manufacturing.

A number of factors explained the growing economic difference between the North and South. Southerners tended to invest their wealth in land and slaves rather than in factories. In addition, the South's dependence on slave labor discouraged European immigrants from settling there. This deprived the region of many consumers and skilled workers.

Free African Americans

Not all African Americans in the South were slaves. By 1860 the region contained about 260,000 free African Americans. Some had taken on extra work while they were slaves and had saved enough money to purchase their freedom. Some had been freed voluntarily by slaveholders. Others were the children of free African Americans and had never been slaves.

Southern whites felt that the institution of slavery was threatened by the mere existence of a free black population, since it served as a constant reminder to slaves that freedom was possible. In a petition to have all free African

Americans banished from South Carolina, a group of whites wrote:

> **"[Slaves] continually have before their eyes, persons of the same color, many of whom they have known . . . freed from the control of masters, working where they please, going whither they please, and expending their money how they please."**

White southerners created legal restrictions that made life very difficult for free African Americans. They generally could not vote, carry guns, travel without a pass, speak at public meetings, or learn to write. Free African Americans also faced the possibility of being kidnapped and sold into slavery. "Though we are not slaves," one African American newspaper explained, "we are not free."

Despite such restrictions, a small number of black southerners managed to buy land and become farmers. Some free African Americans held slaves, and a few even owned plantations.

Other free African Americans mastered skilled trades, such as printing, barbering, bricklaying, and carpentry. A few owned businesses and became wealthy. Many, however, had to accept low-paying, unskilled jobs like ditch digging and street sweeping just to survive.

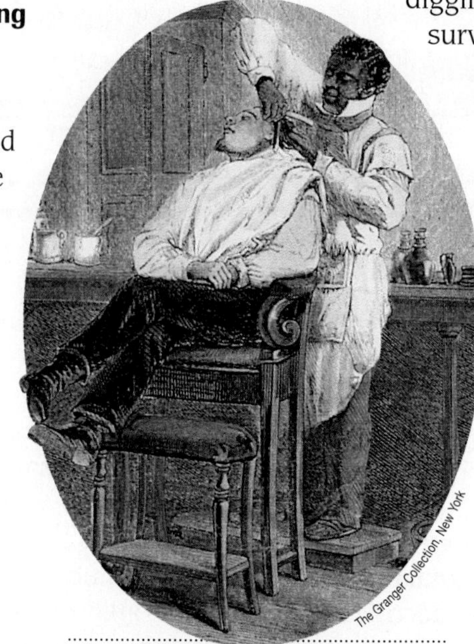

This free African American man ran his own barbershop in Richmond, Virginia. Some free African Americans who remained in the South ran similar businesses.

The Granger Collection, New York

Many free African Americans in the South formed strong communities, and a number of them made important contributions to American life. For example, Norbert Rillieux, who lived in New Orleans, invented a device to extract syrup from sugar and helped make syrup widely available and more affordable.

Although there were some exceptions, the lives of many free African Americans in the South were not much better than those of slaves. Most white southerners thought of them as merely slaves who had no masters.

Section 2 Review

• Glossary

IDENTIFY and explain the significance of the following: planters, William Gregg, Tredegar Iron Works, Norbert Rillieux

REVIEWING FOR DETAILS

1. What different social groups existed within the white southern population?
2. What kind of manufacturing industries existed in the South?
3. How would you describe the lives of free African Americans in the South?

REVIEWING FOR UNDERSTANDING

4. **Writing Mastery:** *Creating* Imagine that you are a reporter for a British newspaper traveling through the South. Write an article describing the region and southern society.
5. **Critical Thinking:** *Drawing Conclusions* Why might the South's dependence on slave labor have discouraged European immigrants from settling there?

Section 3
THE SLAVE SYSTEM

Multimedia Connections

Explore these related topics and materials on the CD–ROM to enrich your understanding of this section:

Media Bank
- African American Spiritual
- Sales Bill
- Sojourner Truth

Readings
- Spirituals
- Nat Turner's Rebellion
- Amistad Mutiny
- Cultural Borrowings
- Narrative of Sojourner Truth

Profiles
- Nat Turner
- Sojourner Truth

In the tense days after a failed Virginia slave revolt, one African American gave a simple reason for his participation—freedom. "I have nothing more to offer than what General Washington would have had to offer, had he been taken by British officers," the man explained. "I have ventured my life . . . to obtain the liberty of my countrymen, and am a willing sacrifice to their cause." What he called a "mockery of a trial" quickly ended, and officials executed more than 30 fighters for their freedom.

As you read this section you will find out:
- **How slaveholders controlled slaves.**
- **How slaves' culture helped them survive slavery.**
- **How enslaved African Americans resisted slavery.**

Treatment of Slaves

By 1850 more than 3 million slaves lived in the South. Many worked in factories or city homes or on small farms, but more than half labored on plantations.

Slave control. Slaveholders' treatment of slaves differed considerably. Some masters tried to treat slaves well while others treated slaves horribly.

Almost all slaveholders used physical punishment to control and discipline slaves. When asked about her previous master, one former slave answered, "Beat women! Why sure he . . . beat women. Beat women jes lak men." Even slave children sometimes felt the lash. Hannah Davidson refused to discuss how her former master treated her. "The things that my sister May and I suffered were so terrible," she said. "It is better not to have such things in our memory."

Slave codes. White southerners also wrote laws called **slave codes** to control slaves. The slave codes outlawed a wide variety of activities: slaves could not testify against whites in court, travel without authorization, hit a white person, carry firearms, and so on. The codes varied from state to state and were not consistently enforced, but their existence helped ensure slaves' obedience.

Under the slave codes, most states made it illegal to teach slaves to read and write. Sometimes, sympathetic whites or other African Americans disobeyed this restriction and educated a few slaves. Even so, by 1860 only about 5 percent of slaves had learned to read.

The slave codes did not recognize marriages between slaves. Some slaveholders, however, allowed slaves to maintain family ties. Of course, slaveholders had the legal right to break up slave families.

Slaves who were separated from their families never stopped hoping to locate and rejoin them. Many ran away in an effort to reach loved ones. Reward notices in southern newspapers, such as this one from South Carolina, described these attempts:

Slave families were often separated by sale. This extended family from South Carolina represents several generations of enslaved people.

"RUN away . . . HAGAR, and her daughter called MARY. . . . I was since informed that the above negroes crossed the Ashley River a few days ago, and suppose they are gone to Mr. William Stoutenburg's plantation, as her relations belong to him."

Many companies like this one in Alexandria, Virginia, earned money by selling American-born slaves after the Atlantic slave trade was banned.

Slave auctions. Perhaps no aspect of slavery brought out its inhumanity more than slave auctions. Slaves waited as buyers looked them over, poking and prodding them as they might a horse or cow. Far worse, buyers were deciding the slaves' fate and often that of the slaves' families. One former slave left this description of an auction in New Orleans:

"[Randall] . . . was made to jump, and run across the floor, and perform many other feats, exhibiting his activity and condition. All the time . . . [his mother] Eliza was crying aloud, and wringing her hands. She besought [pleaded with] the man not to buy him, unless he also bought herself and [her daughter]. . . . The man answered that he could not afford it."

Living Conditions of Slaves

The experiences of slaves living on plantations varied a great deal. Some slaves did chores inside the master's house while others worked in the fields. Slaves also worked as carpenters, blacksmiths, seamstresses, and at other skilled trades.

Plantation slaves generally lived in cabins located in a group near the "big house" of the master. These cabins were small—often two rooms and a narrow hallway for a family—and barely furnished. Many did not have beds. Most had dirt floors and fireplaces for cooking and heat. One former slave described the cabins as "but log huts—the tops partly open."

Slaves' food consisted mainly of corn meal and salt pork or bacon. This did not make for a balanced or tasty diet. Many slaveholders allowed slaves to have small vegetable gardens. Slaves also added to their bland food by fishing and by trapping small forest animals, such as rabbits and raccoons.

Slaves wore simple clothing—cotton and woolen shirts and pants or dresses, work shoes, and a hat or kerchief for protection against rain and summer heat. Such clothing rarely lasted long or protected slaves against cold weather.

The Culture of Slavery

Despite their condition, enslaved African Americans managed to develop a distinct slave culture. African American historian Thomas R. Frazier has declared that "it was in this search for freedom and self-expression that the slaves made their most important contributions to our heritage."

Religion. Although slaveholders often required their slaves to attend white churches, many slaves secretly formed their own churches. Since many of the slave codes outlawed meetings among slaves, religious services frequently occurred "way out in the woods or the bushes somewhere so that the white folks couldn't hear."

Slaves often combined Christian beliefs and traditional African practices to create a unique religion. Slave Christianity often

Slave auctions like this one were usually humiliating experiences for the people who were being sold. Buyers often treated the slaves more like livestock than people.

Slave communities created their own culture, which included music and dances that often blended African and European traditions. This tradition still influences African American music today.

stressed that slaves would find freedom in the afterlife. Many enslaved Africans believed that one day they would be led to a "promised land" that was free of slavery. This gave slaves some comfort in daily life and also reinforced the injustice of slavery to them.

An important part of religious practices among slaves were the deeply moving songs known as **spirituals**. These songs were sung in worship services, at work, and at social gatherings. The spirituals, which also blended Christian and African traditions, provided emotional comfort in the slaves' difficult lives.

Folktales. Slaves also developed other ways of expressing their dignity and humanity. Their **folktales**, or oral stories, reflect this. Some of the stories were moral fables that helped educate and set a standard of behavior for slaves to follow.

Other tales featured an animal trickster, or sneaky character, such as the famous Brer Rabbit. In these stories, the animal represented either a particular slave or a personality type who usually got the better of a more powerful but dim-witted opponent. Slaves often used this sort of folktale to triumph symbolically over a master or over slavery itself.

Rebellion and Resistance

Slave culture provided strength, hope, and a way to resist slavery. Many slaves also engaged in many other forms of resistance, however. Some protested individually, while others joined together in open rebellion.

Slave resistance. Many slaves opposed slavery with individual acts of courage that protested the system and lessened its effects on their lives. This resistance took many forms. Slaves might set fire to barns, disrupting the plantation. They might step on plants while plowing, slowing their own work and cutting into the master's profit. They might slip away at night to visit friends on nearby plantations. Some sought freedom in the North by running away.

Slaves sometimes pretended that they were sick or injured. This was a particularly successful form of resistance, since slaveholders realized that forcing "sick" slaves to work might cause permanent injury and lessen their value.

Slave revolts. A small number of slaves actually rebelled against the slave system. Very few of these revolts succeeded because of the restrictions of the slave codes. Slaveholders feared slave uprisings so much that they usually reacted to them with terrible brutality. When captured, rebellious slaves were nearly always tortured or killed.

One rebel leader was Denmark Vesey of Charleston, South Carolina. Vesey had purchased his freedom after winning some money in a lottery. After his escape, he preached against slavery.

By 1821 Vesey had developed a plot to gather thousands of slaves, steal guns, and kill

American Letters

Incidents in the Life of a Slave Girl

Harriet Jacobs

Harriet Jacobs was born into slavery in North Carolina in 1813. In 1842 she escaped to the North. She published her narrative account of slavery, Incidents in the Life of a Slave Girl, *in 1861. In this selection from her book, Jacobs relates how the slaveholders tried to use religion to control slaves. She was about 18 years old and still enslaved at the time of the events she describes.*

After the alarm caused by Nat Turner's insurrection [rebellion] had subsided [died down], the slaveholders came to the conclusion that it would be well to give the slaves enough of religious instruction to keep them from murdering their masters. The Episcopal clergyman offered to hold a separate service on Sundays for their benefit. . . .

When the Rev. Mr. Pike came, there were some twenty persons present. . . . Pious [Holy] Mr. Pike brushed up his hair till it stood upright, and, in deep, solemn tones, began: "Hearken, ye servants! Give strict heed unto my words. You are rebellious sinners. . . . Instead of serving your masters faithfully, which is pleasing in the sight of your heavenly Master, you are idle, and shirk [avoid] your work. God sees you. . . . Although your masters may not find you out, God sees you; and he will punish you. You must forsake your sinful ways, and be faithful servants. . . . If you disobey your earthly master, you offend your heavenly Master. . . ."

THE

DEEPER WRONG;

OR, INCIDENTS

IN THE

LIFE OF A SLAVE GIRL.

WRITTEN BY HERSELF.

"Northerners know nothing at all about Slavery. They think it is perpetual bondage only. They have no conception of the depth of *degradation* involved in that word, SLAVERY; if they had, they would never cease their efforts until so horrible a system was overthrown."—A WOMAN OF NORTH CAROLINA.

"Rise up, ye women that are at ease! Hear my voice, ye careless daughters! Give ear unto my speech."—ISAIAH xxxii. 9.

EDITED BY L. MARIA CHILD.

LONDON:
W. TWEEDIE, 337, STRAND.

1862.

Harriet Jacobs's life story was published with the help of a northern abolitionist. This edition is from 1862.

We went home, highly amused at brother Pike's gospel teaching. . . . I went the next Sabbath evening, and heard pretty much a repetition of the last discourse [discussion]. . . . I went home with the feeling that I had heard the Reverend Mr. Pike for the last time. . . .

I well remember one occasion when I attended a Methodist class meeting. I . . . happened to sit next a poor, bereaved [grieving] mother. . . . The class leader was the town constable—a man who bought and sold slaves. . . . This white-faced, black-hearted brother came near us, and said to the stricken woman, "Sister, can't you tell us how the Lord deals with your soul? Do you love him as you did formerly?"

She rose to her feet, and said, in piteous tones, "My Lord and Master, help me! My load is more than I can bear. . . . They've got all my children. Last week they took the last one. God only knows where they've sold her. . . . Pray for her brothers and sisters! I've got nothing to live for now. God make my time short!"

She sat down, quivering in every limb. I saw that constable class leader become crimson in the face with suppressed [held in] laughter, while he held up his handkerchief, that those who were weeping for the poor woman's calamity [tragedy] might not see his merriment. . . .

No wonder the slaves sing—
"Ole Satan's church is here below;
Up to God's free church I hope to go."

The Granger Collection, New York

Nat Turner and his followers plotted a massive rebellion against the slave system. Although the revolt failed to end slavery, it did strike fear in the southern white community.

most of the white population of Charleston. At the last minute, one of Vesey's followers betrayed the plan. Officials later hanged Vesey and 35 other participants.

A Virginia slave named Nat Turner organized what proved to be the bloodiest slave uprising in America. As a young boy, Turner had taught himself to read. He eventually became a slave minister, preaching after long days in the field. Turner hated slavery and believed that God had chosen him to seek freedom.

In 1831 Turner and his followers killed about 60 whites before being captured. This episode became known as **Nat Turner's Rebellion**. Some slaveholders responded to the revolt by carrying out their own reign of violence and terror. In the process they killed at least 120 innocent African Americans in the area.

Turner's revolt had widespread results. It fanned fear and rage throughout the white population of the South. White officials increased restrictions on slaves, making it more difficult for slaves to meet in groups outside the presence of whites. The Virginia legislature passed laws that almost completely eliminated slave preachers, slave schools, and slave religious meetings. Nat Turner's Rebellion was a lasting indication of how much slaves despised their condition and how badly they wanted to be free.

Section 3 Review

• Glossary

IDENTIFY and explain the significance of the following: slave codes, spirituals, folktales, Denmark Vesey, Nat Turner's Rebellion

REVIEWING FOR DETAILS

1. What methods did slaveholders use to control slaves?
2. How did enslaved African Americans resist slaveholders?

REVIEWING FOR UNDERSTANDING

3. **Geographic Literacy** How did geographic conditions in the South make it difficult for slaves to escape?
4. **Writing Mastery:** *Creating* Write a folktale, like those told by African Americans in the 1800s, that reflects important elements of slave culture.
5. **Critical Thinking:** *Synthesizing Information* How did the slave codes make it difficult for people like Denmark Vesey and Nat Turner to mount successful revolts against slavery?

Section 4

THE CRUSADE AGAINST SLAVERY

Multimedia Connections

Explore these related topics and materials on the CD–ROM to enrich your understanding of this section:

Biographies

- William Lloyd Garrison

Profiles

- Angelina and Sarah Grimké
- Charles Remond
- Harriet Tubman
- Robert Purvis
- Theodore Weld

Media Bank

- William Lloyd Garrison

Maria Stewart stepped up to the stage. Everyone in the Boston auditorium knew it was a very special day. To hear this inspiring African American abolitionist, the first native-born woman in America to deliver a political lecture—how wonderful! The crowd hushed as she spoke. "All the nations of the earth are crying out for liberty and equality," Stewart explained. "Away, away with tyranny [unjust rule] and oppression [burden]."

As you read this section you will find out:

- **Why some African Americans supported the colonization movement.**
- **How the American Anti-Slavery Society opposed slavery.**
- **Why some northern whites opposed the abolition movement.**

Ideas About Abolition

Even before the American Revolution, small groups of Americans began to call for **abolition**, or an end to slavery. The Quakers, for example, criticized slaveholders for supporting what they believed to be an un-Christian practice. Free African Americans in the North also formed antislavery societies and published newspapers.

The colonization movement. In the early 1800s some people explored the idea of colonizing, or settling, African Americans outside the United States. Most white sponsors of colonization had a low opinion of African Americans. This group wanted to send black people "back" to Africa, even though by this time most black Americans had been born in America.

A small group of African Americans and whites saw colonization as a way for black people to escape prejudice and abuse. Paul Cuffe, a wealthy northern African American, was one of the first to support colonization. In 1815 he transported 38 free black volunteers to West Africa at his own expense. However, Cuffe died before he could send another group.

In 1817 a number of white citizens founded the **American Colonization Society**. They bought land in what became the nation of Liberia and helped free African Americans settle there. In the late 1820s the society also began to purchase slaves, free them, and send them to Africa. By 1830 the organization had persuaded about 1,400 African Americans to make the move to Africa. Most African Americans did not want to live there, however. They viewed America, not Africa, as their home. Their opposition to colonization helped cause the movement to lose strength in the 1830s and 1840s.

Different motives, different goals. Even as support for colonization faded, more people began to consider the situation of African Americans in the United States. Gradually, more people became abolitionists.

Abolitionists opposed slavery for a variety of reasons. Some abolitionists put forth religious arguments, stressing that God saw all human beings as equals. Other abolitionists believed in the ideal of freedom. They quoted the Declaration of Independence to show that slavery violated American principles.

Abolitionists also had different goals. Some wanted African Americans to have the same rights that white people had. Others thought black people should have fewer liberties than white people.

Radical Voices Demand Action

Two radical abolitionists helped to bring attention to the growing movement against slavery. David Walker was a free African American from North Carolina. Over time he educated himself and made his way to Boston, where he operated a used-clothing store.

In 1829 Walker wrote *Appeal to the Colored Citizens of the World,* an influential pamphlet. It urged African Americans—free and slave—to protest for freedom. "Will you wait," he warned America, "until we shall . . . obtain our liberty by the crushing arm of power?" Walker secretly distributed copies of his pamphlet by sewing them into the clothes of sailors heading to the South.

William Lloyd Garrison, a white Massachusetts publisher, soon added his voice to Walker's in the call for freedom. Garrison wanted immediate abolition and criticized not only slaveholders but all Americans who allowed slavery to exist.

In 1831 Garrison began publishing an abolitionist newspaper, *The Liberator*. Supported at first mostly by African American subscribers, *The Liberator* eventually entered the homes of more and more white people, encouraging support for abolition.

Though Garrison used only nonviolent tactics, his radical position alarmed even some more conservative abolitionists. He cried "No Union with Slaveholders," urging northern

The Granger Collection, New York

William Lloyd Garrison's The Liberator *became one of the most widely read abolitionist newspapers in the North.*

• **Abolitionists**

Former slave Harriet Tubman (far left) risked her life to help many others escape from slavery, including the people pictured here with her.

• **Underground Railroad**

states to break away from the nation. He publicly set fire to a copy of the Constitution, claiming that it was "an agreement with Hell."

The Underground Railroad

Like Walker and Garrison, many abolitionists sprang into action for the cause. In the 1830s a small group of abolitionists formed the **Underground Railroad**, an informal network that helped between roughly 50,000 and 75,000 slaves escape to freedom. It used more than 3,000 "conductors," or guides, to help lead slaves along different paths to liberty in Canada or in the North. They stopped at "stations"—barns, stables, and safe houses—to hide escaping slaves.

One of the most famous conductors was Harriet Tubman, who escaped slavery after suffering years of abuse as a field hand. She became a specialist in the dangerous task of helping slaves escape into the northern states. Tubman made at least 19 trips into the South and helped free more than 300 slaves.

The American Anti-Slavery Society

In 1833 Garrison and other abolitionists founded an organization called the **American Anti-Slavery Society**. The group supported abolition and racial equality. The group also called for using nonviolent methods to achieve these goals. The society soon spread throughout the North and the Midwest by creating smaller regional organizations and hiring inspiring speakers.

Through Others' Eyes

The Abolition Movement

After 1833, when Great Britain ended slavery in its empire, many British abolitionists turned their attention elsewhere. Some offered advice to their American friends who were working hard to end slavery. In 1839 British historian Esther Copley reported on efforts to aid American abolition:

> *"We should employ every means in our power to promote the utter annihilation [destruction] of slavery. . . . Such appears to be the duty of Britain towards other nations, especially America, to whom she is most closely allied. . . . Several deputations [groups] have already been sent from Great Britain to America, to promote the great object, particularly by lecturing in the principal cities and towns of the free States, upon . . . the duty, necessity, and advantage of immediate emancipation. . . . It is a matter of heartfelt delight and congratulation, that the good cause seems to be rapidly spreading in America."*

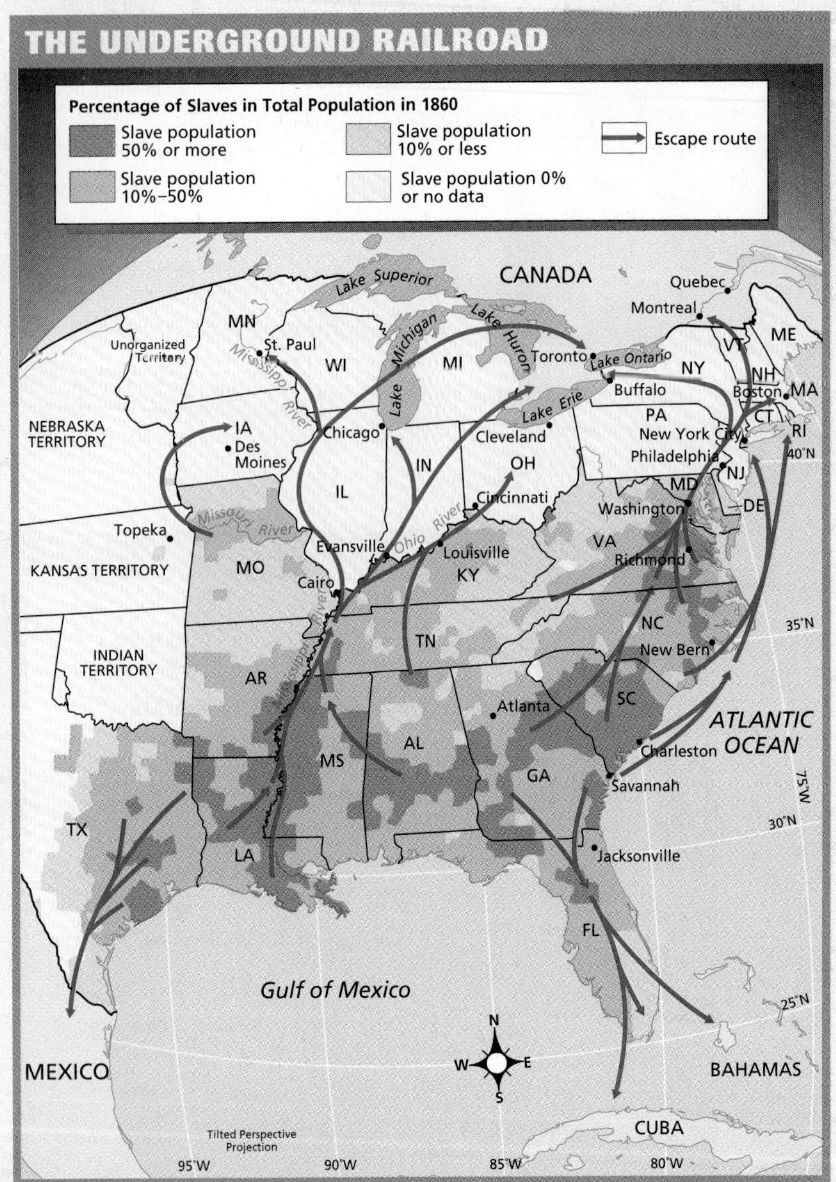

Learning from Maps.
Conductors on the Underground Railroad helped between 50,000 and 75,000 slaves find freedom.

▶ **Movement.** How did a slave's location help determine his or her route to escape on the Underground Railroad?

• Maps

The Grimké sisters. The sisters Sarah and Angelina Grimké, two white abolitionists from South Carolina, traveled through New England for the American Anti-Slavery Society. They demonstrated that even some southerners hated slavery. Angelina Grimké expressed her commitment to abolition:

> **"If persecution is the means which God has ordained [ordered] for the accomplishment of this great end, [freedom]; then . . . LET IT COME; for it is my deep, solemn, deliberate conviction [belief], that this is a cause worth dying for."**

In 1836 Angelina Grimké wrote an "Appeal to the Christian Women of the South," urging southern women to "overthrow this horrible system of oppression and cruelty."

Frederick Douglass. The abolitionist movement soon added another powerful fighter to its ranks. Frederick Douglass had been a slave in Maryland for many years. In 1838 he escaped and eventually settled in Massachusetts.

One day in 1841, Douglass attended a meeting of the Anti-Slavery Society. Without preparation, he delivered a powerful speech. The members of the society were so impressed that they urged him to work full-time for abolition.

Douglass gradually began to engage in political activity. He and Martin Delany also

Former slave Frederick Douglass became a powerful voice in the fight against slavery.

• Narrative

published an abolitionist paper, the *North Star*. In one article he wrote:

> **"The white man's happiness cannot be purchased by the black man's misery. . . . All distinctions founded on complexion [skin color] ought to be . . . abolished, and every right, privilege, and immunity, now enjoyed by the white man, ought to be as freely granted to the man of color."**

Different strategies. As the abolition movement gained strength, two different groups emerged. Garrison and many of his followers favored immediate **emancipation**, or freedom, for slaves. Other abolitionists supported gradual emancipation.

Opposition to Abolition

Most white southerners hated the abolition movement. Many white northerners did as well. Several factors motivated their opposition to abolition. Many white workers feared job competition from freed slaves. Some northern manufacturers thought abolition would destroy the southern economy and eventually hurt their businesses. In addition, many northerners shared a deep prejudice against all African Americans.

Like southerners, some northerners disliked the abolition movement so much that they resorted to harassment and violence. Opponents often tried to break up abolition meetings by shouting or throwing rocks. Sometimes they hurt or even killed individual abolitionists. Several times when Elijah Lovejoy published abolitionist articles in his Illinois newspaper, opponents broke into his shop and destroyed his press. When Lovejoy tried to install another press in November 1837, an angry group murdered him. Some abolitionists became discouraged by this opposition. However, they were slowly convincing the people of the North that slavery was an evil institution.

Section 4 Review

• Glossary

IDENTIFY and explain the significance of the following: abolition, Paul Cuffe, American Colonization Society, David Walker, William Lloyd Garrison, Underground Railroad, Harriet Tubman, American Anti-Slavery Society, Sarah and Angelina Grimké, Frederick Douglass, emancipation

• Time Line

REVIEWING FOR DETAILS

1. Why did some African Americans support the movement for colonization?
2. What were some of the methods the American Anti-Slavery Society used to fight slavery?
3. Why did some northern whites oppose the abolition movement?

REVIEWING FOR UNDERSTANDING

4. **Writing Mastery:** *Persuading* Create a poster for the American Anti-Slavery Society persuading people to support the abolition movement.
5. **Critical Thinking:** *Recognizing Point of View* How did some white northerners' support of the colonization movement reveal their racial prejudice?

The Cotton Kingdom

Throughout the 1800s the South continued to grow the staple crops it had relied on in the 1700s, such as tobacco, rice, and sugarcane, but those crops were quickly overshadowed in importance by cotton. The fluffy white bolls dominated the economy of the region like no other crop. The wealth of the South rose and fell according to the cotton market. It became so important to the southern economy that many people referred to it as "King Cotton."

The rise of the textile industry in the Northeast and in Europe created a huge demand for cotton. By 1860 cotton accounted for about half of the value of all major exports for the United States. This made cotton, and the South, vital to the overall economy of the nation. As tensions increased between the North and the South over slavery, some southerners thought that the importance of cotton would prevent the federal government from interfering with the slave system.

The Cotton Kingdom

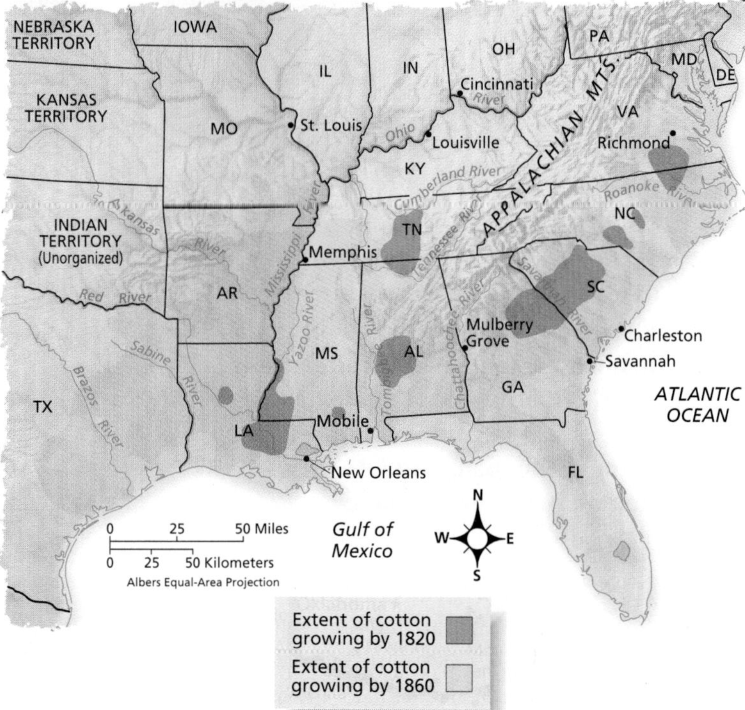

The Cotton Kingdom gradually expanded westward throughout the 1800s. **Region:** What two states began to grow cotton after 1820? What three states accounted for about 60 percent of all cotton production?

Share of Total Cotton Production by State in 1850

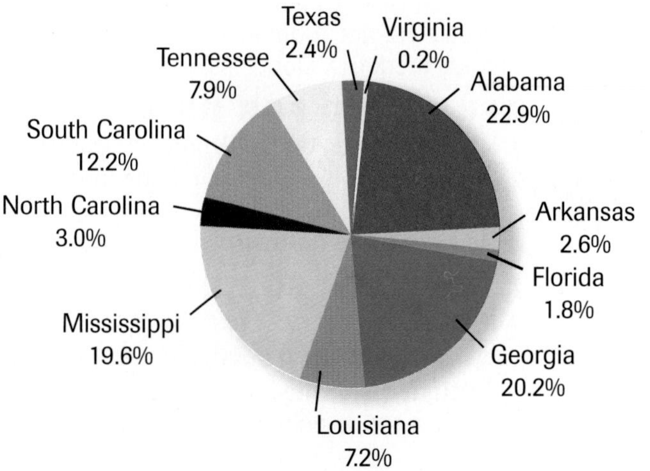

Source: *Historical Statistics of the South, 1790–1970*

Cotton Production and U.S. Exports, 1790–1850

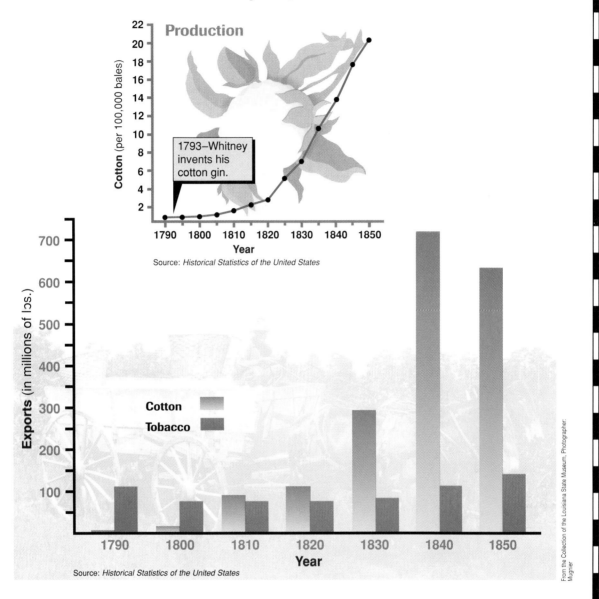

Source: *Historical Statistics of the United States*

Source: *Historical Statistics of the United States*

From the Collection of the Louisiana State Museum, Photographer: Mugnier

Tobacco was the country's leading export crop in 1790. Within 15 years, cotton had exceeded it. While tobacco production rose very slowly throughout the early 1800s, cotton boomed. The vast majority of this cotton was exported to Europe. **Linking Geography and History:** About how many times more cotton than tobacco was exported in 1840?

To learn more *about the Cotton Kingdom, go to the interactive map, "The Cotton Plantation," on the CD-ROM.*

• The Cotton Plantation

unit 4

SEEKING GROWTH AND CHANGE (1820–1860)

Chapter 11
Conflicts and Reform (1820–1860)

Chapter 12
Americans Expand West (1820–1860)

Courtesy Museum of American Political Life, University of Hartford, West Hartford, CT

Campaign items like this image of Andrew Jackson and this frog statue engraved with "Croak for the Jackson Wagon," marked a change in the way people ran for public office.

Linking Past to Present
Campaigning

VOTE MISSY FOR STUDENT COUNCIL PRESIDENT! This was one of the signs supporting a candidate running for office at Mena Middle School. She and her opponents all made signs, flyers, and buttons to encourage other students to vote for them. They even gathered at an assembly to give campaign speeches to the student body.

Students all across the country participate in similar campaigns every year. Their methods of carrying out campaigns reflect many of the methods that politicians use when they try to win public office. Posters, flyers, buttons, and public speeches are standard in almost all elections as each candidate tries to convince voters that he or she is the best candidate for the position. Bill Clinton and Bob Dole used these tactics to woo the voters in the 1996 presidential campaign.

Even though they may be too young to vote, these teenagers are getting involved in politics by campaigning for a candidate in a state election.

American elections were not always carried out in such a manner, however. During the country's first 30 years, most candidates for public office did very little campaigning. What little they did was aimed mostly at leaders of their own political parties. As you read this unit, you will learn that things began to change in the 1820s, a period that set the standard for the way in which political campaigns would be carried out in the future.

Instead of focusing their attention only on party leaders, candidates began to appeal directly to voters. They flooded the countryside with campaign "giveaways" such as buttons, metal tokens, bandannas, cups, and plates. Local campaign committees encouraged voters to get involved in elections by holding high-spirited parades, barbecues, and rallies. These public parties were intended both to make politics "fun" for voters and to get them excited about a particular candidate.

Probably the most significant change brought about in the 1820s was the increasing involvement of ordinary people in politics. As you read this unit, note that even many people who could not vote became active in campaigns and sought other ways of affecting national politics. You will learn that the era of the 1820s ushered in a period of expanding democratic ideals and political participation that are still at work in America today.

CHAPTER 11

The Granger Collection, New York

Conflicts and Reform

(1820–1860)

THEMES IN AMERICAN HISTORY

Constitutional Heritage:
How might the federal and state governments come into conflict?

Geographic Diversity:
Why might people from different regions of the country work together for political change?

Democratic Values:
How does American society reflect a belief in individual rights?

Writer Ralph Waldo Emerson captured the hopeful spirit of America during the presidency of Andrew Jackson:

"It is easy to see that a greater self-reliance must work a revolution in all the offices and relations of men; in their religion; in their education; in their pursuits; their modes [ways] of living; their association; in their property; in their . . . views."

• Video Opener

• Skill Builder

image above: *Andrew Jackson on the road to his inauguration*

Section 1

THE AGE OF ANDREW JACKSON

Multimedia Connections

Explore these related topics and materials on the CD–ROM to enrich your understanding of this section:

Gazetteer

- Maine
- Missouri

Atlas

- Male Suffrage

Profiles

- Andrew Jackson
- Henry Clay

Readings

- Jefferson on Missouri

After his inaugural address, Andrew Jackson held a reception at the White House. The mansion was soon full of people. Some knocked over furniture and tracked mud over the carpets, while others consumed huge amounts of food and drink. One woman reported that "the *majesty of the people* had disappeared, and . . . [had been replaced by] a mob . . . scrambling, fighting, romping." The new president escaped out a side door and slept in a nearby hotel.

As you read this section you will find out:

- **Why the Missouri Compromise was important.**
- **How national politics changed in the 1820s.**
- **How Jacksonian Democracy affected government.**

The Missouri Compromise

During President Monroe's first term, the nation grew rapidly. Settlers swarmed west, and new states joined the Union. This expansion, however, raised the issue of whether slavery should be allowed in the new lands. The issue came to a crisis in 1819, when Missouri applied for admission as a **slave state**, or a state where slavery was permitted. At the time there were 11 free states and 11 slave states in the Union. Missouri would upset this balance.

Government leaders, led by Speaker of the House Henry Clay, created the **Missouri Compromise** in 1820. This agreement admitted Missouri as a slave state and Maine as a free state. The compromise outlawed slavery in the rest of the Louisiana Purchase north of 36°30′ north latitude.

Learning from Maps.
Under the Missouri Compromise, Maine entered the Union as a free state and Missouri as a slave state.

• Maps

Region. After the Missouri Compromise, how many slave territories were there? How many free territories?

The Second President Adams

After the Missouri Compromise, sectional differences played an increasingly important role in national politics. No candidate had opposed President Monroe for re-election in 1820. In the following years, however, the North, South, and West each produced important leaders. When Monroe did not seek a third term, they competed for the presidency.

The election of 1824. One candidate was Secretary of State John Quincy Adams, the son of former president John Adams. The Adams name combined with his long career of public service gave John Quincy advantages, but he had few supporters outside the northeastern states. The favorite in the South was William H. Crawford of Georgia, Monroe's secretary of the treasury. The two other candidates were westerners, Andrew Jackson of Tennessee and Henry Clay of Kentucky.

As a hero of the War of 1812, Jackson was a nationally popular figure. In the heated campaign of 1824, Jackson won the largest share of the popular vote. No candidate received a majority of the electoral votes, however. Therefore, according to the Constitution, the House of Representatives decided the election. Clay strongly opposed Jackson, whom he considered unqualified to become president. Clay encouraged his supporters to back Adams, who then received the votes of a majority of the states and became president. After the election, Adams appointed Clay secretary of state. Jackson and his supporters accused Adams and Clay of making a "corrupt bargain." This turn of events made an angry Jackson very eager for the next election.

Adams's presidency. President Adams was extremely hardworking. He rose every morning at 5:00. Even in the dead of winter, Adams threw open his window and took a sponge bath with ice-cold water to prepare for his day's work. He took office, he said, with:

> **"intentions upright and pure, a heart devoted to the welfare of our country, and the unceasing application of all the faculties allotted [assigned] to me to her service."**

Adams favored a government that put national interests before sectional concerns. He would not use the

Around 1840 John Quincy Adams posed for this daguerreotype, an early form of photography.

• John Quincy Adams

political tactics necessary to get his programs adopted. For example, he refused to replace government officials who resisted his policies with people who supported them. As a result, his administration faced many problems.

The Election of 1828

By 1828 Adams was discouraged and depressed, but he was determined to seek re-election. This time he faced only one opponent—Andrew Jackson.

The campaign of 1828 was bitterly fought and mean-spirited. The race was, however, typical of politics at the time. Jackson's supporters split from the Democratic-Republican Party and began calling themselves Democrats. This was the formal beginning of the modern **Democratic Party**.

The Democrats said little about the political issues of the day. Instead, when they discovered that Adams had bought an ivory chess set and a billiard table for the White House, they charged him with wasting public money on gambling devices. The president's supporters replied with their own accusations. They said that Jackson was a gambler and a murderer. They also told shady stories about his wife, Rachel, and his mother. Neither these accusations nor the political issues probably had much effect on the election. Jackson won mainly because he was so popular.

Jacksonian Democracy

Jackson's victory marked a turning point in American history. He was the first westerner to occupy the White House, and his election signaled the growing importance of the West in the expanding nation.

The election also demonstrated a new democratic spirit in America that many historians have given the label **Jacksonian Democracy**. When he was running for president, Jackson presented himself as being in tune with the common person. Jackson and his supporters claimed that any ordinary person who was intelligent enough

Presidential Lives

Andrew Jackson

President Jackson was a pale, thin man who had a reputation for being very tough. His nickname was "Old Hickory," after a type of tree that produces extremely hard wood.

During the American Revolution, young Andrew had refused to polish a British officer's boots. The angry officer slashed the boy with a sword. Jackson bore the scar the rest of his life.

Later, when he was a general, Jackson showed little mercy for British or American Indian enemies. He was also tough on his personal and political opponents. His reputation as a fighter was widely known. While fighting one duel, he was shot in the chest. The bullet remained lodged there for the rest of his life.

Tough "Old Hickory" had a soft spot when it came to his wife, Rachel, however. When Rachel died just weeks before his inauguration, Jackson felt her loss deeply. He blamed her death on the vicious attacks made on her character during the 1828 campaign. "Those vile wretches," said a grief-stricken Jackson of his wife's critics. "May God Almighty forgive her murderers. . . . I never can."

could be an effective leader. Good leaders did not have to come from the upper classes of society. Jackson summed it up this way:

> **"The duties of all public officers are . . . so plain and simple that men of intelligence may readily qualify themselves for their performance. . . . In a country where offices are created solely for the benefit of the people, no one man has any more intrinsic [basic] right to official station [position] than another."**

Many Americans viewed Andrew Jackson as a man of the people. While he was president, residents of upstate New York sent him a 1,400-pound wheel of cheese. The White House invited hundreds of people to consume this gift at an informal party.

This faith in ordinary people had already led to important reforms. Most state governments had done away with property qualifications for voting and holding office. Presidential electors were increasingly chosen directly by the voters instead of by state legislatures.

Party leaders soon began to hold national meetings. Delegates from all over the nation attended these meetings, called **nominating conventions**, to choose their party's presidential and vice presidential candidates.

After the elections, winners generally appointed their supporters to government jobs. During Jackson's time this practice became known as the **spoils system**, from the phrase "to the victor belong the spoils." While Jackson did not make any more such appointments than most earlier presidents had, the Jacksonians added the idea of **rotation in office**. After a certain time some jobholders were replaced to give the party in power more political control.

Section 1 Review

• Glossary

IDENTIFY and explain the significance of the following: slave state, Henry Clay, Missouri Compromise, John Quincy Adams, Democratic Party, Jacksonian Democracy, nominating conventions, spoils system, rotation in office

REVIEWING FOR DETAILS

1. How did the presidential elections of the 1820s differ from those of earlier years?
2. What effect did Jacksonian Democracy have on government?

REVIEWING FOR UNDERSTANDING

3. **Geographic Literacy** How did the Missouri Compromise temporarily settle regional differences?
4. **Writing Mastery:** *Persuading* Imagine that you are a political leader in the 1820s. Write a short speech persuading members of your party to support a greater role for Americans in their government.
5. **Critical Thinking:** *Drawing Conclusions* What are the disadvantages of political candidates using negative personal attacks in their campaigns?

Section 2

JACKSON AS PRESIDENT

Multimedia Connections

Explore these related topics and materials on the CD–ROM to enrich your understanding of this section:

Media Bank

- Panic of 1837
- Martin Van Buren
- National Debt

Glossary

- balanced budget
- deficit spending
- nullification crisis

Profiles

- Martin Van Buren
- John C. Calhoun

Davy Crockett, a frontier hero, had opposed the presidency of fellow Tennessean Andrew Jackson. He also disliked Jackson's chosen successor, Martin Van Buren. Before the 1836 presidential campaign, Crockett wrote: "I think *all* will agree, that Martin Van Buren is not the man he is cracked up to be." Some people, Crockett added, had even "used the popularity of General Jackson to abuse the country with Martin Van Buren." Crockett's words were an attempt to sway the voters.

As you read this section you will find out:

- **Why the North and the South disagreed about tariffs.**
- **What the nullification crisis was.**
- **How Jackson destroyed the Bank of the United States.**

The Tariff Issue

President Jackson's national popularity was not a strong enough unifying force to end sectional disagreements. The argument over tariffs was particularly troublesome. Many people in the Northeast favored **protective tariffs**, high duties on imported goods that competed with American products.

Much of the enthusiasm for protective tariffs was connected to a plan developed by Henry Clay called the **American System**. While some northerners wanted protective tariffs, many westerners wanted the government to help pay for internal improvements, such as the roads and canals needed to get western goods to market. Clay hoped that these two regions could vote as one on issues—western members of Congress would vote for high tariffs in exchange for northern

By 1821 Henry Clay, then in his mid-forties, was an able politician. His support of the Missouri Compromise had gained him the nickname "Great Pacificator" [peacemaker]. Over the next 30 years, he continued to work toward compromise.

The Granger Collection, New York

votes for internal improvements. Clay explained that America had a:

> **"great diversity of interests: agricultural, planting, farming, commercial, navigating, fishing, manufacturing. . . . The good of each part and of the whole should be carefully consulted. This is the only mode by which we can preserve, in full vigor, the harmony of the whole Union."**

Southern states, however, which had few industries to protect, opposed protective tariffs. These tariffs would raise the price of many manufactured goods southerners had to buy from other countries.

The Nullification Crisis

Further complicating the tariff argument was the belief of some Americans that protective tariffs were unconstitutional. They argued that the Constitution gave Congress the power to tax imports to raise money but not to make foreign goods less competitive in price. Vice President John C. Calhoun of South Carolina insisted that if a state considered a law of Congress unconstitutional, the state could nullify, or refuse to accept, the law and prevent it from being enforced in that particular state.

Many Americans thought **nullification** threatened the Union. In 1830 Senator Daniel Webster of Massachusetts voiced this concern in a speech to the Senate. He closed with these rousing words: "Liberty *and* Union, now and forever, one and inseparable!"

Calhoun had expected that Congress would lower the high tariff of 1828, which many southerners called the **Tariff of Abominations** because they found it hateful. The northern manufacturers' influence in Congress was growing, however, and a new tariff passed in 1832 lowered duties only slightly.

Many southerners were extremely angry over this new tariff, and South Carolina decided to nullify it. Calhoun resigned as vice president and was elected senator from South Carolina. Jackson believed the nation would fall apart if states could reject federal laws. He threatened to march into South Carolina with U.S. troops and hang the nullifiers.

Few Americans were ready to break up the Union over tariffs, so Congress passed a new tariff that lowered duties gradually. South Carolina then repealed the Ordinance of Nullification. With this compromise, the nullification crisis passed, but the fundamental question—whether a state had the right to reject a federal law it believed to be unconstitutional—remained unanswered.

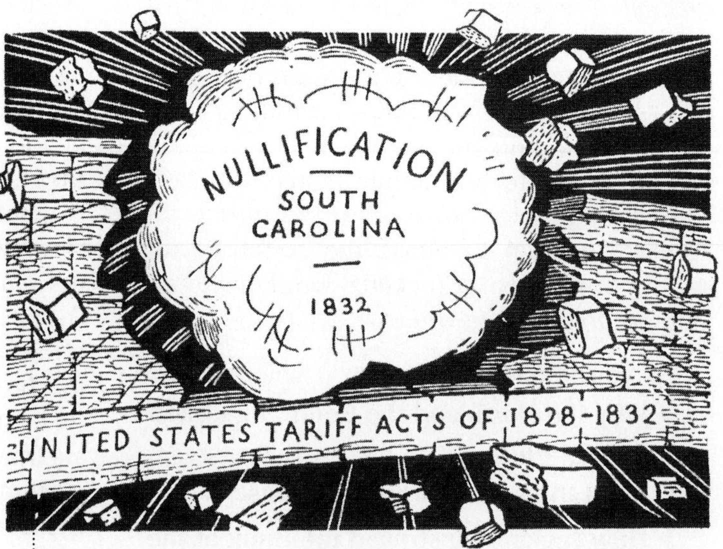

This political cartoon shows the Ordinance of Nullification blowing a hole through the wall built by the protective tariffs.

Jackson and the Bank

One reason Jackson acted so confidently in the nullification crisis was that he had just been overwhelmingly re-elected president in 1832. His popularity had risen in part because of his fight against the establishment of the Second Bank of the United States.

The charter for the First Bank of the United States had expired in 1811. In 1816 Congress had chartered a Second Bank of the United States to operate for a period of 20 years. Many Americans, including Jackson, opposed this Bank. Jackson believed that it had too much power over the nation's economy, and he favored limits on the Bank's operations.

The Bank's supporters in Congress knew that Jackson hoped to destroy it. Therefore, before the presidential election of 1832, they introduced a bill extending the Bank's existence. They hoped Jackson would sign it, or suffer the consequences of a veto in the election. Jackson vetoed the bill, explaining that the Bank had allowed a few wealthy investors to make profits from "the earnings of the American people." Most Americans were impressed by Jackson's attack on wealth. In the 1832 election Jackson defeated Henry Clay, 219 electoral votes to 49.

Jackson then began to withdraw the government's money on deposit in the Bank of the United States. He ordered that the federal government's income from taxes and land sales be deposited in various state banks.

Jackson's opponents charged that the government was showing favoritism in this matter. They called banks that received these deposits "pet banks." Many of these banks began to lend money recklessly. More bank notes were put into circulation. This, combined with other factors, caused enormous inflation. In 1837 this inflationary boom ended in a sudden collapse of prices and business activity, called the **Panic of 1837**. When people refused to accept the bank notes as payment, many banks failed. In addition, many companies throughout the country went out of business. The economies of the West and the South suffered greatly.

Some Americans opposed Jackson's policies. One person criticized Jackson's political leadership by showing "King Andrew the First" holding the presidential veto and standing on a shredded copy of the U.S. Constitution.

President Martin Van Buren

In 1836, with Jackson's strong support, the Democratic Party had nominated Martin Van Buren for president. Van Buren had been secretary of state during Jackson's first term and vice president during his second. This small, red-haired man was such a clever politician that he was frequently called "the Little Magician" or "the Red Fox." Even though three candidates ran against him, Van Buren won with little difficulty.

Van Buren's opponents in 1836 were members of a newly formed political organization known as the **Whig Party**, founded by Henry Clay in 1834. The new party did not present a serious challenge to the more established Democrats in the election of 1836, but they would play an important role in future elections.

Van Buren's presidency was hurt by the economic **depression**—a sharp drop in business activity accompanied by high unemployment—that followed the Panic of 1837. When Van Buren sought re-election in 1840, the Whigs had a sound strategy. They united behind General William Henry Harrison, who was famous for having defeated the great Indian leader Tecumseh at the Battle of Tippecanoe.

During the 1840 campaign the Whigs sang the praises of "Old Tippecanoe." They described Harrison as a simple man who lived in a log cabin and always offered a warm welcome to strangers. In contrast, the Whigs insisted that Van Buren dined off gold plates and wasted the people's money on expensive French wines. When Van Buren tried to discuss such issues as the tariff and banking policy, they shouted, "Van, Van, is a used-up man."

Voter turnout for the election of 1836 had reached close to 1.5 million. In 1840 the number of voters soared to around 2.4 million. Harrison won by an enormous margin—234 electoral votes to 60. The appeal to the common person that the Jacksonians had set in motion in 1828 had proved unbeatable.

The Granger Collection, New York

This image captures the main elements of William Henry Harrison's campaign. To the left, Harrison and his dog give a warm welcome to the one-legged veteran. This represents Harrison's fame as a soldier and host, while atop the roof, the American flag emphasizes his patriotism.

• William Harrison

Section 2 Review

• Glossary

IDENTIFY and explain the significance of the following: protective tariffs, American System, John C. Calhoun, nullification, Daniel Webster, Tariff of Abominations, Panic of 1837, Martin Van Buren, Whig Party, depression

REVIEWING FOR DETAILS

1. Why did the North and the South have different views about protective tariffs?
2. How did the nullification crisis develop, and how was it settled?
3. How did President Jackson deal with the Bank of the United States?

REVIEWING FOR UNDERSTANDING

4. **Geographic Literacy** Why did Henry Clay's American System focus on a compromise between the West and the North rather than the West and the South?
5. **Critical Thinking:** *Making Comparisons* What were the similarities and differences between the presidential elections of 1828 and 1840?

Section 3

INDIAN REMOVAL

Multimedia Connections

Explore these related topics and materials on the CD–ROM to enrich your understanding of this section:

Profiles

- John Ross
- Sequoyah

Gazetteer

- Indian Territory

Media Bank

- Cherokee Trail of Tears

Readings

- Trail of Tears
- Two Views of Indian Removal

Black Hawk and other Sauk returned to their Illinois home, east of the Mississippi River, for the spring planting. The time for the planting came and went, however, while they negotiated and battled with the U.S. Army. Exhausted and starving, Black Hawk and his followers decided to retreat west, back across the river. Troops came upon them and opened fire on the men, women, and children who tried desperately to swim to the safety of the far shore. They would never again return to Illinois.

As you read this section you will find out:

- **Why settlers wanted to remove American Indians.**
- **Where the government moved Indians.**
- **How American Indians resisted removal.**

Jackson's Indian Policy

One of the major issues during Jackson's presidency was the removal of eastern Indians to territory west of the Mississippi River. As the nation expanded, settlers slowly pushed American Indians farther and farther west.

Americans who lived far from the frontier knew very little about Indians other than what they read in novels such as James Fenimore Cooper's "Leatherstocking Tales." Settlers who wanted Indian land had no interest in learning about American Indians or their rights. They often ignored the fact that Indians' right to their land was guaranteed by treaties.

Ever since President Jefferson's time, U.S. presidents had considered relocating eastern Indians onto western territory acquired in the Louisiana Purchase. Under President Monroe, a policy of removal had been adopted to solve "the Indian Problem," and Jackson had been a supporter of Indian removal since the War of 1812. Jackson felt that Indian nations were a threat to the stability of the United States because they were not under the federal government's authority.

Jackson hoped to convince Indians to move by offering to pay eastern tribes for their lands, to transport them west at government expense, and to settle them on the frontier. The place chosen to become **Indian Territory** was in present-day Oklahoma.

Not everyone favored Indian removal. For example, some religious groups strongly objected to uprooting people from their homes. Senator Theodore Frelinghuysen of New Jersey was also a critic of the seizure of Indian lands. "We have crowded the tribes upon a few miserable acres," he said, ". . . and still, like the horse-leech, our insatiated cupidity [unsatisfied greed] cries, give! give! give!" Despite such protests, in 1830 Congress passed the **Indian Removal Act**, providing money to carry out Jackson's policy.

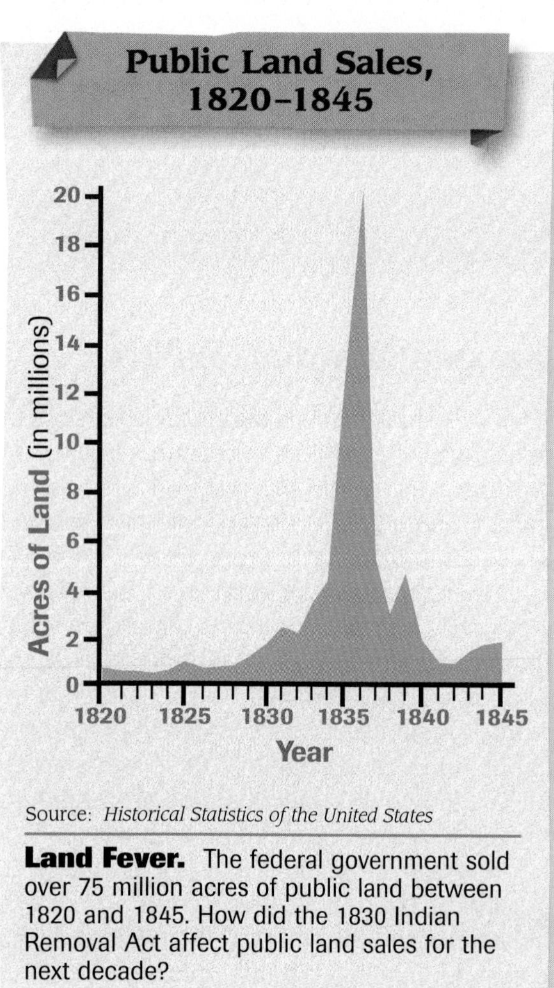

Source: *Historical Statistics of the United States*

Land Fever. The federal government sold over 75 million acres of public land between 1820 and 1845. How did the 1830 Indian Removal Act affect public land sales for the next decade?

Indian Removal Begins

The federal government first approached the Choctaw, who lived primarily in central Mississippi. In September 1830, government agents organized a conference at Dancing Rabbit Creek. Over 5,000 Choctaw attended. The agents distributed gifts, including cash bribes. They promised to provide the Choctaw with land in the West, free transportation, expense money for a year while they were settling in their new home, and annual grants to support the tribal government.

Any Choctaw who wished to remain in Mississippi would be given a plot of land. Agents warned, however, that failure to move could mean destruction of their society. The federal government would offer the Choctaw no protection against the state of Mississippi.

The Choctaw accepted removal in the **Treaty of Dancing Rabbit Creek** and then ceded their homeland—10.5 million acres—to the United States. "Friends, my attachment to my native land is strong—that cord is now broken," one Choctaw chief said. "We must go forth as wanderers in a strange land!"

Jackson was eager to have the removal carried out quickly. The move was badly managed, however. The first Choctaw group set out during the winter of 1831–32. That winter turned out to be bitterly cold, even in Mississippi and Arkansas. Many Choctaw died of exposure and starvation.

For later Choctaw parties, the journey was somewhat better. A Choctaw named Tushpa recalled his last days spent on the eastern side of the Mississippi River.

> **"The party put up some shelter and arranged temporary camps and prepared to stay on the banks of the river until they might**

During his life Sequoyah excelled as a scholar, silversmith, painter, and warrior. He is most noted, however, for developing the Cherokee alphabet and teaching thousands of Cherokee to read and write.

The Granger Collection, New York

cross it. On the second night of their stay a runner had announced that a fire had destroyed their former homes and everything that had been left in them, so that the last hope of remaining in this homeland was rudely snatched away. . . ."

In all, about 15,000 Choctaw settled in Indian Territory.

Resistance to Removal

The removal policy was applied to most Indians east of the Mississippi, including northern tribes. In 1832 a band of Sauk who earlier had moved to Iowa returned to Illinois under Chief Black Hawk. Army and state militia units were immediately dispatched to drive them back. The resulting Black Hawk War was short but very bloody. Black Hawk was soon captured, and his defeated followers were returned back across the Mississippi to Iowa.

More resistance to removal came from the southeastern United States, where some 120,000 American Indians still lived. Resistance was greatest among the Cherokee and the Seminole.

Cherokee resistance. For centuries, the Cherokee had been farmers. They lived in houses grouped in small settlements or towns and worked fields owned by the entire community. Families were assigned specific plots to cultivate.

The Cherokee had adopted many elements of white culture. They had a written alphabet, a newspaper, and a constitution modeled on the U.S. Constitution. Like many white southerners, some Cherokee owned plantations and held slaves.

The Cherokee also maintained their own tribal government. Under a series of treaties with the United States, they were essentially a separate nation within the state of Georgia. It was not long, however, before Georgia authorities informed the Cherokee that they must either give up their government and submit to Georgia law or leave the state. If they refused they would be driven out by force.

Jackson believed the Cherokee should agree to move west because they were unwilling to give up their government. After all, he explained, every year thousands of Americans left family and friends "to seek new homes in distant regions." Jackson's comparison overlooked the fact that most of the settlers *wanted*

Woolaroc Museum, Bartlesville, Oklahoma

Jackson's Indian removal policy meant the dislocation of thousands of American Indians. Forced out of their homes and carrying what possessions they could, American Indians endured terrible conditions on the journey to Indian Territory.

to move west, and the Cherokee did not. Jackson also ignored the fact that the Indians' right to their lands was guaranteed by treaty.

The Cherokee took their battle to the courts. In the 1832 case of ***Worcester* v. *Georgia***, the U.S. Supreme Court ruled in their favor. The Court declared that Georgia law did not extend to the Cherokee Nation. The Cherokee had won their case within the U.S. legal system!

President Jackson, however, did not accept the Supreme Court's ruling. He permitted Georgia, in effect, to nullify the Court's decree and use force against the Cherokee.

The Trail of Tears. In 1835, in the **Treaty of New Echota**, a small group of Cherokee leaders finally agreed to be resettled. This small group clearly did not represent a majority of the Cherokee people, but the U.S. Senate ratified the treaty by a single vote in May 1836. Chief John Ross presented the Cherokee's protest to Congress:

> **"Little did they anticipate that when taught to think and feel as the American citizen, and to have with him a common interest, they were to be despoiled by their guardian, to become strangers and wanderers in the land of their fathers."**

Two years later the Cherokee were driven from their homes by militia and were locked up in stockades. They were then marched 800 miles west through Tennessee and Arkansas to Indian Territory. Along the way, sick and tired people were left in the freezing cold to care for themselves with little or no food. Many did not survive the trip. Of the estimated 17,000 Cherokee who started the journey, about 4,000 died before they reached their destination. The Cherokee called this forced march the **Trail of Tears**.

Seminole resistance. Some Seminole Indians in Florida had also signed treaties agreeing to move west. When the majority of the Seminole refused to leave, however, the government sent in troops. The Seminole, led by Osceola, were experts at striking swiftly and then

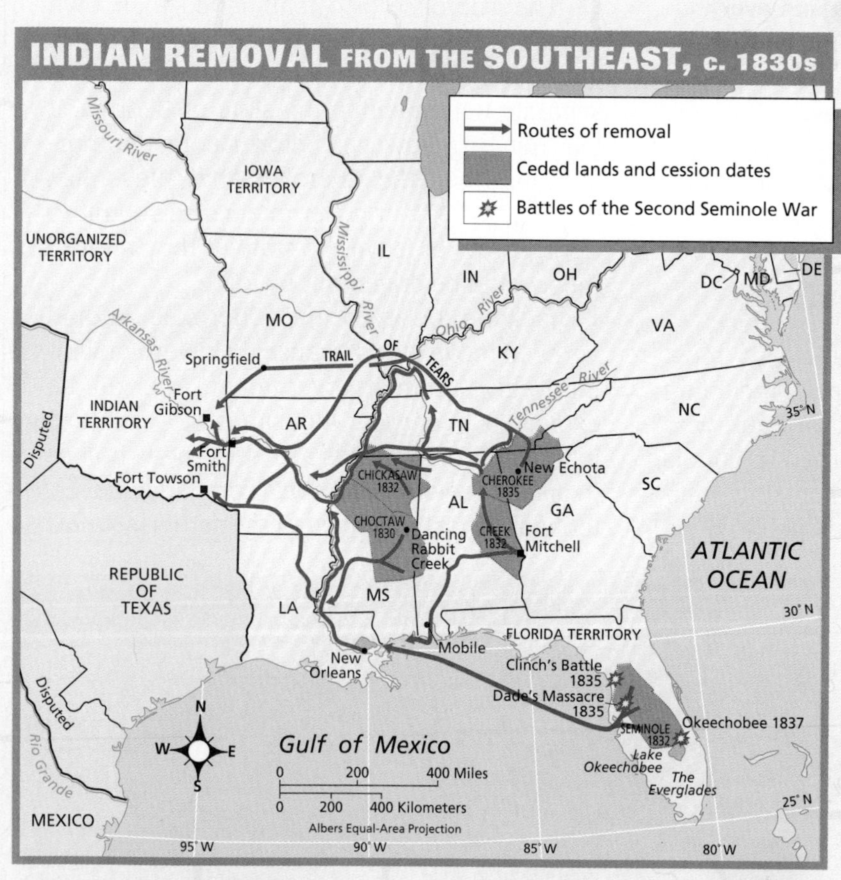

Learning from Maps.
American Indians crossed hundreds of miles and passed through several states on their forced relocation west under the Indian Removal Act.

▶ **Location.** What states bordered Indian Territory?

• **Maps**

melting away into swamps and thickets. For seven years they fought on, retreating deeper into the Everglades but never surrendering, despite their decreasing numbers.

By the time the second of two Seminole wars had come to an end in 1842, fewer than 3,000 Seminole had been sent to Indian Territory. Their resistance finally wore down the federal government, which had lost 1,500 regular army soldiers and $20 million trying to remove the Seminole.

The Seminole, however, were not a typical example of Indian Removal. In just over a decade, the government had resettled about 45,000 southern Indians. Removed tribes suffered heavy loss of lives, and few Indians remained north of Florida. For the time being, the survivors were free to go their own way.

• Osceola

Under Osceola's leadership, the Seminole resisted removal. They continued to fight even after Osceola was captured at a peace conference. He died in an army prison in South Carolina in 1838.

The Granger Collection, New York

Section 3 Review

• Glossary

• Gazetteer

IDENTIFY and explain the significance of the following: Indian Territory, Indian Removal Act, Treaty of Dancing Rabbit Creek, *Worcester* v. *Georgia,* Treaty of New Echota, Trail of Tears, Osceola

REVIEWING FOR DETAILS

1. Why did white settlers support Indian removal?
2. How did Indians resist removal from their lands?

REVIEWING FOR UNDERSTANDING

3. **Geographic Literacy** Where did the government relocate American Indians, and what hardships did Indians face getting there?
4. **Writing Mastery:** *Creating* Write a short story, poem, or song that expresses how a Cherokee might have felt on the Trail of Tears.
5. **Critical Thinking:** *Generalizations and Stereotypes* How did the attitudes of many whites toward American Indians affect the government's Indian policy?

Section 4
An Age of Reform

Multimedia Connections

Explore these related topics and materials on the CD-ROM to enrich your understanding of this section:

Media Bank

- Shakers
- Ralph Waldo Emerson
- Hudson River School
- Seneca Falls Declaration
- Helping the Children
- Educating the Blind
- Social Reform
- Reform and Society

Readings

- American Romantic Poets
- Reform and the Ideal World
- Women Seek Rights

Profiles

- Emily Dickinson
- Mary Lyon
- Emma Willard

Atlas

- Utopian Communities

Biographies

- Ralph Waldo Emerson

Simulation

- Reform: Making a Difference

Reverend Thomas Low Nichols had been to several revivals. The crowded camps always seemed to bubble with excitement. After waking up to prayers, the camp would gather for a hearty breakfast, then more people would arrive and the camp meeting would begin. People became hysterical with joy, rolling on the ground or shouting prayers. A number of them were converted. Most would attempt to maintain the momentum and bring their spirit of reform back to their communities.

As you read this section you will find out:

- **What ministers preached in the Second Great Awakening.**
- **How Americans tried to reform society.**
- **Why women wanted more rights.**

The Second Great Awakening

In the 1790s a **Second Great Awakening** began in various parts of the nation. One of the most influential preachers of the Second Great Awakening was Charles Grandison Finney. He believed that **revivals**, or spirited religious meetings, were essential to spreading the word of God. Finney gave hundreds of sermons in the 1820s and 1830s. In his sermons he described a democratic heaven that seemed rather like the United States of America. "God always allows His children as much liberty as they are prepared to enjoy," Finney explained.

The revival movement swept through upstate New York, Kentucky, and Ohio with great force. People flocked to religious camp meetings, which often lasted for days.

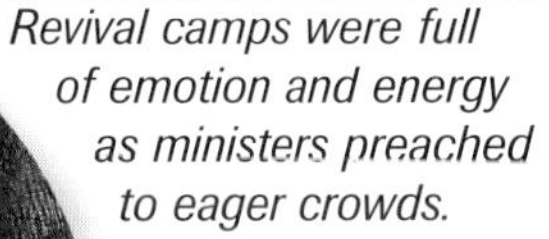

Revival camps were full of emotion and energy as ministers preached to eager crowds.

The Granger Collection, New York

• Southern Camp Meetings

Converts joined several Protestant groups, most notably Presbyterian, Baptist, and Methodist. Church attendance increased throughout the country.

The Second Great Awakening also advanced the cause of moral and social reform, which was a vital function of churches all over America. For example, many ministers outside the South became involved in the abolition movement.

Reforming Society

The hopeful spirit of the Second Great Awakening affected other movements around the country. Some New Englanders, for example, were attracted to **transcendentalism**, a philosophy that stressed an individual's ability to transcend, or rise above, material concerns, such as money or possessions. New England writers Ralph Waldo Emerson, Henry David Thoreau, and Margaret Fuller, and educator Bronson Alcott were important transcendental leaders. Americans also formed **utopian communities**, places where they tried to live out their vision of a perfect society.

• American Romantics

Most Americans were unwilling to live in isolated utopian communities and abandon many of the patterns of everyday life. They were, however, sincerely interested in improving society. Some devoted their energies to helping poor and disadvantaged people.

Through Others' Eyes

The Second Great Awakening

During the Second Great Awakening a young French visitor, Alexis de Tocqueville, toured the United States. He recorded his impressions of the country's religion in his book *Democracy in America*:

> *"It must never be forgotten that religion gave birth to Anglo-American society. In the United States, religion is therefore mingled with all the habits of the nation and all the feelings of patriotism, whence it derives a peculiar force. . . . Religious institutions have remained wholly distinct from political institutions, so that former laws have been easily changed whilst former belief has remained unshaken. Christianity has therefore retained a strong hold on the public mind in America. . . . Christian sects [groups] are infinitely diversified [spread out] and perpetually [continuously] modified; but Christianity itself is an established and irresistible fact."*

Dorothea Dix dedicated her life to social reform.

• Dorothea Dix

The Granger Collection, New York

Aiding the disadvantaged. Dorothea Dix, a Massachusetts schoolteacher and reformer, revolutionized the treatment of people who were mentally ill. One day in 1841 Dix taught a Sunday school class in a jail in Cambridge, Massachusetts. She discovered to her horror that mentally ill people were being kept there and treated like criminals. Dix spent months visiting prisons and then reported her findings to the Massachusetts legislature:

> **"I come to present the strong claims of suffering humanity . . . the miserable, the desolate [deserted], the outcast . . . to call your attention to the *present* state of insane persons confined . . . in *cages, closets, cellars, stalls, pens! Chained, naked, beaten with rods,* and *lashed* into obedience."**

Thereafter, Dix worked hard to improve the care of prisoners and those who suffered from mental illness. She visited prisons all over the country and wrote reports describing conditions within them. Dix insisted that mental illness should not be treated as criminal behavior. Through her efforts, many states investigated the treatment of mentally ill persons and established facilities for their care.

Saving children. As cities grew larger, an increasing number of children and teenagers began to get into trouble with the law. Many orphans, runaways, and children who had been abandoned by their parents wandered homeless in the cities, sometimes begging and stealing to survive. When found, these children were often put into the local poorhouse along with adult debtors, drunkards, and tramps. Some people thought that a different approach should be taken with these children.

Reformers founded houses of refuge in New York, Boston, and Philadelphia. Life in these institutions was hard; discipline was strict. The children rose at dawn, and after passing inspection to make sure they were neat and clean, they had an hour or so of lessons. After breakfast, the rest of the day, except for the noon break, was spent working in shops. The boys made such things as cane chair seats, nails, and candles. The girls spent their time sewing. Evening classes went on until bedtime. Reformers hoped to change the behavior of delinquent children. They also wanted to make sure that the homeless ones were protected and taught a trade.

Attacking "Demon Rum." Still other reformers tried to get citizens to give up what they considered bad habits, such as drinking alcohol and gambling. **Temperance**, the effort to limit drinking, soon became a campaign to eliminate the consumption of alcohol. Other reformers supported the **prohibition**, or outlawing, of

The Granger Collection, New York

Reformers hoped that family life would be improved if adults signed the temperance pledge.

Students like these often found themselves taking exams under difficult conditions. One-room schoolhouses could be overcrowded and physically uncomfortable. Having students of a wide range of ages made it hard at times for teacher and student alike. Nonetheless, Americans took pride in their free public education and in the high literacy rate they achieved as a nation.

the manufacture and sale of alcoholic beverages. Many members of the American Temperance Society, which was founded in 1826, traveled around the country lecturing and distributing pamphlets promoting temperance. The campaign reached a high point in 1851 when the state of Maine outlawed the manufacture and sale of alcoholic beverages.

Educational Reforms

The fight for public education made a great deal of progress in the mid-1800s during the Age of Reform. Educational reformers argued that democracy could not prosper unless all citizens could read and write. Schools would train students to be patriotic, hardworking, and law-abiding citizens. Many Americans also supported public education because they hoped it would enable their children to succeed in the world.

Before 1839 there were no established qualifications for teachers. One man being interviewed for a job as a teacher in a mining town was asked only, "Do you retain a clear recollection of the twenty-six letters of the alphabet?" Apparently that was all the town expected him to know to "educate" the local children!

By modern standards even the best schools of the 1830s and 1840s were very uncomfortable. One-room "little red schoolhouses" were the rule. Students sat on narrow, backless benches. Sixty or more children of all ages were sometimes crowded into one classroom, and a single teacher had to deal with first graders and teenagers at the same time.

The effort to improve public education was particularly strong in Massachusetts. The Puritans had established public elementary schools in all but the smallest colonial towns, and the state built on this foundation. Thanks to Horace Mann, the first secretary of education for Massachusetts, by 1848 there were 50 well-equipped and comfortable public schools throughout the state.

The growth of public education had many far-reaching effects. By the 1860s villages, towns, and cities in other states had established free elementary schools, and most white adults in the United States could read and write. Education had become a public responsibility.

In the early 1800s, however, women had little hope of receiving much education beyond reading and writing. Free African Americans had even fewer opportunities. Many people believed that African Americans were intellectually inferior and that women could not stand the strain of studying such difficult subjects as chemistry and mathematics.

In 1833 Oberlin College in Ohio became the first college to admit women and African Americans. Four years later, Mary Lyon founded the first women's college, Mount Holyoke in Massachusetts. In 1847 the poet Emily Dickinson, then a teenager, described Mount Holyoke's high standards:

> **"Miss Lyon is raising her standard of scholarship a good deal, on account of the number of applicants this year and on account of that she makes the examinations more severe than usual. You cannot imagine how trying they are, because if we cannot go through them all in a specified time, we are sent home."**

The Granger Collection, New York

Horace Mann spent his life calling for education reform—both in public schools and in teaching practices.

• Horace Mann

The Women's Rights Movement

Since the late 1700s many women had grown increasingly dissatisfied with the limitations society placed on their activities. During the 1830s and 1840s, increasing prosperity offered middle- and upper-class women more time to pursue activities outside the home. Many of them became involved in reform movements and began to call for more rights for women.

Women and abolition. Many women became reformers and were particularly interested in the abolition movement. Women such as former slave Sojourner Truth were able to move audiences with their powerful speeches opposing slavery. When women became abolitionists, their activism often raised an awareness of their own limited rights. Female abolitionists frequently found themselves forced into secondary roles. For example, many women who tried to speak in public against slavery were prevented from doing so by male abolitionists.

Both Sarah and Angelina Grimké experienced so much resistance when they made speeches attacking slavery that they became activists for women's rights as well. Angelina Grimké wrote that "the investigation of the rights of the slave has led me to a better understanding of my own [rights]."

One argument abolitionists used against slavery was the statement in the Declaration of Independence that "all men are created equal." Supporters of women's rights argued that if slaves were entitled to equality, surely women were too. Women were still treated as second-class citizens, however. They did not have such civil rights as voting or sitting on juries. Most married women had little or no control over their own property.

The Seneca Falls Convention. Another abolitionist, Elizabeth Cady Stanton, became a women's rights leader after she was not allowed to participate in an antislavery conference in 1840. Eight years later, Stanton and Lucretia Mott organized the first American women's rights convention at Seneca Falls, New York.

In their Declaration of Sentiments at the **Seneca Falls Convention**, the delegates echoed the Declaration of Independence. Just as it had listed complaints of the colonists, the Declaration of Sentiments contained a list of women's grievances. "The history of mankind," the declaration said, "is a history of repeated injuries . . . on the part of man toward woman." These included denials of the right to vote, the right to equal educational opportunity, and the right of married women to own property. The Declaration of Sentiments also demanded that women receive "all the rights and privileges which belong to them as citizens of the United States."

In the 1850s several national women's rights conventions took place. Women were fighting for change. Susan B. Anthony organized campaigns on behalf of equal pay for female teachers and for equal property rights for women. Addressing a women's rights convention in 1855, Lucy Stone described the inspiration for her hard work:

> **"In education, in marriage, in religion, in everything, disappointment is the lot of woman. It shall be the business of my life to deepen this disappointment in every woman's heart until she bows down to it no longer."**

Some states began to grant women more legal rights. In 1860 New York gave women the right to sue in court and to control their earnings and property. The women's rights campaigners had achieved some of their goals, but women were unable to gain the right to vote.

Elizabeth Cady Stanton (left) and Susan B. Anthony (right) were tireless in their pursuit of women's rights.

• Women in Jacksonian American

Section 4 Review

• Glossary

IDENTIFY and explain the significance of the following: Second Great Awakening, Charles Grandison Finney, revivals, transcendentalism, utopian communities, Dorothea Dix, temperance, prohibition, Horace Mann, Mary Lyon, Elizabeth Cady Stanton, Lucretia Mott, Seneca Falls Convention, Susan B. Anthony

• Time Line

REVIEWING FOR DETAILS

1. What ideas did preachers express during the Second Great Awakening?
2. How did Americans try to reform society?
3. Why did women campaign for more rights?

REVIEWING FOR UNDERSTANDING

4. **Writing Mastery:** *Expressing* Write a short essay expressing the benefits of a public education system.
5. **Critical Thinking:** *Drawing Conclusions* How might working for movements such as abolition or educational reform have encouraged women to demand greater rights for themselves?

CHAPTER 12

Americans Expand West (1820–1860)

THEMES IN AMERICAN HISTORY

Geographic Diversity:
How might natural resources stimulate the development of a region?

Cultural Diversity:
How might a people's culture reflect the particular region in which they live?

Global Relations:
In what ways might national expansion affect foreign relations?

In the United States, thousands of men and women of all ages took editor Horace Greeley's advice to "fly, scatter through the country, go to the Great West." The American West was not an empty land waiting to be settled, however. American Indians had lived there for centuries, and Mexicans had migrated north to the Southwest and California.

• Video Opener

• Skill Builder

image above: *Thomas Moran's* Grand Canyon of the Yellowstone

Section 1
Americans in Texas

Multimedia Connections

Explore these related topics and materials on the CD–ROM to enrich your understanding of this section:

Atlas
- Settlements in Texas, 1850

Biographies
- Antonio López de Santa Anna

Media Bank
- Sam Houston, Texas Hero
- Lorenzo de Zavala
- Comanche on Horseback
- Mexican Fandango
- Life in Northern Mexico
- Austin, Republic of Texas
- Texas, 1822–1845

Profiles
- Stephen F. Austin
- Sam Houston

Readings
- Comanche Kidnapping
- Texas

Father Miguel Hidalgo y Costilla reached for the church bells and pulled the rope. Would history remember the bells that rang for independence on September 16, 1810? For it was on this day in the small village of Dolores, Mexico, that Hidalgo summoned Mexicans to throw off Spanish rule, embrace racial equality, and redistribute the land. Thousands of Mexicans answered this *Grito de Dolores* (Cry of Dolores), which signaled the beginning of Mexico's revolt against Spain.

As you read this section you will find out:

- **How Mexico treated settlers from the United States.**
- **Why Texans wanted independence from Mexico.**
- **How Texas won its independence.**

Mexican Texas

Mexico finally won its independence from Spain in 1821. The new country's territory included present-day Mexico and what today are the states of Texas, New Mexico, Arizona, California, Nevada, Utah, and portions of Colorado, Wyoming, Oklahoma, and Kansas.

The struggle for independence had taken its toll on Texas, which was inhabited mainly by Indians and **Tejanos** (tay-HAH-nohs), Texans of Mexican descent. Settlements in east Texas had been destroyed, and the region had lost almost two thirds of its Tejano population. Only about 3,000 Tejanos remained. They lived mainly on sprawling cattle ranches or in old mission towns like San Antonio.

The Mexican government hoped to rebuild Texas's population and settlements by attracting colonists from Europe and the United

States. The newcomers would become loyal citizens and would also help Mexico's economy, which was burdened by a heavy war debt and the loss of Spanish investment.

• New Spain and Mexico

Texas Opens to Americans

Before the Mexican Revolution, a few U.S. citizens had begun to trickle into Texas. Among them was Moses Austin of Missouri, who expected to acquire a fortune by establishing a colony of 300 American families in Texas.

Spain had given Austin a land grant, but he died of pneumonia before he could organize a group. On his deathbed, Austin asked his son Stephen to carry out his dream of establishing a colony in Texas.

In 1821 Stephen F. Austin and a group of 300 families, later known as the "Old Three Hundred," arrived in Texas. Before they could establish their settlement, Austin had to renew his father's land grant with the new Mexican government.

Austin therefore became an ***empresario***—someone who made a business of bringing in settlers. Each *empresario* received thousands of acres of land for bringing families into Texas. Each family also received a grant of land. American settlers began to pour into Texas to take advantage of this offer. Most new colonists were southerners interested in growing cotton. They often brought slaves to work their land.

Austin became a citizen of Mexico, as required by the government, and was the political leader of the American settlement in Texas. He was unsuccessful, however, in persuading other American settlers to be loyal to Mexico. Furthermore, few bothered to learn Spanish or to adapt to Mexican culture. By 1830 some 20,000 Americans had settled in Texas, outnumbering Tejanos by about five to one. Most of these colonists were beginning to feel that Texas should be *their* country, rather than part of Mexico. Others felt that their ties were to the United States.

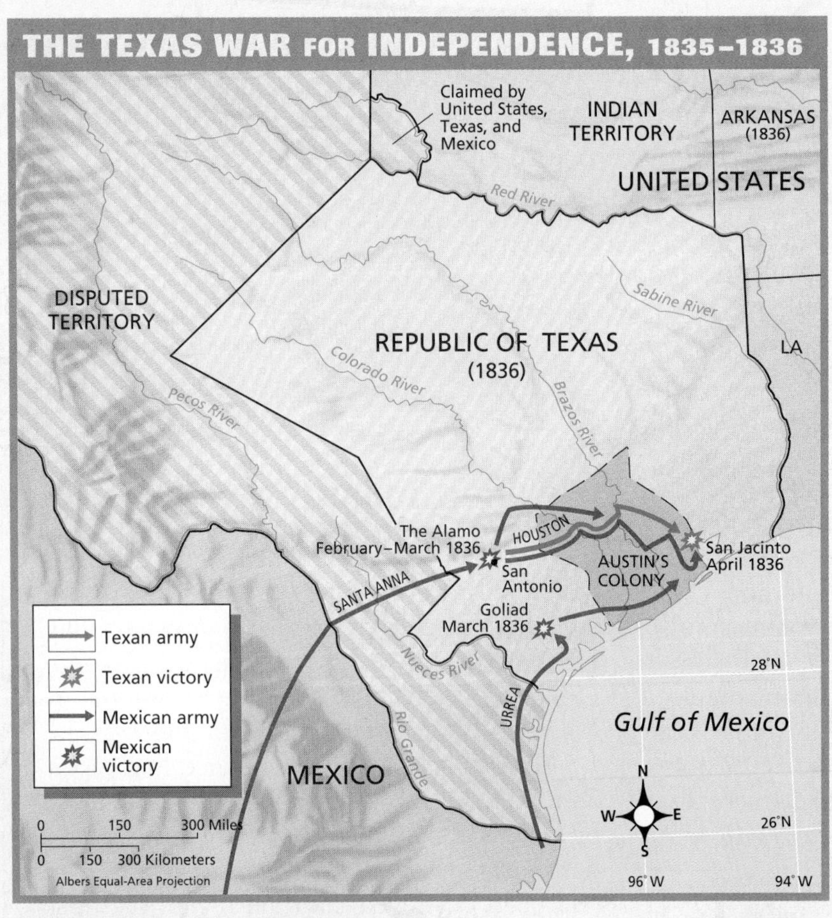

Learning from Maps.
The Texans won their independence from Mexico, but the Republic's border remained in dispute. Mexico considered the Nueces River to be Texas's southern boundary.

Location. How far did the Texans claim that their southern border extended?

• Maps

Stephen F. Austin obtained a large land grant to establish a colony in Texas. He became a Mexican citizen, but his loyalty to Mexico was soon tested.

These developments troubled the Mexican government. One official, General Manuel Mier y Terán, warned:

> **"The department of Texas is contiguous to [borders] the most avid [greedy] nation in the world. The North Americans have conquered whatever territory adjoins them. They incite [encourage] uprising in the territory in question."**

Concerned about the situation in Texas, Mexico decided to reverse its policy and prohibited further immigration from the United States. This restriction, along with a ban on importing slaves, angered most American colonists and even many Tejanos.

Texas Gains Independence

These Texans disliked the national government in Mexico City. Most believed in the Mexican constitution of 1824, which gave the Mexican states a great deal of local control. After a new, strongly centralized Mexican government took control in the early 1830s, Mexican officials began to take away the powers guaranteed to states in the constitution. This angered the residents of Texas, who did not want people in a faraway capital to run their lives. They wanted more local power over such issues as the right to hold slaves.

Government leaders in Mexico City resented the Texans' attitude. When Austin went to Mexico City to explain the Texans' position, he was thrown in jail and held for a year without trial.

The fight for the Alamo. Finally, in 1835, Texans revolted. The Mexican government quickly reacted. President Antonio López de Santa Anna marched northward at the head of an army of 6,000 troops to put down the rebellion. In February 1836 he captured San Antonio. However, 187 rebels and about 30 townspeople retreated into the **Alamo**, an old Spanish mission that had been converted to a fort. They refused to surrender despite the overwhelming odds. In a letter addressed "To the People of Texas & all Americans in the world," rebel leader William Travis vowed "Victory or Death!"

> **"I shall never surrender or retreat. . . . I call on you in the name of Liberty, of patriotism & everything dear to the American character, to come to our aid. . . . If this call is neglected, I am determined to sustain myself as long as possible & die like a soldier who never forgets what is due to his own honor & that of his country."**

The defenders of the Alamo fought off attacks by the Mexican army for nearly two weeks, but eventually Santa Anna's troops successfully stormed the walls. Suzanna Dickenson (above) was one of the few survivors of the Battle of the Alamo.

Fall of the Alamo by Robert Jenkins Onderdonk, Courtesy of Friends of the Governor's Mansion, Austin, Texas

After nearly two weeks of repeated attacks, Santa Anna's army finally overran the Alamo. Every one of its defenders died—only the lives of civilians were spared. The victory cost Santa Anna some 1,500 casualities.

Among the Alamo's dead were Davy Crockett, a colorful frontier character who had represented Tennessee in Congress, and James Bowie, for whom the Bowie knife is named. The battle set Francisco Esparza, who attacked the Alamo, against his brother, Gregorio, who died defending it. Other Tejano families were similarly divided in the conflict.

After the Alamo, another Mexican army captured the town of Goliad. However, the fighting spirit of the rebels was unbroken, particularly after they learned that Santa Anna had ordered the execution of 371 Texans captured at Goliad.

Victory at San Jacinto. On March 2, 1836, the Texans had declared independence. They set up a temporary government for their **Republic of Texas** and appointed Sam Houston commander of its army. For a time Houston retreated eastward. Then, on April 21, 1836, he turned and attacked Santa Anna's pursuing army.

Houston had only about 800 soldiers, Santa Anna about 1,400. "Forward!" Houston shouted. The Texans rushed into the Mexican camp, the battle cry "Remember the Alamo! Remember Goliad!" on their lips. Under the Texans' fierce attack, the Mexicans fell back in disorder and were soon defeated.

Houston's victory was total. "The fierce vengeance of the Texans could not be resisted," he later explained. In less than 20 minutes more than 600 Mexicans were killed. This short **Battle of San Jacinto** had determined who would win the war. After the battle, Santa Anna was captured. Houston set Santa Anna free in exchange for his promise to grant Texas its independence. When the war ended, the Texans set up a permanent government, electing Houston, a former governor of Tennessee, president and Lorenzo de Zavala, who had served in the Mexican congress, vice president.

President Antonio López de Santa Anna led the troops that came to put down the rebellion in Texas.

Section 1 Review

• Glossary

IDENTIFY and explain the significance of the following: Tejanos, Stephen F. Austin, *empresario,* Antonio López de Santa Anna, Alamo, William Travis, Republic of Texas, Sam Houston, Battle of San Jacinto

LOCATE and explain the importance of the following: Texas, San Antonio, Goliad

• Gazetteer

REVIEWING FOR DETAILS

1. How did Mexico deal with American settlers in Texas?
2. Why did people in Texas want independence from Mexico?

REVIEWING FOR UNDERSTANDING

3. **Geographic Literacy** What attracted Tejanos and Americans to Texas?
4. **Writing Mastery:** *Describing* Imagine that you are a soldier in Sam Houston's army. Write several diary entries describing the revolt against Mexico.
5. **Critical Thinking:** *Recognizing Point of View* Imagine that you are a Mexican government official. How might you feel about the Texans' demands?

Section 2
THE FAR WEST

Multimedia Connections

Explore these related topics and materials on the CD–ROM to enrich your understanding of this section:

Gazetteer
- Oregon Country

Atlas
- Oregon Country

Media Bank
- Oregon Settlers
- Trailblazer

Profiles
- Marcus Whitman
- George Caleb Bingham
- George Catlin

Interactive Map
- Mission to Metropolis

Readings
- Two Years Before the Mast
- Settling the Northwest

Many pioneer women were eager to head west. The wagons had to be hitched and the supplies loaded, then the wagon train could get rolling and the adventure would begin. On the trail, some lost their eagerness. Lodisa Frizzel wrote:

> **"That this journey is . . . perilous [dangerous], the deaths of many will testify . . . and often as I passed the freshly made graves, I have glanced at the side boards of the wagon, not knowing how soon it might serve as the coffin for some one of us."**

As you read this section you will find out:

- **Why Americans went west.**
- **What life on the trail was like.**
- **How manifest destiny affected American migration.**

The Fur Trade

While some Americans were heading south to Texas, others were going west. Most of the westward-bound pioneers were involved in the fur trade. The American Fur Company, begun by John Jacob Astor, a German immigrant, controlled most of the western fur trade by the 1820s. Other fur traders built a thriving trade based in St. Louis.

Companies hired rugged **mountain men** to roam the Rocky Mountains and trap beaver and other animals. The life of a mountain man was full of hardships, and only a few got rich. The harsh climate and rugged terrain made the job risky. Trapper James Clyman reported:

> **"I think few men had stronger ideas of their bravery and disregard of fear than I had but . . . to be shot at from behind a**

This 1841 drawing shows trappers and American Indians meeting outside Fort Walla Walla in Oregon Territory. They are probably trading furs for manufactured goods from the East.

picketed Indian village was more than I had contracted for and somewhat cooled my courage."

Trapping was solitary work in remote areas far from white settlements. During the fall and spring, mountain men set and checked their traps. In July or August, they met at a **rendezvous**, a yearly gathering where they sold their furs, exchanged stories, and had a rollicking good time. In the winter, mountain men often lived with friendly American Indians who showed them how to survive and trap in the wilderness.

Beaver pelts, which were extremely popular in Europe, brought the best prices for the fur trappers. After the beaver had been trapped out of one area, the mountain men moved on. Eventually, there was no new trapping land to move on to because the beaver population was nearly extinct from over trapping. Beaver also became less fashionable in Europe. By around the 1840s, the fur trade had collapsed. But the mountain men's role in the West was not over. As one St. Louis newspaper pointed out, some trapping expeditions had clearly demonstrated "that overland expeditions in large bodies [groups] may be made to that remote region [the Far West]."

Trappers had followed Indian trails or cut new ones through the mountains. These paths were later used by westward-bound settlers who hired mountain men to guide them through the wilderness.

Settling Oregon

West of the Rocky Mountains lay Oregon Country, with its magnificent forests, fertile valleys, and rivers full of fish. Oregon, as it was commonly called in the early 1800s, stretched northward from California to the present southern boundary of Alaska. Spain, Russia, Great Britain, and the United States all claimed the region until Spain gave up its claim in 1819, and Russia withdrew in 1825. By this time the United States and Britain had agreed to joint occupation of the region.

Oregon fever. The first U.S. settlers to move to Oregon were a few missionaries who arrived in the Willamette Valley in the 1830s. Among the first to make the six-month journey was Jason Lee, a Methodist minister sent to preach to American

• Narcissa Whitman

Narcissa Prentiss Whitman was one of the first white settlers in Oregon. She, along with her husband, was massacred by Cayuse Indians.

Indians. Two years later Marcus and Narcissa Whitman and another missionary couple arrived in Oregon.

These missionaries had little success in converting local Indians to Christianity. They were successful, however, in attracting more easterners, particularly farmers, to the area. By 1840 some 120 farms could be found in the Willamette Valley.

From such small beginnings came a mass movement westward. All over the eastern states, people caught what they called "Oregon fever." They gathered in groups in western Missouri to make the 2,000-mile trip over the **Oregon Trail**.

National Cowboy Hall of Fame

Hudson River school painter Albert Bierstadt captured the West's landscape in such paintings as this Emigrants Crossing the Plains.

This trail followed the Platte River to Fort Laramie, a fur-trading post in present-day Wyoming, and then crossed the Rockies by way of South Pass before descending to Oregon along the Snake and Columbia Rivers.

Marcus Whitman, who had returned east on church business, led one of the first big groups of pioneers. Nearly 1,000 people set out in the spring of 1843. They rode in 120 canvas-covered wagons pulled by oxen and were accompanied by several thousand farm animals and a small army of pet dogs.

This large group was essentially a community on wheels. Because the journey was full of dangers and hardship, the caravan was ruled like an army. It had an elected council to settle disputes. A guide chose the route and decided where and when to stop for food and rest. A bugler summoned everyone to rise at dawn and begin the long day's journey. Each night the pioneers arranged the wagons in a great circle—in part out of fear of an attack from the American Indians whose lands the settlers crossed.

The group traveled 10 to 15 miles on an average day. Getting the entire company across a river could take as long as five days, for there were no ferries or bridges along the way. Nevertheless, progress was steady. In late November, 1843, the caravan reached the Willamette Valley safely.

Life on the trail. Over the next few years, many more settlers made the trip west. So

The Granger Collection, New York

Pioneers on the Oregon Trail faced many hardships. Crossing a river was dangerous and time-consuming.

Young People In History

On the Trail

About 40,000 children—one out of every five pioneers—made the trek across the country to the Far West. These pioneer children showed great courage and responsibility. Teenagers shared chores with adults. They herded livestock, collected fuel and food, and stood guard at night. Those who lost parents often had to care for younger family members. The journey was not all hard work, however. For many children it was also a great adventure. They met Indians, made new friends, and traveled through dramatic countryside. One young pioneer even kept an antelope, Jennie, as a pet. Many who finally reached the Far West shared the same emotions that Elizabeth Keegan expressed:

> *"the feeling of those who have come that wearisome journey, the joy they feel at once more beholding and mingling with their fellow creatures."*

Children rode on ponies and in wagons on the trek west.

long as they stayed healthy, most pioneers saw the trip as a great adventure. The trek was long, tiring, and hazardous, however. Along the way many died—most from disease, a few from Indian attacks. Settlers feared American Indians, even though they traded with them for food and information. In reality, however, few Indians attacked wagon trains.

Pioneers heading west faced many other dangers. Without the proper tools, a broken wagon wheel or other gear could cause serious problems for travelers. Groups heading west also had to pay careful attention to the weather. Heavy rains or snow could leave pioneers stranded for months at a time. In 1846, for example, heavy snows stranded a group of pioneers known as the Donner party in the Sierra Nevada Mountains. Members of the group were able to survive only by resorting to cannibalism.

Making the trip west required back-breaking labor. Men, women, and children all shared in the work. The men drove the wagons, herded the cattle, and scouted for Indians. Women did the cooking and washing, hauled water, and usually helped load and unload the wagons. Martha Ann Morrison, a girl of 13, remembered:

> **"The women helped pitch the tents, helped unload, and helped yoking up the cattle. . . . Many times the men were off [away from camp]. One time my father was away hunting cattle driven off by the Indians, and that left Mother and the children to attend to everything."**

In addition to the physical hardships, many pioneers also suffered emotionally from leaving friends and family behind. Elizabeth Goltra sadly noted, "I am leaving my home, my early friends and associates never to see them again." Despite these challenges, thousands of pioneers made the trip west. The ruts worn by their wagon wheels can still be seen today.

California

Not everyone on the trail was going to Oregon. Others were making their way to the Mexican province of California. From the late 1700s, American ships had sailed around South America to the California coast. Americans traded with the **Californios**—settlers from Mexico and their descendants—exchanging American manufactured goods for cattle hides and furs.

Few Americans intended to settle in California. Most came only to trade. One of the first such traders was John A. Sutter. Sutter had immigrated to America from Switzerland in 1834 and eventually made his way to Oregon. He then sailed to the Hawaiian Islands. From there he sailed to Alaska and finally to San Francisco.

In 1839 Sutter persuaded the Mexican governor of California to grant him a large tract of land at the junction of the American and Sacramento Rivers. He gradually built a home and a fort, which came to be called **Sutter's Fort**. The entire place was surrounded by a thick wall 18 feet high topped with cannons for protection against Indian attacks.

Sutter, like most of the Americans in California, was a merchant. His fort had an excellent location on the **California Trail**, which branched off south from the Oregon Trail. The fort attracted weary pioneers the way a magnet attracts iron.

After Mexico became independent, some Americans also traded overland following a 780-mile-long route called the **Santa Fe Trail**. This trail ran from Missouri to Santa Fe, in present-day New Mexico. A 19-year-old newlywed, Susan Shelby Magoffin, described the hardships of the trail that she and her husband, a trader, encountered:

> **"Now, about dark, we came into the mosquito regions. . . . Millions upon millions were swarming around me, and their knocking against the carriage *reminded me of a hard rain.* It was equal to any of the plagues of Egypt. I lay almost in a perfect stupor [daze], the heat and stings made me perfectly sick."**

Manifest Destiny

For 200 years moving west had seemed like climbing up a steep hill—slow and difficult work. The pioneers of the 1840s, like the mountain men who had traveled before them, had to cross rugged and dangerous country. Vast prairies, high mountains, and barren deserts lay in their path. Neither the Great Plains nor the Rocky Mountains could stop the determined pioneers, however. One enthusiastic speaker referred to the towering Rockies as "mere molehills."

Americans rushed westward eagerly, excited by the possibility that the entire continent could be theirs! One newspaper editor, John L. O'Sullivan, used the phrase **manifest destiny** to describe this nationwide feeling.

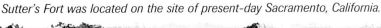

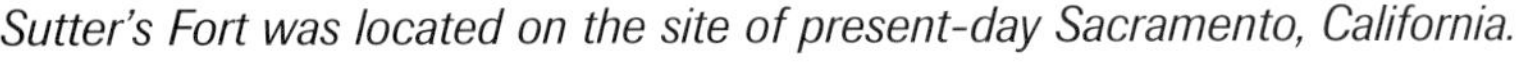
Sutter's Fort was located on the site of present-day Sacramento, California.

The Granger Collection, New York

Detail from National Museum of American Art, Washington, DC/Art Resource, NY

Emanuel Gottlieb Leutze's Westward the Course of Empire Takes its Way *shows Americans' feeling of manifest destiny in the mid-1800s. The scout points the way west for the eager settlers.*

Manifest destiny was the popular belief that the United States was destined to expand across the North American continent to the Pacific Ocean, and possibly even beyond. O'Sullivan explained that the nation was:

> **"to overspread and to possess the whole of the continent which Providence [fate] has given us for the development of the great experiment of liberty and . . . self-government."**

Many Americans agreed with O'Sullivan. Like the U.S. settlers in Texas, the Oregon and California pioneers mostly ignored the fact that they were going to areas not then part of the United States. Those who believed in manifest destiny also gave little thought to the fact that the West was not empty land but was a region alive with cultures that had existed for centuries. On the Oregon Trail people sang:

> **"The hip-hurrah for the prairie life!**
> **Hip-hurrah for the mountain strife!**
> **And if rifles must crack, if swords**
> **we must draw,**
> **Our country forever, hurrah, hurrah!"**

Section 2 Review

• Glossary

• Gazetteer

IDENTIFY and explain the significance of the following: John Jacob Astor, mountain men, rendezvous, Marcus and Narcissa Whitman, Oregon Trail, Californios, Sutter's Fort, California Trail, Santa Fe Trail, manifest destiny

REVIEWING FOR DETAILS

1. Why did many Americans head west?
2. How did the idea of manifest destiny affect American migration westward?

REVIEWING FOR UNDERSTANDING

3. **Geographic Literacy** How would you describe life on the trail west?
4. **Writing Mastery:** *Creating* Imagine that you are a former mountain man. Create an advertisement to drum up business for your new job as a trail guide.
5. **Critical Thinking:** *Synthesizing Information* What supplies do you think someone heading west might need? Why would they need these items?

Section 3
WAR WITH MEXICO

Multimedia Connections

Explore these related topics and materials on the CD–ROM to enrich your understanding of this section:

Profiles

- John Tyler
- Zachary Taylor
- Winfield Scott
- John Frémont

Media Bank

- Texas Admitted to the Union
- Bear Flag Revolt
- Music of the Southwest
- Zachary Taylor and Officers

Readings

- Course of Empire
- Opposition to the Mexican War

In the sleepy town of Sonoma, California, rebellion stirred. A pounding at the door awoke the household. The servant who went to investigate the racket found 30 armed men at the door. They demanded to see Commandante Vallejo, the local top-ranking Mexican official. Doña Francisca Vallejo turned to her husband and begged him to escape, but he refused. They arrested him and put him in jail. Vallejo suffered greatly while in custody: "I left Sacramento half dead, and arrived here [Sonoma] almost without life."

As you read this section you will find out:

- **What events led to war with Mexico.**
- **What course the fighting took during the war.**
- **What consequences the war had.**

Expanding the Nation's Boundaries

In the 1840s westward expansion was both a unifying and a dividing force. Many Americans believed in expanding the nation's boundaries, but each section of the country wanted a different region. Southerners had little interest in Oregon. They wanted Texas, and some even hoped to **annex**, or take control of, Cuba and parts of Central America to expand slave territory even farther. Many northerners were strongly opposed to adding Texas to the Union because that would mean opening more territory to slavery.

This was the situation when James K. Polk was elected president in late 1844. Polk, a Democrat, had promised to bring Texas and Oregon under U.S. control. In December 1845 Texas became a state. Once he took office,

Polk began diplomatic negotiations with the British about Oregon. Polk's Democratic supporters made it clear that if Great Britain did not agree to a satisfactory settlement, they were ready to take the territory by force.

In 1846, after considerable discussion, the negotiators reached a compromise. Oregon was divided by extending the existing boundary along the 49th parallel between the United States and Canada to the West Coast.

Polk also hoped to obtain New Mexico and California. However, he could not claim, as he did with Texas and Oregon, that the lands were already peopled by U.S. citizens. By 1846 there were still very few Americans living in New Mexico or California. Polk would have to find a different way to bring those territories under the control of the United States.

The Mexican War

Although Mexico had not been able to prevent Texas from gaining independence, it had never accepted the Texans' claim to land all the way to the Rio Grande, the "Great River." Mexican officials insisted that Texas extended only to the Nueces, a river farther north and east.

After Texas became part of the United States, Polk sent troops under the command of General Zachary Taylor south of the Nueces River. Then he sent a diplomat named John Slidell to Mexico City to discuss the border dispute. Polk had instructed Slidell to offer Mexico $25 million for both New Mexico and California, as well as for recognition of the United States's border claims to the Rio Grande. Mexican leaders became angry and refused to discuss the boundary issue or even acknowledge that Texas was now part of the United States.

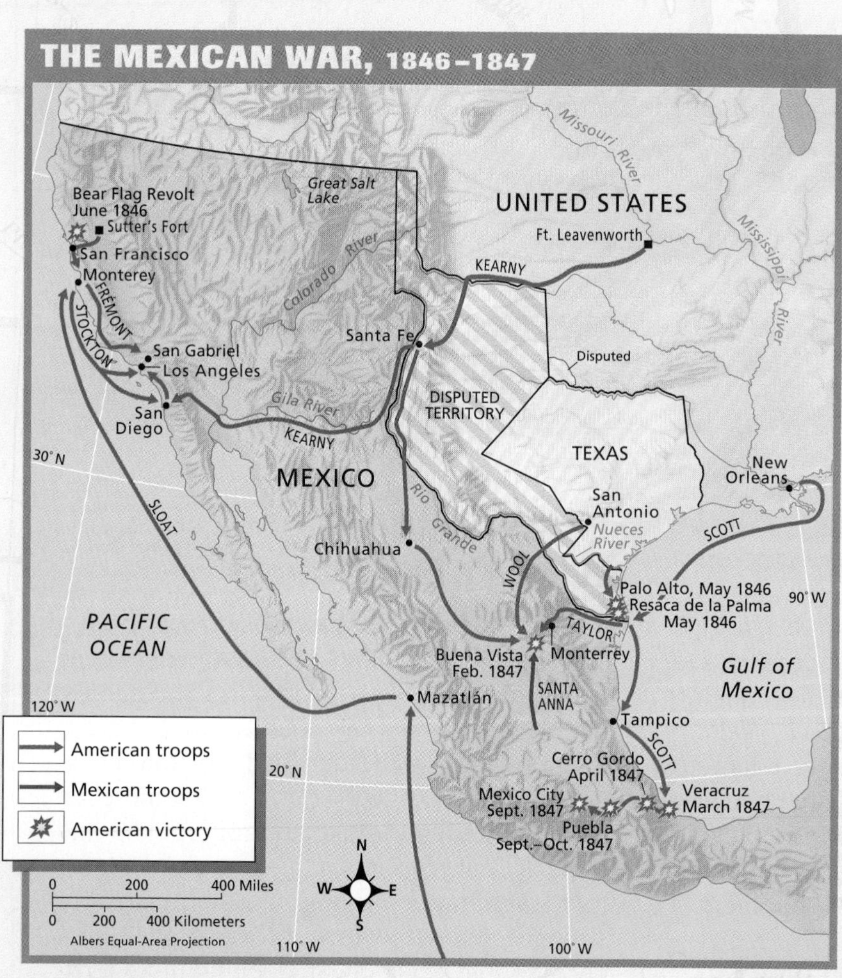

Learning from Maps.
The U.S. troops concentrated on taking the California coast and the major cites on the way to Mexico City.

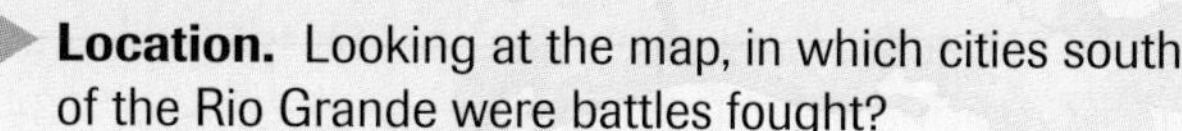
Location. Looking at the map, in which cities south of the Rio Grande were battles fought?

• Maps

Polk announces war. In January of 1846 President Polk ordered General Taylor to advance to the Rio Grande. Shortly after Taylor did so, a Mexican force attacked one of his

James K. Polk

• James K. Polk

patrols. Upon receiving news of the incident, Polk informed Congress:

> **"After reiterated [repeated] menaces [threats], Mexico has passed the boundary of the United States, has invaded our territory and shed American blood upon the American soil. . . . War exists."**

Meanwhile, on May 8 and 9, 1846, in the battles at Palo Alto and Resaca de la Palma, Taylor's troops had driven the Mexican army across the Rio Grande. Later, in the summer, General Stephen Kearny captured Santa Fe, winning control of New Mexico. Kearny's force pushed on to southern California, where it combined with a force under Robert Stockton. This force then captured San Diego, San Gabriel, and Los Angeles.

In northern California, explorer John C. Frémont and his party had joined residents of the area around Sutter's Fort to defeat the local Mexican forces. Then they designed a flag—a grizzly bear over a plain background—and declared the Republic of California. This incident became known as the **Bear Flag Revolt**.

The capture of Mexico City. In February 1847 General Taylor won a major victory over the Mexican forces at Buena Vista. After the battle, much of Mexican territory north of Mexico City was controlled by American troops. These victories contributed to General Taylor's reputation as a hero, but they created a political problem for Polk.

Taylor was a plain, unassuming soldier; his troops affectionately called him "Old Rough and Ready." Polk was afraid that Taylor might run for president on the Whig Party ticket in 1848. Polk did not plan to seek a second term, but as a loyal Democrat, he did not want Taylor to gain too much political advantage from any battlefield successes.

The president therefore put General Winfield Scott in command of the final campaign of the war to capture Mexico City. Scott lacked Taylor's easy-going style. Behind his back Scott's troops called him "Old Fuss and Feathers." Even though Scott was also a Whig, Polk thought he was less of a threat to the Democratic Party than Taylor.

Scott was an excellent general. In March 1847 he ordered 10,000 troops ashore near Veracruz on Mexico's east coast. They captured the city and then marched inland, following the same route that Hernán Cortés had taken in the 1500s. Scott's troops won an important battle at Cerro Gordo and captured the town of Puebla. By September they were at the outskirts of Mexico City.

The battle for Mexico City was brutal. The U.S. soldiers were vastly outnumbered. The Mexicans suffered much higher losses during the battle, however, and Scott's troops were victorious. The Mexicans soon asked for peace.

When General Scott captured Veracruz, he took control of one of Mexico's most important port cities.

National Portrait Gallery, Smithsonian Institution, Washington, DC/Art Resource, NY

The transcendentalist Henry David Thoreau was a critic of the Mexican War. He was imprisoned after he refused to pay his taxes in protest of U.S. actions.

The Treaty of Guadalupe Hidalgo

President Polk had assigned Nicholas P. Trist, a State Department official, to negotiate a peace treaty once Mexico had been defeated. He authorized Trist to offer to buy California and the rest of the Southwest from Mexico. Trist proved to be an excellent negotiator. The negotiations took a great deal of time, however, and Polk became impatient. Officials close to Polk advised him to demand even more territory. In his haste, Polk sent Trist a message ordering him to break off the peace negotiations with Mexico.

Trist ignored the order. He persuaded the Mexicans to cede California, Nevada, and Utah as well as parts of Arizona, New Mexico, Colorado, and Wyoming for a little more than $15 million. This huge U.S. gain of territory became known as the **Mexican Cession**. Trist completed the negotiations with the Mexican government and sent the resulting **Treaty of Guadalupe Hidalgo** back to Polk in the United States. Furious, Polk had Trist fired from his State Department job and refused to pay him for the time he had spent in Mexico.

Nevertheless, Polk had to accept the treaty. The terms, after all, were better than he had hoped for, and the war had become extremely unpopular in some parts of the country. Many people felt that a minor boundary dispute was no reason for seizing so much Mexican territory. Adding more territory where slavery might be established was another concern in the North. Polk therefore swallowed his anger and submitted the treaty to the Senate, which ratified it after heated debate.

Just a few years later, in 1853, the United States completed its territorial expansion in the Southwest when American diplomat James Gadsden negotiated the **Gadsden Purchase** with Mexico. For $10 million, the purchase added a strip of Mexican land to southern New Mexico and Arizona.

A Blending of Cultures

After the Mexican War, more and more Americans moved into the Southwest and the West. They brought their own language, laws, and ways of behaving. The cultural differences between the Americans and the Mexican Americans already in the region created problems, however.

Before the war, about 75,000 Mexicans and more than 250,000 American Indians lived in the Southwest and California. Under the Treaty of Guadalupe Hidalgo, these Mexicans received all the rights of American citizens. However, many Mexican Americans

American Indians and the Spanish worked and lived in missions like San Diego de Alcala.

The Granger Collection, New York

American Letters

The Squatter and the Don

María Amparo Ruiz de Burton

In 1880 María Amparo Ruiz de Burton began writing the novel The Squatter and the Don. *Born in 1832 to a prominent Californio family, she was well positioned to write about the Californios and their struggle to protect their land against American squatters. In the novel Doña Josefa asks, "Is it possible that there is no law to protect us; . . . is there no hope?" Her husband's response highlights the plight of the Californios.*

THE SQUATTER AND THE DON.

A NOVEL DESCRIPTIVE OF CONTEMPORARY OCCURRENCES IN CALIFORNIA.

BY C. LOYAL.

SAN FRANCISCO: 1885

Courtesy The Bancroft Library

Mariá Amparo Ruiz de Burton published her novel under the name "C. Loyal," meaning Ciudadano Leal, *or Loyal Citizen. This name had been a way of signing official correspondence in Mexico.*

"I remember," calmly said Don Mariano, "that when I first read the text of the treaty of Guadalupe Hidalgo, I felt a bitter resentment against my people; against Mexico, the mother country, who abandoned us—her children—with so slight a provision of obligatory stipulations [necessary requirements] for protection. But afterwards, upon mature reflection, I saw that Mexico did as much as could have been reasonably expected at the time. In the very preamble of the treaty the spirit of peace and friendship, which animated both nations, was carefully made manifest [clear]. That spirit was to be the *foundation* of the relations between the conqueror and conquered. How could Mexico have foreseen then that when scarcely half a dozen years should have elapsed the trusted conquerors would, '*In Congress Assembled*,' pass laws which were to be retroactive upon [taking away privileges already granted to] the defenseless, helpless, conquered people, in order to despoil [ruin] them? The treaty said that our rights would be the same as those enjoyed by all other American citizens. But, you see, Congress takes very good care not to enact retroactive laws for Americans; laws to take away from American citizens the property which they hold now, already, with a recognized legal title. No, indeed. But they do so quickly enough with us—with us, the Spano-Americans, who were to enjoy equal rights, mind you, according to the treaty of peace. This is what seems to me a breach [breaking] of faith, which Mexico could neither presuppose [expect] nor prevent." . . .

[Don Mariano:] "We have had no one to speak for us. By the treaty of Guadalupe Hidalgo the American nation pledged its honor to respect our land titles just the same as Mexico would have done. Unfortunately, however, the discovery of gold brought to California the riff-raff of the world, and with it a horde [group] of land-sharks, all possessing the privilege of voting, and most of them coveting [wanting] our lands, for which they very quickly began to clamor [shout]. There was, and still is, plenty of good government land, which any one can take. But no. The forbidden fruit is the sweetest. They do not want government land. They want the land of the Spanish people, because we 'have too much,' they say. So, to win their votes, the votes of the squatters, our representatives in Congress helped to pass laws declaring all lands in California open."

lost their property when newcomers successfully challenged and took away land titles that had been granted by Spanish or Mexican authorities years before. Costly court battles forced other Mexican Americans to sell their land. Ranchers protested to Congress:

> **"Some, who at one time had been the richest landholders, today find themselves without a foot of ground, living as objects of charity."**

Poor Mexican Americans suffered the most. Many were forced to take low-paying jobs on ranches and in mines.

Despite the hostility, however, the different groups borrowed many ideas from one another. Newcomers learned from Mexicans how to mine the ore-rich hills of the Southwest. They also learned that *churros,* the tough Mexican sheep, were better adapted to the dry lands of the Southwest than eastern breeds. Sheep raising had already changed the lives of some Indian tribes. Sheep ranching had become the center of the Navajo economy. Navajo women, who were expert weavers, made beautiful woolen blankets and traded these blankets for horses and other necessary items. Many American newcomers began to raise sheep as well.

In turn, many newcomers brought eastern tools, seeds, and livestock, as well as the latest inventions and business techniques. A new culture was formed in the Southwest that still exists today. It can be found in the local music and art, in laws and architecture, and in the clothes people wear. It is a way of life with roots in three rich cultures—Indian, Mexican, and Anglo American.

Navajo women were skilled weavers. They traded their products with both the Spanish and the Americans.

Section 3 Review

• Glossary

• Gazetteer

IDENTIFY and explain the significance of the following: annex, James K. Polk, Zachary Taylor, Bear Flag Revolt, Winfield Scott, Nicholas P. Trist, Mexican Cession, Treaty of Guadalupe Hidalgo, Gadsden Purchase

LOCATE and explain the importance of the following: Rio Grande, Santa Fe, Buena Vista, Veracruz, Mexico City

REVIEWING FOR DETAILS

1. Why did war break out between the United States and Mexico?
2. How did the United States defeat Mexico?
3. What were the consequences of the war for Mexico and the United States?

REVIEWING FOR UNDERSTANDING

4. **Geographic Literacy** What geographic conditions might have made combat and the movement of troops difficult during the Mexican War?
5. **Critical Thinking:** *Determining the Strength of an Argument* Some Americans argued that it was the nation's manifest destiny to spread into Mexico's territory. Do you think that this reasoning justified war with Mexico? Explain your answer.

Section 4
The Golden West

Multimedia Connections

Explore these related topics and materials on the CD–ROM to enrich your understanding of this section:

Atlas

- Mormons, 1830–1851

Readings

- Westward Ho!

Media Bank

- Clipper Ship
- Indian Wars, 1840–1860

Profiles

- Joseph Smith
- Brigham Young

In 1848 James Marshall brought John Sutter news of a discovery that, Marshall said, "would put both of us in possession of unheard-of wealth—millions and millions of dollars." But how long could they keep Marshall's discovery a secret? They rushed to the new mill on the American River, only to find people already highly excited. Then an Indian worker picked up a shiny object and cried *"Oro! Oro!"*—gold, gold! The secret was out, and California would never be the same.

As you read this section you will find out:

- **Who the Mormons were, and what they achieved in the West.**
- **What life was like in the mining camps.**
- **What impact the California Gold Rush had on the region.**

The Mormons of Utah

One of the most remarkable westward migrations was undertaken by the **Mormons**. Mormons belong to the Church of Jesus Christ of Latter-Day Saints, which was founded in 1830 by Joseph Smith, a New York farmer. Smith attracted several hundred followers, saying he had discovered and translated religious revelations contained on buried golden tablets. From these, he created the Book of Mormon, the basis for the Mormon Church. The Mormons prospered, but their religious practices set them apart from their neighbors. For example, some Mormon men practiced polygamy, which permitted a spouse to have more than one mate at the same time.

Eventually, the Mormons moved to a town they called Nauvoo, in Illinois. Some people in Nauvoo found Smith too strong-willed. He

The Mormons great trek west succeeded in large part because of the organization and leadership of Brigham Young.

organized a Mormon militia and destroyed his critics' printing press. By 1844 opposition to the Mormons in Illinois led to Smith's arrest. Shortly thereafter, a mob attacked the jail and shot Smith.

Mormons head west. After Smith's murder, the Mormons decided to look for a place on the frontier far removed from other people. Brigham Young became their new leader. Young was an excellent organizer. He divided about 12,000 Mormons into small groups and began leading them west in 1846, along what became known as the **Mormon Trail**. The party proceeded slowly, stopping to build camps and to plant crops so that those who followed would have shelter and food.

In July 1847 Young and his followers reached a dry, sun-baked valley near Great Salt Lake in present-day Utah. Young decided, "If nobody on earth wants such a place, then that is the place for my people." There they built Salt Lake City as their permanent home. The Mormon settlement succeeded, largely because of its unity and Young's leadership. As head of both the church and the government, he had almost total control over the Mormon community.

Regulating water rights. The Mormons prospered in this dry country in part because of their intelligent, cooperative use of water. Unlike the East, where water was plentiful, water was scarce in the West. For the Mormon settlers to survive in Utah they had to dam streams and flood land. In addition, they constructed canals and irrigation ditches.

The Mormons believed that the community good outweighed the good of individuals. A limited resource such as water was divided among all the people. Later, other westerners followed the Mormons' example of shared water use, and this principle has become the basis for present-day water law in all western states.

The Gold Rush

By 1848, crossing the continent was a fairly common experience. The trip was still long, tiring, and often dangerous, but the routes were well marked. There were also forts and settlements along the way where travelers could rest.

In the late 1840s California attracted many easterners. Some of them settled around Sutter's Fort on the American River. To supply lumber for new settlers, Sutter decided to build a sawmill about 35 miles up the river.

James W. Marshall was in charge of building the new mill. While inspecting the mill, Marshall noticed bits of shiny yellow metal shimmering in the water. He collected some of the metal and had it tested. It was pure gold.

This discovery took place in January 1848. Soon, other people began to **prospect**, or search for, gold. When they found gold, the miners told friends. By May of that year the town of San Francisco was buzzing with the news.

African Americans joined the forty-niners' rush west. They sifted dirt and panned for gold in streams, hoping to strike it rich.

The Granger Collection, New York

"Gold! Gold! *Gold* from the American River!" Then in December 1848 President Polk announced that the gold in California was "more extensive and valuable" than had been thought. This news triggered the **California Gold Rush** of 1849. In that year at least 80,000 people, called **forty-niners**, flocked to California.

The forty-niners. Most of the forty-niners followed the overland trails across the Rocky Mountains. Others sailed from the East to Panama, crossed the isthmus on foot, and then sailed north to San Francisco.

Still others took the all-water route around South America. Sometimes it took six months to make the long ocean voyage. But for those who could afford it, sleek, three-masted clipper ships made the trip in much less time. In 1851 the clipper *Flying Cloud* sailed from Boston to San Francisco in 89 days—a record time.

Gold fever. In 1849 about $10 million worth of gold was mined in California. By 1852 some 100,000 prospectors were mining there, and they found about $80 million worth of gold. Some miners became extremely wealthy. Two African American miners hit a deposit so rich that the site was named Negro Hill in honor of their find. In four months these two men found gold worth $80,000.

U.S. BOUNDARIES IN 1853

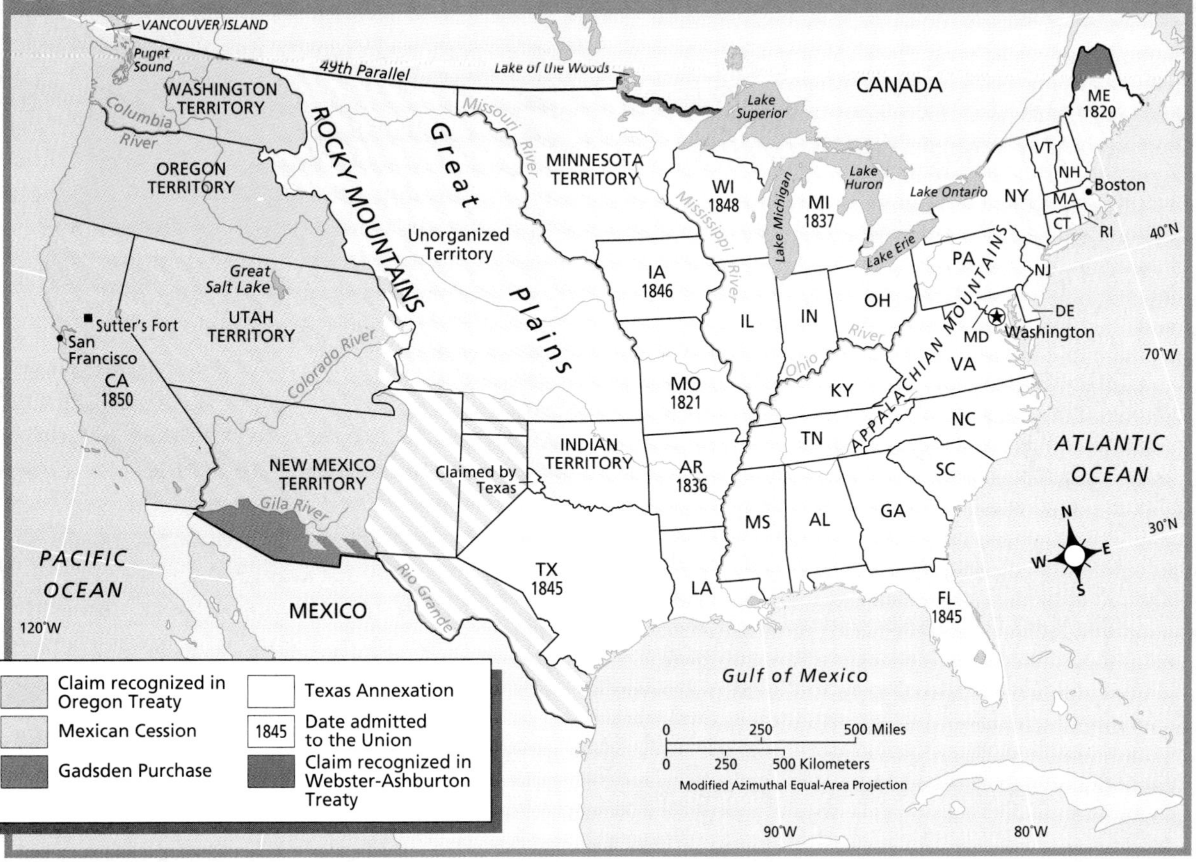

Claim recognized in Oregon Treaty
Mexican Cession
Gadsden Purchase
Texas Annexation
1845 Date admitted to the Union
Claim recognized in Webster-Ashburton Treaty

Learning from Maps. By 1853 the current boundaries of the continental United States were established.

Place. What states were admitted to the Union in 1845?

• Maps

Most miners, however, made little or nothing. Still, they were willing to risk all for a chance at making a fortune. When word of a new strike reached town, people rushed to the gold fields to start prospecting. Forty-niner Alonzo Delano wrote:

> **"In May, 1850, a report reached the settlements that a wonderful lake had been discovered, . . . the shores of which abounded with gold, and to such an extent that it lay like pebbles on the beach. An extraordinary ferment [activity] among the people ensued [began], and a grand rush was made from the towns. . . . Stores were left to take care of themselves, business of all kinds was dropped, mules were suddenly bought up at exorbitant [very high] prices, and crowds started off to search for the golden lake."**

Whenever miners found traces of gold, they staked a claim by driving wooden stakes in the ground to mark the spot. Soon, dozens of other prospectors would flock to the surrounding area to stake out their claims, and disputes about boundaries often broke out.

Life in Mining Camps

Villages called mining camps sprang up wherever gold was found. These camps were given colorful names, such as Whiskey Bar, Hangtown, Poker Flat, and Skunk Gulch. Life in these camps was uncomfortable, expensive, and sometimes dangerous.

A person could be flat broke one day and worth thousands of dollars the next. Such an up-and-down life, combined with the hardships the miners faced, encouraged a live-for-the-day attitude. Many miners were heavy drinkers and reckless gamblers. Fighting in the mining camps with fists, knives, and guns was common.

Mining camps attracted all sorts of thieves and tricksters, as well as clever saloon-keepers and business dealers. Merchants sold the miners everything from pickaxes and tents to fancy clothes and fine horses at sky-high prices. These townspeople made far more money than most miners.

Despite the problems of camp life, most prospectors and storekeepers were eager to build schools and churches and live peacefully. The difficulty was that most of the camps sprang up and died too quickly to establish orderly governments. When the gold ran out, prospectors abandoned camps and rushed off to strikes in other regions. The old camps became ghost towns, inhabited only by stray cats, hermits, or vagabonds.

Global Connections

Chinese Immigration

In the densely populated Guangdong province of southeastern China, the mid-1800s was a time of economic hardship. The expenses of war weakened the Chinese government and resulted in high taxes. Thousands of farmers lost their land when they could not pay these taxes. Landless farmers rarely found employment—hunger and poverty became their way of life. Even more Chinese joined the ranks of the poor when floods devastated the land and crops. In Guangdong this had a disastrous consequence—famine.

Just when conditions seemed at their worst, word spread throughout the province that "gold hills" had been found in California. Soon, young Chinese men were crossing the Pacific, hoping to find gold and return with their riches to China. It seemed as though *gam saan haak* "travelers to the golden mountain" always came back rich. In reality, of the thousands of Chinese who came to California, few found gold and many could never afford to return to their homes in China.

Building the Golden West

The California Gold Rush greatly increased both western development and the economic growth of much of the country. For Indians in California, however, it was a disaster. The movement of white settlers into the gold region crowded many American Indian tribes off their lands. In California, Indians who had not been forced to labor on the great ranches were almost wiped out by the invading settlers and miners.

People from the United States, Mexico, South America, Europe, and as far away as China and Australia flocked to California. Not all newcomers were welcome, however:

> **"The Yankee regarded every man but [an Anglo] American as an interloper [intruder], who had no right to come to California and pick up the gold of 'free and enlightened citizens.'"**

Many Mexicans and Californios were treated badly. They often had their lands seized, suffered violent attacks, and were viewed as second-class citizens. Chinese miners and free African Americans also faced discrimination. A heavy foreign miners tax was placed on Chinese prospectors, and they were not allowed to become naturalized citizens because they were not white.

Despite these obstacles and the hard mining life, the gold fields lured a huge number of people who shared the dream of "striking it rich." In a way, gold made California a land of great cultural diversity.

During the California Gold Rush, people came from as far away as China to make their fortune.

Section 4 Review

• Glossary

IDENTIFY and explain the significance of the following: Mormons, Joseph Smith, Brigham Young, Mormon Trail, prospect, California Gold Rush, forty-niners

REVIEWING FOR DETAILS

1. What was life like in the mining camps?
2. How did the California Gold Rush affect the region?

• Gazetteer

REVIEWING FOR UNDERSTANDING

3. **Geographic Literacy** Who were the Mormons, and what were their accomplishments in the West?
4. **Writing Mastery:** *Creating* Imagine that you are a prospector. Write a journal entry about your experiences in working your mining claim.

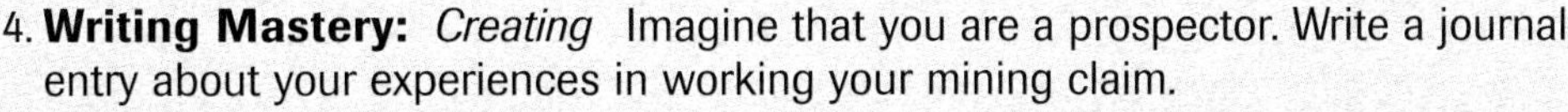

• Time Line

5. **Critical Thinking:** *Making Comparisons* What were the differences between the Mormons and the forty-niners? Describe how those differences affected their settlement patterns.

The Journey West

Although travelers to the West arrived by sailing around South America or crossing the Isthmus of Panama, the more popular routes were overland. Good trails were important in the migration westward. Travelers needed dependable sources of water, game to hunt for food, and enough grass to sustain their livestock. Some trails spread over a wide area, only narrowing to a single path at river crossings and mountain passes. Many trails had been traveled by Indians on foot and horseback long before the first wagons rumbled over the trails.

Some travelers used the southern trails originally made by the Spanish to connect missions and forts in the 1700s. By 1870 almost 400,000 people had traveled the northern routes of the Oregon, California, and Mormon Trails. These trails were longer than some of the southern trails, but were somewhat easier to cross. By the 1880s most of the overland routes had been replaced by railroads.

Major Water Routes from the East Coast to California in 1849

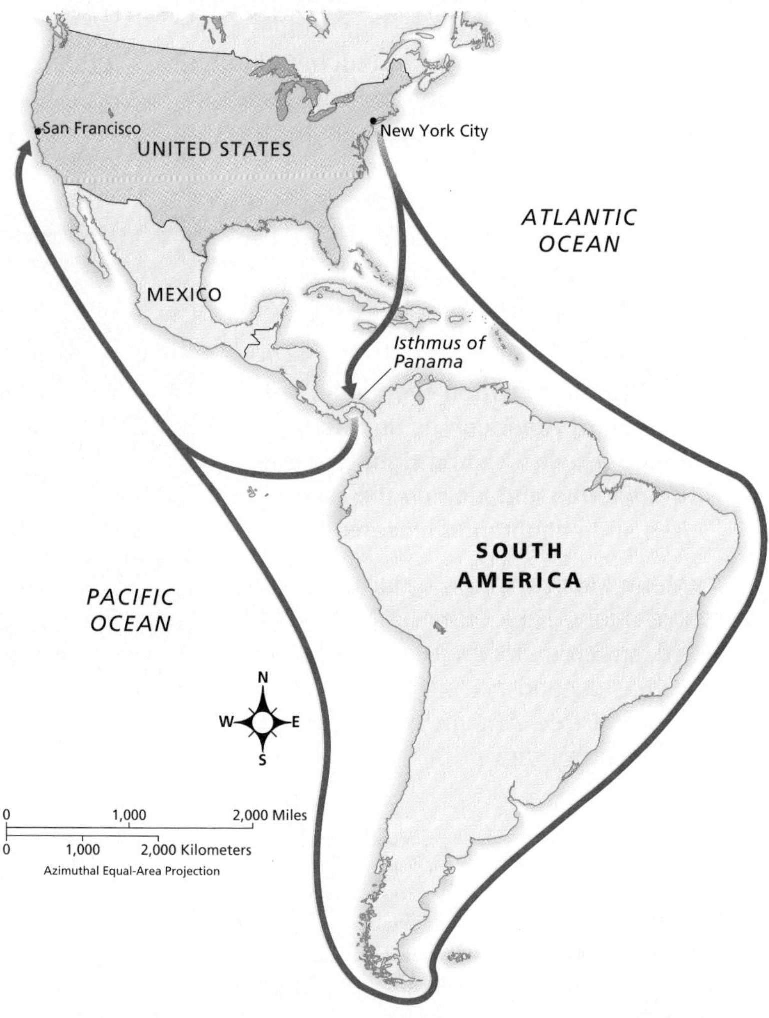

Both of the major water routes to the gold fields of California from the East Coast were long. Although those who went across the Isthmus of Panama had a much shorter trip, they had to travel overland about 50 miles to catch a ship that would take them the rest of the way to San Francisco. Sometimes travelers had to wait in Panama a long time until a ship arrived. Instead of waiting, some impatient travelers journeyed the rest of the way overland through Central America and Mexico. **Movement:** If you were living in New York and wanted to travel to San Francisco by boat, about how long would your trip be if you took the route around South America?

Although the main route from Fort Hall to Sutter's Fort is generally identified as the California Trail, the route actually branched off into several trails that travelers could take. The terrain and lack of a good water supply made travel along the California Trail more difficult than along the Oregon Trail. Some travelers found the route so difficult that they preferred to travel all the way to Oregon, then go south along the West Coast to get to California.

Major Overland Routes to the West in 1860

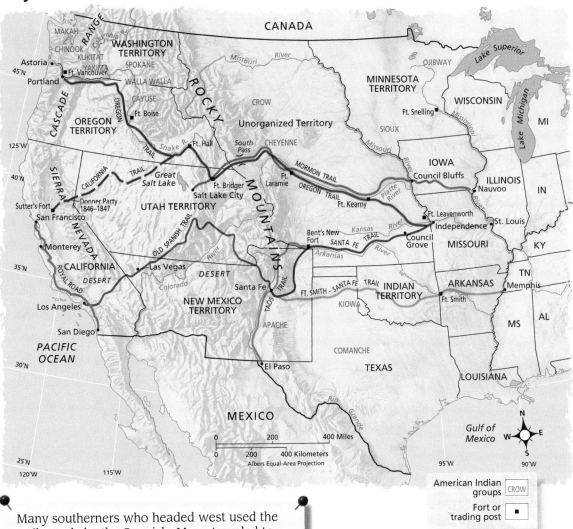

Many southerners who headed west used the trails made by the Spanish. Many traveled to Santa Fe, then followed the Old Spanish Trail, one of the first major trails established in North America. The 1,200-mile Old Spanish Trail went through some of the driest and most difficult terrain of the Southwest. **Movement:** If you were living in St. Louis, Missouri, in 1860 and wanted to travel to Monterey, California, which route would you take to get there? Why?

***To learn more** about the journey west, go to the interactive map, "Mission to Metropolis," on the CD-ROM.*

• Mission to Metropolis

unit 

DIVISION AND REUNIFICATION (1848–1900)

Chapter 13
Breaking Apart (1848–1861)

Chapter 14
The Civil War (1861–1865)

Chapter 15
Reuniting the Nation (1865–1900)

This artwork celebrates the passage of the Fifteenth Amendment to the Constitution giving former slaves the right to vote. It shows some major events in African American history during the Civil War and Reconstruction Eras.

Linking Past to Present
Black History Month

Every February, high school students from Prince George's County, Maryland, participate in the Black Pursuits Quiz Competition. One of the sponsors of the event describes it as "an activity that pits teams . . . in an all-day academic match to determine who knows the most about black . . . history and culture." Since its creation in the 1980s, both the popularity of the contest and students' knowledge of African American history have increased.

Students all across the country focus on the achievements of African Americans during February, which is typically recognized as Black History Month. Some of the activities in which students participate include reading about African American leaders; experiencing aspects of African culture such as songs, dances, and crafts; and viewing films and museum displays on African American history.

Although many students from coast to coast observe Black History Month, the celebration is particularly significant in states like Maryland, which supported slavery in the 1800s. As you read this unit, you will learn what role the southern states played in the increasing conflict over the enslavement of African Americans.

For most people in the 1800s the study of history was the study of those who held power, meaning the study of wealthy white men. Although black labor played a central role in the development of the southern economy and culture, few people would have considered African American contributions to society worthy of study. As long as most African Americans remained property, their heritage as a people was not widely recognized.

As you will learn, this situation slowly began to change in the mid-1800s, as more and more people in power began to oppose the enslavement of African Americans. Although the battle over this issue would tear the country apart, in the end it created a society free of slavery—one that would eventually begin to recognize the important contributions of its many African American citizens.

These teenagers are learning about black history as part of their family's celebration of Kwanza, an African American holiday in December.

CHAPTER 13

Breaking Apart

(1848–1861)

Constitutional Heritage:
How might differing interpretations of the Constitution cause problems?

Democratic Values:
How might individuals use the political system to express opinions?

Geographic Diversity:
Why might slavery have caused controversy when new territory was added to the United States?

• Video Opener

• Skill Builder

A foreign observer of the growing sectional conflict in the United States asked an American what separated northerners and southerners. "The first is slavery; the second the climate. . . . Every ten years the South loses some proportion of its representation," the man observed. "Power is quickly shifting from these old centers." Would these things break up the United States? Americans would soon find out.

image above: *Slave quarters in the South*

Section 1
An Uneasy Peace

Multimedia Connections
Explore these related topics and materials on the CD–ROM to enrich your understanding of this section:

Biographies
- Frederick Douglass

Profiles
- Millard Fillmore
- Harriet Beecher Stowe
- Henry Clay
- Daniel Webster
- John C. Calhoun
- James K. Polk

Readings
- Flight to Canada

The slave catcher marched fugitive Anthony Burns into the Boston courthouse. Angry abolitionists quickly planned to rescue him. One morning several thousand people gathered around the courthouse. The abolitionists rammed the door with a huge log and fired shots. The judge was not swayed, however, and decided to return Burns to slavery. Bostonians watched as Burns marched, chained, to a waiting ship. "The funeral of liberty!" one protest sign read.

As you read this section you will find out:

- **Why the Mexican Cession aroused controversy between North and South.**
- **How the Compromise of 1850 attempted to satisfy all Americans.**
- **Why the Fugitive Slave Act caused controversy in the North.**

Slavery in the Mexican Cession

Victory in the Mexican War had added a huge tract of land to the United States. It also revived a national controversy over slavery in western territories, however.

The Missouri Compromise of 1820 had admitted Missouri as a slave state and Maine as a free state. It also divided the rest of the Louisiana Purchase into free and slave territory. The compromise permitted slavery in the land south of Missouri's southern border, which was marked by an imaginary line at latitude 36° 30′. It prohibited slavery in the land north of this line, with Missouri as the sole exception.

After the Treaty of Guadalupe Hidalgo, which ended the war between the United States and Mexico, some people favored extending the Missouri Compromise line all the way to the Pacific Ocean. This would split the Mexican Cession in two, allowing slavery only in areas south of the line.

Other Americans felt that none of this new territory should be open to slavery. Even before the war with Mexico had ended, Representative David Wilmot of Pennsylvania introduced the **Wilmot Proviso**. It declared that "neither slavery nor involuntary servitude shall ever exist in" any territory taken from the Republic of Mexico. Although the House of Representatives passed the measure, southerners defeated it in the Senate. Many northerners, however, hoped the terms of the Wilmot Proviso would eventually be adopted and settle the debate over slavery in the Mexican Cession.

Still other Americans proposed to end the controversy by applying a principle known as **popular sovereignty**. This process would let voters in a new territory make their own decision about slavery. They would elect proslavery or antislavery representatives, who would then decide the issue. If popular sovereignty were approved, however, it would end the Missouri Compromise.

The Election of 1848

The debate over slavery in the Mexican Cession played an important part in the heated presidential election of 1848. Since President James K. Polk did not seek a second term, the Democrats nominated Lewis Cass, a senator from Michigan. Cass was a supporter of popular sovereignty.

Many northern Democrats were unhappy about the nomination of Cass. They considered popular sovereignty a victory for supporters of slavery because it might allow slaveholders to bring slaves into new territories. Along with some antislavery Whigs, these Democrats founded a new political organization called the **Free-Soil Party**. They picked former president Martin Van Buren as their candidate. Their platform called for "free soil, free speech, free labor, and free men."

The Whig Party nominated war hero Zachary Taylor for president. Taylor refused to express an opinion on slavery, fearing that it would only divide his supporters. During the campaign, the Whigs stressed Taylor's victories in the Mexican War, his courage, and his personal honesty. This approach and the avoidance of the slavery issue worked well, and Taylor won the election.

The Compromise of 1850

The presidential election did not bring the country any closer to solving the controversy over slavery in the Mexican Cession. Developments in California finally forced Congress to resolve this difficult issue.

In 1848 Martin Van Buren and his running mate, Charles Francis Adams, ran on the first presidential ticket to represent the Free-Soil Party.

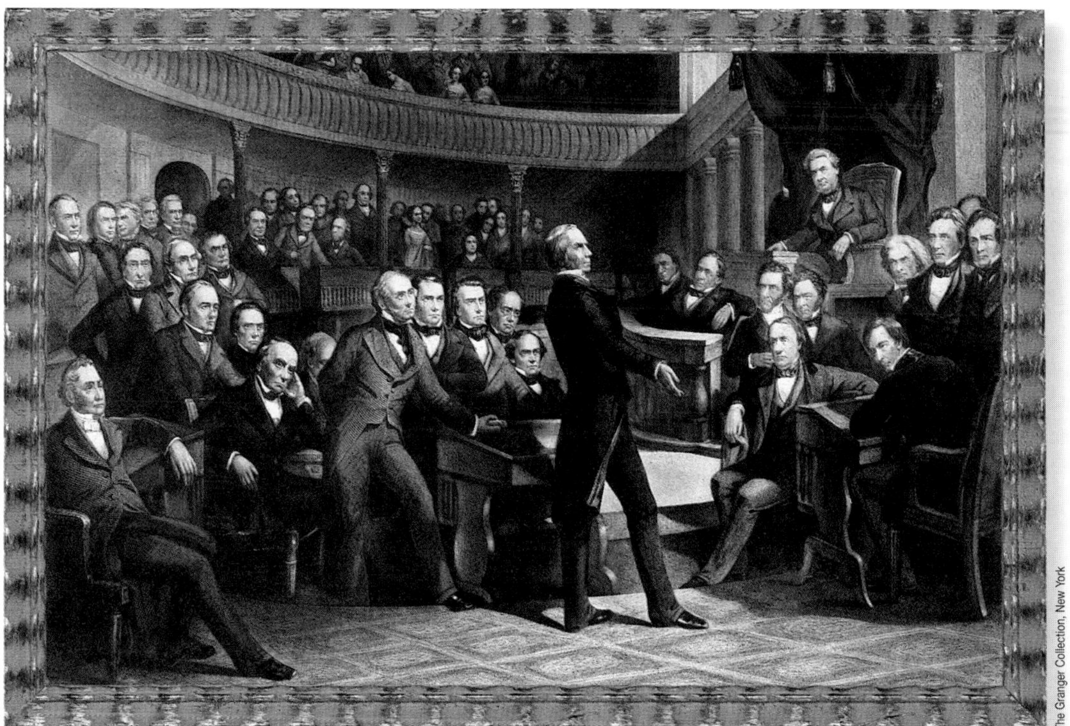

Senator Henry Clay of Kentucky gives a speech convincing Congress to support his compromise plan for balancing the interests of slave and free states.

California demands an answer. The gold rush that began in 1849 greatly increased California's population. It was clear that the region would enter the Union directly as a state rather than through the usual process of territorial development. The question was whether California would be a free state or a slave state.

Most Californians did not want slavery. Few of the Spanish and Mexican families there had ever been slaveholders, and most of the American settlers came from free states. If California became a free state, however, it would upset the balance of free and slave states in the Union.

As political leaders struggled with these issues, other difficult problems complicated their debate. Many northerners had long disapproved of the existence of slavery and the slave trade in the nation's capital. Southerners had complained that the U.S. law requiring the return of fugitive slaves was too weak. Antislavery sentiment in the North made it difficult for southerners to reclaim slaves who had escaped there.

Henry Clay's solution. All the important members of Congress took part in the slavery debate. Kentucky senator Henry Clay offered a series of proposals to settle the situation. Congress should admit California as a free state, Clay urged. To further please northerners, he suggested that the slave trade should be prohibited in the District of Columbia. To satisfy southerners, Clay proposed a harsh fugitive slave bill. He also argued that the rest of the Mexican Cession should be organized into territories where popular sovereignty would decide the slavery issue.

A heated debate. Senator John C. Calhoun of South Carolina bitterly attacked Clay's compromise. His once-powerful voice broken by illness, Calhoun sat grim and silent as another senator read his speech. "How can the Union be preserved?" he asked. Since slaves were a form of property, Calhoun argued, slaveholding citizens had the right to take their "property" into all the territories of the United States. Calhoun threatened that unless Congress allowed slaveholders to bring slaves into the territories, the southern states would leave the Union.

New York senator William Seward also attacked the compromise. He spoke against making any concessions to the slave interests. Clay's compromise, he said, was "radically wrong and essentially vicious."

Daniel Webster of Massachusetts, however, delivered a powerful speech in support of Clay's compromise proposals. He warned Americans to settle their differences:

> **"I wish to speak today, not as a Massachusetts man, nor as a Northern man, but as an American. . . . Is the great Constitution under which we live . . . to be thawed and melted away . . . ? No, sir! No, sir! . . . I see it as plainly as I see the sun in heaven–I see that disruption must produce . . . a war."**

Compromise at last. The debate dragged on for weeks. In the middle of it, both Senator Calhoun and President Taylor died. Vice President Millard Fillmore, who favored Clay's compromise, succeeded Taylor. Clay's proposals finally came to a vote. All passed and together became known as the **Compromise of 1850**. California entered the Union as a free state. The rest of the Mexican Cession was formed into two territories, Utah and New Mexico, where settlers would determine slavery's status through popular sovereignty. The slave trade, but not slavery itself, was prohibited in the District of Columbia, and a stronger fugitive slave law was enacted.

Few Americans approved of all these laws. The Compromise of 1850, however, appeared to put an end to the conflict between the free and slave states. As Illinois senator Stephen A. Douglas put it, a "final settlement" had been reached—or so it seemed to many Americans in 1850.

Slave Catching

The **Fugitive Slave Act** of 1850 quickly proved that the controversy was far from over. The law was enforced even in areas where it was very unpopular. Anyone caught hiding runaway slaves faced six months in jail and a $1,000 fine per slave. All citizens were required to help capture runaway slaves when ordered to do so by a law official. Since many southern slave owners offered rewards for the return of runaway slaves, slave catchers had a good reason to snatch up as many runaways as possible. The law provided that persons accused of being escaped slaves could not testify in their own defense.

During the next few years, law officials seized some 200 African Americans, most of whom were sent into slavery. This was only a small percentage of the number who had escaped, but these cases had a powerful impact on the black community. Runaways

Outraged northerners considered the practices of slave catchers to be kidnapping.

The Granger Collection, New York

Opponents of the Fugitive Slave Act of 1850 feared that it would leave all African Americans at the mercy of dishonest slave catchers.

and even African American northerners who had never been slaves felt threatened, and many left the United States for Canada.

The incidents also influenced northern whites, many of whom were prejudiced against people of African descent, free or slave. Yet in spite of these prejudices, some also sympathized with runaways who had risked their lives to win freedom. An additional concern was that free African Americans in the North would be falsely sent into slavery under the new law.

Both white and black northerners were outraged when they witnessed accused fugitive slaves being dragged off without a chance to defend themselves in court. Even white northerners who remained unmoved by stories of cruelty to slaves usually objected to the law's requirement that they help officials catch escaped slaves.

Abolitionists led the attack on the law. Frederick Douglass, an escaped slave himself, urged resistance. "The only way to make the fugitive slave law dead letter," he wrote, "is to make a half a dozen or more dead kidnappers." In Boston an angry group so threatened one slave catcher that he fled the city in fear for his life. In Pennsylvania a mob actually killed a slave catcher.

Few captured runaways gained their freedom through public protest or force. In most cases they went before a judge as the law provided. Some won freedom, but most were carried off into slavery without the public taking much notice. Nevertheless, more and more northerners were becoming troubled about the existence of slavery.

A Novel About Slavery

Northerners' discomfort with the slavery issue grew after the 1852 publication of ***Uncle Tom's Cabin***, a powerful novel about slavery. The author, Harriet Beecher Stowe, was born in Connecticut but spent many years in Ohio. There she met fugitive slaves and learned about the cruel and unjust nature of slavery. While visiting a Kentucky plantation, Stowe gathered material to write her graphic account of the slave system. *Uncle Tom's Cabin* tells the story of a slave named Tom, who is sold to the cruel master of a Louisiana cotton plantation. This man has Tom beaten, and the long-suffering slave dies from his injuries. "Oh, my country!" Stowe wrote of Tom's death, "these things are done under the shadow of thy laws!"

Harriet Beecher Stowe created much controversy with her book, Uncle Tom's Cabin.

The Granger Collection, New York

Many southerners were deeply offended by *Uncle Tom's Cabin*. One minister called Stowe's novel "a filthy, lying book." The novel, however, shocked many northerners, and it became an immediate popular success. The novel was made into a play and presented in packed theaters all over the free states and territories.

Although it is not known exactly how many of the millions of people who read the book or saw the play became abolitionists as a result, *Uncle Tom's Cabin* had an unquestionable effect on northern attitudes toward slavery. One reader described the impact of the book in an anonymous letter to the author:

> **"I sat up last night long after one o'clock, reading and finishing 'Uncle Tom's Cabin.' I *could not* leave it any more than I could have left a dying child; nor could I restrain an almost hysterical sobbing. . . . This storm of feeling has been raging, burning like a very fire in my bones, all the livelong night, and all through my duties this morning it haunts me,—I *cannot* do away with it."**

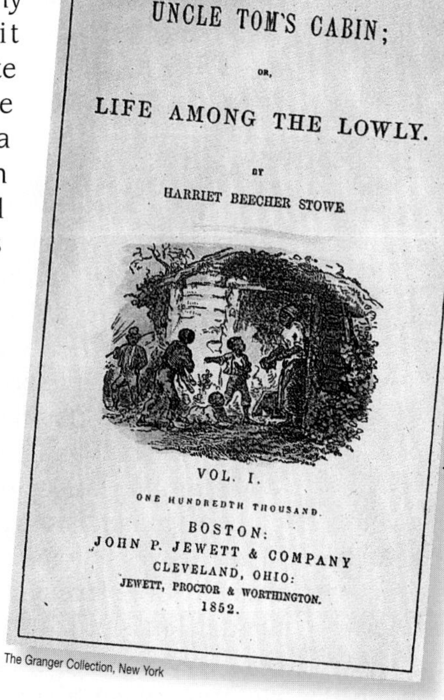
UNCLE TOM'S CABIN;
OR,
LIFE AMONG THE LOWLY.
BY
HARRIET BEECHER STOWE.
VOL. I.
ONE HUNDREDTH THOUSAND.
BOSTON:
JOHN P. JEWETT & COMPANY
CLEVELAND, OHIO:
JEWETT, PROCTOR & WORTHINGTON.
1852.

The Granger Collection, New York

This edition of Uncle Tom's Cabin *was the 100,000th copy of Stowe's popular novel about slavery. Within a short time there were few people unfamiliar with her story.*

Section 1 Review

• Glossary

IDENTIFY and explain the significance of the following: Wilmot Proviso, popular sovereignty, Free-Soil Party, Henry Clay, John C. Calhoun, Compromise of 1850, Fugitive Slave Act, *Uncle Tom's Cabin*, Harriet Beecher Stowe

REVIEWING FOR DETAILS

1. Why did the Mexican Cession cause controversy between northerners and southerners?
2. How did the Compromise of 1850 attempt to solve the problem of slavery in the Missouri Compromise?
3. Why did many northerners object to the Fugitive Slave Act?

REVIEWING FOR UNDERSTANDING

4. **Writing Mastery:** *Creating* Imagine that you are a northerner in the 1850s. Create a short poem, speech, letter, or editorial expressing your reaction to the sensation created by *Uncle Tom's Cabin.*
5. **Critical Thinking:** *Recognizing Point of View* Taking the point of view of a southerner, list from best to worst the three solutions offered to settle the issue of slavery in the Mexican Cession. Then list them as a northerner. Explain why the two lists might differ.

Section 2

THE STRUGGLE FOR KANSAS

Multimedia Connections

Explore these related topics and materials on the CD-ROM to enrich your understanding of this section:

Gazetteer

- Nebraska
- Kansas

Atlas

- Bleeding Kansas

Readings

- Southerners Eye Latin America
- Violence in Congress

Profiles

- Franklin Pierce

Media Bank

- Slavery Compromises, 1820–1854
- John Brown

South Carolina representative Preston Brooks approached Massachusetts senator Charles Sumner. Brooks was furious about Sumner's attack on the Kansas-Nebraska Act and his personal comments about one of Brooks's relatives. The South Carolina man raised his cane and beat Sumner until the wood splintered. Sumner's blood splattered on the floor. The greatest political issue of the day—the question of expanding slavery into new territory—had erupted in violence in the U.S. Senate.

As you read this section you will find out:

- **What plan Stephen Douglas had for the new western territories.**
- **Why northerners protested Douglas's plan.**
- **Why trouble arose in Kansas.**

The Kansas-Nebraska Act

The controversy over slavery in the territories soon erupted again. After California entered the Union, a number of plans for building a railroad to the West Coast sprang up. Northerners generally favored a route from Chicago, while southerners wanted the railroad to run from New Orleans.

No railroad could be built through a region that did not have a territorial government, however. Hoping to secure a northern route for his Illinois voters, Senator Stephen A. Douglas introduced a bill in 1853 to create a territorial government for the region west of Missouri and Iowa.

Douglas's bill ran into trouble, however. Southerners in Congress did not want to create a northern territory. They argued that the railroad could take a southern route and cross

This violent attack on Massachusetts senator Charles Sumner by South Carolina representative Preston Brooks demonstrated how hostile the congressional debate over slavery had become. Sumner never completely recovered from his injuries.

New Mexico Territory, which already existed because of the Compromise of 1850. They also feared that the proposed territory, which was north of the Missouri Compromise line, might eventually become a free state. Southerners refused to vote for Douglas's bill.

Douglas was a clever politician, however. When he realized that southern representatives disliked his bill, he came up with a new plan—allowing the settlers themselves to decide the question of slavery in the new territory. This plan was simply the principle of popular sovereignty that had already been applied in New Mexico and Utah Territories. As a further compromise, Douglas also proposed that the area be split into two territories—Kansas, west of the slave state of Missouri, and Nebraska, west of the free state of Iowa.

Douglas knew that many northerners would dislike this Kansas-Nebraska bill because Kansas might be settled by slave owners. He thought, however, that northerners would merely grumble. Douglas himself believed that the area's climate, which was unsuitable for the most profitable plantation crops, made it unlikely that slavery would be established there.

On January 4, 1854, Douglas introduced his revised bill in the Senate. Antislavery northerners were outraged, and they responded to the proposed law with roars of protest. The bill, in effect, repealed the ban on slavery imposed by the Missouri Compromise. Some antislavery members of Congress called the Kansas-Nebraska bill "an atrocious plot" to make the area "a dreary region . . . inhabited by masters and slaves."

For months Congress debated the bill. Finally, with the votes of southerners who approved of the popular sovereignty provision, the **Kansas-Nebraska Act** passed both houses. President Franklin Pierce, who had won the office in the 1852 election, promptly signed the bill.

Conflicts in Kansas

The northerners who had opposed the Kansas-Nebraska bill grew more angry after it became law. They soon became determined to prevent slavery from spreading from Missouri into Kansas. New York senator Seward said:

> **"Gentlemen of the Slave States, . . . We will engage in competition for the virgin soil of Kansas, and God give the victory to the side which is . . . right."**

Eli Thayer, a Massachusetts abolitionist, organized the Massachusetts Emigrant Aid Company to help pay the moving expenses of antislavery families willing to settle in Kansas.

Encouraged by people like Thayer or prompted by their own beliefs, hundreds of free-soilers rushed to Kansas. They hoped to use popular sovereignty to ban slavery in the territory. Pro-slavery citizens in Missouri also hurried to Kansas.

When the first territorial governor took a census of Kansas late in 1854, he found fewer than 3,000 voters in the territory. After officials held an election for a territorial legislature in March 1855 however, they counted more than 6,300 ballots! Missourians had crossed into Kansas to vote. Their ballots were illegal, of course, since they were not residents of the territory. Still, their votes were counted. As a result, a large majority of the delegates elected

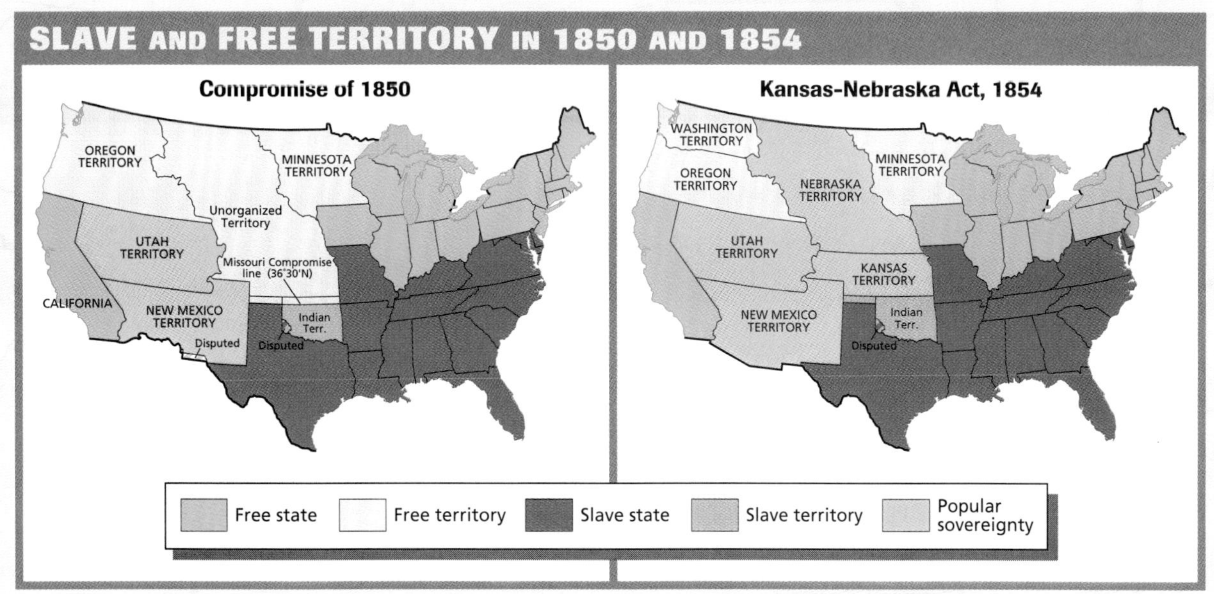

Learning from Maps. The Kansas-Nebraska Act led many northerners to believe that southerners wanted to expand slavery throughout the United States.

▶ **Place.** How did the Kansas-Nebraska Act extend slavery?

• **Maps**

to the territorial legislature were supporters of slavery.

The new legislature moved quickly to pass laws authorizing slavery in Kansas. One law even provided the death penalty for anyone giving help to runaway slaves. Free-soil Kansans were furious. They argued that the new legislature had no right to rule them, and promptly set up their own government.

With two governments claiming to rule the same territory, it is not surprising that fighting soon broke out. Both sides took up arms. Some abolitionists in the East began shipping guns to the antislavery forces so they could defend themselves. One such abolitionist was the Reverend Henry Ward Beecher, a brother of Harriet Beecher Stowe. He was so successful in convincing people to send guns to Kansas that people began to call the weapons "Beecher's Bibles."

In November 1855 a pro-slavery man killed a free-soil settler in an argument. The dead man's friends then set fire to the killer's cabin.

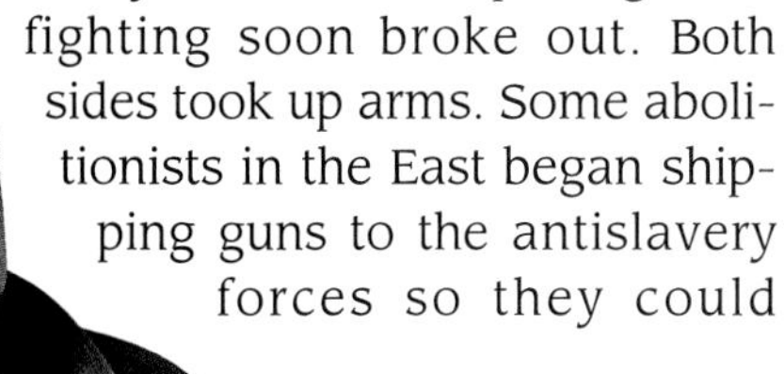

Reverend Henry Ward Beecher was one of the most outspoken abolitionists of his era.

The Granger Collection, New York

John Brown and "Bleeding Kansas"

As other such incidents occurred, the situation in Kansas grew more explosive. In the spring of 1856, antislavery settlers organized their own government and militia in Lawrence, Kansas. On May 21 a pro-slavery sheriff and a large group of armed Missourians marched into Lawrence and attacked the town. An eyewitness described the scene:

> **"The newspaper offices were the first objects of attack. . . . The presses were**

broken down to pieces and the type carried away in the river. The papers and books were treated the same way. . . . From the printing offices the attackers went to the hotel. By evening, all that remained . . . was a part of one wall. The rest was a shapeless heap of ruins."

This engraving shows the attack on Lawrence, Kansas, by supporters of slavery. The attack shocked people throughout the country.

The Granger Collection, New York

One person was killed in the attack. A man named John Brown soon set out to avenge the attack on Lawrence. During his 56 years Brown had tried many businesses but failed time after time. His behavior had often been on the fringes of the law, if not outside it. Yet he sincerely opposed slavery—calling it "the sum of all villainies"—and felt a deep devotion to the cause of racial equality. He had come to Kansas in October 1855 to support the antislavery movement there.

A few days after Brown learned of the attack on Lawrence, he led a party of seven men—four of whom were his sons—to a proslavery settlement near Pottawatomie Creek. In the dead of night Brown and his followers entered the cabins of unsuspecting families and murdered five people simply because they supported slavery.

This incident, known to slavery supporters as the **Pottawatomie Massacre**, brought Kansas to the verge of civil war. Free-soilers and pro-slavery men squared off to fight. Politicians and the press played up the unrest in Kansas. Soon, horror-stricken citizens were reading exaggerated newspaper reports of the situation in "Bleeding Kansas." They grew more worried about the future of the country as they read about Americans fighting each other on the Plains.

Section 2 Review

• Glossary

• Gazetteer

IDENTIFY and explain the significance of the following: Stephen A. Douglas, Kansas-Nebraska Act, Franklin Pierce, Henry Ward Beecher, John Brown, Pottawatomie Massacre

LOCATE and explain the importance of the following: Kansas, Lawrence, Pottawatomie Creek

REVIEWING FOR DETAILS

1. What was Stephen Douglas's controversial plan for the new territories west of Missouri and Iowa?
2. Why did antislavery northerners protest Douglas's plan for the new territories?
3. Why did people refer to the territory as "Bleeding Kansas"?

REVIEWING FOR UNDERSTANDING

4. **Geographic Literacy** Why did both antislavery and pro-slavery forces try to advance their respective positions in Kansas rather than Nebraska?
5. **Critical Thinking:** *Drawing Conclusions* How did the conflict in Kansas represent the issues that were dividing the entire nation?

Section 3
THE ROAD TO DISUNION

Multimedia Connections

Explore these related topics and materials on the CD–ROM to enrich your understanding of this section:

Profiles

- Abraham Lincoln
- Stephen Douglas
- James Buchanan
- Dred Scott

Media Bank

- Congressman Lincoln
- Poster for John C. Fremont
- Attack on Abolitionist Press

Readings

- *Civil Disobedience*

The Michigan sun filtered through a large grove of oak trees as many of the state's leading citizens gathered "to consider . . . the measures which duty demands." So many people came to the meeting that officials moved it from a large hall to the circle of trees outdoors. Speakers criticized the Kansas-Nebraska Act and labeled slavery a great evil. A new political organization—the Republican Party—took shape.

As you read this section you will find out:

- **How the Kansas-Nebraska Act changed American politics.**
- **How the *Dred Scott* decision affected African Americans and the issue of slavery.**
- **How Lincoln and Douglas differed over slavery in new territories.**

Political Changes

The controversy over slavery in the territories produced major shifts in the nation's political parties. The Democratic Party, under the leadership of Stephen Douglas, had supported the Kansas-Nebraska Act. Antislavery Democrats opposed the act, and when it passed, the party lost thousands of supporters throughout the northern states.

The Whig Party, however, shattered completely. Pro-slavery southern members supported the act. Antislavery northern members opposed it. Some Whigs abandoned the party altogether and switched to the new, anti-immigrant American Party, whose members were called the Know-Nothings. The Know-Nothings supported the Kansas-Nebraska Act and won some local elections in the 1850s. The party never had much support, however.

The Republican Party grew very large in a short amount of time. This engraving shows the crowds that gathered at the party's national convention in 1860. The party's main goal was to keep slavery out of the territories.

Many northern Whigs and northern Democrats joined a new organization called the **Republican Party**. It sprang up in the North after passage of the Kansas-Nebraska Act. For Republicans, the most important issue was keeping slavery out of the western territories. Dislike of slavery was not the only reason the party took this stand. In fact, some Republicans shared the racial prejudices of many other white Americans. They feared that small farmers in the territories could not compete if southerners brought their slaves there.

The election of 1856 proved just how unsettled the political situation was. All three parties offered candidates. Democrat James Buchanan won the election, but the Republican Party made a strong showing.

• Election of 1856

The *Dred Scott* Case

Two days after Buchanan took office, a Supreme Court decision produced yet another crisis. Americans had been anxiously awaiting the Court's ruling in an important case involving a slave named Dred Scott. Very little is known about Scott's early life. He was born in Virginia and must have been a very determined person, because he carried on a long struggle for his freedom.

For many years Scott was the slave of John Emerson, an army doctor. Although Emerson lived for a time in Missouri, during the course of his career, he took Scott to live in Illinois, a free state, and Wisconsin Territory, a free region. Emerson eventually sent Scott back to Missouri.

In 1846 Scott sued for his freedom in a Missouri court. He argued that since slavery was illegal in Illinois and the Wisconsin Territory, he had become free when Dr. Emerson took him to those places. Scott claimed that he could not be re-enslaved just because he had been returned to Missouri. Therefore, he believed that he was legally still free. The case eventually came to the Supreme Court for final settlement. On March 6, 1857, the Court announced the ***Dred Scott* decision**. Seven of the nine justices ruled against Scott.

Dred Scott fought unsuccessfully against slavery through the courts.

The Granger Collection, New York

The Chief Justice of the Supreme Court, Roger B. Taney (TAW-nee), explained the majority position. "The Negro race," he said, "were not regarded . . . as citizens" by the Constitution of the United States. Since Scott was not a citizen, he had no right to bring a suit in a federal court. Taney's statement alone was enough to keep Scott a slave. Taney, however, did not leave it at that.

Living in Illinois, he argued, had not made Scott free. Nor did his stay in Wisconsin Territory, because the Missouri Compromise, which had banned slavery in that territory, had been unconstitutional!

Taney reasoned that slaves were not persons, but property. The Fifth Amendment to the U.S. Constitution states that no person "shall . . . be deprived of life, liberty, or property, without due process of law"—that is, action by a court. Therefore, a law that prevented slaveholders from taking slaves into a territory violated the slaveholders' Fifth Amendment rights.

Slaveholders cheered the Court's decision in the *Dred Scott* case. "What are you going to do about it?" they asked northerners. Northerners responded to the *Dred Scott* decision with a storm of criticism. Abolitionists and other opponents of slavery argued that the Court was using part of the Bill of Rights to keep people in chains! Black abolitionist Robert Purvis spoke for many when he said:

> **"This atrocious [horrible] decision furnishes final confirmation of the already well-known fact that, under the Constitution and government of the United States, the colored people are nothing and can be nothing but an alien, disfranchised [powerless], and degraded class."**

Even worse to many northerners was the Court's ruling that the Missouri Compromise was unconstitutional. That law had been canceled, of course, by passage of the Kansas-Nebraska Act. The Court's action, however, implied that Congress did not have the power to stop the advance of slavery into the West. Republicans particularly objected to this part of the decision. It made their main goal—to keep slavery out of the territories—illegal.

The Lincoln-Douglas Debates

The national controversy over the *Dred Scott* decision played an important role in an 1858 Senate race in Illinois. The Republican Party nominated Abraham Lincoln to oppose

The Granger Collection, New York

The Supreme Court decision in the Dred Scott *case shocked many northerners opposed to slavery. They felt it allowed slavery to expand throughout the United States.*

Senator Douglas. Lincoln was a prosperous lawyer who had once served a term in Congress. He had always been a loyal member of the Whig Party and seemed a rather ordinary local politician.

Lincoln takes a stand. Lincoln's status changed when the Kansas-Nebraska Act revived the question of slavery in the territories. "If slavery is not wrong," Lincoln later said, "then nothing is wrong." Still, he was not an abolitionist. Slavery was like a cancer, he said, but cutting it out might cause the patient—the United States—to "bleed to death." He was, however, firmly opposed to the extension of slavery. By 1856 Lincoln had joined the new Republican Party.

Lincoln was an excellent speaker with a remarkable gift for words. His strong position and good judgment called him to the attention of Republican leaders. Although Lincoln hated slavery, he did not hate slaveholders, and he did not blame them for the existence of the institution. He even admitted that he did not know how to do away with slavery in states where it already existed. These views appealed to moderates in the North.

A challenge. Lincoln's fine mind and clever tongue were important because Douglas was a brilliant speaker and an expert on the issues of the day. Lincoln knew it would be difficult—but not impossible—to remove Douglas from his long-held Senate seat. To boost his prospects, Lincoln challenged Douglas to debate him in different sections of Illinois. Douglas agreed. Their seven encounters around the state eventually became known as the **Lincoln-Douglas debates**.

These meetings attracted large crowds, for each was a great local occasion. Families piled into wagons and rumbled for miles over dusty roads to hear the two men speak. Because of the issues involved, newspapers all over the country reported on the debates in detail.

Douglas's side. Douglas tried to persuade the voters that Lincoln and the Republicans were dangerous radicals. He accused them of being abolitionists and of favoring equality for African Americans. Lincoln "thinks that the Negro is his brother," Douglas sneered.

As for the western territories, Douglas defended popular sover-

History Makers

Stephen A. Douglas
(1813–1861)

Stephen Douglas was full of energy and determination. He usually got what he wanted. Before the Illinois legislature elected him to the Senate, Douglas made a fortune in business and served as a state legislator, a judge, and a U.S. representative. Since he was quite short with a wide chest and booming voice, observers called him the "Little Giant." Douglas attributed his political success to his extraordinary closeness with voters.

National Portrait Gallery, Smithsonian Institution, Washington, DC/Art Resource, NY

"I live with my constituents [voters]," he once boasted. "Drink with them, lodge with them, pray with them."

Douglas had a deep commitment to national unity. When it appeared that slave states might leave the Union as a result of the election of 1860, he went on a tour to beg southerners to reconsider. His noble effort failed. Douglas died of typhoid fever soon after.

Throughout Illinois, Abraham Lincoln and Stephen Douglas debated the issue of slavery.

eignty. He also believed that climate and soil conditions would not support slavery in the western territories. Allowing slaveholders to settle in Kansas, he told the crowds, did not mean they would necessarily do so.

Lincoln's reply. Hoping to appeal to Illinois voters, Lincoln responded by distancing himself from then-radical racial beliefs: "I have no purpose to introduce political and social equality between the white and the black races." But, he added, all people had the "natural rights" described in the Declaration of Independence: the right to life, liberty, and the pursuit of happiness. Unlike Douglas, who appealed to the racism of his audience, Lincoln urged white Americans to show sympathy for African Americans and respect for their human rights.

Lincoln also stood firm on the issue of slavery's expansion. Republicans viewed "the institution of slavery as a wrong," he told audiences. "One of the methods of treating it as a wrong is to *make provision* [be sure] *that it shall grow no larger*."

The Freeport Doctrine

During a debate at Freeport, Illinois, Lincoln attempted to use the issue of slavery in the territories against Douglas. He reminded the senator that the *Dred Scott* decision had determined that slavery could go into any territory. Since this was the case, Lincoln asked, then how could the people of a territory possibly

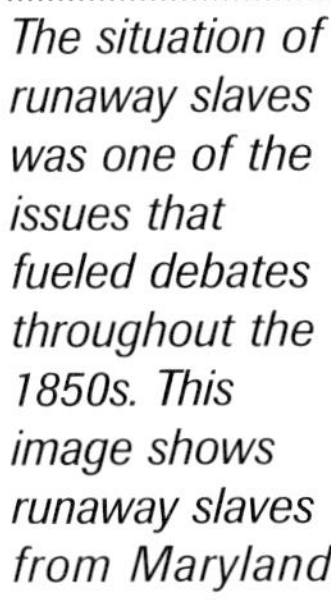

The situation of runaway slaves was one of the issues that fueled debates throughout the 1850s. This image shows runaway slaves from Maryland.

keep slavery out of their region even through popular sovereignty?

Douglas's answer became known as the **Freeport Doctrine**. He replied:

> **"It matters not what way the Supreme Court may . . . decide [about slavery]; the people have the lawful means to introduce it or exclude it as they please. . . . If the people are opposed to slavery, they will elect representatives to that body [the local legislature] who will by unfriendly legislation effectually [effectively] prevent the introduction of it into their midst. If, on the contrary, they are for it, their legislation will favor its extension."**

National Portrait Gallery, Smithsonian Institution, Washington, DC/Art Resource, NY

This doll was used by supporters of Stephen A. Douglas during one of his campaigns.

Douglas meant that since territorial legislatures had the power to write local laws, they could either support slavery or make it impossible for the institution to exist.

This argument helped Douglas in Illinois, where many voters wanted to believe that popular sovereignty could work in the territories despite the *Dred Scott* decision. Douglas's speeches hurt him in the South, however, where slaveholders felt betrayed by the Freeport Doctrine. Thus, Douglas's strategy reduced his chances of achieving his greatest goal—the presidency.

On election day the Democrats carried the Illinois legislature by a small majority. Douglas was therefore re-elected to the Senate. But Lincoln probably benefited from the debates more than Douglas did. His effective speeches attracted much national attention. "It [the campaign] gave me a hearing," he said of the political race. "I believe I have made some marks."

Section 3 Review

• Glossary

IDENTIFY and explain the significance of the following: Republican Party, Dred Scott, *Dred Scott* decision, Abraham Lincoln, Lincoln-Douglas debates, Freeport Doctrine

REVIEWING FOR DETAILS

1. What impact did the Kansas-Nebraska Act have on political parties?
2. How did the *Dred Scott* decision affect African Americans and the issue of slavery in general?
3. How did Lincoln and Douglas differ in their views on the expansion of slavery into western territories?

REVIEWING FOR UNDERSTANDING

4. **Writing Mastery:** *Creating* Imagine that you are working for either the Lincoln or Douglas campaign in Illinois. Create a campaign poster expressing your candidate's ideas on slavery.
5. **Critical Thinking:** *Cause and Effect* Why had many pro-slavery southerners supported Douglas, and why did they stop supporting him after he stated his Freeport Doctrine?

Section 4
THE SECESSION CRISIS

Multimedia Connections

Explore these related topics and materials on the CD–ROM to enrich your understanding of this section:

Gazetteer

- South Carolina

Media Bank

- Harpers Ferry
- Secession
- Last Moments of John Brown
- Candidate Lincoln

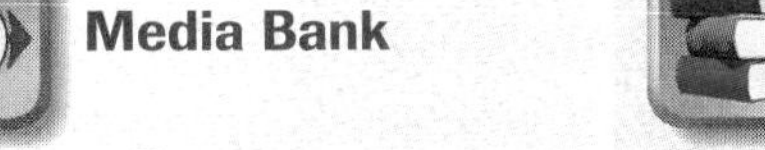

Readings

- South Carolina's Declaration

Two men pushed through the snowdrifts outside the mansion. They spoke in low tones of a bold, dangerous scheme—John Brown's plan to attack an arsenal in the South and to free slaves. "We cannot give him up to die alone," one man pleaded. "I will raise so many hundred dollars for him; . . . ask [your friends] to do as much." The other man finally agreed. They and their associates became the "Secret Six," a tiny group that funded Brown's raid.

As you read this section you will find out:

- **How Americans reacted to John Brown's raid.**
- **How Abraham Lincoln became president.**
- **Why many southerners wanted to leave the United States.**

John Brown's Raid

In October 1859 John Brown again appeared on the national scene. Outraged by the continuing existence of slavery, he decided to organize a band of armed followers and break into an arsenal in Virginia. With the captured weapons, he planned to free nearby slaves and seize land in the mountains. Apparently Brown expected slaves from all over the region to join him. With their help he would organize uprisings and launch raids to rescue more slaves.

Brown soon persuaded six important Massachusetts abolitionists to give him enough money to organize and supply his group, which included about 20 white and African Americans followers. Brown and his force targeted the federal arsenal in the town of Harpers Ferry, Virginia.

A midnight attack. On the evening of October 16, 1859, Brown and his men splashed across a stream near the arsenal. In what became known as **John Brown's raid**, they overpowered a guard and occupied both the arsenal and a government rifle factory. Brown then sent some of his followers off to capture several local slaveholders as hostages. When workers arrived at the arsenal in the morning, Brown also took some of them prisoner. Then he waited for the slaves in the area to rise up and join his rebellion.

Not one slave did so, but the local authorities reacted promptly. In a matter of hours they pinned down Brown's force in the arsenal. A detachment of U.S. Marines under the command of Colonel Robert E. Lee arrived from Washington. Brown refused to surrender. On October 18 Lee ordered his forces to attack.

Ten of Brown's men died in the attack, but Brown was taken alive. Officials charged him with conspiracy, treason, and murder. After a fair but swift trial, Brown was convicted and sentenced to be hanged.

Brown's raid might have been dismissed as the work of a lunatic had he acted like a disturbed person after his capture. But he did not do so. Instead, Brown behaved with remarkable dignity and self-discipline. When he was condemned to death, Brown said that he had acted in the name of God:

> **"I believe that to have interfered as I have done . . . in behalf of His despised poor, was not wrong, but right. Now, if it is deemed necessary that I should forfeit my life for the furtherance of the ends of justice . . . let it be done! . . . I feel no consciousness of guilt."**

A short time later Brown was hanged.

The debate over John Brown. Although most moderate northerners condemned Brown, he was a hero to the opponents of slavery. "Our heart may grow more hopeful for humanity when it sees [his] sublime [great] sacrifice," a young African American woman wrote to Brown's wife. Many abolitionists considered Brown a noble freedom-fighter. They conveniently forgot about the bloody murders Brown had committed in Kansas.

Brown's attack terrified and enraged people throughout the South. "Our peace has been disturbed; our citizens have been imprisoned . . . ; their property has been seized by force of arms," the Virginia governor protested in a message to the state legislature. When some northerners practically made Brown a saint, southerners became even more concerned. They began to fear that northerners intended

Through Others' Eyes

John Brown's Raid

Most African Canadians responded to John Brown's attack on Harpers Ferry with enthusiasm and praise. They regarded his effort as an admirable move for freedom. Harvey C. Jackson posted the following notice just five days after Brown was executed:

> *"You are all aware of the excitement recently created at Harper's Ferry . . . by Captain John Brown and a few others. . . . You are also aware that their attempt was a failure. . . . But that bold attempt to liberate the slaves will be attended with the most important results. It has already enlightened public opinion more than all the anti-slavery speeches made for the last ten years. . . . Some persons may brand Brown's effort as 'rash, futile [useless], and wild,' but they must acknowledge that it will be productive of much good. . . . Brown and his confederates are martyrs to the cause of Liberty."*

Believing he was called to carry out violence for the cause of abolition, John Brown made a lasting impression on the country. This mural of him was painted on the Kansas statehouse.

to destroy slavery, not merely limit its expansion. Once again, northerners and southerners looked at each other with suspicion, fear, and even hatred.

The Election of 1860

As the 1860 presidential election drew near, the Democrats became even more sharply divided over slavery. Their first nominating convention broke up after the delegates could not agree on a candidate. They gathered again a few months later, but once more they failed to agree. After the convention nominated Stephen Douglas, southern Democrats broke away. They nominated President Buchanan's vice president, John C. Breckinridge of Kentucky.

In the meantime, the Republican convention took place. To broaden the party's appeal, leaders drafted a program of economic reforms to go along with their position that slavery be kept out of the territories. New York senator Seward was the leading presidential candidate. Many, however, thought Seward was too antislavery for most northern voters. After much political "horse trading," or intense back-and-forth bargaining, the Republican delegates nominated Abraham Lincoln.

Fearing that the South might leave the Union if a Republican won the election, some southerners formed yet another political organization. They called it the **Constitutional Union Party**. Its platform was simple—"the Union as it is and the Constitution as it is." Though many members of this party supported slavery, they did not want the country to break apart over the issue.

The Constitutional Unionists nominated John Bell from Tennessee, who had served in both houses of Congress. Although he held slaves, Bell had opposed the Kansas-Nebraska Act, which made him attractive to many moderates.

The November election showed just how fragmented the nation had become. With four candidates running, no one could hope to get a majority of the popular vote. The electoral vote was a different matter. Lincoln and Douglas fought it out in the heavily populated free states. Lincoln won in most of these states, taking 180 electoral votes to Douglas's mere 12.

In the less populated slave states Breckinridge and Bell divided the vote. Breckinridge took all the states of the Lower South and some of those in the Upper South, winning 72 electoral votes. Bell carried the states of Tennessee, Kentucky, and Virginia, which netted him 39 electoral votes.

These results gave Lincoln a solid majority, 180 of the 303 electoral votes. Although he received much less than half the popular vote, he had won the presidency.

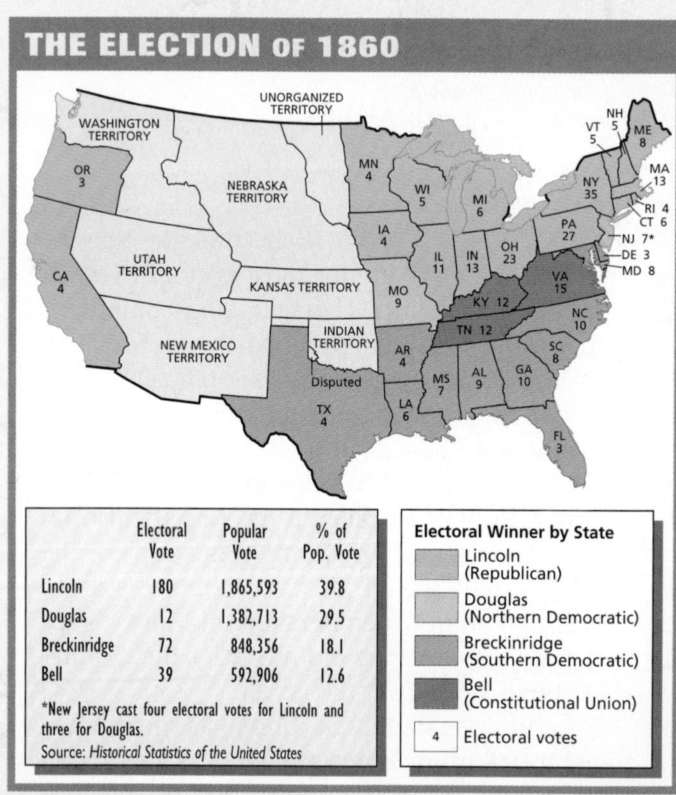

	Electoral Vote	Popular Vote	% of Pop. Vote
Lincoln	180	1,865,593	39.8
Douglas	12	1,382,713	29.5
Breckinridge	72	848,356	18.1
Bell	39	592,906	12.6

*New Jersey cast four electoral votes for Lincoln and three for Douglas.
Source: *Historical Statistics of the United States*

Learning from Maps.
Lincoln's victory in the election of 1860 increased pre-existing regional tensions and soon led to secession.

▶ **Place.** How did the election results reflect regional interests?

• **Maps**

The Lower South Secedes

Lincoln's victory alarmed many southerners. He had not carried a *single* slave state. Southerners recognized that Lincoln had been legally elected, but they questioned the fairness of a political system that allowed him to govern people who had not chosen him. A New Orleans newspaper editorial expressed the typical viewpoint:

> **"The history of the . . . Republican party of the North is a history of repeated injuries and usurpations [things taken without right], all having in direct object the establishment of absolute tyranny over the slaveholding States. . . . [The North has] capped the mighty pyramid of unfraternal [unfriendly] enormities by electing Abraham Lincoln . . . on a platform and by a system which indicates nothing but the subjugation [enslavement] of the South and the complete ruin of her . . . institutions. The South has compromised until she can compromise no farther."**

For several years southerners had talked of possibly withdrawing from the United States if an antislavery Republican was ever elected president. Now southern radicals prepared to act on that threat. Within days of Lincoln's election, the legislature of South Carolina summoned a special convention to consider the question of **secession**, the act of formally withdrawing as part of the nation. Before the end of the year the delegates voted to withdraw their state from the United States of America.

Two views of secession. Though some southerners did not want to leave the Union, others used the idea of states' sovereignty to justify secession. They pointed out that the original 13 states had existed separately before they had joined together to form the United States. Representatives from the states had drafted and then approved the U.S. Constitution, southerners noted. Surely, they reasoned, each state then had the right to cancel its allegiance if its citizens so desired.

Many northerners saw secession as a challenge to the basic principles of the Constitution. The Constitution bound all the states together by mutual consent, they argued. The states had agreed to recognize the Constitution as the supreme law of the land. They had also accepted federalism—the sharing of power by the national and state governments—and the responsibility of thc national government to oversee certain government functions. After years of accepting the system the slave states now proposed to cast the Constitution aside in favor of states' rights. This angered northerners.

Protecting the South. Southerners' belief in states' sovereignty formed their constitutional basis for secession. This does not, however, account for why so many people in the South were willing to leave the Union. Their loyalty to the region and to the slave system explain their desire for separation. The prolonged controversy over slavery had weakened southerners' loyalty to the nation as a whole.

Even though Lincoln and other moderates had no intention of trying to get rid of slavery where it already existed, southerners could not accept the idea that slavery itself was "wrong." When Lincoln's point of view triumphed and he became president of the United States, many southerners no longer wished to be part of the nation.

CHARLESTON

MERCURY

EXTRA:

Passed unanimously at 1.15 o'clock, P. M., December 20th, 1860.

AN ORDINANCE

To dissolve the Union between the State of South Carolina and other States united with her under the compact entitled "The Constitution of the United States of America."

We, the People of the State of South Carolina, in Convention assembled, do declare and ordain, and it is hereby declared and ordained,

That the Ordinance adopted by us in Convention, on the twenty-third day of May, in the year of our Lord one thousand seven hundred and eighty-eight, whereby the Constitution of the United States of America was ratified, and also, all Acts and parts of Acts of the General Assembly of this State, ratifying amendments of the said Constitution, are hereby repealed; and that the union now subsisting between South Carolina and other States, under the name of "The United States of America," is hereby dissolved.

THE

UNION

IS

DISSOLVED!

The Granger Collection, New York

A South Carolina newspaper published this broadside on December 20, 1860, to announce that the state had seceded.

Section 4 Review

• Glossary

• Time Line

IDENTIFY and explain the significance of the following: John Brown's raid, Constitutional Union Party, secession

REVIEWING FOR DETAILS

1. How did Abraham Lincoln win the presidency?
2. Why did so many southerners want to secede?

REVIEWING FOR UNDERSTANDING

3. **Geographic Literacy** How did the election of 1860 show that the nation was divided?
4. **Writing Mastery:** *Describing* Write a short newspaper article describing reactions to John Brown's raid.
5. **Critical Thinking:** *Determining the Strength of an Argument* How did both northerners and southerners defend their positions on secession? Which position seems stronger to you?

America's Geography

Balancing Political Power

Maintaining a balance of political power between the slave and free states had been a major concern in the United States since the Constitutional Convention. The balance of power in Congress was of particular concern. The free states had always had a greater representation in the House of Representatives because of their larger populations. Representation in the Senate, however, was kept in balance by ensuring that as each new free state came into the union, so did a slave state. This balance of slave and free states was upset in the 1850s when three new free states joined the Union without any new slave states being added. When Abraham Lincoln was elected president in 1860, many southerners believed that they had lost their voice in the federal government.

Distribution of Population Counted for Representation

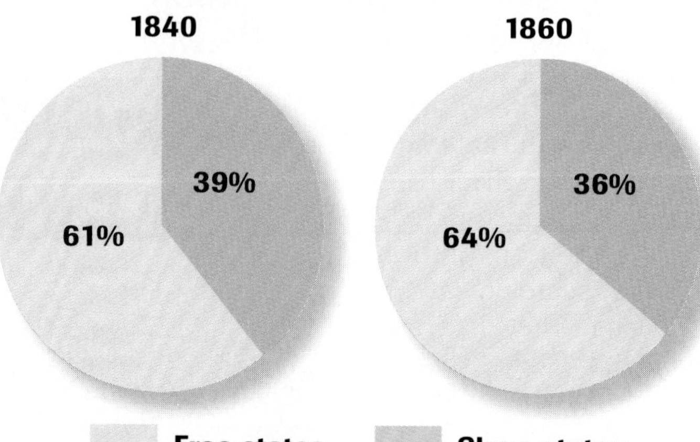

Free states / Slave states

The delegates to the Constitutional Convention had agreed that only three fifths of the slave population would count in determining how many representatives each state would be allowed in the House. At that time, the well-populated free states enjoyed a small numerical advantage over the slave states. In the 1800s the population grew at a faster rate in the free states than in the slave states. This meant that the number of representatives for the free states increased more quickly than the number of representatives for the slave states. As a result, it became more difficult for the slave states to win decisions in the House. **Linking Geography and History:** How many seats did the free states gain in the House of Representatives between 1840 and 1860?

Representatives in the House

	Slave States	Free States
1840	88	135
1860	85	155

Admission of New States

Free States ▶ Illinois • 1818

1820 1830

Slave States ▶ Missouri • 1821

Stephen Douglas had good reason to believe that slavery was unlikely to become popular in the territories. Although the territories were the cause for much of the debate over the expansion of slavery in the 1850s, there were few slaves in the region. From the political standpoint of the South, however, the issue of whether slavery would be allowed in the territories was extremely important.

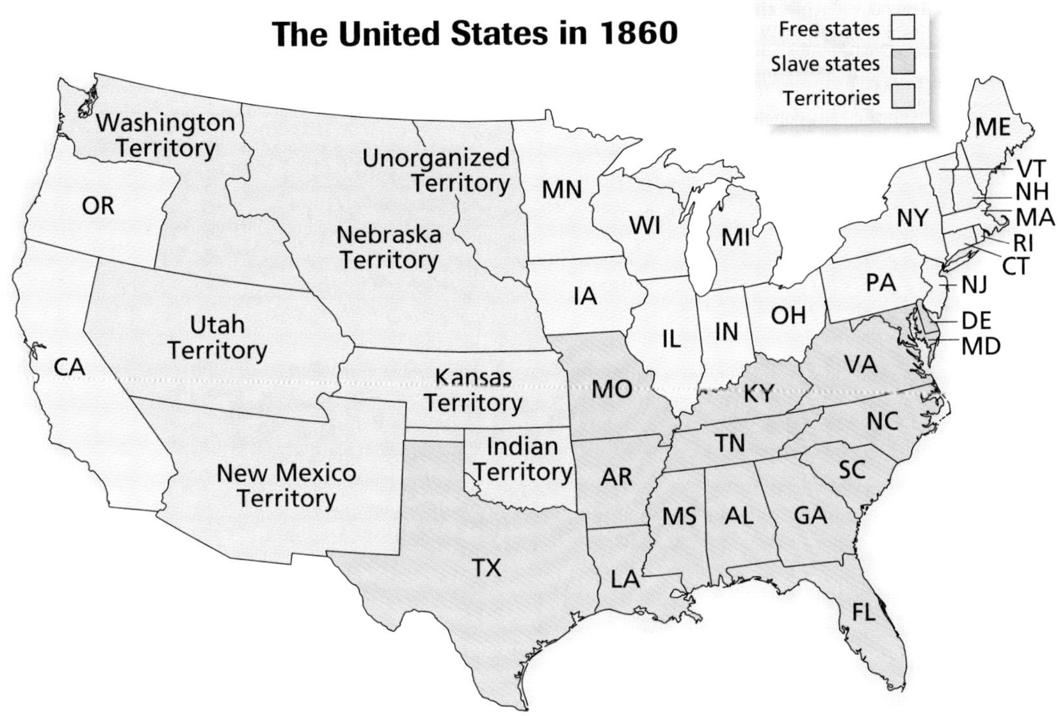

The makeup of the Senate ensured equality among the states by allowing each state two senators. The system did not ensure equality between regions, however. Initially, the greatest concern was over equality between large and small states, but soon the struggle between slave and free states took center stage. **Linking Geography and History:** What would the total number of senators have been for the free states in 1860? For the slave states?

To learn more *about balancing political power, go to the interactive map, "Balancing Political Power," on the CD–ROM.*

• Balancing Political Power

Michigan • 1837
Iowa • 1846
Wisconsin • 1848
California • 1850
Minnesota • 1858
Oregon • 1859

1840 **1850** **1860**

Arkansas • 1836
Florida • 1845
Texas • 1845

CHAPTER 14

The Connecticut Historical Society, Hartford, Connecticut

The Civil War

(1861–1865)

THEMES IN AMERICAN HISTORY

Geographic Diversity:
How might geography affect the outcome of a war?

Economic Development:
How might a nation's economy affect its ability to wage war?

Constitutional Heritage:
How might a period of rebellion affect a people's civil rights?

• Video Opener

• Skill Builder

While many Americans feared the coming of the Civil War, others were thrilled. Abolitionist Frederick Douglass saw it as a chance to end slavery, "the monster evil of the nineteenth century." "Friends of freedom," he cried, "now is your time." To many southerners the war offered a different freedom—independence from the United States! Americans on both sides soon learned the high cost of these goals.

image above: *Antisecession cartoon, 1861*

Section 1
THE WAR BEGINS

Multimedia Connections

Explore these related topics and materials on the CD–ROM to enrich your understanding of this section:

Media Bank

- Union Soldiers' Occupations
- Road to the Civil War
- Civil War Recruitment Poster
- Union and Confederate Soldiers
- Elizabeth Blackwell
- Civil War Nurses
- Susie King Taylor
- Nurse Tending a Soldier

Readings

- Raising the Regiments

Profiles

- Elizabeth Blackwell
- Dorothea Dix
- Abraham Lincoln
- Susie King Taylor

On December 20, 1860, the people of Charleston, South Carolina, went wild with excitement. Their state had seceded from the Union! People poured out into the streets to spread the word. The celebrations lasted through the day and into the night. Back in Washington, President James Buchanan was at a reception. Suddenly, a South Carolina congressman rushed in with the fateful news from Charleston. The shaken president quickly left the gathering when he heard the account of South Carolina's secession.

As you read this section you will find out:

- **How the Confederacy was formed.**
- **What incident sparked the Civil War.**
- **What the strengths and weaknesses of each side were when the war began.**

The Confederate States of America

By February 1, 1861, Mississippi, Louisiana, Alabama, Georgia, Florida, and Texas had joined South Carolina in seceding from the Union. On February 4, delegates from the seceding states met in Montgomery, Alabama, to create their own central government, called the **Confederate States of America**—or the Confederacy for short. It took the delegates just four days to draft a constitution. This was possible because the document was based on the U.S. Constitution.

After writing their constitution, the delegates chose Jefferson Davis of Mississippi as president of the Confederacy and Alexander Stephens of Georgia as vice president. In an election later that year, southern voters confirmed their delegates' choice.

The Granger Collection, New York

Jefferson Davis had served in both the U.S. military and government.

• Jefferson Davis

Davis was a tall, slender man with high cheekbones, fair hair, and blue gray eyes. He was 52 years old when he became president of the Confederacy. Like Abraham Lincoln, he was born in Kentucky, the child of a pioneer family. He graduated from the United States Military Academy in 1828, but he resigned his commission in 1835 and became a cotton planter in Mississippi.

In 1845 Davis was elected to the House of Representatives. When the Mexican War broke out, however, he gave up his seat to serve as a colonel in the army. Although wounded in the Battle of Buena Vista, Davis recovered fully. In 1847 he was appointed to the U.S. Senate. When Franklin Pierce became president in 1853, he named Davis secretary of war.

Davis was an extremely hard worker, but he did not get along well with people, and he often quarreled with government officials. These traits would later create problems in the Confederate government.

Lincoln Becomes President

In early 1861, however, Davis's strengths seemed much more obvious than his weaknesses. Indeed, when Abraham Lincoln was inaugurated as president of the United States on March 4, 1861, many people thought him a far less inspiring leader than the president of the new Confederacy.

Lincoln had chosen a cabinet that included his four main Republican rivals for the presidency. His attempt to unite his party was understandable at a time of national crisis, but many people wondered whether this backwoods lawyer could control such a powerful group. Lincoln appointed one of the best-known Republicans in the United States, William H. Seward, as secretary of state. Seward did not think Lincoln was capable of

Presidential Lives

Abraham Lincoln

Shortly after the Civil War began, Abraham Lincoln faced a devastating crisis at home—the death of his beloved young son, William. Sadly, Lincoln and his wife had experienced a similar loss before. In February 1850 their three-year-old son, Edward, had died of tuberculosis. The Lincolns barely survived this tragedy, but they soon had another child.

William, their newborn son, was a smart and handsome boy. Many observers thought he was Lincoln's favorite child, though the president showed no outward preference. In January 1862 William fell sick with "bilious fever." This harsh illness might have been caused by polluted water in the White House. He died a few weeks later, plunging both the Lincolns into a deep depression. "My boy is gone—he is actually gone!" Lincoln cried upon learning the terrible news. "We loved him so," the president later reflected.

The Granger Collection, New York

The Civil War left little time for grief, however. Lincoln struggled to lead the Union even as he mourned his son.

being president. Seward was ready, he told his wife, "to save freedom and my country" by making the major decisions necessary to run the country himself.

Lincoln, however, did not intend to be dominated by Seward or anyone else. In his inaugural address, his words to the divided nation made his position clear:

> **"I have no purpose, directly or indirectly, to interfere with the institution of slavery in the states where it exists. I believe I have no lawful right to do so, and I have no inclination [intention] to do so. . . .**
>
> **We are not enemies but friends. We must not be enemies. Though passion may have strained, it must not break our bonds of affection."**

In hopes that the southern states might be persuaded to change their minds, Lincoln assured the South that he would not rush troops into the region to prevent secession. Many northerners believed that the secession crisis could be solved by yet another compromise. Nevertheless, Lincoln warned that secession was illegal. "No state, upon its own mere motion," he said, "can lawfully get out of the Union."

The immediate problem facing Lincoln was the situation at Fort Sumter. The fort was located on an island in South Carolina's Charleston Harbor. The commander of Union forces in Charleston, Major Robert Anderson, had kept control of the fort when South Carolina seceded. Anderson and his men could not hold out forever without fresh supplies, however. After considering the fort's position, Lincoln decided to send food—but no reinforcements or ammunition—to the fort. He then informed the governor of South Carolina of his intentions.

After months of standoff, the Confederates decided to capture the fort before supplies could arrive. On April 12, they began to bombard Fort Sumter. By the next day, they had nearly destroyed the fort. When the Union's ammunition was almost exhausted, Major Anderson and his weary troops surrendered. The Civil War had begun.

Preparing for War

After the attack on Fort Sumter, Lincoln called for 75,000 volunteer soldiers. The Confederate Congress quickly responded with a call for 100,000 men. News that Lincoln intended to use force against the Confederacy convinced Virginia, North Carolina, Tennessee, and Arkansas to secede and to join the other Confederate states.

Choosing sides. To strengthen support for secession in Virginia, the Confederacy shifted its capital from Montgomery, Alabama, to Richmond, Virginia. The people of western Virginia, however, held few slaves and preferred to remain in the Union. Several western counties seceded from Virginia. In 1863 they were admitted to the Union as the state of West Virginia.

Four additional slave states—Delaware, Maryland, Kentucky, and Missouri—remained in the Union. Both sides wanted the loyalty of these strategic states. Kentucky and Missouri were important for control of the Ohio and Mississippi Rivers. If Maryland seceded, the

More than 3,000 shells poured down onto Fort Sumter during the 34-hour bombardment. Miraculously, no one on either side was killed or seriously wounded in the battle.

Confederacy would surround Washington! Delaware, which had few slaves, showed the strongest support for the Union. Many people in the other three states, however, openly supported the South. Soldiers from these **border states** fought on both sides.

At times, the war set brother against brother, husband against wife, and father against son. Four of Henry Clay's grandsons fought for the South and three others fought for the North. First Lady Mary Todd Lincoln, a native of Kentucky, had four brothers in the Confederate army.

The volunteers. In both the North and the South, the recruiting of troops was left to the states. In most places, recruits came forward enthusiastically. Even a few women enlisted in the army, disguised as men. The majority of recruits, however, were men hoping for an exciting adventure that would take them far from the farm or the factory. Most southerners fought to defend what they saw as their rights, while many northerners signed up to preserve the Union. In Boston, Mary Ashton Livermore reported:

> **"Hastily formed companies marched to camps of rendezvous, the sunlight flashing from gun-barrel and bayonet. . . . Merchants and clerks rushed out from stores, bareheaded, saluting them as they passed. . . . I had never seen anything like this before."**

Soldiers were not the only type of volunteers needed by the North and South. Some civilians served as spies. One important spy for the Union was Mary Elizabeth Bowser, a slave who worked in the home of Confederate president Jefferson Davis.

Many other men and women volunteered to care for the armies' sick and wounded. Before the war, most Americans considered nursing a male profession. During the war, however, thousands of women served this role. Catholic nuns turned their convents into hospitals and treated soldiers on both sides. The well-known reformer Dorothea Dix volunteered her services and was appointed superintendent of nurses for the Union armies. To train nurses and to improve the overall state of medical conditions, Dr. Elizabeth Blackwell helped found what became the U.S. Sanitary Commission.

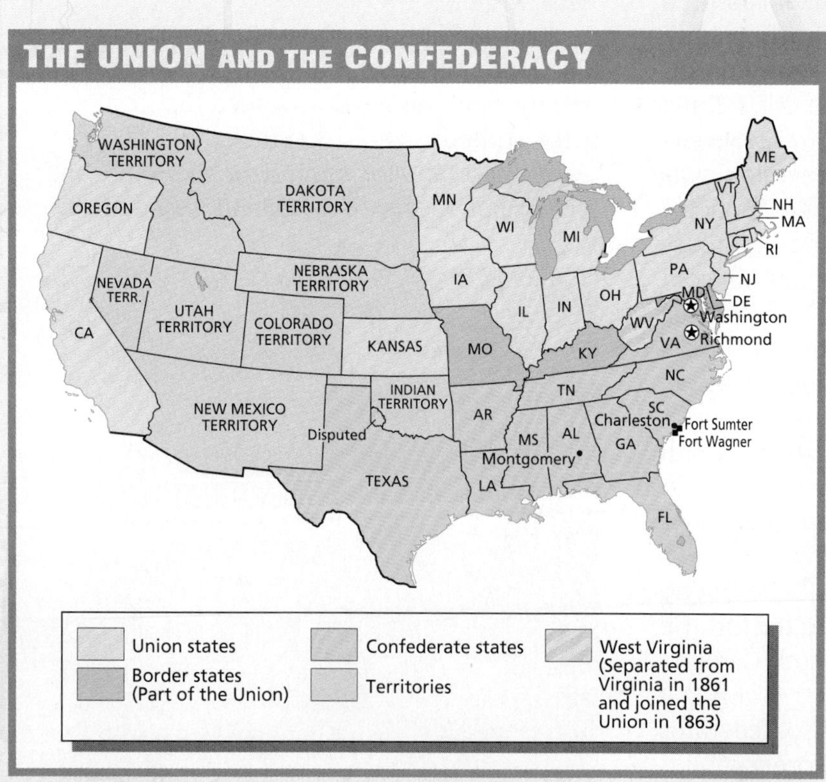

Learning from Maps.
Washington was surrounded by slave states.

Region. What states made up the Confederacy? What states made up the Union?

• Maps

North Versus South

In numbers, the Confederacy was no match for the Union. The North had about 22 million people, the South about 9 million. About 3.5 million of the southerners were slaves. Because southerners were unwilling to arm slaves, the Confederate army could only draw from around 1 million men.

In 1860 about 85 percent of the nation's factories were in the northern states. New York, Pennsylvania, and Massachusetts each had more factories than the entire South. There were only two small gun factories in the South, and no southern factory was capable of handling the need for uniforms and shoes.

In addition, the North had more than twice as many miles of railroad tracks as the South and almost twice the number of horses, donkeys, and mules. Thus, the Union could easily move its troops and supplies. The United States already had an army and navy, as well as established ways of raising money. The Confederacy had to create these institutions from scratch.

The Confederacy, however, had important strategic advantages over the Union. The South's military tradition provided it with brilliant generals. In addition, the South did not have to *defeat* the North. Instead, it just had to defend itself until the people in the North grew tired of fighting. Southern armies also had the advantage of usually fighting on familiar land and among friendly civilians. These factors added to their determination to fight and helped make up for the shortage of troops and supplies.

Women on both sides made valuable contributions to the war effort. They labored on farms, in government, and in factories. Making cartridges in arsenals was dangerous work.

• **Rating the North and South**

Section 1 Review

• **Glossary**

IDENTIFY and explain the significance of the following: Confederate States of America, Jefferson Davis, Abraham Lincoln, border states, Elizabeth Blackwell

REVIEWING FOR DETAILS

1. What steps did southerners take to form a new nation?
2. How did the Civil War begin?

REVIEWING FOR UNDERSTANDING

3. **Geographic Literacy** Why would the support of Maryland, Delaware, Kentucky, and Missouri have been important to each side in the Civil War?
4. **Writing Mastery:** *Expressing* Take the role of a general for the North or South and, in a short essay, explain why you think your side had the most advantages at the beginning of the Civil War.
5. **Critical Thinking:** *Drawing Conclusions* Why do you think people chose to side with the North or the South? Explain your answer.

Section 2
The War: East and West

Multimedia Connections

Explore these related topics and materials on the CD-ROM to enrich your understanding of this section:

Atlas

- War in New Mexico
- Theaters of War, 1861–1865
- War in Missouri and Arkansas
- Southern Railroads, 1862–1865

Media Bank

- Civil War Music 1
- Civil War Battles
- Second Battle of Bull Run
- Mary Boykin Chesnut
- Family Store
- Johnny Shiloh
- Wounded Union Soldiers
- Stonewall Jackson

Profiles

- Mary Boykin Chesnut
- George McClellan

Biographies

- Stonewall Jackson

It takes time to raise and train an army, but people in the North were impatient for action. "On to Richmond" was the popular cry in Washington. In July 1861, long before the Union troops were ready, General Irvin McDowell ordered them into Virginia. Laughing and joking along the way, the soldiers were joined by carriages filled with politicians, newspaper reporters, and curious onlookers. Some carried picnic lunches, anticipating an afternoon of entertainment.

As you read this section you will find out:

- **What the Union's war goals were in the East, and why it did not achieve them.**
- **How the Union pursued its war goals in the West.**
- **Why the Mississippi River and the city of Vicksburg were important.**

The First Battle of Bull Run

On July 21, 1861, some 35,000 poorly trained Union troops met the Confederate army of about 22,000 soldiers along a small stream called Bull Run at Manassas railroad junction in northern Virginia. The Confederates, who were not much better prepared, held the high ground above the stream. The Union general, Irvin McDowell, circled west, guessing that the Confederate line was weakest there. When he attacked, the Confederates fell back.

The Union soldiers broke the Confederate line, but Confederate troops under General Thomas J. Jackson stopped the Union advance cold. At the peak of the **First Battle of Bull Run**, a southern officer cried, "There is Jackson standing like a stone wall! Rally behind the Virginians!"—winning for Jackson the nickname "Stonewall."

When the southerners counterattacked, the Union army panicked. Hundreds of Union soldiers dropped their weapons and fled north toward Washington. The Confederates might have captured the Union capital if they had not been so disorganized. As southern General Joseph E. Johnston commented, "Our army was more disorganized by victory than that of the United States by defeat."

Following the battle, a government clerk named Clara Barton saw that many of the wounded went untreated because the army lacked medical services. Thereafter, she provided first aid and distributed supplies to Union soldiers. The soldiers labeled her "Angel of the Battlefield" because she even gave aid in the midst of battle. After the war, Barton eventually organized the American Red Cross.

After Bull Run, Americans on both sides realized that winning the war might be difficult. Southerner Mary Chesnut worried that the victory would mislead "us into a fool's paradise of conceit at our superior valor [courage]." She had cause for concern. In the North, Lincoln's secretary wrote, "The preparations for the war will be continued with increased vigor by the Government." Indeed, Congress authorized Lincoln to raise a force of 1 million soldiers to serve for three years.

The War in the East

Lincoln replaced McDowell with George B. McClellan. General McClellan then prepared to attack Richmond, located only about 100 miles south of Washington. Union leaders believed that by capturing the Confederate capital, the war would come to a quick end.

McClellan was a skilled organizer and was popular with ordinary soldiers, but he had serious weaknesses as a leader. He was vain and had too high an opinion of his own abilities. McClellan also often overestimated the strength of his enemies. Despite his dashing appearance and bold talk, he never seemed ready to march against the enemy.

After the disastrous loss at the First Battle of Bull Run, McClellan's cautious approach seemed the right policy. The Union army had to be trained and disciplined before it was ready to fight again. Yet even when this task had been accomplished, McClellan still delayed. Finally, in March 1862 he was ready to advance.

McClellan on the move. McClellan's plan for capturing Richmond was complicated but sensible. He moved his army by boat down the Potomac River and through Chesapeake Bay to the Virginia coast southeast of Richmond. He planned to take the Confederates by surprise by attacking where their defenses seemed weakest. Instead of striking swiftly as his plan called

Clara Barton

• Clara Barton

The Granger Collection, New York

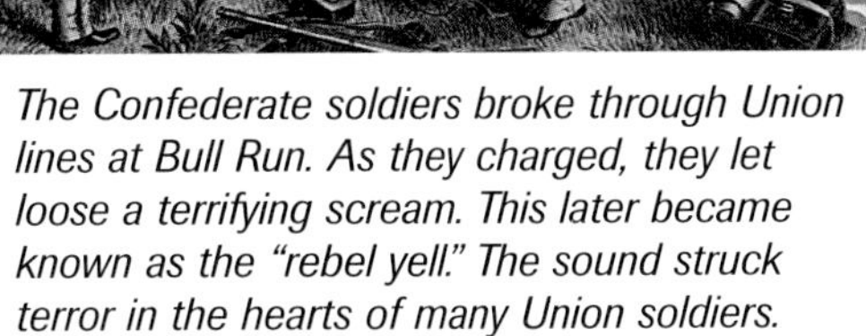

The Confederate soldiers broke through Union lines at Bull Run. As they charged, they let loose a terrifying scream. This later became known as the "rebel yell." The sound struck terror in the hearts of many Union soldiers.

for, however, McClellan hesitated. He had more than 100,000 men—a force that was much larger than the Confederates'—yet he pleaded for more troops. Impatient for action, President Lincoln wrote an urgent letter to McClellan on April 9, 1862:

> **"[Your] hesitation to move upon an intrenched [entrenched] enemy is but the story of Manassas [Bull Run] repeated. . . . I have never written you, or spoken to you, in greater kindness of feeling than now. . . . *But you must act.*"**

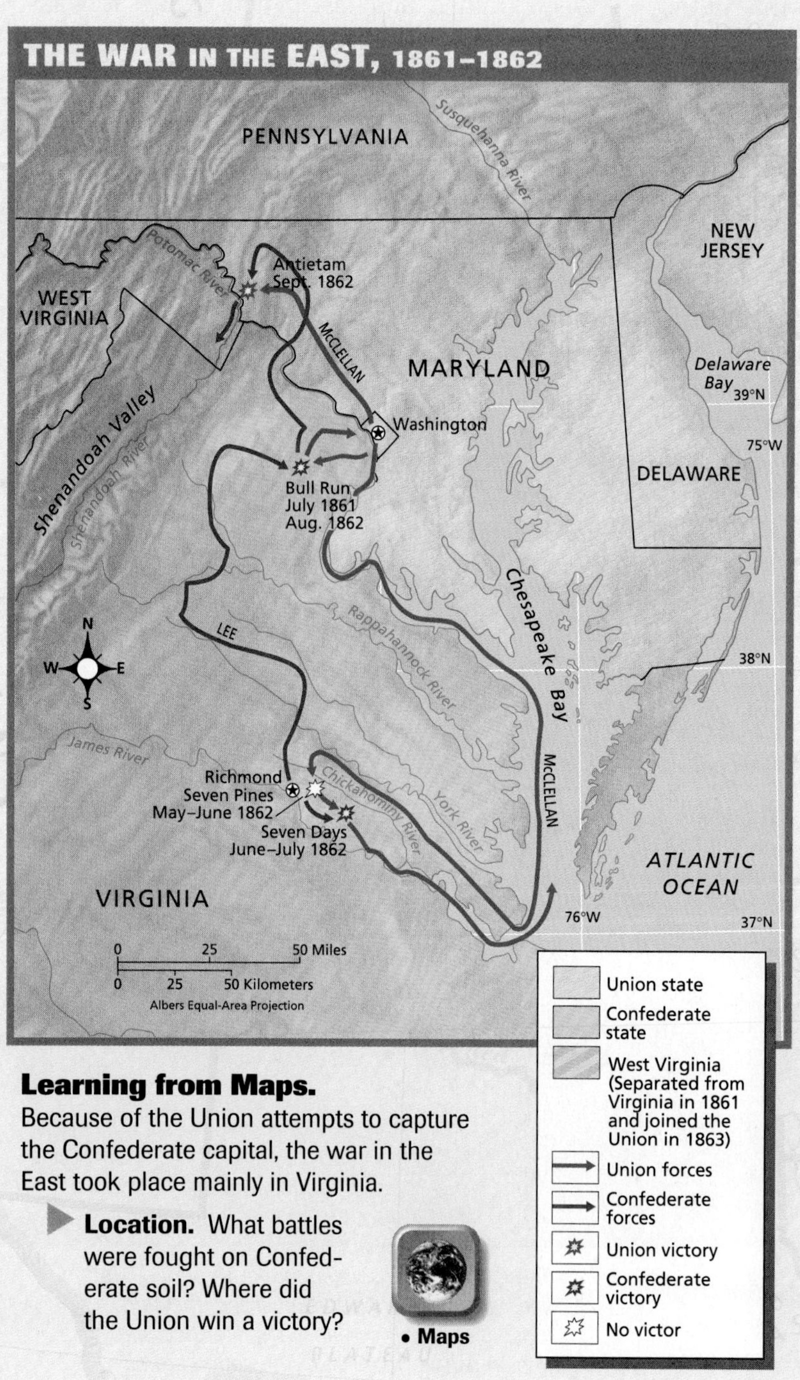

Learning from Maps.
Because of the Union attempts to capture the Confederate capital, the war in the East took place mainly in Virginia.

▶ **Location.** What battles were fought on Confederate soil? Where did the Union win a victory?

In early May, McClellan finally began a slow-moving advance. On May 31, while the Union army was crossing the Chickahominy River, Confederate general Joseph E. Johnston launched a fierce attack. Despite heavy loss of life in this **Battle of Seven Pines**, neither side gained an advantage.

Johnston was wounded in this battle and had to give up his command. Robert E. Lee, the officer who had led the 1859 capture of John Brown at Harpers Ferry, became the new commander of the southern armies.

Lee takes command. Lee, who had served brilliantly during the Mexican War, had been Lincoln's first choice to lead the Union army. He had declined. Although he opposed secession, Lee decided that his first loyalty was to his home state of Virginia.

Lee was a great addition to the Confederate army. With McClellan threatening Richmond, Lee daringly sent Stonewall Jackson's troops in northern Virginia up to threaten the defenses of Washington. Lincoln became alarmed at the southern army's presence so near the capital. He canceled the

Robert E. Lee was beloved in the South and respected in the North. His horse, Traveler, was nearly as celebrated. After the war, visitors kept hairs from his tail as souvenirs.

• Robert E. Lee

reinforcements requested by McClellan and ordered them to protect Washington instead. This was what Lee had wanted.

In June 1862 Lee launched an all-out attack on McClellan's forces. After a series of clashes, the Union army fell back. Lee had won the **Seven Days Battles**. More than 16,000 Union soldiers were killed or wounded, and the South lost nearly 20,000 men.

The Second Battle of Bull Run.

A discouraged Lincoln ordered General McClellan to withdraw and to combine his troops with a new army that had been formed south of Washington under the command of General John Pope.

As McClellan pulled back, Lee moved northward. He wanted to destroy this new army before McClellan's could join it. In a daring maneuver, Lee sent Stonewall Jackson's troops to hit Pope's army from the rear. Jackson marched swiftly and then struck hard, destroying Pope's supplies and supply lines. In desperation, on August 29, Pope attacked the Confederates.

This **Second Battle of Bull Run** was fought on almost the same ground as the first. Again, the Confederates drove the Union troops back toward Washington. Dismayed by Pope's failure, Lincoln gave McClellan command of Pope's army.

The War in the West

At the same time the war was raging in the East, Union forces were on the move in the West. After the First Battle of Bull Run, the Union focused on its chief objective in the West—to control the Mississippi River. This would take away the South's most important trade route to the sea and would make movement of troops and supplies within the South difficult. The South would be cut in two.

Grant on the move. The struggle for the river was long and bitter. Out of this struggle came the Union's greatest general, Ulysses S. Grant. Although Grant had been just an average student at West Point, he served well in the Mexican War. After the war, however, he found his army posting in the West lonely and boring, and he began to drink heavily.

In 1854 Grant left the army. He tried a number of different careers but succeeded in none. When the Civil War began, he quit his job in a leather shop and joined an Illinois regiment. Because of Grant's performance, he was quickly promoted to the rank of brigadier general.

Grant was a shy, small man who constantly chewed cigars

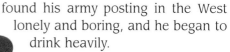

General Ulysses S. Grant

• Ulysses S. Grant

and rarely stood up straight. His uniforms were rumpled and ill fitting. Grant did not look like a general, yet he was brave and determined, and he turned out to be an excellent military strategist.

Grant decided that the best way to get control of the Mississippi River, which the Confederates had heavily fortified, was to attack the more vulnerable but strategically important Tennessee River. In February 1862 he organized a successful land-and-river attack on Fort Henry, a Confederate outpost on the Tennessee. Union gunboats pounded the fort into surrender before moving on to attack Fort Donelson, on the Cumberland River. When the fort's commander asked Grant the terms for surrender, Grant replied, "No terms except an unconditional and immediate surrender can be accepted." This won him the nickname "Unconditional Surrender" Grant.

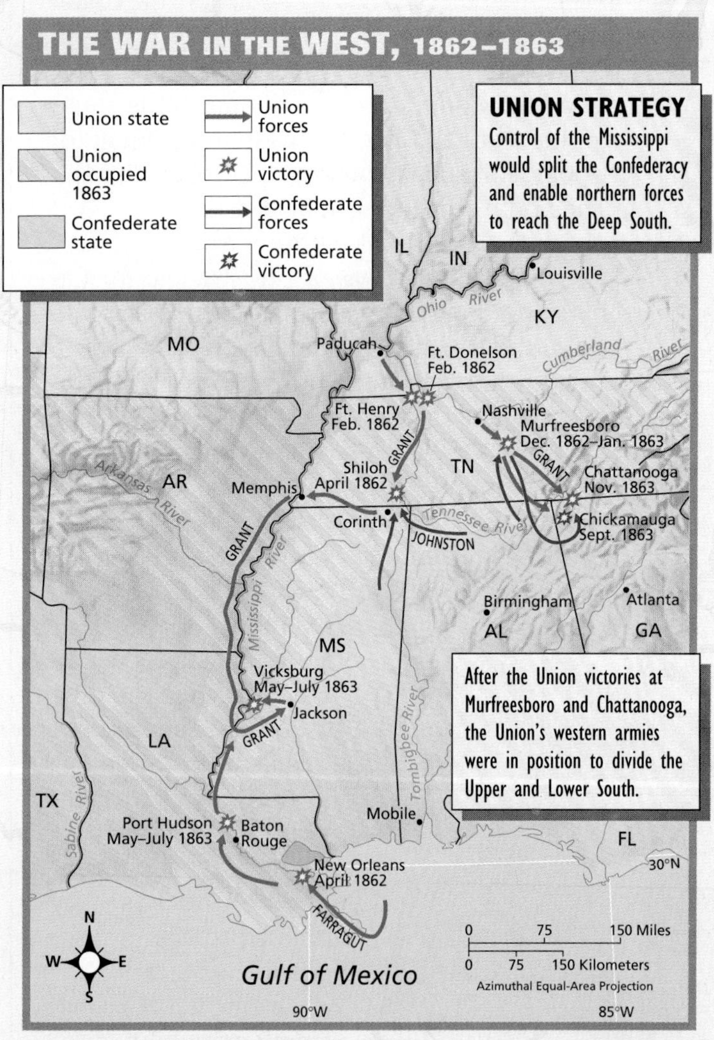

Learning from Maps.

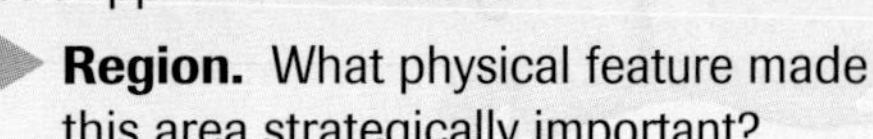

The war in the West was fought largely in Mississippi and Tennessee.

▶ **Region.** What physical feature made this area strategically important?

The Battle of Shiloh. Grant next marched his men farther south along the Tennessee River. He intended to capture a Confederate railroad center at Corinth, Mississippi. However, on April 6, 1862, about 20 miles north of Corinth, the Confederates surprised Grant's army at Shiloh Church in southern Tennessee. During the first day of this **Battle of Shiloh**, the Confederates drove Grant's army back.

Fortunately for Grant, 25,000 fresh Union troops arrived during the night. The next day, the Union army forced the Confederates back, but Shiloh was an extremely costly victory. In just two days, the Union suffered some 13,000 casualties. Confederate casualties were some 11,000.

The huge losses suffered by both sides had a sobering effect on the troops, their generals, and the public. After the battle one soldier reflected, "I saw more of human agony and woe than I trust I will ever again be called on to witness."

The Capture of Vicksburg

While Grant was fighting to gain control of the Tennessee River, a Union fleet commanded by Captain David Farragut captured New Orleans and Baton Rouge, Louisiana. By autumn, only a 200-mile-long stretch of the Mississippi River between Vicksburg, Mississippi, and Port Hudson,

Confederate guns in Vicksburg, high over the Mississippi River, shell Union gunboats on the river below.

Louisiana, was still in Confederate hands. Grant then decided to attack Vicksburg, a city high on the cliffs overlooking the river. A small Confederate force, commanded by General John C. Pemberton, defended the city.

Grant first approached Vicksburg from the north in November 1862, but he soon discovered that the marshy land around the city made an infantry attack impossible. Instead, he pinned down Pemberton's troops inside Vicksburg and waited for them to surrender—a military strategy known as a **siege**. The siege of Vicksburg began in mid-May. Grant's army shelled the city almost continuously. As the Confederates ran short of food, a resident wrote in her diary:

• War in Indian Territory

> **"We are utterly cut off from the world, surrounded by a circle of fire. . . . The fiery shower of shells goes on day and night. . . . People do nothing but eat what they can get, sleep when they can, and dodge the shells."**

On July 4, 1863, Pemberton surrendered to Grant. Shortly afterward, Port Hudson, the last remaining southern position on the Mississippi River, also surrendered.

Even after the fall of Vicksburg and Port Hudson, the Confederates continued to control much of Louisiana, Arkansas, and Texas. However, these states were cut off from the rest of the Confederacy!

Section 2 Review

• Glossary

• Gazetteer

IDENTIFY and explain the significance of the following: First Battle of Bull Run, Stonewall Jackson, George B. McClellan, Battle of Seven Pines, Robert E. Lee, Seven Days Battles, Second Battle of Bull Run, Ulysses S. Grant, Battle of Shiloh, siege

LOCATE and explain the importance of the following: Richmond, Potomac River, Vicksburg, Port Hudson

REVIEWING FOR DETAILS

1. What did the Union hope to accomplish in the war in the East, and why was it unable to achieve these goals?
2. How did Union forces go about winning the war in the West?

REVIEWING FOR UNDERSTANDING

3. **Geographic Literacy** Why were the Mississippi River and the city of Vicksburg important in the West?
4. **Writing Mastery:** *Describing* Imagine that you are a newspaper reporter at one of the major battles of the Civil War, such as Second Bull Run or Shiloh. Write a short article describing what you have seen.
5. **Critical Thinking:** *Making Comparisons* Compare the attempts of Generals McDowell and McClellan to capture the Confederate capital. What difficulties did each commander face?

Section 3
THE PEOPLE'S WAR

Multimedia Connections

Explore these related topics and materials on the CD–ROM to enrich your understanding of this section:

Atlas
- Emancipation, 1863

Profiles
- Charlotte Forten
- Robert Smalls

Readings
- Emancipation Proclamation
- Emancipation Reactions

Simulation
- Global Politics & the Civil War

Media Bank
- Celebrating Emancipation
- Southern Plantation
- Northern Machine Shop

As the Civil War dragged on, most Americans—men and women, soldiers and civilians—began to feel its terrible effects. "God grant these things may soon end and peace be restored. Of this war I am heartily sick and tired," complained a Pennsylvania soldier. Confederate Mary Chesnut voiced the feelings of many civilians on both sides: "Is anything worth it? This fearful sacrifice—this awful penalty we pay for war?"

As you read this section you will find out:

- **How the Emancipation Proclamation changed the war.**
- **Why some northerners opposed the war.**
- **How the war affected the economy of the South.**

Antietam

General Lee believed that the South had to do more than simply defend Richmond. To end the war, it had to deliver such a stinging defeat that northerners would grow tired of the costly conflict and would lose the will to fight. So Lee decided to march north, around the defenses of Washington. On September 4, 1862, he crossed the Potomac River and entered Maryland.

Union general McClellan was unsure of Lee's exact position. Then on September 13, one of McClellan's soldiers found a copy of Lee's battle plans wrapped around some cigars in an abandoned Confederate camp. With this information, McClellan was able to track down Lee's army. The armies met in battle on September 17 at Antietam Creek, near Sharpsburg, Maryland. Lee had about

Confederate soldiers lie dead beside the ruins of a cannon following the Battle of Antietam. The high casualties at Antietam made it the bloodiest single day of the entire war.

40,000 soldiers, McClellan nearly twice that number.

The **Battle of Antietam** began at dawn. When it ended at twilight, the Confederates had lost nearly 14,000 men, the Union forces more than 12,000. Then the next night, the Confederates retreated across the Potomac River. The North could finally claim a victory in the East.

Emancipation

Even before Antietam, the high cost of lives and money had started to change northerners' view of the war. Many began to believe that the war had to do more than preserve the Union—it also had to put an end to slavery. Otherwise, a northern victory would be in vain because future conflict would be inevitable. Lincoln also believed that slavery should not continue, but he was aware of the obstacles to ending slavery. He knew that many white northerners remained prejudiced against African Americans, whether enslaved or free. He also realized that a president did not have the constitutional authority to simply end slavery.

Lincoln was a clever politician. To emancipate, or free, the Confederates' slaves, he issued a military order declaring an end to slavery in the Confederacy in order to weaken the rebels' ability to fight the war. Lincoln felt he could do this under his constitutional powers as commander-in-chief of the armed forces.

Lincoln waited to issue the **Emancipation Proclamation** until after the Union victory at Antietam. He then announced that after January 1, 1863:

> **"all persons held as slaves within any state or designated part of a state, the people whereof shall then be in rebellion against the United States, shall be then, thenceforward, and forever free."**

Of course, the Emancipation Proclamation did little to free slaves until the Union defeated

Global Connections

The Civil War

Neither Great Britain nor France entered the Civil War, but both nations leaned toward supporting the South. French ruler Napoleon III saw the war as a chance to obtain an empire in Mexico. While the North and South were fighting, French troops were overthrowing Mexico's government. Lincoln protested France's actions, but Davis did not.

Some British believed that an independent South would be a better market for industrial products. By mid-1862, Confederate victories in Virginia had increased Britain's confidence in the South. British leaders began to discuss pressuring Lincoln to end the war.

Lincoln's Emancipation Proclamation, however, ended whatever real hopes the South had for outside intervention. Slavery was illegal in Britain and France, and the British abolitionist movement was strong. Both countries might have supported southerners in a war strictly for independence. Neither nation, however, would side with a government fighting to defend its right to enslave people.

the Confederacy. Nonetheless, it was an important step. "The dawn of freedom which it heralds [declares] may not break upon us at once; but it will surely come," rejoiced abolitionist Charlotte Forten.

African Americans and the War

President Lincoln also ordered that freed slaves be encouraged to enlist in the army. Enlisting former slaves, he told General Grant, "works doubly, weakening the enemy and strengthening us."

From the beginning of the war, free African Americans and **contrabands**—escaped slaves who crossed Union lines—had tried to join the Union army. It was not until July 1862, however, that Congress authorized African Americans to join the armed forces. Furthermore, it was only after Lincoln issued the Emancipation Proclamation that African Americans officially were encouraged to enlist in fighting units. Frederick Douglass described the motivation of many of the tens of thousands of African American volunteers:

> **"Once let the black man get upon his person the brass letters, U.S.; let him get an eagle on his button, and a musket on his shoulder and bullets in his pocket, and there is no power on earth which can deny that he has earned the right to citizenship."**

African American troops first saw major action in Port Hudson, Louisiana, in early July 1863. Later that same month, the **54th Massachusetts Infantry** won an honored place in U.S. military history during the battle for Fort Wagner, in South Carolina's Charleston Harbor. After days of trying to take the fort, the Union commander ordered a desperate frontal attack. Knowing the risks, the 54th led the charge under a storm of Confederate cannon fire. The soldiers reached the top of the fort's walls before being turned

Under steady cannon fire, the 54th Massachusetts Infantry bravely led the charge to take Fort Wagner. Over half the regiment was wounded or killed during the charge.

• African American Soldiers

back in fierce fighting. As leader of the charge, the 54th had the highest casualty rate of the battle. The regiment lost nearly half its men.

In all, some 180,000 black soldiers fought for the Union. By the end of the war there were 166 all-black regiments, and one Union soldier in eight was an African American. For much of the war, black soldiers were paid less than white soldiers, even though they performed with equal bravery. Twenty-one African Americans won the Congressional Medal of Honor and more than 30,000 gave their lives for the cause of freedom.

The Granger Collection, New York

Liberty with her Union shield defends herself against the Copperheads, represented as snakes in this 1863 political cartoon.

Northern Opposition to the War

Not everyone in the North, however, welcomed the Emancipation Proclamation. Some northerners were unwilling to support a war to free slaves or to prevent the southern states from seceding.

The Copperheads. Northern Democrats who opposed the war were known as **Copperheads**. Many Copperheads were sympathetic to the South. Radical Copperheads organized secret societies, through which they persuaded Union soldiers to desert and helped Confederate prisoners to escape.

To stop the activities of the Copperheads and other critics of the war, Lincoln at times suspended ***habeas corpus***, a constitutional protection that prevents authorities from unlawfully jailing people. Lincoln hoped to quiet criticism of the Union war effort by imprisoning protesters. During the war, the government jailed some 13,000 Americans without formal charges.

The draft. A few months after the Emancipation Proclamation went into effect, Congress established a **draft**, a system requiring men to serve in the military. Like the Confederate draft law passed in 1861, this measure allowed draftees to hire substitutes. Draftees could even avoid military service by paying the government $300. Poor men could not possibly raise $300, which was as much as some laborers earned in a year.

Draft riots soon broke out throughout the North. The worst occurred in New York City, where rioters ran wild for four days in July 1863. They burned buildings, looted shops, and attacked local African Americans. African Americans were the target of the rioters because many blamed the draft on the Emancipation Proclamation and resented having to risk their lives to free slaves. Union troops were rushed from the battlefront to New York, but more than 100 people were killed before order was restored.

Southern Shortages

While the North was facing opposition to the war, the South was struggling with economic problems. Paying for the war was among its most difficult tasks. Because the South could not raise enough funds by borrowing or taxing, it simply printed money—more than $1.5 billion. This resulted in tremendous inflation. Salt rose from $2 a bag before the war to $60 in some places by the fall of 1862. Near the end of the war, 50 Confederate paper dollars were worth less than one gold dollar.

Confederate blockade runners tried to slip past Union ships. As the blockade tightened, fewer Confederate ships were successful in their attempts.

In addition, the South's tradition of growing cotton instead of food crops resulted in food shortages in some areas. Clothing was also scarce in the South. Confederate soldiers wore ragged uniforms and sometimes marched without shoes.

Manufactured products were also scarce in the South. The region was mostly agricultural and was largely cut off from trade with Europe. Early in the war, Lincoln had established a naval blockade of southern ports. About 6,000 ships had entered and left southern ports in 1860. By the next year, however, only 800 ships managed to slip past the blockade. Each year fewer and fewer slipped through. The capture of New Orleans also cut off the whole interior of the South from international trade.

The South's shortages encouraged some ship captains to try to break through the ever-tightening northern blockade. The blockade runners' ships were small and fast. The British island of Bermuda, in the western Atlantic Ocean, was among their favorite destinations. There they exchanged cotton or other farm products for guns, medicines, blankets, and coffee, as well as for silks and other luxuries.

The volume of these imports was too small to have much effect on the South's needs, however. In addition, the blockade runners carried whatever goods they thought would sell for the best price. Because most blockade runners were private citizens, the Confederate government could not force them to import the war supplies that southern armies so badly needed.

• Wartime Economy

Section 3 Review

• Glossary

IDENTIFY and explain the significance of the following: Battle of Antietam, Emancipation Proclamation, contrabands, 54th Massachusetts Infantry, Copperheads, *habeas corpus*, draft

REVIEWING FOR DETAILS

1. What changes did the Emancipation Proclamation bring in the war?
2. Why did some northerners object to the war?
3. How did the war affect the South's economy?

REVIEWING FOR UNDERSTANDING

4. **Writing Mastery:** *Expressing* Imagine that you are a member of the 54th Massachusetts Infantry. Write a letter back home telling why you feel it is important to fight for the Union.
5. **Critical Thinking:** *Determining the Strength of an Argument* President Lincoln believed that the need to win the war and save the Union permitted him to suspend the rights of some Americans. Do you think this was a convincing argument? Explain your answer.

Section 4
VICTORY AT LAST

Multimedia Connections
Explore these related topics and materials on the CD–ROM to enrich your understanding of this section:

Profiles
- George Meade
- Jeb Stuart

Readings
- Gettysburg Address

Media Bank
- Fredericksburg
- Chancellorsville
- Wilderness
- Spotsylvania Court House
- Cold Harbor
- Sherman's Army in Atlanta
- Ruins of Atlanta
- Jeb Stuart
- Draft of Gettysburg Address

Glossary
- Andersonville Prison

Confederate general James B. Longstreet studied the Union troops on the hills outside of Gettysburg. Convinced that the enemy's position was too strong, he urged Robert E. Lee not to force a fight in this place. But Lee had confidence in his soldiers. "The enemy is there," he said, "and I am going to attack him there." Longstreet remained worried, however. He sensed that Lee would not win the victory he needed outside this small Pennsylvania town.

As you read this section you will find out:

- **Why the Battle of Gettysburg was significant.**
- **What General Grant's strategy was to win the war.**
- **How General Sherman's march affected the South.**

The Battle of Gettysburg

By the spring of 1863 the war had raged for two long years, and the North seemed no closer to restoring the nation than when Fort Sumter fell. Reports from the front did little to raise northern spirits. On Virginia battlefields like Fredericksburg and Chancellorsville, the Confederates continued to beat back the Union armies. As the casualties continued to mount, Lincoln searched for a general who could defeat Lee and put an end to the terrible war.

- Southern Victories

Lee on the move. Lee invaded the North for a second time in June 1863. He still hoped to gain a decisive victory on northern soil and make the Union give up the struggle. As gray-clad Confederates marched through Maryland

and into Pennsylvania, Union troops raced cross-country to intercept them. General George G. Meade was in command, the fifth officer to head the Union forces in less than a year.

On July 1, some of Meade's cavalry made contact with Confederate infantry outside of Gettysburg, Pennsylvania. The southerners had come to the town looking for some much-needed shoes. Both sides quickly concentrated their armies at Gettysburg.

Meade positioned his troops south of town on Cemetery Ridge. Lee's forces occupied Seminary Ridge, almost a mile away. For the next two days, the Confederates tried to capture Cemetery Ridge. As the sun set on July 2, Union troops had turned back fierce attacks on the northern and the southern ends of their position.

On average, Civil War soldiers spent about 50 days in camp for every day they spent in battle. Like many men on both sides, this soldier from the 31st Pennsylvania Infantry is joined in camp by his wife and children.

• Soldiers of the Civil War

Pickett's Charge. On the afternoon of July 3, Confederate artillery shelled Cemetery Ridge. Around 3:00 P.M. General George E. Pickett led a charge at the center of the Union line. Howling the eerie "rebel yell," some 15,000 southern soldiers started at a trot across about a mile of open ground into heavy Union gunfire.

For a brief moment, a handful of southerners reached the Union trenches, but the Union forces rallied and drove back **Pickett's Charge**. In 30 bloody minutes, almost half the Confederate attackers had been killed or wounded. Pickett described his "overwhelming heartbreak" in a letter to his wife:

> **"Well, it is over now. The battle is lost, and many of us are prisoners, many are dead, many wounded, bleeding and dying. Your soldier lives and mourns. If it were not for you, my darling, he would rather . . . be back there with his dead, to sleep for all time in an unknown grave."**

The **Battle of Gettysburg** was indeed over. The Confederates lost more than 20,000 men,

Union forces (left) defend themselves against the Confederates (right) during Pickett's Charge.

• Battle of Gettysburg

the Union forces some 23,000. On July 4, 1863, the very day that Vicksburg surrendered in the West, Lee began his retreat from Gettysburg. Had General Meade pursued, he might have destroyed Lee's army and ended the war. Instead, Meade delayed, and the war dragged on.

Grant Versus Lee

In March 1864 Lincoln called Grant to Washington and named him commanding general of all Union armies. Grant decided to try to end the war by mounting two great offensives. He would lead an advance toward Richmond, seeking a showdown battle with Lee's army in northern Virginia.

Another Union army commanded by General William Tecumseh Sherman would march from Chattanooga, Tennessee, into Georgia to capture the important railroad center of Atlanta. Then the two armies would march toward each other, crushing any Confederate resistance that remained.

Grant's march into Virginia met fierce resistance. In May 1864 Grant and Lee clashed in a series of bloody battles. Lee's soldiers fought hard to keep the Union forces from advancing. Grant's army, however, pressed on toward Richmond.

As Union and Confederate forces hammered away at each other, the death count rose. In seven weeks of fighting, Grant had lost

THE FINAL CAMPAIGNS

Union state; Union occupied; Union forces; Union victory; Confederate state; Confederate forces; Confederate victory; No victor; Union blockade

Union forces shatter the Confederacy's major western army.

Johnston fails to stop Sherman and accepts final surrender terms on April 26, 1865.

Lee surrenders to Grant on April 9, 1865.

SHERMAN'S CAMPAIGN

THE TIDE TURNS IN THE EAST

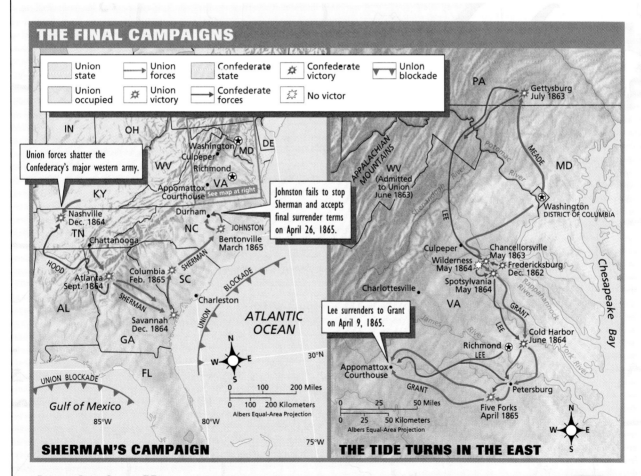

Learning from Maps. After Gettysburg, Lee retreated south and concentrated on stopping Grant's advance toward Richmond.

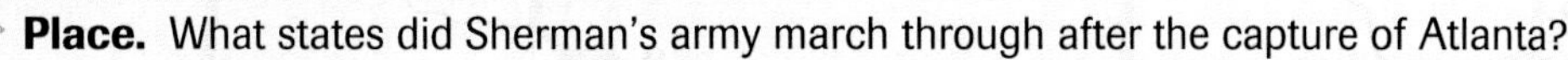

▶ **Place.** What states did Sherman's army march through after the capture of Atlanta?

• Maps

Mathew Brady, perhaps the greatest photographer of the Civil War, took this photograph of William Tecumseh Sherman.

• William T. Sherman

some 65,000 men to Lee's 35,000. Despite the high cost in lives, Grant was wearing down Lee's tired army. The Confederates were running short of men and equipment. Lee could no longer replace all his casualties.

In contrast, Grant was supported by a steady stream of recruits. In addition, Uion factories were turning out almost unlimited amounts of supplies. The larger population and greater resources of the North were finally tipping the scales toward the Union.

In June 1864 Grant crossed the James River and approached the town of Petersburg, an important railroad junction a few miles south of Richmond. If Grant captured Petersburg, most supplies to Richmond and to Lee's army would be cut off.

Lee's weary veterans managed to stop the Union army outside Petersburg, but Grant placed the town under siege. Trenches stretched for miles as both sides dug in. Snipers and artillery attacks took Union and Confederate lives almost daily. For nearly 10 desperate months, the Confederate defenses held firm.

Sherman's March to the Sea

While Grant was stalled outside Petersburg, Sherman advanced toward Atlanta with a force of more than 100,000 troops. Like the Shawnee chief for whom he was named, William Tecumseh Sherman was a tough and relentless soldier. John B. Hood, the Confederate general resisting him, had only 60,000 men. Hood twice attacked Sherman's advancing troops. Both attacks failed, and on September 2, the Union army marched triumphantly into Atlanta.

News of Sherman's victory reached the North during the 1864 presidential campaign. Lincoln had been renominated by Republicans and prowar Democrats on a "National Union" ticket. The vice presidential candidate was Andrew Johnson, a Tennessee Democrat who had remained loyal to the Union. The Democratic Party's presidential candidate was General McClellan. With the war dragging on, Lincoln feared he would lose the election. Sherman's success helped Lincoln, however, and he was re-elected in a landslide victory—212 electoral votes to 21.

After the election, on November 15, Sherman's army began marching eastward from Atlanta toward Savannah, Georgia, on the Atlantic coast. As he left Atlanta, Sherman set fire to the city. He was waging what is called **total war**—a strategy to break an enemy's will to fight by destroying the

The fires ordered first by Confederate general Hood and then by Union general Sherman destroyed much of Atlanta.

• Burning of Atlanta

American Letters

Hospital Sketches

Louisa May Alcott

Louisa May Alcott is best known for her famous novel Little Women, *published in 1868. However, it was another novel,* Hospital Sketches, *published in 1863, that first brought her to the attention of the American public. During the Civil War Alcott worked as a volunteer nurse in a military hospital near Washington. There she helped care for the casualties that poured in from the battlefields of Virginia.* Hospital Sketches *is a fictional version of her experiences. Her descriptions were a sharp contrast to the idealistic views many Americans held about the war in its early years.*

Louisa May Alcott helped support her father and family with her writing.

• Civil War Nurses

"They've come! they've come! hurry up, ladies—you're wanted."

"Who have come? the rebels?"

This sudden summons in the gray dawn was somewhat startling to a three days' nurse like myself, and, as the thundering knock came at our door, I sprang up in my bed. . . .

"Bless you, no child; it's the wounded from Fredericksburg; forty ambulances are at the door, and we shall have our hands full in fifteen minutes."

. . . I had rather longed for the wounded to arrive . . . ; but when I peeped into the dusky street lined with what I at first had innocently called market carts, now unloading their sad freight at our door, . . . I indulged in a most unpatriotic wish that I was safe at home again, with a quiet day before me. . . .

. . . There they were! "our brave boys," as the papers justly call them, for cowards could hardly have been so riddled with [full of] shot and shell, so torn and shattered. . . . In they came, some on stretchers, some in men's arms, some feebly staggering along propped on rude crutches, and one lay stark and still with covered face, as a comrade gave his name to be recorded before they carried him away to the dead house. All was hurry and confusion; the hall was full of these wrecks of humanity, for the most exhausted could not reach a bed till duly ticketed and registered; the walls were lined with rows of such as could sit, the floor covered with the more disabled. . . .

. . . The house had been a hotel before hospitals were needed, and many of the doors still bore their old names; some not so inappropriate as might be imagined, for my ward was in truth a *ball-room,* if gun-shot wounds could christen it. . . . Round the great stove was gathered the dreariest group I ever saw—ragged, gaunt [very thin] and pale, mud to the knees, with bloody bandages untouched since put on days before; many bundled up in blankets, coats being lost or useless; and all wearing that disheartened [discouraged] look which proclaimed [showed] defeat. . . . I pitied them so much, I dared not speak to them, though, remembering all they had been through since the rout [defeat] at Fredericksburg, I yearned to serve the dreariest of them all.

resources of the opposing civilian population and its army. When this harsh policy was questioned, Sherman simply said, "War is cruelty."

As Sherman's army marched through Georgia, it left behind a path of destruction 60 miles wide. His troops destroyed or consumed everything in their path that could aid the southern war effort.

The Union soldiers slaughtered chickens and cattle for food. They burned barns and houses. When the troops crossed a railroad line, they tore up the tracks, burned the ties, and twisted the rails so that they were useless.

On December 21 the Union army entered Savannah, Georgia. Then Sherman marched north, destroying large sections of South Carolina and North Carolina with the same cold-blooded efficiency.

Surrender at Appomattox

On March 4, 1865, Lincoln began his second term as president. The war still raged, but it now seemed clear that the long and tragic conflict was drawing to a close. In his second inaugural address, Lincoln outlined the policy he intended to follow toward the South:

> **"With malice [hatred] toward none, with charity for all, with firmness in the right as God gives us to see the right, let us strive on to finish the work we are in, to bind up the nation's wounds, to care for him who shall have borne the battle and for his widow and his orphan—to do all which may achieve and cherish a just and lasting peace among ourselves and with all nations."**

In early April 1865, Grant finally overran the Confederate defenses at Petersburg. Lee had to abandon both Petersburg and Richmond and retreat westward. His last hope was to escape into North Carolina and to join with the Confederate army that Sherman was driving before him. When Grant's pursuing troops sealed off his escape route, Lee made the painful decision to surrender.

Lee and Grant met at the home of Wilmer McLean in the Virginia town of Appomattox Courthouse on Sunday, April 9. It was a moving scene. Lee was dignified in defeat, Grant gracious in victory. "I met you once before, General Lee, while we were serving in Mexico," Grant said after they had shaken hands. "I think I should have recognized you anywhere."

The two generals talked briefly about that old war when they had been comrades. Then Grant sat down at a little table and wrote out the terms of surrender. Considering the loss of life on both sides—more than 350,000 Union soldiers and more than 250,000 Confederates—and the completeness of the Union

Over 40,000 Union soldiers filled the cramped and unsanitary quarters of Andersonville prison camp in Georgia. The poor living conditions resulted in the deaths of over 10,000 of its prisoners.

• Casualties of War

Lee and Grant signed the surrender papers at Appomattox. Grant then provided food rations to the starving Confederate troops and ordered his army not to celebrate, saying, "the rebels are our countrymen again."

• Civil War Music 2

victory, the terms were generous. The Confederates were merely to surrender their weapons and flags and depart in peace.

When General Lee hinted that his men needed to keep their horses for the spring planting, Grant said that every man who claimed to own a horse or mule could take the animal home with him. Both men signed the surrender papers. Then Grant introduced Lee to his staff. As he shook hands with Colonel Ely Parker, a Seneca Indian, Lee observed, "I am glad to see one real American here." Colonel Parker replied, "We are all Americans." Union bugler Seth M. Flint described what happened after the meeting concluded:

"Out came General Lee, his soldierly figure erect, even in defeat. We stiffened and gave him a salute, and the man in gray courteously [politely] returned it. . . .

After the departure of General Lee, we quickly learned the happy news of the surrender and it spread like wildfire through the army. That night was one of the happiest I have ever known.

When I sounded taps, the sweetest of all bugle calls, the notes had scarcely died away when from the distance—it must have come from General Lee's headquarters—came, silvery clear, the same call. The boys on the other side welcomed peace."

Section 4 Review

• Glossary

• Gazetteer

• Time Line

IDENTIFY and explain the significance of the following: George G. Meade, Pickett's Charge, Battle of Gettysburg, William Tecumseh Sherman, total war

LOCATE and explain the importance of the following: Petersburg, Atlanta, Savannah, Appomattox Courthouse

REVIEWING FOR DETAILS

1. How did the Battle of Gettysburg affect the war?
2. How did General Grant plan to win the war?

REVIEWING FOR UNDERSTANDING

3. **Geographic Literacy** How did Sherman's total war policy affect the South?
4. **Writing Mastery:** *Persuading* Imagine that you are a Confederate soldier or civilian. Write a letter to General Lee to persuade him either to surrender or to continue fighting.
5. **Critical Thinking:** *Drawing Conclusions* What did Lee hope to gain by invading the North?

CHAPTER 15

Reuniting the Nation

(1865–1900)

Constitutional Heritage:
How might amending the U.S. Constitution protect people's rights?

Democratic Values:
Why might some groups want to keep others from voting?

Economic Development:
How might people try to reshape their economy after a defeat in war?

• Video Opener

• Skill Builder

African American poet Frances Watkins Harper described life for former slaves in the South after the Civil War:

"Well, the Northern folks kept sending
The Yankee teachers down;
And they stood right up and helped us,
Though Rebs did sneer and frown. . . .
Then I got a little cabin,
A place to call my own—
And I felt as independent
As the queen upon her throne."

image above: *Former slaves during Reconstruction*

Section 1

RECONSTRUCTING THE SOUTH

Multimedia Connections

Explore these related topics and materials on the CD–ROM to enrich your understanding of this section:

Profiles

- Thaddeus Stevens
- Ulysses S. Grant
- Andrew Johnson

Readings

- Oh Captain! My Captain!
- Andrew Johnson's Impeachment

Media Bank

- Lincoln's Assassination
- Reconstruction Amendments

On the evening of April 14, 1865, less than a week after the South's surrender, Abraham and Mary Todd Lincoln were attending a play at Ford's Theater in Washington. Suddenly, a shot rang out. John Wilkes Booth, an actor sympathetic to the South, had slipped into the president's box and fired a bullet into Lincoln's head. The president died the next day. Northerners were shocked and grief-stricken. For southerners, Lincoln's death heightened uncertainty about the future.

As you read this section you will find out:

- **What the main goal of President Johnson's Reconstruction plan was.**
- **What the Radical Republicans wanted from Reconstruction.**
- **Why Congress impeached President Johnson.**

President Andrew Johnson

President Lincoln's death left a terrible void. For months he had been involved in planning for **Reconstruction**, the rebuilding of the South's government and society after the end of the Civil War. Much now depended on Vice President Andrew Johnson, who became president after Lincoln's assassination.

Before the Civil War, Johnson had served in both houses of Congress and as governor of Tennessee. Although he was a Democrat, the Republicans had picked him to run for vice president in 1864 because he was one of the few pro-Union politicians who came from a Confederate state.

Most Republican politicians expected Johnson to make a fine president. Some disagreed, however, over how he should treat the defeated South. Many moderate Republicans

Apprenticed to a tailor as a young boy, President Andrew Johnson never had any formal education. Through hard work and the help of his wife, Eliza, he succeeded in politics, winning his first local office at the age of 19.

believed that Lincoln's idea of "malice [hatred] toward none" was the best policy. They hoped, as Lincoln had once said, "to bind up the nation's wounds" quickly.

Johnson pleased the moderate Republicans and Democrats by issuing **amnesty**, or forgiveness, to southerners who would take an oath of loyalty to the United States. The states of the former Confederacy would then eventually be allowed to hold elections and send representatives and senators to the U.S. Congress. Under Johnson's plan, southern states could still deny African Americans the right to vote.

Radical Republicans were concerned that the president's plan put too much power in the hands of former slaveholders. They were determined to protect the rights of the newly freed slaves. Radical Republicans wanted Johnson to punish the planters severely.

Congressman Thaddeus Stevens of Pennsylvania was one of the Radical leaders. He demanded that the United States seize the property of the large former slaveholders and divide it among the former slaves. There would be plenty of "rebel land," he said, to give a 40-acre farm to every adult male former slave in the South.

The Black Codes

Radicals like Stevens were deeply concerned about the way former slaves, or freedpeople, were being treated in the South. By April 1866 all the southern state governments established under President Johnson's amnesty plan had ratified the new **Thirteenth Amendment** to the Constitution, which officially abolished slavery. However, powerful white planters still formed the majority of leaders in the South and easily controlled the new governments. These "white" governments did not allow freedpeople to vote. Southern state legislatures swiftly passed regulations called **Black Codes**. These codes were designed to keep freedpeople in a slavelike condition.

The Black Codes often barred African Americans from any kind of work except farming and household service. Some states forced African Americans to sign labor contracts with landowners at the beginning of each year. If they left their jobs, they received no pay for what they had done. If they did not sign, they were charged with being vagrants. When convicted, the "sentence" often included having

Under the Black Codes, this African American man was arrested for vagrancy simply because he did not have a job. To pay his fine he was "sold" as a servant to the highest bidder.

The Granger Collection, New York

the freed person work for a landowner for a full year without pay.

The Black Codes alarmed many northerners, and the results of southern elections alarmed them even further. Southern voters chose for office many of the people who had led them during the Civil War. Several former Confederate generals were elected to Congress. In 1866 the Georgia legislature sent Alexander H. Stephens, former vice president of the Confederacy, to represent the state in the U.S. Senate, even though Stephens had only recently been paroled from prison.

Most of the newly elected representatives were members of the Democratic Party. Both houses of Congress voted not to allow them to take their seats. Even moderate Republicans were furious. Johnson's plan for bringing southern states back into the Union was rejected.

Johnson and the Republicans

The Radical Republicans in Congress then began to reconstruct the South according to their own ideas. Shortly before the end of the war, Congress had created the **Freedmen's Bureau**, an agency run by the army. Its main assignment was to care for freedpeople and **refugees**, people who had fled their homes to avoid danger. Early in 1866 Congress passed a bill increasing the ability of the Bureau to protect freedpeople. President Johnson vetoed this bill, hoping to control Congress.

In April both houses of Congress passed the **Civil Rights Act of 1866**. The bill forbade southern states from passing laws such as the Black Codes restricting freedpeople's rights. Johnson vetoed the bill, but Congress

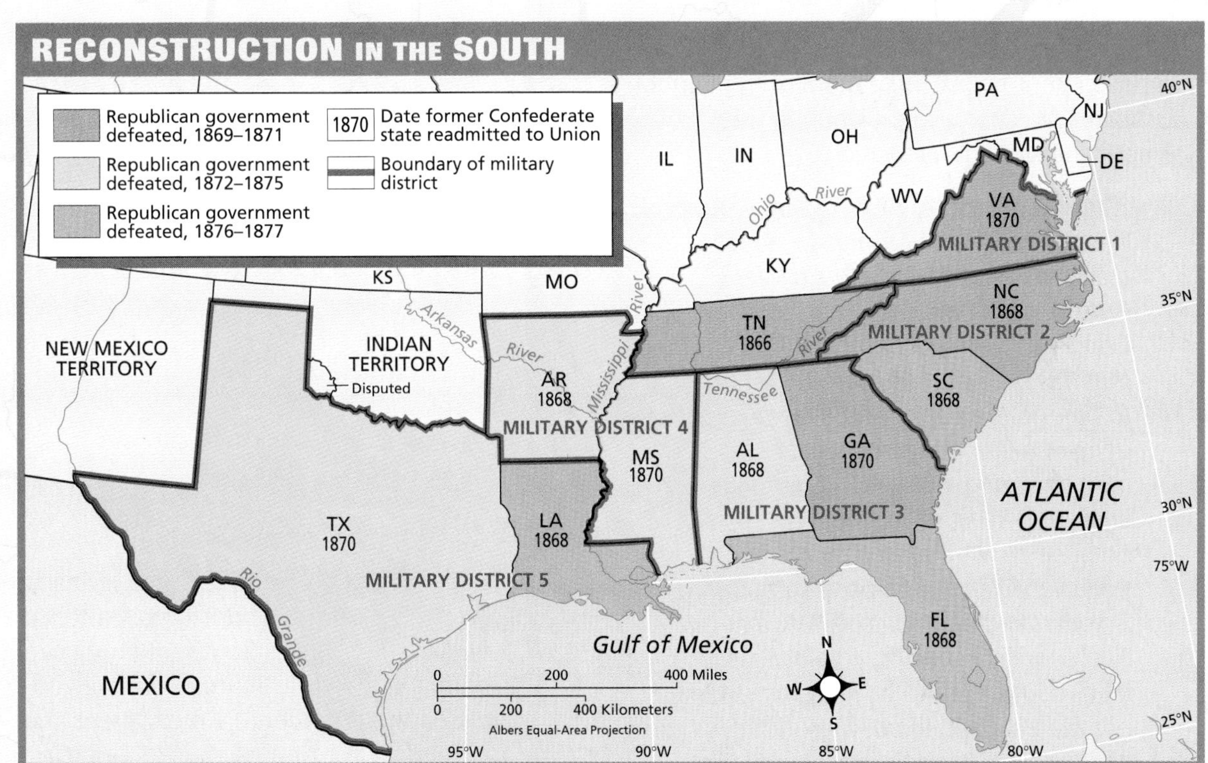

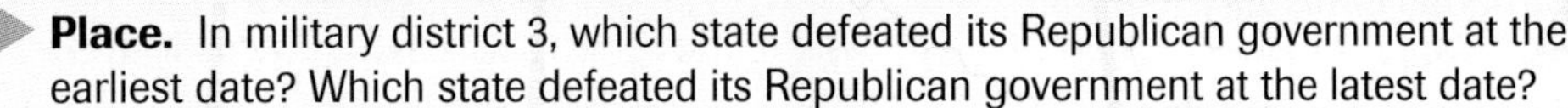
Learning from Maps. As northern support for Reconstruction declined, southern states began to vote out their Republican governments.

Place. In military district 3, which state defeated its Republican government at the earliest date? Which state defeated its Republican government at the latest date?

• Maps

obtained the two-thirds majority necessary to override the veto.

Congress next passed the **Fourteenth Amendment** to the Constitution. In many ways this measure was even more important than the Thirteenth Amendment. "All persons born or naturalized [admitted as citizens] in the United States," the amendment read, ". . . are citizens of the United States and of the State wherein they reside." This gave citizenship to all African Americans in the United States. Then the amendment struck down the Black Codes by declaring:

> **"No State shall make or enforce any law which shall abridge [reduce] the privileges or immunities [freedoms] of citizens of the United States; nor shall any State deprive any person of life, liberty, or property, without due process of law; nor deny to any person . . . the equal protection of the laws."**

Most white southerners strongly objected to the Fourteenth Amendment. The southern states refused to ratify it. Without their votes, it was impossible to get the required approval of three fourths of the states. When it became clear that the southern states would not ratify the Fourteenth Amendment, Congress passed a series of **Reconstruction Acts** to pressure them. These stern measures strengthened military control of the South. They divided the former Confederacy into five military districts and stationed troops in each district.

To end army rule, each state would have to draw up a new constitution that guaranteed African Americans the right to vote. Each southern state would also have to ratify the Fourteenth Amendment. In other words, Congress ordered a military occupation of the South. Lincoln's hope that the nation could quickly bind up its wounds would not be fulfilled.

Through Others' Eyes

A British View of the Impeachment Crisis

Foreign journalists paid close attention to the impeachment crisis. The editors of the London *Examiner,* for example, praised the way Americans settled political differences:

> *"We, for our parts, think the men of 1789 were wiser Constitution builders than the Republican leaders of 1868. . . . But we have never yet heard of the Constitution of a country worth studying that has not been subjected from time to time to temporary and even perilous derangement [dangerous madness]. It may go wrong, but it will come right again. . . . Injustice for the moment may be done to Mr. Johnson by the uncontrollable violence of a party vote. But it is something after all to reflect that our descendants, when they go politically mad, do not take to political murder, as our fathers used to do. The official life of President Johnson may possibly be shortened by a few months, but even his enemies do not dream of imbruing [soaking] their hands in his blood, in this frenzy of political rage."*

President Johnson on Trial

Republicans blamed President Johnson for much of the stubborn resistance of white southerners to the Republican plan for Reconstruction. Johnson opposed the Fourteenth Amendment and vetoed every one of the Reconstruction Acts.

Most Republicans finally became convinced that Reconstruction would never be successful unless Johnson was no longer president. In February 1868, angry congressional leaders decided to try to remove him from office, They began the official process of **impeachment**—bringing formal charges of wrongdoing against a public official. In all, they brought 11 charges against the president. He was spared in his Senate trial because the senators fell one vote short of conviction on the strongest charges. The threat, however, was enough to end Johnson's resistance to the Radicals.

The presidential election of 1868 led to a dramatic change in the political situation. The federal troops stationed in the South prevented whites from interfering with the voting process. Naturally, African Americans overwhelmingly cast their ballots for the Republican candidate, Ulysses S. Grant. Grant won an easy victory in the electoral college—214 votes to 80 for the Democratic candidate, Horatio Seymour.

At last, in the spring of 1868, African Americans were allowed to participate in southern governments. These governments ratified the Fourteenth Amendment. The final state to complete the process was Georgia, in July 1870—more than five years after the end of the Civil War.

Early in 1869 the overwhelmingly Republican Congress drafted still another constitutional amendment that guaranteed that "the right of citizens of the United States to vote shall not be denied . . . on account of race, color, or previous condition of servitude." Within about a year this **Fifteenth Amendment** was ratified by the states. While the Fifteenth Amendment was a great victory for the rights of African American men, many women were deeply disappointed that the amendment did not extend the vote to them.

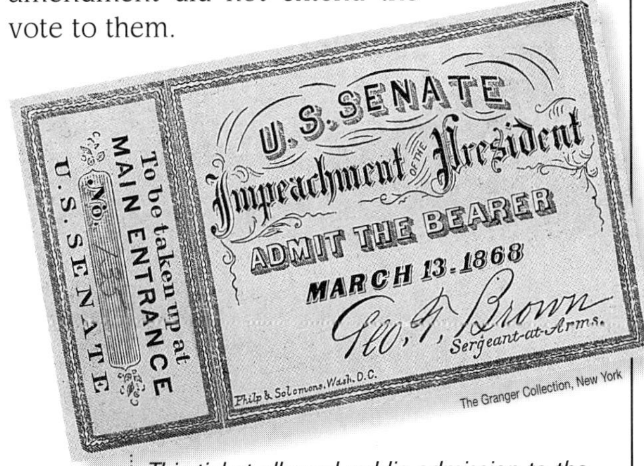

The Granger Collection, New York

This ticket allowed public admission to the gallery box in the U.S. Senate to observe President Johnson's impeachment trial.

Section 1 Review

• Glossary

IDENTIFY and explain the significance of the following: Reconstruction, Andrew Johnson, amnesty, Radical Republicans, Thirteenth Amendment, Black Codes, Freedmen's Bureau, refugees, Civil Rights Act of 1866, Fourteenth Amendment, Reconstruction Acts, impeachment, Fifteenth Amendment

REVIEWING FOR DETAILS

1. What was President Johnson's main goal for Reconstruction?
2. What did the Radical Republicans hope to gain from Reconstruction?
3. Why did some members of Congress want to impeach President Johnson?

REVIEWING FOR UNDERSTANDING

4. **Writing Mastery:** *Describing* Write a brief paragraph describing the differences between Johnson's approach to Reconstruction and the Radical Republicans' approach.
5. **Critical Thinking:** *Determining the Strength of an Argument* Some Radical Republicans argued that Reconstruction could not be successful with Johnson in office. Was this argument valid? Explain your answer.

Section 2

Freedom After Slavery

Multimedia Connections

Explore these related topics and materials on the CD–ROM to enrich your understanding of this section:

Atlas
- African American Colleges

Media Bank
- The First Vote
- African American Home Scene
- Freedmen's Bureau Office
- Fisk Jubilee Singers
- Fisk Jubilee Singers slide show

Profiles
- Blanche K. Bruce
- Hiram Revels

Like the American Revolution, the Civil War marked a great turning point in American history. From it a dramatically different society arose. The war had destroyed the South's economy and the lifestyle of many white southerners. The social and economic positions of the former slaves also had changed. African Americans were eager to explore the boundaries of their new freedom.

As you read this section you will find out:

- **What changes freedpeople experienced during Reconstruction.**
- **Who served in Reconstruction governments.**
- **Why the sharecropping system was developed and what effects it had.**

The Privileges of Freedom

The Thirteenth, Fourteenth, and Fifteenth Amendments brought former slaves freedom first of all to decide what to do with their own time. It meant freedom to move about. In many cases, families that had been separated under slavery were reunited. For example, in Alabama, Nelson and Phoebe Humphrey and their five children were reunited after living on two separate plantations. The Humphreys, who had been field hands, each started their own businesses after emancipation. Phoebe Humphrey took in laundry while Nelson Humphrey did odd jobs.

Most other former slaves continued to work the land, but now their work was for their own gain, not someone else's. Older people labored less and rested more. Mothers devoted more time to their children and

homes, less to planting, hoeing, and harvesting. Caroline Jones, a former house slave, reported shortly after the war that her occupation was now "caring for her family."

Another privilege of freedom was that former slaves could seek education. Very few could read and write because it had been against the law in most southern states to teach slaves to read. The Freedmen's Bureau set up schools in the South as soon as the war ended. In Charleston, South Carolina, for example, schools were established as soon as the Union army captured the city.

African American students of all ages responded eagerly to opportunities for schooling. All over the South, elderly freedpeople could be seen learning their ABCs alongside their grandchildren. Charlotte Forten, a northern African American woman who taught freed slaves in South Carolina, wrote:

> **"Many of the grown people are desirous of learning to read. It is wonderful how a people who have been so long crushed to the earth . . . can have so great a desire for knowledge."**

By 1870 there were more than 150,000 students in Freedmen's Bureau schools. In addition to these schools, several new colleges were established for African American students. Included among these were Howard University, Fisk University, and Hampton Institute.

Freedpeople also founded new churches that attracted large congregations. Many white religious groups from the North contributed time, money, and teachers to help educate former slaves. Northern African American congregations also recruited large numbers of teachers and sent clergy to help establish new schools and churches for former slaves. Methodist, Presbyterian, and Baptist churches expanded rapidly in the South. By 1870 one of the most influential new groups, the Colored Methodist Episcopal Church, had grown large enough to appoint its first bishops, W. H. Miles and R. H. Vanderhorst. Many leaders of the black churches also played influential roles in politics.

Reconstruction Governments

The occupation of the South by the U.S. Army helped African Americans vote and hold office in all the states of the former Confederacy. Nothing made most white southerners more

Many former slaves studied at this Freedmen's Bureau school in Charleston, South Carolina.

- **Reconstruction Programs**

The Granger Collection, New York

The first African American members of Congress: (left to right) Hiram Revels, Benjamin Turner, Robert DeLarge, Josiah Wells, Jefferson Long, Joseph Rainey, and Robert Elliott.

bitter and resentful than to be "ruled" by the very people they had dominated for so long.

African American politicians. "Rule" is not, however, the proper word to describe the role of African Americans in southern politics during Reconstruction. Between 1869 and 1901, only 22 African Americans ever served in Congress. African Americans did hold many local offices, but the only state legislature to have a black majority between 1868 and 1877 was South Carolina's.

Like their white counterparts, black politicians in the South varied widely in ability and devotion to their duties. During the 1870s white southerners who objected to African Americans holding office called attention to any cases of corruption or mistakes that came to light involving black politicians.

In reality, many African American legislators were men of great character and ability. The Reverend Henry M. Turner, who had been a Union army chaplain during the war, was elected to the Georgia legislature and later served as a postmaster. Another minister, Hiram Revels, who was born free in North Carolina and moved north, helped recruit several black regiments during the Civil War. In 1866 he settled in Natchez, Mississippi, and became active in politics. He served briefly in the U.S. Senate, filling the unexpired term of Confederate president Jefferson Davis for the state of Mississippi. Later, Revels became president of Alcorn College.

Carpetbaggers and scalawags. Most of the officeholders in the "Black Republican" governments, as their opponents called them, were white. Those who came from the northern states were called **carpetbaggers** because travelers of the period often carried their belongings in soft-sided bags made of carpeting. Many southerners believed that these "invaders" had come south not to put down roots but only to get rich.

Southern white Republicans were referred to scornfully by their Democratic neighbors as **scalawags**—good-for-nothing rascals. In reality, however, many of the "scalawags" were conservative, high-minded community leaders. The Confederate governor of Georgia, Joseph E. Brown, became a Republican and served as chief justice of the Georgia Supreme Court during Reconstruction.

"Carpetbaggers" and "scalawags" came from all walks of life. Some genuinely wanted

The Granger Collection, New York

In this cartoon by James Wales, the defeated South is shown carrying the heavy burden placed on it by evil "carpetbaggers" and federal troops during the Reconstruction Era.

to improve schools for former slaves and to help them achieve political influence. Others were employees of the federal government stationed in the South. Still others hoped to obtain state political offices by attracting black votes. Most "carpetbaggers" mainly wanted to improve themselves economically. Only after establishing themselves in their new homes did some of them become involved in local politics.

The southern state governments accomplished a great deal during the Reconstruction Era. They raised taxes in order to improve public education, which had been badly neglected before 1860. They also spent large sums on roads, bridges, railroads, and public buildings damaged during the war, and they expanded public support for social services. The biggest challenge for southerners, however, was constructing a new economy that was not based on slave labor.

History Makers

Blanche K. Bruce
(1841–1898)

One of the most famous African American politicians of the Reconstruction era was Mississippi senator Blanche K. Bruce, who was born a slave in Virginia. Unlike most slaves, he received a good education. During the Civil War Bruce ran away to Kansas, where he opened a school for African Americans. After the war he attended Oberlin College, then moved to Mississippi, where he became a wealthy planter.

Bruce was highly respected in the Republican Party. He held many elected and appointed positions in addition to serving in the Senate from 1875 to 1881. He worked tirelessly on issues such as economic and political reform and civil rights. In one of his most famous speeches, Bruce expressed his hopes that freedpeople would eventually be able to succeed despite racism. "I have confidence," he declared, ". . . in the endurance, capacity, and destiny of my people."

Sharecropping

Most black southerners had been farmworkers before emancipation. Nearly all former slaves continued to work on the land after they became free. Efforts by Radical Republicans like Thaddeus Stevens to carve up the large plantations and give each black family "forty acres and a mule" never attracted much support among northern whites, however.

According to a law passed in 1862, each former slave could get a free 160-acre farm in the West. Only a handful managed to do so, however, because the price of land was just a small part of the cost of starting a farm. Most freed families lacked the tools, seed money, and the transportation to the frontier. Therefore, most of the former slaves continued to farm land owned by whites. At first they worked for wages, but most landowners were short of cash, and freedpeople wanted to be more independent of plantation control.

A new system called **sharecropping** was soon created. Sharecropping means sharing the crop. The landowners provided the farmers with houses, tools, seeds, and other supplies. The sharecroppers provided the skill and labor needed to grow the crops. When the harvest was gathered, it was supposed to be shared, usually half to two thirds for the landowner, the rest for the sharecropper.

This system freed black workers from the close daily supervision they had endured under slavery. Each family generally had its own cabin and tilled its own plot of land as a separate unit. At first, the system allowed freedpeople the opportunity to choose what crop to grow, rather than being forced to grow cotton or tobacco. For these reasons, many families became sharecroppers instead of working the land for wages. Sharecroppers could at least hope that by working hard and saving they might someday have enough money to buy a farm of their own someday. Then they would be truly free.

In practice, it was very difficult for sharecroppers to buy their own farms. Sharecroppers ran up bills at the general store during the growing season. When the crop was sold in the autumn, they planned to use the money to pay off this debt. If they experienced bad weather or sold their crops for less than expected, they could not pay their bills. In addition, local storekeepers often cheated sharecroppers. Frequently, the merchant added items the farmers had never purchased to the bill. Some landowners also cheated the sharecroppers when the harvest was divided. At the end of the season, many sharecroppers often found themselves much deeper in debt than they had been before the crop was planted in the spring!

Most sharecroppers who objected to the system were threatened with the loss of credit in the future, or with violence. Even when they dealt with honest landowners and merchants, it was hard to make a decent living as a sharecropper. Prices were high in the stores because the storekeepers also had to borrow to get the goods they sold. The South's economic problems and racial prejudice kept most African American sharecroppers from acquiring land of their own.

In sharecropping families, everyone had to help out with the work in the fields. These children are helping their family to pick cotton around 1870.

The Granger Collection, New York

Section 2 Review

• Glossary

IDENTIFY and explain the significance of the following: Henry M. Turner, Hiram Revels, carpetbaggers, scalawags, sharecropping

REVIEWING FOR DETAILS

1. What were some of the privileges freedpeople enjoyed during Reconstruction?
2. Who governed the states of the former Confederacy during Reconstruction?
3. Why was the sharecropping system developed? What were some of the results of this system?

REVIEWING FOR UNDERSTANDING

4. **Writing Mastery:** *Expressing* Write a poem, song, or short story expressing how you think freedpeople might have felt about life under Reconstruction.
5. **Critical Thinking:** *Making Comparisons* How would you compare life for southern African Americans before and after emancipation?

Section 3

The End of Reconstruction

Multimedia Connections

Explore these related topics and materials on the CD–ROM to enrich your understanding of this section:

Media Bank

- "Exodus" Movement
- Slave Narrative

Profiles

- Rutherford B. Hayes
- John Harlan

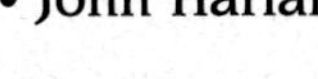

Glossary

- southern Democrat

Readings

- *Plessy* v. *Ferguson*

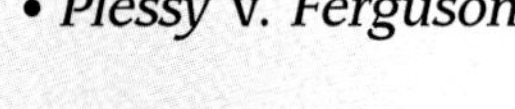

The grandson of former slave Charlotte Fowler cried: "Oh, grandma, they have killed my poor grandpappy!" Moments earlier Fowler's unarmed husband, Wallace, had been shot by white men in hoods. Wallace Fowler, a 70-year-old former slave, had been an open supporter of the Radical Republicans. This loyalty cost him his life. Fowler's death was just one example of how some southern whites resisted the changes brought by Reconstruction.

As you read this section you will find out:

- **How some southern whites resisted Reconstruction.**
- **Why the election of 1876 led to the end of Reconstruction.**
- **How the case of *Plessy* v. *Ferguson* affected society.**

Resistance to Reconstruction

The great majority of white southerners strongly resisted the changes forced upon them during Reconstruction. They did so in many ways, sometimes openly, sometimes secretly in the dead of night. In 1866 some white southerners began to form secret organizations that used violence to hold back African Americans.

The most notorious of these organizations was the **Ku Klux Klan**. Klan members were determined to intimidate white Republican leaders and to keep African Americans from voting. They tried to frighten potential voters by galloping through the night dressed in white robes, hoods, and masks, claiming to be the ghosts of Confederate soldiers. They burned black churches and schools, and

In this 1874 cartoon, artist Thomas Nast portrays the harassment African Americans faced after emancipation as worse even than life had been under slavery.

The Granger Collection, New York

threatened terrible tortures against African Americans who dared to exercise their right to vote.

When these scare tactics did not work, the Klan often resorted to physical violence. Many hundreds of southern African Americans were assaulted. Statistics on the Reconstruction Era reveal that in one North Carolina judicial district there were 12 murders, 14 cases of arson, and more than 700 beatings. During this same period more than 150 African Americans were murdered in Jackson County, Florida.

The federal government sent troops to stop the worst Klan violence. By the early 1870s, the power of the Klan had been broken. Gradually, however, more and more white southerners joined in efforts to keep African Americans from voting. Groups in Mississippi, South Carolina, and Louisiana even formed private military companies and marched around in broad daylight. They beat African Americans whom they believed to be "uppity" or rebellious. When some victims resisted, bloody battles broke out.

This Alabama member of the Ku Klux Klan poses in his robe for a formal portrait in 1868. Klan hoods hid the wearers' identities.

In 1876 Senator Blanche K. Bruce of Mississippi denounced such violence against African Americans:

> **"It is an attack by an aggressive, intelligent, white political organization upon inoffensive, law-abiding fellow-citizens; a violent method for political supremacy, that seeks . . . the destruction of the rights of the party assailed [attacked]."**

The Election of 1876

For the most part, Senator Bruce's protests went unheeded. By 1876 many white northerners had begun to lose interest in trying to control southern affairs. As long as the white southerners did not actually try to re-enslave African Americans, northerners were prepared to put Klan activities in the South out of their minds. They grew more concerned about other issues such as the condition of the national economy.

Gradually, the number of troops stationed in the southern states was reduced. Without military protection, many African Americans were afraid to vote or exercise their other rights. In state after state during the 1870s, all-white conservative parties took control of the government away from the Republicans. These political organizations resisted the changes Republicans had proposed for the South. Many of their leaders were former Confederate officials who took advantage of the Amnesty Act of 1872, which ended the Fourteenth Amendment ban on former Confederate leaders holding office.

The Republican Party was further weakened by President Grant's failure to live up to the people's expectations. Grant proved to be as poor a chief executive as Andrew Johnson, but in a different way. His administration was marked by serious scandals and corruption. Although he was easily re-elected in 1872, by 1876 the Republicans remained in control of just three southern states—Louisiana, Florida, and South Carolina.

In the heated presidential election of 1876 Democratic governor Samuel J. Tilden of New York faced Republican governor Rutherford B. Hayes of Ohio. Tilden narrowly won the popular vote. He also led in electoral college votes, but 20 of these—the electoral votes of South Carolina, Louisiana, Florida, and one single vote in Oregon—were in dispute. If all 20 votes went to Hayes, he would then have an electoral majority. Charges of election tampering flew wildly as both Tilden and Hayes claimed victory in these disputed states.

After weeks of debate, Congress appointed a special electoral commission made up of eight Republicans and seven Democrats to study the matter. The commission, voting along party lines, gave all the disputed votes to Hayes. Thus, Hayes won with 185 electoral votes to Tilden's 184. The Democrats felt cheated. Many remained ready to fight to make Tilden president.

• Contested Election

In this crisis, leaders of the two political parties worked out what is known as the **Compromise of 1877**. If the Democrats would agree to accept the electoral commission's decision, Hayes would remove all the remaining federal troops stationed in the South.

In exchange, the Democrats promised to guarantee African Americans their rights and not to prevent them from voting. After all these details had been settled, the Democrats agreed to go along with the electoral commission's decision, and Hayes was inaugurated.

Second-Class Citizens

After the Compromise of 1877, white northerners turned their backs on black southerners. At the same time, white leaders in the southern states broke their promise to treat African Americans fairly. Step-by-step, they deprived black southerners of the right to vote

The election of 1876 between Hayes and Tilden threatened another civil war as Tilden supporters were ready to use violence to make sure that he became president.

Faced with increasing persecution and more limited opportunities after the Compromise of 1877, some rural African Americans, like the group pictured here, moved to southern cities hoping to find a better life.

and reduced them to second-class citizens. White southern leaders started by requiring voters to pay **poll taxes**, or taxes on individuals, which were often collected at the time of an election. In other places they required voters to pass **literacy tests**, which limited voting to those who could read well. Although these laws should have disqualified many white voters, they were directed primarily against African Americans.

One way this was done was by using so-called **grandfather clauses** as part of voting requirements. These clauses stated that literacy tests and poll taxes did not apply to persons who had been able to vote before 1867, or to their descendants. Almost all white male southerners fell into this category, but no black southerners did. Once black southerners ceased to have an influence on elections, officials paid little attention to their other rights and desires.

Along with political discrimination, the legal **segregation**, or forced separation, of the races became widespread. Starting in 1881 with Tennessee, southern states began to pass what became known as **Jim Crow laws**, which enforced segregation.

When African Americans were segregated at public places like theaters, some went to court to seek their constitutional rights. In one case, W. H. R. Agee protested against being denied a hotel room in Jefferson City, Missouri. In another case, Sallie Robinson sued because she and her nephew were forced to ride in a second-class car while traveling on a southern railroad, even though they had first-class tickets.

These and other suits, known as the *Civil Rights Cases*, were decided by the Supreme Court in 1883. The majority of the justices ruled that a previous civil rights act, which had been passed in 1875, was unconstitutional and furthermore that the Fourteenth Amendment protected against actions by state governments, not by private persons. It was therefore legal for private businesses to practice racial segregation.

In 1896 the Supreme Court heard the case of ***Plessy* v. *Ferguson***. Homer A. Plessy, an African American from Louisiana, was arrested for taking a seat in a railroad car reserved by Louisiana law for whites. His attorneys argued that the law under which he was arrested was unconstitutional. The Court ruled against Plessy on the grounds that the railroad provided separate but equally good cars for black passengers.

Justice John Marshall Harlan objected to this separate-but-equal idea. Harlan's family had held slaves. The experiences of

Reconstruction, however, had changed his views of racial issues. In his dissent Harlan wrote:

> **"[I]n the eye of the law, there is in this country no superior, dominant, ruling class of citizens. There is no caste [social class] here. Our Constitution is color-blind and neither knows nor tolerates classes among citizens. In respect of civil rights, all citizens are equal before the law."**

In 1896 Harlan's was a minority opinion not only on the Court but also among white citizens in all parts of the country. Efforts to prevent segregation practically ended. African American travelers could not stay at hotels used by white guests. Theater owners herded black audiences into separate sections, usually high in the balcony. Black streetcar riders had to sit or stand in the rear sections. They could not enter "white" parks or swim at "white" public beaches. Even cemeteries were segregated. Although segregation was enforced most strongly in the South, it was also found in some northern cities.

The schools, parks, and other facilities open to black people were almost never as good as those for white people. For example, in 1876 some southern states were spending the same amount on the education of every child, black or white. By the late 1890s, however, most southern schools were required to be segregated, and most southern states were spending several times more on each white child than on each black child. The "equal" part of the separate-but-equal ruling was ignored practically everywhere.

The Granger Collection, New York

In this drawing an African American man is asked to leave the "white" section of a segregated railroad car.

Section 3 Review

• Glossary

IDENTIFY and explain the significance of the following: Ku Klux Klan, Blanche K. Bruce, Compromise of 1877, poll taxes, literacy tests, grandfather clauses, segregation, Jim Crow laws, *Plessy* v. *Ferguson*, John Marshall Harlan

REVIEWING FOR DETAILS

1. How did some southern whites resist Reconstruction policies?
2. How did the election of 1876 put an end to Reconstruction?
3. What was the impact of *Plessy* v. *Ferguson*?

REVIEWING FOR UNDERSTANDING

4. **Writing Mastery:** *Persuading* Imagine that you are a southern African American in the late 1800s. Write a letter to your state legislator persuading him to vote against a Jim Crow law.
5. **Critical Thinking:** *Cause and Effect* How did the changing attitude of many northerners affect people in the South?

Section 4
THE NEW SOUTH

Multimedia Connections

Explore these related topics and materials on the CD–ROM to enrich your understanding of this section:

Profiles

- Booker T. Washington

Biographies

- Ida B. Wells-Barnett

Media Bank

- New South Rises from Ashes
- Commerce in the South
- Illiteracy in the South
- Wade Hampton
- Crop Lien System

Readings

- A Sharecropper's Story
- Atlanta Compromise

With the following words in 1886 Atlanta journalist Henry Grady expressed what many hoped would be a better future for the troubled South after Reconstruction:

> **"The new South presents a perfect democracy . . . a hundred farms for every plantation, fifty homes for every palace–and a diversified [varied] industry that meets the complex need of this complex age."**

As you read this section you will find out:

- **How the crop-lien system affected the southern economy.**
- **How the Redeemers tried to improve the southern economy.**
- **What Booker T. Washington advised African Americans to do to succeed.**

The Crop-Lien System

By the late 1800s the sharecropping system dominated southern society. Although the system started among former slaves, soon roughly half of all southern sharecroppers were white. In general, there was little difference in the standard of living among black and white sharecroppers. Before the war there had been few landless whites in the South. Economic hard times after the war, however, caused many small landowners to lose their holdings. Many turned to sharecropping. Few would ever own land again.

The shortage of money in the South made nearly everyone—landowners, sharecroppers, merchants, and manufacturers—dependent on bankers and other people with funds to invest. In order to ensure that farmers' loans were repaid after the crops had been harvested, these investors demanded that the landowners put up the future crop as security for the loan. This gave investors a claim, called a **crop lien**, against the harvest before the crop was even planted. If the borrower was unable to pay when the loan came due, the lender could take possession of the crop.

On the surface, the crop-lien system seemed fair enough. However, it had an unfortunate side effect. The lenders insisted that the borrowers grow one of the South's major cash crops, particularly cotton. There was a world market for these crops, and they could be converted into cash anywhere, anytime. If the price was low, the crops could often be stored until market conditions improved.

Both the landowners and the sharecroppers would have been better off if they could have grown vegetables and fruits as well as cash crops. This concentration on just one crop rapidly exhausted the fertility of the soil. In addition, if farmers had an unusually large harvest, the price of the cash crops fell steeply because supply was greater than demand.

Everyone was caught up in the system. The bankers put pressure on the landowners and storekeepers, who in turn forced the sharecroppers to plant what the bankers wanted. Some might argue that the bankers were greedy and shortsighted, but from the bankers' point of view it would have been extremely risky to lend a farmer money to grow tomatoes, for example. Such crops had to be sold locally when they were ripe or they would rot and become worthless within a few days.

The Redeemers

Because of conditions under the crop-lien and sharecropping systems, southern agriculture remained depressed for years. Although the region was generally tied to farming, a few business leaders called for the creation of a "New South" based on industry.

As a result of the Compromise of 1877, by the late 1870s political power was as much in the hands of southern whites as it had been before the Civil War. The new white leaders in most states called themselves **Redeemers**.

Cotton Production and Cotton Prices, 1876–1896

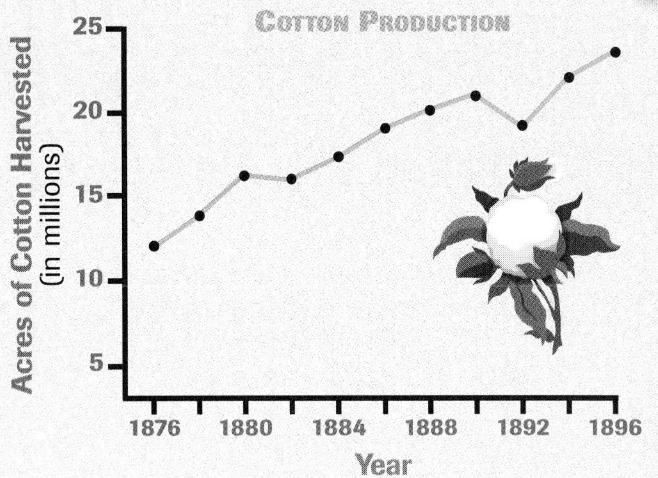

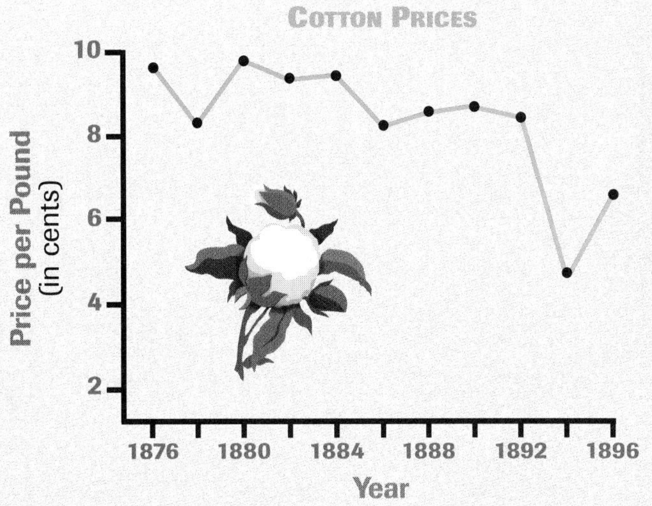

Source: *Historical Statistics of the United States*

A Cash Crop. As the sharecropping system expanded, more southern land was used to grow cotton. What general trend do you notice between the expansion of cotton production and the price of cotton from 1876 to 1896?

Redeemers hoped that the expansion of industries like this southern ironworks would improve the overall economy of the South. Agriculture would continue to dominate the southern economy, however.

They claimed that they were redeeming, or taking back, powers and duties their class had exercised before Reconstruction.

The Redeemers were forward-looking when it came to economic questions. They hoped to increase industrial production and improve the South's railroad network.

There was a great deal of talk about "out-Yankeeing" the Yankees. The South had large supplies of both cotton and poor people. Why not combine them in order to manufacture cotton goods? Between 1880 and 1900 the number of textile mill workers in the South jumped from 17,000 to 88,000. The output of these mills, most of which were in the Southeast, increased even more rapidly. The South's tobacco production also expanded rapidly because of the invention of machines that produced cigarettes in huge numbers.

Many black southerners did not benefit from the "New South." Most mill jobs were closed to African Americans. Some policies of the Redeemers led to more racial discrimination. For example, the Redeemers also made steep cuts in state taxes. Then, to balance state budgets, they reduced spending on social services and education, particularly for African Americans.

The Atlanta Compromise

Faced with these handicaps, many black southerners took the advice of Booker T. Washington. Washington founded Tuskegee Institute, an African American trade school in Alabama. Washington was born a slave. Through dedication and study he obtained an education while also working to pay for his schooling. During Reconstruction Washington had seen firsthand what happened to most African Americans who openly fought against racial prejudice.

These experiences convinced him that African Americans could hope for fair treatment only if they made themselves essential to the South as a reliable, trained, and capable

Noted African American scientist George Washington Carver observes his chemistry students at Tuskegee Institute. Founded in 1881, the school blossomed under Booker T. Washington's leadership as he gained funding and attracted teachers like Carver.

workforce. Until they elevated themselves to this level, Washington believed that African Americans should not struggle for equal rights, particularly equal political rights. Washington became highly skilled at obtaining the financial support of wealthy whites who agreed with his philosophy. As a result of Washington's efforts, and because of its high-quality graduates, Tuskegee Institute prospered.

Washington was already well known when, in an 1895 speech at Atlanta, Georgia, he proposed what became known as the **Atlanta Compromise**. In it he argued that African Americans should accept the American system and try to get ahead within it. Thus, African American students should learn skilled trades so that they could earn more money and improve their lives. Washington believed that there was nothing shameful about working with one's hands, as he explained:

> **"In the great leap from slavery to freedom . . . we shall prosper in proportion as we learn to dignify and glorify common labor. . . . The opportunity to earn a dollar in a factory just now is worth infinitely more than the opportunity to spend a dollar in an opera-house."**

Washington asked whites only to be fair. Help African Americans, he argued, by making sure that what was separate was really equal.

Ida B. Wells-Barnett was born into slavery in 1862. Educated in a Freedmen's Bureau school, she first became a teacher. She went into journalism after losing her teaching job for protesting discrimination. She spent the rest of her career fighting racism.

Some black leaders, such as journalist Ida B. Wells-Barnett, criticized Washington. She argued that African Americans should do all they could to oppose segregation, which was never truly equal. They should insist on receiving all their rights as citizens. Most white southern leaders, however, were delighted with the Atlanta Compromise, in part because it discouraged African Americans from challenging the system.

Section 4 Review

• Glossary

• Time Line

IDENTIFY and explain the significance of the following: crop lien, Redeemers, Booker T. Washington, Atlanta Compromise, Ida B. Wells-Barnett

REVIEWING FOR DETAILS

1. How did the crop-lien system affect the economic situation in the South?
2. What did the Redeemers try to do to improve the southern economy?

REVIEWING FOR UNDERSTANDING

3. **Geographic Literacy** How did the crop-lien system affect southern land?
4. **Writing Mastery:** *Describing* Imagine that you are in the audience during Booker T. Washington's Atlanta speech. Write a letter to a friend describing Washington's advice to African Americans.
5. **Critical Thinking:** *Fact and Opinion* Booker T. Washington argued that whites would support separate but equal segregation. Why might some black leaders have questioned his opinion?

unit 6 

THE RISE OF MODERN AMERICA (1850–1900)

Chapter 16
Western Crossroads (1850–1900)

Chapter 17
Becoming an Industrial Nation (1865–1900)

The Granger Collection, New York

This painted photograph shows an immigrant family making garments around 1900. The United States experienced one of its largest periods of immigration around this time.

Linking Past to Present
Ethnic Traditions

It is Christmas time in Texas, and Phyllis Salazar is gathering with her family to make tamales. Making tamales is an annual tradition that is practiced in many Mexican American families. When Phyllis was young, her mother taught her the tradition. At that time the family boiled a hog's head to get the pork needed to make the tamales. This did not appeal to young Phyllis, who now uses pork roast and chicken to fill the tasty tamales she makes.

The process for making the tamales usually takes an entire day. Sometimes cooks experiment by filling the tamales with sweet-flavored raisins or nuts and seeds. "If a new filling tastes good," says Salazar, "we use it again next year."

On New Year's Eve, some Mexican American families celebrate by making *buñuelos*, pastry items that are sometimes called "Mexican doughnuts." They are often eaten with Mexican hot chocolate, a rich, frothy drink. In recent years more and more Americans not of Mexican descent have come to enjoy such foods as well.

Food represents just one of the many items from different cultures that enrich American life. The popularity of restaurants that specialize in Chinese, Italian, Greek, and other ethnic foods illustrates how diverse American tastes have become. Mexican food in particular has become one of the most popular types of ethnic foods consumed in the United States.

As you read this unit, you will learn that many ethnic groups whose cultures influence American life today did not come to the United States in large numbers until the late 1800s. You will also learn about how Americans spread into the Southwest and were influenced by its Spanish and Mexican heritage of the region.

This Mexican American family gathers to make tamales for a Christmas celebration.

CHAPTER 16

Western Crossroads

(1850–1900)

Cultural Diversity:
Why might conflict arise between new settlers and people already living in an area?

Technology and Society:
How might technological advances affect new areas of settlement?

Economic Development:
What conflicts might arise between individuals and big business?

• **Video Opener**

• **Skill Builder**

When forty-niner Jasper Hixson crossed the Great Plains, he noted that "in the best map we can get hold of, this is called the Great American Desert." Unlike many people in the United States, he saw the land's potential and predicted:

"The land is too fertile and possesses too many inducements [attractions] for settlement to remain in possession of the Indians forever."

image above: *Plains Indians' tepees*

Section 1
THE GREAT PLAINS

Multimedia Connections

Explore these related topics and materials on the CD–ROM to enrich your understanding of this section:

Glossary

- cultural assimilation
- nomad
- Sun Dance

Gazetteer

- Great Plains
- Oregon Country

Atlas

- Great Plains

Media Bank

- Bison Population
- Great Plains Landscape

The men returned from the successful summer buffalo hunt, pleased that there would be food for the fall and winter. The night would be a time of feasting and celebration. A lot of hard work still lay ahead for the women, however. A mature buffalo could weigh up to 2,000 pounds, and every part of the buffalo would be used. The women had to cut off the meat, stretch it, and dry it. The fat would be boiled and saved for soup. The hide had to be scraped and dehaired before it could be tanned.

As you read this section you will find out:

- **How Plains Indians were organized.**
- **How the horse introduced by Europeans changed Plains Indian life.**
- **In what ways the Plains Indians were dependent on the buffalo.**

The "Great American Desert"

Today the region known as the Great Plains extends from western Texas north to the Dakotas and then on into Canada. In the 1800s, endless acres of grassland rolled westward across the Plains, gradually rising until they reached the Rocky Mountains.

The various American Indian groups that lived in this region became known as **Plains Indians**. The Blackfoot Indians, who lived in the northern Plains, described the land as being full of animal and plant life. In the Blackfoot creation story, the "Old Man" made the land and then:

> **"covered the plains with grass for the animals to feed on. He marked off a piece of ground, and in it he made to grow all kinds**

For years, Plains Indians saw only a few explorers and fur traders cross their land. Then wagon trains filled with pioneers heading for Oregon and California began to roll across the Plains.

of roots and berries–camas [bulbs], wild carrots, wild turnips, sweet-root, bitter-root, sarvis berries, bull berries, cherries, plums, and rosebuds. He put trees in the ground. He put all kinds of animals on the ground. . . . [He] took the antelope down on the prairie, and turned it loose; and it ran away fast and gracefully."

Some early explorers had called the Plains region the "Great American Desert." Most people who had never visited the Plains thought that the region was home only for the coyote, the donkey-eared jackrabbit, the prairie dog, the antelope, and the great, shaggy buffalo. The buffalo in particular seemed the masters of the Great Plains. About 12 million buffalo were grazing there at the end of the Civil War. Despite all the active life there some reports—based on the Plains' limited rainfall and mostly treeless landscape—described the region as "a country destined to remain forever an uninhabited waste."

The Plains Indians

The Plains, of course, were not uninhabited. Nearly 30 Plains Indian tribes lived there. The Apache lived in present-day western Texas, Arizona, and northern Mexico. The Comanche lived in parts of present-day Oklahoma and Texas. The Pawnee occupied western Nebraska, and the Sioux were scattered from Minnesota to the Dakotas and Montana. The Cheyenne and Arapaho were the principal groups of the central Plains.

In 1850 the American Indian population of the Plains was over 150,000. Although the many groups of the Plains spoke different languages, they had developed a complex and efficient sign language so that all could communicate with one another.

The Plains Indians differed from group to group. Some groups were divided into bands. The Cheyenne, for example, consisted of bands with names like the Hairy Band, the Scabby Band, and the Dogmen Band. The bands were governed by chiefs and councils of elders. Although each band was a separate community, bands at times joined together for religious ceremonies or to fight enemies.

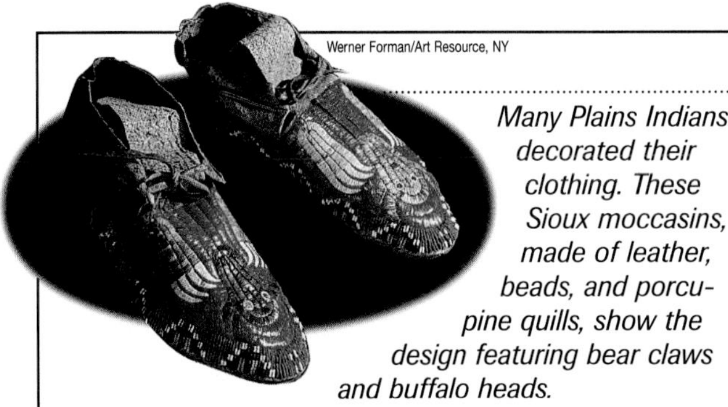

Werner Forman/Art Resource, NY

Many Plains Indians decorated their clothing. These Sioux moccasins, made of leather, beads, and porcupine quills, show the design featuring bear claws and buffalo heads.

Small groups of warriors called **soldier bands** settled disputes between band members, punished those who broke tribal laws, protected the group against attacks, and led hunting expeditions. Within each band, warriors tried to prove their courage and daring on the battlefield. To touch an enemy or capture his weapon—called "**counting coup**"—was proof of a warrior's highest bravery.

The Plains Culture

Most of the Plains groups shared a common culture based on the use of the buffalo and other large game. When Europeans arrived with their horses, guns, and metal tools, the Plains Indians incorporated these new elements into their lives.

Horses on the Plains. Spanish explorers had brought the first horses to America. Some of these animals escaped and ran wild. Eventually, large herds roamed parts of the West, living off the fertile grass of the prairies. Beginning in the mid-1600s the Plains Indians captured and tamed wild horses. Sometimes these horses even came to them, as a Sioux oral history tells of the event that marked the winter of 1781:

"This year while they were in camp with their ponies in the center of the circle, many wild horses came down from the hills and joined their ponies; so they divided up the wild horses."

Many of the Plains Indians, both men and women, became expert riders. On horseback they could cover large distances swiftly and run down buffalo and other game. Horses became so important to the Plains Indians that many groups went to war against their neighbors to obtain them. Many counted their wealth in horses. Some even paid their debts with horses.

Following the buffalo. Before Europeans came to America, Indians had lived in the hills on the edges of the Plains and would venture down onto the Plains to hunt on foot. They hunted some buffalo, but still relied heavily on agriculture for food. With the introduction of the horse, the Plains Indians were able to hunt buffalo far more successfully. They could travel great distances and spend much more time on the Plains than before. They depended on game of many kinds, but none more than the buffalo to support their way of life.

Hunting parties followed the thundering buffalo herds across the Plains. Men were usually the hunters, although in some groups women also participated. Many Plains Indians carried bows made of wood. Their arrows had

Mounted on a horse and armed with a bow and arrows, a Plains Indian would go track down a buffalo herd. It required courage and skill to face a buffalo.

points made of bone, flint, or metal. Galloping on horseback at a high speed, they could shoot arrows so fast that the next would be in the air before the first had found its target. These arrows struck with great force. At short range a hunter could sink the entire shaft of an arrow into the body of a buffalo.

Western artist George Catlin spent years sketching and painting life on the Plains. In this painting he illustrated the Sioux moving with their tepees.

Using the buffalo. After a successful hunt, women were responsible for preserving the meat and processing the hides. This was quite a task because the Plains Indians used all parts of the buffalo. As well as providing fresh meat, the buffalo flesh was dried for future use. They called this dried meat **jerky**. Plains Indian women used buffalo skin to make clothing. The thick buffalo fur made robes that provided protection against the harsh winters. They used tanned buffalo leather to make the shelters, called tepees, that were widely used on the Plains. Tepees consisted of many buffalo skins that were wrapped around poles. They were highly practical and were often beautifully decorated. Hunting tepees were small and portable.

The Plains Indians used other parts of the buffalo, such as bones, for tools and weapons. Some warriors were armed with long, stone-tipped lances and round shields made of buffalo hide. These shields were smoked and hardened with glue made from buffalo hooves. They were so tough that bullets striking them at an angle would not go through the shields.

With the buffalo providing for most of their needs, the Plains Indians prospered. For close to 100 years, from around 1780 to 1880, the Plains Indians lived and hunted in the midst of an immense grassland, moving freely on their swift ponies.

Section 1 Review

• Glossary

IDENTIFY and explain the significance of the following: Plains Indians, soldier bands, counting coup, jerky

REVIEWING FOR DETAILS

1. How were Plains Indian societies organized?
2. How did the horse change the lives of the Plains Indians?

REVIEWING FOR UNDERSTANDING

3. **Geographic Literacy** In what ways were the Plains Indians dependent on the buffalo?
4. **Writing Mastery:** *Describing* Imagine that you are an early explorer staying overnight at a Plains Indian village. Write a report to the president describing the Plains Indians and their way of life.
5. **Critical Thinking:** *Synthesizing Information* How did the members of Plains Indian societies work together for survival?

Section 2

THE WARS FOR THE WEST

Multimedia Connections

Explore these related topics and materials on the CD–ROM to enrich your understanding of this section:

Profiles

- Chief Joseph
- Helen Hunt Jackson
- Susette La Flesche
- Sitting Bull

Media Bank

- Massacre at Wounded Knee
- Ghost Dance
- Sitting Bull
- Chief Joseph
- Slaughtering the Buffalo
- Geronimo
- Crazy Horse
- Sarah Winnemucca

Biographies

- Geronimo

Readings

- Nez Percé

The young Cheyenne woman was bathing in the Greasy Grass stream near a Sioux camp when she heard the shouting. "Soldiers are coming!" Kate Bighead liked to watch battles—and her nephew would be fighting in this one—so she hurried to the battle scene. There were about 20 warriors for every soldier. The warriors rained arrows down on the U.S. soldiers for whom there was no escape.

As you read this section you will find out:

- **How incoming miners and settlers disturbed American Indian culture.**
- **What attempts the U.S. government made to end conflict between Plains Indians and settlers.**
- **How the Sioux response to the expansion of settlement changed over time.**

New Treaties

Before the 1850s the Plains Indians seldom came into contact with whites, other than fur traders. For the most part, only the Spanish in the Southwest and the Mormons in Utah had made permanent white settlements in this huge area. In the early 1850s, however, settlers and miners began moving into the Plains. They demanded that the U.S. government remove the Plains Indians.

Much of the Great Plains consisted of land that the United States had recognized as the property of American Indians. To secure safe passage west for settlers and future railroads, the federal government sent agents to negotiate with the Plains Indians. In 1851 the agents met with the northern Plains tribes at Fort Laramie, in present-day Wyoming. The meeting ended with both sides agreeing to the

Many Plains Indians did not want pioneers to cross their territory. In this painting, an Indian leader refuses to let a wagon train pass through tribal land.

• U.S. Indian Policy

Fort Laramie Treaty. Two years later, the government signed a treaty with the southern Plains Indians at Fort Atkinson.

Under these treaties, most of the Plains remained Indian land. The treaties encouraged Indians to live in particular areas and paid them fees to do so. The treaties' terms also stated that settlers could pass freely through the territories and that Indian groups would be held responsible for any attacks. In turn, the U.S. government promised to pay for any damages caused by travelers. It was not long before problems arose. The pioneers who crossed the Plains used wood—a scarce resource—for their campfires and killed local game along the trails. The Shoshoni chief Washakie complained:

> **"Since the white man has made a road across our land and has killed off our game, we are hungry, and there is nothing for us to eat. Our women and children cry for food and we have no food to give them."**

Broken Treaties

The Plains Indians soon found that the U.S. government would not keep its promises. People moving west demanded more and more land for settlement. The treaties were broken first on the southern Plains. The trouble began north of the Pikes Peak area of Colorado, where gold was discovered. By 1859 a seemingly endless stream of wagons was rolling across the Plains. Many of these prospectors, called "fifty-niners," had the slogan "Pikes Peak or Bust!" lettered on their canvas wagon covers.

Close to 100,000 of these "fifty-niners" pushed their way onto Cheyenne and Arapaho land. The Colorado territorial government persuaded federal officials to make new treaties that would move, and restrict, these Indians to **reservations**—federal lands set aside specifically for American Indians. The federal government's **Bureau of Indian Affairs** supervised the reservations and promised money and supplies to support this new way of life. The reservation system would mean the end of the buffalo-hunting culture because it required freedom of movement.

Some Cheyenne and Arapaho agreed to move to reservations. Others fiercely resisted, and between 1861 and 1864 they clashed several times with settlers and miners. Then in November 1864 Colonel John M. Chivington led a surprise attack on a peaceful Cheyenne encampment at Sand Creek in the Colorado Territory. The Cheyenne, under Chief

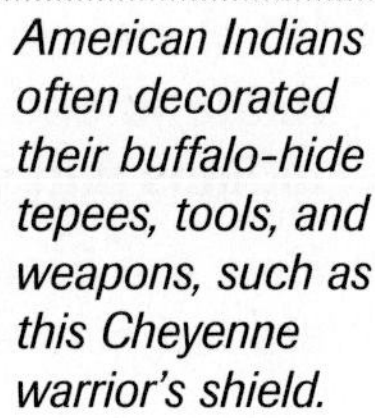

American Indians often decorated their buffalo-hide tepees, tools, and weapons, such as this Cheyenne warrior's shield.

The Granger Collection, New York

Black Kettle, tried to surrender by first raising an American flag and then a white flag of truce.

Chivington ignored these flags. "Kill and scalp all, big and little," he ordered. The U.S. soldiers killed around 200 Cheyenne during this **Sand Creek Massacre**. Others, including Black Kettle, escaped. Some of the Cheyenne bands later struck back with equally bloody attacks on settlers.

Global Connections

European Expansion in Southern Africa

Much like American Indians, the native peoples of southernmost Africa battled to save their homelands from European settlers. When the first Europeans came, many native Africans fell victim to European diseases. Then in the 1800s, many native Africans lost their land to German, Dutch, British, French, and other European settlers.

At first British settlers and Afrikaners, descendants of the early Dutch settlers, lived on the coast. Over time, mining and farming interests drew them inland. As these pioneers moved onto native Africans' land, conflicts broke out. Native Africans gained some ground when they used rifles, but few had access to European weapons. In the end the settlers and their weapons overpowered native Africans. Entire groups of some native peoples, such as the San and the Khoikhoi, were wiped out. By 1900, many native Africans had been killed, and those that remained had lost most of their power and their lands.

War on the Plains

The Sand Creek Massacre enraged many American Indians throughout the Plains. As more whites crossed Indian land, the conflict intensified. Soon, many other Plains Indians were at war with the U.S. Army and settlers.

The Indian Wars then spread to the northern Plains after the Pikes Peak gold rush that had triggered the conflict on the southern Plains proved to be a bust. About half the miners returned East. This time the signs on their wagons read "Busted, By Gosh!" The miners who remained in the West spread north through the mountains. Many followed the route pioneered by John M. Bozeman, a prospector from Georgia. This **Bozeman Trail** branched off the Oregon Trail west of Fort Laramie and ran north into Montana. It cut through the rolling foothills of the Big Horn Mountains, the hunting grounds of the western Sioux.

Red Cloud, a Sioux chief, protested angrily when miners and settlers began to appear on the trail. Red Cloud warned that the Sioux would fight to protect their hunting grounds, which were alive with deer, buffalo, elk, antelope, and bear.

In 1865 Sioux warriors made repeated attacks on trespassing white parties. The U.S. Army responded by building forts along the trail. In December 1866 Ta-sunko-witko (tuh-SUHN-koh WIT-koh), known as "Crazy Horse," led an attack on an army supply caravan. When a troop of soldiers commanded by Captain W. J. Fetterman appeared, the Sioux retreated. Fetterman followed them and fell right into their well-laid trap. The Sioux defeated Fetterman, killing him and every man in his troop. A few months later John Bozeman was killed crossing the Yellowstone River on the very trail he had marked.

Prospectors stopped crossing Sioux land. Both sides were ready to end the fighting. In 1867 the southern Plains Indians had signed the **Treaty of Medicine Lodge**, agreeing to give up their lands and move to reservations in Indian Territory. The Sioux signed a second

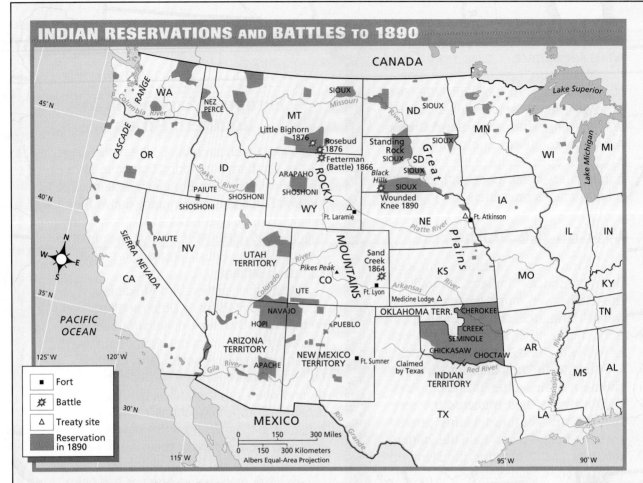

INDIAN RESERVATIONS AND BATTLES TO 1890

Learning from Maps. Despite early treaties that guaranteed American Indians full control of their lands, later agreements relocated many tribes to reservations.

▶ **Location.** In which state did federal officials and southern Plains Indians sign the treaty of Fort Atkinson?

• **Maps**

treaty at Fort Laramie in 1868. The federal government agreed to abandon its forts along the Bozeman Trail in exchange for an end to Sioux raids. To ensure that the government kept its word, the Sioux burned down all the forts. Then they agreed to live on a reservation in the Black Hills of the Dakota Territory.

Sioux chief Red Cloud and his great-granddaughter, Burning Heart

The Sioux War of 1876

This move to the reservation did not end the fighting, however. In 1869 Civil War hero General William Tecumseh Sherman became commander of the U.S. Army. He pursued a policy of total war against the Plains Indians. Between 1869 and 1875 more than 200 clashes between Plains Indians and army units took place.

Sitting Bull. Tatanka Iyotake (tuh-TAHN-kuh ee-yuh-TAH-kay), also known as Sitting Bull, was one of the most important leaders of the northern Plains Indians. He was a **shaman**, or

American Letters

Ten Bears's Speech from 1867

The Comanche of the southern Great Plains fought to keep their lands and stay off of reservations. Ten Bears was an important chief of the Yamparika Comanche. In this 1867 speech, Ten Bears describes the conflicts in Texas.

My people have never first drawn a bow or fired a gun against the whites. There has been trouble on the line between us, and my young men have danced with war dance. But it was not begun by us. It was you who sent out the first soldier and we who sent out the second. Two years ago I came upon this road, following the buffalo, that my wives and children might have their cheeks plump and their bodies warm. But the soldiers fired on us, and since that time there has been a noise like that of a thunderstorm. . . . The blue-dressed soldiers and the Utes came from out of the night when it was dark and still, and for campfires they lit our lodges. Instead of hunting game they killed my braves, and the warriors of the tribe cut short their hair for the dead. So it was in Texas. They made sorrow come in our camps, and we went out like buffalo bulls when their cows are attacked. When we found them we killed them, and their scalps hang in our lodges. The Comanches are not weak and blind, like the pups of a dog when seven sleeps old. They are strong and farsighted, like grown horses. We took their road and we went on it. The white women cried and our women laughed.

. . . You said that you wanted to put us upon a reservation, to build us houses and make us medicine lodges [places of religious practice]. I do not want them. I was born upon the prairie, where the wind blew free and there was nothing to break the light of the sun. I was born where there were no enclosures and where everything drew a free breath. I want to die there and not within walls. I know every stream and every wood between the Rio Grande and the Arkansas. I have hunted and lived over that country. I lived like my fathers before me, and, like them, I lived happily.

This 1875 photograph was taken in Indian Territory. Comanche and Kiowa Indians are in the process of painting their history on buffalo robes.

When I was at Washington the Great White Father told me that all the Comanche Land was ours, and that no one should hinder us in living upon it. So, why do you ask us to leave the rivers, and the sun, and the wind, and live in houses? Do not ask us to give up the buffalo for the sheep. . . .

If the Texans had kept out of my country, there might have been peace. But that which you now say we must live on is too small. The Texans have taken away the places where the grass grew the thickest and the timber was the best. Had we kept that, we might have done the things you ask. But it is too late. The white man has the country which we loved, and we only wish to wander on the prairie until we die.

medicine man, of the Sioux. Fiercely proud and independent, Sitting Bull urged the Sioux to keep their lands and customs. He refused to sign a treaty with the United States no matter how favorable the terms seemed. He firmly believed that compromise was impossible with a people he did not trust. "What treaty that the whites have kept has the red man broken? Not one. What treaty that the white man ever made with us have they kept? Not one." Sitting Bull's views made him extremely popular with many Plains Indians.

The Battle of the Little Bighorn. In 1874 Sioux territory was invaded again, this time by prospectors looking for gold in the Black Hills. Sitting Bull advised the Sioux to resist any attempts to be moved from their sacred Black Hills, and war soon broke out.

Lieutenant Colonel George Armstrong Custer was in command of the U.S. 7th Cavalry when it rode into southern Montana in search of the Sioux. American Indians called Custer "Long Hair" because of his long, flowing blond hair. Custer often wore buckskin trousers, red-topped boots, and a broad-brimmed hat. A Civil War veteran, Custer was sometimes too daring, deliberately leading his troops into dangerous situations in hopes of winning what he called "glory."

On June 25, 1876, Custer led a troop of around 250 men toward what he believed to be a small Sioux camp. Instead, at a site near the Little Bighorn River, called Greasy Grass by the Sioux, he stumbled upon a very large group of Sioux.

The war chiefs Crazy Horse and Gall commanded the Sioux that now surrounded Custer's force. Racing around and around on their ponies, the Sioux warriors poured a deadly fire upon the troops. The desperate soldiers dismounted and tried to keep their horses from running away. In a short time, the entire company, including Custer, was dead. Sitting Bull's vision of a great Sioux victory was fulfilled. Often called Custer's Last Stand, the **Battle of the Little Bighorn** was the U.S. Army's worst defeat in the West.

The Sioux triumph at the Little Bighorn was short-lived, however. A few months later, the U.S. Army defeated the Sioux. When Crazy Horse surrendered with 900 other Sioux, he was stabbed fatally in the back with a bayonet. Sitting Bull led a group of Sioux into Canada and held out until 1881. He finally surrendered because the Sioux were starving—white hunters had killed off most of the buffalo on which the Sioux depended. In 1883 Sitting Bull was confined to Standing Rock Reservation in the Dakota Territory.

At the Battle of the Little Bighorn, a troop from the U.S. 7th Cavalry was quickly surrounded and suffered an overwhelming defeat at the hands of the Sioux.

• George Armstrong Custer

Many of the U.S. Army troops assigned to the West were Civil War veterans. Among these soldiers were several African American regiments. These African American troops were nicknamed "buffalo soldiers" by American Indians.

The Ghost Dance

The final bloodshed in the wars on the Plains took place in South Dakota. In 1889 an American Indian religious movement, which whites called the **Ghost Dance**, swept through the Plains. Plains Indians performed this Ghost Dance to fulfill the prophecy of a Paiute Indian named Wovoka. The prophecy said that an Indian leader would come to drive white settlers from Indian lands, bring back the great buffalo herds, and unite Indians with their ancestors.

The Ghost Dance spread rapidly among Plains Indians. Government agents, alarmed by the energy and the mystery of the ritual dance, ordered the army to put an end to the Ghost Dance and also to arrest Sitting Bull, who had joined the Ghost Dance movement. When reservation police came to arrest Sitting Bull, they shot and killed him.

Many Sioux fled the reservation with the U.S. Army in pursuit. In December 1890, at Wounded Knee Creek in South Dakota, the U.S. 7th Cavalry encountered a band of Sioux families who were traveling in search of food. Suddenly, a shot rang out. Without warning the U.S. troops opened fire with rifles and Hotchkiss guns, a type of cannon. They massacred around 300 men, women, and children.

Many settlers saw Wounded Knee as revenge for Custer's earlier defeat. Other Americans, however, were horrified by it and demanded an investigation into the massacre. This **Massacre at Wounded Knee** marked the end of more than 25 years of the Plains Indians' armed resistance.

Section 2 Review

• Glossary

IDENTIFY and explain the significance of the following: Fort Laramie Treaty, reservations, Bureau of Indian Affairs, Sand Creek Massacre, Bozeman Trail, Treaty of Medicine Lodge, Sitting Bull, shaman, George Armstrong Custer, Battle of the Little Bighorn, Ghost Dance, Massacre at Wounded Knee

REVIEWING FOR DETAILS

1. How did the U.S. government try to end conflicts between Plains Indians and settlers who were moving west?
2. How did the Sioux gradually change their response to the settlers' expansion?

REVIEWING FOR UNDERSTANDING

3. **Geographic Literacy** How did incoming miners and settlers disturb the Plains Indians' relationship with the land?
4. **Writing Mastery:** *Persuading* Imagine that you are a Sioux chief. Prepare a speech to the Sioux tribal council persuading them either to return to their reservations or to continue resisting the U.S. Army.
5. **Critical Thinking:** *Fact and Opinion* Considering the policies tried by the U.S. government, was war with the Plains Indians unavoidable? Explain your answer.

Section 3

MINERS AND COWBOYS

Multimedia Connections

Explore these related topics and materials on the CD–ROM to enrich your understanding of this section:

Atlas

- Mining Centers

Profiles

- Annie Oakley

Readings

- Cowboy Songs
- Mining Camps and Cattle Towns

Simulation

- The Gold Rush

Media Bank

- Cowboy Life
- Prospectors
- Nevada Mining Town
- Nat Love

Mrs. Lee Whipple-Haslam was a young girl when her family moved to the wilderness and built a snug log cabin. There the family was warm, well fed, and full of hope. Before long, however, prospectors found gold near the cabin. Word soon spread that gold had been discovered, and a mining town quickly sprang up, attracting all types of people, including criminals. Less than a year later, Wipple-Haslam's father was found murdered.

As you read this section you will find out:

- **How new technology changed the role of the individual prospector.**
- **In what ways the cattle industry borrowed from Spanish-Mexican culture.**
- **What factors contributed to the end of open-range ranching.**

The Mining Boom

After the California Gold Rush in 1849, the next important strike was in Nevada in 1859. One center of this activity was Gold Canyon, a sagebrush-covered ravine on the southern slope of Mount Davidson in western Nevada. At first the miners panned for gold in the gravel beds of streams. When their yields declined, they moved up the mountain.

The Comstock Lode. Henry Comstock, known as "Old Pancake," and his partner, James Fennimore, called "Old Virginia," began digging at the head of Gold Canyon on a small rise known as Gold Hill. Another pair, Peter O'Riley and Patrick McLaughlin, started digging at Six Mile Canyon, on the northern slope.

O'Riley and McLaughlin soon came upon a dark, heavy soil sprinkled with gold. Just as

These mining cars are coming out of a shaft in the Comstock Mine in the late 1860s.

they were shouting news of their discovery, Comstock came riding by. Jumping from his horse, he quickly examined the find. "You have struck it, boys!" he said. Then the old prospector bluffed his way into a partnership:

> **"This spring was Old Man Caldwell's. You know that. . . . Well, Manny Penrod and I bought this claim last winter, and we sold a tenth interest to Old Virginia the other day. You two fellows must let us in on equal shares."**

At first O'Riley and McLaughlin said no. Then they were afraid that they might lose everything, so they agreed. The partners went to work at once. They found very little gold. Instead, they struck large deposits of heavy, bluish sand and blue-gray quartz. Not knowing what that "blasted blue stuff" was, they simply piled it beside the mine. A Mexican miner, however, gathered up a sack of the blue quartz and had it **assayed**, or tested.

The assayers' reports exceeded the partners' wildest dreams. They had hit upon a silver **bonanza**, a large find of extremely rich ore. News of the discovery brought some 15,000 people swarming into the region. Comstock gained everlasting fame by naming the find the **Comstock Lode**.

New mining technology. Most of the gold and silver was buried deep in veins of hard quartz rock and required heavy machinery to dig it out. Steam-powered drills gouged out massive chunks of earth. Newly developed steam shovels moved the chunks to waiting wagons or rail cars, which carried them to smelters. Huge rock crushers and smelters then separated the ore from the rock. By 1872 a railway wound through the mining communities, bringing coal to fuel the smelters.

Mine owners realized that large smelters, located in Golden or Denver, were more efficient. So the railroad hauled the ore—rich with silver, copper, lead, and gold—to these plants. Tunneling operations called for experienced mining engineers. Powerful pumps were needed to remove groundwater that seeped in as the shafts grew deeper. Miners like Comstock, O'Riley, and McLaughlin did not have the skill or the money that such operations required. Comstock eventually sold his share of the mine for a mere $11,000.

Prospectors went from one mountain to the next in search of a mining claim that would make them rich. Miners worked hard, but few succeeded in their search for a bonanza.

The Cattle Kingdom

While miners were searching for gold and silver, other pioneers were seeking their fortunes in cattle. The land that stretched from Texas into Canada and from the Rockies to eastern Kansas eventually formed the **Cattle Kingdom**. This area, which spanned roughly one quarter of the United States, became dotted with cattle ranches.

Cattle in the Southwest. Spanish explorers had brought the first cattle into Mexico in the 1500s. Over the years their herds had increased enormously. Many ran wild, and new breeds developed. These great herds spread northward as far as Texas. By the mid-1860s, about 5 million wild cattle were grazing in Texas. Many of these were Texas longhorns, so named because their horns had a spread of as much as seven feet. Longhorns thrived on the Plains because they could survive with little water or grass.

After the Civil War there was a growing demand for beef in eastern cities. Cattle that were worth from \$3 to \$5 a head in Texas could be sold in the East for \$30 to \$50 a head. The problem was transporting the herds to the East. Railroads had not yet come to Texas. Joseph G. McCoy, an Illinois meat dealer, thought he had a solution. He hoped to make his fortune by establishing a convenient meeting place for buyers and Texas cattle ranchers.

Cattle towns. McCoy chose the town of Abilene, Kansas, as this meeting place. There he built a hotel for the cowhands and dealers and built barns, pens, and loading chutes for the cattle. He persuaded officials of the Kansas Pacific Railroad to ship cattle to Chicago—the meat-packing center of the United States—at special low rates.

At first, Abilene was a quiet town, coming to life only during the few months that the ranchers brought in their cattle. Local men and women saw new opportunities for opening businesses such as saloons, restaurants, hotels, and stores. Even children could find work in the rapidly growing town. What had been little more than a railroad station with stockyards for cattle became a town with businesses, schools, and churches. Soon Abilene faced competition from other Kansas cattle towns, such as Ellsworth and Dodge City.

Cattle drives. To get Texas longhorns to cattle towns meant herding them slowly northward over the Plains. This long trip, called a **cattle drive**, was a journey of several months over hundreds of miles. On the first drive, Texans herded some 35,000 longhorns over the Chisholm Trail to Abilene. Soon ranchers blazed other routes, such as the Goodnight-Loving, Western, and Shawnee Trails. During the next 25 years about 10 million head of cattle were driven north over these trails of open grasslands.

The Granger Collection, New York

Cowboys herded Texas longhorns north on the long drive to market. The drive ended at cattle towns like Dodge City, where the railroad would pick up the cattle and ship them east. In this engraving, Dodge City is suddenly filled with the cowboys driving the longhorns to market.

• **Cowhands and Cattle Drives**

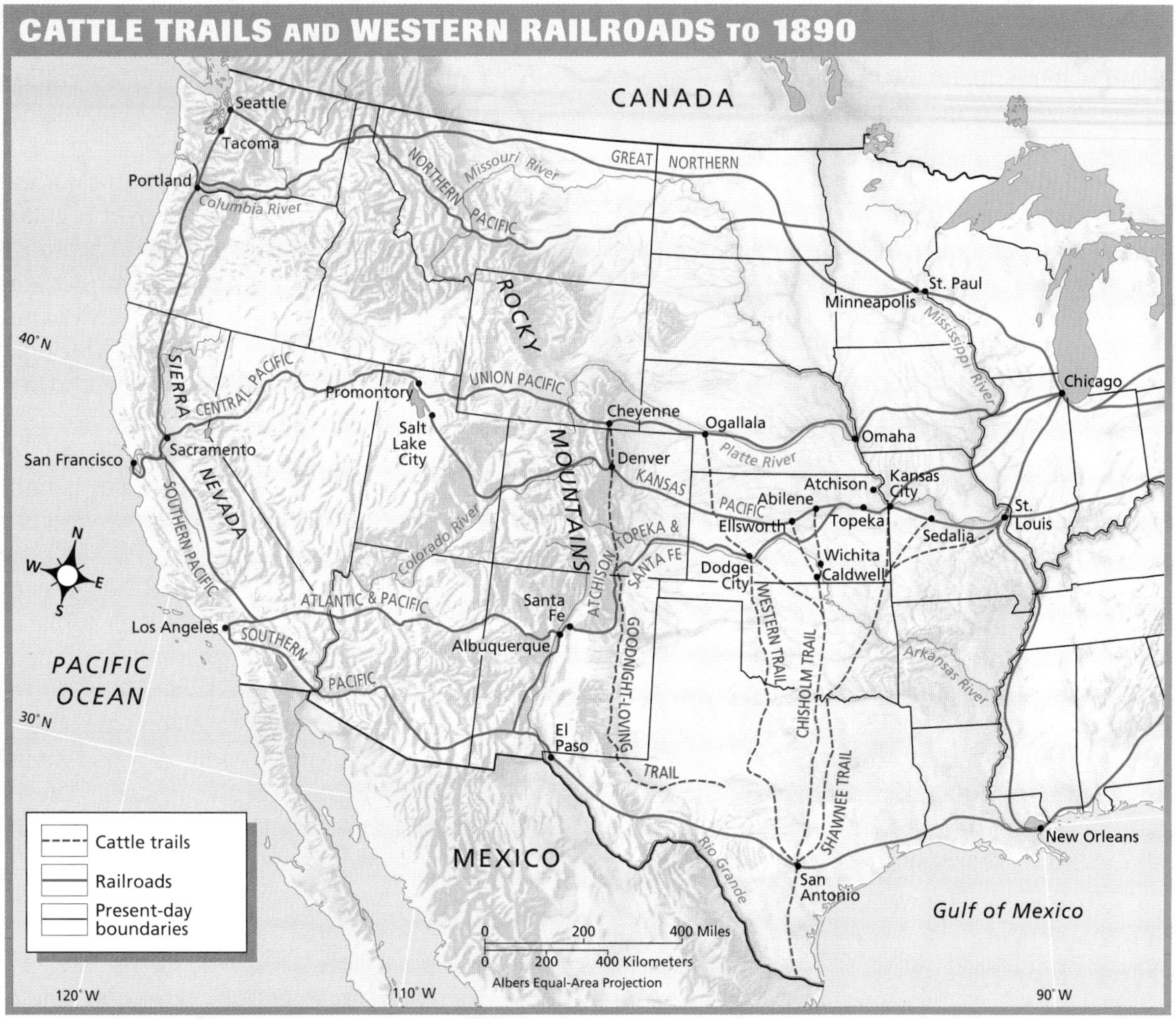

CATTLE TRAILS AND WESTERN RAILROADS TO 1890

Learning from Maps. By the mid- to late 1800s, cattle trails and railroads had crossed much of the West.

▶ **Movement.** About how many miles was it from New Orleans to Los Angeles on Southern Pacific's railroad route?

• **Maps**

Open-Range Ranching

The key to the success of the cattle drive was the **open range**, or grass on the public lands, along the trails. Ranchers discovered that prairie grass made an excellent food for their cattle and that the longhorns got along very well in the harsh winters of the Plains.

When the U.S. government turned former Indian land into public lands, cattle ranching spread west and north of Texas. Cattle roamed freely across the unfenced land that was by now nearly empty of buffalo. Ranchers grazed millions of cattle on the Plains without paying a cent to the federal government. Cattle ranching became highly profitable, and soon it attracted investors from the East Coast and Europe who acquired huge ranches.

Range rights. Cattle ranchers needed access to water. **Range rights**, or water rights, along a stream meant control of all the land around it. Ranchers, individually or in a group, quickly bought up all the land around their water supply. By owning a few acres along a river, ranchers could control thousands of acres of surrounding grassland without actually owning it. Although the rest of the range was public property, no other rancher for miles around could graze cattle there because the access to water was on private property.

Roundup. The ranchers who owned the banks of the stream let their cattle mix together. Each spring and fall, cowhands gathered all the animals to a central place—an event known as a **roundup**. Next they sorted each rancher's cattle from the rest by checking every animal's **brand**, or marking. This brand was a scar made by pressing a red-hot branding iron onto the animal's hide. Each rancher's brand had a distinct shape, so it was easy to determine who owned which cattle.

The Granger Collection, New York

The vaqueros *wore large hats and leather chaps in their work.*

The Cowhand

The success of the drive and the roundup depended upon that colorful figure, the cowboy or cowhand. Many cowhands came from poor families. About one third of the cowhands who worked the herds of cattle on the open range were either Mexican Americans or African Americans.

• Cowboy Music

American Indians and Mexican Americans were the first cowhands. These *vaqueros,* as they were called in Spanish, invented almost all the tools of the cowhands' trade, including the broad-brimmed felt hat, the cotton bandanna, the rope lariat, and the special western saddle.

Every item of the cowhands' clothing and equipment served a necessary function. The wide brims of their hats could be turned down to shade their eyes or drain off rainfall. Their bandannas could be tied over their noses and mouths to protect them from the dust raised by the pounding hooves of countless cattle. The bandanna could also serve as a towel, napkin, bandage, and handkerchief.

Cowhands sometimes wore leather protectors, called chaps, over regular pants. Chaps were fastened to a broad belt buckled at the back. They protected a rider's legs from injury if a cowhand fell from a horse or had to ride through cactus, sagebrush, or other thorny plants.

The cowhands' western saddle was heavy but comfortable. It had a sturdy horn, for help in roping powerful steers and horses. At night the saddle could become a pillow and the saddlecloth a blanket when the cowhand stretched out beside the campfire. Before settling down to sleep, the cowhands often sang songs, such as "Home on the Range." These songs have become a rich part of American music.

Most cowhands' had hard lives. They worked from sunup to sundown and received lower wages than most factory workers. Their legs often became bowed from long days in the saddle. They developed permanent squints from peering into the glaring sunlight of the treeless Plains. Their faces were lined and leathery, their hands callused from constantly handling coarse ropes. The time spent on the open range made for a lonely life.

The End of the Open Range

By the end of the 1880s the days of the open range were coming to an end. Ranchers had overstocked the range. As a result, there was a shortage of good grazing land and a surplus of beef, which drove down prices.

Farmers were glad to see the end of the open range. Cattle herds often trampled

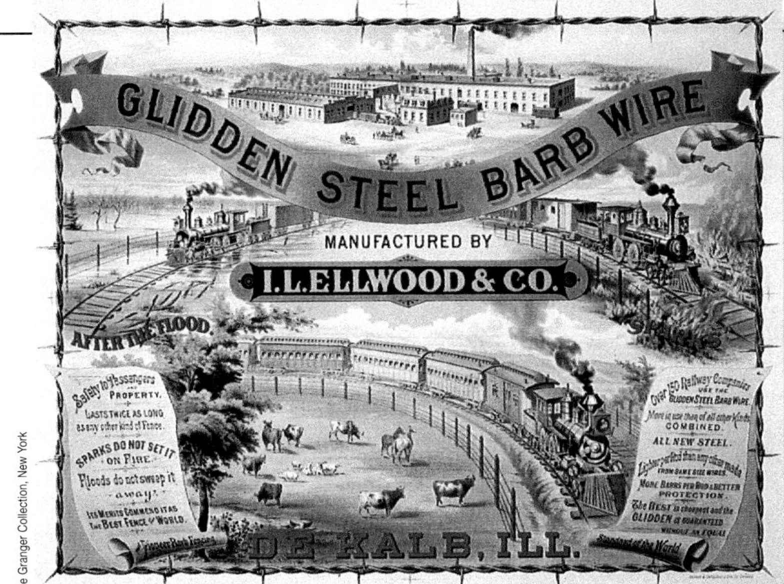

The Granger Collection, New York

Barbed wire made fencing off western farmland easier and more affordable, and as a result, put an end to open-range ranching.

farmers' crops. The farmers also feared that the free-roaming herds would infect their dairy cows with a disease called "Texas fever." The invention of **barbed wire**, a relatively cheap method of fencing, allowed farmers and ranchers to close off their land, thus shrinking the amount of open land for cattle grazing.

In the foothills of the Rockies, sheepherders squared off against local cattle ranchers because sheep cropped the grass so close to the roots that cattle could no longer graze. Many range wars broke out between cattle ranchers and sheep ranchers for control of the grasslands.

Two terrible winters in a row added to the decline of the open range. In 1885–86 and in 1886–87 blizzards howled across the Plains. Theodore Roosevelt, then a "gentleman rancher" in Dakota Territory, wrote:

> **"Furious gales blow down from the north, driving before them the clouds of blinding snow-dust, wrapping the mantle of death around every unsheltered being."**

When spring came in 1887, ranchers discovered that the storms had wiped out a large percentage of their herds. The boom times were over. Cattle ranchers had to fence in their herds and feed them hay in the winter. Thus cattle ranchers became cattle feeders, and the days of the long cattle drives came to an end.

Section 3 Review

• Glossary

• Gazetteer

IDENTIFY and explain the significance of the following: assayed, bonanza, Comstock Lode, Cattle Kingdom, cattle drive, open range, range rights, roundup, brand, barbed wire

LOCATE and explain the importance of the following: Abilene, cattle trails

REVIEWING FOR DETAILS

1. How did new mining technology change the role of the prospector?
2. What elements of Spanish-Mexican culture were used by cowhands?

REVIEWING FOR UNDERSTANDING

3. **Geographic Literacy** Why did open-range ranching come to an end?
4. **Writing Mastery:** *Describing* Imagine that you are the sheriff in a western town in 1884. Write an editorial for the local newspaper describing the conflicts between farmers, cattle ranchers, and sheepherders in the region.
5. **Critical Thinking:** *Synthesizing Information* What effects did mining and the cattle industry have on the growth of towns in the West?

Section 4

SETTLEMENT ON THE GREAT PLAINS

Multimedia Connections

Explore these related topics and materials on the CD–ROM to enrich your understanding of this section:

Media Bank

- U.S. Government and the West
- Cost of Establishing a Farm
- Union and Central Pacific Meet
- Pony Express Rider
- Harvesting Wheat
- "Exodus" Movement

Atlas

- Oklahoma Land Rush

Readings

- *A Lantern in Her Hand*

Profiles

- Willa Cather

Everyday life in the West was often quite difficult. Anne Howard Shaw described her experiences when she was a 15-year-old teacher in a one-room schoolhouse:

> **"The school was four miles from my home. . . . During the first year I had about fourteen pupils, of varying ages, sizes, and temperaments, and there was hardly a book in the school-room except those I owned. One little girl, I remember, read from an almanac, while a second used a hymn-book."**

As you read this section you will find out:

- **Why settlers moved to the Great Plains.**
- **What natural obstacles farmers faced on the Great Plains.**
- **How farmers adapted to the unique conditions of the Great Plains.**

Railroads Reach West

The federal government encouraged economic growth in the West through important legislation passed in 1862, particularly the **Pacific Railway Act**, the **Homestead Act**, and the **Morrill Act**. These acts gave western land grants to promote the building of a transcontinental railroad, settlements, and educational facilities, respectively.

As miners, ranchers, and settlers went west, companies and individual investors became increasingly interested in the region. It still took people several months to reach California by wagon or clipper ship, however. Faster transportation to the Pacific seemed more important than ever.

Soon after passage of the Railway Act, the Union Pacific Railroad and the Central Pacific Railway began the great task of building a

The Central Pacific Railroad saved millions of dollars by hiring Chinese workers at a rate two thirds of that paid to a white laborer. Chinese railroad gangs of 12 to 20 men usually had a Chinese cook who prepared native dishes.

railroad across the West. In 1869 these companies completed the first transcontinental railroad, meeting at Promontory, Utah.

Other railroad companies soon built more transcontinental lines. These new railroads connected with eastern railroads at Chicago, St. Louis, and New Orleans. This meant a traveler could go from the Atlantic coast to San Francisco and other Pacific coast cities in about a week's time, which was much quicker than ever before.

• Building the Railroads

To offset their building costs, the railroad companies sold their free government land grants—about 130 million acres of public lands. The railroad companies advertised these lands in the East and in Europe and offered discounted and free tickets to settlers who would buy land.

The railroad boom in the West also led to improved communications. Railroad companies often stretched **telegraph** lines alongside tracks. The telegraph, which had been invented by Samuel F. B. Morse in 1837, used a system of dots and dashes to transmit messages over wires. During the late 1800s, businesses came to rely on telegraph communications to make orders and to fix schedules. By 1866 Western Union, the nation's largest telegraph company, had over 2,000 offices.

The Plains Farmers

Settlers came by the thousands to buy land from the railroad companies. Others claimed their 160 acres under the Homestead Act. Although Homestead land was practically free, settlers needed some financial resources to make the trip west—buying and transporting supplies to start up a farm or a business was quite costly.

Civil War veterans and New England farmers looking for better soil were among those who headed west. Many more settlers came from states such as Illinois, Indiana, and Wisconsin.

Political oppression drove other Americans west. For example, Benjamin Singleton led some 20,000 or more African Americans west from the South in 1879. They hoped to leave behind violence and racial prejudice. These black settlers became known as **Exodusters**.

Other western settlers were emigrants from Europe. Hundreds of thousands of Irish, Germans, Czechs, Ukrainians, Russians, and Scandinavians settled on the Plains. Writer O. E. Rölvaag described one Norwegian family who moved to Dakota Territory because there was "no lack of opportunity in that country!"

Daily Life on the Plains

In the past many people decided against farming and settling on the Plains because there was too little rain to raise crops and no wood to build houses or fences. On the

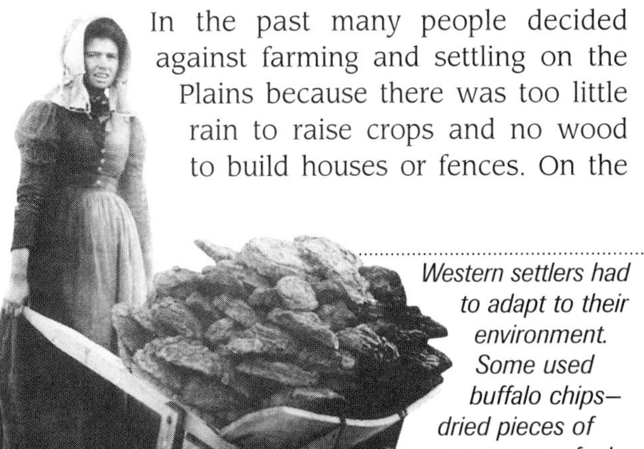

Western settlers had to adapt to their environment. Some used buffalo chips—dried pieces of manure—as fuel.

treeless Plains the pioneers had to build their first homes out of the earth itself. The thick roots of the wild grasses made it possible to cut sod into bricklike chunks. Usually, only the roofs of these sod houses were made of wood. Sod houses were smoky and damp, but they provided shelter until the railroads brought in affordable lumber for building better homes.

Many found that the hardships overshadowed the advantages of free land. The environment offered one of the biggest challenges. In winter, blizzards roared out of Canada. In summer, the thermometer frequently soared above 100 degrees, and tornadoes sometimes swept across the Plains. In addition, pests such as great swarms of grasshoppers descended on the land, eating everything in sight.

Neighbors lent each other their support in this harsh environment. In Willa Cather's novel, *My Ántonia,* the narrator describes a visit to a Czech family who had a new log house:

> **"The neighbors had helped them [the family] to build it in March. It stood directly in front of their old cave, which they used as a cellar. The family were now fairly equipped to begin their struggle with the soil. They had four comfortable rooms to live in, a new windmill—bought on credit—a chicken-house and poultry."**

Farming was hard and risky work. Each member of the family had countless chores. These ranged from plowing, to milking cows, to planting a garden, to taking care of the children. Women often found that their work expanded beyond traditional roles of tending the house and the family. Children also had important duties.

Young People In History

Sodbuster Kids

Life on the Plains was hard for young people. They often lived in very cramped quarters with as many as 10 brothers and sisters. Some could attend school. Many, however, spent long, tiring days working in the fields. Despite the hard work, these young pioneers found ways to have fun. Author Laura Ingalls Wilder wrote many novels based on her own childhood on the Plains. In one book, she described the main character, Laura, joyfully riding her pony after the daily chores were done.

Nebraska State Historical Society

Children on the Plains found enjoyment in simple things.

"She and the pony were going too fast but they were going like music and nothing could happen to her until the music stopped. . . . That was a wonderful afternoon. Twice Laura fell off. . . . Her hair came unbraided and her throat grew hoarse from laughing and screeching, and her legs were scratched from running through the sharp grass and trying to leap onto her pony while it was running."

Farming the Plains

Farming on the Great Plains was difficult, but the soil was very fertile. The biggest problem facing the farmers of western Nebraska, Kansas, and the Dakotas was the lack of rainfall. In some years there was plenty of rain to grow wheat and other grain crops. Often, however, there were dry years, and even **droughts**, when almost no rain fell. Well water could be used to irrigate a small plot or a vegetable garden, but it was not enough for any large-scale farming.

Nebraska State Historical Society

The Granger Collection, New York

Pioneers went west in search of cheap land offered by the government and the railroads. Settlers established farms and built their houses out of sod.

Hardy W. Campbell, a farmer in Dakota Territory, promoted a technique called **dry farming** that made it possible to raise certain crops with very little water. Campbell plowed the land deeply and repeatedly. Rain thus was absorbed easily into the soil, where the roots of the plants could use it. Campbell also planted special varieties of wheat that needed less water than other types. Using dry-farming methods, farmers could raise crops in dry years.

By the 1880s the average Plains farmer was using a great deal of machinery. In 1868 James Oliver of Indiana had begun manufacturing a new type of iron plow. This plow, which later became known as a **sodbuster**, could easily slice through the tough sod of the Plains. In the 1870s John Appleby invented a twine binder. This machine gathered up bundles of wheat and automatically bound them with twine or string, greatly reducing the time needed for harvesting. In 1890 about 5 million people were living on the Great Plains. By the 1890s the land west of the Mississippi Valley had become the breadbasket of America and the greatest wheat-producing region in the world.

Section 4 Review

• Glossary

• Time Line

IDENTIFY and explain the significance of the following: Pacific Railway Act, Homestead Act, Morrill Act, telegraph, Exodusters, droughts, dry farming, sodbuster

REVIEWING FOR DETAILS

1. Why did settlers move to the Great Plains?
2. How did farmers adapt to the conditions of the Plains?

REVIEWING FOR UNDERSTANDING

3. **Geographic Literacy** What geographic challenges did farm families face on the Great Plains?
4. **Writing Mastery:** *Expressing* Imagine that you are a teenager who has recently moved to the Great Plains. Write a letter to one of your friends in the East expressing your feelings about life in your new home.
5. **Critical Thinking:** *Determining the Strength of an Argument* What were the advantages and disadvantages of the U.S. government granting land to companies in exchange for railroad construction?

CHAPTER 17

Becoming an Industrial Nation (1865–1900)

Technology and Society:
How might new scientific discoveries change people's lives?

Economic Development:
How might industrialization lead to the growth of cities?

Cultural Diversity:
How might large numbers of immigrants affect a society's culture?

In the late 1800s the United States was a land of incredible contrasts. In New York City, mansions stood just blocks away from run-down apartment buildings. Wealthy business owners sat comfortably in fancy offices while their workers labored in dangerous factories. "Never before have the rich been so rich and the poor been so poor," one observer noted.

• Video Opener

• Skill Builder

image above: *A city in the late 1800s*

Section 1

INVENTIONS AND THE RISE OF BIG BUSINESS

Multimedia Connections

Explore these related topics and materials on the CD–ROM to enrich your understanding of this section:

Media Bank

- Inventions, 1850–1900
- Mail-Order Catalog
- Advertising
- Vanderbilt Family

Glossary

- bankruptcy

Readings

- The Making of Consumer Culture
- Mark Twain's Criticisms
- Leisure Activities

Profiles

- Alexander Graham Bell
- Cornelius Vanderbilt
- Elijah McCoy
- Granville Woods
- Thomas Edison

The late 1800s were a time of inventions and industrial expansion. Businesspeople ruled America, and those who controlled the production of essential goods had enormous power. Many Americans hoped the new breed of businessperson would help the country make a successful transition to what some observers called a "modern age."

As you read this section you will find out:

- **What new scientific and technological discoveries fueled the Second Industrial Revolution.**
- **How entrepreneurs encouraged the growth of business.**
- **Why the growth of big business led to government regulations.**

Building the New Industrial Society

Between 1865 and 1900 the United States went through one of the most dramatic periods of change the country had ever seen. Several factors were responsible for this amazing transformation.

Changing iron into steel. Steel was the basic building material of what many called the Second Industrial Revolution. In the 1850s a British inventor named Henry Bessemer perfected an inexpensive way to make steel. The **Bessemer process**, as it was called, made possible the mass production of steel.

Steel had many uses in America's rapidly developing industrial society. After steel rails for railroad tracks came steel skeletons for tall buildings and bridges. Nails, wire, and other everyday objects were also made of steel.

The railroad network. Steel production particularly helped American railroads. The first rails were made of cast iron, but they often wore out quickly. Steel rails lasted much longer than iron rails.

Even after the introduction of steel rails, however, problems in the railroad industry remained. Railroads had been built primarily to serve local transportation needs. Most railroads in the United States were short, averaging only about 100 miles. In 1860, passengers and freight traveling between New York and Chicago, for example, had to change lines 17 times!

Business leaders set out to connect these lines into networks. Cornelius Vanderbilt was a pioneer in this work. Although he quit school at age 11, he had a good head for business. Vanderbilt bought up separate railroad routes and combined them. By 1870 his railroad system extended from New York to Chicago. Passengers could travel between the two cities in less than 24 hours!

Inventions and new practices also contributed to the expansion of railroads. George Westinghouse invented a compressed air brake that made larger, faster, and safer trains possible. Another inventor, African American Granville Woods, improved the design of air brakes and created other useful products as well, including a new telegraph system.

Railroads stimulated the national economy in countless ways. They functioned as a major employer, supplying thousands of new jobs. Railroads also created many other jobs in related industries, such the manufacturing of railroad cars and other materials needed for railroad operation. In addition, railroads allowed for the quick, easy, and inexpensive movement of goods and passengers over long distances. Finally, railroads encouraged urban growth.

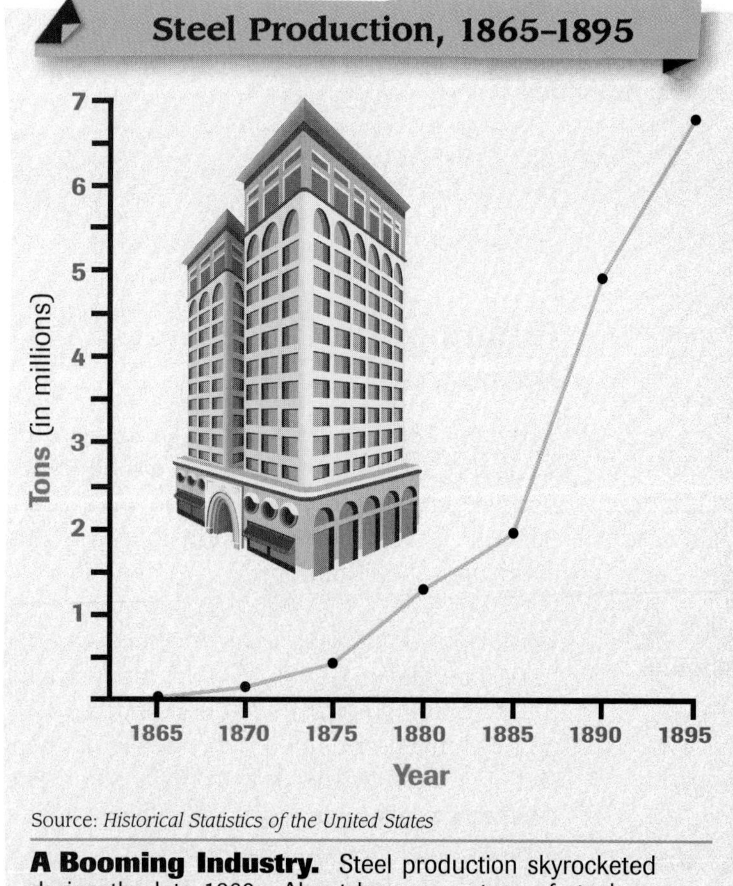

A Booming Industry. Steel production skyrocketed during the late 1800s. About how many tons of steel were produced in 1885? In 1895?

Powering the New Industrial Society

Steel and railroads served as the building blocks of the Second Industrial Revolution. Other products and industries powered the new society.

"Black gold." Americans had known about crude oil, or petroleum, for hundreds of years. Oil was very difficult to collect, though, so few people made much use of it. Then in 1859 a retired railroad conductor named E. L. Drake began drilling for petroleum in Pennsylvania. The idea seemed so impractical that

The Granger Collection, New York

The expansion of railroad networks in the late 1800s greatly changed the way Americans did business. The Illinois Central Railroad, shown here, was one of the many lines that ran through Chicago.

onlookers called it "Drake's Folly," but when he had drilled down about 70 feet, Drake struck oil. In just a few years, "wildcatters," or adventurous people who searched for oil, flooded into western Pennsylvania to drill for what they called "black gold."

Oil quickly became a big business. By 1861 around 2 million barrels of oil were being pumped from western Pennsylvania annually. Businesspeople opened refineries to purify the crude oil. They sold such finished petroleum product as kerosene to other businesses and communities for use in lighting. Several inventions made oil even more valuable. Elijah McCoy, the son of runaway slaves, invented a lubricating cup that fed oil to parts of a machine while it ran. This breakthrough helped all kinds of machines operate more smoothly and quickly. In the 1890s the internal combustion engine, which burned petroleum in the form of gasoline or diesel fuel, turned oil into one of the nation's major sources of power.

The revolution in communications. Advances in communications also furthered thc growth of American industry. Alexander Graham Bell invented the telephone in 1876. At first, many people considered Bell's invention a joke. Fortunately, others realized its usefulness. Telephone wires soon rose up across the skies. The telephone became an essential part of industrial society, allowing rapid, cheap, long-distance communication by voice.

The Wizard of Menlo Park. In the same year that Bell invented the telephone, Thomas Alva Edison established the nation's first industrial research laboratory in Menlo Park, New Jersey. Although he had received only about five years of on-and-off formal schooling, Edison became known as the greatest inventor of the age because he developed so many products.

Edison's first major invention was the quadruplex telegraph. It could send four messages over one wire at the same time. He also invented the phonograph and made several improvements on Bell's telephone. Edison's early inventions fascinated many Americans.

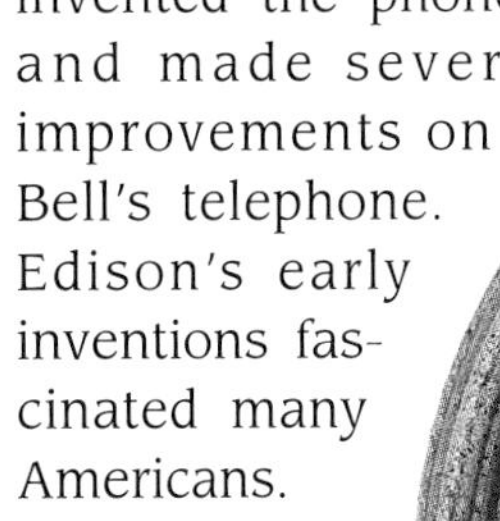

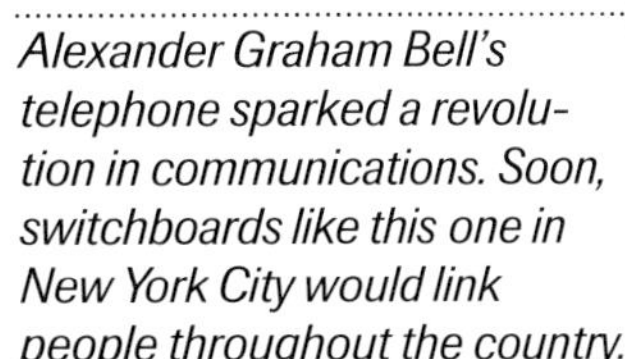

The Granger Collection, New York

Alexander Graham Bell's telephone sparked a revolution in communications. Soon, switchboards like this one in New York City would link people throughout the country.

The Granger Collection, New York

One writer celebrated the products of Edison's "invention factory" in a popular magazine:

> **"If this can be done . . . what is there that cannot be? . . . We feel that there may, after all, be a relief for all human ills in the great storehouse of nature."**

Edison's most important invention came in the late 1870s, when he developed an electric lightbulb. Edison's basic idea was to pass electricity through a thin wire inside an airless glass globe. The electricity heated the wire, causing it to glow brightly. The wire could not burn up because there was no oxygen in the globe. Soon the "Wizard of Menlo Park" was setting up city lighting companies and power stations to generate electricity. He also sold light bulbs by the millions. In just a few years, electric lights were replacing gas lights in cities across the country.

The Leaders of Big Business

Entrepreneurs (ahn-truh-puh-NUHRZ), or risk-taking businesspeople, played an important role in the Second Industrial Revolution. Some were "robber barons"—rough, greedy businesspeople who cheated and mistreated others to enrich themselves. Some were honest, public-spirited citizens. All were eager to take advantage of the opportunities they saw opening up around them.

New business practices. The entrepreneurs of the late 1800s developed new ways to make more money and operate more efficiently. At around this time, businesspeople began to question traditional forms of business organization. In the early 1800s most businesses were owned by individuals or partners. However, it took huge amounts of money to construct and run a railroad, oil refinery, or research lab.

Therefore, entrepreneurs set up their new businesses as **corporations**. They sold shares called stock certificates to investors. These investors, called **stockholders**, made money when the corporation did well.

Corporations offered a number of advantages over other types of business organization. By selling stock certificates, entrepreneurs could raise a lot of money. Investors benefited as well because they had limited liability. They risked only the money that they had paid for their stock. In a partnership, on the other hand, all the partners were responsible for all the debts of the firm. In addition, corporations allowed a small group of directors to control a very large business operation.

Carnegie and steel. One of the most important business leaders of the late 1800s was Andrew Carnegie. He came to the United States from Scotland as a youth and worked 12 hours a day in a cotton mill. By the time he was 17, he had become the private secretary to a railroad company's superintendent. He soon became a railroad superintendent himself and made a great deal of money from various investments.

Carnegie eventually concentrated his investments in the steel industry. He built the

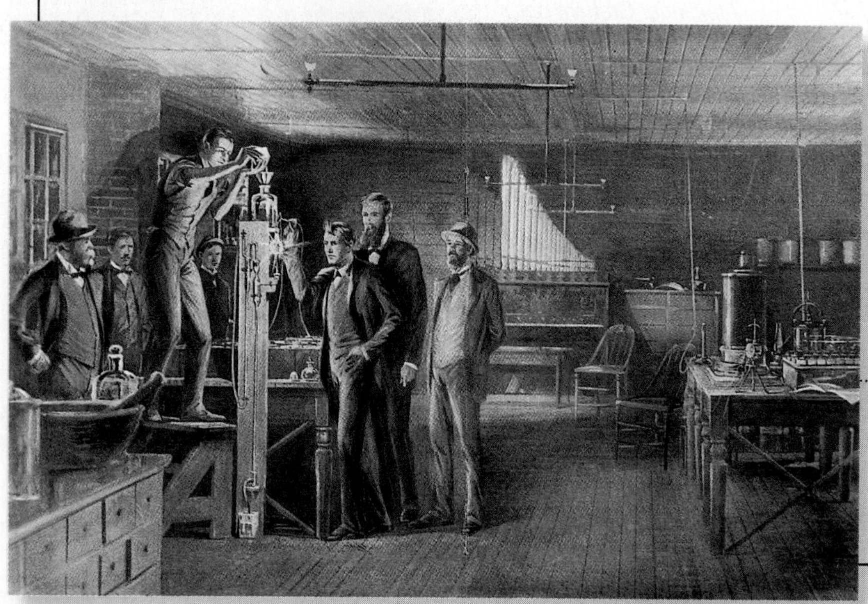

The Granger Collection, New York

Thomas Edison experiments with an electric lightbulb in his Menlo Park laboratory.

• Thomas Edison in Lab

Life in a New Country

Like the old immigrants, those who came in the late 1800s believed in the golden dream of American opportunity. When a 13-year-old Russian girl learned that her father had asked the rest of the family to join him in America, she wrote:

> **"So at last I was going to America! Really, really going, at last! The boundaries burst. The arch of heaven soared. A million suns shone out for every star. The winds rushed in from outer space, roaring in my ears, 'America! America!'"**

Entering a new home. Immigrants' first glimpse of America came at the processing centers where they officially entered the United States. Many European newcomers passed through Ellis Island in New York Harbor, where they were awed by the sight of the Statue of Liberty. Most Asian immigrants stopped at Angel Island in San Francisco Bay. The processing centers were crowded and noisy. Tired workers interviewed the immigrants and examined them for disease. Sometimes they could not pronounce immigrants' names and thus changed them. A name like Martinisian, for example, might be shortened to Martin.

Although many immigrants thought that the United States was much better than their native land, others wondered if America would live up to their hopes. Another young Russian girl, Anzia Yezierska, wrote:

> **"Between the buildings that loomed like mountains, we struggled with our bundles. . . . I looked about the narrow streets of squeezed-in stores and houses, ragged clothes, dirty bedding oozing out of the windows, ashcans and garbage cans cluttering the sidewalks. A vague sadness pressed down on my heart—the first doubt of America."**

Harsh realities. The backgrounds of many old immigrants helped them adjust to their new home. British and Irish immigrants spoke English. Many German immigrants were well educated and skilled in useful trades. Scandinavians usually knew how to farm and often came with enough money to buy land in the West. Except for the Irish and some of the Germans, most of the old immigrants were Protestants, as were the majority of native-born Americans.

The backgrounds of those who came to America in the late 1800s differed considerably. Unlike the old immigrants, the new immigrants often had little education and few special skills. Most knew no English. Their habits, cultures, and religions were different from those of most native-born Americans. These factors made it difficult for the new immigrants to adjust to life in the United States. Most could get only low-paying jobs. Whole families worked to survive.

Charitable organizations often set up **benevolent societies** to help immigrants.

Courtesy The Bancroft Library

Many Asian immigrants found work on farms on the Pacific Coast.

These groups offered all kinds of assistance, like business loans and money for health care. In addition, local politicians often aided newly arrived immigrants.

Immigrants also created their own communities, which provided assistance and comfort. Newcomers from particular countries or areas tended to cluster together in the same neighborhood. In 1890 a New York reporter imagined a city map that used different colors to represent inhabitants' nationalities. He said it would have "more stripes than the skin of a zebra, and more colors than any rainbow." These ethnic neighborhoods were like cities within cities. They offered immigrants a chance to hold on to a few fragments of the world they had left behind. There they could find familiar foods, people who spoke their language, and churches and clubs based on old-country models.

• Immigrants and Political Machines

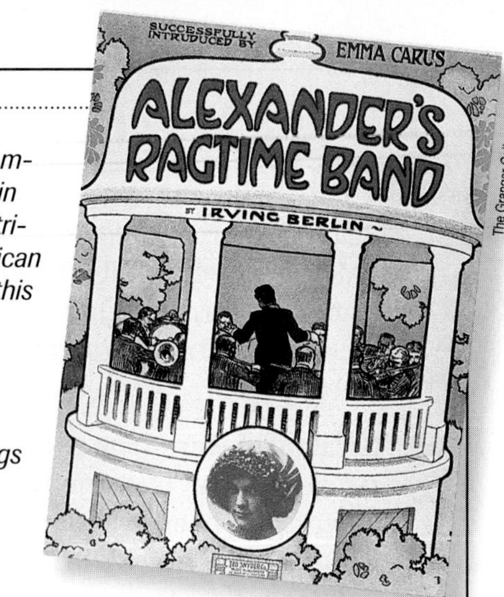

Immigrants like Russian-born composer Irving Berlin made many contributions to American music, such as this popular tune, "Alexander's Ragtime Band." One of Berlin's best-known songs is "God Bless America."

The Granger Collection, New York

Efforts to Limit Immigration

Many native-born Americans disliked immigrants. Nativist workers resented their willingness to work long hours for low wages. Nativists believed that this massive new immigration would weaken their political, social, and religious power. In addition, they also claimed that the immigrants were physically and mentally inferior. The nativists said immigrants were dangerous radicals who wanted to destroy American democratic institutions. In his poem "Unguarded Gates," writer Thomas Bailey Aldrich expressed these fears. "Wide open and unguarded stand our gates," he claimed, "And through them presses a wild motley throng [rowdy group]."

As the number of immigrants grew, nativists launched efforts to limit immigration or end it completely. Some Americans targeted Chinese immigrants. When a depression swept the country, native-born Californians worried that Chinese workers would steal their jobs. In 1882 Congress responded to these fears by passing the **Chinese Exclusion Act**. This law prohibited Chinese

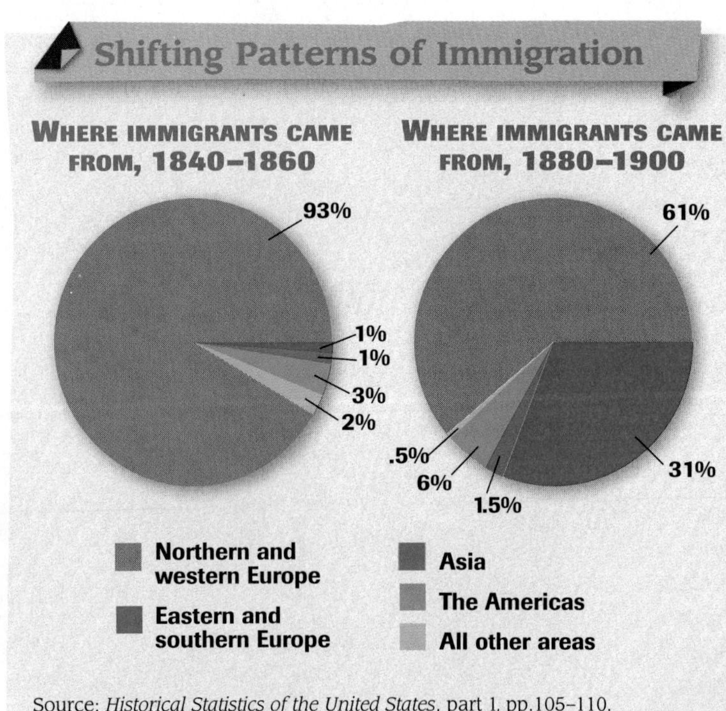

Source: *Historical Statistics of the United States*, part 1, pp.105–110.

The New Immigrants. Toward the end of the 1880s immigration patterns changed drastically. What immigrant group experienced the largest increase between 1840-1860 and 1880-1900?

• Graphs

workers from entering the United States for a period of 10 years. The ban was later extended well into the 1900s. It caused a sharp drop in the Chinese population in the United States.

In the 1890s some nativists formed the **Immigration Restriction League**. This group called for a law preventing immigrants who could not read or write any language from entering the United States. A literacy test would keep out many people from southern and eastern Europe, where public schools were scarce.

Congress passed a literacy test bill in 1897, but President Grover Cleveland vetoed it. He insisted that the United States should continue to be a place of refuge for the world's poor and persecuted. Many employers, for less humane reasons, opposed any check on immigration. They favored unlimited immigration because it would assure a steady source of low-paid but hardworking laborers.

The Rise of American Cities

The growth of cities after the Civil War was both rapid and widespread. In 1865 places like Denver and Seattle were no more than small towns. By 1900, however, they were major urban centers. In that year there were 38 American cities that had 100,000 or more inhabitants.

A number of factors contributed to urban growth. Immigrants, of course, played an essential role, but thousands of native-born Americans also flooded into the cities. Some southern African Americans tried to escape prejudice and limited economic opportunities by moving to northern cities such as Chicago, Detroit, and New York. In addition, many rural whites headed for cities.

Troubling living conditions. The new city-dwellers faced a serious shortage of housing and other facilities. As more people streamed into towns, land values soared. Because of the high cost of property, builders put up large overcrowded apartments called **tenements**. These tenements were crowded so closely together that they blocked out the sunlight and air.

A five- or six-story tenement usually had four apartments on each floor. Front apartments contained four rooms, rear apartments three. Many of the rooms had no windows. In most cases, two families had to share a single

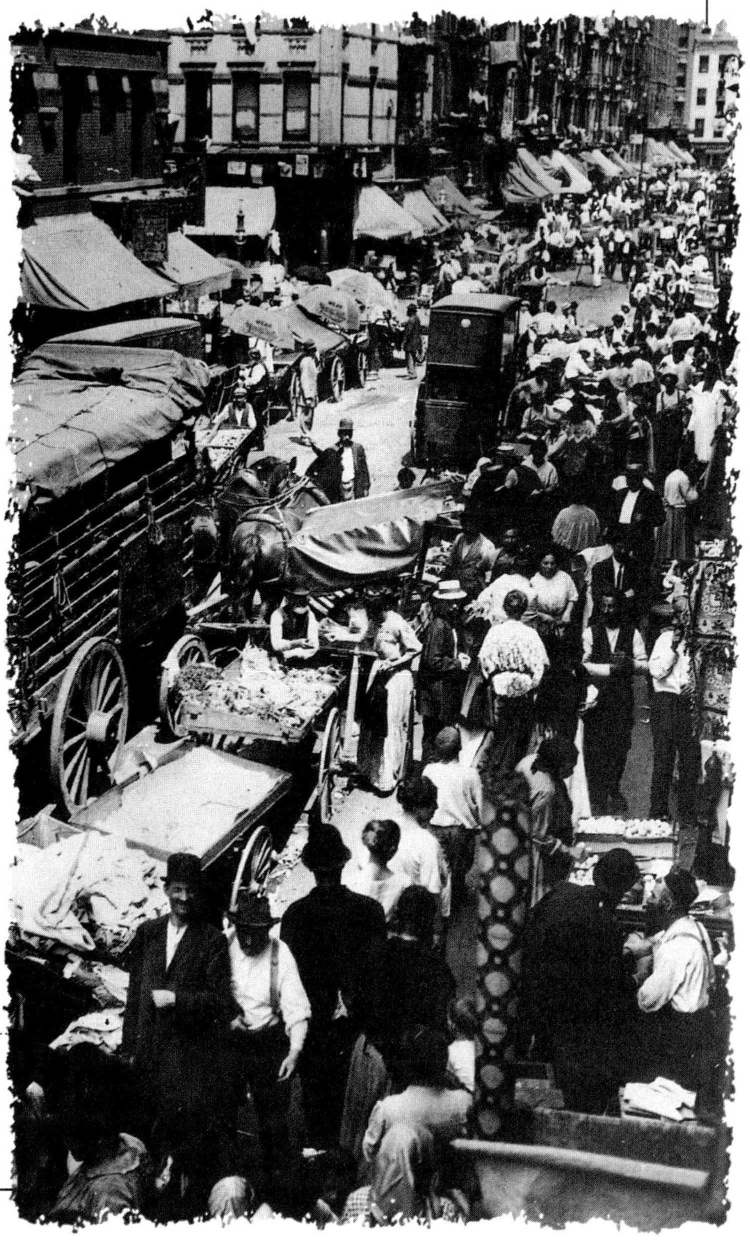

Urban immigrant neighborhoods like this one were often overcrowded, but they helped immigrants preserve ties to their heritage and culture.

bathroom located in a dark, narrow hallway. Musty, garbage-cluttered "air shafts" separated one tenement building from the next and often caused health problems. As one resident told the New York State Tenement House Commission in 1900, "the air shaft is a breeder of disease."

The Granger Collection, New York

This cartoon expressed the sentiments of many opponents of immigration, who wanted to keep foreigners off American soil. Many of those who were opposed to immigration blamed the new immigrants for the many problems facing the growing cities.

Jacob Riis, a social reformer, wrote *How the Other Half Lives* to describe the terrible living conditions of poor people. He had this to say about one New York City tenement:

> **"Suppose we look into [a tenement] on Cherry Street. . . . Here is a door. Listen! that short hacking cough, that tiny helpless cry–what do they mean? . . . The child is dying of measles. With half a chance it might have lived. But it had none. That dark bedroom killed it."**

Many cities lacked basic public services. Police and fire protection remained inadequate in most cities. Garbage collection was infrequent at best, and city water was often impure. Open sewers, clogged with trash, trickled slowly through the streets. Disease could spread quickly under these conditions.

Improving the cities. Many people were disturbed by books like *How the Other Half Lives* and what they saw around them every day. These people tried to improve urban living conditions. Boards of health made studies and established standards for sewage and garbage disposal. Elaborate systems of pipes and reservoirs brought pure water from distant lakes and rivers. Bit by bit, cities started to improve.

Section 3 Review

• Glossary

IDENTIFY and explain the significance of the following: old immigrants, new immigrants, benevolent societies, Chinese Exclusion Act, Immigration Restriction League, tenements, Jacob Riis

REVIEWING FOR DETAILS

1. Why did many immigrants come to America?
2. How did the U.S. government attempt to limit immigration?

REVIEWING FOR UNDERSTANDING

3. **Geographic Literacy** What were some positive and negative factors for immigrants living in large cities?
4. **Writing Mastery:** *Describing* Write a short story describing the life of a typical immigrant to the United States in the late 1800s.
5. **Critical Thinking:** *Synthesizing Information* How did America live up to the expectations of many immigrants? In what ways was it a disappointment?

Section 4

POLITICAL REFORM AND POPULISM

Multimedia Connections

Explore these related topics and materials on the CD–ROM to enrich your understanding of this section:

Atlas

- Agricultural Regions, 1900

Profiles

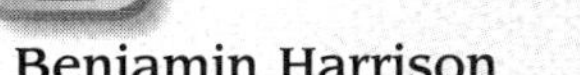

- Benjamin Harrison
- Chester Arthur
- Grover Cleveland
- James Garfield
- William McKinley

Media Bank

- Mark Twain

Putting pencil to paper, an African American farmer addressed those who criticized the new Populist Party. "We don't want to rule the government; we don't want to come into your family," he reassured them. Then he went on to outline a list of supposedly "radical" demands—good wages, equality, a life free of crippling debt. Like many others, he believed that active membership in a new political party could accomplish these goals.

As you read this section you will find out:

- **What issues caused farmers to form a political movement.**
- **How the Populist movement affected government decisions.**
- **What effect the Populist movement had on presidential elections.**

Calls for Political Reform

National, state, and local politics after the Civil War were often characterized by scandal and corruption. Many politicians used their positions to gain wealth for themselves and their friends.

Several scandals developed during the presidency of Ulysses S. Grant, for example. One of the most serious scandals involved Grant's vice president, Schuyler Colfax. Colfax and several members of Congress collected huge sums of money from a railroad company that had greatly overcharged on a government contract. Many critics claimed that the scandal was caused in large part by the well-established spoils system—the practice of awarding civil service (government) jobs to loyal political supporters.

- Civil Service Reform

Throughout the 1880s, the issue of civil service reform increasingly divided national politics. When Republican James A. Garfield was elected president in 1880, many people hoped that reform would soon follow. They were shocked, however, when Garfield was assassinated only a few months after taking office. In 1883 Chester Arthur, Garfield's successor, signed the **Pendleton Civil Service Act**, which established competitive examinations as the basis for awarding some government jobs.

The fight for civil service reform was not over. When Democrat Grover Cleveland won the presidency in 1884, he pushed for further civil service reform. After Cleveland lost the election of 1888, however, his successor, Republican Benjamin Harrison, reversed Cleveland's efforts, and the Republicans appointed many supporters to public office.

Presidential Lives

Grover Cleveland

The Granger Collection, New York

Many Americans referred to Grover Cleveland as "ugly-honest." The term referred to his principles, not his physical appearance. During his long political career, Cleveland acquired a reputation for careful, absolute honesty. The *New York World* convinced many readers to vote for Cleveland with this short list: "1. He is an honest man; 2. He is an honest man; 3. He is an honest man; 4. He is an honest man."

In the harsh world of American politics, Cleveland's honesty sometimes brought him cruel enemies. Quiet and determined, he normally suffered them in silence. A friend glimpsed his true feelings, however, when a stray dog bounded into Cleveland's home in New Jersey. People started to run and shout, assuming that Cleveland would be upset. As his friend ran to get the dog out of the house, Cleveland joked, "No, let him stay. He at least likes me."

Farmers Seek Change

It is not surprising that in the years following the Civil War, many Americans felt ignored by national politicians, who seemed concerned only with their own wealth. Small farmers in particular looked for ways they could have more voice in their government.

In addition, economic conditions in the late 1800s were extremely hard for American farmers. As the number of farms grew, huge amounts of food flooded the market, causing prices to fall. This resulted in serious financial problems for farmers. Many had to borrow money just to keep going; some lost their homes when they could not repay these debts.

In the 1870s many farmers joined the **National Grange** for assistance. The Grange was originally a social club, but it soon became a political organization as well. Branches sprang up all over the country, particularly in the Midwest. The organization founded banks and campaigned for local politicians. It also set up cooperatives, which allowed farmers to buy supplies wholesale and sell directly to stores, thus avoiding costly middlemen.

Granger members also criticized what they saw as the unfair practices of railroads. They believed that freight and storage rates were too high. An angry rural newspaper editor explained:

> **"There are three great crops raised in Nebraska. One is a crop of corn, one is a crop of freight rates, and one is a crop of interest. One is produced by farmers who by sweat and toil farm the land. The other two are**

The Granger Collection, New York

In an increasingly industrial world, the Grangers celebrated the agricultural way of life. They wanted the government to regulate big business to promote a fair and competitive environment.

produced by men who sit in their offices and behind their bank counters and farm the farmers."

Granger leaders demanded government regulation of freight charges. In several states, their efforts led to the passage of laws that helped protect farmers.

The Granger laws led to a debate over whether state governments could regulate businesses like railroads for "the public interest." In the 1877 case of *Munn* v. *Illinois* the Supreme Court ruled that state governments could indeed regulate businesses such as railroads. The Court reasoned that companies that provided broad public services could not be considered completely private.

After a later Supreme Court decision scaled back *Munn* v. *Illinois*, Congress passed the **Interstate Commerce Act** to help farmers. This 1887 law provided that railroad rates must be "reasonable and just." To oversee the affairs of railroads and to hear complaints from shippers, Congress also established the **Interstate Commerce Commission** (ICC), a board of examiners appointed by the president. This was the first of the many modern federal regulatory agencies. However, the ICC had no real power to enforce the regulations it established.

The Money Issue

In addition to criticizing high freight charges, farmers also came together to fight a political battle over the nation's money supply. Before the Civil War, both gold and silver had been minted into coins and used to back bank notes. In 1873, however, Congress voted to stop coining silver. This left only the **gold standard**, a monetary system in which the government backed each dollar with a set amount of gold. The amount of gold in the U.S. Treasury determined the supply of money. The gold standard tended to keep the quantity of money in public circulation fairly low because the supply of gold was limited.

Farmers, however, wanted as much silver coined as possible in order to increase the money supply. They hoped this would create inflation, thus raising the prices for farm products while easing their debt burden. These farmers urged **free coinage**—that is, a law requiring the government to coin silver freely. If this was done, farmers reasoned, there would finally be enough money in circulation.

The Populist Party

Even as they fought for the silver cause, farmers looked for other ways out of their financial hard times. First in Texas, and then elsewhere in the South and Midwest, a new movement, called the **Farmers' Alliance**, was spreading. Like the National Grange before it, the Alliance quickly became an important political force. Its leaders campaigned against high railroad freight rates and high bank interest rates.

Attorney William Jennings Bryan became an outspoken supporter of Populist causes, particularly the coining of silver. Bryan and others felt that poor farmers would never be able to survive in business unless there was more money in circulation.

• William Jennings Bryan

Alliance members also began to run for local and national offices. In 1890 more than 50 Alliance supporters were elected to Congress. Encouraged by these successes, Alliance officials decided to establish a new political party and run a candidate for president. To broaden their appeal, they persuaded labor unions to join them. They named their new organization the People's Party, or **Populist Party**.

In July 1892 the first Populist nominating convention met in Omaha, Nebraska. The delegates adopted a platform that called for government ownership of railroads and the telegraph and telephone network. They also supported a federal income tax and government loans for farmers. To win the support of native-born industrial workers, they called for immigration restrictions and the eight-hour workday. Populists politicians also demanded the "free and unlimited coinage of silver and gold."

The Populists chose James B. Weaver of Iowa, a former Union general, as their candidate for president. Weaver faced Republican President Benjamin Harrison and Democrat Grover Cleveland.

The 1892 election was an exciting one. Though Cleveland won, Weaver received more than 1 million votes, a large number for a third-party candidate. In addition, the Populist Party won many local contests.

The End of an Era

Shortly after the 1892 election, the United States entered perhaps the worst period of economic hard times it had ever experienced in what became known as the Panic of 1893. Business activity slowed, and unemployment dramatically increased. Farmers had trouble selling their products at almost any price. President Cleveland found something to blame for the economic decline—silver.

An election approaches. The money issue continued to play an important role in national politics. As the presidential election of 1896 drew near, the Democrats had to make a difficult decision. The Populist Party was making large gains in several areas by calling for free coinage. If the Democrats again chose Cleveland, who defended the gold standard, they seemed sure to lose.

The Republican Party nominated Ohio governor William McKinley for president. The Republicans' platform was simple—they "opposed . . . the free coinage of silver." This position infuriated farmers. Since many farmers normally voted Republican, Democrats saw a chance to hold on to the presidency.

The money question was the key issue at the Democratic convention. In a formal debate on the topic, former Nebraska congressman William Jennings Bryan gave a speech in support of free coinage. He praised western farmers as "hardy pioneers" who had "made the desert to bloom." He concluded by likening the supporters of the silver standard to Jesus Christ, saying to the defenders of the gold standard: "You shall not crucify mankind upon a cross of gold."

After cheering this "Cross of Gold" speech, the Democrats adopted a platform calling for the free coinage of both silver and gold and nominated the "Great Commoner," Bryan, for the presidency. After much debate the Populists also nominated Bryan. The fact that many Democrats and Populists agreed on several important issues effectively ended the Populist Party. Bryan ran as a Democrat and the Populists ran no other candidate, hoping that Bryan's popularity would carry him to victory.

The election of 1896. The election reflected major shifts in voting patterns. Populists in the South and West solidly voted for Bryan. In the mountain states, where silver mining was important, Bryan won easily. However, thousands of formerly Democratic industrial workers now voted Republican. McKinley had convinced them that free silver would be bad for the economy.

The election was a solid Republican triumph. The electoral vote was 271 for McKinley, 176 for Bryan.

Activist Mary Elizabeth Lease fought for many political causes, but she was best known for her work on behalf of Populists. She wrote about her views in the1895 book The Problem of Civilization Solved.

The Granger Collection, New York

Section 4 Review

• Glossary

IDENTIFY and explain the significance of the following: Pendleton Civil Service Act, National Grange, Interstate Commerce Act, Interstate Commerce Commission, gold standard, free coinage, Farmers' Alliance, Populist Party, William McKinley, William Jennings Bryan

• Time Line

REVIEWING FOR DETAILS

1. Why did people see a need for civil service reform?
2. How did farmers influence government decisions?
3. What role did the Populist movement play in the presidential elections of 1892 and 1896?

REVIEWING FOR UNDERSTANDING

4. **Writing Mastery:** *Persuading* Imagine that you are a farmer living in the late 1800s. Write a letter to your senator explaining the conditions you are currently facing, the need for free silver, and what you feel the government should do to help you.
5. **Critical Thinking:** *Determining Cause and Effect* How did the wide diversity of American voters affect the 1896 election? How might political parties try to appeal to a widely diverse voting public?

AMERICA'S GEOGRAPHY

Immigrants and Cities

The growth of American industry in the late 1800s brought millions of immigrants to the United States. By 1900 huge numbers of immigrants–including Greeks, Italians, Russians, Czechs, Poles, and Hungarians–had begun arriving from southern and eastern Europe. Thousands of Chinese and Japanese immigrants also arrived from Asia.

Most immigrants flocked to America's cities seeking factory jobs and a chance for a new start. Many settled in cities that already had immigrant communities. The largest numbers of immigrants, and the greatest variety, were concentrated in New York City and Chicago. In 1860 Chicago's population was just a little more than 100,000. By 1900 it was nearly 1.7 million. Immigrants accounted for much of this growth. Other major industrial cities that benefited from the growth of their immigrant communities included Philadelphia, Detroit, and Boston.

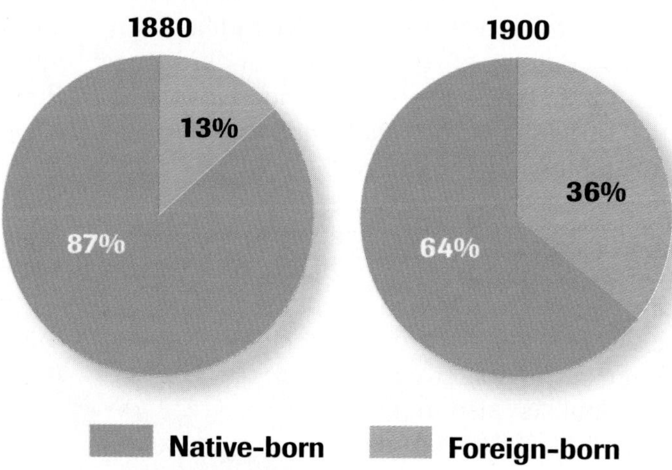

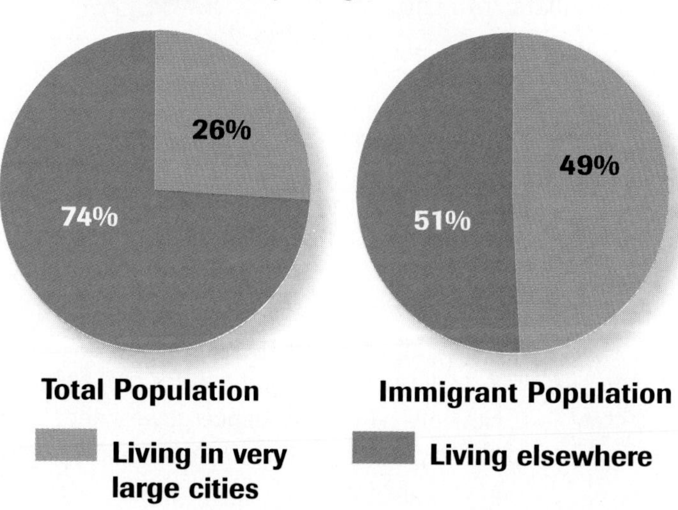

By 1900 around 75 percent of all foreign-born residents of the United States were living in urban areas. Although the majority of Americans still resided in rural areas, few of the new immigrants had enough money to buy land.

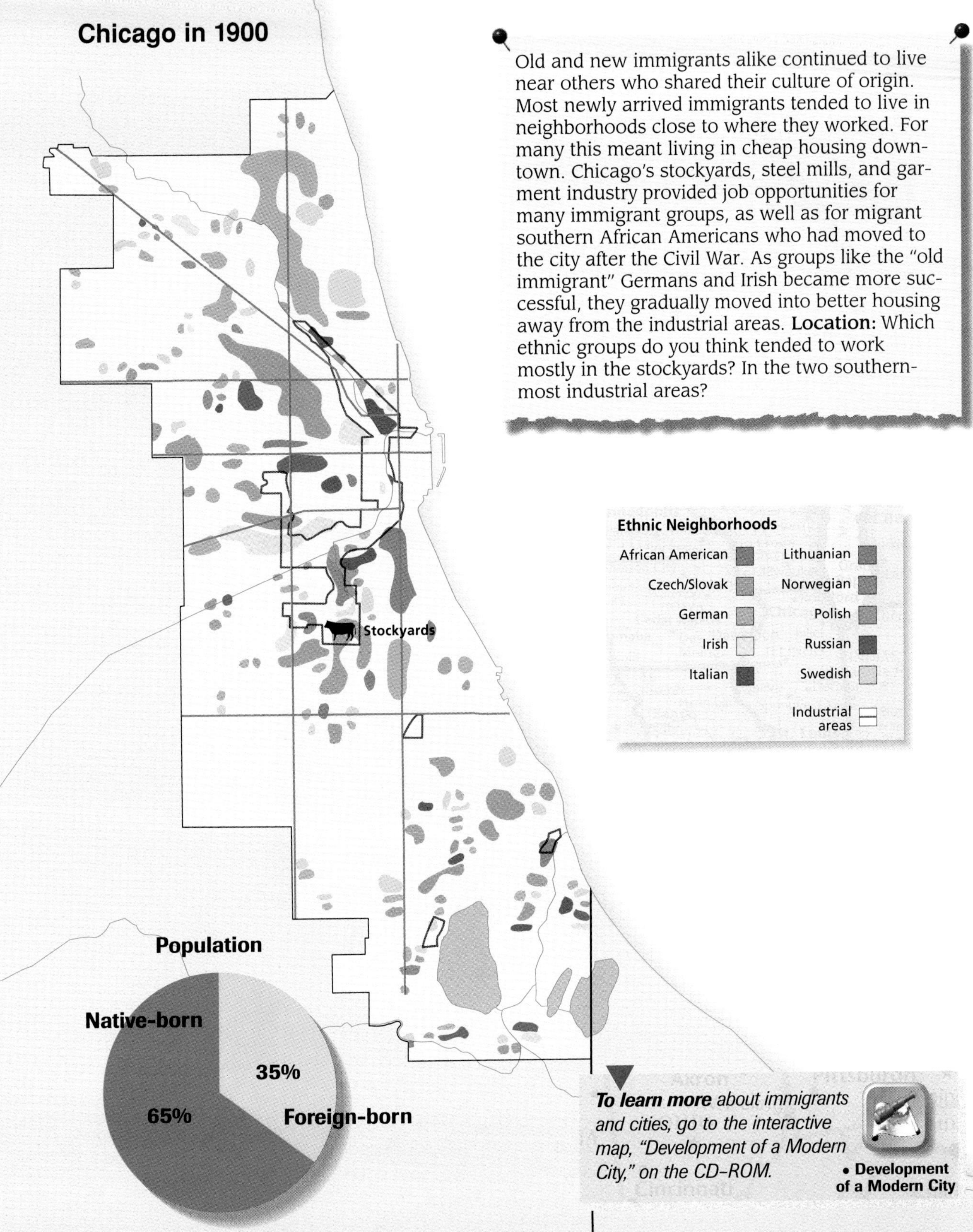

Old and new immigrants alike continued to live near others who shared their culture of origin. Most newly arrived immigrants tended to live in neighborhoods close to where they worked. For many this meant living in cheap housing downtown. Chicago's stockyards, steel mills, and garment industry provided job opportunities for many immigrant groups, as well as for migrant southern African Americans who had moved to the city after the Civil War. As groups like the "old immigrant" Germans and Irish became more successful, they gradually moved into better housing away from the industrial areas. **Location:** Which ethnic groups do you think tended to work mostly in the stockyards? In the two southernmost industrial areas?

To learn more *about immigrants and cities, go to the interactive map, "Development of a Modern City," on the CD-ROM.*

• Development of a Modern City

unit 7

AMERICA BECOMES A WORLD POWER (1865–1920)

Willard Clay/FPG International

The Grand Canyon is one of the most beautiful sights on the American landscape. Reformers in the late 1800s and early 1900s fought to preserve such scenic beauty for future generations.

Section 2
The Progressive Agenda

Multimedia Connections

Explore these related topics and materials on the CD–ROM to enrich your understanding of this section:

Media Bank

- Union Membership, 1864–1921
- Art of the Reform Movement
- Ashcan School Depiction
- Immigrant Workers on Strike
- Louis Brandeis

Profiles

- Louis Brandeis
- Lugenia Burns Hope
- Joseph Mayer Rice

Gazetteer

- Ohio
- Wisconsin
- Oregon

Readings

- Reform Efforts

Glossary

- political machines

Simulation

- The Political Machine

The "army" wound through the streets of Philadelphia. Its soldiers, however, carried no guns. They were children, many under 10 years of age. These child toilers were on their way to see the president of the United States. They wanted to tell him about working in mines and on factory lines, and show him their twisted shoulders and scarred hands. As the protestors moved forward, they wondered if progressives would do something to end "the enslavement of children."

As you read this section you will find out:

- **How progressives worked to improve city life.**
- **How progressives made state governments more democratic.**
- **What legal changes led to improved working conditions in factories.**

Reforming the City

Many progressives concentrated their efforts on reforming the poor living and working conditions that were common to many American cities. Progressive activist Jane Addams described the problems cities faced:

> **"Insanitary housing, poisonous sewage, contaminated water, infant mortality, the spread of contagion [disease], adulterated [contaminated] food, impure milk, smoke-laden air, ill-ventilated factories, dangerous occupations, juvenile crime, unwholesome crowding . . . are the enemies which the modern city must face and overcome would it survive."**

Alarmed and determined to make a difference, progressives soon developed different ways to improve city life.

The fight for better living conditions. Some progressives established community centers called **settlement houses** to help slum-dwellers better their lives. The settlement houses provided day nurseries for children, gymnasiums and social activities for young and old, English classes for immigrants, and many other services.

Perhaps the most famous American settlement house was **Hull House** in Chicago, founded by Jane Addams. The daughter of a wealthy businessman and dedicated abolitionist, Addams had a deep commitment to social reform from a young age. In 1889 she opened Hull House, which served as a model for later settlement houses.

Many of the workers in Hull House were young female college graduates. They lived in the building and tried to become members of the neighborhood. They believed that they could benefit personally and also help others by getting involved in local affairs.

Jane Addams is shown here celebrating the 40th anniversary of Hull House with children from the settlement house. Many people were served by settlement houses throughout the country.

• Jane Addams

Progressives also campaigned for laws to improve the health and housing of poor city-dwellers. In New York City, for example, progressives fought for a stronger tenement house law. One was passed in 1901 that required better plumbing and ventilation in all new tenements. Older buildings had to be remodeled to meet the new standards. During the Progressive Era more than 40 other cities passed similar laws.

The drive for better governments. Progressives also tried to reform city governments, by becoming politicians or by working as reformers. Progressives hoped to destroy the power of the corrupt political machines that controlled many cities. Samuel M. Jones was one notable progressive mayor. He was a Welsh immigrant who grew up poor but eventually made a fortune drilling for oil. Then he became a manufacturer of oil-drilling equipment in Toledo, Ohio.

Jones set out to apply the Golden Rule—"Do unto others as you would have them do unto you"—in his factory. He raised wages and reduced the workday of his employees to eight hours. He offered employees paid vacations and annual bonuses. He created a park and gave picnics for his employees.

In 1897 "Golden Rule" Jones became mayor of Toledo. His election was a victory for honest government. He stressed political independence rather than party loyalty. He established the eight-hour workday for many city employees. He also built playgrounds and provided kindergartens for children.

Other progressives organized reform movements in such cities as Philadelphia, Cleveland, Chicago, and Los Angeles. In San Francisco a newspaper editor named Fremont Older and Rudolph Spreckels, the son of a wealthy sugar manufacturer, led local reformers. Spreckels's family had once held a monopoly on the sugar business.

Samuel "Golden Rule" Jones set a precedent for running an honest city government.

A movement for better utilities. Progressives put pressure on local and state governments to play active roles in solving urban problems. Some city politicians responded with a form of **socialism**, the idea that the government should own all the means of production—the raw materials, factories, and money required to produce goods. Some city leaders took over waterworks that had been privately owned, hoping to lower the cost of water to customers. A few socialist progressives extended this policy to the public ownership of gas and electric companies and streetcar lines. Those progressives who believed in socialist ideas thought the best way to protect the public against high charges and inefficiency was to have their local governments own all public utilities and even some public transportation.

Reforming State Governments

Progressives also worked on the state level. They tried to make state governments more democratic by putting more power in the hands of the people.

Wisconsin sets an example. Many progressives admired the Wisconsin Idea, a set of policies established by Governor Robert M. La Follette. To give voters more control over who ran for public office, La Follette persuaded the legislature to pass a direct primary law. Instead of being chosen by politicians, candidates had to campaign for party nominations in primary elections. The people selected the candidates who would compete in the final election.

La Follette also worked to limit the amount of money candidates for office could spend and to restrict the activities of **lobbyists**, or people hired to influence legislators on behalf of special interests.

La Follette had great faith in the good judgment of the people. He also realized that state governments had to perform many tasks that called for considerable technical knowledge. He therefore created commissions of experts to handle complicated matters such as the determination of tax rates and the regulation of railroads. There were railroad and public utility commissions in many states before 1900, but such organizations spread rapidly during the Progressive Era.

More states enact progressive reforms. Other states copied the Wisconsin Idea to try to expand democratic practices to more people. Many passed direct primary laws. Others authorized important voting practices—the initiative, the referendum, and the recall. The **initiative** enables voters to initiate, or propose, laws. If a certain number of voters in a state sign a petition in favor of a particular proposal, the legislature has to consider it. Under the **referendum**, a legislative proposal is put before the citizens, who vote for or against the measure at a regular election. The **recall** allows voters to remove an elected politician from office before the person's term expires.

Robert M. La Follette's Wisconsin Idea was copied by other state governments across the nation.

Global Connections

The Secret Ballot

One progressive reform—the secret ballot—came to the United States from Australia. Until the 1850s, Australia had used a system of "oral voting." At the public polls, voters would simply call out the name of a candidate, and officials would record it. Many Australians believed this method led to "bribery, a great deal of rioting, and broken heads."

In 1856 the state of South Australia approved a ballot on which voters made a cross in a box beside a particular candidate's name. This ballot later became widespread in the United States. The Australians also developed other ways to ensure voting privacy. They used ballots that contained only candidates' legal names and that listed all of the candidates on one sheet. The Australian government also appointed election officials to hand out the ballots, which further helped to guarantee secrecy in the voting process.

American progressives eventually looked to the Australian secret ballot to decrease corruption and increase democracy. In 1888 Massachusetts became the first state to widely use the secret ballot. Most of the states followed within 10 years.

Amending the Constitution. Another progressive attempt to expand democracy was the **Seventeenth Amendment**. The Constitution had provided that U.S. senators would be elected by members of the state legislatures. However, the Seventeenth Amendment, ratified in 1913, changed the system by providing that the people of a state would elect senators. Supporters of the amendment believed that this would give more political power to the people rather than to the local political machines.

Reforming Society

Progressives were deeply moved by the problems of industrial workers. Many progressives tried to reform working conditions for American laborers by lobbying state legislatures. Progressives also brought cases before state and federal courts to accomplish these goals.

The workplace and workers. A terrible tragedy known as the **Triangle Fire** highlighted the need for workplace reform. In March 1911 a fire broke out in the upper floors of the Triangle Shirtwaist Company factory in New York City. The workers, mostly female immigrants, tried to escape. Many of the exit doors were locked, however, and there had been little preparation for fighting a fire. More than 140 women died in the blaze.

Rose Schneiderman, a local union organizer, blamed the Triangle Fire on greedy employers and an uncaring society:

> **"This is not the first time girls have been burned alive in the city. Each week I must learn of the untimely death of one of my sister workers. Every year thousands of us are maimed. The life of men and women is so cheap and property is so sacred. There are so many of us for one job it matters little if 143 of us are burned to death."**

Despite Schneiderman's fear that the women's "blood" would go unnoticed, the Triangle Fire did lead to reform. New York State responded by passing numerous new factory inspection laws. Other states also approved stronger laws improving the safety of factories. Many states began requiring manufacturers to insure their workers against accidents.

Progressives also fought to change child labor laws. They argued that employing children

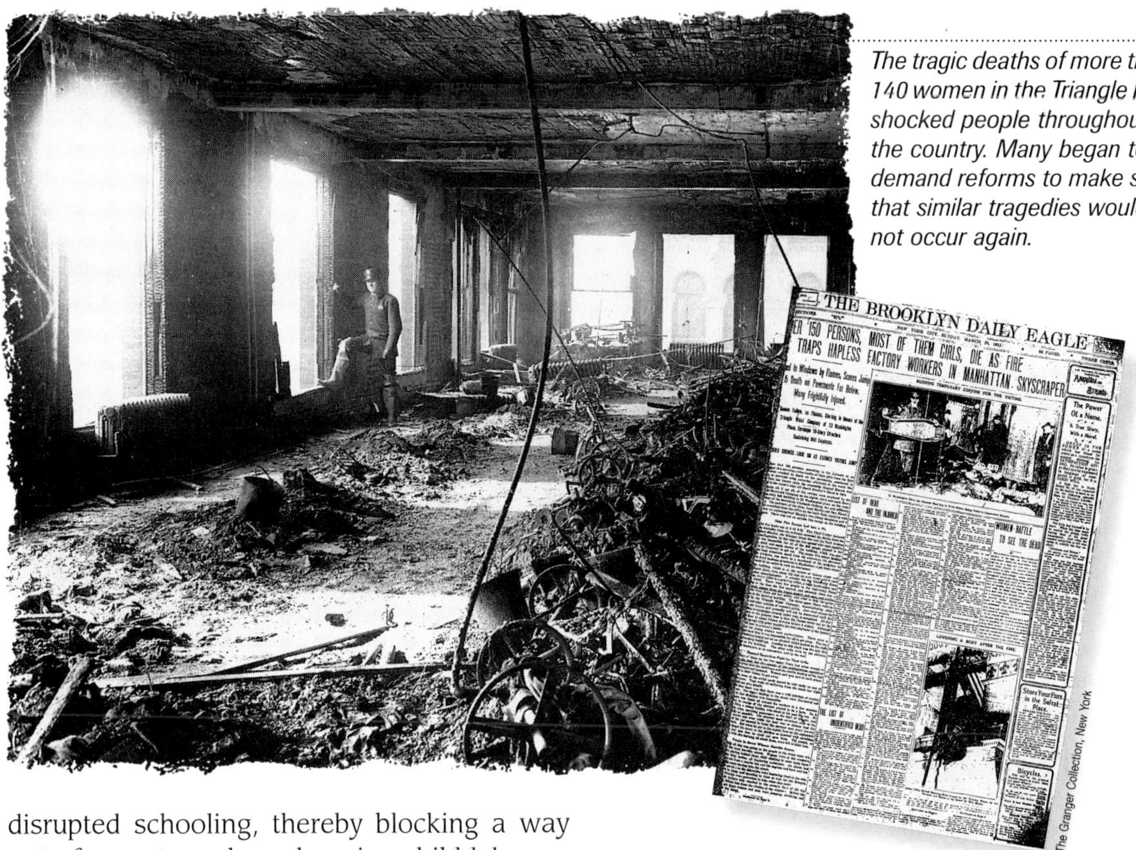
THE BROOKLYN DAILY EAGLE

ER 150 PERSONS, MOST OF THEM GIRLS, DIE AS FIRE TRAPS HAPLESS FACTORY WORKERS IN MANHATTAN SKYSCRAPER

The tragic deaths of more than 140 women in the Triangle Fire shocked people throughout the country. Many began to demand reforms to make sure that similar tragedies would not occur again.

The Granger Collection, New York

disrupted schooling, thereby blocking a way out of poverty and condemning child laborers to a life of often backbreaking work. Urged on by progressives, most states eventually outlawed the employment of young children, but many businesses simply ignored the laws.

A shorter workday. Many states also limited the hours that women, older children, and people in certain dangerous occupations could work. Many employers and some workers claimed that these laws were unconstitutional. They noted that the Fourteenth Amendment says a state may not "deprive any person of life, liberty, or property." Business executives insisted that laws placing restrictions on their operating practices took away their "property." Some employees claimed that such laws deprived them of their "liberty."

Progressives were concerned about the many children who worked instead of going to school, like this West Virginia boy who worked in a coal mine.

Progressives and others who favored reforms responded by stressing the power of the state to protect the public. They argued that laws preventing people from working long hours or under unhealthy conditions protected their families and society in general, not just the workers themselves.

The Court's response. Business owners and employees eventually challenged the new laws in court. Some of these cases went to the U.S. Supreme Court. In the 1905 case of *Lochner* v. *New York,* the Court decided that a New York law limiting bakers to a 10-hour workday was unconstitutional. Such laws represented "meddlesome interferences with the rights of the individual," the justices ruled.

Three years later, however, the Court took a different position. This time the case involved an Oregon law that limited female laundry workers to a 10-hour workday. Louis Brandeis served as the head lawyer for the state of Oregon. He presented a detailed brief, or argument, showing that long workdays injured the health of women and thus damaged the public welfare. Two progressives, Florence Kelley and Josephine Goldmark, did much of the research for this "Brandeis brief."

In the 1908 case *Muller* v. *Oregon,* the Court decided that the law was a proper use of the state's power. Many female laundry workers were also mothers. If working too long injured their health, their children's health might also suffer. Therefore, said the Court, "the physical well-being of woman becomes an object of public interest and care."

This case was particularly important. For the first time the Court paid attention to economic and social statistics, in addition to legal arguments. This changed the way future cases of this type were argued and decided but did not end the controversy about the power of a state to protect its citizens. By the end of the Progressive Era, many more laws had been passed to help workers and the poor.

These women canned olives at a factory in California. Progressives argued that many female workers and their unborn children were put at great risk by the long hours and harsh conditions in some factories.

Section 2 Review

• Glossary

IDENTIFY and explain the significance of the following: Jane Addams, settlement houses, Hull House, Samuel M. Jones, socialism, Robert M. La Follette, lobbyists, initiative, referendum, recall, Seventeenth Amendment, Triangle Fire, Louis Brandeis

REVIEWING FOR DETAILS

1. How did progressives change state governments to make them more democratic?
2. What legal changes improved conditions for industrial workers?

REVIEWING FOR UNDERSTANDING

3. **Geographic Literacy** How did progressives work to improve people's lives in the cities?
4. **Writing Mastery:** *Persuading* Imagine that you are the owner of a New York City garment factory in 1912. Write a letter to the newspaper to justify the working conditions in your factory or to explain how and why you plan to change these working conditions.
5. **Critical Thinking:** *Synthesizing Information* Why do you think progressives had so much success in improving conditions on a local level?

Section 3

The Progressive Presidents

Multimedia Connections

Explore these related topics and materials on the CD–ROM to enrich your understanding of this section:

Atlas
- National Parks

Media Bank
- Bull Moose Party
- Meatpacking Plant

Profiles
- Theodore Roosevelt
- William Howard Taft

The messenger rushed toward Vice President Theodore Roosevelt. "The president appears to be dying," the messenger relayed sadly, "and members of the cabinet . . . think you should lose no time coming." Roosevelt climbed down the mountain and traveled through a terrible thunderstorm. When he finally made it to a railroad station, he was informed that President William McKinley was dead. America had a new president who was a progressive. The nation would never be the same again.

As you read this section you will find out:

- **How Theodore Roosevelt carried out his progressive ideas.**
- **Why Roosevelt ran for president in 1912 as a third-party candidate.**
- **How Woodrow Wilson tried to limit the power of big business.**

Roosevelt Becomes President

Progressives found a colorful ally in the new president, Theodore Roosevelt. He loved hunting, boxing, and writing history books. He also loved politics and had served in many city, state, and national offices.

One newspaper reporter explained why Roosevelt had so much success in politics and life in general:

> **"Roosevelt, more than any man I ever knew, is 'energizing' to the full extent of his capacities. . . . In talking with many people who have met Roosevelt for the first time I have been impressed by their comments upon his 'familiarity.' . . . The marvelous thing in his career is the way in which he has used his commonplace qualities—in every possible direction."**

Presidential Lives

Theodore Roosevelt

The public admired Theodore Roosevelt for his enormous stores of energy. "Get action," he told Americans, and he set a fine example.

As a child, Roosevelt had suffered frequent asthma attacks. He later remembered his father "carrying me in my distress, in my battles for breath, up and down a room all night." After his father advised him to "make your body," Roosevelt began a physical fitness plan and became quite strong.

As president, he loved to go on "obstacle walks," or rough hikes, with important foreign visitors. The French ambassador appeared in formal dress and a silk hat for one such outing. Roosevelt showed up in a "tramping suit" and promptly led the Frenchman across an overgrown field. When they came to a river, the president took off all his clothes "so as not to wet our things in the creek." Shocked but determined to uphold the honor of France, the ambassador removed everything but a pair of purple leather gloves. Then they crossed the river, dressed, and continued their walk.

In 1900 Roosevelt had been elected vice president under William McKinley. When an assassin killed McKinley in 1901, Roosevelt became president.

Roosevelt's approach to the presidency. Roosevelt, whom Americans called "TR" or Teddy, believed that the president should play an active role in politics and society. Early in his presidency he demonstrated his approach to the office.

In 1902 Roosevelt got involved in a national coal strike by forcing mine owners and miners into **arbitration**, or negotiations led by a neutral party. He threatened to take over the mines unless the owners agreed to a settlement. Then he appointed a commission to arbitrate the dispute.

Roosevelt takes on the trusts. Roosevelt soon developed a reputation for being a "trust buster." He accused a railroad organization, the Northern Securities Company, of violating the Sherman Antitrust Act. The Northern Securities Company controlled three railroads, whose lines carried most of the rail traffic between the Midwest and the Pacific Northwest. Roosevelt argued that the combination blocked the natural course of trade and should be broken up. He instructed the attorney general to start legal proceedings against the company.

When the *Northern Securities* case reached the Supreme Court in 1904, the justices ordered the combination dissolved. Roosevelt then brought antitrust suits against such giants as the meatpackers, the tobacco, and the Standard Oil trusts.

Roosevelt did not want to break up all trusts, however. There were, he insisted, "good" trusts and "bad" trusts. "Bad" trusts were those that did nothing for the public good. Roosevelt believed that all large companies had to operate under government regulations.

Roosevelt's other reforms. Roosevelt continued to fight for progressive reforms after he won a second term in 1904. Like many others, he had been horrified by *The Jungle,* Upton Sinclair's novel about conditions in the Chicago stockyards. At Roosevelt's urging,

Progressive President Theodore Roosevelt "tames" the lions of trusts and other unfair business practices.

Congress passed the **Pure Food and Drug Act** of 1906 as well as a meat inspection law. The act provided for federal control of the quality of most foods and drugs. It also called for the regulation of slaughterhouses.

Taft Becomes President

After he completed his second term, Roosevelt used his influence to get the Republican presidential nomination for his secretary of war, William Howard Taft. Taft easily defeated Democrat William Jennings Bryan in the election of 1908.

Taft tried to continue the progressive policies of the Roosevelt administration. He supported a law increasing the powers of the Interstate Commerce Commission. He also continued Roosevelt's policy of attacking "bad" trusts under the Sherman Antitrust Act.

However, Taft also allowed conservative Republicans to influence his policies in many ways. He mismanaged a well-meaning attempt to get Congress to lower the tariffs on manufactured goods, for example.

Taft's actions angered many progressives. Eventually, they persuaded Roosevelt to run for the presidency again in the 1912 election. He sought the Republican nomination, but when the nomination went to Taft, Roosevelt formed a new political organization—the Progressive Party—and secured its nomination. The Democrats selected New Jersey governor Woodrow Wilson. The socialists selected Eugene V. Debs, a labor leader. The election was an exciting one, and Wilson came out on top.

• Presidential Election of 1912

Wilson as President

When he took office, President Wilson first urged Congress to lower the high protective tariff. The resulting **Underwood Tariff** of 1913 decreased tariffs significantly. It provided for an income tax to make up lost revenue. This step was possible because the **Sixteenth Amendment**, a progressive reform that authorized a federal income tax, had just been added to the Constitution.

Wilson next targeted the banking system for improvement. He explained the need for a new structure:

> **"Control of the system of banking . . . which our new laws are to set up must be public, not private, [and] must be vested in [the responsibility of] the Government itself, so that the banks may be the instruments, not the masters, of business and of individual enterprise and initiative."**

Although President Taft supported many progressive policies, he appeared to struggle with issues more than the confident Roosevelt, as this cartoon shows.

In 1913 Congress passed the **Federal Reserve Act**. This law created 12 Federal Reserve banks in different sections of the nation. These were banks for banks, not for businesses or individuals.

The Federal Reserve Board in Washington, D.C., supervised these banks. The board regulated the country's money supply by controlling interest rates. When the board members believed the economy was expanding too rapidly, they encouraged banks to increase the interest rate they charged on loans to businesses. This would discourage borrowing and slow down economic expansion. During depressions or slumps, the Board could lower interest rates so that businesses could borrow money more cheaply. This would encourage businesses to expand.

In practice, the Federal Reserve system often did not work quite so smoothly. It was not always easy to know whether to stimulate the economy or slow it down. However, the system was a great improvement over the old national banking system. It is still an important part the national economy today.

In 1914 Congress passed the **Clayton Antitrust Act**. This law made it illegal for directors of one corporation to be directors of other corporations in the same field. It also stated that labor unions were not to be considered "combinations . . . in restraint of trade under the antitrust laws," meaning that labor unions were legal organizations.

Congress also established the **Federal Trade Commission** in 1914. This commission conducted investigations of large corporations. If the commission found a corporation acting unfairly toward competitors or the public, it issued a "cease and desist order" to stop the corporation's activities.

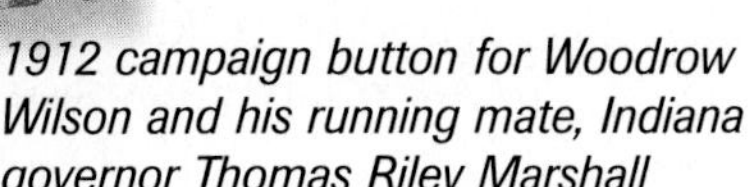

1912 campaign button for Woodrow Wilson and his running mate, Indiana governor Thomas Riley Marshall

• Election of 1912

Section 3 Review

• Glossary

IDENTIFY and explain the significance of the following: Theodore Roosevelt, arbitration, Pure Food and Drug Act, William Howard Taft, Woodrow Wilson, Underwood Tariff, Sixteenth Amendment, Federal Reserve Act, Clayton Antitrust Act, Federal Trade Commission

REVIEWING FOR DETAILS

1. How did Theodore Roosevelt advance progressive ideas?
2. Why did Roosevelt form a third party for the election of 1912?
3. What federal legislation did Woodrow Wilson pass to limit the power of big business?

REVIEWING FOR UNDERSTANDING

4. **Writing Mastery:** *Persuading* Imagine that you are a speech writer for one of the candidates in the 1912 election. Write a short speech convincing people that your candidate deserves to be elected.
5. **Critical Thinking:** *Drawing Conclusions* How might Roosevelt's formation of a third political party have hurt Taft's chances of re-election?

Section 4

Successes and Shortcomings

Multimedia Connections

Explore these related topics and materials on the CD–ROM to enrich your understanding of this section:

Atlas

- Lynchings, 1890–1920

Biographies

- Susan B. Anthony
- Ida B. Wells-Barnett

Media Bank

- Suffragettes Marching
- American Suffragette Parade

Glossary

- suffragette
- suffragist

Profiles

- Booker T. Washington
- Elizabeth Cady Stanton
- W. E. B. Du Bois
- Annie Bidwell

Alice Paul and Lucy Burns sighed with excitement and relief. They had received permission to hold a suffrage parade on the day before Woodrow Wilson's presidential inauguration! They flew into action, hoping the event would persuade Americans to support full voting rights for women. When Wilson rolled into town for his opening ceremonies, he discovered that his "greeters" had gone to see the women's rights parade. Paul and Burns had succeeded. But would women's suffrage triumph as well?

As you read this section you will find out:

- **How women sought more political power.**
- **Why and how prohibition came about.**
- **How some progressives worked for African Americans' rights.**

The Suffrage Movement

Female progressives like Jane Addams played a large part in bringing about many progressive reforms. Even so, male progressives often attempted to limit women's roles and influence in particular organizations and even in the government itself.

Many progressives—some men, but mostly women—hoped to accomplish reform by giving American women the right to vote. They faced powerful opposition. Many people of both sexes agreed with former president Grover Cleveland, who felt women's suffrage would create "social confusion and peril [danger].

Most progressives insisted that women deserved suffrage. "Give the women a Square Deal," they demanded. Some also argued that women would help "purify" the political process if allowed to vote. One female minister,

Reverend Anne Garlin Spencer, wrote:

> **"The instant . . . the State took upon itself any form of educative, charitable, or personally helpful work, it entered the area of distinctive feminine training and power, and therefore became in need of the service of woman."**

In 1890 a group of women founded the **National American Woman Suffrage Association** (NAWSA) to lead the fight for the right to vote. First run by Elizabeth Cady Stanton and then by Susan B. Anthony, the organization worked primarily on the local level. It tried to use progressive reforms like the initiative and referendum to place the suffrage issue before state legislatures and voters. Early on, the NAWSA found little support for its ideas among local politicians.

Carrie Chapman Catt worked out a successful strategy that slowly won support for the women's suffrage movement by working up from the local and state levels.

A dynamic leader named Carrie Chapman Catt helped revive the suffrage group. She had worked for women's rights in her home state of Iowa and became president of the NAWSA in 1900. Catt encouraged suffragists to broaden their base of support by rallying lower-middle-class and poor women to the cause of women's suffrage. Her strategy worked, and many more people began to support suffrage rights for women. By 1912 women had full voting rights in nine states.

A then-radical group of suffragists soon stepped up the call for political equality. They were led by Alice Paul. She had left the NAWSA in 1913 and founded what became the **National Woman's Party**. This group called for a constitutional amendment guaranteeing women's suffrage. Members of the organization used attention-getting techniques such as parades, hunger strikes, and picketing to achieve their goal.

With both the National Woman's Party and the NAWSA working hard for suffrage, the tide slowly turned. In 1918, women had full voting rights in 15 states. The following year Congress passed the **Nineteenth Amendment** to give women voting rights. The amendment was ratified in 1920.

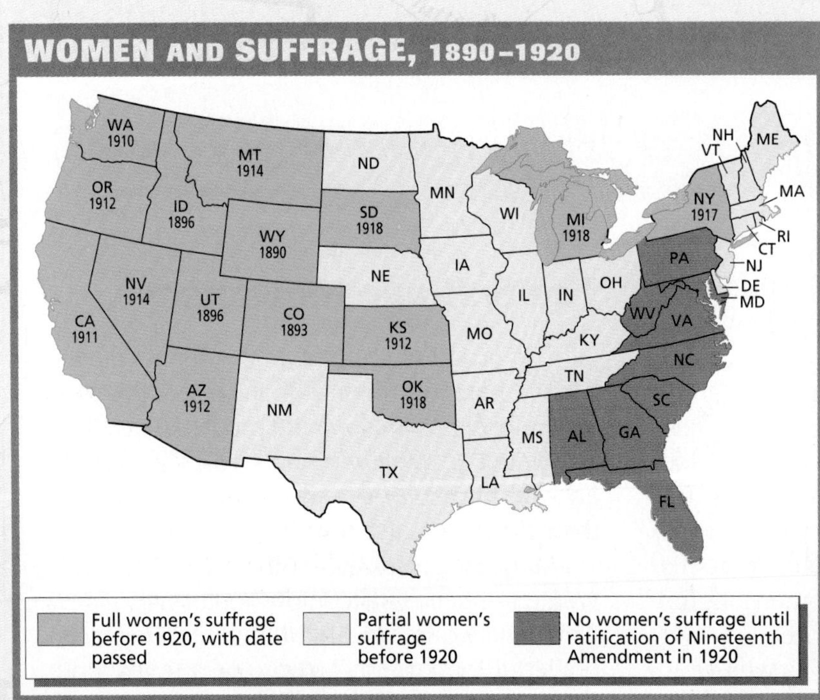

Learning from Maps.
Organizations such as the National American Woman Suffrage Association and the National Woman's Party led a successful battle for women's suffrage.

▶ **Region.** In which region of the United States did women first win full suffrage?

• Maps

The Temperance Movement

Female progressives also played a large role in the temperance movement. Joined by some male progressives, they worked for prohibition, or an end to the manufacture, transportation, and sale of alcoholic beverages. They argued that drinking caused immorality, family troubles, poverty, and social disorder.

Progressives joined organizations to work for prohibition. The **Women's Christian Temperance Union**, begun in 1874 and led by Frances Willard, staged protests against very heavy drinking. The **Anti-Saloon League**, begun by progressives in 1895, urged state legislatures to pass prohibition measures.

Individual reformers, such as Carry Nation, fought for the cause as well. She first supported temperance with public prayer sessions. Then she attacked what she saw as the heart of the problem—saloons. With her ax in hand, she entered bars across the country and chopped beer kegs and liquor bottles to bits.

This temperance poster shows the positive qualities of a life without alcohol.

• Dry States

The prohibition movement gradually gained strength. By 1915 more than a quarter of the states had enacted prohibition laws. These "dry" states, as they were often called, were located mostly in the South and West. In 1919 the states ratified the **Eighteenth Amendment** to make the entire nation dry. The **Volstead Act** gave the government the power to enforce the amendment.

Because they attacked and destroyed supplies of alcoholic beverages, Carry Nation and other temperance leaders were often compared to fierce warriors on a holy crusade.

Progressives and Immigrants

Progressives accomplished many other political, social, and economic reforms. They had prejudices and blind spots, however, that limited their achievements. Most had mixed feelings about immigrants, for example.

Some progressives who felt alarmed about corruption in politics blamed this problem on the immigrants who supported big-city political bosses and machines. Social workers and others who tried to help the poor argued that the country could not absorb so many immigrants so quickly. More generally, many progressives feared that immigrants were destroying the special character of American life.

Some progressives worked to slow or end immigration. Others attempted to assimilate, or absorb and familiarize, immigrants with

American culture and values. These progressives wanted immigrants to be like native-born white Americans.

Some African American leaders, like Harvard-educated W. E. B. Du Bois, argued that greater political freedom was needed to improve life for African Americans. Du Bois expressed many of his ideas in his well-known book The Souls of Black Folk.

Racial Equality in the Progressive Era

The most glaring weakness of the progressive reformers was their attitude toward race relations. Very few progressives believed in racial equality. Most thought that nonwhite racial groups, including Asian Americans and African Americans, deserved second-class citizenship at best. Many progressives shared the attitude of an Alabama reformer who said that African Americans were meant "to be protected by Government, rather than to be the directors of Government."

Clashes over strategy. African American leaders created their own reform agenda during the Progressive Era. Booker T. Washington remained an important figure. He raised a great deal of money for African American schools. He also worked behind the scenes to fight racial discrimination and to help African Americans gain access to political jobs.

Washington believed that the key to African Americans gaining more rights lay in their economic improvement. Washington argument was that African Americans must first learn trades and skills, which would help them hold good jobs and improve their living conditions. Only through economic progress, he insisted, could African Americans seek more political and social equality with whites.

Younger leaders took a different approach to race relations, however. W. E. B. Du Bois was the most important of the new African American figures. He had grown up in Massachusetts and was a brilliant and hardworking student. He won scholarships and eventually earned a doctorate degree in history from Harvard University. Du Bois was proud to be an African American. "Beauty is black," he said. He urged other African Americans to be proud of their African origins and culture.

At first Du Bois admired Washington and supported his policies. Du Bois, however, soon became convinced that more radical action was necessary. Washington "apologizes for injustice," Du Bois wrote in 1903. He argued that African Americans would never get their "reasonable rights" unless they stopped "voluntarily throwing them away." He explained the danger of Washington's approach:

> **"Mr. Washington is especially to be criticized. His doctrine [belief] has tended to make the whites, North and South, shift the burden of the problem to the Negro's**

As head of Tuskegee Institute, Booker T. Washington became one of the best-known African American leaders in the country. He worked tirelessly to promote economic improvement for the African American community.

shoulders and stand aside as critical and rather pessimistic spectators; when in fact the burden belongs to the nation."

Du Bois encouraged all African Americans to speak up for their rights.

African American progressives form organizations. At a 1905 meeting in Niagara Falls, Canada, Du Bois and other African American leaders founded the **Niagara Movement** to work for a variety of issues. They demanded equal economic and educational opportunities, an end to segregation, and protection of voting rights. Four years later, Du Bois joined with Jane Addams and other progressives to form a new organization—the **National Association for the Advancement of Colored People** (NAACP). Du Bois became editor of its journal, *Crisis*. The NAACP attempted to end lynching, or mob murder. Lynching had a long history in the United States. Ku Klux Klan mobs had killed many African Americans since Reconstruction.

After the Civil War lynching became a means of controlling and frightening African Americans. Throughout the Progressive Era about 80 percent of lynch victims were African American. In the 1890s Ida B. Wells-Barnett, a black journalist, studied the records of many lynchings. She found that most of the victims were killed for "no offense, unknown offense, offenses not criminal, misdemeanors, and crimes not capital [those which did not call for the death penalty]."

The NAACP did not succeed in significantly reducing the number of lynchings, which remained high until the early 1920s. Yet the organization grew rapidly both in members and influence. It also won impressive court victories that affected voting rights and housing codes in the South. By the end of the Progressive Era more African Americans started to speak out for their rights.

Though the pace of progressive reform had slowed by the 1920s, progressivism did not come to an end. Indeed, many of the progressives' basic beliefs still influence American life today.

Section 4 Review

• Glossary

• Time Line

IDENTIFY and explain the significance of the following: National American Woman Suffrage Association, Elizabeth Cady Stanton, Susan B. Anthony, Carrie Chapman Catt, Alice Paul, National Woman's Party, Nineteenth Amendment, Women's Christian Temperance Union, Anti-Saloon League, Eighteenth Amendment, Volstead Act, W. E. B. Du Bois, Niagara Movement, National Association for the Advancement of Colored People

REVIEWING FOR DETAILS

1. What methods did women's suffrage organizations use to achieve their goals?
2. What ideas and events led to the passage of the Eighteenth Amendment?
3. In what ways did progressives try to achieve more rights for African Americans?

REVIEWING FOR UNDERSTANDING

4. **Writing Mastery:** *Describing* Imagine that you are a moderator for a debate between Booker T. Washington and W. E. B. Du Bois. Write a brief transcript for a dialogue between the two leaders on the issue of improving rights for African Americans.
5. **Critical Thinking:** *Cause and Effect* How might the success of earlier progressive legislation have influenced the supporters of women's suffrage, prohibition, and equality for African Americans?

CHAPTER 19

The Granger Collection, New York

Involvement in World Affairs (1865–1914)

THEMES IN AMERICAN HISTORY

Economic Development:
What economic influences might lead a country to expand its power?

Global Relations:
What might be some advantages and disadvantages of controlling colonies?

Cultural Diversity:
How might territorial expansion increase cultural diversity?

• Video Opener

• Skill Builder

During the late 1800s, while many European powers were building overseas empires, the United States tended to keep to itself. Some Americans, however, came to believe that the country had a special duty to expand. "We cannot retreat from any soil where Providence [divine guidance] has placed our flag," declared Senator Albert J. Beveridge in 1898. "It is up to us to save that soil for liberty and civilization."

image above: *Spreading America's Wings*

Section 1

EXTENDING AMERICA'S INFLUENCE

Multimedia Connections

Explore these related topics and materials on the CD–ROM to enrich your understanding of this section:

Media Bank

- U.S. Foreign Trade, 1865–1915
- Political Cartoon on Expansion

Gazetteer

- Hawaii
- Alaska

Profiles

- William McKinley

Biographies

- Liliuokalani

Readings

- Viewpoints: Alaska and Hawaii

In March 1893 a ship docked in New York Harbor. Aboard the ship was 17-year-old Princess Kaiulani of the Hawaiian Islands. The princess had recently received news that a group of Americans had overthrown Hawaii's monarchy in a peaceful revolt. She came to New York to plead for her country's right to rule itself. She asked Americans to "refuse to let their flag cover . . . mine." However, the princess could not stop the new voices of expansion that were slowly growing louder in the United States.

As you read this section you will find out:

- **Why the United States did not expand its territory much in the late 1800s.**
- **How the country acquired Alaska.**
- **What events led to the annexation of Hawaii.**

Isolationism and Expansionism

By the 1850s the American people had spread more than 3,000 miles across the North American continent. By the late 1800s, however, the open frontiers on the continent had almost entirely disappeared. What did the closing of the frontier mean to America?

Many powerful European nations, particularly Great Britain, greatly expanded their overseas empires during the late 1800s. For most of this period, American officials called for **isolationism**—keeping out of foreign affairs and halting further expansion of U.S. borders.

By 1900 some people believed that the western frontier was closing because of increasing white settlement. These Americans came to believe that the same manifest destiny that had brought the West into the Union should eventually bring much more of North and South America under the Stars and Stripes. Some argued that this might even include some islands of the Pacific Ocean. This attitude was known as **expansionism**.

Alaska's beautiful scenery and natural resources would come to be highly valued by many Americans, though some originally considered its purchase to be a bad deal.

Anchorage Museum of History and Art

The Purchase of Alaska

One of the few territorial additions to the United States in the late 1800s was Alaska. Americans knew little about Alaska when Secretary of State William H. Seward purchased it from Russia in March 1867 for $7.2 million.

News of the Alaskan purchase surprised almost everyone in the United States. Congress knew little about the negotiations until it was presented with the treaty. To win support for the purchase, Seward launched a nationwide campaign. Alaska's fish, furs, and lumber were very valuable, he claimed. Gaining control of Alaska would increase U.S. influence in the northern Pacific. As Seward explained in one of his speeches:

> **"Alaska has been as yet but imperfectly explored; but enough is known to assure us that it possesses treasures. . . . The entire region of Oregon, Washington Territory, British Columbia, and Alaska seems thus destined to become a shipyard for the supply of all nations."**

Arguments such as these persuaded Congress to approve the deal, even though many Americans thought buying Alaska was a mistake. They called the new territory "Seward's Folly," "Frigidia," and "President Andrew Johnson's Polar Bear Garden."

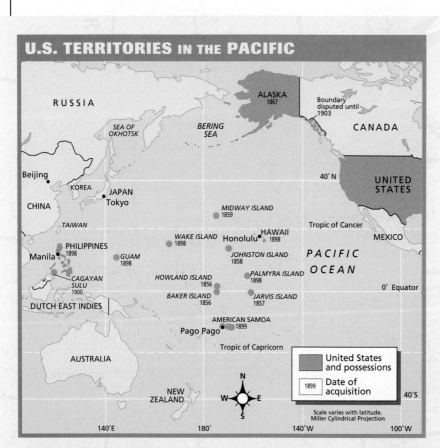

U.S. TERRITORIES IN THE PACIFIC

RUSSIA
SEA OF OKHOTSK
BERING SEA
ALASKA 1867
Boundary disputed until 1903
CANADA
UNITED STATES
Beijing
KOREA
JAPAN
Tokyo
CHINA
TAIWAN
MIDWAY ISLAND 1859
Tropic of Cancer
HAWAII 1898
Honolulu
MEXICO
WAKE ISLAND 1898
PHILIPPINES 1898
Manila
GUAM 1898
JOHNSTON ISLAND 1858
PACIFIC OCEAN
CAGAYAN SULU 1900
HOWLAND ISLAND 1856
PALMYRA ISLAND 1898
0° Equator
BAKER ISLAND 1856
JARVIS ISLAND 1857
DUTCH EAST INDIES
AMERICAN SAMOA 1899
Pago Pago
Tropic of Capricorn
AUSTRALIA
United States and possessions
1899 Date of acquisition
NEW ZEALAND
40°S
40°N
Scale varies with latitude. Miller Cylindrical Projection
140°E
180°
140°W
100°W

Learning from Maps.
In the mid- to late 1800s, the United States acquired many territories in the Pacific.

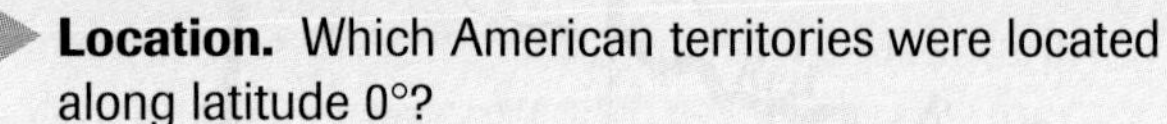

Location. Which American territories were located along latitude 0°?

• **Maps**

Still, Seward made quite a bargain. For about two cents an acre he obtained a region twice the size of Texas. Alaska contained huge amounts of lumber, gold, copper, and other metals. A gold rush in the 1890s brought thousands of eager miners to Alaska. More recently, rich deposits of oil and natural gas have been discovered there.

Hawaii

Some Americans also became interested in the Hawaiian Islands, located in the Pacific about 2,000 miles southwest of San Francisco. The first Americans to reach these beautiful, sunny islands had been New England traders and whalers. Beginning in the late 1700s, they stopped in Hawaii on their lonely Pacific voyages for rest and fresh supplies.

American influence. These sailors were followed by missionaries who came to the islands hoping to convert Hawaiians to Christianity. Most of the missionaries settled down, built houses, and raised various crops. In the mid-1800s the second generation of these American missionary families began to cultivate sugar. By the time of the U.S. Civil War, the missionary families dominated the islands' economy and government.

The Hawaiians were ruled by a monarch. Originally, he or she made all the decisions and owned all the land. As foreign influence increased, however, the power of the monarchy declined as rulers adopted American practices. In 1840 Hawaii established a constitution that drew from parts of the U.S. Constitution.

By the 1870s, however, many Hawaiians were becoming concerned with foreign influence in the islands. King Kalakaua (kah-LAH-KAH-ooh-ah) had close ties to the American sugar planters, and his own government was corrupt. Whenever the king's advisers opposed his decisions, he usually replaced them with foreigners.

In 1875 the United States and Hawaii signed a treaty allowing Hawaiian sugar to enter the United States without payment of a tariff. In exchange, King Kalakaua agreed not to give territory or special privileges in the islands to any other nation.

This treaty greatly stimulated sugar production and further increased U.S. power in the islands. The leading American families formed corporations and imported thousands of low-paid Chinese and Japanese workers to toil on their plantations.

History Makers

Queen Liliuokalani (1838–1917)

For many years former Hawaiian ruler Queen Liliuokalani [li-lee-uh-woh-kuh-LAHN-ee] continued to hope that her country would regain its independence. In 1894 she was placed under house arrest for supporting a counterrevolution. Two years later she traveled to Washington, D.C., to voice her opposition to annexation.

In her later years Queen Liliuokalani became somewhat of a celebrity. The Hawaiian government continued to support her with a generous pension. She lived in Honolulu until her death in 1917. For many Hawaiians she was a symbol of traditional Hawaiian culture. Her autobiography, published in 1898, only increased public fascination with her. So did the many popular songs she wrote, such as "Aloha Oe" (Farewell to Thee).

Between 1875 and 1890 the amount of Hawaiian sugar shipped to the United States increased dramatically. The sugar boom came to a sudden end, however, when Congress passed the **McKinley Tariff** of 1890, a law that, in effect, took away the special advantage of the Hawaiians. The law granted sugar producers in the United States a **subsidy**, or government bonus, of two cents per pound. Prices fell, and the Hawaiian economy suffered.

Courtesy of the Hawaii Agriculture Research Center

Workers labor in the fields of a Hawaiian sugar plantation.

Political disputes. Along with Hawaii's economic crisis came a political crisis. A group of U.S. businessmen formed a secret organization to ensure that the United States eventually annexed Hawaii. In 1887 the group forced King Kalakaua to accept a new constitution that essentially put all the power of the government in American hands.

In 1891 the king died. The new ruler was his sister, Queen Liliuokalani (li-lee-uh-woh-kuh-LAHN-ee). Liliuokalani was fiercely patriotic and resented the influence Americans were having in her country. Her attitude was expressed in the slogan "Hawaii for the Hawaiians." She pleaded:

> **"Americans, . . . hear me for my downtrodden [oppressed] people! Their form of government is as dear to them as yours is precious to you. Quite as warmly as you love your country, so they love theirs."**

The queen was determined to break the power of the foreign-dominated Hawaiian legislature. In January 1893 she announced a new constitution that strengthened the power of the monarchy. In the meantime, the Americans were organizing a revolution.

John L. Stevens, the U.S. minister to Hawaii, ordered 150 U.S. Marines ashore from an American warship in Honolulu Harbor. They did not have to fire a shot to persuade Liliuokalani and her supporters not to resist. With U.S. military support, the revolutionaries promptly raised the American flag. Because of objections to the revolution, however, the United States did not annex the islands until 1898.

Section 1 Review

• Glossary

IDENTIFY and explain the significance of the following: isolationism, expansionism, William H. Seward, McKinley Tariff, subsidy, Queen Liliuokalani

REVIEWING FOR DETAILS

1. Why was there little U.S. territorial expansion in the late 1800s?
2. How did Alaska become part of the United States?
3. How did the United States take control of Hawaii?

REVIEWING FOR UNDERSTANDING

4. **Geographic Literacy** What characteristics made Alaska so appealing to Americans such as William Seward?
5. **Critical Thinking:** *Recognizing Point of View* Why might Queen Liliuokalani have resented American influence in her country?

Section 2
THE SPANISH-AMERICAN WAR

Multimedia Connections
Explore these related topics and materials on the CD–ROM to enrich your understanding of this section:

Profiles
- José Martí
- Joseph Pulitzer
- Lola Rodríguez de Tió

Media Bank
- José Martí
- Yellow Kid
- Female Revolutionary

Readings
- Rough Riders

Gazetteer
- Cuba
- Spain

In January 1898 riots swept Havana, in the Spanish colony of Cuba. To protect U.S. citizens, President William McKinley sent in a battleship, the USS *Maine*. On February 15, while the *Maine* lay at anchor in Havana Harbor, an explosion rocked the ship. Of the 350 men aboard, some 260 were killed. Demands for war against Spain swept across the United States. "Remember the *Maine*!" became a battle cry similar to "Remember the Alamo!" during the Texas Revolution of the 1830s.

As you read this section you will find out:
- **Why Cubans rebelled against Spain.**
- **What led the United States to enter the conflict.**
- **What course the fighting took in the Spanish-American War.**

Cuba and Spain

Cuba was one of the few Spanish colonies that had not rebelled in the early 1800s. It was Spain's last important colonial possession in the Americas. In 1868 a revolution had begun on the island that lasted 10 years. The revolution had failed, but in 1895 Cuban patriots took up arms once again.

With independence as their objective, the rebels engaged in surprise attacks and guerrilla warfare. They burned sugarcane fields, blocked railroads, and ambushed small parties of Spanish soldiers.

The Cuban patriots were inspired by José Martí, a tireless critic of Spanish rule in Cuba. He had been forced out of Cuba in 1879 for opposing colonial rule. Living in exile in New York, he wrote many poems, articles, and speeches that were printed in numerous

American newspapers. In these works, Martí urged other exiled Cubans to return home to support the revolution:

> **"Nations are not founded upon mere hopes in the depths of a man's soul! . . . Down there is our Cuba, smothered in the arms that crush and corrupt it for us! . . . Let us rise up for the true republic, those of us who . . . know how to preserve it."**

When the fighting broke out, Martí returned to Cuba to help but was soon killed. He instantly became a national hero.

In an effort to regain control over the Cuban countryside, the Spanish governor-general, Valeriano Weyler, began herding farmpeople into what were called *reconcentrados*, or concentration camps. He imprisoned several hundred thousand Cubans in these camps. Weyler did this so that Cubans in the camps could not supply the rebels with food and assistance. At least 100,000 Cubans died in the concentration camps. Most were victims of disease and malnutrition.

Swaying Public Opinion

Most people in the United States sympathized with the Cubans' wish to be independent and were horrified by the stories of Spanish cruelty. Encouraged by American support, Cuban revolutionaries established committees called ***juntas*** in the United States to raise money, spread propaganda, and recruit volunteers for the struggle.

This cartoon calls on the United States to save Cuba from the evil ruler Spain.

The Granger Collection, New York

• Fighting Spanish Imperialism

As tension mounted, the publisher of the *New York Journal,* William Randolph Hearst, sent artist Frederic Remington to Cuba to draw pictures of the revolution. Hearst supported the idea of the United States entering a war with Spain on behalf of Cuba. Remington complained that he could find no signs of revolution and asked to be allowed to come home. Hearst telegraphed him:

> **"PLEASE REMAIN. YOU FURNISH THE PICTURES AND I'LL FURNISH THE WAR."**

On February 9, 1898, Hearst published a letter written by the Spanish minister to the United States. The private letter had been intercepted by a Cuban spy. In it the minister insulted President McKinley, calling him "a would-be politician." Americans were outraged by the letter.

Less than one week later the USS *Maine* exploded in Havana Harbor. To this day the cause of the explosion remains a mystery. The Spanish government claimed the disaster was caused by an explosion inside the *Maine.* Many Americans assumed that the Spanish had sunk the ship with a mine, a kind of underwater bomb. Emotions ran high on both sides.

$50,000 REWARD.—WHO DESTROYED THE MAINE?—$50,000 REWARD.

EDITION FOR GREATER NEW YORK

NEW YORK JOURNAL AND ADVERTISER.

NEW YORK, THURSDAY, FEBRUARY 17, 1898.—16 PAGES.

PRICE ONE CENT

DESTRUCTION OF THE WAR SHIP MAINE WAS THE WORK OF AN ENEMY.

$50,000! $50,000 REWARD! For the Detection of the Perpetrator of the Maine Outrage!

Assistant Secretary Roosevelt Convinced the Explosion of the War Ship Was Not an Accident.

The Journal Offers $50,000 Reward for the Conviction of the Criminals Who Sent 258 American Sailors to Their Death. Naval Officers Unanimous That the Ship Was Destroyed on Purpose.

$50,000! $50,000 REWARD! For the Detection of the Perpetrator of the Maine Outrage!

American reporters, like those who wrote for the New York Journal, *helped stir up American anger against Spain after the explosion aboard the USS* Maine.

In the United States, support for war grew. However, President McKinley, a Civil War veteran, wanted to avoid war. He told a friend, "I have been through one war. I have seen the dead piled up, and I do not want to see another." McKinley did not let the sinking of the *Maine* cause an immediate diplomatic break with Spain.

War Is Declared

McKinley was still determined to stop the fighting in Cuba. He believed the Spanish must do away with the concentration camps and negotiate a truce with the Cuban rebels. He also felt that more self-government should be granted to Cuba. After the sinking of the *Maine,* Spain seemed at last willing to take these steps in order to avoid going to war with the United States.

The rebels, however, wanted total independence. The Spanish government did not dare give in completely. Any government that "gave away" Cuba would surely be overthrown. Perhaps the king himself would be deposed. These thoughts made the Spanish stand firmly against Cuban independence.

McKinley finally decided that Spain would never give up control of Cuba voluntarily. On April 11, 1898, the president told Congress that he had "exhausted every effort" to end the "intolerable" situation in Cuba. He then asked Congress to give him the power to secure a stable government on the island.

Congress had been thundering for war for weeks. By huge majorities, Congress passed a

THE SPANISH-AMERICAN WAR IN 1898

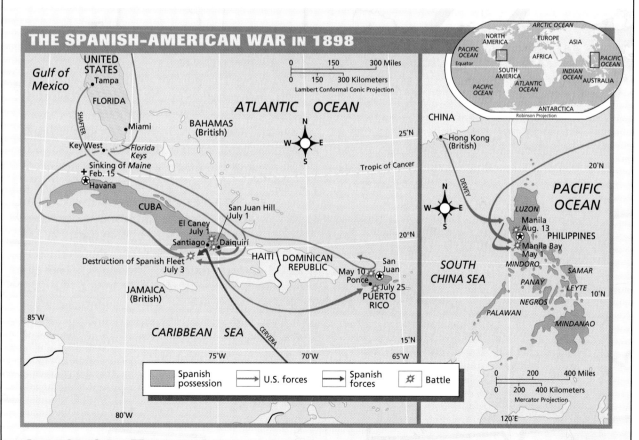

Learning from Maps. Naval warfare and strategy played an important role in the Spanish-American War.

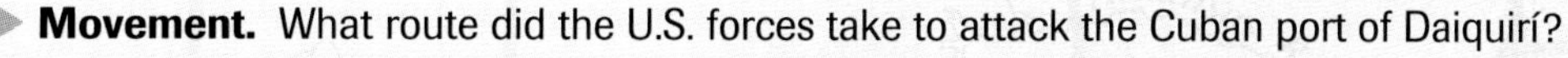

▶ **Movement.** What route did the U.S. forces take to attack the Cuban port of Daiquirí?

• **Maps**

joint resolution stating that the people of Cuba "ought to be free and independent." If the Spanish did not withdraw from the island "at once," the president should use "the entire land and naval forces of the United States" to drive them out.

Congress then tried to protected itself against being accused of going to war for selfish reasons by approving a resolution proposed by Senator Henry M. Teller of Colorado. The **Teller Amendment** stated that the United States had no intention of taking Cuba for itself or trying to control its government. McKinley gave the Spanish government three days to accept his terms or face war. Unwilling to yield, the Spanish broke off relations with the United States.

Battling the Spanish

The two powers did not limit their conflict to the Caribbean. In fact, the first important battle of the Spanish-American War was fought not in Cuba but on the other side of the world in the Spanish-held Philippines.

The Philippines. The United States had a naval squadron led by Commodore George Dewey stationed in Hong Kong. Weeks before war had been declared, Assistant Secretary of the Navy Theodore Roosevelt had ordered Dewey to prepare for battle. As soon as war broke out, Dewey steamed swiftly across the China Sea to the Philippine capital of Manila.

Dewey's fleet entered Manila Bay late on the night of April 30, 1898. Early the next morning, Dewey gave the captain of his flagship the command "You may fire when you are ready, Gridley." The U.S. fleet far outgunned the Spanish warships guarding Manila. By half past noon the Spanish fleet had been smashed, yet not one single American sailor had been killed.

Fighting in Cuba. The war in Cuba did not begin so quickly. President McKinley called for volunteers to fight and received an enthusiastic response. Some 200,000 recruits soon enlisted. Theodore Roosevelt resigned his position as assistant secretary of the navy to organize a regiment to fight in Cuba. He was appointed a lieutenant colonel in the 1st Volunteer Cavalry.

Roosevelt's call for volunteers brought forth many eager applicants. The colorful colonel enlisted several hundred cowboys, several American Indians, some Texas Rangers, lumberjacks, ranchers, hunters, and a number of Harvard and Yale graduates. The chaplain of the regiment was a former football player. The outfit became known as the **Rough Riders**. One observer noted that this odd assortment of soldiers represented, "the character of its founder." Theodore Roosevelt drew on his experience as a Harvard graduate, western adventurer, athlete, and politician to bring the group together. After a brief training period the Rough Riders were ready to fight the Spanish. Before the land invasion of Cuba could begin, however, the Spanish fleet in the Atlantic had to be located and defeated.

The Battle of Manila Bay secured U.S. control of the Spanish Philippine Islands.

The 9th and 10th Colored Cavalry lent support to the Rough Riders as they took San Juan Hill, near the important harbor of Santiago.

The Spanish commander, Admiral Pascual Cervera, tried to avoid the American navy by seeking shelter in the harbor of Santiago, on the southeastern coast of Cuba. By late May an American squadron had discovered this fleet and blockaded the entrance to the harbor.

American strategy called for an attack on Santiago. The U.S. invasion force, commanded by General William R. Shafter, landed first at Daiquirí, a town to the east of Santiago. Once ashore, it began its advance, assisted by Cuban rebels. The U.S. and Cuban forces soon met stiff Spanish resistance. Major battles were fought at El Caney and San Juan Hill. At El Caney a member of the U.S. 2nd Massachusetts regiment reported:

> **"[The Spaniards] are hidden behind rocks, in weeds and in underbrush, and we just simply can't locate them. They are shooting our men all to pieces."**

The Rough Riders and African American soldiers of the 9th and 10th Cavalries took San Juan Hill by storm on July 1. Now U.S. artillery could be moved within range of Santiago Harbor, but the Spanish fleet had sailed. When it did, the powerful American fleet swiftly destroyed every one of the Spanish vessels.

On July 17 the Spanish army commander surrendered Santiago. Less than two weeks later another U.S. force completed the occupation of the Spanish island of Puerto Rico, about 500 miles east of Cuba. Within a month after the battle at Santiago, the remaining Spanish forces in Cuba surrendered. The war was over.

• The United States and Cuba

Section 2 Review

• Glossary

• Gazetteer

IDENTIFY and explain the significance of the following: José Martí, *juntas*, William Randolph Hearst, Teller Amendment, Rough Riders

LOCATE and explain the importance of the following: Philippines, Santiago, El Caney, San Juan Hill

REVIEWING FOR DETAILS

1. Why did Cubans launch a revolution against Spain?
2. What events prompted the United States to enter the war on Cuba's behalf?

REVIEWING FOR UNDERSTANDING

3. **Geographic Literacy** Where did most of the early fighting in the Spanish-American War take place, and why did the fighting occur there?
4. **Writing Mastery:** *Expressing* Imagine that you are a Cuban political writer like José Martí. Write a poem expressing why you feel Cuba should gain its independence.
5. **Critical Thinking:** *Drawing Conclusions* Do you think the news media influenced U.S. entry into the Spanish-American War? Explain you answer.

Section 3

America Expands Further

Multimedia Connections

Explore these related topics and materials on the CD-ROM to enrich your understanding of this section:

Media Bank

- Great White Fleet
- Public Schools in Puerto Rico
- Perry in Japan
- Filipino Patriots

Gazetteer

- Puerto Rico
- Guam
- Japan
- China
- Beijing

Profiles

- Emilio Aguinaldo
- Yung Wing
- Luis Muñoz Marin

At relatively little cost in money and lives, the United States had met its goal of freeing Cuba from Spanish control. But the thrill of victory encouraged some Americans to now create a colonial empire, starting with the Philippines. President McKinley argued that this was necessary "to educate the Filipinos, and uplift them and civilize and Christianize them." The Philippines, however, had already been shaped by centuries of Spanish rule. And the vast majority of Filipinos were already Christians!

As you read this section you will find out:

- **Why some people opposed the treaty that ended the Spanish-American War.**
- **How Filipinos reacted to the treaty.**
- **How the United States expanded its influence in East Asia.**

The Treaty Controversy

In late July 1898, President McKinley sent his peace terms to the Spanish government. At the peace conference the U.S. delegates demanded possession of the Philippines in addition to the islands of Puerto Rico and Guam. The Spanish strongly objected, but finally gave in. To make it easier for them, the United States agreed to pay $20 million for the islands.

Many people in the United States opposed the treaty with Spain. They insisted that **imperialism**—controlling overseas colonies by force—was un-American. Some Americans who opposed U.S. colonization formed the **Anti-Imperialist League** to oppose the proposed treaty. Despite their objections, the Senate approved the treaty.

• Treaty Fight

Fighting in the Philippines

The Filipino people would not agree to American rule. After his victory at Manila Bay, Commodore Dewey had helped the exiled leader of the Filipino patriots, Emilio Aguinaldo, return to the islands. Dewey also encouraged Aguinaldo to resume his fight against Spanish rule. Aguinaldo thus assumed that the United States intended to help liberate his country.

After the Spanish forces had been defeated, Aguinaldo declared the Philippines independent and started drafting a new constitution. When it became clear that the United States was planning to take over the islands, Aguinaldo organized a revolt against U.S. rule. He warned that if U.S. troops invaded, "upon their heads will be all the blood which may be shed."

Bloody jungle fighting broke out as 70,000 U.S. troops were sent to the islands. Many Americans opposed the war. Peace was not fully restored until 1902. By that time, more than 4,000 American troops and at least 200,000 Filipinos had been killed. The revolt was over, but opposition to imperialism was growing in the United States.

Global Connections

Roosevelt and Japan

By 1907 President Theodore Roosevelt had become concerned that Japan, an emerging world power, might be getting too strong. He was particularly worried that the Japanese might try to take control of the Philippines away from the United States. To remind Japan of America's military might, Roosevelt sent a fleet of U.S. naval ships on a 46,000-mile global cruise. All of the ships were painted a brilliant white. When this "Great White Fleet," as it was nicknamed, sailed into a Japanese harbor it sent a stern but silent warning.

Earlier that same year Roosevelt had negotiated a secret "Gentleman's Agreement" to limit informally Japanese immigration to the United States. Roosevelt promised to try to stop discrimination against Japanese Americans if Japan halted immigration to the United States. Both the Gentleman's Agreement and the Great White Fleet sent a message that the United States wanted the Japanese to stay within their present boundaries.

The Open Door Policy

Despite such growing opposition, controlling the Philippines made the United States a power in East Asia. Most importantly, it gave the country a base near China. For many years Great Britain, France, Germany, and Russia had been seizing **spheres of influence**—regions where foreign countries controlled trade and natural resources—in China. If this trend continued, Americans feared that they might not be able to expand their share of the Chinese market.

• Opening of Japan

The Granger Collection, New York

This cartoonist made fun of the American imperialists' appetite for more land, showing President McKinley ready to take their order.

In the 1850s the United States had reacted to the situation by forcing Japan open to U.S. trade and creating its own sphere of influence. The United States, however, was unable to gain such influence in China.

In 1899 Secretary of State John Hay asked the European nations and Japan to agree that all countries should be allowed to trade with China on equal terms. Hay's so-called Open Door note was intended to protect U.S. trade. None of these discussions included the Chinese, whose trade and territory were being carved up. To protest, members of a secret society of Chinese nationalists known as the "Fists of Righteous Harmony," or Boxers, launched an attack on foreigners in the capital city of Beijing (Peking) and in other parts of China.

Armed with swords and spears, the Boxers destroyed foreign property and killed missionaries and businesspeople. Frightened foreigners fled for protection to the buildings that housed their governments' representatives in Beijing. They remained there for weeks, basically prisoners cut off from the outside world.

The Western nations organized an international army to put down this **Boxer Rebellion**. A force that included some 2,500 Americans was rushed to the area. They rescued the trapped foreign civilians and defeated the Boxers.

Snark International/Art Resource, NY

These participants in the Boxer Rebellion opposed foreign interference in China.

Hay feared that the European powers would use the rebellion as an excuse to expand their spheres of influence. He sent off a second Open Door note stating that the United States opposed any further carving up of China by foreign nations. The **Open Door Policy** thus stated that all nations would have equal trade rights in China. None of the European nations officially rejected these principles. American businesses were able to trade freely throughout the Chinese Empire.

Section 3 Review

• Glossary

IDENTIFY and explain the significance of the following: imperialism, Anti-Imperialist League, Emilio Aguinaldo, spheres of influence, John Hay, Boxer Rebellion, Open Door Policy

REVIEWING FOR DETAILS

1. Why did some people in the United States oppose the treaty that ended the Spanish-American War?
2. How did the United States expand its trade in East Asia?

REVIEWING FOR UNDERSTANDING

3. **Geographic Literacy** How might the location of the Philippines have influenced the decision to retain American control of the islands?
4. **Writing Mastery:** *Expressing* Imagine that you are a Filipino shortly after the end of the Spanish-American War. Write a letter to the U.S. president expressing your reaction to the peace treaty.
5. **Critical Thinking:** *Determining the Strength of an Argument.* Was John Hay justified in calling for the Open Door Policy? Why or why not?

Section 4

Policing the Western Hemisphere

Multimedia Connections

Explore these related topics and materials on the CD-ROM to enrich your understanding of this section:

Media Bank

- Fighting Mosquitos in Panama

Atlas

- Panama Canal Zone
- U.S. Interests in Latin America

Profiles

- Francisco "Pancho" Villa

Gazetteer

- Panama
- Dominican Republic
- Veracruz

In 1913 American writer Frederic Haskin described what would become one of the seven wonders of the modern world, thanks to American politics:

> **"Now stretches a man-made canyon across the backbone of the continent; now lies a channel for ships through the barrier; now is found . . . the gate through the West to the East. . . . It is majestic. It is awful. It is the Canal."**

As you read this section you will find out:

- **Why the Panama Canal was built.**
- **How the Roosevelt Corollary and "dollar diplomacy" shaped foreign policy.**
- **What policy Woodrow Wilson followed toward Mexico.**

The Panama Canal

The Spanish-American War increased interest in linking the Atlantic and Pacific Oceans with a canal across Central America. During the war, one U.S. battleship had to steam 12,000 miles from the West Coast around South America in order to get to Cuba. At top speed that voyage took 68 days. A canal would have shortened the trip down to 4,000 miles.

In the 1880s a private French company had obtained the right to build a canal across Panama, which was then part of the Republic of Colombia. The company had spent a fortune but had made little progress and ended up bankrupt. The company then offered to sell to the United States its right to build a canal for $40 million.

In 1903 Secretary of State John Hay and a Colombian representative negotiated a treaty

The Granger Collection, New York

In this cartoon Philippe Bunau-Varilla is shown sparking Colombia to release Panama. The free Republic of Panama then hands over control of the canal zone to President Roosevelt.

in which Colombia would lease a canal zone across Panama to the United States. Colombia would receive $10 million up front and a rent of $250,000 a year.

The U.S. Senate approved this treaty, but the Colombians rejected it. They wanted more money. President Theodore Roosevelt was furious with the Colombians. Roosevelt got word to Philippe Bunau-Varilla, a representative of the now bankrupt French canal company that he would not look unfavorably on a rebellion in Panama. Bunau-Varilla soon led the Panamanians in a revolt against the Colombian government.

When Colombian troops landed at the port of Colón to put down the revolt, they found themselves faced by the guns of the USS *Nashville.* The Colombians were forced to return to their base without firing a shot.

Thus was born the Republic of Panama. Three days later, on November 6, 1903, the U.S. government officially recognized Panama. On November 18, Secretary of State Hay signed a canal treaty with Bunau-Varilla, now the representative of the new nation. The **Hay–Bunau-Varilla Treaty** granted the United States a 10-mile-wide canal zone under the same financial agreement Colombia had turned down. Work on the long-awaited canal could now begin.

From 1906 to 1914, a large force of workers drilled, blasted, dug, and scooped. They had to cut a long channel through mountains of solid rock. To remove the 105 million cubic yards of earth required about 6 million pounds of dynamite each year. Writer Frederic Haskin described how the difficult task progressed:

> **"Here the great barrier of the continental divide resisted to the utmost the attacks of the canal army; here disturbed and outraged Nature conspired with gross [huge] mountain mass to make the defense stronger and stronger. . . . Grim, now, but still confident, the attackers fought on. The mountain was defeated."**

It took many years to dig out the land for the Panama Canal. The task took some 43,000 workers, of which about 6,000 died during the project from disease and accidents.

• Building of the Panama Canal

The Granger Collection, New York

The Granger Collection, New York

President Roosevelt enforces his policy to "speak softly and carry a big stick" in the Caribbean by ordering the U.S. Navy to patrol the area and keep foreigners out.

The **Panama Canal** was finally finished in 1914, a truly magnificent achievement. Some people in the United States and in many Latin Americans, however, believed that Roosevelt had stolen the canal zone away from Colombia. In 1921 Congress gave Colombia $25 million to make up for the loss of Panama.

Involvement in the Americas

The Panama Canal was one of the many ways in which President Roosevelt expanded U.S. involvement throughout the Americas. Roosevelt was particularly interested in keeping European nations from interfering in the domestic affairs of Latin American governments. Increasing numbers of American and European businesspeople looked to Latin America as a source of investment. These investments often took the form of high-risk loans. When these governments did not make their loan payments, European governments sometimes sent in troops to force the countries to pay.

Roosevelt decided that any European interference in nations in the Western Hemisphere violated the Monroe Doctrine. He believed that if a nation in the Western Hemisphere could not pay its debts, then the United States must make it do so. This policy became known as the **Roosevelt Corollary** to the Monroe Doctrine.

Early on, Roosevelt said that he applied the Corollary with great reluctance. Before he sent marines into the Dominican Republic in 1905, he insisted that he had no more desire to make that nation a colony of the United States than a snake would have to swallow a porcupine backward.

After William Howard Taft became president in 1909, the United States began to try to control the nations of the region indirectly. By investing money in countries like Cuba and the Dominican Republic, more stable economies and governments might result. This policy came to be known as "**dollar diplomacy**" since it focused on using economic methods more than military force.

Wilson and Mexico

Even before his election to the presidency in 1912, Woodrow Wilson held strong opinions about how to deal with foreign nations. He reasoned that the United States did not need any more territory since it had no foreign enemies. Wilson also believed that the United States had a duty to help its neighbors.

One of Wilson's first foreign policy challenges came from America's closest neighbor to the south—Mexico. A revolution had begun there in 1910. The **Mexican Revolution** was against the dictator Porfirio Díaz, who had allowed foreign companies to take advantage of his country's resources. The revolution concerned U.S. officials because American investments were threatened by the troubles. Also, many Mexican refugees were crossing the border illegally into the United States.

In 1911 a reform-minded rebel leader, Francisco Madero, forced Díaz to resign and leave Mexico. Madero became president but early in 1913 he was murdered by General Victoriano Huerta, who set up a military dictatorship. President Wilson called Huerta's government "a government of butchers" and refused to recognize him as the official leader of Mexico.

Many Mexicans agreed with President Wilson. A new revolt soon broke out, led by Venustiano Carranza. Wilson asked Huerta to order free elections and to promise not to be a candidate himself. If Huerta agreed, the United States would then try to persuade the Carranza forces to stop fighting.

Supporters of both Huerta and Carranza resented Wilson's interference. If Mexicans agreed to U.S. interference, said an official of the Huerta government, "all the future elections for president would be submitted to the veto of any president of the United States."

In April 1914 a group of U.S. sailors were arrested in Mexico. They were soon released, but their arrest flared into an international incident that further divided the United States and Mexico. Wilson tried to use the incident to overthrow Huerta. He sent a naval force to seize the port of Veracruz.

Wilson expected his "show of force" to lead to the downfall of Huerta. Unfortunately, 19 American sailors and more than 100 Mexicans were killed before Veracruz was captured. Again, Carranza joined his enemy, Huerta, in speaking out against the interference of the United States in Mexican affairs.

Fortunately, a group of ambassadors from the **ABC Powers**—Argentina, Brazil, and Chile—offered to find a peaceful settlement. Wilson eagerly accepted their offer, and the crisis ended. By August Carranza had forced Huerta from power. The United States then withdrew its naval force from Veracruz.

The Pursuit of Pancho Villa

No sooner had Carranza defeated Huerta than one of his own military commanders, Francisco "Pancho" Villa, rebelled against him. Resenting Carranza's criticism of the U.S. policy, Wilson supported Villa. Villa also seemed to be interested in improving the lives of poor Mexicans.

Supporting Pancho Villa soon became a serious

Mexican rebel leader Pancho Villa (third from right) inspects the rifles of his troops. Although the United States supported Villa at first, he soon became the country's sworn enemy.

problem for the Wilson administration. Villa was strongly anti-American, and Carranza's forces were considerably stronger than Villa's. Carranza's troops soon drove the Villistas into the mountains of northern Mexico.

In October 1915 Wilson realized that the best policy for the United States was to let the Mexican people decide for themselves how they wanted to be governed. Thus, he officially recognized the Carranza government.

This decision angered Pancho Villa, who quickly planned his response:

> **"We have decided not to fire a bullet more against Mexicans, our brothers, and to prepare and organize ourselves to attack the Americans in their own dens and make them know that Mexico is a land for the free and a tomb for thrones, crowns, and traitors."**

In January 1916 Villa's forces stopped a train in northern Mexico and killed 18 Americans on board. Then in March, Villa and his men crossed the border and attacked the town of Columbus, New Mexico. They killed 17 more Americans and set the town on fire.

President Wilson then ordered troops under General John J. Pershing to capture Villa. This meant invading Mexico. Pershing's men pursued Villa vigorously, but they could not catch him on his home ground. This U.S. interference again angered Carranza. Wilson finally called off the invasion in 1917, the same year Carranza introduced a new national constitution for Mexico.

The Granger Collection, New York

General John J. "Black Jack" Pershing leads American troops into Mexico to try to capture Pancho Villa. The pursuit turned out to be both a military and political failure.

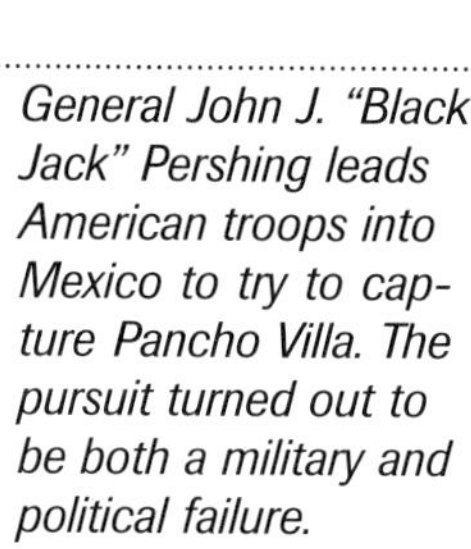

Section 4 Review

• Glossary

• Time Line

IDENTIFY and explain the significance of the following: Hay-Bunau-Varilla Treaty, Panama Canal, Roosevelt Corollary, dollar diplomacy, Mexican Revolution, Victoriano Huerta, Venustiano Carranza, ABC Powers, Pancho Villa

REVIEWING FOR DETAILS

1. How did the Roosevelt Corollary and dollar diplomacy influence U.S. foreign policy?
2. How did President Wilson respond to the Mexican Revolution?

REVIEWING FOR UNDERSTANDING

3. **Geographic Literacy** Why would the construction of a canal across Panama be a benefit to the United States?
4. **Writing Mastery:** *Persuading* Imagine that you are a member of Woodrow Wilson's cabinet. Write a memo to Wilson explaining why the United States should or should not get involved in Mexican affairs.
5. **Critical Thinking:** *Making Comparisons* How did the role of the United States in the revolution in Panama differ from its role in the Mexican Revolution?

Imperialism

The rapid industrialization that occurred during the late 1800s and early 1900s was closely tied to imperialism. As their industries expanded, the United States and other industrial nations hoped to dominate foreign regions to gain sources of raw materials and new markets for their products. The resource-rich continent of Africa was quickly taken over by European nations looking to build overseas empires. By 1914 Liberia, the country founded by American abolitionists, and Ethiopia stood alone as the only independent nations left on the continent.

Although the United States possessed few overseas colonies, it invested millions of dollars in overseas business ventures and trade. Likewise, European countries continued to invest in businesses in North and South America. The Monroe Doctrine helped prevent Europeans from trying to build new colonies in the Americas, but it did not prevent them from investing money there. With such economic influence often came political influence over foreign governments.

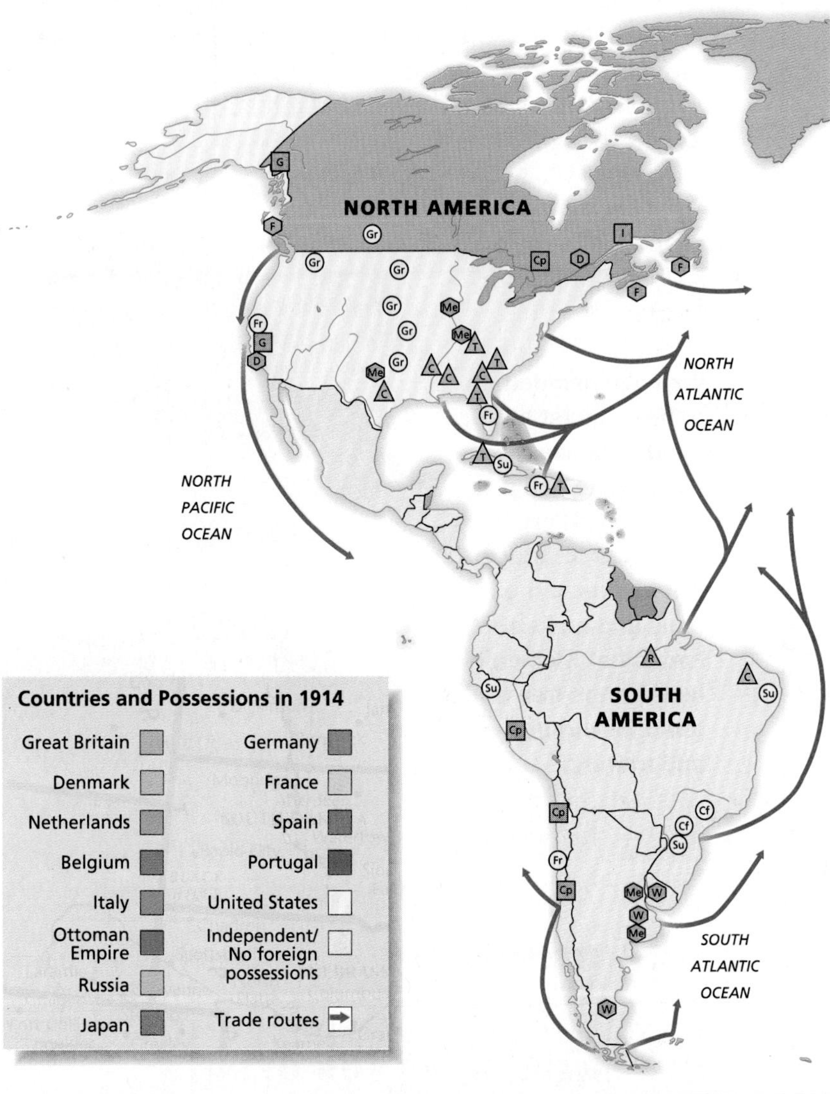

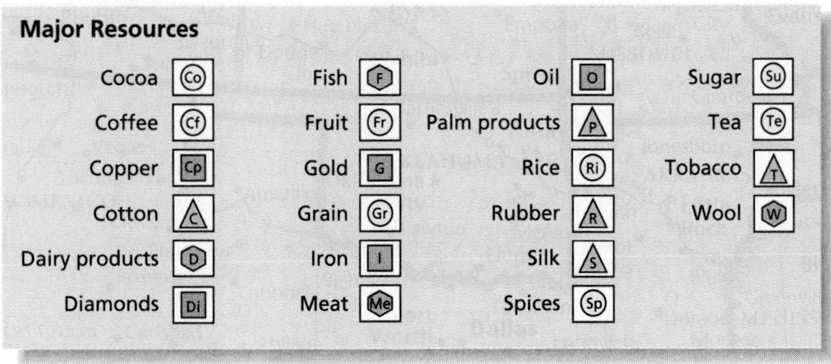

Global Possessions in 1914

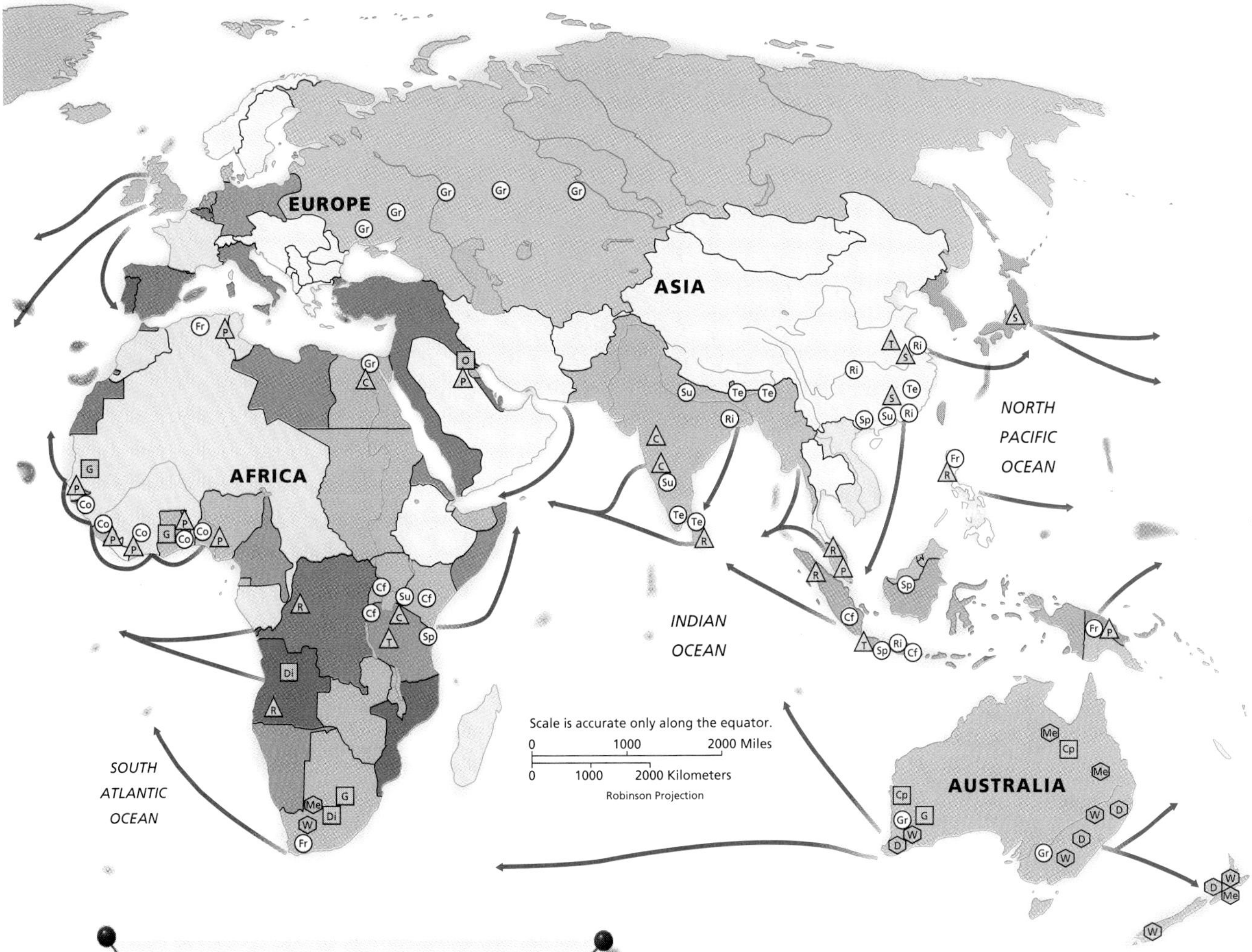

EUROPE
ASIA
AFRICA
AUSTRALIA
NORTH PACIFIC OCEAN
INDIAN OCEAN
SOUTH ATLANTIC OCEAN

Scale is accurate only along the equator.
0 1000 2000 Miles
0 1000 2000 Kilometers
Robinson Projection

The United States benefited greatly from the resources of its colonies and areas of financial investment. For example, its major possession in Asia—the Philippine Islands—was rich in rubber used to supply U.S. industries. Financially, the United States focused its attention on Latin America, as U.S. businesses invested more money in South America than in any other continent. **Region:** What were the three major resources of South America? What other areas had these same resources?

To learn more *about imperialism, go to the interactive map, "U.S. Imperialism in Latin America," on the CD-ROM.*

• **U.S. Imperialism in Latin America**

EPILOGUE

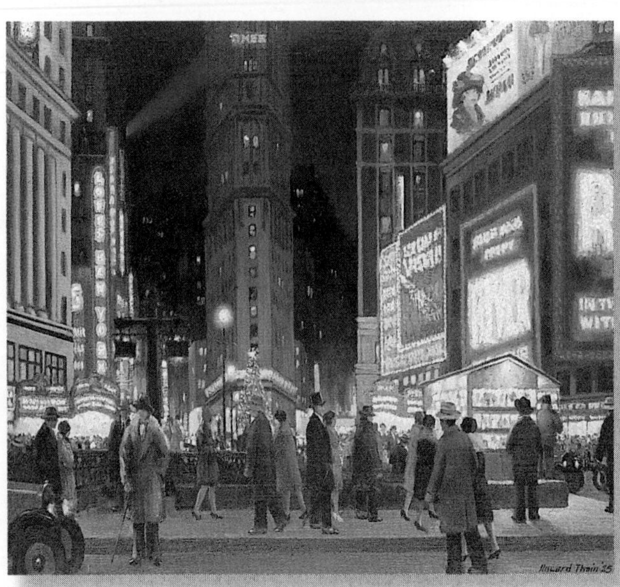

Modern America
(1914–Present)

THEMES IN AMERICAN HISTORY

Economic Development:
What might a government do to help economic growth?

Democratic Values:
How might democratic values shape a country's foreign policy?

Global Relations:
Why might a country be drawn into an international conflict when its safety is not directly threatened?

• Video Opener

• Skill Builder

The 20th century has been a time of great changes in America. The United States became involved in several foreign wars and faced new domestic challenges. After Bill Clinton was sworn in as president in 1993, he said, "As we stand at the edge of the 21st century, let us begin anew with energy and hope, with faith and discipline." As Americans reflected on their past, they looked forward to the new century.

image above: *Howard Thain's* The Great White Way

Section 1
America at War and at Peace

Multimedia Connections

Explore these related topics and materials on the CD–ROM to enrich your understanding of this section:

Media Bank
- Jazz Age Music
- Personal Income, 1929–1941
- Unemployment, 1929–1941
- Events of WWI
- American Troops in Europe
- Hooverville
- Radio Show
- Second New Deal

Atlas
- Convoy System
- Trench Warfare

Readings
- *The Grapes of Wrath*
- Life in the Trenches
- World War I Aviators
- The Lost Generation
- Wilson's Fourteen Points

Profiles
- Henry Ford
- Franklin D. Roosevelt
- John Pershing
- Jeannette Rankin
- George "Babe" Ruth
- Woodrow Wilson

Biographies
- Bernard Baruch

Although a long and bloody conflict, World War I finally came to an end in late 1918. This was the first true "world" war, because the United States and most of the major European nations were involved. Americans hoped that this would be "the war to end all wars." For a short time, that seemed a possibility. The 1920s brought many people peace and prosperity. However, the 1930s ushered in a worldwide depression and enormous suffering.

As you read this section you will find out:

- **Why World War I erupted, and how the United States became involved.**
- **What life was like in the United States during the 1920s.**
- **How Americans coped with the economic depression in the 1930s.**

World War I Begins in Europe

In the early 1900s, southeastern Europe was a political powder keg that was ready to be ignited by any incident. Nationalism, or a strong sense of loyalty to one's country or culture, had gained strength across the continent. Many Europeans united with others who shared the same language or customs. During the late 1800s, nationalism had brought together the many German-speaking states to form both the German and the Austro-Hungarian empires. At the same time, nationalism was uniting the Slavic peoples of eastern Europe in their desire to break free of Austrian rule.

Another factor in the growing tensions in Europe was the rise of **militarism**—the idea that a prepared and aggressive military force was a good solution to international crises. Wilhelm II, Germany's kaiser, or emperor, wanted to make Germany the strongest nation in Europe. He believed the best way to do this was through strengthening Germany's military. Other European nations expanded their military power as well.

Various European governments also joined together in alliances, agreeing to help their allies should any one of them come under an attack. For example, Germany, Austria-Hungary, and Italy formed one alliance, and in response, Great Britain, France, and Russia created another.

Nationalism, militarism, and the alliance system set the stage for war. When war finally broke out, it erupted on a worldwide scale. On June 28, 1914, Archduke Franz Ferdinand, the heir to the Austrian throne, and his wife were visiting the Bosnian city of Sarajevo (sahr-uh-YAY-voh). A terrorist from the neighboring country of Serbia, motivated by Slavic nationalism, emerged from a crowd of onlookers and shot the archduke and his wife to death. The incident eventually brought all the major nations of Europe into war.

By August 1914 the Central Powers—Germany, Austria-Hungary, and their allies, Bulgaria and the Ottoman Empire—were at war with the Allied Powers—Great Britain, France, Russia, and their allies.

At first, it seemed that the war might end quickly. The German army rolled across Belgium into France, crushing everything in its path. Then French and British troops stopped the German advance in northeastern France. Neither side advanced more than a few yards for months at a time.

To protect themselves from flying bullets and artillery shells, soldiers from both sides dug a vast network of trenches that stretched from northern France to Switzerland. When the soldiers finally crawled out of the trenches to attack the enemy, the slaughter was terrible. Rows of barbed wire entangled the men, while poisoned gas and machine guns killed or wounded thousands.

The Granger Collection, New York

French troops march through the muddy trenches in World War I.

America Enters the War

Americans were horrified that Europeans went to war without first trying to settle their differences peacefully. Most Americans believed that the United States should practice neutrality. President Woodrow Wilson declared that all Americans should "act and speak in the true spirit of neutrality" by demonstrating "fairness and friendliness" toward all the warring nations. For many Americans, however, it become increasingly hard to remain neutral. The war made it difficult for U.S. ships to continue trading with Europe. Both sides refused to accept America's view of neutrality.

The situation grew more tense when a German submarine torpedoed the British passenger liner *Lusitania* in May 1915. Among the 1,200 passengers killed were 128 Americans. Then in March 1916, a German submarine attacked the *Sussex,* another vessel with Americans on board. President Wilson warned the German military to stop these attacks. The German government agreed to the ***Sussex* pledge**, a promise to stop attacking unarmed ships. When the Germans broke the agreement less than a year later, the United States declared war on Germany.

The home front. Wilson tried to convince Americans that the war was for a good cause. He told them that the United States had a responsibility to restore democracy and freedom to Europe. "The world," said Wilson, "must be made safe for democracy."

In America, millions of men, women, and children worked together to supply the U.S. troops. The president created the **War Industries Board** to make sure factories produced what the nation needed during wartime and the **Food Administration** to encourage Americans to produce enough food for themselves, the troops, and the Allies.

The war brought an increased need for factory workers. To help fill the new positions, some 1.5 million women entered the workforce. About 500,000 African Americans and thousands of Mexican Americans flocked to northern cities to work in factories.

The battlefront. By the time American soldiers arrived in France in the summer of 1917, British, French, and Russian troops had been fighting the Germans for nearly three years. "Doughboys," or U.S. soldiers, were shocked at the terrible conditions in the trenches. One soldier, Norman Roberts, described the fear he and others faced:

> **"Oh, what a morning. Machine gun bullets flying past you as the wind. . . . Dead and wounded all around you. Comrades falling**

WORLD WAR I IN EUROPE, 1914–1917

Allied Powers, 1916
Central Powers, 1916
Neutral countries
Allied Powers forces
Central Powers forces
British naval blockade
Farthest Russian advance (1914)
Farthest Central Powers advance
Trench line, western front
Battle
German submarine activity

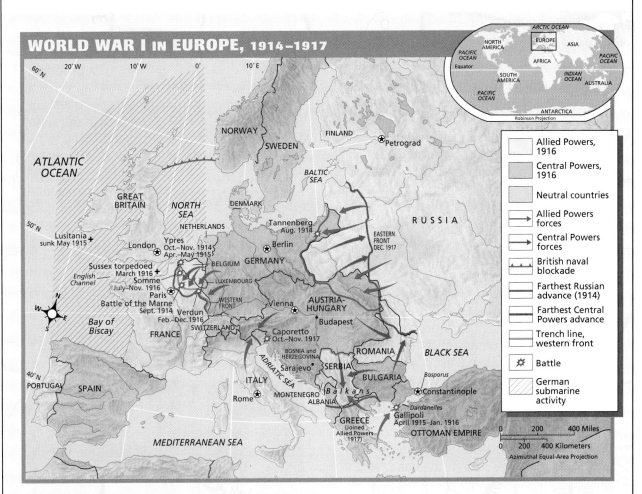

Learning from Maps. The British established a naval blockade that stretched from Spain into the Atlantic Ocean north of Great Britain. The British hoped their blockade would cut off Germany from the supplies it needed to continue the war.

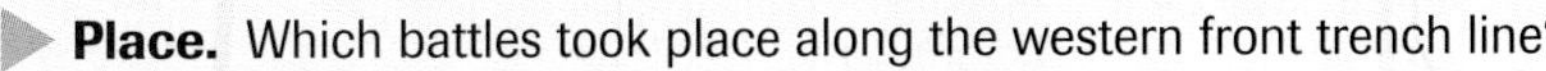

▶ **Place.** Which battles took place along the western front trench line?

• **Maps**

Collection Claus Bergen, Bergen, Germany, Photograph by Erich Lessing/Art Resource, NY

German U-boats like this one, the U 53, attacked many merchant ships during World War I. Here the U 53 attacks a British ship.

directly in front and you not allowed to assist them. . . . Every minute looking for the next to be gone to the great beyond."

After a year and a half more of bloody fighting, the United States and the Allies finally defeated the Central Powers. On November 11, 1918, Germany signed an **armistice**, or agreement, to stop fighting. Peace had come at last, but at a terribly high price. Millions of soldiers and civilians had been killed, and much of Europe's countryside was destroyed. Although it entered the war late, America lost some 112,000 soldiers with more than 200,000 others wounded.

After the war, the victorious Allies met at the French palace of Versailles to work out a peace treaty. President Wilson had proposed Fourteen Points he felt were necessary to build a lasting peace. The last of these points was the establishment of a League of Nations to help resolve international disputes. Some of Wilson's Fourteen Points, including the creation of the League, were incorporated into the Treaty of Versailles. Republicans in the U.S. Senate, worried that the League would require the United States to commit troops to foreign conflicts without congressional consent, refused to approve the treaty.

The 1920s: A Decade of Change

When World War I ended, Americans celebrated their role in restoring peace to Europe. Americans soon faced serious problems at home, however. With the war over, factories cut back on production. Many of the more than 4 million U.S. soldiers returning to civilian life had difficulty finding employment. In addition, millions of women and minority workers lost their jobs. Workers protested layoffs and pay cuts by holding strikes.

After the war, many Americans feared that **Communists** were trying to destroy the U.S. government and economy. Communists, also called "Reds," believed that workers should own the factories and that all citizens should share society's wealth equally. Because Communists claimed that workers should take control by force, many Americans felt threatened. A **Red Scare** swept the country. Anyone suspected of being disloyal to the government was harassed, jailed, or deported.

Politics in the 1920s. The presidential election of 1920 was the first national election in which women could vote. During the 1920s, Americans elected several conservative Republicans to the presidency. These presidents

These women went to work in a munitions factory in Detroit, Michigan, to help with the war effort. War industries helped boost the economy and provide jobs for many people who previously had trouble finding employment.

enacted policies that favored the strong growth of business and industry. President Calvin Coolidge, for example, believed that the government's priority should be helping business grow and prosper. "The business of America is business," Coolidge said.

A booming economy. The U.S. economy boomed during the 1920s. Factories turned out all kinds of new products, from household appliances to construction equipment. Because factories were expanding production, most Americans found jobs. This gave them more money to buy new products, so factories increased output further in a cycle of prosperity and growth.

Advertising also helped stimulate the economy. Advertisers created images of success, popularity, and glamour to sell their goods. Those who could not pay cash could purchase products on the **installment plan**, which allowed customers to pay the amount, plus interest, over time.

A nation on wheels. Of all the new products available, the automobile had the greatest impact on America. The first gasoline-powered vehicles in the United States were built in the 1890s but had been mere toys for the wealthy. Then in the early 1900s an inventor named Henry Ford opened a factory that made cars affordable for many Americans. "I will build a motor car for the great multitude," said Ford—and he did. Ford reduced the cost of his Model T, or "Tin Lizzie," to $290 by using an **assembly line**, a system in which workers stand in one place, adding one or two parts to a product as it passes by on a conveyor belt.

The automobile quickly became a major force in shaping the American economy. As the auto industry boomed, it stimulated other industries, such as steel, glass, rubber, and oil. By the end of the decade, 25 percent of American jobs were in either the auto industry or one of its related industries.

The Roaring Twenties. The 1920s also brought great cultural change in the United States. Movies and radio became very important to American culture. Americans began to dress, talk, and act like their favorite movie stars. A drop in price allowed most American families to own radios, which brought information, entertainment, and advertising directly into people's homes.

The Granger Collection, New York

By 1921 this Model T had already been around for more than 10 years. Many Americans were eager to try out a different type of automobile.

Radio also allowed Americans to "attend" sporting events without actually being there. This helped make sports one of the country's favorite pastimes and turned sports figures into national heroes. Radio introduced the country to important changes taking place in music. **Jazz**, a new type of music that grew from African American blues and ragtime, became very popular among young people.

American literature also flourished during the 1920s. "Lost Generation" writers, such as Ernest Hemingway, criticized what they considered the public's shallow search for happiness through money and possessions. One such writer, Malcolm Cowley, complained that "life in [the United States] is joyless and colorless" and "given over to the worship of wealth and machinery." African American writers and artists participated in a movement known as the **Harlem Renaissance**. It celebrated the rich heritage and many contributions African Americans had made to American society.

Blues singer Bessie Smith and jazz great Louis Armstrong

Conflicts of the 1920s. Despite the general prosperity of the 1920s, Americans disagreed strongly on certain issues, including immigration and moral values. Congress passed laws restricting the number of immigrants allowed into the United States. During the 1920s, the membership of the Ku Klux Klan grew, and the group began attacking immigrants as well as African Americans.

Crime increased as bootleggers smuggled alcohol into the country, violating prohibition, which had outlawed the production, sale, and transportation of alcohol. Americans also broke the law by drinking liquor at home or in "speakeasies"—secret clubs that served alcohol. Armed with guns, gangsters and criminal gangs fought for territory and control of this illegal market until the Twenty-first Amendment repealed prohibition.

Science and religion clashed in the 1925 trial of school teacher John T. Scopes. Many Americans followed the trial as arguments addressed the issue of whether schoolchildren should be taught the Biblical story of creation or the theory of natural selection.

The Dawn of the Great Depression

In 1928 Americans elected Republican Herbert Hoover president. Riding high on the prosperity of the 1920s, Hoover was hopeful about the country's future. "We in America today . . . ," said Hoover, "shall soon . . . be in sight of the day when poverty will be banished [driven] from this nation." In less than a year, however, the stock market collapsed, and the United States and the entire world were plunged into a decade of tremendous economic suffering.

The crash. Americans wondered why the prosperous 1920s had ended in such disaster. Throughout the 1920s, there had been serious economic problems. Although the auto industry boomed, several other industries slowed down, throwing millions of Americans out of work. In addition, the great wealth generated during the decade had been unevenly distributed. While the richest Americans grew richer,

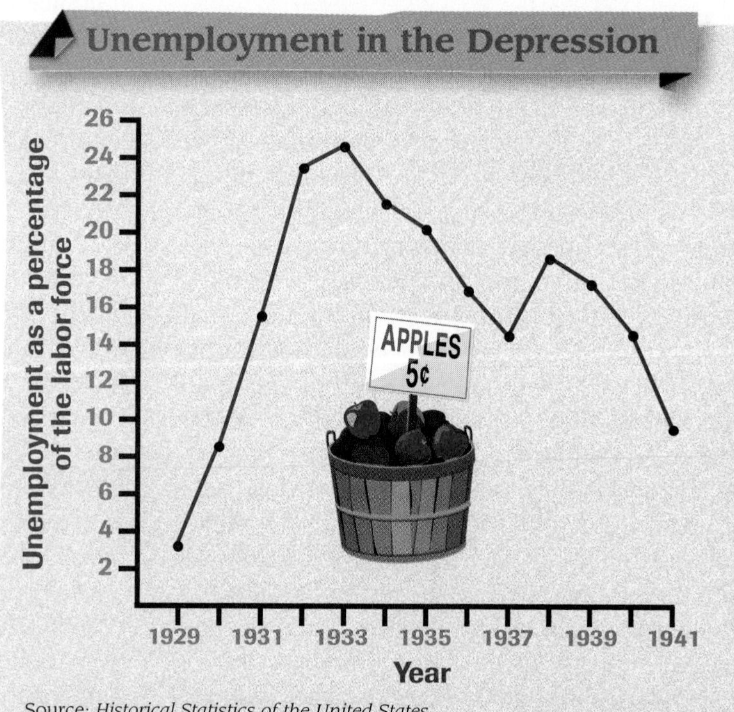

Source: *Historical Statistics of the United States*

Jobless Americans. At the peak of the depression, more than 12 million Americans were unemployed. During what year was unemployment highest?

most Americans stayed about the same or went into deeper debt.

Perhaps the most serious problem, however, was the widespread speculation, or risky investment, in stocks, which investors hoped would increase in value. By late 1929, many realized they had paid too much for their stocks. When they started to sell their investments, other investors panicked. On October 29, known as "Black Tuesday," investors sold off their stocks in record numbers. As more and more people got rid of their holdings, stock prices began a rapid downward spiral.

When the stock market crashed, the economy began to collapse. Many banks failed because of their loans to speculators. Fearing they might lose their savings, millions of Americans withdrew their money from the banks. More banks, as well as factories and businesses across the country, were forced to close. From 1932 to 1935, more than 20 percent of American workers were unemployed. Americans and people around the world were feeling the full impact of what came to be known as the **Great Depression**.

Hoover responds to the depression. Hoover tried to help the economy by urging Congress to lower taxes and create jobs through **public works** projects, such as road or bridge construction. He also supported some federal assistance to banks and large corporations. Hoover believed the companies could use the money to produce goods and earn profits, and then repay their loans. As the depression worsened, people called on the federal government to give relief, or direct aid, to the needy and unemployed. The president refused to give relief, fearing it would make Americans dependent on the government.

Hoover's policies failed to end the depression, and fewer and fewer people believed his prediction that "prosperity is just around the corner." In fact, some Americans had to resort to sleeping in parks or abandoned buildings. Millions got their meals from soup kitchens, often run by churches or charities. One hungry teenager recalled waiting in food lines:

> **"We'd ask the guy that was putting the soup into the buckets . . . to please dip down to get some meat and potatoes from the bottom of the kettle. But he wouldn't do it."**

As the depression dragged on and more Americans went hungry and became homeless, Hoover grew increasingly unpopular.

A New Deal

In 1932 the Democratic governor of New York, Franklin D. Roosevelt, defeated Hoover in the presidential election. Roosevelt was very hopeful. He reassured Americans that the country could recover from the terrible depression. "This great nation . . . will revive, and will prosper . . . ," declared Roosevelt. "The only thing we have to fear is fear itself."

Roosevelt in action. Roosevelt went to work right away. He called his program the **New Deal**, because he believed that most Americans were ready for new ideas and a break with the old policies of the 1920s.

The new president's first goal was to restore public confidence in the banking system. He closed all the banks and allowed only the financially healthy ones to reopen. Roosevelt then went on the radio to reassure everyone that it was safe to redeposit money in the banks. For the first time in nearly three years, Americans started putting more money into banks than they were taking out of them. Congress later created the **Federal Deposit Insurance Corporation** (FDIC) as a government insurance program to protect depositors' savings.

Roosevelt soon pushed his New Deal program of relief, recovery, and reform through Congress. For relief,

Franklin D. Roosevelt

Congress founded the Federal Emergency Relief Administration (FERA) to bring aid directly to poor Americans. The Civil Works Administration (CWA) created jobs, which provided a source of dignity and hope for many people. For recovery, Congress established such programs as the National Recovery Administration. It encouraged manufacturers to cooperate with the government to keep prices, wages, and production stable. These were just a few of the many New Deal agencies.

Roosevelt also wanted long-term reform to prevent a future depression. In 1933 Congress passed the Federal Securities Act to put the stock market under federal regulation. In 1935 Roosevelt pushed the **Social Security Act** through Congress to provide older Americans with a guaranteed monthly income through taxes paid by workers and their employers.

The limits of the New Deal. Roosevelt was popular with many Americans, but some thought he had become too powerful. His critics complained about his creation of a large **welfare state**, in which the government was committed to caring for all needy citizens.

Despite New Deal programs, millions of people remained in poverty throughout the 1930s. African Americans and Mexican Americans faced particularly tough conditions. When jobs were scarce, they were often the first to be fired and the last to be hired. Minorities did make important progress during the 1930s, however. For example, Roosevelt placed some women and African Americans in his administration. Under the Indian Reorganization Act, American Indians gained greater legal protection.

The Great Depression was a difficult time for most Americans. The fact that the nation survived such ecomomic hardship without more social disorder is an indication of the great endurance and adaptability of the American people and the American political system.

Migrant Mother, *Dorothea Lange's most famous photograph, shows the dignity with which people lived through the difficult times.*

Section 1 Review

• Glossary

IDENTIFY and explain the significance of the following: militarism, *Sussex* pledge, War Industries Board, Food Administration, armistice, Communists, Red Scare, installment plan, assembly line, jazz, Harlem Renaissance, Herbert Hoover, Great Depression, public works, Franklin D. Roosevelt, New Deal, Federal Deposit Insurance Corporation, Social Security Act, welfare state

REVIEWING FOR DETAILS

1. What started World War I, and why did the United States get involved?
2. What was life like in America during the 1920s?
3. What challenges did Americans face in the 1930s?

REVIEWING FOR UNDERSTANDING

4. **Writing Mastery:** *Creating* Write a poem, folk song, or short story about life during the Great Depression.
5. **Critical Thinking:** *Synthesizing Information* How did World War I affect the lives of Americans at home and overseas?

Section 2
WORLD WAR II

Multimedia Connections

Explore these related topics and materials on the CD–ROM to enrich your understanding of this section:

Media Bank

- World War II Radio Bulletin
- WW II Alliances
- African American Fighter Pilots
- Concentration Camp Survivors
- Japan's Invasion of China
- Leaders at Potsdam Conference

Profiles

- Winston Churchill
- Hirohito
- Adolf Hitler
- Douglas MacArthur
- Benito Mussolini
- Joseph Stalin

Biographies

- Norman Mineta

Readings

- *Diary of Anne Frank*
- Soldier's Story
- Survivors' Voices

Atlas

- D-Day Invasion
- German Concentration Camps

In late 1939 a second world war, which would prove to be even more destructive than the first, erupted in Europe. On the other side of the globe, Japanese aggression threatened the peace of East Asia and the Pacific region. Before long, the United States found itself drawn into this war, sending troops across both the Atlantic and Pacific Oceans. Millions of lives would be lost and countries ruined before the war came to an end. This terrible conflict changed the United States and the world forever.

As you read this section you will find out:

- **How World War II began.**
- **What role the United States played in World War II.**
- **What effect World War II had on the nation.**

World War II Begins

Most people had hoped the 1919 Treaty of Versailles would prevent future wars from breaking out. The treaty, however, had left many people in Italy, Germany, and Japan feeling angry and cheated out of territory. The Italian leader, Benito Mussolini, built his power on a political system called **fascism**, in which the nation-state dominated public and private life. Mussolini began a campaign to expand Italy's power by invading the African nation of Ethiopia.

The Treaty of Versailles had forced the Germans to admit guilt for starting World War I. It also required Germany to give up large parts of its territory and pay millions of dollars to the countries it had attacked. As a result, Germans suffered humiliation and economic hardship. Then the Great Depression hit.

The Granger Collection, New York

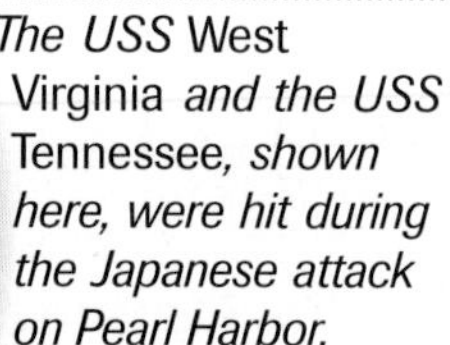

The USS West Virginia *and the USS* Tennessee, *shown here, were hit during the Japanese attack on Pearl Harbor.*

• Pearl Harbor

The Germans turned to Adolf Hitler to lead them. He promised to restore German pride as well as the nation's economic strength. By 1933 Hitler and his National Socialists, or **Nazis**, had taken control of the country. Like Mussolini, Hitler ruled as a dictator.

After Hitler gained power, he began to violate the Versailles Treaty. In 1938 he annexed Austria and retook parts of Czechoslovakia. In 1939 Germany invaded Poland. In response, France and Great Britain, later known as the Allies, declared war on Germany. Just 20 years after the Versailles Treaty, another world war had begun. In the spring of 1940, Nazi troops took control of most of Europe, including Denmark, Norway, France, Belgium, and the Netherlands. The next year Germany invaded the Soviet Union, which then joined the war on the side of the Allies.

In Japan powerful military leaders, who also ran the government, were determined to expand the nation's territory. The Japanese army invaded China and continued to expand its control over East Asia. In 1940 Germany, Japan, and Italy formed a pact and together became known as the Axis Powers.

Americans were shocked by the Axis Powers' aggression, but few were willing to become involved in another foreign war. The United States pursued a policy of neutrality. By 1940, however, Great Britain was desperate for help. It was running short on money, and the Nazis had destroyed many British ships. The British, under the leadership of Winston Churchill, turned to America for aid. In early 1941 President Roosevelt persuaded Congress to pass the **Lend-Lease Act**, which allowed the United States to help resupply the British war effort. Some Americans feared Roosevelt's Lend-Lease program would draw the country into war.

What finally brought the United States directly into World War II was a Japanese surprise attack on the U.S. naval base at Pearl Harbor, Hawaii. President Roosevelt had halted exports of aviation fuel to Japan and had frozen all Japanese funds in the United States. He hoped this would convince the Japanese to stop their expansion in Asia. Instead, it only angered Japanese leaders. They planned an air raid on Pearl Harbor. The devastating attack came on December 7, 1941. Cornelia MacEwen Hurd, a civilian eyewitness, described the destruction:

> **"I saw the most dreadful thing I ever saw in my life. The fire, the blasting of the ships, just one after the other, in flames! . . . A Japanese plane passed right in front of my yard, not more than forty feet from where I was sitting. . . . It was so vivid I could see the face, the profile, and the rising sun on the plane."**

The Home Front

The day after the attack, Congress declared war on Japan. Germany and Italy then declared war on the United States. The bombing of Pearl Harbor united most Americans in their determination to win the war. Millions of men and women volunteered for military service. Industry rapidly converted to wartime production. As had been the case during World War I, the government oversaw war-related industries and also rationed certain vital materials and scarce food products. The high level of wartime production and employment finally ended the depression.

Tens of thousands of Americans poured into factories to help produced the needed weapons and supplies for the war effort. As U.S. soldiers prepared to go overseas, many women replaced them in defense plants. In addition, African Americans and Mexican Americans found new and better-paying jobs in many large American cities.

Despite such patriotic cooperation, not all Americans received equal or fair treatment during World War II. About 1 million African Americans served in the military, some of

WORLD WAR II IN EUROPE, 1942–1945

0 200 400 Miles
0 200 400 Kilometers
Azimuthal Equal-Area Projection

The German defeat at Stalingrad marked the turning point in the war in the East.

Axis controlled, June 1944	Farthest Axis advance, 1942
Allied controlled, June 1944	Allied advances
Neutral countries	Major battles
	Allied air attacks

Learning from Maps. In late 1942, the Allies began their campaign to take control of North Africa. Once North Africa was secure, they planned to launch an attack on Italy from the south. The push to retake France and land in eastern Europe would come later.

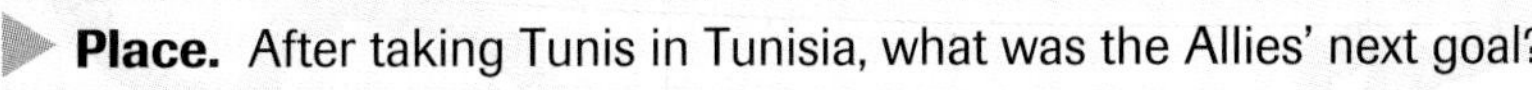

Place. After taking Tunis in Tunisia, what was the Allies' next goal?

• **Maps**

whom were among the most highly decorated soldiers. Nevertheless, they faced discrimination, as did many of the 400,000 Hispanic Americans who served during the war.

Japanese Americans in particular suffered abuses of their civil rights. Some 112,000 Japanese Americans were forced into internment, or detention, camps because of fear that they might spy for Japan. Many lost their homes and businesses.

Allied Victory

With the help and the hard work of Americans on the home front, the United States and its allies started to win the war in Europe. On June 6, 1944, Allied troops launched the enormous **D-Day** invasion of France. After months of fierce fighting, Allied troops finally defeated the Germans in May 1945. As Allied soldiers occupied the areas formerly controlled by

WORLD WAR II IN THE PACIFIC, 1941–1945

Japan (Axis Power)
Controlled by Japan, July 1942
Allied advances
Major battles
Allied air attacks
Atomic bombings

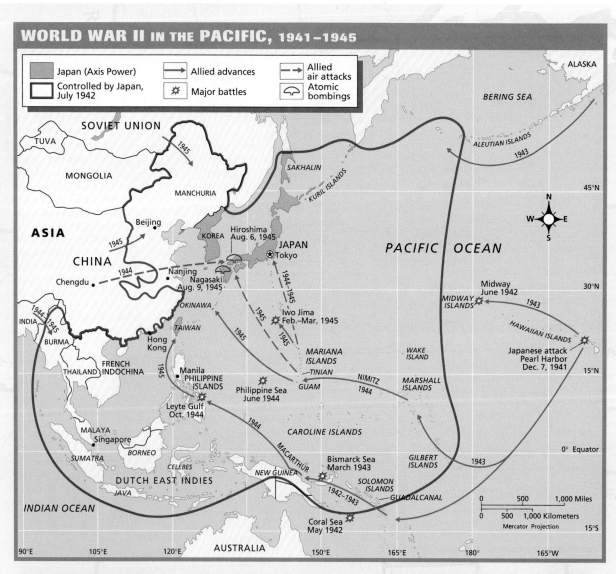

Learning from Maps. By 1942 Japan's control stretched far into the Pacific and stretched across much of East Asia, including Manchuria and other areas in China. Countries under British, French, and Dutch colonial rule had also fallen to the Japanese.

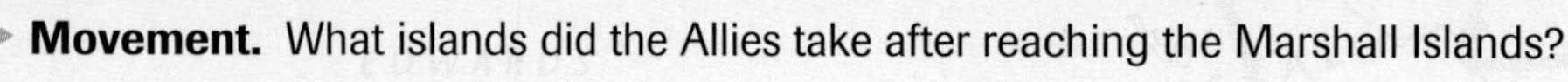

Movement. What islands did the Allies take after reaching the Marshall Islands?

• **Maps**

Germany, they were horrified to discover a network of concentration camps built by the Nazis. These were part of Hitler's plan to eliminate all Jews and other "undesirables" in what is known as the **Holocaust**, a massive extermination campaign. Concentration camp survivor Sophia Litwinska recalled how she almost died in the gas chamber before being saved at the last moment:

> **"We were led into a room which gave me the impression of a shower-bath. . . . Suddenly I saw fumes coming in through a very small window at the top. I had to cough very violently, tears were streaming from my eyes, and I had a sort of feeling in my throat as if I would be asphyxiated [suffocated]."**

Although Germany had surrendered, Japan continued to fight. After President Roosevelt had died of a stroke in April 1945, Vice President Harry Truman had become president. The war in the Pacific had been brutal—the long fight to retake island after island was resulting in high casualties on both sides. While the United States was winning the war, a full-scale invasion of Japan had not yet been attempted. Truman decided that the best way to end the war quickly and save American lives was to use a new secret weapon scientists had developed. On August 6, 1945, the United States dropped this weapon, the **atomic bomb**, on the Japanese city of Hiroshima.

The bomb's incredibly powerful explosion killed 75,000 Japanese in a blinding flash. When the Japanese still refused to give up, the United States dropped another atomic bomb on the city of Nagasaki. Within days, Japan agreed to surrender, and on September 2, 1945, Japan signed a peace agreement. At the cost of millions of lives and billions of dollars, World War II was over at last. Its impact, however, would be felt for decades to come.

U.S. Marines raise the American flag above the Pacific island of Iwo Jima. This photograph has become one of the most famous images of the war.

Section 2 Review

• Glossary

IDENTIFY and explain the significance of the following: Benito Mussolini, fascism, Adolf Hitler, Nazis, Lend-Lease Act, D-Day, Holocaust, Harry Truman, atomic bomb

REVIEWING FOR DETAILS

1. What were the causes of World War II?
2. What part did America play in the war?
3. How did World War II affect the lives of Americans?

REVIEWING FOR UNDERSTANDING

4. **Writing Mastery:** *Describing* Imagine that you are a teenager in 1943. Write several diary entries describing how the war is affecting your life.
5. **Critical Thinking:** *Drawing Conclusions* What might have happened if the United States had not aided Great Britain or entered World War II?

Section 3
FROM WORLD WAR TO COLD WAR

Multimedia Connections
Explore these related topics and materials on the CD-ROM to enrich your understanding of this section:

Media Bank

- Baby Boom
- Civil Rights in the Truman Era
- Little Rock Nine
- Berlin Airlift
- Cartoon of the Arms Race
- Cold War Movie Poster
- Rock 'n' Roll in Action
- Thurgood Marshall

Profiles

- Alger Hiss
- George C. Marshall
- Joseph R. McCarthy
- Rosa Parks
- Ethel and Julius Rosenberg
- Harry Truman

Biographies

- Martin Luther King, Jr.

Readings

- Eisenhower's Domestic Policies
- Integrating Central High
- Intelligence Agencies
- Beat Generation

Atlas

- Nuclear Technology

Once World War II was over, the United States faced a new and difficult challenge—keeping the peace. This soon proved impossible. The world was now divided into spheres of influence dominated by new superpowers—the United States and the Soviet Union. These nations became locked in a tense standoff that would last some 45 years. This struggle for world domination changed U.S. relations with other countries and affected the way many Americans viewed one another.

As you read this section you will find out:

- **How and why the Cold War began.**
- **How the Cold War affected U.S. relations with other countries.**
- **What life was like for many Americans during the 1950s.**

Returning to Peace

Tens of millions of people had been killed during World War II. Much of Europe and parts of Asia were in ruins. Both would have to be rebuilt if peace and prosperity were to be restored. During the war, the Allied Powers had begun organizing the **United Nations** (UN), a body designed to settle disputes between nations peacefully. In addition, in February 1945, leaders of the United States, Great Britain, and the Soviet Union met at the **Yalta Conference**. There, the **Big Three**—President Roosevelt, British prime minister Winston Churchill, and Soviet leader Joseph Stalin—discussed how to end the war and establish lasting world peace.

In July 1945 Churchill, Stalin, and President Truman met at the Potsdam Conference. They agreed to divide Germany into four zones, with the United States, Great Britain, France, and the Soviet Union each controlling a zone. Berlin, the capital city, would be located in the Soviet zone, but it too would be divided.

Truman and Churchill disagreed with Stalin over several important issues. The Soviet Union wanted control of Poland to prevent future invasions. Truman and Churchill believed this was an excuse for Stalin to spread communism throughout Europe.

The Cold War

These growing tensions between the United States and the Soviet Union brought about the **Cold War**—a long power struggle over world domination. As the Soviet Union expanded its influence across Eastern Europe, Churchill accused the Soviets of building an "Iron Curtain" between the East and West.

Truman was convinced that it was primarily up to the United States to stop the spread of communism. In 1947 he announced his **Truman Doctrine**, which said that the United States would aid any country resisting takeover by communist forces. That same year, Congress approved the **Marshall Plan**, through which the United States provided about $13 billion to help Europe rebuild. This was partly a humanitarian gesture. U.S.

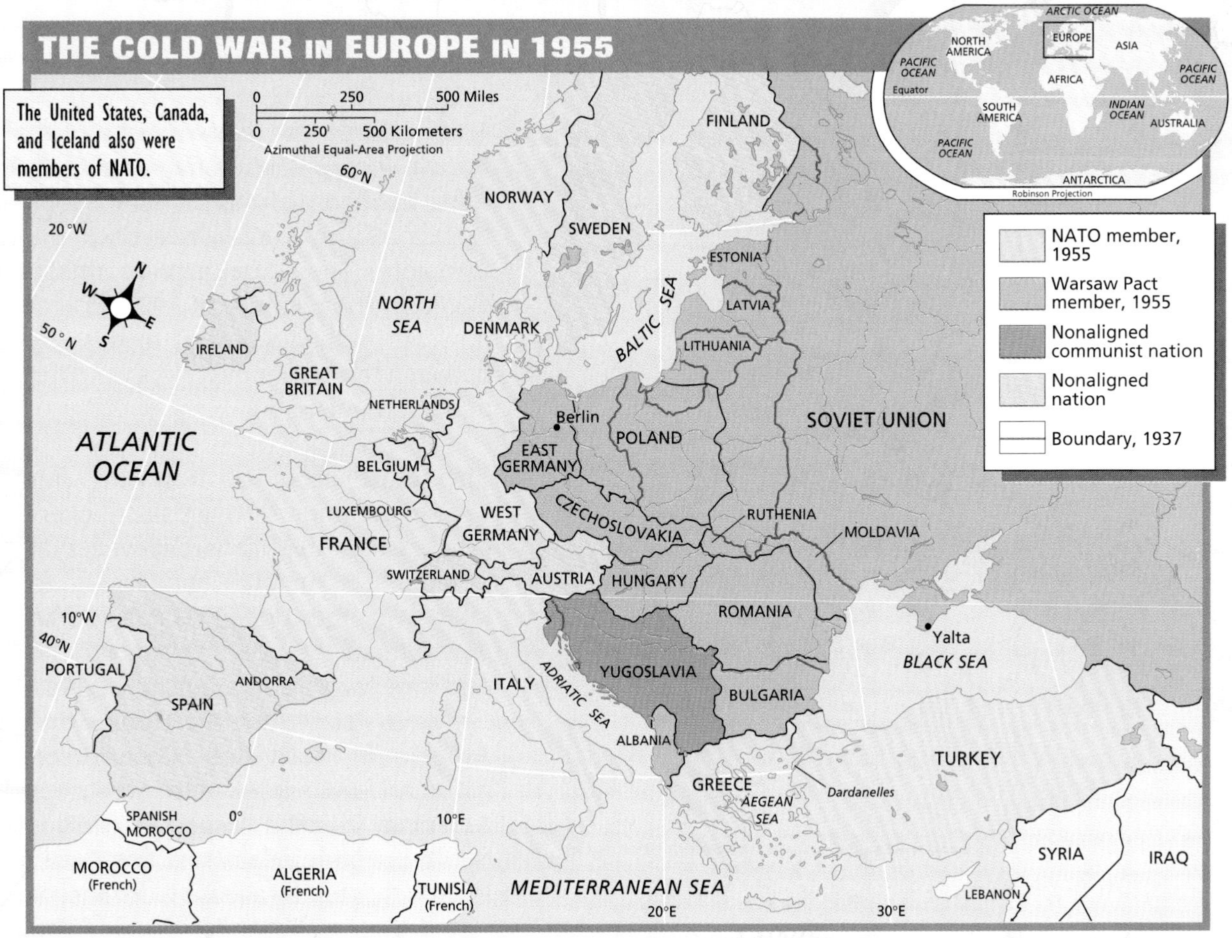

THE COLD WAR IN EUROPE IN 1955

The United States, Canada, and Iceland also were members of NATO.

0 250 500 Miles
0 250 500 Kilometers
Azimuthal Equal-Area Projection

NATO member, 1955
Warsaw Pact member, 1955
Nonaligned communist nation
Nonaligned nation
Boundary, 1937

ARCTIC OCEAN, NORTH AMERICA, EUROPE, ASIA, PACIFIC OCEAN, Equator, AFRICA, SOUTH AMERICA, INDIAN OCEAN, AUSTRALIA, ANTARCTICA, Robinson Projection

60°N, 20°W, 50°N, 10°W, 40°N, 0°, 10°E, 20°E, 30°E

FINLAND, NORWAY, SWEDEN, ESTONIA, LATVIA, LITHUANIA, NORTH SEA, DENMARK, BALTIC SEA, IRELAND, GREAT BRITAIN, NETHERLANDS, Berlin, POLAND, SOVIET UNION, ATLANTIC OCEAN, BELGIUM, EAST GERMANY, LUXEMBOURG, WEST GERMANY, CZECHOSLOVAKIA, RUTHENIA, MOLDAVIA, FRANCE, SWITZERLAND, AUSTRIA, HUNGARY, ROMANIA, Yalta, BLACK SEA, PORTUGAL, ANDORRA, SPAIN, ITALY, ADRIATIC SEA, YUGOSLAVIA, BULGARIA, ALBANIA, TURKEY, GREECE, AEGEAN SEA, Dardanelles, SPANISH MOROCCO, MOROCCO (French), ALGERIA (French), TUNISIA (French), MEDITERRANEAN SEA, SYRIA, IRAQ, LEBANON

Learning from Maps. The majority of European nations were allied with either NATO or the Warsaw Pact.

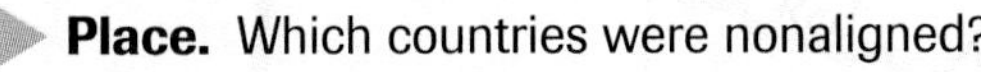

Place. Which countries were nonaligned?

• **Maps**

leaders also believed that Europeans would support capitalism instead of communism if Europe's prosperity could be quickly restored. The Soviet Union refused to participate in the Marshall Plan and refused to let its satellite nations—those states it controlled in Eastern Europe—participate. The countries that took part in the plan quickly rebuilt their economies and soon enjoyed tremendous prosperity.

The Cold War turns hot. In 1948 Stalin tried to block supplies from reaching the Western zones of Berlin. American and British air forces solved this problem by flying in goods. For nearly a year, planes flew more than 270,000 missions into Berlin to feed its 2 million residents. The Soviets eventually lifted their blockade, but the tensions heated up again when they tested their first atomic bomb. The nuclear arms race had begun.

In 1949 the United States, Great Britain, and 10 other nations joined together to form the **North Atlantic Treaty Organization** (NATO). Members of NATO pledged to defend each other in case of attack. The Soviets later formed their own defensive alliance known as the **Warsaw Pact**.

Also in 1949, communist forces won control of the Chinese government. Now the United States faced two great communist powers—the Soviet Union and China. In 1950, American leaders' fear that communism was spreading was reinforced by the invasion of South Korea by communist North Korean forces. The United States and other members of the UN sent troops to help South Korea drive back the invasion. The Korean War finally ended in the summer of 1953. Korea, however, remains divided to this day between the communist North and the anticommunist South.

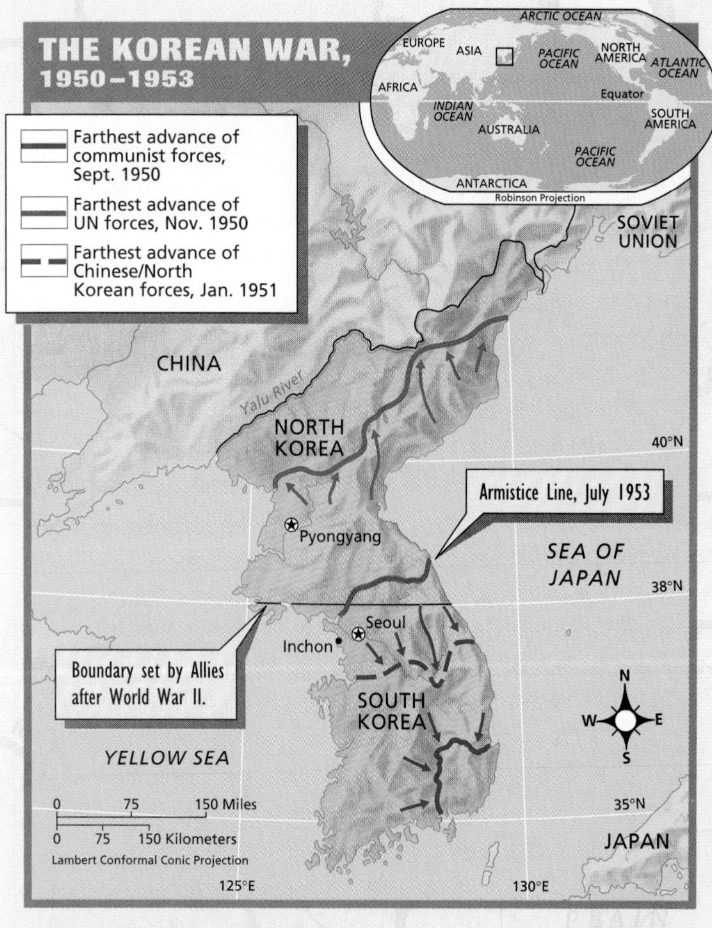

Learning from Maps.

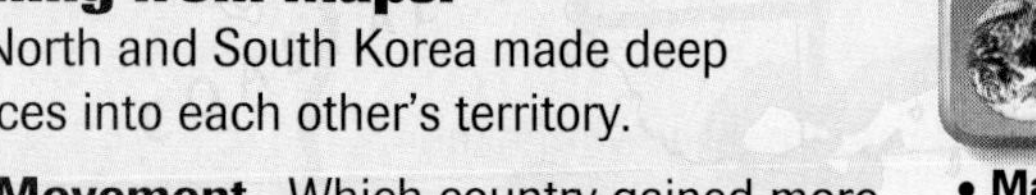
Both North and South Korea made deep advances into each other's territory.

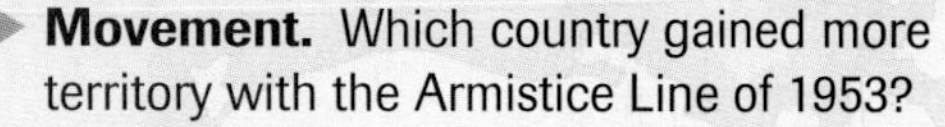
Movement. Which country gained more territory with the Armistice Line of 1953?

The Cold War at home. After seeing communist aggression overseas, many Americans believed that Communists might eventually try to take over the United States. Some government officials played on the public's fear of communism. In 1947 Congress established the **House Un-American Activities Committee** (HUAC). HUAC's job was to investigate American citizens suspected of supporting communism in any way. HUAC eventually accused dozens of Americans of disloyalty. Those who refused to cooperate and those who could not defend themselves were often blacklisted, or could no longer find jobs in their chosen professions.

These U.S. troops march to stop further North Korean advances while South Korean women and children flee the fighting in August 1950.

This fear of communism turned into mass hysteria in 1950 when Wisconsin senator Joseph McCarthy claimed that he knew of 205 Communists working for the U.S. government. McCarthy never offered any solid proof to support his charges, but this did not seem to matter to many people. Although McCarthy was eventually discredited, he and HUAC ruined the lives and careers of many people.

The Eisenhower Presidency

In the midst of the Cold War, Americans wanted a leader who was strong, capable, and very confident. Dwight D. Eisenhower, commander of the Allied forces in Europe during World War II, seemed an ideal choice. In his election campaign Eisenhower, nicknamed "Ike," promised to go to Korea to end the war. After he became president, negotiations resulted in a truce.

Eisenhower and the Cold War. The new president and his secretary of state, John Foster Dulles, developed their own strategy for fighting the spread of communism. This policy, called **massive retaliation**, contained the threat that the United States might use nuclear weapons against the Soviet Union. Dulles stated that, if necessary, the United States would "retaliate instantly against open aggression by Red armies."

By the mid-1950s, the United States and the Soviet Union each had enough nuclear weapons to destroy each other many times over. The fear of being completely wiped out in a war probably helped convince leaders on both sides not to launch an attack. Although they avoided all-out war, serious Cold War tensions placed tremendous economic and psychological strain on the people of both the United States and the Soviet Union.

The space race. One area in which Americans and Soviets competed was in exploring outer space. In 1957, Soviet scientists launched ***Sputnik***, the world's first artificial space satellite. Americans were shocked that the Soviets were leading in the space race. The U.S. government quickly attempted to close this gap by creating the **National Aeronautics and Space Administration** (NASA) to expand scientific research and development on space exploration. The government also supported increased educational funding in the sciences and mathematics.

A Changing America in the 1950s

America experienced other changes after World War II. Despite some fears of a postwar

World War II hero Dwight D. Eisenhower inspired many Americans who felt that his skills as a general would make him a fine president.

• Dwight Eisenhower

recession like the one that had followed World War I, the U.S. economy boomed. Factories soon began turning out items that had been unavailable in wartime. Many Americans had saved their money during the war, and now they were ready to spend it.

In addition to an economic boom in the 1950s, the United States experienced a **baby boom**, or rapid rise in the birthrate. As families grew, millions of young couples bought homes in newly developed suburbs around big cities. In the suburbs, families found that they had greater space and more affordable housing. They filled these homes with the latest in appliances and furniture. Many Americans had reached a higher standard of living than their parents had ever imagined.

Discontent in the suburbs. For many, however, this supposedly ideal life in the suburbs was not very fulfilling. People often found themselves competing with neighbors to buy the newest consumer goods in order to show how successful they were. When television became widespread in people's homes, they began to turn to new shows to see how other Americans looked and behaved. In many ways, suburban living encouraged conformity, or trying to look and act like everybody else.

Some suburban wives began to resent being at home all day while their husbands were away at work. Women were expected to be "content in a world of . . . kitchen . . . babies, and home." Although women had been expected to return to their roles as homemakers after World War II, many continued working outside the home. One female steelworker expressed what more and more women had come to believe:

> **"If [women] are capable, I don't see why they should give up their position to men. . . . The old theory that a woman's place is in the home no longer exists. Those days are gone forever."**

Many poets and writers of the 1950s criticized the suburbs, descibing them as unoriginal and boring. Many American teenagers also found middle-class life too confining. In part as a way of rebelling against conformity, many young Americans turned to a new style of music known as rock 'n' roll, which drew heavily on African American rhythm and blues music. However, its danceable beat and sometimes wild lyrics caused many adults to disapprove of the music.

The movement for equal rights. Most African Americans did not share in the prosperity of the 1950s. Few could afford to live in the suburbs, where there were almost no houses or apartments to rent. A higher percentage of African Americans than ever before worked in factories, but they were usually paid less than white workers for the same jobs.

Nevertheless, African Americans had made some progress against discrimination. Under pressure from African American leaders, President Truman had ended racial segregation in the armed forces in 1948. For the most part, however, African Americans had to push for civil rights without the support of the federal government.

In many places, African American and white children attended segregated schools. In 1952 a young African American girl named Linda Brown and her father argued that she should be allowed to attend the all-white school near their home

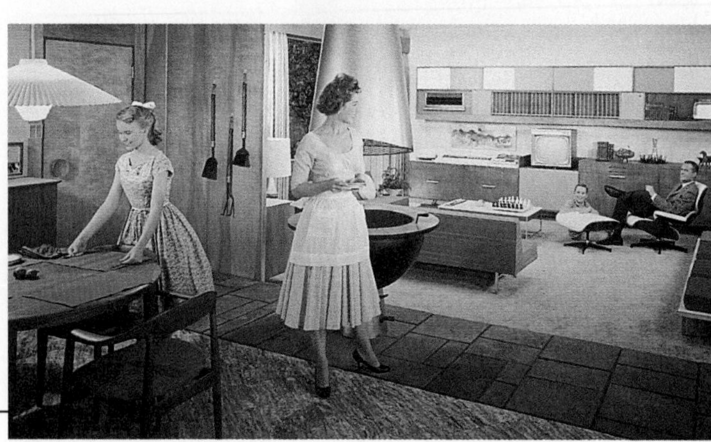

Popular images in the 1950s often expressed the idea that the main role of women should be taking care of the home.

in Topeka, Kansas. In the 1954 court case ***Brown* v. *Board of Education***, the Supreme Court agreed. With its ruling in the case, the Supreme Court ordered the desegregation of educational facilities.

Despite the Court's decision, many schools continued to discriminate against African American students. For example, in 1957, when nine African American teenagers tried to attend Central High School in Little Rock, Arkansas, the governor ordered National Guard troops to block the way. Angry white students screamed and threw things at the black students. President Eisenhower responded by sending federal troops to escort the students into the school, explaining that no state had the authority to ignore a federal court order. Despite such incidents, African Americans succeeded in gaining greater rights during the 1950s.

In December 1955 an African American woman named Rosa Parks helped launch the **Montgomery Bus Boycott** in Montgomery, Alabama. Parks refused to give up her seat on a city bus to a white passenger. Her arrest for breaking a discriminatory law convinced local African Americans to quit riding the city buses until the city ordinance no longer required African Americans to sit at the back of the buses or give up their seats to white riders. After a year, the boycott succeeded. One very important African American leader to emerge from the Montgomery boycott was a young clergyman named Martin Luther King, Jr. He became one of the most powerful leaders in the campaign to guarantee equality and opportunity for all Americans.

Rosa Parks after her arrest

Section 3 Review

• Glossary

IDENTIFY and explain the significance of the following: United Nations, Yalta Conference, Big Three, Cold War, Truman Doctrine, Marshall Plan, North Atlantic Treaty Organization, Warsaw Pact, House Un-American Activities Committee, Joseph McCarthy, Dwight D. Eisenhower, massive retaliation, *Sputnik*, National Aeronautics and Space Administration, baby boom, *Brown* v. *Board of Education*, Montgomery Bus Boycott

REVIEWING FOR DETAILS

1. What events contributed to the Cold War?
2. How would you describe U.S. relations with other countries during the Cold War?
3. What were some positive and negative aspects of American society in the 1950s?

REVIEWING FOR UNDERSTANDING

4. **Writing Mastery:** *Persuading* Imagine that you are a woman who worked in a factory during World War II. Write a speech to persuade factory owners that you should be allowed to keep your job after the war.
5. **Critical Thinking:** *Drawing Conclusions* Why do you think African American leaders believed that a boycott of city buses would be an effective protest?

Section 4

THE TURBULENT 1960s

Multimedia Connections

Explore these related topics and materials on the CD-ROM to enrich your understanding of this section:

Profiles

- John F. Kennedy
- Lyndon Johnson
- Malcolm X
- Richard Nixon

Atlas

- Election of 1968
- Urban Unrest

Media Bank

- Berlin Wall
- 1968 Campaign
- Nurse with Vietnamese Child
- Counterculture
- Cuban Missile Crisis
- Free Speech Movement
- Faces of Poverty
- U.S. Troops in Rural Vietnam

Readings

- Soldiers' Diaries
- America After the Vietnam War
- Johnson's Great Society
- Women's Movement of the 1960s

Biographies

- Dith Pran

The 1960s brought sweeping social unrest and change in the United States. Several important public figures, including a president, were assassinated. In addition to these tragedies, the United States became involved in a bloody war in Southeast Asia. At home, Americans protested against the war, and various groups in society demanded more rights and a greater voice in how the country was run.

As you read this section you will find out:

- **What important policies President John F. Kennedy pursued in the 1960s.**
- **What events marked Lyndon Johnson's presidency.**
- **What changes American society underwent during the 1960s.**

The Torch Is Passed

In the 1960 presidential election, Americans had two seemingly very different choices. Republican candidate Richard Nixon promised to continue the peace and prosperity of the 1950s. Democratic candidate John F. Kennedy promised not only to increase the nation's prosperity but also to make sure all Americans shared in it. By a very narrow margin, voters chose Kennedy, the nation's first Catholic president. In his inaugural address, Kennedy challenged Americans to make the United States, and the world, better places for everyone:

> **"The torch has been passed to a new generation of Americans. . . . The energy, the faith, the devotion which we bring to this endeavor [task] will light our country and all who serve it—and the glow from that**

The Kennedys displayed style and elegance in all their public appearances. Here they are returning from dinner with the president and first lady of France.

fire can truly light the world. And so, my fellow Americans–ask not what your country can do for you–ask what you can do for your country."

Almost as soon as he took office, Kennedy faced serious problems abroad. In 1959 communist leader Fidel Castro had taken over the government of Cuba, a small island nation roughly 90 miles south of Florida. Many Americans and Cubans disliked Castro, and U.S. officials feared the establishment of a communist base so close to home. Hundreds of Cubans who had fled to the United States wanted to return to Cuba and overthrow Castro. With the approval of President Kennedy, a force of Cuban refugees launched an attack against Castro's government at the Bay of Pigs in April 1961. Kennedy refused to provide U.S. air support, however. Castro's forces quickly defeated the invading Cuban exiles. Kennedy's inaction angered many Cuban Americans. In addition, many other Americans questioned whether he was strong enough to stand up to communist leaders around the world.

In August 1961 Kennedy's leadership was tested once again. Soviet premier Nikita Khrushchev (kroosh-CHAWF) ordered a wall of concrete and barbed wire built across the German city of Berlin. This **Berlin Wall** prevented East Germans from escaping to the West in search of greater personal and economic freedom. In a 1963 visit to West Berlin, Kennedy criticized the Soviets for dividing the city. "All free men, wherever they may live, are citizens of Berlin," declared Kennedy. "And therefore, as a free man, I take pride in the words *'Ich bin ein Berliner'* ['I am a Berliner']."

Kennedy's toughest foreign policy challenge—and the most dangerous moment of the Cold War—again involved Cuba. In October 1962, U.S. spy planes discovered that the Soviets were building nuclear missile bases in Cuba. Kennedy demanded that the Soviets remove the bases. When they refused, the president set up a naval blockade around Cuba. During this **Cuban missile crisis**, the whole world watched nervously, afraid that the standoff between the United States and

The building of the Berlin Wall created a great deal of tension between the Western world and the Soviet Union. The wall would remain standing for almost 30 years as a symbol of a divided Europe.

the Soviet Union might erupt into another world war. After a very tense week, the Soviets agreed to remove the missile bases if the United States promised not to invade Cuba. The crisis was resolved peacefully, but it left Americans painfully aware of how close the world was to nuclear war.

President Kennedy was not as successful in dealing with domestic issues as he was with foreign affairs. He urged Congress to pass measures to fight poverty and improve civil rights. He also encouraged Congress to pass a large tax cut, hoping that this would boost consumer spending and help the economy. Most of these measures, however, became stalled in Congress.

Kennedy's presidency came to an abrupt and tragic end on November 22, 1963, when an assassin's bullet took his life while he was visiting Dallas, Texas. The assassination shocked the nation. It was now up to Vice President Lyndon Johnson to follow through on Kennedy's challenge to the country.

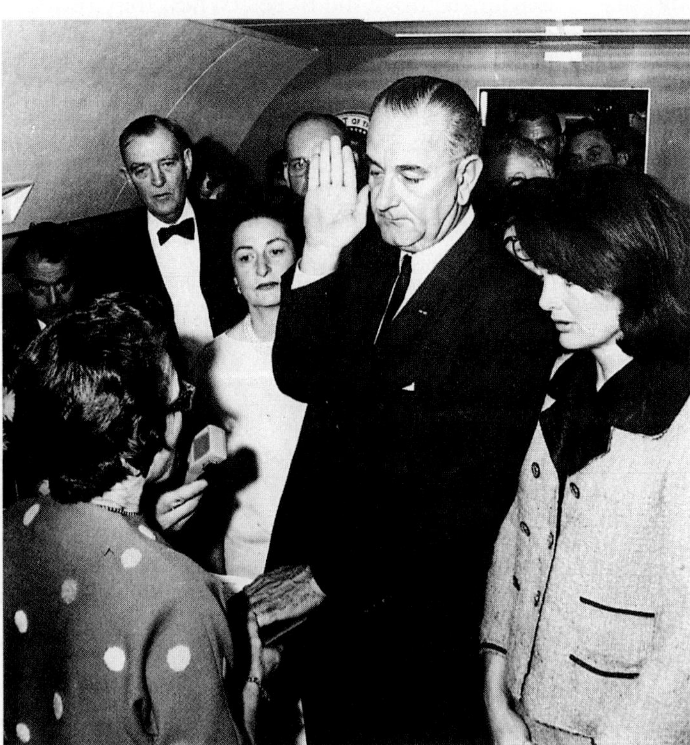

Lyndon Johnson is sworn in as president after Kennedy's assassination. Standing next to him are his wife, Lady Bird Johnson (left), and Jacqueline Kennedy (right).

A Decade of Change

Lyndon Johnson was sworn in as president within hours of Kennedy's death. His calm and confident manner during this tragedy reassured the nation. President Johnson quickly set to work getting Kennedy's domestic bills passed into law. Johnson was able to persuade Congress to pass many of these proposals because he had been a skilled and respected legislator. He also urged the public and Congress to support the policies as a tribute to the slain president.

The War on Poverty. One of Johnson's main goals was ending poverty in America. He believed the United States had the potential to be the greatest society in human history. Studies showed, however, that some 40 million Americans, or about 20–25 percent of the population, lived below the poverty line. Johnson called this a national disgrace that robbed the country of its strength, creativity, and opportunity. Johnson's many proposals to change this national problem became known as the **Great Society**. Part of this Great Society program was what Johnson termed a **War on Poverty**, designed to help poorer Americans become educated, find jobs, and escape from poverty. For example, the Medicare program provided many Americans with affordable health care. Some of Johnson's critics charged that many of his programs made the poor dependent on the government.

The civil rights movement. Johnson had a long record of helping minorities. As president he pushed hard for civil rights legislation. He also hoped his War on Poverty would improve conditions for minorities.

Since the 1950s, more women, minorities, and young people had been resisting traditional roles they believed were too confining. Women

Martin Luther King, Jr., waves to the hundreds of thousands of people who gathered for the March on Washington

• "I Have a Dream"

pushed for more legal rights and economic equality. Young Americans demanded more of a voice in how government and educational institutions were run.

Throughout the 1960s, African Americans became increasingly active in fighting for their civil rights through such organizations as Martin Luther King, Jr.'s **Southern Christian Leadership Conference** (SCLC). African Americans staged nonviolent **sit-ins**, protesting segregation by sitting down in public areas reserved for whites, such as lunch counters, and refusing to leave. Another group, the **Congress of Racial Equality** (CORE), recruited black and white college students from the North to go into the South and campaign for equal rights. These students organized **Freedom Rides**, in which they traveled in buses across the South, protesting segregated facilities. The attacks of angry whites on the Freedom Riders focused national attention on the problems of racial segregation.

In August 1963 more than 200,000 people gathered in Washington, D.C., to hear Martin Luther King, Jr., speak on civil rights and equality for all Americans. This rally was known as the **March on Washington**. Addressing the large crowd, King gave one of his most famous and moving speeches:

> **"I have a dream that one day this nation will rise up and live out the true meaning of its creed: 'We hold these truths to be self-evident, that all men are created equal.'"**

In the mid-1960s Congress passed several important pieces of civil rights legislation. Before the decade's end, however, the nonviolent civil rights movement lost its leader. King was assassinated in Memphis, Tennessee, on April 4, 1968.

The War in Southeast Asia

As the 1960s progressed, the United States became increasingly involved in a war in

Protesters in Birmingham, Alabama, brace themselves as they are sprayed with fire hoses by police. Press coverage of the Birmingham protesters—many of them young children—being attacked with fire hoses and dogs, was widespread across the country. This helped increase national support for the movement.

President Nixon tours the Great Wall of China during his historic 1972 visit to China.

Washington, D.C. Newspaper reporters investigating the break-in uncovered connections leading to high White House officials. Congress started its own investigation into the **Watergate** affair. Before long, several top Nixon administration officials admitted that the president in fact knew about the break-in and had ordered a cover-up.

At first, Nixon denied this. He refused to give Congress certain tape recordings that were thought to contain evidence against him. The Supreme Court finally ruled that Nixon had to hand over the tapes. Facing all but certain impeachment, Nixon resigned from the presidency on August 8, 1974. Many Americans were angry when Nixon's successor, Gerald Ford, granted a full pardon to Nixon. The Watergate scandal shook many Americans' confidence in their government.

Gerald Ford faced many difficult problems when he became president. The energy crisis and rising inflation continued to plague the economy. Ford disagreed with many members of Congress over economic issues. In foreign affairs, however, Ford did make important gains by improving relations with the Soviet Union and several Middle Eastern nations.

Domestic changes. In the 1970s, African Americans made progress in the struggle for equality—more went to college, found good jobs, and entered into politics. One reason for these advances was **affirmative action**—the practice by some businesses and government agencies of giving special consideration to minorities and women to make up for past discrimination when applicants' qualifications are roughly equal.

American Indian activists formed a campaign for equal rights known as the **American Indian Movement** (AIM). AIM sometimes staged radical public demonstrations to pressure the government to improve conditions for American Indians.

Mexican American leaders started the **Chicano movement** to demand better economic, educational, and political opportunities for Hispanics. They were inspired by César Chávez who founded what would become the United Farm Workers, a union of Mexican American migrant workers. After launching strikes and other protests, Chávez's union eventually won more rights for farmworkers.

César Chávez

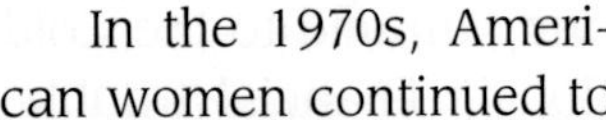

In the 1970s, American women continued to fight for equality with men. The **National Organization for Women** (NOW) and other groups tried to win passage of the **Equal Rights Amendment** (ERA). Although Congress passed the ERA, the amendment failed to gain support from enough states to win ratification.

The Carter Presidency

In 1976, voters elected the Democratic candidate Jimmy Carter president in part because of his open, honest attitude toward politics. Carter's administration also had its problems.

Women's rights march

Like Nixon, Carter could not end the energy crisis or inflation. Carter also had trouble dealing with Congress, which rejected many of his proposals.

In foreign policy, Carter worked hard to bring peace between Israel and its Arab neighbors in the Middle East, particularly Egypt. In 1979, Islamic revolutionaries overthrew the U.S.-backed shah of Iran. In November a mob in Tehran, Iran's capital, overran the embassy and took 53 Americans hostage. As the hostage crisis dragged on for more than a year, many Americans blamed Carter.

Republicans in Power

In 1980 Republican candidate Ronald Reagan won the presidential election. He promised to restore the country's dignity and projected an image of strong, no-nonsense leadership.

The Reagan presidency. President Reagan's victory reflected a growing conservative reaction against the more liberal policies of the past, particularly those that had greatly expanded the role of the federal government. To reduce the power of the federal government, Reagan cut spending on several social welfare programs and lifted many regulations on industry. He also cut taxes and introduced **supply-side economics**, a theory that lower taxes would stimulate stronger economic growth. Most Americans who saved through these tax cuts did not invest their savings back into the economy as Reagan had hoped, and the economy fell into a steep slump.

President Reagan and Congress also spent billions of dollars to build up the U.S. military. As a result of massive spending, the deficit—the money borrowed by the federal government each year—increased dramatically in the 1980s.

Reagan's foreign policy. Reagan firmly believed in a strong national defense. For example, he urged Congress to fund the **Strategic Defense Initiative** (SDI), an advanced, space-based system designed to destroy incoming missiles before they could reach the United States. He focused much of the nation's military might on defeating what he believed were communist movements around the world.

Reagan's adminstration provided money and weapons to groups trying to overthrow the pro-Soviet government in Nicaragua. Some of the president's top aides, however, got into trouble for illegally selling weapons to Iran in order to fund anticommunist troops in Nicaragua.

U.S. relations with the Soviet Union began to change when Mikhail Gorbachev became

(left to right) Nancy Reagan, Ronald Reagan, former Soviet leader Mikhail Gorbachev, and his wife, Raisa, relax at the Reagans' California ranch in 1992. President Reagan's friendship with Gorbachev during and after their time in office surprised many people, since Reagan had been a long-time enemy of the Soviet Union.

its new leader in 1985. He worked to restructure the Soviet government and economy and to allow more political openness. Reagan and Gorbachev also negotiated to reduce the number of nuclear weapons on each side and to improve relations between their countries. In this way, Reagan helped end the Cold War. Despite the problems of his administration, Reagan remained extremely popular with many Americans.

The Bush presidency. Reagan's vice president, George Bush, was elected president in 1988. Bush waged a **War on Drugs**—a campaign at home and abroad to try to stop the flow of illegal drugs into the country. Unfortunately, the drug supply only increased.

In early 1991 the United States fought another war, this time in the Persian Gulf region. Iraq had invaded its tiny oil-rich neighbor, Kuwait. Allied forces, led by the United States, launched an all-out attack on Iraq, known as **Operation Desert Storm**. Bush addressed the American people and Congress:

> **"In the life of a nation, we're called upon . . . to stand up for what's right and condemn what's wrong—all in the cause of peace. . . . If history teaches us anything, it is that we must resist aggression or it will destroy our freedoms."**

After six weeks of intense bombing, U.S. and allied forces defeated the Iraqis. Many Americans were upset that Iraqi leader Saddam Hussein had not been removed from power. He refused to step down or obey UN orders. Although victory in the Persian Gulf War helped Bush's popularity, many Americans grew increasingly dissatisfied with the slow-moving national economy. While the richest Americans had enjoyed a dramatic increase in wealth during the 1980s, America's poor had grown significantly poorer. The bulk of Americans in between also saw their economic standing decline.

• George Bush

President George Bush and his wife, Barbara, wave to supporters at a gathering in their hometown of Houston, Texas.

Clinton in Office

In the 1992 presidential election, Democrats hoped to take advantage of Bush's economic policies. President Bush, a veteran of World War II, was again the Republican candidate. Arkansas governor Bill Clinton, born after the end of World War II, ran as the Democratic nominee. A third candidate, Texas billionaire Ross Perot, ran as an independent.

Both Clinton and Perot promised to revive the economy. Many dissatisfied Bush supporters voted for Perot. This gave Clinton enough of an edge to win, even though he received only 43 percent of the popular vote.

Clinton had grown up admiring the policies of John F. Kennedy and Lyndon Johnson. Clinton worked to ensure equal rights for all Americans and placed several women and minority members in important positions in his administration. He tried to cut the deficit and revive the economy through spending cuts and a tax increase. Eventually, the economy did begin to recover. Clinton's wife, Hillary Rodham Clinton, helped him design a national health care program, but it was defeated in Congress because many believed it was unworkable and would be too expensive.

Clinton faced difficulty in passing his legislative program after Americans elected dozens of new Republicans to Congress in 1994. The Republicans offered their own program, which was known as the **Contract with America**. This included the promise to cut taxes and spending, reduce the size of the government, and limit the time

(left to right) Republican President George Bush, independent candidate Ross Perot, and Democratic nominee Governor Bill Clinton debate each other in 1992.

politicians could serve in office. The Republicans had mixed success in fulfilling the Contract. In 1996, Clinton was re-elected to serve a second term as president.

The 1990s

Although the Cold War had ended, Americans faced new challenges during the 1990s. In April 1995 a powerful bomb destroyed a federal building in Oklahoma City, killing 168 people and wounding many others. This tragedy awakened Americans to the fact that attacks on the U.S. government could come from within the country as well as from abroad.

The United States sent troops and aid to several troubled countries during the 1990s, including Somalia, Haiti, and Bosnia. Such aid missions were often dangerous and controversial, but they usually helped bring stability and reduce human suffering in those places.

Young people in the 1990s encountered a variety of challenges—a tight job market, a rising cost of living, and an increase in racial tensions. Nevertheless, there were also tremendous opportunities with newly developing technology, improvements in health care, a recovering economy, and an end to the Cold War anxieties that had troubled their parents' and grandparents' generations before them.

Section 5 Review

• Glossary

IDENTIFY and explain the significance of the following: energy crisis, Watergate, Gerald Ford, affirmative action, American Indian Movement, Chicano movement, César Chávez, National Organization for Women, Equal Rights Amendment, Jimmy Carter, Ronald Reagan, supply-side economics, Strategic Defense Initiative, George Bush, War on Drugs, Operation Desert Storm, Bill Clinton, Contract with America

REVIEWING FOR DETAILS

1. What challenges did Nixon, Ford, and Carter face during their presidencies?
2. What important changes occurred under Presidents Reagan and Bush?
3. What opportunities and challenges face Americans in the 1990s?

REVIEWING FOR UNDERSTANDING

4. **Writing Mastery:** *Describing* Imagine that you are celebrating your 100th birthday. Write a speech you might give to a group of students describing the changes you have seen throughout your life.
5. **Critical Thinking:** *Synthesizing Information* Do you think foreign or domestic affairs were more influential in presidential elections between 1976 and 1992? Give reasons to support your answer.

Booker T. Washington

George Washington oversees the Constitutional Convention.

Immigrant neighborhood

Freedman's school in Charleston, South Carolina

Plains Indians watch as settlers cross their lands.

Cheyenne warrior's shield

The Granger Collection, New York

Exploring America's Past

Beginnings to 1914

Reference Section

Elizabeth Cady Stanton (left) and Susan B. Anthony (right)

Civil War camp life

President Franklin D. Roosevelt

The World: Political

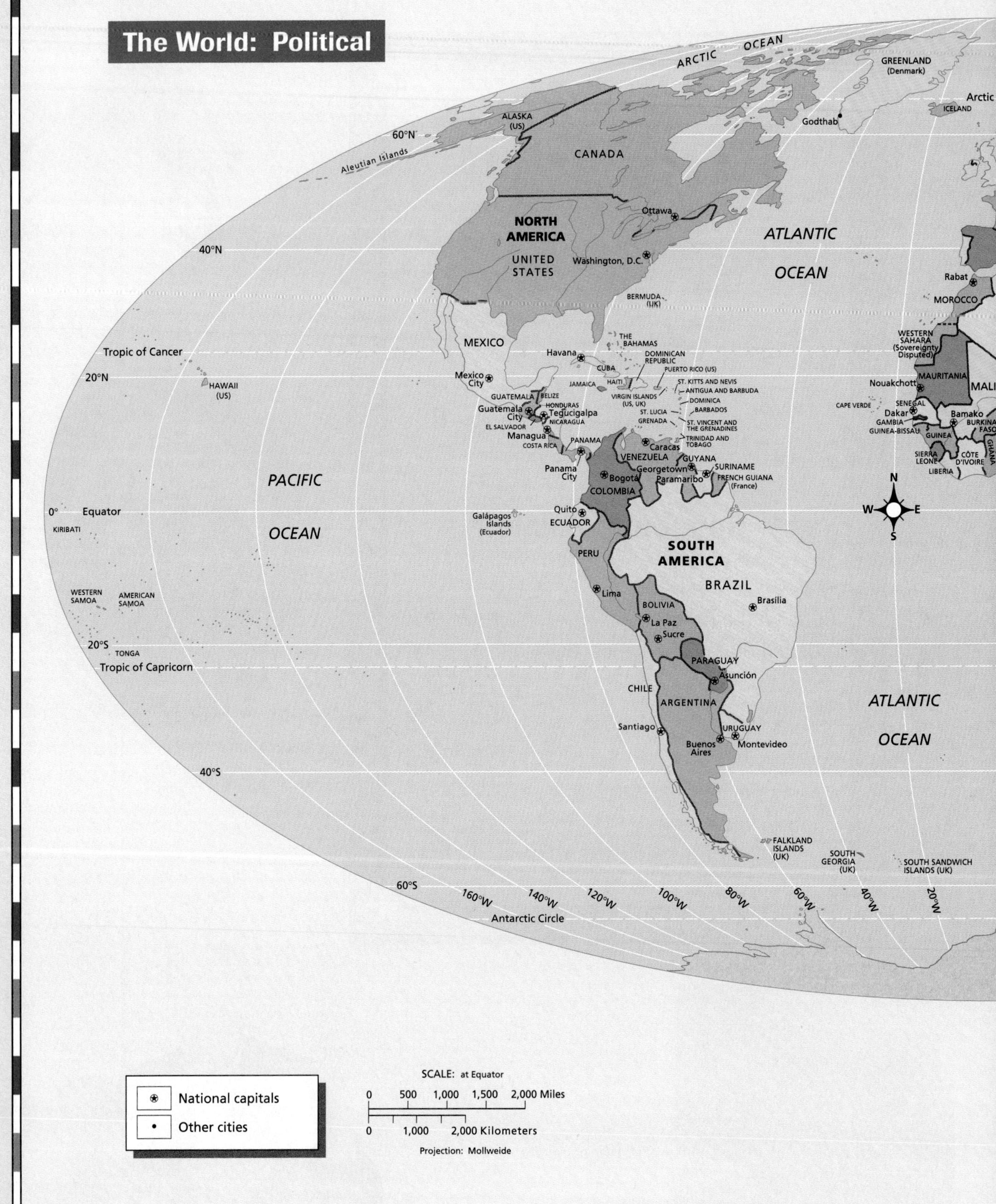
ARCTIC OCEAN
GREENLAND (Denmark)
Arctic
ICELAND
Godthab
ALASKA (US)
60°N
Aleutian Islands
CANADA
Ottawa
NORTH AMERICA
UNITED STATES
Washington, D.C.
40°N
ATLANTIC OCEAN
Rabat
MOROCCO
BERMUDA (UK)
THE BAHAMAS
MEXICO
Havana
DOMINICAN REPUBLIC
PUERTO RICO (US)
CUBA
Tropic of Cancer
WESTERN SAHARA (Sovereignty Disputed)
MAURITANIA
MALI
Nouakchott
20°N
HAWAII (US)
Mexico City
JAMAICA
HAITI
ST. KITTS AND NEVIS
ANTIGUA AND BARBUDA
DOMINICA
BARBADOS
ST. VINCENT AND THE GRENADINES
TRINIDAD AND TOBAGO
VIRGIN ISLANDS (US, UK)
ST. LUCIA
GRENADA
GUATEMALA
BELIZE
HONDURAS
Guatemala City
Tegucigalpa
NICARAGUA
EL SALVADOR
Managua
COSTA RICA
PANAMA
Caracas
VENEZUELA
GUYANA
Georgetown
SURINAME
Paramaribo
FRENCH GUIANA (France)
Panama City
Bogotá
COLOMBIA
CAPE VERDE
SENEGAL
Dakar
GAMBIA
GUINEA-BISSAU
GUINEA
Bamako
BURKINA FASO
SIERRA LEONE
LIBERIA
CÔTE D'IVOIRE
GHANA
PACIFIC OCEAN
0°
Equator
KIRIBATI
Galápagos Islands (Ecuador)
Quito
ECUADOR
N
W
E
S
SOUTH AMERICA
PERU
BRAZIL
Brasília
Lima
BOLIVIA
La Paz
Sucre
WESTERN SAMOA
AMERICAN SAMOA
20°S
TONGA
Tropic of Capricorn
PARAGUAY
Asunción
CHILE
ARGENTINA
Santiago
URUGUAY
Buenos Aires
Montevideo
40°S
FALKLAND ISLANDS (UK)
SOUTH GEORGIA (UK)
SOUTH SANDWICH ISLANDS (UK)
60°S
160°W
140°W
120°W
100°W
80°W
60°W
40°W
20°W
Antarctic Circle
National capitals
Other cities
SCALE: at Equator
0 500 1,000 1,500 2,000 Miles
0 1,000 2,000 Kilometers
Projection: Mollweide

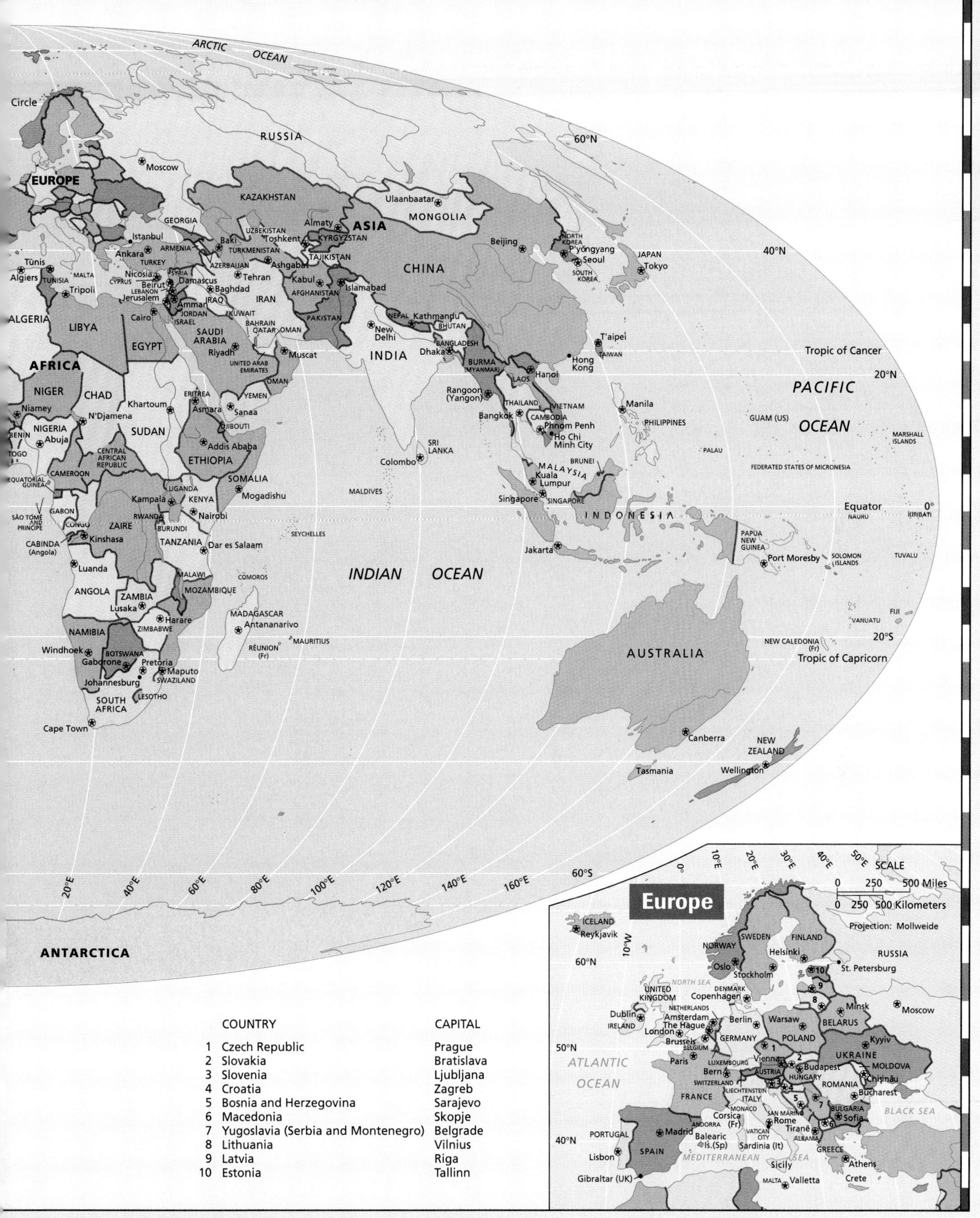

	COUNTRY	CAPITAL
1	Czech Republic	Prague
2	Slovakia	Bratislava
3	Slovenia	Ljubljana
4	Croatia	Zagreb
5	Bosnia and Herzegovina	Sarajevo
6	Macedonia	Skopje
7	Yugoslavia (Serbia and Montenegro)	Belgrade
8	Lithuania	Vilnius
9	Latvia	Riga
10	Estonia	Tallinn

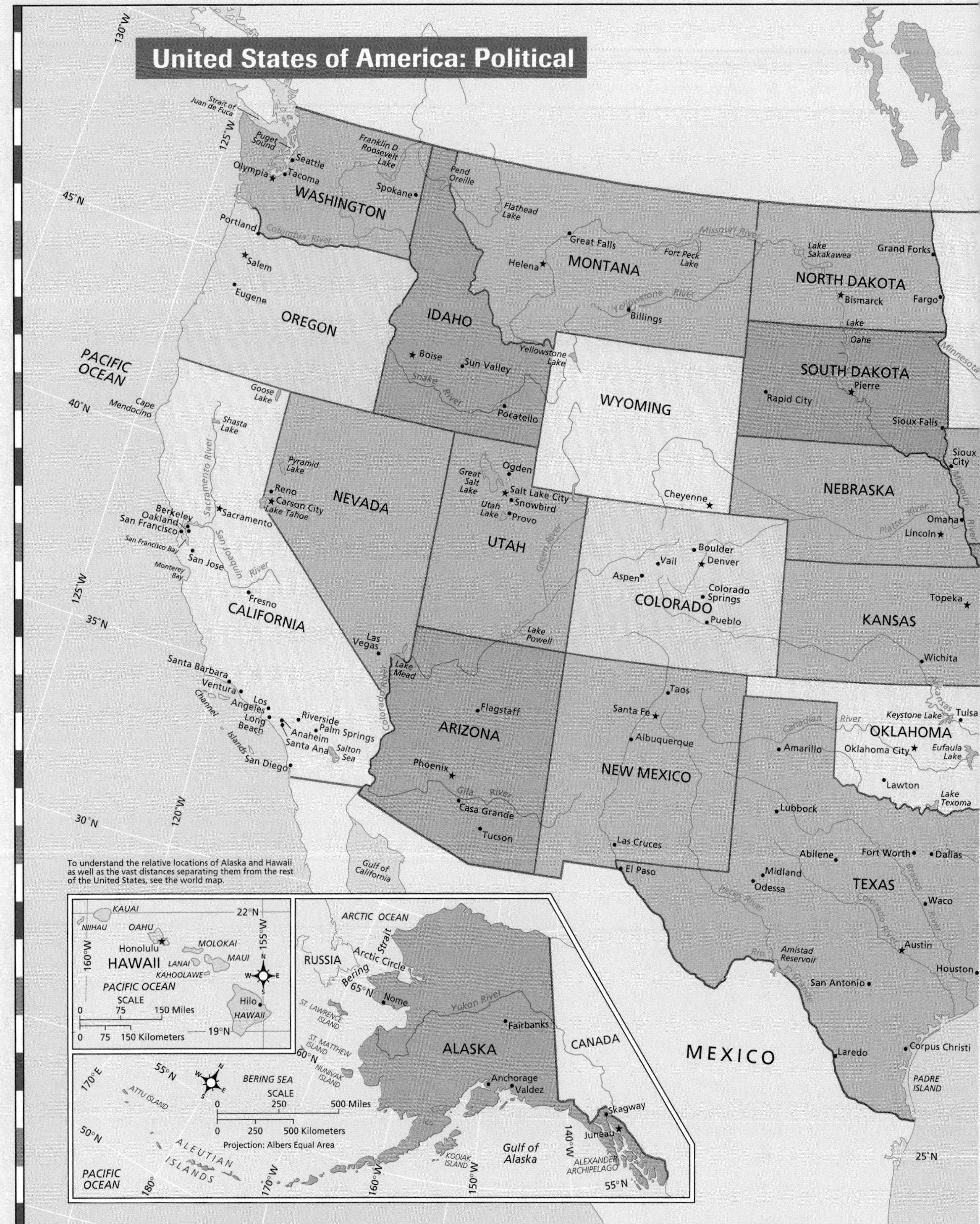
United States of America: Political
WASHINGTON
OREGON
CALIFORNIA
NEVADA
IDAHO
MONTANA
WYOMING
UTAH
COLORADO
ARIZONA
NEW MEXICO
NORTH DAKOTA
SOUTH DAKOTA
NEBRASKA
KANSAS
OKLAHOMA
TEXAS
MEXICO
PACIFIC OCEAN
Seattle
Olympia
Tacoma
Spokane
Portland
Salem
Eugene
Boise
Sun Valley
Pocatello
Helena
Great Falls
Billings
Bismarck
Grand Forks
Fargo
Pierre
Rapid City
Sioux Falls
Sioux City
Omaha
Lincoln
Cheyenne
Ogden
Salt Lake City
Snowbird
Provo
Reno
Carson City
Lake Tahoe
Sacramento
Berkeley
Oakland
San Francisco
San Jose
Fresno
Santa Barbara
Ventura
Los Angeles
Long Beach
Riverside
Palm Springs
Anaheim
Santa Ana
San Diego
Las Vegas
Flagstaff
Phoenix
Casa Grande
Tucson
Boulder
Denver
Vail
Aspen
Colorado Springs
Pueblo
Taos
Santa Fe
Albuquerque
Las Cruces
El Paso
Topeka
Wichita
Tulsa
Oklahoma City
Lawton
Amarillo
Lubbock
Abilene
Fort Worth
Dallas
Midland
Odessa
Waco
Austin
Houston
San Antonio
Laredo
Corpus Christi
To understand the relative locations of Alaska and Hawaii as well as the vast distances separating them from the rest of the United States, see the world map.
HAWAII
KAUAI
NIIHAU
OAHU
Honolulu
MOLOKAI
LANAI
MAUI
KAHOOLAWE
Hilo
PACIFIC OCEAN
SCALE
0 75 150 Miles
0 75 150 Kilometers
ALASKA
RUSSIA
CANADA
ARCTIC OCEAN
Arctic Circle
Bering Strait
Nome
Fairbanks
Anchorage
Valdez
Skagway
Juneau
BERING SEA
Gulf of Alaska
ALEUTIAN ISLANDS
SCALE
0 250 500 Miles
0 250 500 Kilometers
Projection: Albers Equal Area

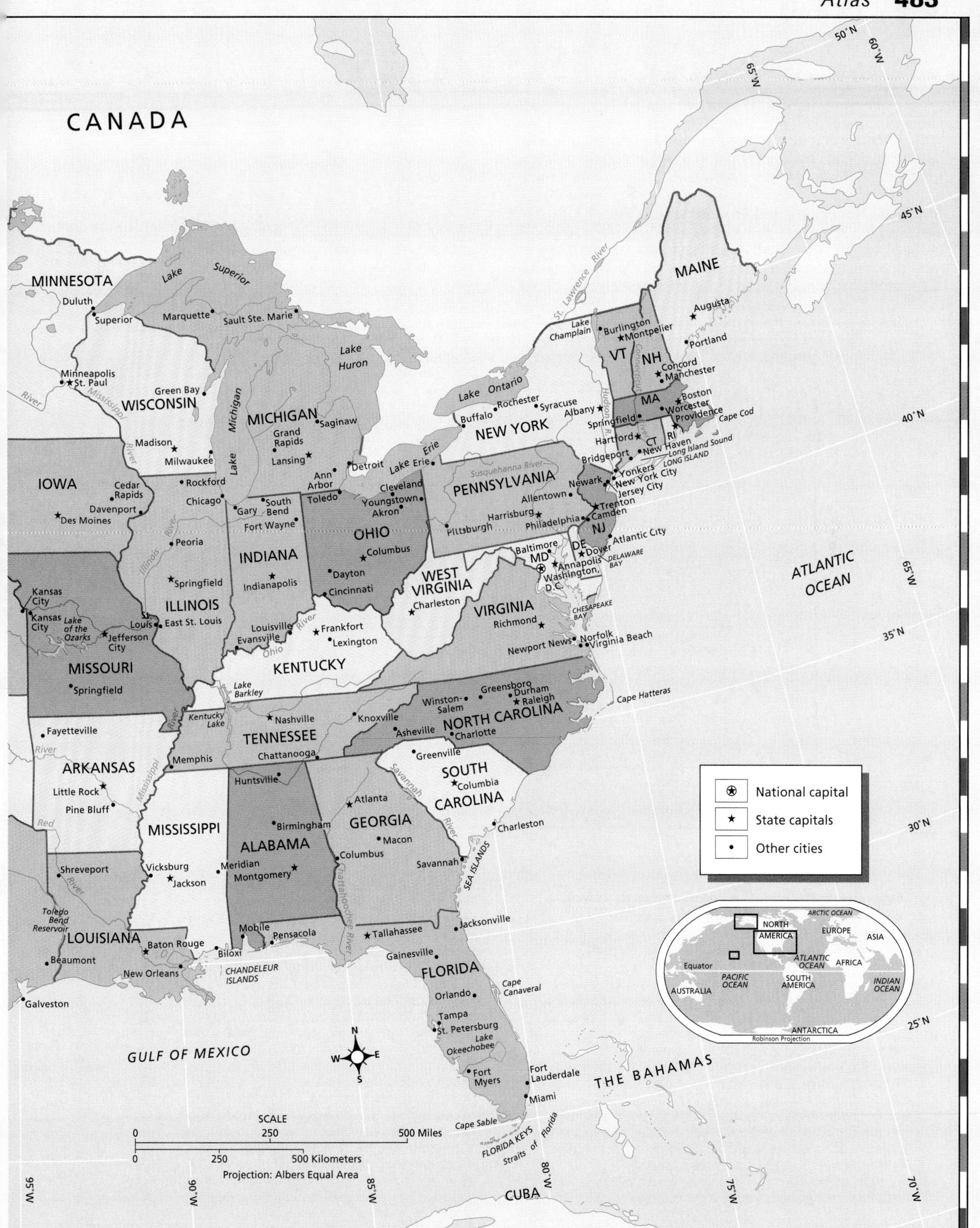
CANADA
MINNESOTA
WISCONSIN
MICHIGAN
IOWA
ILLINOIS
INDIANA
OHIO
PENNSYLVANIA
NEW YORK
MAINE
VT
NH
MA
CT
RI
NJ
DE
MD
WEST VIRGINIA
VIRGINIA
KENTUCKY
MISSOURI
TENNESSEE
NORTH CAROLINA
SOUTH CAROLINA
ARKANSAS
MISSISSIPPI
ALABAMA
GEORGIA
LOUISIANA
FLORIDA
ATLANTIC OCEAN
GULF OF MEXICO
THE BAHAMAS
CUBA
Lake Superior
Lake Michigan
Lake Huron
Lake Erie
Lake Ontario
Lake Champlain
St. Lawrence River
Mississippi River
Ohio River
Lake Okeechobee
Cape Cod
Cape Hatteras
Cape Canaveral
Cape Sable
FLORIDA KEYS
Straits of Florida
National capital
State capitals
Other cities
SCALE
0 250 500 Miles
0 250 500 Kilometers
Projection: Albers Equal Area
N E S W
NORTH AMERICA
EUROPE
ASIA
AFRICA
ATLANTIC OCEAN
PACIFIC OCEAN
INDIAN OCEAN
SOUTH AMERICA
AUSTRALIA
ANTARCTICA
ARCTIC OCEAN
Equator
Robinson Projection
50° N
45° N
40° N
35° N
30° N
25° N
95° W
90° W
85° W
80° W
75° W
70° W
65° W
60° W

GLOSSARY

This Glossary contains terms you need to understand as you study American history. After each term there is a brief definition or explanation of the meaning of the term as it is used in *Exploring America's Past.* The page number refers to the page on which the term is introduced in the textbook.

Phonetic Respelling and Pronunciation Guide

Many of the key terms in this textbook have been respelled to help you pronounce them. The letter combinations used in the respellings throughout the narrative are explained in the following phonetic respelling and pronunciation guide. The guide is adapted from *Webster's Tenth New College Dictionary, Webster's New Geographical Dictionary,* and *Webster's New Biographical Dictionary.*

MARK	AS IN	RESPELLING	EXAMPLE
a	alphabet	a	*AL-fuh-bet
ā	Asia	ay	AY-zhuh
ä	cart, top	ah	KAHRT, TAHP
e	let, ten	e	LET, TEN
ē	even, leaf	ee	EE-vuhn, LEEF
i	it, tip, British	i	IT, TIP, BRIT-ish
ī	site, buy, Ohio	y	SYT, BY, oh-HY-oh
	iris	eye	EYE-ris
k	card	k	KAHRD
ō	over, rainbow	oh	oh-vuhr, RAYN-boh
u̇	book, wood	ooh	BOOHK, WOOHD
ȯ	all, orchid	aw	AWL, AWR-kid
ȯi	foil, coin	oy	FOYL, KOYN
au̇	out	ow	OWT
ə	cup, butter	uh	KUHP, BUHT-uhr
ü	rule, food	oo	ROOL, FOOD
yü	few	yoo	FYOO
zh	vision	zh	VIZH-uhn

**A syllable printed in small capital letters receives heavier emphasis than the other syllable(s) in a word.*

A

ABC Powers Argentina, Brazil, and Chile. **442**

abolition An end to slavery. **233**

aces Fighter pilots who shoot down many enemy planes. **462**

Adams-Onís Treaty (1819) An agreement in which Spain gave up its claims to West Florida and Oregon Country and ceded the rest of Florida to the United States. **195**

affirmative action Practice by some businesses and government agencies of giving special consideration to nonwhites and women when applicants' qualifications are roughly equal to make up for past discrimination. **474**

Alamo Old Spanish mission-fort in San Antonio, Texas, that was the site of the most famous battle of the Texas war for independence in 1836; the Mexican victory resulted in the deaths of all the Texan defenders. **265**

Albany Plan of Union (1754) Proposal drafted by Benjamin Franklin for permanently uniting the colonies. **113**

Alien and Sedition Acts (1798) Series of laws passed by Federalists aimed at foreigners in the United States and at Republicans who were supposedly trying to weaken the government. **173**

amendments Official changes to a constitution. **118**

American Anti-Slavery Society Group founded in 1833 by William Lloyd Garrison and other abolitionists to support abolition and racial equality. **235**

American Colonization Society Group organized in 1817 by white citizens to relocate about 1,400 African Americans to what became the African nation of Liberia. **234**

American Federation of Labor (AFL) Union founded in the 1880s consisting only of skilled workers. **389**

American Indian Movement (AIM) Protest organization formed in 1968 that used confrontational tactics to draw attention to abuses against American Indians. **474**

American System Plan developed by Henry Clay to get western members of Congress to vote for high tariffs in exchange for eastern votes for internal improvements. **247**

amnesty Forgiveness. **338**
annex To take control of land. **273**
Antifederalists Opponents of the U.S. Constitution who tended to come from rural areas and were generally less wealthy than Federalists. **127**
Anti-Imperialist League Organization formed in June 1898 by Americans opposed to U.S. colonization. **436**
Anti-Saloon League Organization begun by progressives in 1895 to urge state legislatures to pass prohibition measures. **423**
arbitration Negotiations led by a neutral party. **418**
armistice Cease-fire agreement. **450**
arsenal Place where weapons are stored. **119**
Articles of Confederation America's first national constitution, drafted in 1777, that stressed the independence of the separate states. **113**
artisans People who craft items by hand. **13**
assayed To have minerals tested for value. **371**
assembly line Method of mass production in which a product is assembled by moving along a conveyer belt past a line of workers. **451**
astrolabe An instrument that helped sailors in the 1400s figure out a ship's latitude. **14**
Atlanta Compromise (1895) Proposal by Booker T. Washington that African Americans should accept American society and try to get ahead within it by learning skilled trades. **355**
atomic bomb Weapon developed by American scientists during World War II that released enormous amounts of energy by breaking the atomic bonds that hold together radioactive elements. **459**

B

baby boom Leap in the birthrate following World War II. **464**
Bacon's Rebellion (1676) Virginia movement led by Nathaniel Bacon to rid the colony of American Indians, in defiance of the royal governor. **54**
balance of trade The relationship between what a nation buys from and what it sells to foreign countries, not including its own colonies. **64**
bank notes Paper money produced by banks to represent the money they have on deposit. **162**
Bank of the United States A national bank with branches in major American cities, first proposed by Alexander Hamilton. **162**
bankruptcy A state of extreme financial ruin. **385**
barbed wire A relatively cheap method of fencing that allowed farmers and ranchers to close off their land. **375**
Battle of Antietam (1862) Civil War battle that resulted in the first major victory for the Union in the East. **325**
Battle of Bunker Hill (1775) Revolutionary War battle in which more than 1,000 British soldiers and some 400 American militiamen were killed or wounded in British victory. **92**
Battle of Fallen Timbers (1794) Battle between U.S. troops led by General "Mad Anthony" Wayne and an Indian confederacy led by Blue Jacket that ended the Indian confederacy's campaign to halt white settlement west of the Appalachian Mountains. **167**
Battle of Gettysburg (1863) One of the bloodiest battles of the Civil War in which the Confederates lost more than 20,000 troops and the Union forces some 23,000. **330**
Battle of Horseshoe Bend (1814) Defeat of Creek Indian forces allied with the British by the Tennessee militia, led by Andrew Jackson, in the War of 1812. **191**
Battle of Lake Erie (1813) U.S. victory led by Oliver Perry in the War of 1812. **190**
Battle of New Orleans (1815) Greatest victory for the United States in the War of 1812, even though it actually took place after the war was officially over. **192**
Battle of San Jacinto (1836) Final battle of the Texas war for independence in which Sam Houston led 800 Texas soldiers to victory against 1,400 Mexican troops led by Santa Anna. **266**
Battle of Saratoga (1777) Turning point of the Revolutionary War in which Americans, led by General Horatio Gates, delivered a crushing blow to British forces led by General John Burgoyne. **105**
Battle of Seven Pines (1862) Civil War battle in which neither side gained an advantage. **320**
Battle of Shiloh (1862) Civil War battle in Tennessee that resulted in Union victory, but a huge loss of life on both sides. **322**
Battle of the Little Bighorn (1876) Custer's Last Stand; the U.S. Army's worst defeat in the West when Sioux Indians, led by Sitting Bull, defeated troops led by General George Armstrong Custer. **368**
Battle of the Thames (1813) U.S. victory in the War of 1812 led by William Henry Harrison; allowed the United States to gain back the Great Lakes region and resulted in the death of Tecumseh, which ended the British-allied Indian confederacy. **190**
Battle of Tippecanoe (1811) Indiana battle between Americans, led by William Henry Harrison, against Indian confederacy, led by Tecumseh, that opposed American settlement in the Northwest Territory; defeat weakened the Indian confederacy. **188**
Battle of Trenton (1776) New Jersey battle of the Revolutionary War in which American soldiers overwhelmed Hessians fighting for the British, taking 900 prisoners. **102**
Battle of Yorktown (1781) Final major battle of the Revolutionary War that ended with the surrender of British general Cornwallis. **107**
Bear Flag Revolt (1846) Revolt against Mexico by California settlers who declared the Republic of California during the Mexican War. **275**
benevolent societies Groups set up by charitable organizations to help immigrants. **393**
Berlin Wall Concrete and barbed wire wall built between East Berlin and West Berlin by the Soviets in 1961. **467**
Bessemer process Inexpensive way to make steel, developed by Henry Bessemer in the 1850s. **381**
bicameral Two-house legislature. **121**
Big Three British prime minister Winston Churchill, U.S. president Franklin Roosevelt, and Soviet leader Joseph Stalin; leaders of the Allied Powers who met at Yalta in 1945 to plan for the end of World War II. **460**
Black Codes Regulations passed by southern state legislators to keep freedpeople in a slavelike condition after the Civil War. **338**
Black Death A deadly disease that first struck in the 1300s and swept across Europe, killing between 25 and 50 percent of the population. **13**
blockade Naval measure that uses ships to cut off a country's trade and supplies. **92**
bonanza A large find of extremely rich ore. **371**
bonds Treasury certificates that represent money the federal government has borrowed from citizens. **160**
border states Delaware, Maryland, Kentucky, and Missouri; the slave states that did not join the Confederacy. **316**
Boston Massacre (1770) Incident when British soldiers fired into a crowd protesting at a customs house, killing five colonists. **86**
Boston Tea Party (1773) Protest against the Tea Act in which colonists disguised as Mohawk Indians boarded tea ships and threw all the tea overboard. **87**
Boxer Rebellion (1900) Attack on foreigners in Beijing and other parts of China by Chinese nationalists known as the "Fists of Righteous Harmony," or Boxers; an international

army organized by Western nations put down the rebellion. **438**

Bozeman Trail Trail for miners, founded by John M. Bozeman, that branched off the Oregon Trail west of Fort Laramie and ran north into Montana. **365**

boycott To refuse to buy goods. **85**

brand Scar made by pressing a red-hot branding iron onto a cow's hide. **374**

Brown v. Board of Education (1954) Supreme Court case that overturned the "separate but equal" doctrine established in *Plessy* v. *Ferguson* and desegregated public schools. **465**

Bureau of Indian Affairs Government agency that supervised American Indian reservations and promised money and supplies to support their new way of life. **364**

C

cabinet Heads of federal departments who advise the president. **158**

California Gold Rush Rush of people to California to prospect for gold after a major gold discovery in 1848. **281**

California Trail Trail to California that branched off south from the Oregon Trail. **271**

Californios Mexican settlers and their descendants in California. **271**

canals Artificial waterways used for transportation. **214**

carpetbaggers Name given to northerners who moved to the South after the Civil War. **344**

causalties People killed, wounded, or missing in combat. **90**

cattle drive Long journey northward to get Texas longhorns to cattle towns. **372**

Cattle Kingdom Area from Texas into Canada and from the Rocky Mountains to eastern Kansas that became dotted with cattle ranches. **372**

cede Surrender. **195**

charter Document granting certain rights and powers to form colonies. **35**

Chicano movement Movement mostly among college students to increase awareness of Hispanic culture and political strength.**474**

Chinese Exclusion Act (1882) Legislation prohibiting Chinese workers from entering the United States for a period of 10 years, which was later extended well into the 1900s. **394**

circumnavigate To travel around the entire world. **24**

Civil Rights Act of 1866 Legislation forbidding southern states from passing laws, such as the Black Codes, restricting freedpeople's rights. **339**

Clayton Antitrust Act (1914) Law that made it illegal for directors of one corporation to be directors of other corporations in the same field. **420**

Cold War Long-lasting struggle for global power between the United States and the Soviet Union after World War II. **461**

collective bargaining Process in which union leaders negotiate with employers to determine employee working conditions and benefits. **389**

colonists People who leave their home countries to establish new settlements. **30**

Columbian Exchange The transfer of ideas, plants, animals, and diseases between the Eastern and Western Hemispheres. **36**

Commercial Revolution A rapid growth in the European economy during the 1400s. **13**

Committees of Correspondence Group organized by Samuel Adams to share information throughout the American colonies about resistance to the British. **86**

common A plot of public grazing land around which English colonists in North America centered their towns. **48**

Communists People who want to overthrow the capitalist economic system and replace it with a society where all individuals share wealth equally and where private ownership is abolished. **450**

Compromise of 1850 Proposal by Henry Clay to allow California to enter the Union as a free state, while the rest of the Mexican Cession would be divided into two new territories where the residents would determine the status of slavery; also prohibited the slave trade in the District of Columbia and created a stronger fugitive slave law. **292**

Compromise of 1877 Proposal that grew out of disputed presidential election of 1876; Democrats agreed to let Republican Rutherford B. Hayes become president if he would remove all federal troops stationed in the South. **349**

Comstock Lode Silver bonanza struck in western Nevada in 1859. **371**

Confederate States of America The Confederacy, central government created by delegates of states that seceded from the Union in 1861. **313**

Confederation Congress Single national governing body created by the Articles of Confederation. **113**

Congress of Racial Equality Organization which recruited black and white college students from the North to campaign in the South for equal rights. **469**

conquistadores Soldier-explorers who helped Spain establish and expand its empire in the Americas. **22**

constitution A set of laws that defines the basic structure and powers of a government. **112**

Constitutional Convention (1787) Meeting of state delegates to draw up the Constitution of the United States. **121**

Constitutional Union Party Group formed in 1860 by southerners who wanted to preserve "the Union as it is and the Constitution as it is." **307**

Continental Army Official colonial military force created by the Second Continental Congress and led by George Washington. **91**

contrabands Escaped slaves who crossed Union lines during the Civil War. **326**

Contract with America (1994) Republican document that put into effect a 10-point program for redirecting the government and the economy. **476**

Convention of 1818 Agreement that set the boundary between the Louisiana Purchase and British Canada at 49° north latitude from northern Minnesota to the Rocky Mountains; also called for joint control of the disputed area of Oregon Country. **194**

Copperheads Northern Democrats who opposed the Civil War. **327**

corporations Businesses in which entrepreneurs sell shares called stock certificates to investors. **384**

cotton belt A huge agricultural region largely devoted to the production of cotton. **221**

cotton gin Machine produced by Eli Whitney in 1793 that separated cotton seeds from the fibers. **220**

Council of the Indies Group of royal assistants in Spain that nominated colonial officials and drafted and administered laws relating to Spain's colonies in the Americas. **27**

counting coup To touch an enemy or capture his weapon; proof of an American Indian warrior's highest bravery. **361**

covenant Sacred agreement. **49**

creditors People to whom money is owed. **119**

crop lien Investors' claim against a crop before it is even harvested. **353**

Crusades A series of religious wars fought between Christians and Muslims for control of Palestine, an area in Southwest Asia that was sacred to Muslims, Jews, and Christians. **12**

Cuban missile crisis (1962) Standoff between the Soviet Union and the United States over missiles in Cuba; resulted in decreasing likelihood of nuclear war. **467**

culture Common values and customs of a society. **4**
culture area A geographic region in which residents share common cultural traits; used to group American Indian societies. **5**

D

D-Day June 6, 1944; beginning of Allied invasion of France during World War II. **458**
debtors People who owe money. **118**
Declaration of Independence Statement by members of the Second Continental Congress, signed on July 4, 1776, explaining the need for independence by the colonies. **95**
Democratic Party Political party formed in 1828 by Andrew Jackson's supporters who split from the Democratic-Republican Party. **245**
Democratic-Republican Party Republicans; political party led by Thomas Jefferson and formed in the 1790s by those who opposed Alexander Hamilton. **170**
deport To order a person out of a country. **173**
depression A sharp drop in business activity accompanied by high unemployment. **250**
diplomats Officials who conduct government relations with foreign countries. **113**
dissenters People who disagree with commonly held opinions. **50**
dollar diplomacy President William Howard Taft's policy of trying to control nations in the Western Hemisphere indirectly by using economic methods rather than military force. **441**
Dominion of New England Unified group of colonies organized by King James II in 1686 and led by Sir Edmund Andros; was overthrown in 1689. **62**
draft A system requiring people to serve in the military. **327**
***Dred Scott* decision** (1857) Supreme Court ruling that declared African Americans were not citizens and that the Missouri Compromise had been unconstitutional. **300**
droughts Dry periods when almost no rain falls. **378**
dry farming Technique promoted by Hardy W. Campbell that made it possible to raise certain crops with very little water. **379**
duties Import taxes. **84**

E

Eighteenth Amendment (1919) Constitutional amendment that made prohibition legal throughout the nation. **423**
emancipation Freedom. **237**
Emancipation Proclamation Order issued by President Abraham Lincoln to announce that as of January 1, 1863, all slaves in the states rebelling against the Union would be free. **325**
embargo A government order prohibiting trade. **185**
Embargo Act (1807) Law that prohibited all exports from the United States. **185**
empresario Someone who made a business of bringing settlers into the American West. **264**
enclosure movement Process in Great Britain by which many tenant farmers were thrown off their land when owners fenced the land to raise sheep; many of these farmers went to work in factories. **205**
energy crisis Situation in the 1970s when the cost of electricity and gasoline soared due to rising oil prices. **473**
Enlightenment Movement in the 1700s that grew out of the Scientific Revolution and encouraged the use of reason to investigate and try to improve government and society. **112**
entrepreneurs Risk-taking businesspeople. **384**
enumerated articles Products that colonial producers could sell only within English-controlled territory. **64**
Equal Rights Amendment (ERA) Proposed constitutional amendment stating that equality of rights could not be denied on the basis of gender; passed by Congress in 1972, but failed to be ratified. **474**
Erie Canal Canal completed in 1825, running from the Hudson River across New York to Lake Erie. **215**
escalation Increase. **471**
excise taxes Taxes on goods produced and consumed inside a country. **161**
executive branch Branch of government that carries out laws. **123**
Exodusters Some 20,000 or more African Americans who moved west from the South in 1879. **377**
export To sell products to another country. **64**

F

54th Massachusetts Infantry African American Union troops that won an honored place in U.S. military history during the Civil War battle for Fort Wagner. **326**
fascism Totalitarian political system founded in Italy in the 1920s by Benito Mussolini. **455**
Farmers' Alliance Political group in the late 1800s that opposed high railroad rates and high bank interest rates. **399**
Federal Deposit Insurance Corporation (FDIC) Organization established by Congress in the 1930s to prevent another banking crisis by insuring deposits up to $5,000. **453**
Federal Reserve Act (1913) Legislation that created 12 Federal Reserve banks in different sections of the nation; these banks were for banks, not for businesses or individuals. **420**
Federal Trade Commission Organization established in 1914 to conduct investigations of large corporations. **420**
federalism System established by the U.S. Constitution of dividing power between the state and national governments. **125**
Federalist Party Political party organized in the 1790s by members of Congress who favored Alexander Hamilton's financial policies. **170**
Federalists Supporters of the U.S. Constitution who tended to be wealthy lawyers, merchants, and planters. **126**
Fifteenth Amendment (1869) Constitutional amendment guaranteeing that the right to vote could not be denied on the basis of race, color, or previous condition of servitude. **341**
First Battle of Bull Run (1861) First major battle of the Civil War; afterward, Americans on both sides realized that winning the war might be difficult. **319**
First Continental Congress (1774) Meeting of representatives from all colonies (except Georgia) to express loyalty to Britain but demand the repeal of all British taxation laws and to ban all trade with Britain until Parliament met its demands. **88**
folktales Oral stories that help to educate and set a standard of behavior for people. **230**
Food Administration Organization headed by Herbert Hoover during World War I to make sure that enough food was produced and that it was distributed fairly. **449**
Fort Laramie Treaty (1851) Agreement signed between the U.S. government and Plains Indians to allow settlement in the West. **364**
forty-niners At least 80,000 people who flocked to California in 1849 to prospect for gold. **281**
Fourteenth Amendment (1866) Constitutional amendment that gave citizenship to all African Americans in the United States. **340**
free coinage Policy requiring the government to coin silver freely, increasing the money in circulation. **399**
Freedmen's Bureau Agency created by Congress shortly before the end of the Civil War to take care of freedpeople and refugees. **339**

Freedom Rides Plan developed by CORE to challenge segregation in interstate commerce by having white and black Freedom Riders travel through the South on buses, intentionally ignoring signs in segregated stations. **469**
Freeport Doctrine (1858) Statement by Stephen A. Douglas during the Lincoln-Douglas debates arguing that the people of a territory could outlaw slavery by passing local laws making it impossible for slavery to exist. **304**
Free-Soil Party Political organization founded by antislavery Whigs and northern Democrats to prevent slavery in the new territories. **290**
French Revolution Revolution against the French monarchy that began in 1789. **164**
Fugitive Slave Act (1850) Allowed slave catchers more power to capture suspected runaways. **292**

G

Gadsden Purchase (1853) Agreement that added a strip of Mexican land to southern New Mexico and Arizona for $10 million. **276**
Ghost Dance (1889) American Indian religious revival that swept through the Plains. **369**
glaciers Vast ice fields that formed during the Ice Age and caused the water level of the world's oceans to drop sharply. **3**
Glorious Revolution (1688) Revolt against pro-Catholic King James II by Parliament that resulted in James's Protestant daughter Mary and her husband, William of Orange, being crowned queen and king of England. **63**
glyphs System of picture writing used by the Maya around A.D. 300–800. **5**
gold standard Monetary system in which the government backs each dollar with a set amount of gold. **399**
grandfather clauses Laws stating that literacy tests and poll taxes did not apply to persons who had been able to vote before 1867 or to their descendants. **350**
Great Awakening A series of events that began in the 1730s and sparked new interest in Christianity in the American colonies. **71**
Great Compromise (1787) Agreement establishing that population would determine representation in the national legislature's lower house, while each state would have an equal vote in the legislature's upper house. **122**
Great Depression Worldwide economic downturn that began with the stock market crash of 1929. **453**
Great Migration Large movement of English Puritans to the Americas in the 1600s. **49**
Great Society Vast effort by President Lyndon Johnson to transform society by eliminating many long-standing social and economic problems. **468**
guerrillas Fighters who use hit-and-run tactics. **106**

H

habeas corpus A constitutional protection that prevents authorities from unlawfully jailing people. **327**
Harlem Renaissance Movement among black writers in the 1920s who urged respect for African American culture. **451**
Hay-Bunau-Varilla Treaty (1903) Agreement granting the United States a 10-mile-wide canal zone across Panama. **440**
Haymarket Riot (1886) Bombing during a union meeting at Chicago's Haymarket Square in which seven police officers were killed; turned public opinion against unions. **389**
headright Land grant of 50 acres per head, or person, given by the London Company to colonists who paid their own way and that of others to America. **53**
Holocaust Hitler's "Final Solution," or plan to rid Europe of Jews by placing them in concentration camps, where millions were killed. **459**
Homestead Act (1862) Federal law that gave western land grants to promote settlement. **376**
Homestead Strike (1892) Strike against Andrew Carnegie's steel factory in Homestead, Pennsylvania, which led to violence between strikers and private police from the Pinkerton Detective Agency. **390**
horizontal integration The attempted ownership of all the companies in a particular field. **385**
House of Burgesses The first elected English governing body in the colonies. **54**
House of Representatives Lower house of the United States legislature; assumed to act on behalf of the people. **123**
House Un-American Activities Committee (HUAC) Congressional committee that began a series of hearings in 1947 to investigate citizens who belonged to a number of liberal organizations. **462**
Hull House The most famous American settlement house, founded in 1889 by Jane Addams in Chicago. **412**
hunter-gatherers Groups that hunted game and gathered wild plants, traveled in small groups, and lived in caves or tepees. **5**

I

Ice Age Ancient period during which the weather was much colder than it is now, causing snow to fall and form glaciers. **3**
immigrants Foreign-born people who move to another country. **208**
Immigration Restriction League Organization formed by nativists in the 1890s to call for a law preventing immigrants who could not read or write any language from entering the United States. **395**
immunity Resistance to disease. **26**
impeachment Bringing formal charges of wrongdoing against a public official. **341**
imperialism Controlling overseas colonies by force. **436**
import To buy products from another country. **64**
impressment British practice of forcing sailors suspected of being British soldiers to serve in the Royal Navy; strained relations between the United States and Great Britain in the early 1800s. **185**
indentured servants People who signed contracts to work for others for a set period of time, usually four or five years. **53**
Indian Removal Act (1830) Federal law that provided money to carry out President Andrew Jackson's policy for removing eastern Indian tribes to Indian Territory. **252**
Industrial Revolution Period of great industrial expansion that began in Britain in the late 1700s. **200**
Indian Territory Place chosen to relocate eastern Indian tribes in the early 1800s; later became Oklahoma. **252**
inflation A sharp rise in prices. **32**
initiative Voting practice that enables voters to initiate, or propose, laws. **413**
installment plan Program allowing customers to make monthly payments, along with interest, on a product until it is paid in full. **451**
interchangeable parts Process developed by Eli Whitney in the 1790s to allow broken items to be fixed more quickly by making parts of certain models of an item exactly the same. **203**
interstate commerce Business and trade between states. **114**
Interstate Commerce Act (1887) Law that required railroad rates to be "reasonable and just." **399**
Interstate Commerce Commission (ICC) Federal board of examiners who oversaw railroads. **399**
Intolerable Acts (1774) Four laws passed by Parliament in reaction to the Boston Tea Party to reclaim its control over the colonies and to punish Massachusetts. **87**

Iroquois League The Five Nations; an alliance formed by tribes of the Northeast culture area in what is now New York State. **7**
isolationism Keeping out of foreign affairs and halting further expansion of U.S. borders. **427**
isthmus Small neck of land that connects two larger land masses. **22**

J

Jacksonian Democracy New democratic spirit in America ushered in by the election of President Andrew Jackson in 1828. **245**
Jay's Treaty (1994) Treaty negotiated by John Jay between the United States and Great Britain to ease tensions over trade, western territory, and British seizure of U.S. merchant ships. **166**
jazz Music created in the late 1800s by African American musicians primarily in New Orleans. **451**
jerky Dried meat. **362**
Jim Crow laws Laws that enforced segregation in the South. **350**
John Brown's raid (1859) Incident in which John Brown and his followers took control of an arsenal and government gun factory in Harpers Ferry, Virginia, hoping to spark a slave rebellion. **306**
joint-stock companies Businesses owned by many stockholders who shared in the profits and losses. **41**
judicial branch Branch of the government that interprets laws. **123**
judicial review The right of the courts to declare an act of Congress unconstitutional. **180**
juntas Committees established by Cuban revolutionaries in the United States to raise money, spread propaganda, and recruit volunteers for the struggle for Cuban independence from Spain. **432**

K

Kansas-Nebraska Act (1854) Federal law allowing residents of each of the territories to decide whether slavery would be legal there. **296**
Knights of Labor One of the first large unions to emerge in the United States after the Civil War; founded by Uriah Stephens in 1869. **388**
Know-Nothings Members of the American Party, formed in 1849 by nativists opposed to immigration. **209**
Ku Klux Klan A secret organization that emerged after the Civil War and used violence and threats to hold back African Americans. **347**

L

labor unions Organizations workers form to improve their conditions. **206**
Land Ordinance of 1785 Congressional plan for the orderly sale of the western territories. **116**
latitude The distance north or south of the equator. **14**
legislative branch Branch of government that writes laws. **123**
Lend-Lease Act (1941) Federal law giving the president authority to sell or lend war supplies to any nation whose defense was considered to be essential to America's security. **456**
Lewis and Clark expedition Expedition led by Meriwether Lewis and William Clark starting in 1804 to explore land in the Louisiana Purchase. **183**
Lincoln-Douglas debates Series of debates between Illinois candidates for the U.S. Senate, Republican Abraham Lincoln and Democrat Stephen A. Douglas. **302**
Line of Demarcation Line established by Pope Alexander VI that divided the ocean about 400 miles west of the Azores. Lands west of the line were to belong to Spain, those east to Portugal. **19**
literacy tests Tests limiting voting to those who could read well; were used primarily against African Americans in the South after Reconstruction. **350**
lobbyists People hired to influence legislators on behalf of special interests. **413**
loose construction Argument that congressional action is constitutional as long as the U.S. Constitution does not clearly forbid it. **162**
Louisiana Purchase (1803) Large American purchase of French land west of the Mississippi River that doubled the size of the United States. **181**
Lowell girls Female employees in Francis Lowell's Massachusetts textile factory. **206**
Loyalists Tories; colonists who strongly supported the British and opposed the Declaration of Independence. **95**

M

maize Corn; the most important food crop grown in ancient America. **5**
manifest destiny Phrase used to describe some Americans' feeling that the entire North American continent could belong to the United States. **271**
manors Sections of land in Europe that were ruled by nobles known as lords. **9**
Marbury* v. *Madison (1803) Supreme Court case that established the Court's power of judicial review. **180**
March on Washington (1963) Gathering of more than 200,000 people to demonstrate peacefully for civil rights. **469**
Marshall Plan (1948) Economic plan, proposed by Secretary of State George C. Marshall, of providing monetary help to war-torn European nations if they asked for it. **461**
Massacre at Wounded Knee (1890) Killing of 300 Sioux by the U.S. Army; ended armed Indian resistance to white settlement in the West. **369**
massive retaliation Cold War strategy of Secretary of State John Foster Dulles calling for the free world to develop the will and organize the means to retaliate instantly against open aggression by communist armies. **463**
mass production Process of producing large numbers of identical goods more efficiently. **202**
Mayflower Compact (1620) Document drawn up by the Pilgrims to provide a legal basis for Plymouth, their colony in North America. **47**
McClure's Magazine One of many important muckraking periodicals. **410**
McKinley Tariff (1890) Measure that took away the special advantage of Hawaiians by granting sugar producers in the United States a payment of two cents per pound on sugar; as a result, sugar prices fell and the Hawaiian economy suffered. **430**
mercantilism Economic program designed to achieve a favorable balance of trade by tightly controlling traded goods. **64**
mercenaries Hired soldiers. **102**
Mexican Cession Territory that Mexico ceded to the United States after the Mexican War. **276**
Mexican Revolution Revolution begun in Mexico in 1910 against dictator Porfirio Díaz. **442**
middle class New social class between the rich and the poor that developed in the 1840s as a result of industrialization. **211**
Middle Passage The transportation of enslaved Africans to the Americas during which many Africans died. **69**
migration Movement from one place to another. **4**

militarism Belief that the use of military force is a good solution to international problems. **447**
militia A group of citizens organized for military service. **78**
Minutemen Colonial members of rebel militias who were ready for action on a minute's notice. **90**
missions Church communities founded by Catholic priests. **30**
Missouri Compromise (1820) Agreement that admitted Missouri to the Union as a slave state and Maine as a free state; it also outlawed slavery in the rest of the Louisiana Purchase north of 36°30′ north latitude. **243**
monopoly Complete domination of an industry. **385**
Monroe Doctrine (1823) Statement issued by President James Monroe declaring that European countries could no longer establish colonies in the Americas and that the United States would stay out of European affairs. **196**
Montgomery Bus Boycott (1955–56) Boycott in Montgomery, Alabama, in which African Americans stayed off city buses until the city changed the law requiring them to sit in the rear and give up their seats to white passengers. **465**
Mormon Trail Trail on which 15,000 Mormons led by Brigham Young traveled to Utah. **280**
Mormons Members of the Church of Jesus Christ of Latter-Day Saints, founded in 1830 by Joseph Smith. **279**
Morrill Act (1862) Federal law giving western land grants to promote educational facilities. **376**
mountain men Men hired by fur companies to roam the Rocky Mountains and trap beaver and other animals. **267**
muckrakers Progressive journalists who saw the "filth on the floor" and tried to "scrape [it] up with a muck-rake." **408**
Muslims Followers of Islam, the religion established by Muhammad in 610. **11**
mutiny Rebellion against the captain of a ship by the crew. **23**

N

National American Woman Suffrage Association (NAWSA) Organization founded in 1890 to lead the fight for women's right to vote. **422**
National Aeronautics and Space Administration (NASA) Agency founded by the U.S. government in the 1950s to expand scientific research and development on space exploration. **463**
National Association for the Advancement of Colored People (NAACP) Progressive organization that attempted to end lynching, or mob murder, and that worked for African Americans' civil rights. **425**
national debt Debt accumulated by the federal government. **160**
National Grange Political organization that represented farmers in the 1870s. **398**
nationalism A spirit of national pride. **197**
National Organization for Women (NOW) Group founded by Betty Friedan in 1966 to fight for women's rights. **474**
National Road Federal road project on which construction started in 1811 in Cumberland, Maryland; the road crossed over the mountains in southwestern Pennsylvania and ended at present-day Wheeling, West Virginia (later extended to Vandalia, Illinois). **214**
National Woman's Party Organization founded by Alice Paul in 1913 to call for a constitutional amendment guaranteeing women's suffrage. **422**
Nat Turner's Rebellion (1831) Failed Virginia slave revolt, led by Nat Turner, that resulted in the deaths of 60 whites and at least 120 African Americans. **232**
Navigation and Trade Acts Series of laws passed by Parliament from 1651 to the mid-1700s regulating the buying and selling of goods. **64**
nativists Americans opposed to unlimited immigration because they believed that too many newcomers would destroy American institutions. **209**
Nazis National Socialists; political party led by Adolf Hitler that established a totalitarian government in Germany in 1933. **456**
Neutrality Proclamation (1793) Statement issued by President George Washington to warn Americans not to favor either side in the war between France and Great Britain. **165**
New Deal President Franklin Roosevelt's policy for dealing with the Great Depression. **453**
new immigrants People who came to the United States after the 1880s, mainly from southern and eastern Europe. **392**
New Jersey Plan Rejected set of resolutions written by delegates to the Constitutional Convention from small states that would have continued the one-state, one-vote system of government used under the Articles of Confederation. **121**
Niagara Movement Movement founded by W. E. B. Du Bois and other African American leaders in 1905 to demand equal economic and educational opportunities, voting rights, and an end to segregation. **425**
Nineteenth Amendment (1920) Constitutional amendment that gave women the right to vote. **422**
nominating conventions Meetings of delegates to choose a political party's presidential and vice-presidential candidates. **246**
Non-Intercourse Act (1809) Federal law that replaced the Embargo Act by restoring trade with all foreign countries except Great Britain and France. **186**
North Atlantic Treaty Organization (NATO) Alliance between the United States and Western European nations in which members pledged to defend one another in case of attack and to form a unified military force for this purpose. **462**
Northwest Ordinance The Land Ordinance of 1787; a plan to create a government for the region north of the Ohio River and west of Pennsylvania. **116**
nullification Idea supported by John C. Calhoun that if a state considered a federal law unconstitutional, it could refuse to accept the law and prevent it from being enforced in that state. **248**

O

old immigrants Immigrants mainly from western and northern Europe who came to the United States before the 1880s. **392**
Olive Branch Petition (1775) Offer sent by the Second Continental Congress to King George III to ask him to protect the colonies against further actions by Parliament until a compromise could be worked out. **92**
Open Door Policy (1898) Statement by U.S. secretary of state John Hay saying that all nations would have equal trade rights in China. **438**
open range Grass on public lands in the West. **373**
Operation Desert Storm (1991) UN military attack on Iraq to drive back Saddam Hussein's invasion of Kuwait. **476**
Oregon Trail 2,000-mile trail from western Missouri to Oregon. **269**

P

Pacific Railway Act (1862) Federal law giving western land to promote the building of a transcontinental railroad. **376**
Panama Canal Waterway completed in 1914 linking the Atlantic and Pacific Oceans across the Isthmus of Panama; controlled by the United States. **441**
Panic of 1837 Sudden collapse of prices and business activity after an inflationary boom, followed by many bank and business failures, particularly in the West and South. **249**
Parliament The lawmaking body of Great Britain. **61**
Patriots Colonists who favored independence. **95**

Pendleton Civil Service Act (1883) Law that established examinations as the basis for awarding some government jobs. **398**
Pickett's Charge (1863) Final, failed Confederate charge, led by General George E. Pickett, in the Battle of Gettysburg. **330**
Pinckney's Treaty (1795) Treaty negotiated by Thomas Pinckney between the United States and Spain establishing a western border for Florida and recognizing American rights on the Mississippi and in New Orleans. **167**
pilgrimage A religious journey. **11**
Pilgrims The first English Separatists to come to America seeking religious freedom. **47**
Plains Indians American Indians who lived on the Great Plains, from western Texas to the Dakotas and then on into Canada, in the 1800s. **359**
plantations Large farms. **44**
planters People who owned plantations and who held more than 20 slaves. **222**
Plessy* v. *Ferguson (1896) Supreme Court case that established the doctrine of "separate but equal" facilities for different races. **350**
political parties Groups of people who organize to help elect government officials and to try to influence government policies. **170**
poll taxes Taxes on individuals, which were usually collected at the time of an election. **350**
Pontiac's Rebellion (1763) American Indian rebellion led by Ottawa chief Pontiac to drive white settlers back across the Appalachian Mountains; halted after failed siege on Fort Detroit. **84**
popular sovereignty Principle that would let voters in new territories make their own decisions about slavery. **290**
Populist Party Political party in the 1890s that called for government ownership of railroads, telegraph, and telephone systems, a federal income tax, and loans to farmers. **400**
Pottawatomie Massacre (1856) Incident in which John Brown and his followers murdered five members of a pro-slavery settlement in Kansas. **298**
precedents Earlier examples. **157**
prejudice Unreasonable opinion unsupported by facts. **122**
privateers Armed private vessels authorized to attack enemy shipping. **165**
Privy Council Group of English royal advisers who made colonial policy and were subject to Parliament. **61**
Proclamation of 1763 Order issued by the British government to close the area west of the Appalachians to colonial settlement. **84**
progressives Americans who worked for reform around 1900. **408**
prohibition The outlawing of the manufacture and sale of alcoholic beverages. **258**
proprietor Single owner of a colony. **55**
prospect To search for. **280**
protective tariffs High duties on imported goods that compete with American products. **247**
public works Government projects such as constructing roads or building dams. **453**
pueblos "Towns"; what European explorers called homes of Native Americans in the Southwest culture area. **7**
Pure Food and Drug Act (1906) Law that provided for federal control of the quality of most foods and drugs and for the regulation of slaughterhouses. **419**
Puritans English Protestants who wanted to "purify" the Anglican Church by removing all traces of Catholicism from it. **47**

Q

Quakers Members of a religious sect that settled in Pennsylvania and stressed religious tolerance, simplicity, and kindness toward others. **58**

R

Radical Republicans Members of Congress who were concerned that President Andrew Johnson's plan for Reconstruction would put too much power in the hands of former slaveholders. **338**
range rights Water rights on western lands. **373**
ratification Formal approval by states. **114**
recall Practice that allows citizens to remove an elected politician from office before the person's term expires. **413**
Reconstruction The rebuilding of the South's government and society after the end of the Civil War. **337**
Reconstruction Acts (1867) Series of stern measures strengthening military control of the South. **340**
Red Scare Fear of Communists and anarchists, as well as socialists, following World War I. **450**
Redeemers New southern white leaders who claimed they were taking back the powers and duties their class had exercised before Reconstruction. **353**
referendum Practice that allows citizens to vote on a legislative proposal, then vote for or against the measure at a regular election. **413**
Reformation Protestant religious movement of the 1500s that challenged the power of the Catholic Church. **46**
reforms Improvements. **120**
refugees People who flee their homes to avoid danger. **339**
repeal Officially withdraw. **85**
Republic of Texas Government established on March 2, 1836, by Texans who wanted independence from Mexico. **266**
republican Form of government in which the people hold the power and give elected representatives the authority to make and carry out laws. **112**
Republican Party Political organization formed in the North after the passage of the Kansas-Nebraska Act to oppose the spread of slavery into the western territories. **300**
rendezvous Yearly gathering of mountain men where they sold their furs, exchanged stories, and had a rollicking good time. **268**
reservations Federal lands set aside specifically for American Indians. **364**
revivals Spirited religious meetings. **256**
right of deposit The right to transfer goods without paying a duty. **167**
Roosevelt Corollary (1904) President Theodore Roosevelt's policy that considered any European interference in nations in the Western Hemisphere a violation of the Monroe Doctrine. **441**
rotation in office Practice of replacing government jobholders to give the party in power more political control. **246**
Rough Riders U.S. regiment in the Spanish-American War made up of an odd assortment of soldiers led by Theodore Roosevelt. **434**
roundup Event that occurs each fall and spring when cattle hands gather all cattle together, then separate them by brand. **374**
Rush-Bagot Agreement (1817) Agreement signed between the United States and Great Britain providing that neither country would maintain a fleet of warships on the Great Lakes. **194**

S

Sand Creek Massacre (1864) Attack led by Colonel John Chivington on a Cheyenne encampment in Colorado Territory in which some 200 Cheyenne were killed. **365**
Santa Fe Trail 780-mile-long route from Missouri to Santa Fe, New Mexico. **271**
scalawags "Good-for-nothing rascals"; name given to southern white Republicans during Reconstruction. **344**

Scientific Revolution A movement that began in the 1500s in Europe and encouraged people to improve themselves and the world around them by careful study. **72**
seadogs English sailors who preyed on Spanish ships in the 1500s. **34**
secession The act of withdrawing as part of a nation. **308**
Second Battle of Bull Run (1862) Civil War battle that resulted in Confederate victory. **321**
Second Continental Congress (1775) Group of delegates who met in Philadelphia after battles of Lexington and Concord; decided not to break with Britain, but did create an official military force. **91**
Second Great Awakening Series of religious revivals that began in the 1790s. **256**
sects New religious groups. **47**
segregation Forced separation. **350**
Senate Upper house of the United States legislature, intended to give the executive advice and consent on appointments and foreign treaties. **123**
Seneca Falls Convention (1848) First American women's rights convention. **261**
Separatists Radical English Protestants who wanted to break with the Church of England. **47**
serfs Peasants who worked for lords on European manors. **9**
settlement houses Community centers established by progressives to help slum-dwellers improve their lives. **412**
Seven Days Battles (1862) Civil War battles that resulted in Confederate victory. **321**
Seventeenth Amendment (1913) Constitutional amendment that allowed the people of a state to elect U.S. senators. **414**
shaman American Indian medicine man. **366**
sharecropping "Sharing the crop"; system in which landowners provide farmers with houses, tools, seeds, and other supplies while the sharecroppers provide the skill and labor to produce a crop, which is split at harvest season. **345**
Shays's Rebellion (1786–87) Revolt of Massachusetts farmers led by Daniel Shays, sparked by rising taxes and seizure of farms to pay back-taxes. **119**
Sherman Antitrust Act (1890) Federal law banning business combinations "in the form of trust or [that] otherwise restricted interstate trade or commerce." **386**
siege Military strategy of pinning down troops inside a city and waiting for them to surrender. **323**
Silk Road Network of trade routes that connected China and the Arab world. **12**
Sixteenth Amendment (1913) Constitutional amendment that authorized a federal income tax. **419**
slave codes Laws written by white southerners in the early 1800s to control slaves. **228**
slave state A state where slavery was permitted. **243**
socialism The idea that the government should own all the means of production. **413**
Social Security Act (1935) Federal law that set up a system of old-age insurance, which was paid for by workers and their employers. **454**
societies Groups of people who live and work together and who have common values and customs. **4**
sodbuster Plow that could easily slice through the tough sod of the Great Plains. **379**
soldier bands Small groups of warriors who settled disputes between different bands of American Indians. **361**
Southern Christian Leadership Conference (SCLC) Organization founded in the late 1950s by Martin Luther King, Jr., and others who believed that nonviolence was the only way to win civil rights for African Americans. **469**
Spanish Armada Spanish fleet defeated by England in 1588, opening the way for English settlement in the Americas. **34**
speculators Investors who buy bonds, stocks, or land, gambling that they will be able to make huge profits when they can sell these things at a later date. **161**
spheres of influence Regions where foreign countries control trade and natural resources. **437**
spirituals Deeply moving religious songs that blended Christian and African traditions and provided emotional comfort to slaves. **230**
spoils system Practice by election winners of appointing their supporters to government jobs. **246**
Sputnik The first artificial satellite, sent into space by the Soviets in 1957. **463**
Stamp Act (1765) Law approved by Parliament to enable the British to collect money by selling stamps, which had to be purchased and attached to all printed material in the colonies. **84**
staple crops Crops that farmers raise in large quantities to sell. **66**
states' rights Belief that the states, not the federal government, hold ultimate political power. **174**
stockholders Investors in corporations who buy shares and make money when the corporations do well. **384**
Strategic Defense Initiative (SDI) An advanced space-based system designed to destroy incoming missiles before they could reach the United States. **475**
strict construction Argument that congressional action is constitutional only if the U.S. Constitution specifically says that Congress has the power to carry out that action. **162**
strike A refusal to work until workers' demands for improved conditions are met. **207**
subsidy A government bonus in the form of a payment. **430**
suffrage Voting rights. **112**
supply-side economics A complex theory suggesting that lower tax rates will lead to economic growth. **475**
***Sussex* pledge** (1916) German promise not to torpedo any more passenger or merchant ships without warning. **448**
Sutter's Fort Fort built at the junction of the American and Sacramento Rivers by John A. Sutter. **271**

T

Tariff of Abominations Name given to a high 1828 tariff by southerners who disliked it. **248**
tariffs Taxes on imported goods. **118**
Tea Act (1773) Law passed by Parliament to allow the British East India Company to sell tea directly to the American colonies; sparked the Boston Tea Party. **86**
technology The use of tools to produce goods or to do work. **202**
Tejanos Texans of Mexican descent. **263**
telegraph Invention by Samuel F. B. Morse in 1837 that used a system of dots and dashes to transmit messages over wires. **377**
Teller Amendment (1898) Proposals stating that the United States had no intention of taking Cuba for itself or trying to control its government. **434**
temperance The effort to limit drinking. **258**
tenements Large overcrowded apartments. **395**
Tet Offensive (1968) Attack by the NLF that turned American public opinion against the Vietnam War. **471**
textiles Cloth. **200**
Thirteenth Amendment (1865) Constitutional amendment that officially abolished slavery. **338**
Three-Fifths Compromise (1787) Agreement that established a system of counting all free persons and only three fifths of all other persons in figuring a state's population. **122**
total war A strategy to break an enemy's will to fight by destroying the resources of the opposing civilian population and its army. **332**

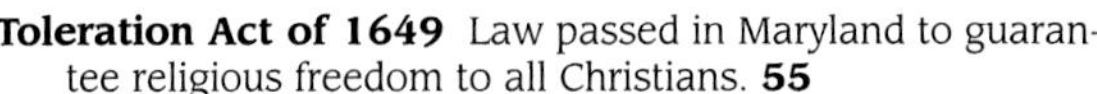

Toleration Act of 1649 Law passed in Maryland to guarantee religious freedom to all Christians. **55**

Townshend Acts (1767) Laws passed by Parliament to put duties on some items that colonists imported from Great Britain. **85**

Trail of Tears (1838) 800-mile forced march of the Cherokee, from the east to Indian Territory, in which 4,000 people died along the way. **254**

transcendentalism Philosophy that stresses an individual's ability to transcend, or rise above, material concerns. **257**

Transportation Revolution Period of rapid growth in transportation during the 1800s that made it easier for people in one region to meet one another and to do business with people in other regions. **217**

Treaty of Dancing Rabbit Creek (1830) Treaty in which the Choctaw accepted removal and ceded their homeland of 10.5 million acres to the United States. **252**

Treaty of Ghent (1814) Agreement signed between the United States and Great Britain, officially ending the War of 1812. **193**

Treaty of Greenville (1795) Agreement signed after the Battle of Fallen Timbers by more than 90 Indian chiefs, turning over the entire southern half of present-day Ohio to American settlers. **167**

Treaty of Guadalupe Hildago (1848) Treaty between the United States and Mexico that ended the Mexican War and gave the United States the Mexican Cession. **276**

Treaty of Medicine Lodge (1867) Agreement signed by Sioux who lived along the Bozeman Trail, agreeing to give up their lands and move to reservations in Indian Territory. **365**

Treaty of New Echota (1835) Agreement signed by a small group of Cherokee leaders agreeing to resettlement. **254**

Treaty of Paris of 1783 Agreement officially ending the Revolutionary War; signaled Britain's recognition of U.S. independence, and enlarged American territory. **115**

Treaty of Tordesillas (1494) Agreement signed by Spain and Portugal to move the Line of Demarcation about 700 miles farther west. **19**

Tredegar Iron Works The largest iron works in the South during the early 1800s, located in Richmond, Virginia. **225**

Triangle Fire (1911) Fire at the Triangle Shirtwaist Factory in New York in which more than 140 women died. **414**

Truman Doctrine U.S. policy under President Harry Truman to support peoples resisting communism. **461**

trust Legal agreement under which several companies group together to regulate production and eliminate competition. **385**

turnpikes Toll roads that used a pike as a tollgate to block the road until travelers paid the fees to use them. **214**

U

Uncle Tom's Cabin Novel written by Harriet Beecher Stowe in 1852 that increased controversy over slavery. **293**

unconstitutional In violation of the Constitution. **180**

Underground Railroad An informal network that helped between roughly 50,000 and 75,000 slaves escape to freedom. **235**

Underwood Tariff (1913) Federal law decreasing tariffs significantly and providing for an income tax to make up for the lost revenue. **419**

United Nations (UN) International organization formed in 1945 to promote world peace and settle international disputes. **460**

utopian communities Places where transcendentalists tried to live out their vision of a perfect society. **257**

V

vertical integration The attempted ownership of companies that provide the material and services for the attempted owner's company. **385**

viceroy Representative of the Spanish monarch who oversaw Spain's colonies in the Americas. **19**

Vietcong Pro-communist South Vietnamese guerrillas. **470**

Virginia and Kentucky Resolutions (1798–99) Statements supported by Thomas Jefferson arguing that the Alien and Sedition Acts were unconstitutional. **174**

Virginia Plan Proposal drafted in part by James Madison and presented at the Constitutional Convention by Edmund Randolph to provide for a central national government with three separate branches. **121**

Volstead Act (1919) Federal law giving the government the power to enforce the Eighteenth Amendment. **423**

W

War Hawks Members of Congress in the early 1800s who favored going to war with Great Britain; led by John C. Calhoun and Henry Clay. **186**

War Industries Board Agency established during World War I to oversee the production and distribution of manufactured goods; headed by Bernard Baruch. **449**

War on Drugs A comprehensive effort, announced by President George Bush, to eliminate the production and use of illegal narcotics at home and abroad. **476**

War on Poverty Program by President Lyndon Johnson to prevent, remedy, and eliminate poverty in America. **468**

Warsaw Pact (1955) Cold War alliance among the Soviet Union and its satellite nations pledging mutual defense against attack. **462**

Watergate Scandal that resulted in the resignation of President Richard Nixon in 1974. **474**

welfare state System of government institutions that provides for basic social needs of citizens. **454**

Whig Party Political party founded in 1834 and led by Henry Clay. **249**

Whiskey Rebellion (1794) Rebellion by western Pennsylvania farmers protesting a new whiskey tax; quickly put down by militia organized by President George Washington. **168**

Wilmot Proviso (1846) Resolution proposed by David Wilmot of Pennsylvania to declare that "neither slavery nor involuntary servitude shall ever exist in" any territory taken from the Republic of Mexico; passed by the House of Representatives, but defeated in the Senate. **290**

Worcester* v. *Georgia (1832) Supreme Court case that ruled Georgia law did not extend to the Cherokee; ignored by President Andrew Jackson and the state of Georgia. **254**

Women's Christian Temperance Union Prohibition organization begun in 1874 and led by Frances Willard. **423**

writs of assistance Special search warrants used by colonial customs officials. **85**

X

XYZ affair (1797) Scandal in which French agents reported that the French foreign minister would not negotiate with U.S. representatives until he received a large bribe; sparked undeclared naval war between the United States and France. **172**

Y

Yalta Conference (1945) Meeting between Winston Churchill, Franklin Roosevelt, and Joseph Stalin in which Stalin agreed to enter the war in the Pacific in exchange for a large part of eastern Poland. **460**

INDEX

A

D

I

J

K

L

M

N

INDEX

Q

R

S

INDEX

T

U

V

W

X

Y

Z